Routledge Handbook of Religious Laws

Much has been written on specific religious legal systems, yet substantial comparative studies that strive to compare systems, identifying their analogies and differences, have been relatively few. This absence undermines the capacity to understand religions and becomes particularly serious when the faithful of these religions live together in the same geographical space, as happens today with increasing frequency. Both interreligious dialogue and dialogue between States and religions presuppose a set of data and information that only comparative research can provide.

This book seeks to address this gap in the literature by presenting a comparative analysis of Christian, Jewish, Islamic and Hindu laws and traditions. Divided into five parts, the first part of the book offers the historical background for the legal analysis that is developed in the subsequent parts. Part II deals with the sources of law in the four religions under discussion. Part III addresses the dynamics of belonging and status, and Part IV looks at issues relating to the conclusion of marriage and its dissolution. The fifth and final part discusses how each religion views the legal other. Each part concludes with exploring what we can learn from a comparative examination of the topic that is dealt with in that part.

Written by leading experts in the field, this book presents a clear and comprehensive picture of key religious legal systems along with a substantial bibliography. It provides a state of the art overview of scholarship in this area accompanied by a critical evaluation. As such, it will be an invaluable resource for all those concerned with religious legal systems, multiculturalism and comparative law.

Rossella Bottoni is a Researcher and an Adjunct Professor at the Catholic University of Milan, Italy. She has published extensively in both English and Italian on aspects relating to law and religion.

Silvio Ferrari is Professor of Law and Religion at the University of Milan, Italy. He has been Visiting Professor at the University of California, USA (1994 and 2001), the Institute for Advanced Legal Studies, London (1998–99), the Ecole Pratique des Hautes Etudes, Sorbonne, Paris (2004) and the CTI, Princeton (2014).

Routledge Handbook of Religious Laws

Edited by Rossella Bottoni and Silvio Ferrari

Routledge
Taylor & Francis Group
LONDON AND NEW YORK

First published 2019 by Routledge
2 Park Square, Milton Park, Abingdon, Oxon OX14 4RN

and by Routledge
605 Third Avenue, New York, NY 10017

First issued in paperback 2021

Routledge is an imprint of the Taylor & Francis Group, an informa business

British Library Cataloguing-in-Publication Data
A catalogue record for this book is available from the British Library

Library of Congress Cataloging-in-Publication Data
Names: Bottoni, Rossella, author. | Ferrari, Silvio, editor.
Title: Routledge handbook on religious laws / Rossella Bottoni and Silvio Ferrari. Other titles: Handbook on religious laws
Description: New York, NY: Routledge, 2019. | Series: Routledge international handbooks
Identifiers: LCCN 2018048172| ISBN 9781138698437 (hbk) | ISBN 9781315518978 (ebk)
Subjects: LCSH: Religious law and legislation. | Religion and law. | Comparative law. | Church and state.
Classification: LCC KB197 .B68 2019 | DDC 208/.4—dc23
LC record available at https://lccn.loc.gov/2018048172

ISBN 13: 978-1-03-209306-2 (pbk)
ISBN 13: 978-1-138-69843-7 (hbk)

Typeset in Bembo
by Swales & Willis, Exeter, Devon, UK

Contents

Contributors

Roberta Aluffi is an Associate Professor in the Department of Law at the University of Turin, Italy.

Gary F. Bell is an Associate Professor in the Faculty of Law at the National University of Singapore and Director of the Asian Law Institute.

Burkhard J. Berkmann is a Professor of Canon Law in the Faculty of Catholic Theology at the Ludwig-Maximilian University, Germany.

Rossella Bottoni is a Researcher and an Adjunct Professor in the Faculty of Political and Social Sciences at the Catholic University of Milan, Italy.

Joseph E. David is an Associate Professor of Law and Religion at the Law School of Sapir Academic College, Israel.

Norman Doe is a Professor of Law at the School of Law and Politics and Director of the Centre for Law and Religion at Cardiff University, UK.

Anver M. Emon is a Professor of Law in the Faculty of Law at the University of Toronto, Canada.

Silvio Ferrari is a Professor of Law at the University of Milan, Italy.

Domenico Francavilla is an Associate Professor in the Department of Law at the University of Turin, Italy.

Zoe Headley is a Researcher at the National Centre for Scientific Research, France.

Kalindi Kokal is a Research Partner in the Department of Law and Anthropology at the Max Planck Institute for Social Anthropology, Germany.

Werner Menski is an Emeritus Professor in the School of Law at the SOAS University of London, UK.

Francis Messner is a Professor at the University of Strasbourg, France.

Agustín Motilla is a Professor of Law and Religion at the University Carlos III of Madrid, Spain.

Kenneth Pennington is an Emeritus Professor in the School of Canon Law at the Catholic University of America, USA.

Russell Sandberg is Head of Law and Professor of Law at the School of Law and Politics at Cardiff University, UK.

Adam B. Seligman is a Professor of Religion and a Research Associate at the Institute on Culture, Religion and World Affairs at Boston University, USA.

Yüksel Sezgin is an Associate Professor of Political Science in the Maxwell School of Citizenship and Public Affairs at Syracuse University, USA.

Gopika Solanki is an Associate Professor in the Department of Political Sciences at Carleton University, Ottawa, Canada.

Suzanne Last Stone is a Professor of Jewish Law and Contemporary Civilization and Director of the Center for Jewish Law and Contemporary Civilization in the Benjamin N. Cardozo School of Law at Yeshiva University, USA.

John Tolan is a Professor of History at the University of Nantes, France, and a Member of the Academia Europæa.

Knut S. Vikør is a Professor of the History of the Middle East and Muslim Africa at the University of Bergen, Norway.

Avishalom Westreich is a Senior Lecturer at the College of Law and Business, Ramat Gan and a Research Fellow at the Shalom Hartman Institute, Jerusalem, Israel.

Elimelech Westreich is a Professor of Law in the Buchman Faculty of Law at Tel-Aviv University, Israel.

Introduction

Religious laws and their comparison

Theoretical and methodological issues

Rossella Bottoni, Silvio Ferrari and Russell Sandberg

In the twenty-first century, the interaction of law and religion has rarely been far from the global news headlines. Academics have paid increased attention to the international and national laws affecting religion, extending attention beyond constitutional provisions concerning religion to explore human rights, discrimination law, criminal law and other provisions that affect individual and collective religious freedom.[1] Some consideration has also been given to the laws, rules and norms generated by religious groups themselves, which may be referred to for convenience as 'religious law'. However, most of this literature has focused on the interaction and compatibility of religious laws with international and national laws.[2] Less attention has been given to the study of religious laws in their own right as systems of law. In addition, where such work has taken place it has tended to focus upon one religious tradition in isolation. There are important works on Islamic law, Jewish law, Christian law and Hindu law as well as works focusing upon traditions within each faith.[3] However, to date, in the Anglo-American legal literature, there has been little attempt to provide a comparative study of religious laws; to take a step back from the detailed study of particular religious traditions to reflect upon the similarities and differences between religious legal systems and whether it is useful to talk of a category of religious law.[4] More attention to this issue has been devoted in legal texts written in other languages, but they have had limited circulation among Anglophone academic circles.[5]

This chapter argues that, in a religiously diversified society, knowing different religious legal systems is not enough to build a legal framework that grants religious freedom and helps the faithful of various religions to live together in peace. Comparing different religious laws is necessary. The first question that needs to be addressed is what the added value of this comparative approach is. It can be argued that the comparative study of religious law is required for three main reasons. First, and this may be sufficiently persuasive to close the discussion, it may be said that knowledge presupposes comparison. As Müller (1893: 13) and later Neusner and Sonn (1999: 1) have argued, 'who knows only one religion, knows no religion'. To really understand a religion it is necessary to compare it with other religions, since only then 'do we gain perspective, a sense of proportion and balance, an account of the choices a religion makes: for example, why one makes choices the contrasting religion may well reject'.

In other words, understanding religion involves not only knowing the religious dimensions of another person's cultural universe but also constantly comparing them with those of other cultural universes. Only through this comparative work (and not just from the, albeit necessary, knowledge of the cultural universe of the other, including its religious dimensions) is it possible to translate correctly the meaning from one context to another. This method of comparison is familiar to us from other contexts. We are only able to choose which coffee to order, for instance, by comparing and contrasting it with others. From these differences and similarities we are able to identify the precise attributes of the coffee we select. This comparative method is commonplace in the academy. It is used regularly in the natural sciences, for instance. If, among the many types of beetles that exist in nature, the scientists had studied only one, they would not have realized the similarities and differences with the others, would not have understood why these similarities and differences exist and what function they have. In other words, they would not have been able to understand and explain an item in a category without putting it into the context of that category. It is, of course, much more difficult to compare religions than beetles because the category of 'religions' is more contested than the category of 'beetles' (or, indeed, 'coffees'). However, all categories are to some degree contestable; all are human constructs, the meaning of which will mutate over time and space. Nevertheless, the point stands that studying a phenomenon in isolation is likely to be insufficient. As Neusner and Sonn note, 'in the study of religion we are not yet able to explain very much'. This is in part because it is unknown what light the act of comparison might shed. Aspects of one type of religious law may appear to be more significant when they are compared. If, as the anthropologist Gregory Bateson wrote, difference is information (1972: 315, 459), comparison is a method of learning that goes far beyond the boundaries of the laws of particular religions. This does not mean it is less necessary to understand these laws; it simply means that such laws need to be understood within their context, within their category or, perhaps we could say, their family.

Second, it is clear that comparative study of religious laws has many benefits for developing a 'secular' order[6] that is able to include people of different religious (and non-religious) persuasions. By identifying what religions have in common and how they differ, light is shed upon the likely points of tension between particular religions and 'secular' authorities as well as upon general tensions between religion and such authorities. Developing this understanding is likely to offer both practical and political advantages, helping to provide answers to all-important questions such as how to manage cultural and religious conflicts, how to build an inclusive society and what model of integration should be implemented. More specifically, a comparative approach also brings legal benefits, especially in relation to religion. Concepts, understandings and meanings differ significantly in different contexts both when comparing the religious with the non-religious and also when comparing different religions. A comparative approach is therefore needed so that State and international regulators can take into account these differences, developing an inclusive vocabulary that attempts to reduce the likelihood of unintended side-effects. For example, if legislators and judges are only aware of Christianity then they may well unwittingly create or interpret laws that define religion too narrowly (say) by reference to a divine being which would exclude some adherents of religion from the legal protection.[7] Moreover a comparative approach can be used to develop effective legal solutions that are religiously and culturally sensitive. Different religious legal systems are frequently confronted with similar problems. Taking into consideration family law, the definition of the relations between the spouses and between them and their children, the regulation of interreligious marriages, the dissolution of marriage in case of apostasy of one spouse – just to take a few examples – are issues that are faced by all religious legal systems. The ways to solve these problems are not unlimited: on closer inspection, it is possible to see that they replicate a limited number of models that are applied in different ways by each religious legal system. Comparing the rules that the different religious legal systems apply to the same case allows the secular lawmaker to develop an informed and sensible legal framework, where the claims of different religious groups can be accommodated as long as they do not conflict with some fundamental rules of the secular legal order.

What has been said regarding law-makers applies also to judges. There is no general agreement on the benefits that courts could gain through the comparison of religious laws. It has recently been contended that work on comparative religious law:

> [i]s unlikely to help the secular courts to solve the difficult questions which come before them . . . [because] . . . what judges need to understand is what the individuals before them actually believe and whether that belief is freely and sincerely held. Judges are not concerned with whether it is doctrinally right or wrong, or what, if anything, the Church's rule book has to say about it.
>
> *(Hale, 2016: 229)*

These remarks should not be overlooked. It is correct to state that judges are concerned with the particular claim in front of them and that individual religious freedom should protect adherents who have a different interpretation of their faith from that found in written sources or that expressed by their co-religionists.[8] Studies of comparative religious law should not be used to determine what a claimant can or cannot believe, whether the claim is genuine, or whether it should constitute a manifestation of religion. Studies of comparative religious law can, however, shed light upon the context of the claim, highlight religious aspects of the claim that have become sidelined by the legal arguments advanced and show the likely effect of the decision upon the community of which the claimant is part and other religious communities. It is correct to state that judges are concerned with the particular claim, but judicial decisions do not exist in a vacuum. In the same way that comparative religious law can inform (but not dictate) the decisions of legislators and policy-makers, it can have a similar role in relation to judicial decisions. The knowledge of the laws of different religions is required to understand the questions that emerge from the social body; the formulation of an adequate answer to these questions requires the comparison between these laws on the one hand, and between them and the State legal system on the other. It is therefore not enough to know the laws of different religions; it is necessary to develop the capacity to compare them. This comparative approach is even more necessary in an age of religious pluralism. The good governance of a plural society presupposes the ability to find a balance between the claims advanced by the different individual and collective subjects that co-exist in the same territory. A religiously plural society needs to safeguard the uniqueness of these subjects giving them adequate spaces of autonomy and recognizing structures of self-organization, without triggering a process of fragmentation that would frustrate any possibility of dialogue and co-existence among collective subjects that express different identities and without crushing the individual rights under the weight of collective or 'group' rights. This can be achieved through a complex mechanism of balances and compromises that requires not only the knowledge of different religious laws but also the ability to compare their content and to assess their compatibility with the State legal system. The importance of comparative analysis is only too clearly shown in the focus upon Islam in recent years, which all too often has failed to place the claims made by the Islamic communities within the context of other religions. For instance, the furore that erupted in recent years about Sharia law and Sharia courts in some Western countries invariably ignores the fact that in the same countries other religions too have long had their own laws and courts. The failure to contextualize has repeatedly made more difficult the development of inclusive societies, capable of accepting and building on religious diversity. It has led to the unhelpful stereotyping of adherents of some (or at times all) religions as the 'other' whose beliefs and actions cannot be understood by the majority of the population.

Third, comparative study benefits religious groups themselves, especially in providing a basis for interreligious dialogue. Like all identities, religious identities are 'defined by relation to differences: if we do not know exactly what distinguishes us from the others, we are not able to find what unites us in a collective "we"' (Ferlito, 2005: 75). Comparative approaches can highlight the challenges and pressure points that are common to religious groups allowing them to share experiences and to work together, where appropriate, upon solutions. Moreover Doe's (2013) study of the laws of Christian churches has shown that it is possible to induce common principles from the similarities found in such laws.[9] One can wonder whether something similar can happen within other religions and also among different religions. In particular, comparative religious law is relevant for ecumenism where 'juridical ecumenism' may provide 'the missing link' in interreligious dialogue (Doe, 2013: 10). Interreligious dialogue has been developed mainly on theological grounds, by comparing and discussing the doctrinal tenets of different religions. The focus of this dialogue is on the truth of each religion, and this is also its limit because truth is not negotiable. As a result, the closer we get to the heart of the problem, the doctrinal nucleus of each religion, the more the dialogue becomes difficult and slows almost to a halt. Lawyers ask a different and more mundane question: how can different truths be translated into behaviours and practices that are compatible with each other, and, conversely, how is it possible to work together starting from different truths? It is a dialogue focused more on the human activities that result from religions than on the ideas and beliefs themselves. A legal analysis leads to the practical question of what we can do together, without giving up our principles and faith. Obviously, the problem of truth cannot be circumvented and resurfaces at every step. However, the lawyers' pragmatic and operational approach is less naive than it seems at first sight. It implies the intuition that there is an area of relationships and activities to which human beings can contribute starting from different religious backgrounds, because there are principles and values that everybody – Jew, Christian, Muslim, Hindu, atheist, and so on – is able to recognize and for whose implementation cannot fail to cooperate with the faithful of other religions.

The process of comparison therefore has significant advantages that render it necessary for the understanding of religious law at a scholarly, practical, political, legal and personal level. Comparing religious laws remains, however, a risky endeavour. It is important that the results of comparative work are not used to produce a homogenized understanding of a religious adherent or to exclude from protection manifestations of religion that are unique and novel. Despite the similarities that might exist when laws are compared in abstract, differences invariably emerge when it comes to their real life application. It is also the case that, as we have noted, the category of religious law is a disputed one. It may be questioned whether the comparison should only occur within a particular denomination or religion. It may be questioned whether it is meaningful or a reductionist act of simplification to talk of 'Islamic law', 'Jewish law', 'Christian law' or 'Hindu law' as an entity. Furthermore, these objections increase when the talk extends to 'religious law'. The remainder of this introductory chapter will attempt to address these concerns contending that comparison at the level of religious laws ought to occur. It will begin by exploring how religious law can be understood as an identifiable category before explaining the intention and structure of this volume as a whole in providing a first step for the study of comparative religious law and an agenda for its further development.

The nature of religious laws

A huge library has been written on the topic of the definition and nature of law. Like the definition and nature of religion, it is one of the topics on which much ink has been used without reaching a significant agreement. Without wanting to add to that literature, however, it may be observed that a general distinction can be drawn in such work that attempts to understand the definition or nature of law. This distinction is between the theories that attempt to define law regardless of the content of the rules and those which deem it impossible to develop a meaningful notion of law without reference to a core of legal principles that the rules enacted by the lawmaker must respect. This is, in a nutshell, the difference between positivist and natural law theories as to the nature of law (Ferrari, 2008: 37–39).

The basic conceptual difference between these two theories lies in the way that positivist theories see the status of law as depending upon the fact that it has been laid down in a certain way recognized by the legal system, while natural law theorists, to varying extents, reject the notion that a law must be obeyed simply because it has been created through the mechanisms of the particular legal system (Sandberg, 2017). As Alexy (2002: 3–4) has written, the difference between the two schools of thought is that positivistic theories defend the 'separation thesis', that 'there is no conceptually necessary connection between law and morality, between what the law commands and what justice requires, or between the law as it is and the law as it ought to be' while natural law theories support the 'connection thesis', that 'the concept of law is to be defined such that moral elements are included'. For positivists, the two questions of 'is it law?' and 'is it good law?' are essentially different. As stated by John Austin, 'The existence of law is one thing; its merit or demerit is another. Whether it be or be not is one enquiry; whether it be or be not conformable to an assumed standard, is a different enquiry' (1995: 157). Positivist legal theory contends that whether something is law simply depends upon whether it is the product of certain structures of governance. Such theories focus on the authority that enacts the rules, the procedures that are to be followed to create them and their coactivity or their effectiveness (that is the observance that they receive in social life). They all strive to define law regardless of the content of the rules. The latter may be right or wrong, but nevertheless they remain legal rules. This does not mean that the supporters of these theories disregard the problem of justice: on the contrary, many of them pay great attention to the conditions that are necessary for a legal system to approach the ideal of justice as much as possible. However, these scholars believe that it is impossible to define law starting from the values that are conveyed by the rules and that the only scientifically sound way to define law is based on axiological neutrality (Ferrari, 2008: 37–39).

By contrast, natural law theorists suggest that there are universal standards found in nature which are discoverable in a similar manner to the physical laws of nature. These standards are normative and are often reflected in 'positive law', the rules and regulatory instruments of international, national and sub-national bodies. The development of universal human rights standards can therefore be seen as being underwritten with natural law assumptions. Natural law theories often directly oppose positivist ideas by stating that whether something is law also depends upon whether it is good law, adopting the maxim *lex injusta non est lex*, 'an unjust law is not law' (Davies, 1994: 59, 66). They share the conviction that law must comply with certain legal principles of absolute and universal validity. Within this broad field there are many differences, particularly concerning the relationship between these immutable principles and their historical translations. However, in one way or another, all these theories revolve around three fundamental assumptions:

> a) the existence of a meta-positive law; b) that is considered inherently valid, even if it is not recognized by the lawmaker; c) that is axiologically superior to positive law and therefore must be obeyed even in case an irreducible contrast arises between its requirements and those posed by the lawmaker.
>
> *(D'Agostino, 1993: 219)*

To the supporters of natural law theories, then, the definition of law cannot be separated from the notion of justice, because law's content is justice and the obligation to respect justice is not ultimately grounded on human law but 'on the very nature of the relationship between human beings' (Ghirlanda, 2000: 60).

The distinction, some would say battle, between positivist and natural law theories is ongoing. While numerous classical authors are typically cited as early proponents of the natural law approach, such as Plato, Aristotle and Cicero, most accounts of natural law begin with Christian writers, such as Augustine and Aquinas. Such approaches were seen to be widely superseded by the development of rationalist and secular approaches to law through the work of Comte, Austin, Bentham, Kelsen and Hart among others. However, natural law approaches did not disappear. Rather, since the seventeenth century, most of the natural law theories that have developed in Europe have been founded on human reason and conscience, gradually marginalizing any reference to God. The work of Grotius, Hobbes and Locke can be seen as examples of this approach. The twentieth century witnessed 'a revival of interest in natural law' as the horrors of the Second World War led to the determination to avoid future bloodshed through the development of international human rights standards seeking to protect basic fundamental rights such as the right to be free from torture, the right to a fair trial and so on (Freeman, 2014: 107). The work of Finnis and Fuller among others provides many examples of modern natural law theories, and it has been asserted that 'positivists today are less positivistic than they were a few years ago' (Freeman, 2014: 113). Even Hart (1984: 193) has developed a 'minimum theory of natural law', contending that to survive as a community certain fundamental rules need to exist based on the need to protect persons and property given the existence of universal human frailties.

As Alexy (2002) has argued, an element relating to natural law is a necessary feature of all legal systems in terms of the resolving of disputes. His work recognizes a tripartite distinction of three elements that can be found in legal communications (2002: 13). The first, 'authoritative issuance', defines a statement as law if certain procedural or status-based requirements are met. This is the classic positivist approach, discussed earlier. The second, 'social efficiency', defines a statement as law by reference to how it is observed to function in society (2002: 14–16). This includes 'external aspects' such as the Weberian understanding that law exists as law where there is a possibility of it being enforced by 'coercion through action aimed at enforcing compliance or punishing violation' (Weber, 1978: 34). It also includes 'internal aspects', which comprise subjective approaches whereby law is law if people recognize it as such. The third, 'correctness of content', defines a statement as law if it is 'rationally justifiable' within the context of the legal system (Alexy, 2002: 16): 'There is no claim that the normative statement asserted, proposed, or pronounced in judgments is absolutely rational, but only a claim that it can be rationally justified within the framework of the prevailing legal order' (Alexy, 2002: 214). For Alexy (2002: 125), law is a system of norms 'that are not themselves unjust in the extreme'. He points out that positivist approaches to law are based solely on 'authoritative issuance' and / or 'social efficiency' while natural law accounts are those which attach significance only to 'correctness of content' (2002: 13). His work concludes that all three of these requirements are needed.

Although Alexy's approach definition has been criticized (see, for example, Bertea 2003: 224–225), it helpfully redefines law as an argumentative practice. In doing so it provides a 'procedural model' for legal validity – a legal decision is to be considered to be correct 'so long as the procedural rules have been obeyed' and provided 'there is no reason to believe that the procedure by which it was reached was not fair' (Gordon, 1995: 53). This reference to fairness means that argumentation theory goes further than traditional positivist accounts provided that fairness is understood in absolute terms. The common binary depiction of natural law and positivist theories is undermined by Alexy's insistence that legal argumentation necessarily includes both positivist and natural law. This correctly reflects the fact that ideas and assumptions from both theories are found in the day to day life of all legal systems. Both natural law and positivist ideas have long informed and been expressed both explicitly and implicitly by judges in court rooms. Historical research has shown that positivist ideas have long existed alongside natural law ideas, and concepts that we attribute to the law of equity actually have a long history in the common law courts (Doe, 1990; Seipp, 2016). Indeed, even the accounts that place most stress on the autonomy of law – such as the systems theory of Luhmann (2004, 2014) – nevertheless accept that law is influenced by wider societal influences. Many authors, most notably Dworkin (1978, 1986), have written of the way in which morality infuses law as it is applied and interpreted.

For current purposes, the importance of the positivist-natural law distinction is to stress that natural law ideas are even more prevalent within the legal systems of most religions than within the legal systems of most States or other social groups. It is especially true for religious legal systems that their laws reflect rules that precede humanity and that humans must follow. Put simply, the 'correctness of content' in religious laws is often regarded as something that is determined by something or somebody that is external to human beings and precedes them. The form in which natural law ideas are expressed will vary from tradition to tradition even within one religion (as shown by the essays in Doe, 2017a). Sometimes natural law is understood to be the law divinely implanted in nature that rational creatures can discern through the use of natural reason; sometimes natural law is considered to be directly revealed by the divine. Sometimes a distinction is made between natural law and divine law; sometimes the two terms are considered to be synonymous. This means that natural law thinking is evident not only in the case of religions based on revelation, such as Judaism, Christianity and to a lesser extent Islam,[10] but also in traditions where the notion of revelation has less significance or is absent, such as Hinduism and Buddhism, where there is still the idea of an order that pervades everything and is the yardstick to measure whether human behaviour is or is not appropriate (Ferrari, 2008: 39–41).

There is, however, a difference between religious and non-religious natural law theories, and this relates primarily to the origins of the natural order and the way it can be understood by human beings. Since the seventeenth century, most of the natural law theories that have developed in Europe have been founded on human reason and conscience, gradually marginalizing any reference to God. The idea that some fundamental legal principles are rooted in the conscience of every man have become dominant, followed by the conviction that they can be understood through the correct use of reason and are sufficient to lead a good life and build a just society. Religious laws do not share this approach to natural law and do not place their ultimate foundation in human reason and conscience. Instead, they refer, in different ways, to '"something" ("the sacred") or somebody (superhuman beings, gods, God) that transcends the human dimension and, at the same time, lays at its roots' (Filoramo, 2004: 76). This is the distinctive characteristic that differentiates religious law from non-religious conceptions of natural law. The ultimate foundation of the rule is neither human reason nor human conscience but a reality external to the individual: religious rules must be obeyed simply because they are dictated by God (for some religions) or rooted in the cosmic order (for others). The Jewish prohibition of eating meat and milk together may have had, at its origins, motivations of a practical nature, but today is respected only because observant Jews consider it is the will of God, not because it has a rational basis or responds to an ethical imperative. Similarly, in the Hindu tradition, the duty to perform certain acts can be explained only through a reference to revelation and cannot be grasped by way of reason (Ferrari, 2008: 43). This different foundation of natural law in religious and non-religious legal theories reflects also on the ability of human reason to grasp fully the content of natural law. In different ways all religious legal systems tend to affirm that reason alone cannot reach an exhaustive understanding of the natural law rules and needs to be complemented by something else such as revelation and faith.[11] The following sections will explore how religious legal systems can be distinguished from other legal systems by reference to their religious and legal nature. Although this discussion presupposes a distinction between law and religion which is, according to some, Christian and Western centric, our purpose here is to suggest that a definitional attribute of religious legal systems is not only the existence of both religious and legal phenomenon but also their fusion. It is impossible to neatly distinguish law and religion within religious legal systems. They are characterized by being both religious and legal.

Religious nature

The discussion of religious and non-religious natural law theories suggests that one means by which religious law can be distinguished from other types of law is by reference to its sources and to the ability of human reason to grasp fully its content. Although natural law thinking is present in all types of law, in religious law legal rules are not exclusively grounded on human reason or conscience and therefore cannot be understood only through human faculties. This is not to say, however, that religious law is limited to the rules that the faithful know through sacred texts or cosmic laws. The label 'religious law' refers to the 'internal' laws or other regulatory instruments that govern the activity of a religious group. It includes also the more practical rules, norms and laws – formal and informal, written and unwritten – that are constantly developed by group members to regulate their everyday life. These modern rules are often seemingly indistinguishable from the rules of other social groups or indeed State law. In the Anglican context, the *Principles of Canon Law* (2008) distinguishes between 'fundamental authoritative sources of law' namely 'Scripture, tradition and reason' and 'formal sources' such as 'constitutions, canons, rules, regulations and other instruments'. It might be thought that only the 'fundamental authoritative sources' of religious law are distinctive since the 'formal sources' of religious law have much in common with other forms of law. However, this would ignore the way in which some 'formal sources' of religious law are seen to be divinely inspired and that all of them are oriented to a supernatural goal (be it called salvation, eternal life and so on). To take just one example, the Roman Catholic Canon law ends its code with a rule (canon 1752) stating that the salvation of souls is the supreme law to which all other canons must be subordinate.

It follows that, in addition to reference to sources, religious law can be defined and distinguished from other types of law by reference to its purposes or functions (Sandberg, 2011: 172). The purpose of religious law, like other forms of law, is to facilitate and order everyday life.[12] As Madrid (2004: vi) has noted in relation to Catholic Canon law, the Church 'needs canon law the way a freeway needs lane stripes'. However, religious law is distinctive in that, unlike other types of law it includes a 'soteriologic dimension through which the religious legal system opens to a "beyond" that becomes relevant and decisive for the fate of the faithful in this world' (Mazzola, 2007: 320). Although categories and terminology vary from religious tradition to religious tradition (salvation, eternal life, restoration of the cosmic order, reincarnation and so on), they are related to a transcendent reality that introduces new perspectives into the legal system, stressing the legal significance of the 'internal forum', the connection between law and morality and so on.[13] These transcendent dimensions are not unknown in State law or international law but do not carry the same weight. Religious law can also be defined by reference to the subjects it covers. Beckford and Richardson (2007: 397) identify 'the codification of beliefs, tests of orthodoxy, the training and certification of leaders, and the disciplining of deviants' as 'forms' of what they refer to as 'religious self regulation'. The subjects that religious laws cover tend to be different from 'secular' laws because religious groups tend to face unique issues which they have in common with one another and differ from those regulated by State or international law. For Anglicans, for instance, 'the principal subjects with which laws deal are ecclesiastical government, ministry, discipline, doctrine, liturgy, rites, property, and ecumenical relations'.[14] However, it is important not to overstate this. Many of the subjects dealt with by religious law are not uniquely its preserve and are also regulated by State law. This is true, for instance, of laws concerning property rights.

Although religious laws will often have much in common with other laws, reference to their sources, purposes and (to same extent) subject matter show that religious laws are distinctive because of their religious nature and context (Sandberg, 2011: chapter 9). The fact that religious law can be defined and distinguished from other types of law means that this expression is epistemologically sound and can be used to include particular systems of religious law such as Islamic law, Jewish law, Hindu law and Christian law (or indeed, labels that describe particular denominations, traditions or schools within a religion). This is not to deny, however, that the use of the label religious law is controversial. Its use has been criticized on a number of grounds: the focus on religion excludes legal systems based on cultures and beliefs which have much in common with religious legal systems (Hussain, 2015); it is unproven what particular systems of religious law such as Islamic law, Jewish law and Christian law have in common; and talk of religious law often invokes an understanding that such phenomena are largely historical relics (Constantinesco, 1983: 168). This view is taken by Huxley (2002: 1) who preferred to refer to religious law as 'Old World Law texts' or 'Obsolescent Written Law'. He argued that emphasis is to be given to the 'O' word in both of these formulations since 'what critically differentiates these . . . systems from the normal Comparative Law fodder is oldness, obsolescence or, if you prefer, history'. This approach, however, underplays the dynamic nature of religious law: the way in which religious laws are created, interpreted and applied in the day to day life or faith communities. These criticisms, though important, do not require the rejection of religious law as a category for comparison.

Legal nature

In discussing the legal nature of religious law, two caveats need to be made at the outset. First, it should be noted that the distinction between 'religious' and 'secular' law is far from simple. The distinction between the two is by no means obvious, and comparative law scholars sometimes wonder whether the law of ancient China is a religious law or, to make another example, whether the law that the 1789 French revolutionaries promulgated under the protection of the Goddess of Reason should also be counted as a religious law. These questions arise from the observation that many secular legal systems contain religious rules and many religious legal systems contain rules which, at least in the Western legal tradition, we would not hesitate to define as secular. However, a legal system is not religious because it presents one or more religious components: if that were the case, all legal systems (including those of modern liberal States) should be considered religious because all contain, implicitly or explicitly, rules related to religion. A legal system only qualifies as religious because it is produced by a religious community. Also, not all rules produced by a religious community should be properly classified as law, at least in the sense this term is used in State and international law (Ferrari, 2002b: 37–47, 263–273). This brings us to our second caveat. It should be emphasized that when applied to religions, the word 'law' assumes a meaning that is different from the meaning it has in reference to States. Dharma, shari'a, halacha, the terms used in the Hindu, Islamic and Jewish traditions, can only be translated as 'law' provided it is accepted that there is no automatic distinction between law and rules of conduct (ethical, ritual, social) and between law and politics, ethics and religion (Ferrari, 2002b). The label 'law' is incorrectly applied to systems of religious law if State law is taken either explicitly or implicitly 'to represent the epitome of law' (Tamanaha, 2001: 178). Such an approach should not be taken given that the pre-eminent status it affords State law is incorrect both historically and sociologically. Rather, a legal pluralist approach needs to be adopted that accepts that 'it is normal for more than one "legal" system to co-exist in the same social arena' (Tamanaha, 2001: 171) and that laws should not be defined in analogy with State law.

The problem with such an approach, however, is that it becomes difficult to draw a line between law and forms of social control. Tamanaha (2001: 171) has argued forcibly that the concept of legal pluralism is 'fundamentally flawed' despite the popularity of the term. He criticizes the legal pluralist literature as a whole on the basis that scholars have tended to hold 'essentialist assumptions' about law: they have assumed that law consists of a singular phenomenon which can be defined but have then failed to agree upon a definition of law meaning that their work suffers 'from a persistent inability to distinguish what is legal from what is social' (2001: 174). Muñiz-Fraticelli (2014: 139) agreed that the legal pluralist tradition has 'failed to provide criteria either for distinguishing legal from non-legal phenomena or for recommending for or against the recognition of a normative system as law'. Even the founders of modern legal pluralism have seemingly turned their backs on the term (Tamanaha, 2008: 393). John Griffiths (2005: 63–64) has subsequently argued that the word 'law' should be 'abandoned altogether for purposes of theory formation in sociology of law' with the terms 'normative pluralism' or 'pluralism in social control' as his preferred candidates to replace 'legal pluralism', while Sally Falk Moore (2005: 357) has written that distinctions must be made between governmental and non-governmental norms of social control. The failure of legal pluralism is that, while it asserts the normality of there being more than one 'legal' system co-existing in the same social arena, it does not provide a means whereby such 'legal' norms can be identified and distinguished from other forms of social control.

This does not mean, however, that we should abandon any attempt to distinguish law from other forms of social control (Sandberg, 2016a). If we conflate law with social control then the width of the definition makes it difficult to say anything meaningful about law in particular. In the same way that not all forms of social control operated by the State constitute State law, not all forms of social control operated by religious groups constitute religious law. This raises the question of where (and how) the line is to be drawn. Malik's (2012: 23) distinction between legal norms 'where an individual or group can point to distinct norms that regulate normative social order' and legal orders 'that indicate that there are mechanisms for institutionalized norm enforcement', may prove useful. Religious legal systems exist wherever there is a legal order; where there is not only a norm but also any mechanism, however informal, for resolving disputes about validity, interpretation and enforcement.[15] Religious legal systems exist where norms are produced and where disputes are resolved by the application of those norms. There are echoes here of Hart's (2012) distinction between primary and secondary rules.

Malik's definition of a legal order is objective. For Malik (2012: 24), the term is said to 'exclude diffuse mechanisms for normative regulation even if their adherents insist that these are "law"'. She calls for 'objective criterion' to determine whether the mechanisms are diffuse, but it is unclear what criterion would be used. It would be possible to identify such standards. An obvious candidate would be the 'five basic techniques' by which law discharges social functions identified by Robert S. Summers (1971): it could be said that enforcement by law consists of actions that remedy grievances, prohibit forms of antisocial behaviour, regulate socially desirable activities, regulate the provision of services and provide for the private arranging of affairs. Religious laws perform these functions: they always contain provisions providing the members of the religious community with legal remedies against the activities and decisions of other members; sanction behaviours that contradict the tenets and practices of the community; regulate recommended activities (fasting and prayer for example); provide services such as marriage and burial; and define the scope and limits of the private initiatives that the faithful can take. Similarly, Karl Llewellyn's (1940) four 'law-jobs' or basic functions of law could be evoked: a legal order could be defined as providing the orderly resolution of disputes, the preventive channelling and reorientation of conduct and expectations to avoid conflict, the allocation of authority in the group and what Llewellyn called the 'net drive', that is, the organization and harmonization of group activity to provide direction and incentive to group members. Again, there is copious evidence of religious laws providing such functions. This can be seen by focusing on the Roman Catholic Code of Canon Law which clearly provides for the orderly resolution of disputes within the church,[16] the preventive channelling to avoid ecclesiastical conflict,[17] the allocation of authority within the church,[18] and the organization and harmonization of church activities.[19] However, the use of objective standards is questionable given that such conditions are prone to suffer from three defects. First, they are likely to be overly conservative, excluding novel or different mechanisms. Second, they may be culturally specific, perpetuating a Westernized notion of law. Third, they may fail to take into account changing understandings of what people regard as law. This would include failing to take into account, or at least being slow to take into account, social change.

The pitfalls with an objective approach may lead to the conclusion that a subjective approach is required. This is the approach taken by Tamanaha's (2001: 162) 'social theory of law' which recognizes that law is a 'social construction'.[20] His 'methodology of socio-legal positivism' states that 'the activities of private citizens and legal officials (if any) cannot be understood without attention to their internal point of view' and that: 'Law is whatever people identify and treat through their social practices as "law" (or droit, Recht etc.)' (2001: 163, 166). He asserts that something is considered to be law, 'if sufficient people with sufficient conviction consider something to be "law", and act pursuant to this belief, in ways that have any influence in the social arena' (2001: 167).[21] The problem with a wholly subjective approach has much in common with the problems raised by a subjective definition of religion. Subjective approaches perpetuate the problem of legal pluralism discussed earlier: they fail to provide a means by which to distinguish legal norms from social norms. If law becomes law when people identify and treat it as such, then it becomes impossible to identify law as a phenomenon separate from social control. It follows that a wholly subjectivist approach should be rejected.

However, rather than taking a purely subjective or objective approach, a middle way should be adopted: the notion of law as communication should be used to distinguish legal norms from other forms of social control (Sandberg, 2016a). This approach suggests that the definition of law, or at least its distinguishing features, can come from law itself. By emphasizing the role of legal reasoning as a linguistic activity, such an approach provides an analysis of how law itself can distinguish legal from social norms. This can be illustrated by reference to Niklas Luhmann's social systems theory. Put simply,[22] Luhmann's social systems theory states that modern society is functionally differentiated into autonomous social systems such as law, religion, politics, science and the media.[23] Luhmann sees these social systems as reproducing themselves by communication, rather than following the classic social theory of Durkheim and Weber in seeing them as being the product of labour divisions or social action. For Luhmann, social systems are self-referential: he came to refer to them as 'autopoietic' systems on the grounds that they produce and reproduce their own unity (Luhmann, 2014: 281). Social systems, therefore, define themselves based on self-description: as systems reproduce themselves, they also define themselves by distinguishing themselves from other social systems. Social systems are operationally closed because they are self-referential; their individual operations 'are identified as such by themselves' (Luhmann, 2004: 86). However, they are 'cognitively open' in that they require 'the exchange of information between system and environment' (Luhmann, 1990: 229). For Luhmann, law is one social system and, like other social systems, law reproduces itself by communication. It is 'neither structure nor function' that defines what law is (Teubner, 1997: 14–15). Neither 'law' nor 'the legal system' is defined by institutions, individuals or 'organized legal practice' (King and Thornhill, 2003: 35). The legal system defines and distinguishes itself. This shifts the focus from debates on the 'true nature of law' towards asking how law defines its own boundaries and where they are drawn (King and Thornhill, 2003: 42) This approach has the benefit of being able to keep in line with social change without either having to resort to an external objective definition with set criteria or a wholly subjective approach that allows individuals to define what is law on a case by case basis. Law, like every other social system (law, religion, politics, science and so on), becomes distinct and autonomous by developing its own functional specification. Each social system becomes differentiated by having its own function and its own binary code (Luhmann, 2013: 45). This is 'the basic distinction that a social system applies in order to communicate' (Moeller, 2006: 216). The code allows the system 'to determine which communications "belong to" the system' (King and Thornhill, 2003: 24). Coding is always binary in nature, 'imposing a distinction between two opposing values and effectively excluding third values' (King and Thornhill, 2003: 25).[24] The social system's function and binary code provides the means by which each system will self-define and therefore perpetuate itself.

Law's function is the 'stabilization of normative expectations' in the face of disappointment and its binary code is legal / illegal (Luhmann, 2004: 98–99, 147–148).[25] As Teubner (1991: 1451) noted, this means that 'law' includes any phenomenon which is communicated using the distinction legal / illegal that has the function of the stabilization of normative expectations. Any communication that has this function and uses the legal / illegal code becomes part of the social system of law. Law is a system of communications which 'extends to all those communications that are understood as directly relating to the issue of legality or illegality' (King and Thornhill, 2003: 35, 36). Law is not defined as being part of the State; indeed, for Luhmann, the very concept of the State is 'a paradox or fiction which the political system itself produces (for simplicity's sake)' in order to perpetuate itself (King and Thornhill, 2003: 77).[26] Only law itself can decide what law is. This shifts the focus from debates on the 'true nature of law' towards asking how law defines its own boundaries and where they are drawn (King and Thornhill, 2003: 42).

Applying social systems theory, religious legal systems produce both legal and other (most notably religious) communications, but whenever they produce legal communications (that is, communications that use the legal / illegal code and fulfil the function of law) then that is law. A systems theory approach, therefore, allows social norms to be distinguished from legal norms. It provides a means by which we can recognize legal pluralism but yet still distinguish law from social norms. A legal communications approach, understanding that law itself defines what law is and that law exists wherever there is legal communication, is a preferable approach to wholly objective approaches that are invariably conservative and to entirely subjective approaches that breed uncertainty. Rather than assessing the question of what law is against agreed standards or asking people whether they think it is law, it is preferable to determine how legal systems regard themselves. As Nobles and Schiff (2013: 130) observe, this provides 'the possibility of what pluralist motivation has not yet produced – a common theoretical endeavour, not based on a common conception of law, but a sociologically informed understanding'. The quest should not be for manifestations of something that resemble State law; rather, it should be accepted that law can take various different forms of which State law is simply one.

Such an approach underlines that religious laws do not form a homogenous group. Their heterogeneous nature can be seen from religion to religion and within each religion. The existence of a category of religious law simply requires the existence of a similarity or common feature between category members that allows a comparison to take place, while noting the differences that also exist. It has been argued that the common feature found in religious laws is their dual religious and legal nature. First, religious law is religious in that it has distinct sources, purposes and subject matters than other forms of law. Second and concurrently, religious law is legal not because it resembles State law but because under a legal pluralist approach religious legal systems are just one of the many legal systems that co-exist in the social arena. The definition of law is met once the legal /illegal code is met: where there is a legal order; where there is not only a norm but also any mechanism, however informal, for resolving disputes about validity, interpretation and enforcement. Laws become designated as religious law where the immanent / transcendent code also applies. Religious laws exist wherever both codes are employed. They exist at the meeting point of two orders, a legal order (based on the code legal / illegal) and a religious order (based on the code immanent / transcendent). The specificity of religious law (and its difference from State law) consist of the use at the same time of the two codes. The religious and legal dimensions of religious law overlap; a neat line between the two cannot be drawn. It is also the case that it is often difficult to distinguish between religious laws and forms of social control used by religious groups. Objective and subjective approaches to distinguishing law are both problematic, but religious law can be defined and distinguished by means of a middle way approach that regards law as communication and sees law as defining and distinguishing itself. Applying and developing social systems theory, it can be said that religious law exists where religious groups directly or indirectly produce communications that are based on the binary code legal / illegal and which has the function of stabilizing normative expectations. The dual religious and legal nature of religious law is its key definitional attribute. It underscores that the study and analysis of religious law is necessarily an interdisciplinary activity, requiring the insight of different scholars, both those trained in the study of the particular religious tradition and those trained in the study of law.

Comparative religious law

This book furthers and facilitates this interdisciplinary dialogue by bringing together experts in the legal systems of four religions (Judaism, Christianity, Islam and Hinduism) to begin a comparative analysis of religious law in relation to five areas of religious laws. Each part includes a discussion by an expert on each of the religious traditions before concluding with 'Comparative remarks', which explore the similarities, differences and potentials for future research.

The first part, 'History', introduces and considers religious laws in their historical context, placing them in the broader framework of the belief and practice system of each religion and providing a picture of their development. Each contributor explores how law arose in the sacred texts of the religion itself and the importance placed upon that in the early development of the religion, examining the meaning and function of the law that emerged. Contributors then explore the historical evolution of their respective religious legal systems, looking at how the religious legal tradition evolved under the pressure of internal and external elements with recognition of how the legal tradition has developed in different geographical contexts. They also focus on central characteristics by examining the key features of each particular religious legal tradition as it has evolved and explaining, if possible, how it is distinguishable from other legal traditions (religious and non-religious). Last but not least, given our understanding of religious law as containing those rules (including non-written rules) / norms / laws found in sacred texts and those generated by religious groups in the past and today, contributors in this part explore the role of law in the religious tradition today, examining how religious laws / norms continue to be adjudicated, interpreted and created. This often involves discussion of how the tradition operates in different geographical terrains (international, local, regional) and the different schools of thought / denominations currently found under each religious tradition.

The second part, 'Sources of law', describes and compares the sources of law in the four religions. Each contributor discusses the sources of law found in their legal traditions, which often requires a distinction to be made between laws at the international, national and local level. Contributors discuss the instruments of regulation that are used (codes, covenants, constitutions and so on), exploring both formal and informal rules. They also examine the subject matters that are dealt with by the concerned laws. This discussion returns to a theme of this introductory chapter, the consideration of 'natural law and divine law', exploring the relationship and interplay of human / non-human sources. This includes an analysis of the meaning, role and types of natural law as well as the role of theology. Contributors also focus on the mechanisms of legal change, discussing who can change the law, how it can be changed, what is the legitimate scope of interpretation, including the role played by the faithful community, as opposed to the institutional leadership, in changing the law. This part considers the role of courts / tribunals / legal experts / commentators within the religious tradition both historically and today.

The third part, 'Dynamics of belonging and status', explores the legal framework concerning how adherents enter and leave the religion in question, including the extent to which the religious law determines questions of status and affords rights to adherents, including 'minorities within minorities' with particular reference to the position of women. As regards entering the religion, contributors examine the legal rules within the religion concerning how the faithful adhere to the religion, whether by birth or conversion, the religious laws governing the associated religious rites and any particular points of tension or controversy. The issue of leaving the religion is dealt with within the legal rules concerning, inter alia, changing religion, apostasy and excommunication. This includes an analysis of the systems of discipline for comprising the structures in place, the matters that give rise to discipline and the sanctions that are imposed. Contributors also focus on the rights and obligations that the religious legal system places upon adherents, which includes discussion of the extent to which being an adherent of the religion in question limits the rights that the adherent would otherwise be entitled to under national and international law, encompassing the right to freedom of religion, freedom of expression and the right not to be discriminated against on grounds of sex and sexual orientation.

The fourth part, 'Marriage', focuses upon a particular rite of passage that involves many religious groups. The focus here is upon the religious laws concerning marriage rather than upon State laws concerning marriage. However, where appropriate, contributors consider where religious rules have effect under State laws and areas of tension and controversy surrounding different understandings of marriage as between the State and the religion in question, especially in the context of the recognition of same sex marriages or unions by several States. Contributors discuss the formation of marriage, the rules within the religion concerning who can marry (including the age of the parties and any restrictions on the marriage of relatives and so on), the rules that need to be complied with in order for the marriage to be valid, where and when marriages can take place and who can conduct marriage ceremonies. They also explore the nature of marriage as understood by the religion in question, as well as particular issues that apply in relation to the religion they are contributing on such as the issues of mixed marriages and of equal rights of men and women. Further, contributors discuss the rules within the religion concerning the termination of religious marriages. This will include discussion of the rules and mechanisms in place concerning divorce, repudiation and nullity.

The fifth and final part, 'The legal other', explores how each religious legal system considers other normative orders and how they relate to individuals who are not members of the religious group. Contributors discuss other religious traditions and their laws, considering if and how and to what extent the laws of the religious legal system recognize other religious groups and their laws. This includes discussion of the treatment of dissenting groups and of any laws concerning or recognizing ecumenical and / or interfaith collaboration as well as rules that may restrict such cooperation including, for instance, the non-recognition of religious orders within other traditions. Another topic that is dealt with by contributors in this part is the issue of the rights and obligations of non-adherents, including what they may gain in the after-life. This comprises the extent to which non-adherents can make use of the ministry of the religion (including participation in worship and rites of passage) and places that belong to the religion (including the visiting of places of worship and their use for non-religious purposes). Contributors further examine if and how the laws of the religious legal system recognize the laws of the State and international human rights obligations. This includes discussion of how the religion operates in various different countries, outlining the main features of religion–State relations and highlighting particular areas of cooperation and conflict as well as the extent to which international human rights laws are reflected within the religious legal system: the perception, doctrine and teaching on human rights within the tradition, the extent to which religious laws and rules are compatible with these standards and the extent to which adherents can rely upon human rights arguments.

The coverage of this book is selective. Much is omitted, not least due to space limitations. We have chosen to focus on subjects that are shared by the four different religions, that have a significant impact on their relations (mixed marriages, for example) and that are relevant for the relations between religions and States. This has meant difficult decisions to exclude topics that are important (ritual laws, for example) but which do not meet these criteria. We hope, however, that this book is just the beginning of a line of research. We do not aim to be exhaustive, but rather to set a model and a standard. Our objective is to demonstrate the need and to show the value of a comparative approach to religious law.

Further reading

Alexy, R. 1989. *A Theory of Legal Argumentation*. Oxford University Press.
Briden T. and Hanson, B. 1992. *Moore's Introduction to English Canon Law*. 3rd ed. Mowbray.
Coriden, J. A. 2000. *Canon Law as Ministry*. Paulist Press.
Doe, N. 2008. 'Modern Church Law' in J. Witte Jr. and F. S. Alexander (eds) *Christianity and Law*. Cambridge University Press. 271.
Helmholz, R. H. 2017. 'Natural Law and Christianity: A Brief History' in Doe N. (ed.) *Christianity and Natural Law*. Cambridge University Press.
Hill, M. 2007. *Ecclesiastical Law*. 3rd ed. Oxford University Press.
Murphy, L. 2014. *What Makes Law*. Cambridge University Press.
Ombres, R. 1974. 'Why Then the Law?' 55 *New Blackfriars*. 296.
Waldron, J. 2001. *Law and Disagreement*. Oxford University Press.

Notes

1 It has been suggested that these laws may be said to form a body of law called 'religion law' (Sandberg, 2011).
2 See, for instance, the essays in Sandberg (2015a) and Bottoni et al. (2016).
3 There are also a small number of works on the laws of other Eastern religions such as Buddhism, see Hussain (2015) and Redwood French and Nathan (2014).
4 There are, of course, exceptions to this trend such as the works of Neusner and Sonn (1999, 2000), Huxley (2002) and, in relation to Christianity, Doe (2013).
5 See, for example, Ferrari (2002b), Puza (2000) and Berkmann (2018). See also the articles published in *Daimon. Annuario di diritto comparato delle religioni* (now a special issue of the *Quaderni di diritto e politica ecclesiastica*) and in *Revue de droit canonique*.
6 The problematic nature of the word 'secular' will be explored later.
7 This occurred under English law following the judgment in *R v Registrar General, ex parte Segerdal* [1970] 2 QB 679 and was not corrected until the decision in *R (on the Application of Hodkin) v Registrar General of Births, Deaths and Marriages* [2012] EWHC Admin 3635. See Sandberg (2014a).
8 This was stressed by the European Court of Human Rights in *Eweida and Others v United Kingdom* (2013) 57 EHRR 8, para 82.
9 As Baroness Hale has recognized, Doe's work has a clear ecumenical purpose 'to challenge the assumptions of difference which have stood in the way of greater cooperation' between religious groups (Hale, 2016: 230). Indeed, Doe has argued that 'given the Christian genius for doctrinal divisions, it is a particular challenge for both theologians and lawyers to justify the continued significance of doctrinal disagreements when the law of churches converse so profoundly around norms of conduct shared by all Christians' (2013: 7).
10 See, however, the differences between natural law thinking in Judaism, Islam and Christianity discussed by Emon et al. (2014), Doe (2017b) and Ferrari (2002a: 54–56).
11 For example, Roman Catholic Canon law affirms that after the original sin human beings have an imperfect knowledge of natural law and require Church guidance to understand it correctly; the majority position in Orthodox Judaism is that, were the seven Noah's principles not been revealed by God, human beings would not have been able to discover all of them; many Islamic lawyers claim that what we call principles of natural law are integrally contained in God's revelation and ultimately can be known through revelation only. See Ferrari (2002: 133–150).
12 For discussion of the facility and order theories, see Doe (1996: 33ff).
13 For a discussion of the impact of this soteriologic dimension on the law of the Roman Catholic Church, see Ferrari (2002a: 52–54).
14 Principle 3(5) of *The Principles of Canon Law*.
15 Compare Malik (2012: 23): 'If there is some mechanism, albeit informal, for resolving disputes about validity, interpretation and enforcement, then this institutional aspect will make it more likely that there is a minority legal order'.
16 See Book VII of the *Code of Canon Law* entitled 'Processes'.
17 See Book VI of the *Code of Canon Law* entitled 'Sanctions in the Church'.
18 See Book II of the *Code of Canon Law* entitled 'The People of God'.
19 See Book IV of the *Code of Canon Law* entitled 'The Sanctifying Office of the Church'.
20 See also Tamanaha (1997: chapters 5 and 6).
21 Tamanaha's 'social theory of law' has much in common with some approaches to legal pluralism such as Kleinhans and MacDonald's (1997) 'critical legal pluralism' which understands legal knowledge as 'the project of creating and maintaining self-understandings' and Codling's (2012, 2015) concept of 'subjective legal pluralism' which requires the narrative accounts of people to be captured and analysed.
22 For an accessible guide, see King and Thornhill (2003), and for further discussion of Luhmann's theory in relation to law and religion, see Sandberg (2015b, 2016b).
23 This concept of differentiation is much discussed in sociological theories of secularization: see Sandberg (2014b: 64).
24 For Luhmann, coding is complemented by programming, which 'fills it with content' (2004: 203). Programming provides 'the conditions, which that system establishes for when it is appropriate to apply the negative or positive side of the code' (Nobles and Schiff, 2004: 17).
25 Religion has the 'function of transforming the indeterminable into the determinable' and the binary code of immanence / transcendence. This enables the system to 'perceive what can (and cannot) be adapted as religious communication' (Luhmann, 2013: 249–250, 73).

26 Several critics, however, point out that Luhmann's concept of law is 'openly parasitic upon the State law model' given that the operation of the binary code rests upon common legal centralist ideas about the notion of law: Tamanaha (2001: 103) and Kleinhans and Macdonald (1997: 39).

References

Alexy, R. 2002. *The Argument from Injustice: A Reply to Legal Pluralism*. Oxford University Press.
Austin, J. 1995. *The Province of Jurisprudence Determined*. Cambridge University Press.
Bateson, G. 1972. *Steps to an Ecology of Mind*. Ballantine Books.
Beckford, J. A. and Richardson, J. T. 2007. 'Religion and Regulation' in J. A. Beckford and N. J. Demerath (eds) *The Sage Handbook of the Sociology of Religion*. SAGE. 396.
Berkmann, B. J. 2018. *Internes Recht der Religionen. Einführung in eine vergleichende Disziplin*. Kohlhammer.
Bertea, S. 2003. 'Legal Argumentation Theory and the Concept of Law' in F. H. van Eemeren et al. (eds) *Anyone Who Has a View: Theoretical Contributions to the Study of Argumentation*. Kluwer. 213.
Bottoni, R., Cristofori, R. and Ferrari, S. (eds) 2016. *Religious Rules, State Law, and Normative Pluralism – A Comparative Overview*. Springer.
Codling, A. R. 2012. 'A Critical Pluralist Analysis of *R (on the application of Begum) v Headteacher and Governors of Denbigh High School*'. 169 *Law & Justice*. 224.
Codling, A. R. 2015. 'What Do You Believe? Taxonomy of a Subjective Legal Pluralism' in R. Sandberg (ed.) *Religion and Legal Pluralism*. Ashgate. 199.
Constantinesco, L.-J. 1983. 'Traité de droit compare. Tome III. La science des droits comparés'. *Economica*.
D'Agostino, F. 1993. 'Diritto naturale' in E. Berti and G. Campanini (eds) *Dizionario delle idee politiche*. AVE. 219.
Davies, M. 1994. *Asking the Law Question*. Sweet & Maxwell.
Doe, N. 1990. *Fundamental Authority in Late Medieval English Law*. Cambridge University Press.
Doe, N. 1996. *The Legal Framework of the Church of England*. Clarendon Press.
Doe, N. 2013. *Christian Law*. Cambridge University Press.
Doe, N. (ed.) 2017a. *Christianity and Natural Law*. Cambridge University Press.
Doe, N. 2017b. 'Natural Law in an Interfaith Context: The Abrahamic Religions' in N. Doe (ed.) *Christianity and Natural Law*. Cambridge University Press. 184.
Dworkin, R. 1978. *Taking Rights Seriously*. Harvard University Press.
Dworkin, R. 1986. *Law's Empire*. Harvard University Press.
Emon, A., Levering, M. and Novak, D. 2014. *Natural Law: A Jewish, Christian, and Islamic Trialogue*. Oxford University Press.
Falk Moore, S. 2005. 'Certainties Undone: Fifty Turbulent Years of Legal Anthropology, 1949–1999' in S. Falk Moore (ed.) *Law and Anthropology: A Reader*. Wiley. 346.
Ferlito, S. 2005. *Le religioni, il giurista e l'antropologo*. Rubbettino.
Ferrari, S. 2002a. 'Canon Law as a Religious Legal System' in A. Huxley (ed.) *Religion, Law and Tradition. Comparative Studies in Religious Law*. Routledge. 49.
Ferrari, S. 2002b. *Lo spirito dei diritti religiosi. Ebraismo, cristianesimo e islam a confronto*. Il Mulino.
Ferrari, S. (ed.) 2008. *Introduzione al diritto comparato delle religioni*. Il Mulino.
Filoramo, G. 2004. *Che cos'è la religione. Temi metodi problemi*. Einaudi.
Freeman, M. 2014. *Lloyd's Introduction to Jurisprudence*. 9th ed. Sweet & Maxwell.
Ghirlanda, G. 2000. *Il diritto nella Chiesa mistero di comunione*. San Paolo – Ed. Pont. Univ. Gregoriana.
Gordon, T. F. 1995. *The Pleadings Game*. Kluwer.
Griffiths, J. 2005. 'The Idea of Sociology of Law and its Relation to Law and to Sociology'. 8 *Current Legal Issues* 49.
Hale, B. 2016. 'Religious Freedom and Law' in F Cranmer et al. (eds) *The Confluence of Law and Religion*. Cambridge University Press. 218.
Hart, H. L. A. 2012. *The Concept of Law*. 2nd ed. Oxford University Press.
Hussain, A. 2015. 'Legal Pluralism, Religious Conservatism' in R Sandberg (ed.) *Religion and Legal Pluralism*. Ashgate. 151.
Huxley, A. 2002. 'Introduction' in A. Huxley (ed.) *Religion, Law and Tradition: Comparative Studies in Religious Law*. Routledge. 1.
King, M. and Thornhill, C. 2003. *Niklas Luhmann's Theory of Politics and Law*. Palgrave Macmillan.
Kleinhans M. M. and Macdonald, R. A. 1997. 'What is a *Critical* Legal Pluralism?' 12(2) *Canadian Journal of International Law and Society*. 25.

Llewellyn, K. N. 1940. 'The Normative, the Legal and the Law Jobs: The Problem of Juristic Method'. 49 *Yale Law Journal*. 1355.
Luhmann, N. 1990. *Essays on Self-Reference*. Columbia University Press.
Luhmann, N. 2004. *Law as a Social System*. Oxford University Press.
Luhmann, N. 2013. *A Systems Theory of Religion*. Stanford University Press.
Luhmann, N. 2014. *A Sociological Theory of Law*. 2nd ed. Routledge.
Madrid, P. 2004. 'Foreword' in P. Vere and M. Trueman (eds) *Surprised by Canon Law*. St Anthony Messenger Press.
Malik, M. 2012. *Minority Legal Orders in the UK*. The British Academy.
Mazzola, R. 2007. 'Metodologia ed "esperimento mentale" nello studio del diritto comparato delle religioni'. *Daimon. Annuario di diritto comparato delle religioni*. 315.
Moeller, H. 2006. *Luhmann Explained*. Open Court.
Müller, F. M. 1893. *Introduction to the Science of Religion*. Longmans, Green, and Co.
Muñiz-Fraticelli, V. M. 2014. *The Structure of Pluralism*. Oxford University Press.
Neusner, J. and Sonn, T. 1999. *Comparing Religions through Law. Judaism and Islam*. Routledge.
Neusner, J., Sonn T. and Brockopp, J. E. 2000. *Judaism and Islam in Practice: A Sourcebook*. Routledge.
Nobles, R. and Schiff, D. 2004. 'Introduction' in N. Luhmann (ed.) *Law as a Social System*. Oxford University Press. 3.
Nobles, R. and Schiff, D. 2013. *Observing Law Through Systems Theory*. Hart.
Principles of Canon Law. n.d. www.anglicancommunion.org/media/124862/AC-Principles-of-Canon-Law.pdf.
Puza, R. 2000. 'Die Religionen und das Recht. Grundlagen, Prinzipien und Strukturen des religiösen Recht im Judentum, Islam und Christentum'. 9 *Informationes theologiae Europae*. 273
Redwood French R. and Nathan M. A. 2014. *Buddhism and Law: An Introduction*. Cambridge University Press.
Sandberg, R. 2011. *Law and Religion*. Cambridge University Press.
Sandberg, R. 2014a. 'Defining the Divine'. 16 *Ecclesiastical Law Journal*. 198.
Sandberg, R. 2014b. *Religion, Law and Society*. Cambridge University Press.
Sandberg, R. (ed.) 2015a. *Religion and Legal Pluralism*. Ashgate.
Sandberg. R. 2015b. 'Religious Law as a Social System' in R. Sandberg (ed.) *Religion and Legal Pluralism*. Ashgate. 249.
Sandberg R. 2016a. 'The Failure of Legal Pluralism'. 18 *Ecclesiastical Law Journal*. 137.
Sandberg R. 2016b. 'A Sociological Theory of Law and Religion' in F. Cranmer et al. (eds) *The Confluence of Law and Religion*. Cambridge University Press. 66.
Sandberg, R. 2017. 'Towards a Jurisprudence of Christian Law' in N. Doe (ed.) *Christianity and Natural Law*. Cambridge University Press. 220.
Seipp, D. J. 2016. 'Trust and Conscience in Early Common Law' in F. Cranmer et al. (eds) *The Confluence of Law and Religion*. Cambridge University Press. 48.
Summers, R. S. 1971. 'The Technique Element in Law'. 59 *Californian Law Review*. 733.
Tamanaha, B. Z. 1997. *Realistic Socio-Legal Theory*. Oxford University Press.
Tamanaha, B. Z. 2001. *A General Jurisprudence of Law and Society*. Oxford University Press.
Tamanaha, B. Z. 2008. 'Understanding Legal Pluralism: Past to Present, Local to Global'. 30 *Sydney Law Review*. 375.
Teubner, G. 1991. 'The Two Faces of Janus: Rethinking Legal Pluralism'. 13 *Cardozo Law Review*. 1443.
Teubner, G. 1997. '"Global Bukowina": Legal Pluralism in the World Society' in G. Teubner (ed.) *Global Law without a State*. Ashgate. 3.
Weber, M. 1978. *Economy and Society*. University of California Press.

Part I
History

1

The Jewish tradition

A history

Joseph E. David

Giving an account of a legal tradition that goes back some millennia is by its nature a pretentious task. Depicting the history of Jewish law, of which there is no unitary or trans-historical conception, is even riskier, because each of its components – 'history', 'Jewish' and 'law' – is highly contested and subject to intensely held ideological perspectives. The manifold comprehensions of and attitudes towards Jewish law and its nature, content and meanings raise severe doubts about the possibility of providing a neutral or at least consensual account of its history. Our point of departure, however, is that sketching the history of Jewish law is possible given adherence to the 'own terms' of the traditional discourses and an acute awareness of their ideological, theological and academic predispositions. As a starting point, it will be worthwhile to outline the a priori difficulties posed by our task.

History

I suspect that the history of Jewish law is more a matter of historiosophy, i.e., of interpretation and meaning, rather than descriptive historiography, than are the histories of other religio-legal traditions. The historical narration of Jewish law is itself a disputed matter across the generations and one indispensable to ideologies and views concerning the Jewish religion. Tales and theories about the origins of Jewish law, its evolution and its mutability have been, and still are, at the heart of theological and ideological rifts among Jews and non-Jews alike. As a result, we face a variety of contesting histories of Jewish law, each of which is deeply reliant upon a different conception of the essence of Jewish law and Judaism writ large.

Jewish

The juxtaposition 'Jewish law' seemingly alludes to an intrinsic link between a law and the attribute – Jewishness[1] – that designates its character, orientation or addressees. Yet this link is evidently a nontrivial statement and definitely not an exclusive one.[2] Alternate expressions, it must be noted, avoid this connotation and either suggest an independent vocabulary (e.g., *mitzvah, din, torah, halakhah*) or designate different semantic referents: the origins of the law and its value ('divine law'[3]), its constitutive figures ('Mosaic Law'[4]), territory ('the law of the God of the land')[5] or events ('Sinaitic law'), its bygone status ('Old Law') or its literary sources ('biblical law', 'Hebrew law', 'talmudic law'), etc. The meaning of the 'Jewishness' of Jewish law, its weight and its content is therefore a crucial question that hovers over any account of the history of Jewish law.

In what sense is Jewish law in fact Jewish? This question is profoundly dependent on even more complex, and in fact open-ended, questions. Who is a Jew? What is the essence of Judaism as a religion? The variety of answers to these questions certainly reflects diverse ideological perspectives, but even among the differing views it might be agreed that the semantic of adjective 'Jewish' is diffusive, fluid, interchangeable and to be perceived differently in different contexts.

Law

Even this seemingly straightforward term is quite debatable. There is no consensual term or designation that stands for the 'law' of Jewish law (Davies, 2001). A range of rich terminological variations are in use; some of these preserve an original vernacular (e.g., *din, mishpat, ḥoq*), while others express an equation with, or rather translation to, analogous nomenclature (e.g., *nomos, shariah, Gesetz*). Understanding the history of Jewish law in its own terms requires attention to the conceptual vocabulary that is used to denote the 'law' of Jewish law in each particular context.

In point of fact, the very phrase 'Jewish law' is somewhat misleading and might fail to represent our topic in its own terms. The very use of 'law' is burdened by a reductive fallacy on two counts. First, using the word 'law' simplifies its complexity and narrows the conceptual abundance of the category. Second, so long as the question of what *law* is remains an open question in Western legal theory, using this term with regard to Jewish law charges that concept with the theoretical baggage of Western understandings and debates about law. In our case, the problem of translation is even more complex, and the affiliation between original vocabulary and external translation is subject to not a little instability. In various discourses, the subjugation of Jewish law to external meanings and conceptions was a choice intentionally made by Jewish thinkers and jurists, so that in such contexts it became the authentic and authoritative manifestation of Jewish law. Further, the entire body of Jewish law never fully reflected a praxis and thus generally was not fully applied, and even those parts that were practiced were not enforced in the common sense, as a materialization of political will and power.

There is no simple and coherent response to these challenges. One might wonder whether these comments could but lead to relativist answers or immense skepticism about the prospect of delineating any historical framework of Jewish law. One might ask whether the history of Jewish law is fundamentally limited to the 'law on the books', its doctrines and rules, as well as to whether a linear, systematic and coherent history of Jewish law would be superficial for a history of a 'law on the books'.

I nevertheless am optimistic about the possibility of providing a plausible account of the history of Jewish law. Still, in light of the above concerns and reasons, I prefer to circumvent the narration of Jewish law and instead focus on the history of the conceptions of it. Avoiding the question of the structural meaning of the history of Jewish law, I will offer a conceptual sequence, rather than portray an evolutionary scheme. Preferring polythetic to monothetic organization,[6] I will outline a conceptual genealogy of Jewish law based on observable discursive frameworks, suggesting six genealogical layers each of which has at its core a conceptual framework encapsulating a network of ideas and concepts: (a) the biblical framework, (b) the Second Temple Era, (c) Late Antiquity, (d) the Middle Ages, (e) modernity and (f) the twentieth century. Evidence of the coherency of each framework will be offered in correspondence with commonly accepted periodization.

The Bible: a covenantal law

The biblical conception of Jewish law must be understood against the backdrop of ancient Mesopotamian law, which greatly differed from the legal notions of the ancient Greeks. The Western notion of law has roots in both conceptual worlds, which over the ages converged and merged to varying extents.[7] Even taken as divine law, these two sources are set apart by crucial differences, particularly the meaning of the law's divinity[8] (divine inspiration vs. divine origins and authorship) and its aim (application of order and stability vs. fulfilling a divine will). The Greek idea of law focused on relations within a political realm, and although law was considered to be inspired by gods, it was essentially a human-made social device that aimed to cure social deficiencies, impose order and improve communal efficiency.[9] The validity of Greek law, as a social and communicative vehicle, was dependent on its promulgation, applicability and persuasive capacity. Mesopotamian law meanwhile was understood in terms of divine authorship and heavenly origins. Thus in principle Mesopotamian law was not legislated, but revealed and given – not promulgated, but commanded.[10]

Fashioned upon Mesopotamian patterns of engagement with vassals and suzerains,[11] the biblical conception presents a given and commanded law that governs relations with the divine superpower. In addition to imposing order and stability, biblical law situates the Israelites in a politico-divine universe, orienting them in relation to YHWH on the one hand, and other nations on the other. Within the biblical covenantal framework, the law gives rise to the belonging of its adherents and designates their singularity, as a chosen people, against the alienness of different peoples, who are taken as consummate 'others' to the covenantal community. It is this logic that draws the contour of biblical law. Covenantal commitments precede the law and shape its style and content: the obligatory power of biblical law stems from, and is dependent on, the covenantal relationship between YHWH and the Israelites (Vroom, 2017). Moreover, the main function of the biblical law accordingly is to preserve an existing alliance that otherwise would break apart. To remain valid, therefore, biblical law requires occasional ratifications and timely reaffirmations.

Set within the dynamic of a covenant, divine actions and reactions are indispensable to the law and to its prescriptive power. Obedience to the law and fulfillment of its demands consequentially promise protection, redemption and salvation, while violation of the law is taken as a personal outrage, nothing less than a betrayal, against YHWH Himself. Breaching the law therefore earns expulsion from the communal body (*karet*)[12] or from the Promised Land, as well as abandonment and loss of power.

The biblical conception of Jewish law thus is that of a divine commandment (*mitzvah*)[13] that illustrates the relationship between the Israelite, as protégé, and YHWH, as omnipotent mentor and patron. This conception is pivotal to later articulations and conceptualizations of Jewish law. At some points it merged with additional concepts, and in certain other contexts it was eroded and became peripheral to accompanying conceptions.

The Second Temple Period: an ethnic law

In contrast to classical biblical discourse, throughout the Second Temple Period (530 BCE–CE 70) there is a well-defined ethnic identification of Jews and the Jewish people. In the absence of political independence for most of this period – a time when Jews nevertheless were generally permitted to retain, observe and practice their tradition – Jewish law was chiefly the law designated for the Jews or else deemed an imperial law incumbent upon them. Jewish law through this period was therefore an aspect of the existence of the Jews as ostensive race (*genos*) or nation (*ethnos*), and so it was acknowledged as the Jews' law to the extent the Jews were tolerated and accommodated as a civic body.

The terminology accompanying this conception took several forms in Aramaic and Greek vernacular. Ezra's royal commission to reconstitute the Jewish community and religious presence in Achaemenid Judea privileged the Jews with a personal choice between the laws of Ezra's God and the royal laws, given as two exclusionary options, and 'whoever does not obey the *law of your god* (דָּתָא דִי-אֱלָהָךְ) and the *law of the king* (דָּתָא דִּי מַלְכָּא), let judgment be strictly executed on him.'[14] Three centuries later, the charter of the Seleucid king Antiochus III authorized the Jews in Jerusalem to live in accordance with their 'ancestral laws' (πατρίους νόμους),[15] and papyrological evidence from the second century BCE reflects a reality in which Alexandrian Jews followed the 'civic law of the Jews' (νόμον πολιτικὸν των Ιουδαίων) (Modrzejewski, 2004).

At its core, the conception of Jewish law as the law of the Jews did not vary from the biblical conception. At its heart is the idea of the law as the will of God, expressed as divine commandment and commanded to His chosen people. In this respect, Jewish law remained an exclusive law specifically addressing the Jewish people and reflecting Jewish covenantal loyalty. Nevertheless, unlike the biblical portrayal, the ethnic conception of Jewish law here is part of a global, even imperial, framework that acknowledges and at times also legitimizes legal pluralism. In this respect, this conception resituates Jewish law in generic terms.

During this period, remarkable endeavors to converge the Mesopotamian legal notion with Greek notions took place. Judeo-Hellenic culture of the Second Temple Period created the conditions for a potential turn toward a conception closer to the Greek *nomos*, a viable possibility in Hellenized Jewish circles that stressed the identification of the biblical *torah* with *nomos*. This identification, found in various writings from the second century BCE, was certainly a mindful translation[16] – much more than a lexical choice – that evolved novel views of the Pentateuch and its fundamental messages through the lens of Greco-Roman political ideas and values. Yet far beyond a mere conceptual analogy, the *torah–nomos* correlation opened up the possibility of defining Jewish law in a way that transcended the covenantal paradigm, i.e., in universal and political terms. No wonder then that this translational option fascinated the imagination of Jewish elites thoroughly integrated within Hellenic culture!

We can only speculate as to why the *torah–nomos* identification failed to be assimilated as a dominant influence in the history of Jewish law, but it surely was an elitist intellectual endeavor that was not welcomed by the priestly establishment and the common folk. What is more, acceptance of the identification would have blurred Jewish particularity at a time when such a prospect probably was regarded by many Jews as undesirable.

Although this paradigm shift did not strike root in the historical development of Jewish law, it profoundly affected the religious imagination of the early centuries of the Common Era and played a pivotal role in Pauline criticism of the Old Testament and the assimilation of natural law doctrine in Christian theology. The conceptualization of Jewish law as political law, though subdued, was not suppressed. From time to time, the equation of *torah* and *nomos* reappeared to challenge Jewish reflective thought.

Late Antiquity: jurists' imagined law

Even as the Judeo-Hellenic translation of Jewish law as *nomos* failed to gain permanence, a dramatic departure from the conception of divine commandment was executed by rabbinic circles with a totally new conception of Jewish law.[17] The rabbinic conception of Jewish law can be characterized on an elementary level by comparison to the 'jurists' law' of the late Roman Republic and the Principate (second century BCE to third century CE).[18] The rabbis, a new, emerging elite still secondary to the Jerusalem priesthood, created a jurists' law independent of that class, so that the further the priestly establishment dissolved, the more the rabbis and their construction of Jewish religion developed and expanded.

Yet the rise of rabbinic culture was much more than the development of a social elite. It was a trend that reflected changes in Jewish awareness and social structure, as well as a transformation of religious values and understanding. Through these changes, temple-centric rites, administration and social leadership were replaced by schools and scholastic values that celebrated intellectual merit and expertise – an evolutionary step with far-reaching ramifications for religious perceptions and expectations. While previously access to the divine had been available through prophetic revelation or the priestly temple, rabbinic culture introduced *halakhah*[19] and its authorities, the rabbis, as the *sine qua non* of communion with the divine.

Under the rabbinic paradigm shift, the conception of Jewish law and its operative meaning were reformulated. The rabbis replaced the covenantal affinity with God with a framework built around *halakhah* and redefined the division of roles and powers between the human and the divine. *Halakhah*, as a body of laws and knowledge, supplanted the covenantal relationship, and literacy took the place of priesthood.[20] This shift dramatically empowered the human dimension of the law and inevitably altered the inner mechanisms and outer contours of Jewish law and the means by which it was represented.

The sophisticated halakhic conception is reflected in literary corpora comprising three distinct genera – *mishnah, midrash* and *talmud*.[21] Notwithstanding the differences between them, they are united by a common conception of Jewish law as an elaborate set of instructions that are self-consistent yet detached from external antecedent. More than an extension of preexisting collections of rules and directives, *halakhah* came about as a reorganization and systematization of an all-encompassing body of law. Few significant features characterize the conception of Jewish law as a close and systematized body of the – *halakhah*.

Professional scholasticism

The conceptual transition from divine commandment to a sophisticated, systematic body of law generated and simultaneously justified legal professionality. Manipulation and execution of the law required scholastic expertise, and so the halakhic project naturally generated professional scholastic enterprises such as interpretation, debate and rhetorical technique. The more *halakhah* expanded and became a broad and intricate field of knowledge, the greater was its need of legal experts. The formulation of Jewish law as *halakhah*, or jurists' law, thus reflected and accelerated a culture of professional scholasticism.

Self-canonization

The redefinition of Jewish law as a closed legal corpus was in fact a process of canonization, the ascription of official and authoritative status to a complete collection of laws and legal knowledge.[22] Yet in contrast to canonization borne of political authorization (e.g., the *Corpus Juris Civilis*), the canonization of rabbinic *halakhah* was a self-canonization – a theo-legal project that proclaimed and created its own canonical status. In other words, the self-canonization of rabbinic *halakhah* constructed the binding and normative standing of *halakhah* through religious devotion rather than through political power.

The *mishnah* is a notable example of this self-canonization. Composed in Hebrew and redacted in Palestine ca. CE 200, the *mishnah* represents virtually the entire body of *halakhah* in a uniform and thematically coherent format[23] with no reference to any prior such source. The fact of self-canonization is evident from the very name *mishnah*, which originally meant 'second law,' i.e., one second and parallel to that of Moses.[24] Similarly, from an editorial perspective, the *mishnah* is not only a collection of the rabbis' rulings and legal definitions but also a reorganization of the learned law as a closed and self-sufficient system.[25]

Legal imagination

The comparison of rabbinic *halakhah* to the Roman jurists' law sheds light on the uniqueness of *halakhah* as a theoretical or imaginary legal system. From its beginning, rabbinic *halakhah* was not created as a practical law at the service of a political power. It was rather a construction of virtual law through which the rabbis created an alternate world consistent with their values and worldviews. Unlike the Roman jurists' law, rabbinic *halakhah* lacked executive mechanisms and factually was not a part of legal reality but a reaction to prevailing legal systems and political realities. It was not created of an urge to resolve complicated situations and to apply order and stability, but was driven by idealism and moral visions of a perfect society. As a comprehensive project, the creation of *halakhah* can be fairly labelled a 'legal phantasm' – an endeavor to produce an alternate legal vision to the priestly political structure, on the one hand, and the imperial legal system, on the other. Many discussions of rabbinic *halakhah* resonate with actual rulings of the Roman or Sassanian legal system. Yet as a complete body of imagined law, it represents the law of a temple state[26] as defined in the Pentateuch and realized by Ezra and Nehemiah.[27]

The model that prevailed in the initial centuries of the Common Era thus contrasted strongly with the Judeo-Hellenic conception of Jewish law as *nomos*. The *torah–nomos* identification played a pivotal role in the developing theologies of Jewish-Christian circles, but it was rejected, or totally ignored, by the rabbis, who employed their own approaches in shaping the human relationship with scriptural law. Nonetheless, just as the *torah–nomos* identification suggested an alternative to the covenantal conception of divine commandment, rabbinic *halakhah*, as a closed and systematic body of law, also marked a momentous turn from the biblical conception of Jewish law. By any measure, the rabbinic conception of Jewish law as a jurists' imagined law of the temple state was a far-reaching innovation that would dominate Jewish legal thought in the centuries to come.

The Middle Ages: divine law

The history of Jewish law in the Middle Ages is associated with broader debates about the legitimacy of talmudic law and rabbinic *halakhah* at large. Briefly, the conception of Jewish law was the core of the multifaceted dispute between the Karaites[28] and the post-talmudic rabbis. The Karaites strongly rejected talmudic law, not because they necessarily challenged the rulings of the talmudic rabbis, but because they objected fundamentally to the rabbinic legal conception and its premises. They could not tolerate the idea of *halakhah* as a self-consistent body of law. The self-canonization of the rabbis' rulings seemed to the Karaites no less than a scandalous contempt of the scriptures' revelational value, and they accused the rabbis of pushing aside prophetic legal content in favor of their own, human-made laws.[29]

The polemics between the two camps were essentially a matter of legal epistemology, which is to say, a concern with the conditions ensuring that existing legal content and knowledge are indeed authentic. The Karaites emphasized the fallibility of any tradition, condemned the Rabbinites' practice of blindly following rabbinic teachings and in principle discredited the human capacity to transmit authentic knowledge without abusing it. The Karaites took a skeptical and critical approach to Rabbinite jurisprudence and in contrast invested their own intellectual efforts in systematic legal methodology, reasoned accounts of legal logic and exegesis.

Contrary to the Rabbinite claim of loyalty to talmudic law as a comprehensive and independent legal corpus, the Karaites aspired to preserve scriptural law and insisted on obedience to it. The Rabbinites meanwhile saw themselves as preserving the scholastic *Geist* of talmudic law, and their responses to Karaite critiques included idealization of the epistemology of blindly following authority (Lobel, 2000) and arguments in favor of tradition as a reliable source of knowledge (Jacobs, 2010).

However, though post-talmudic Rabbinites justified the premises of rabbinic *halakhah* and declared themselves the genuine successors of the talmudic rabbis, they distinguished themselves from the sages of the *talmud* in several ways. First, unlike their predecessors, post-talmudic rabbinic rulings were not self-canonized. On the contrary, the later Rabbinites stressed their essential inferiority to talmudic figures. In contrast to the boundless scope of talmudic legal discourse, post-talmudic Rabbinites limited the authoritativeness of their discourse to the talmudic framework, defined in literary and historical terms, and distinguished between legal and extra-legal talmudic content. Unlike the self-canonization of the rabbis' legal discourse, the canonization of talmudic law – the 'sealing' of the *talmud*[30] – was an external act of canonization that situated the *talmud* as a fixed body of law, any further extension of which was essentially secondary and inferior. Post-talmudic legal literature changed and developed accordingly, taking various forms – methodological compendia, collections of religious customs, codes, thematic monographs, responsa, commentaries on the talmudic text and novellae – all of which were based on the canonical status of the *talmud* as a closed body of law.[31]

Second, the legal imagination of post-talmudic Rabbinites incorporated different values and aspirations from those of the talmudic rabbis. Their self-perception and presuppositions were much more diasporic than their predecessors and all the more distanced from the founding imagery of the law of the temple state.[32]

This genealogical phase also introduced and consolidated a solid notion of divine law. A notable feature of the medieval conception of Jewish law is its distance from the notion of political law. In conjunction with the diasporic worldview and the reintroduction of Greek heritage, the relationships between Jewish law and the Greek *nomos* reemerged. Like their Islamic counterparts, Jewish thinkers involved with philosophical and theological reflections on the law consciously declined the equation of *torah* and *nomos* and articulated the former by reference to the concept of divine law as essentially differing from political law. In contrast to *nomos*, or political law, the aim of the divine law (*shariah*,[33] *mishpat ha-torah*,[34] *dat elohit*[35]) is to lead individuals towards spiritual and intellectual perfection, rather than to safeguard interpersonal relations or to impose order and social justice.

Articulating Jewish law as divine law and stripping it of any political features traditionally ascribed to *nomos* were the aims of enormous intellectual efforts, such as demoting the legal value of religious content, dislodging the law from the sociopolitical realm and treating the law as a means for higher ends.[36] This depoliticization of the conception of Jewish law evidently took place independently in various geographic and cultural contexts[37] in a process that prepared the ground for the Jews, as minorities, to be simultaneously loyal to local civil laws and their own religious laws – a crucial condition under the dual jurisdiction of Jewish diasporic existence.

However, there was more to the conception of Jewish law as divine law than simply diasporic depoliticization. Because Jewish law was seen as a means of achieving personal perfection, transcending ethnic belonging and history, its particularity to the Jews and its very Jewishness were questioned. The universality of Jewish law was suggested and discussed by Rabbinites and Karaites alike (Erder, 1994; Kellner, 2015: 77–106). Overall, even though less reflective statements, the medieval depoliticized conception of Jewish law and its potential universality were profoundly acknowledged to be bequeathed to later generations.

The Modern era: law, religion and identity

Modern conceptions of Jewish law developed against the background of medieval conceptions, in an era when dramatic changes in the European political and theological setting significantly affected reflective understandings of Jewish law. The rise of the nation-state, the construction of state law and emerging concerns of secularization, citizenship and identity problematized anew the relationship between law and belonging in general, including as they related to Jewish law.

Intriguingly, despite these momentous political changes, the medieval depoliticized conception of Jewish law did not vanish, but grew stronger. In contrast to medieval thought, though, modern conceptions of Jewish law were indispensable to the phenomenology of the Jewish religion and the conceptual nexus of law, religion and identity.[38] This link was not only a theoretical development but also an outcome of the novel political experiences of European Jews and the influence of the ideas of the Protestant Reformation and the Enlightenment.

Beyond the medieval distinction between divine law and political law, early modern Jewish thinkers were concerned with the relationship between divine law, as an abstract category, and the particular ceremonial laws of the Jewish religion.[39] A bridging phase between the two frameworks can be seen in the writings of Benedict (Baruch) Spinoza (1632–1677), who played a key role in articulating the parameters of modern discourse on Jewish law. More than his predecessors, Spinoza refined the concept of divine law, which he defined as universal, ahistorical and apolitical,[40] and accordingly established the distinction between 'ceremonial law' and divine law.

The division of divine law into 'ceremonial,' 'juridical' and 'moral' laws had been acknowledged by medieval Christian theologians (Ross, 2010) and Jewish thinkers. But only Protestant reformers associated this legal typology with differing theo-political ideologies. The typology of laws was a significant factor in the 'economy of religious differences' that was initiated and then intensified by Lutheran theology with the argument that Catholicism and Judaism mistakenly preserved the ceremonial law and ignored the eternal components of the biblical law.

Through the eighteenth century, the equation of the Mosaic Law with ceremonial law was approved by and internalized into Jewish self-perception as a positive phenomenology of the Jewish religion, and the identification of Judaism with legalism and ceremonial laws was embraced by Jews themselves (Breuer, 1992; Fenves, 2001: 90). The political theology of Moses Mendelssohn (1729–1786), for instance, is built on the linkage of ceremonial law (*Zeremonialgesetz*) (Weber, 2007: 527–528) and the Jewish religion, stressing that the latter, in contrast to Christianity, is 'divine legislation.' Mendelssohn idealized the function of Jewish ceremonial laws as a symbolic script and vehicle for unifying the Jewish people as a religious community.[41]

Both the correlation of Jewish identity and Jewish law and the view of Jewish law as a signifier of the Jewish religion were broadly accepted by various Jewish theologians and ideologists. They were embraced not only by Reform followers of Mendelssohn's ideas who demanded changes and revision of the traditional laws but also by Orthodox Jews who insisted that Jewish law is not only apolitical but also trans-historical and immutable. Depiction of Jewish law as the core of the Jewish religion became a leitmotif of Orthodox Jewish ideology and of Jewish philosophers reflecting on the essence of the Jewish religion. The Ultra-Orthodox ideologist Moses Schreiber (*Ḥatam Sofer*, 1762–1839) elevated the conception of Jewish law to unprecedented heights of imaginative metaphysics,[42] and the founder of German Orthodoxy, Samson Raphael Hirsch (1808–1888), described loyalty to the Jewish religion with the term

Gesetzestreue Judentum ('Judaism that is faithful to the law'). The progressive thinker Hermann Cohen (1842–1918) likewise stressed the equation of Jewish law and Jewish monotheism as the cornerstone of other monotheistic religions, and Leo Strauss (1899–1973) exalted Judaism (and Islam) for preserving the idea of the 'word of God' as divine legislation even as Christianity reduced revelation to philosophy.

Generally, the modern conception of Jewish law diverges from the idea of divine instructions that lead to spiritual and intellectual perfection, while preserving its apolitical character. In its representation of Jewish religion and nationality, the modern conception of Jewish law marks the shift from divinity to ceremony and from the personal to the communal.

The twentieth century: law, nationalism and politics

For the bulk of the Jewish world, the arrival of the twentieth century did not affect conceptions of Jewish law. The ideological trends that emerged in Europe before the wars expanded and developed beyond the continent. Simultaneously, this period witnessed the appearance of strong nationalist tendencies that eventually came to be embodied in the Zionist project, which laid the foundations for new existential conditions for the Jewish nation. These deep changes also heralded a new chapter in the conceptual history of Jewish law, one in which its apolitical, diasporic and divine dimensions are being melded and marginalized.

A profound departure from the depoliticized conception of Jewish law was ushered in with the growth of the Zionist movement. Most versions of Zionism were political visions of the establishment of a modern Jewish *politeia* for the Jewish people, accompanied by ideological revivalism that aimed to redeem the nation's latent resources and capacities. This trend is demonstrated by the successful revival of Hebrew, a dead language that was revitalized and became the spoken language of emerging Jewish communities in the future State of Israel. The lingual renaissance and resurging nationalist ideologies inspired endeavors to transform Jewish law from apolitical law to the living law of the renewed Jewish commonwealth and later the State of Israel.

However, despite the analogy to the Hebrew language, the modification of the law was a very different project from the start. While the revival of the language was basically a cultural change extending the use of Hebrew beyond ceremonial books, the aim of actualizing Jewish law and rearticulating it as a black-letter law for the Jewish state was a much more venturesome project. It required two shifts, each challenging enough on its own. First, it aimed to extract the political instructions contained in the traditional body of Jewish law, and, second, it aspired to politicize Jewish law itself.

In the 1920s and 1930s, secular Zionists who believed that the renewal of Jewish law went hand-in-hand with secularizing it became the first to press and campaign for its politicization. They presumed that in order for Jewish law to be applied to modern circumstances, it had to be articulated as a secularized state law. This secular-Zionist move was represented by the coinage 'Hebrew law' (המשפט העברי), with which they replaced the traditional terms – a change meant to avoid the religious aspects of exilic Jewish law. The Hebrew law campaign, however, did not succeed. Despite partial acknowledgement under the British Mandate, the founding fathers of the State of Israel preferred to base nascent Israeli law on common law rather than Hebrew law (Shamir, 2000).

An ideological twist came a few decades later, when the vision of Hebrew law was embraced by religious-Zionist ideology. Despite the use of the same term – 'Hebrew law' – this project was very different from the first. Religious Hebrew law was about politicizing Jewish law while preserving its terms and character as a religious law. With the Zionist movement as a whole viewed in religious terms, as a fulfillment of the prophetic promise of the Return to Zion, this politicization of Jewish law sought to retrieve it from its diasporic conception as an apolitical law.

The interconnection of Jewish law and the Zionist project thus filters past features of Jewish law. It exhibits opposing tendencies toward either theocracy or secularization. Simultaneously, it can enrich the preexistent conceptual inventory and in so doing more sharply plot an alternate legal discourse that reacts to, reflects and criticizes statist political power and invites reconsideration of the links between law, power and religion.

Conclusion

The history of Jewish law from biblical to contemporary times (Roszler, 2017) is not a history of a law legislated, adjudicated and administered, but that of a constructed combination of idea and ideal. Conceptions of Jewish law across the generations range from a covenant with God to a private case of nomic order, the imagined law of a temple state, a prescription for personal perfection and finally the law of a nation-state. In every historical context, Jewish law was much more than a legal system, and each conception of it encapsulated normative guidelines describing how to comprehend and how to approach imperfect existential conditions.

The history of Jewish law in this respect is obviously not limited to the political domain. As an expression of an all-inclusive worldview, it was situated time and again in different contexts – between divine decrees and social orders, between reality and imagined visions, between the universal and the particular, between glorified past and wishful future – none of which corresponds strictly to our contemporary understanding of law and its operation. As our brief outline has shown, the history of Jewish law is inseparable from the history of the Jewish religion and Jewish existence in various settings and under various conditions.

Notes

1 The variance of 'Jew' and 'Israel' is traceable to the biblical split between the Northern Kingdom, or Israel, and the Southern Kingdom, Judah. Through the Hellenistic Period, however, 'Jew' and 'Jewish' were generally neutral terms designating ethnic identity associated with the territory of Judea. The term 'Hebrew,' initially associated with 'Abraham the Hebrew' (Gen. 14:13), through various historical moments was often a self-designation of those who changed or challenged tradition while claiming that their actions in some way corresponded to some more authentic tradition. Throughout rabbinic literature, the term 'Israel' is a contrast to gentiles. See Harvey (2001).

2 The linkage between 'law' and 'Jewish' also is incompatible with the view that the applicability of *torah* is not exclusive to the Jewish people, as has been argued in a range of contexts, including by rabbis and in New Testament theology. See Hirshman (2000). For later periods see later.

3 See recent discussions: Hayes (2017); David (2017). God's law (תורת האלהים; Josh 24: 26), 'the book of God's law in Moses' hand' (ספר תורת ה' ביד משה; 2 Chron. 33:8; 34:14; 35:6).

4 *Legum Mosaicarum*. See Frakes (2011). The biblical term 'Moses' law' (תורת משה; Josh. 23:6; 1 Kings 2:3; 2 Kings 14:6; 23:25).

5 The idiom 'the law of the God of the land' (משפט אלהי הארץ; 2 Kings 17:26) is atypical and even exceptional. Essentially, biblical law is not mediated through territory: its territoriality is derivative of the God–Israel covenant. Thus, the Israelites' settlement in Canaan both is the fulfillment of the covenant and is conditioned upon the covenant's observance. Endeavors to engage territorial jurisdiction with Jewish law, in both theory and practice, are apparent only in later contexts (medieval and modern).

6 A 'monothetic' (or 'Aristotelian') classification is defined in terms of the necessary and sufficient characteristics of its members, so that members are identical. A 'polythetic' classification is defined in terms of a broad set of criteria, neither of which is necessary or sufficient. Thus each member of the polythetic class possesses a certain minimum number of defining characteristics not necessarily found in all members of the category (a model associated with Ludwig Wittgenstein's concept of family resemblance). See Bailey (1989).

7 The identification of the biblical *torah* and the Greek *nomos* (see endnote 16) is an example of an attempt to converge the Mesopotamian and the Greek notions of law.
8 On the difference between a 'law's divinity' and 'divine law,' see our discussion later regarding the medieval conception of the Jewish law.
9 The laws of the Spartan lawgiver Lycurgus, for instance, were considered to enjoy divine imprimatur because he was inspired at the Oracle of Delphi, but both Plutarch (*Lycurgus* 4.1) and Herodotus (1.65, 66) subscribe to the notion that his laws may have come from Crete. Draco's laws were superseded by those of Solon, which it was hoped would be obeyed for 100 years (Aristotle, *Athen. Const.*, 7.1–2; Plutarch, *Solon*, 25.1). Plutarch (*Solon*, 15.2) recounts that when asked whether he had 'enacted the best laws for the Athenians,' Solon replied, 'the best they would receive.' See Bréhier (1908: 16–18); Brague (2008: 121–156).
10 Thus, for example, the stele of Hammurabi's Code (ca. 1792–1750 BCE) portrays Hammurabi as receiving the laws directly from Shamash, the sun god. These differences are related as well to the fact that the Greeks trusted their gods much less than did the Mesopotamians. Thus the Greek ideal of the 'rule of law' is fundamentally based on mistrust of both humans and gods. See Bers and Lanni (2014).
11 Among the most important such treaties are those of the Hittite Empire of the second millennium BCE, to which many scholars look for the origin of the genre as a whole, and the Neo-Assyrian vassal treaties, especially those of Esarhaddon (early seventh century BCE). See Weinfeld (2004).
12 The Hebrew term *karet* ('cutting off') connotes punishment by death or exclusion from the community.
13 The original meaning of the biblical *mitzvah* is 'a commandment commanded by YHWH.'
14 Ezra 7:26.
15 Josephus Flavius, *Antiquitates Judaicae*, 12:140.
16 See Richardson and Westerholm (1991). Indeed, some modern scholars view the translation as misleading and erroneously depicting Jewish tradition as a legalistic ideology, in the guise of which Christianity fought Jewish tradition from the time of Paul of Tarsus to Martin Luther and beyond.
17 Late ancient rabbinic circles consisted of the Jewish sages, mostly in Palestine, between the second century BCE and the fifth century CE, the initial generations of whom (ca. 150 BCE–CE 200) were known as Tanna'im (lit., 'those who recite' or 'teach') and the latter as Amora'im (lit., 'those who say' or 'speak'). Through most of this period the rabbis lacked any form of institutionalized power, but rather were a self-proclaimed elite whose recognition was based on their social positions, wealth, education and charisma. Their main involvements were in teaching and instructing, and thus they established schools of learning, known as *yeshivot* (lit., 'sittings'). See Goodblatt (2006).
18 During this period, a body of law was developed by non-official jurists to support the processes of drafting documents (*cavere*), advising on procedural matters (*agere*) and responding to questions of law (*respondere*).
19 The term *halakhah* (lit., 'the way to walk') in pre-modern Hebrew is one peculiar to rabbinic literature that expresses a deep conceptual change. See Urbach (1996). Traditional accounts ignored the religious mindfulness of the rabbinic world and took an interest only in the failure of the Jewish revolt against Rome and the need to develop modes of existence for survival after the destruction of Jerusalem in CE 70. Recent accounts have given more weight to the conscious motivation of the rabbis to create an alternative to temple-centered religion. Halbertal describes the construction of *halakhah* as a dramatic evolutionary jump, a shift from a law based on commandment (*mitzvah*) to a dense, systemized network of instructions (*halakhah*) expressing a new religious sensitivity. See Halbertal (2013).
20 E.g., 'there is no covenant but *torah*' (*Mekhilta, Pisḥa* 5, et al.); 'Since the day the Temple was destroyed, God is [present] in His world only within the four cubits of *halakhah*' (BT *Berakhot* 8a).
21 The *mishnah* (lit., 'that which is repeated' or 'secondary') is a redacted assemblage of the rabbis' sayings and rulings organized as a thematic code (redacted ca. CE 200). *Midrash* (lit., 'exposition' or 'investigation') is a hermeneutical method and a body of commentaries on the Scriptures that use this method. The Hebrew term *talmud* and its Aramaic parallel *gemara* (lit., 'study' or 'learning') refer to two literary compilations (the Palestinian Talmud, redacted in the late fourth or early fifth century, and the Babylonian Talmud, redacted between the late fifth and the late sixth century) of commentaries and elaborations of the *mishnah* alongside additional scholastic discussions, teachings and discursive reasoning.
22 Homological to the canonization of the Hebrew Scriptures, also by the rabbis.
23 Divided into six orders (*sedarim*), each order into tractates (*massekhtot*), and each tractate into chapters (*peraqim*).
24 The sense of *mishnah* as 'second law' is evident in its Greek name, *deuteroseis*, or 'second in rank.' St. Jerome, for example, denounces the *mishnah* while accusing the rabbis of seeking to replace the

Mosaic Law: '[they are] despising the law of God, and following the traditions of men, which they call *deuteroseis*.' See Simon (1996: 91). This meaning is not contradicted by rabbinic tradition, and some medieval rabbinic authorities indeed embraced it.

25 Unlike the *mishnah*, the *midrash* and *talmud* do not present a holistic image of *halakhah* as a closed system. Both are presented and structured as commentaries on superior and primary texts – scripture in the case of the *midrash* and the *mishnah* in that of the *talmud*.

26 It should be noted that to characterize rabbinic *halakhah* as a law of the temple state is not to argue that it is a territorial law. On the contrary, the imaginative aspect of rabbinic law dilutes the law's spatial binding and in fact legitimizes its existence and validity as diasporic law. On the diasporic aspect of the *talmud*, see Boyarin (2015).

27 Only the third of the six mishnaic divisions, which focuses on family law, discusses non-temple issues. The first division is concerned with priestly dues, the second with the festivals celebrated at the Temple, the fourth with civil and criminal laws subject to the judicial system centered at the temple, the fifth with sacrifices and the sixth with purity of private homes and the Temple. For further analyses on the imaginative aspects of the rabbinic literature, see Fraade (2011).

28 For a general extract of Karaism see Lasker et al. (2007). The Karaites trace their origins to the first split of the Judean kingdom. Rabbanite sources, however, ascribe the emergence of the Karaism to days of Anan b. David (eighth century). The term 'Karaites' was not applied until the ninth century; the precursor of the sect was known as 'Ananites' – the followers of the Anan. Generally, the Karaites' doctrine is characterized primarily by independency and denial of the talmudic-rabbinic tradition. Karaism viewed scripture as the sole manifestation of divine content that is self-explanatory and intelligible. Accordingly, the Karaites rebutted the rabbinic idea of 'oral *torah*' and disproved tradition as a reliable source of religious knowledge. The literary expressions of medieval Karaism began with the eighth-century scholar Anan b. David and his followers (Ananites). Through the 'golden age' of Karaism (c. 900–1100) the movement flourished socially and intellectually to the point that Karaites comprised some 40% of world Jewry.

29 They rebuked the rabbinates' devaluation of revelation and prophecy, a position explicitly expressed in the talmudic maxim 'a sage is greater than a prophet' (BT *Bava Batra* 12a). Karaite authors commonly termed the rabbis 'people of the *mishnah*' (Heb. בני משנה), a contrast to the Karaites, termed 'people of Scripture' (Heb. בני מקרא), and the Karaites' insistent adherence to scriptural meaning.

30 The jurisprudential significance of historical events is illustrated by a parallel conception in Sunni legal theory establishing that the 'gates of *ijtihad*' were 'closed' in the tenth century. On the meaning of this phrase, see Hallaq (1984).

31 Though these literary developments certainly should be seen in the context of concurrent literary genera among neighboring legal traditions, they often entail far more than mere adoption of external trends. At times, the similarities between these literatures reflect a vigorous intellectual interplay with the legal content and jurisprudential thought of the other (as with the Geonim and Islamic jurisprudence, or the Tosafists and Latin Scholasticism).

32 The Geonim made clear that priestly Jerusalem had been replaced by the Babylonian academies; in the words of Pirkoi b. Bavoi (early ninth century), 'Zion is the academy.' See David (2014: 139–150).

33 On Jewish use of the term *shariah* to denote the Jewish divine law, see e.g., Kraemer (1986).

34 Lit., 'the law of the *torah*.'

35 Lit., 'divine law.'

36 Even Moses Maimonides (1138–1204), the great codifier of Jewish law, balked at viewing the *torah* as a case of *nomos*. He addresses the fundamental differences between political laws (*nomoi*) and divine laws (*al-awamir al-ilahiyyah*) in the *Treatise on Logic*, among his earliest writings. (The word *amr* can be translated as 'affair,' 'order,' 'decree,' 'command' or 'purpose.' In this context, I believe that the most precise sense of *al-amr al-ilahi* is 'divine standards.' See Kraemer (1986).

37 Comprehensive accounts of the essential distinctions between political laws and divine laws appear as well in Christian contexts, such as in the writing of the talmudist Nissim of Girona (1320–1376) and the Spanish philosopher Joseph Albo (1380–1444). See Lorberbaum (2002).

38 No doubt this conceptual link is associated with the Protestant typology identifying Judaism with legalism, based on which Jewish law is cast as the signifier of the Jewish religion. For a different account of the modern shaping of Judaism as religion, see Batnitzky (2011).

39 The concept of 'ceremonial laws' is originated in early Christianity and is based on the distinction between 'moral laws', which are universal justice-aimed laws, and 'ceremonial laws', which are binding only on God's people as a symbol of separation and which the New Testament had abolished. See Ross (2010).

40 Spinoza argued accordingly that the Mosaic Law could be considered a private case of divine law: 'in this sense the law of Moses, although it was not universal, but entirely adapted to the disposition and particular preservation of a single people, may yet be called a law of God or Divine law . . . the nature of natural Divine law . . . is (1) . . . universal or common to all men, for we have deduced it from universal human nature. (2) . . . does not depend on the truth of any historical narrative whatsoever . . . (3) . . . does not demand the performance of ceremonies and (4) . . . the highest reward of the Divine law is the law itself, namely, to know God and to love Him of our free choice, and with an undivided and fruitful spirit' (*Tractatus Theologico-Politicus*, IV, 61).

41 'Letter to Naftali Herz Homberg,' in Gottlieb (2011: 114).

42 The leading uncompromising opponent of the Reform Movement in modern Judaism, Moses Schreiber (1762–1839) coined the idiom 'nature is subordinated to the divine law (*torah*).' See *Responsa of Ḥatam Sofer* (Bratislava, 1841), I:14, pp. 6a–6b.

References

Bailey, K. D. 1989. 'Constructing Typologies through Cluster Analysis'. 25(1) *Bulletin of Sociological Methodology*. 17.

Batnitzky, L. 2011. *How Judaism Became a Religion*. Princeton University Press.

Bers, V. and Lanni, A. 2014. 'Disqualified Olympians: The Skeptical Greek View of Divine Judges' in A. Memelstein and S. E. Holtz (eds) *The Divine Courtroom in Comparative Perspective*. Brill. 128.

Boyarin, B. 2015. *A Traveling Homeland: The Babylonian Talmud as Diaspora*. University of Pennsylvania Press.

Brague, R. 2008. *The Law of God: The Philosophical History of an Idea*. The University of Chicago Press.

Bréhier, E. 1908. *Les Idées Philosophiques et Religieuses De Philon D'Alexandrie*. Librairie Alphonse Picard.

Breuer, E. 1992. 'Politics, Tradition, History: Rabbinic Judaism and the Eighteenth-Century Struggle for Civil Equality'. 85 *Harvard Theological Review*. 357.

David, J. E. 2014. *Jurisprudence and Theology: In Late Ancient and Medieval Jewish Thought*. Springer.

David, J. E. 2017. 'Divinity, Law, and the Legal Turn in the Study of Religions'. 32(1) *Journal of Law and Religion*. 172.

Davies, P. R. 2001. '"Law" in Early Judaism' in J. Neusner, A. J. Avery-Peck and B. Chilton (eds) *Judaism in Late Antiquity*. Brill. 3.

Erder, Y. 1994. 'Early Karaite Conceptions about Commandments Given before the Revelation of the Torah'. 60 *Proceedings of the American Academy for Jewish Research*. 101.

Fenves, P. D. 2001. *Arresting Language: From Leibniz to Benjamin*. Stanford University Press.

Fraade, S. D. 2011. *Legal Fictions: Studies of Law and Narrative in the Discursive Worlds of Ancient Jewish Sectarians and Sage*. Brill.

Frakes, R. M. 2011. *Compiling the Collatio Legum Mosaicarum et Romanarum in Late Antiquity*. Oxford University Press.

Goodblatt, D. 2006. 'The Political and Social History of the Jewish Community in the Land of Israel, c. 235–638' in S. T. Katz (ed.) *The Cambridge History of Judaism IV – The Late Roman-Rabbinic Period*. Cambridge University Press. 404.

Gottlieb, M. (ed.) 2011. *Moses Mendelssohn. Writings on Judaism, Christianity, and the Bible*. Brandeis University Press.

Halbertal, M. 2013. 'The History of Halakhah and the Emergence of Halakhah'. 29 *Dine Israel*. 1.

Hallaq, W. B. 1984. 'Was the Gate of Ijtihad Closed?' 16(1) *International Journal of Middle East Studies*. 3.

Harvey, G. 2001. *The True Israel: Uses of the Names Jew, Hebrew, and Israel in Ancient Jewish and Early Christian Literature*. Brill.

Hayes, C. 2017. *What's Divine About Divine Law? Early Perspectives*. Princeton University Press.

Hirshman, M. 2000. 'Rabbinic Universalism in the Second and Third Centuries'. 93(2) *The Harvard Theological Review*. 101.

Jacobs, J. A. 2010. *Law, Reason, and Morality in Medieval Jewish Philosophy: Saadia Gaon, Bahya ibn Pakuda, and Moses Maimonides*. Oxford University Press.

Kellner, M. 2015. *Maimonides' "True Religion": For Jews or All Humanity?* Brill.

Kraemer, J. L. 1986. 'Namous and Shari'a in Maimonides' Thought' (in Hebrew). 4 *Te'udah*. 185.

Lasker, D. J. et al. 2007. 'Karaites' in M. Berenbaum and F. Skolnik (eds) *Encyclopaedia Judaica*. 2nd ed. Vol. *11*. Macmillan. 785.

Lobel, D. 2000. *Between Mysticism and Philosophy: Sufi Language of Religious Experience in Judah Ha-Levi's 'Kuzari'*. State of New York University Press.
Lorberbaum, M. 2002. *Politics and the Limits of Law: Secularizing the Political in Medieval Jewish Thought*. Stanford University Press.
Modrzejewski, J. M. 2004. 'The Septuagint as Nomos: How the Torah became a "Civic Law" for the Jews of Egypt' in J. W. Cairns and O. F. Robinson (eds) *Critical Studies in Ancient Law, Comparative Law and Legal History*. Hart. 183.
Richardson, P. and Westerholm, S. 1991. *Law in Religious Communities in the Roman Period: The Debate Over Torah and Nomos in Post-Biblical Judaism and Early Christianity*. Wilfried Laurier University Press.
Ross, P. S. 2010. *From the Finger of God: The Biblical and Theological Basis for the Threefold Division of the Law*. Christian Focus Publications.
Roszler, I. 2017. 'Law as a Prism into National Identity: The Case of Mishpat Ivri'. 38(2) *University of Pennsylvania Journal of International Law*. 715.
Shamir, R. 2000. *The Colonies of Law: Colonialism, Zionism, and Law in Early Mandate Palestine*. Cambridge University Press.
Simon, M. 1996. *Verus Israel: A Study of the Relations between Christians and Jews in the Roman Empire A.D. 135–425*. Liverpool University Press.
Urbach, E. E. 1996. *The Halakhah: Its Sources and Development*. Yad La Talmud.
Vroom, J. 2017. *Law, Authority, and Interpretation in the Ancient World: The Origin of Legal Obligation in Early Judaism*. PhD Dissertation: University of Toronto.
Weber, E. 2007. 'Fending Off Idolatry: Ceremonial Law in Mendelssohn's Jerusalem'. 122(3) *Modern Language Notes*. 522.
Weinfeld, M. 2004. *The Place of the Law in the Religion of Ancient Israel*. Brill.

2

The Christian tradition

A history

Kenneth Pennington

Origins

Two major sources of jurisprudence and norms shaped European legal systems: Roman law as it was organized in the sixth century under the Eastern Roman emperor Justinian, and the religious law of the Roman Catholic Church that evolved from the time of the first Christian Roman Emperor Constantine to the seventeenth century. Both were important sources of Christian religious law. The reason why an ancient, dead legal system and a system of religious law became important for shaping European jurisprudence is both institutional and the result of a unique series of unforeseeable developments. Forgotten, abbreviated, neglected, and scattered in various pieces, Justinian's codification of Roman law (529–534) attracted the attention of a shadowy group of men who reassembled it in Italy at the end of the eleventh and the beginning of the twelfth century. The improbability of this rebirth was underlined a century ago by a legal historian who called it a ghost story (Vinogradoff, 1909: 4). A few decades later in the twelfth century, a man named Gratian joined the teachers of Roman law in Bologna and began introducing students to the Church's law with a revolutionary textbook that he called the *Concordia discordantium canonum*, the *Concord of discordant canons*. The jurists shortened his unwieldly title to the *Decretum*.

During the twelfth century both laws were established in the emerging law schools in Italy as the fundamental teaching texts of the legal curriculum and became, in the parlance of the jurists, the 'libri legales'. By the thirteenth and fourteenth centuries law schools all over Europe used the same sources, the same commentaries, and the same language (Latin) to teach law. Their graduates received a law degree with the title *Utriusque iuris* doctor, a doctor of both laws. European law schools continued to grant that title to law graduates until the eighteenth century.

The medieval and early modern jurists created a universal jurisprudence that penetrated every crack and crevice of every courtroom in Christendom. They called this jurisprudence that evolved from teaching and commentaries on these texts the *Ius commune*. The *Ius commune* existed side by side with local, territorial customary law that the jurists called the *Ius proprium*. Manlio Bellomo has used the imagery of the sun and the planets to explain the relationship between the *Ius commune* and the *Iura propria* in the Middle Ages. He explained that the sun influences the planets but does not destroy or supplant their local environments.

The *Ius commune* and the various *Iura propria* have a similar relationship (Bellomo, 1994: 192). The law schools did not begin teaching the *Iura propria* until the early modern period. Until then a law student's legal education was suffused with the religious norms and values found in Justinian's codification and ecclesiastical legal texts.

To understand how Christian religious law evolved and became institutionalized in European society we must look at the context of its origins. The basic texts that informed the entire Christian legal tradition were the New Testament and the Old Testament. The earliest Christian texts drew upon them in one way or another. Consequently, Jewish legal traditions were also part of its DNA. Jurists cited texts from the New and Old Testaments again and again to justify basic norms, and in later papal and conciliar legislation they were called upon to justify and to validate significant changes in the legal system (Helmholz, 1996: 20–22 et passim).

The Christian legal tradition was also born in a civilization that had the most sophisticated jurisprudence and legal system yet developed by any society. The Roman Empire had a universal body of norms that did not distinguish between religious and secular norms. Although Roman jurisprudence primarily dealt with secular law, the jurists did not make a clear distinction between secular and religious law. Roman law contained much material on marriage and other fields that was useful to Christians, particularly their notions and definitions of law. The Roman jurists called fundamental principles of religious law *fas*, which was defined as a norm of divine origin. That law was of divine origin was a fundamental principle of all Christian law. The Romans has two terms for what we in English call law: *ius* and *lex*. *Lex* is accurately translated into English as 'law', that is a norm promulgated by a legislative body. *Ius* was a much more complicated term with significant ethical if not precisely religious resonances. At the beginning of Justinian's *Digest* the compilers placed a series of quotations from the Roman jurist Ulpian (ca. 170–223) (Justinian, *Digest* 1.1.10.2 and 1.1.11): 'Jurisprudence is the understanding of divine and human affairs, and the skill of recognizing justice and injustice . . . In one way "ius" means what is always equitable and good, as natural law (Ius naturale)'. The Roman orator Cicero (106–43 BC) had summed up an important strand of ancient thought when he argued in his *De republica* that 'true law was right reason that was congruent with nature'. He concluded that 'there was one eternal, immutable, and unchangeable law' and that God had established it as the Emperor and Master of all humankind. Cicero's vision of law sank deep roots in Roman legal thought. Consequently, by the fourth century, Christians found much in Roman law that was compatible with Christian doctrine, and it was not difficult for the first Christian Emperor Constantine to embrace Roman law. His legislation touching the Christian Church and its doctrine became part of his legacy. The Roman conception of a natural or divine law was especially attractive. It was congruent with a Christian conception of the universe. Law's legitimacy was not, as it is in the modern world, determined by the authority of the legislator. An unjust law could be promulgated, but its provisions could be contested if it violated reason, justice, or natural law. This remained a fundamental principle of Christian jurisprudence until the age of legal positivism, i.e., the modern legal world. The 'rule of law' was far from absolute in Roman and ecclesiastical law (Pennington, 2004: 417–420; 2011: 227–253).

If one were to judge their thought on the basis of their language, early Christians were ambivalent about secular Roman law. Greek culture, language, and the Jewish scriptures shaped early Christian thought and institutions, not Roman law. Christian texts and early church councils did not use the vocabulary of Roman law. As Christian and Jewish diaspora radiated out from Palestine to all parts of the Mediterranean, the structures of Greco-Roman cities formed the institutional character of Christian communities. St. Paul wrote to Roman Christians who knew and lived under the law created by the Roman state and reminded them that faith in Christ replaces secular law with a quest for salvation (Romans 7:1–12 and 10:1–11). Law, he sharply reminded the Galatians, cannot make a man worthy to God; only faith can bring life to the just man. In the early Church, 'canon law' (a Greek term) as a system of written norms that governed the Church or even a large number of Christian communities, did not exist. This is not surprising. The Roman state regulated religious practice and quite naturally legislated for the Christian Church after the Empire became Christian at the beginning of the fourth century (Pennington, 2007: 386–402; Wessel, 2012: 3–17).

The attitudes of the first Christian emperors after Constantine can be seen in their legislation. To take only the imperial statutes in Justinian's *Codex* as a guide, there are 41 imperial statutes dating between 313 and 399 that deal with ecclesiastical discipline and practice (Titles 2–13 of Justinian's *Codex*). The Roman emperors had exercised authority over Roman religious institutions, and it was only natural that Constantine would continue this assertion of imperial authority. Gradually, the Church in the West did begin to conceive itself as a corporate body that had the authority to produce rules to govern itself and exercise a separate judicial role in society. That 'separation' of the Church from the state, however, would not begin in earnest until the second half of the eleventh century.

An attenuated form of Caesaropapism was the primary principle unconsciously followed by all early medieval Christian rulers in the Latin West and the Greek East (Pennington, 2010: 183–185). In the East the Roman emperors who ruled over Greek Constantinople continued to legislate and regulate ecclesiastical institutions until its collapse in AD 1453. Byzantine canon law began to merge with civil law in the sixth century. The first Byzantine legal collections contained only ecclesiastical norms (κανόνες; 'canons') or secular norms (νόμοι; 'laws'). In the late sixth and early seventh centuries Byzantine canonists combined these two sources: These collections were named *nomokanons* (νομοκάνονες), although the name did not become common until the eleventh century (Troianos, 2012a: 115–214).

After the ascension to the imperial throne Constantine began to produce canons that were publicly promulgated and that were recognized as authoritative by all the Christian communities. Constantine also elevated the authority of bishops in Christian communities. Although it is not clear how broad his mandate was, he issued a law that bishops could hear legal cases between Christians. Most scholars think that the episcopal court, the *audientia episcopalis*, originated because of this legislation. Constantine also used the Church council to deal with doctrinal and disciplinary problems within the Church. By the fourth century bishops had established themselves as administrators of local churches. They also recognized their role in governing the affairs of nearby churches in councils as well as their responsibility to confront questions that touched upon the interests of the universal Church. In the East and the West councils became the main vehicles for promulgating norms that regulated the lives of clergy and the organization of the churches. It is during this period that the enactments that these assemblies produced became called 'canons', from the Greek word κανόνες ('canons'), which became 'canon' in Latin. In Greek canon did not mean 'law' but simply a 'straight rod' or a 'rule'. As we shall see, the primary focus of conciliar legislation in the fourth century was on the structure of Church and clerical discipline.

The first significant councils whose canons would become important in the canonical tradition were held in the Greek East. In 325 Constantine summoned an imperial council in the East to settle the doctrinal controversies raised by the Arian heresy, particularly the issue of the relationship of the Father and Son in the Trinity. A number of local episcopal synods were held in the East in preparation for the council. The emperor originally planned to hold the council in Ancyra but moved it to Nicaea. He opened the council in June 325. It was very much a Greek council. Only a few Western clergy were present. The 20 Greek canons of the council became universal norms in the Christian Church even though a Latin translation was made only many years after the council ended. Other early councils established laws and a pattern of governance in the Church that lasted until the end of the ninth century.

Local synods met regularly in the East and the West and were significant sources of law until the twelfth century. A council could be a court or a legislative body. As courts, they decided difficult and contentious problems in the Church, and as legislative bodies, they promulgated canons that regulated the affairs of the provinces. Numerous local synods were supplemented by ecumenical councils that were held exclusively in the East until the Second Council of Nicaea in 787. In the eleventh century the papacy asserted its exclusive right to convene an ecumenical or general (that is papal) council. The sites of all subsequent general councils were in the West. The age of councils whose canons united the Latin and Greek churches came to an end in the ninth century (Tanner, 1990).

Until the fourth century the Old and New Testaments, real and apocryphal Apostolic traditions, custom, and conciliar and synodal canons constituted the four main sources of ecclesiastical norms. During the course of the fourth century two other sources of authoritative Christian law emerged in the Christian Church: The writings of the Fathers of the Church and the letters of the bishops of Rome. In the Eastern Church the 'Canons of the Fathers' were recognized as norms sometime between 381 and 451. They consisted of letters or other writings directed to specific persons by the Eastern Fathers. In the Latin West a parallel development during the fourth and fifth centuries gave papal decretal letters (that were often rescripts, that is responses to questions) an equal place with conciliar canons. These decretal letters were responses to requests that asked for answers from the pope to problems of ecclesiastical doctrine, discipline, and governance. The form of the requests was based on similar letters (rescripts) sent to the Roman emperors on specific questions of law. In imitation of secular practice, in the fourth century bishops in the Western Church began to turn to Rome for answers to questions about discipline and doctrine. Pope Siricius' (384–399) letter to Bishop Himerius of Tarragona was a first step in the long road to the age of the papal decretal in the second half of the twelfth century.

Before the twelfth century, canon law existed as a body of norms embedded in many sources. The collections of canon law included conciliar canons, papal decretals, the writings of the Church fathers, and to a more limited extent, Roman and secular law. These collections did not contain any jurisprudence because they existed in a world without jurists. There were no jurists to interpret the texts, to place a text into the context of other norms of canon law, and to point out conflicts in the texts written at various times.

Historical evolution

Jurists arrived in the late eleventh and early twelfth centuries. They began working and teaching in the city of Bologna in north-central Italy. The first on the scene were the teachers of Roman law, Pepo and Irnerius, and they were succeeded by a cadre of teachers who raised the city to unprecedented intellectual heights. Their first task was to reassemble Justinian's codification and his later legislation. Justinian's *Digest* circulated in three pieces, and the jurists maintained that division even though they learned of the Pisan-Florentine manuscript in which there were no divisions by the middle of the twelfth century. The *Digest* was of crucial importance because it contained the jurisprudence of the Romans. The *Codex* was a compilation of the statutes of the Roman emperors until Justinian, circulated in two parts. The *Institutes* was an elementary teaching text for all of Roman law. It had been circulating in the early Middle Ages (Lange, 1997: 8–35; Radding and Ciaralli, 2007).

Justinian's codification provided the jurists who taught Roman law with a very good vehicle for teaching law. Irnerius made a significant contribution to these texts. He excerpted Justinian's voluminous legislation (*Novellae*) after he had promulgated his codification and added them to the margins of *Codex* manuscripts. Many of these excerpts were added to chapters in the *Codex* dealing with religious issues, marriage, and matters of ecclesiastical discipline. Although the papacy had begun to claim sole jurisdiction and authority to regulate the church and its members, Justinian's Roman jurisprudence continued to be an important source of Christian norms. Emperor Frederick Barbarossa visited Bologna in 1155 and promulgated the *Authentica Habita*, with which the emperor took the masters and students at Bologna under imperial protection. He ordered that his decree be placed in Justinian's *Codex*, a collection of Roman imperial constitutions. The emperor recognized the teachers and students of a flourishing law school. He also understood the importance of the School for his realm. Barbarossa added other legislation to the *Codex* as well (Pennington, 2012: 35–53).

The eleventh-century canonists emphasized papal judicial and legislative primacy as never before in the canonical tradition. They created a muscular Petrine ecclesiology. Yet, by and large, their canonical collections reflect a fiction that the Pseudo-Isidorian had created in the ninth century. These forgers had drafted a series of papal decretals that they attributed to the first three centuries. From these letters later canonists could conclude that the *ius antiquum* of the Church had provided more than enough evidence that popes had achieved judicial and doctrinal primacy in the first three centuries of the Christian era. The men of the age fervently believed that 'old law was good law'. The compilers of the canonical collections endorsed this maxim. They did not have to turn to the contemporary papal legislation to establish the new ecclesiastical order. A small number of papal decretals did find their way into the canon law collections of the eleventh century, and they justified key elements of the reformers' program: Gregory VII's justification of his deposition of Henry IV and his legislation in the Roman council of 1080 that condemned the investiture of clerics by laymen. But these two examples were the exception. The tacit conclusion that could be drawn from a careful study of the sources of the eleventh-century canonical collections was that the papacy did not make new law except out of necessity or utility. The final paradox is that the canonical collections of the reform period prepared the way for a revolution in the sources of canon law that took place in the twelfth and thirteenth centuries. As we will see, by the middle of the thirteenth century, papal decretals will push aside the rich and variegated sources of the first millennium of canon law. Papal decretals became the primary source, if not the exclusive source, of canonical norms.

The eleventh century was also a key moment in the Church. A reform movement emerged that had clerical discipline as a primary goal. For Christian law Pope Gregory VII adopted these earlier reforms and added crucial elements for which historians have given his name to the entire era: 'The Gregorian Reform Movement'. Gregory's pontificate (1073–1085) inaugurated a sea change in the relationship between secular and ecclesiastical authority (Blumenthal, 2001). The reform movement that preceded him was focused on reforming the Church. Gregory embarked on a program that would redefine the relationship of ecclesiastical and lay authority. Secular and ecclesiastical jurisdiction, office, and law were not, as we have seen, clearly separated during the previous 1000 years. Gregory focused on the issue of the practice of lay princes' investing clerics with ecclesiastical offices as a step to delineate the boundaries between lay and ecclesiastical authority. Gregory excommunicated and deposed the Christian emperor and other princes, setting a precedent that future popes would warmly embrace. The conflict and movement he started, called the 'Investiture Controversy', between the papacy and secular princes lasted well into the twelfth century (Blumenthal, 1988; Hartmann, 1993). In the end, however, by 1200, although there were areas of contention, there was a generally agreed upon model that should inform the structure of the Church and the secular state. Caesaropapism in all its even attenuated forms died a quiet death in the Latin West. The next centuries would deal with the growing power of papal monarchy (Tierney, 1988).

It is not without irony that the fusion of religious and secular jurisprudence in the West began at the beginning of the twelfth century, without conflict and devoid of opposition. A teacher named Gratian began to teach canon law in Bologna in ca. 1125. For the development of religious law Gratian was a crucial figure. The pre-twelfth-century canonical collections were not suited for teaching. The Roman law jurists taught Justinian's codification in its Medieval format. Until recently the only secure fact that we knew about Gratian was that he compiled a collection of canons entitled the *Concordia discordantium canonum*, later called the *Decretum*. Very quickly it became the most important canonical collection of the twelfth century and later became the foundation stone of the entire canonical tradition. It was not replaced as an introductory handbook of canon law until the promulgation of the *Codex iuris canonici* of 1917.

Gratian's first recension of his book was fairly short, but he expanded it twice over approximately 20 years. The differences between the recensions mean that Gratian must have been teaching at Bologna for a significant amount of time before he produced his first recension and that there was a significant period of time between the first and second recensions. Some evidence points to Gratian's having given his first lectures in the 1120s. In any case, Gratian's last recension of the *Decretum* was finished in the late 1130s or early 1140s and immediately replaced all earlier collections of canon law in the schools (Pennington, 2014: 25–60).

Gratian became the 'Father of Canon Law' because his final collection was encyclopedic but most importantly because he provided a superb tool for teaching. The *Decretum* was a comprehensive survey of the entire tradition of canon law. Gratian drew upon the canonical sources that had become standard in the canonical tradition and assembled a rich array of canons from many sources, about 4000 in all. He drew most his material from four major eleventh- and early twelfth-century canonical collections that circulated in Italy. Gratian's *Decretum* became a source book for Christian religious texts from the late antique and early Middle Ages for theologians and polemicists.

Gratian introduced jurisprudence into canonical thought. His first innovation was to insert his voice into his collection to mingle with those of the Fathers of Nicaea, St. Augustine, and the popes of the first millennium. He did this with *dicta* in which he discussed the texts in his collection. He pointed to conflicts within the texts and proposed solutions. His *dicta* made the *Decretum* suitable for teaching, and it became the basic text of canon law used in the law schools of Europe for the next five centuries.

In addition to the novelty of his *dicta*, Gratian created a collection of canon law that was organized differently from any earlier collection. At the core of his collection he constructed 36 cases (*causae*). In each case he formulated a problem with a series of questions. He then would answer each question by providing the texts of canons that pertained to it. When the text of the canon did not answer the question without interpretation, or when two canons seemed in conflict, Gratian provided a solution in his *dicta*. Gratian's hypothetical cases were effective teaching tools that were ideally suited to the classroom.

Perhaps the most important parts of his work for the beginnings of European jurisprudence were the first 20 distinctions of the 101 distinctions (*distinctiones*) of the first section. In these 20 *distinctiones* he treated the nature of law in all its complexity. Justinian's codification of Roman law that was being taught in Bologna at the time Gratian was working on his *Decretum* defined the different types of law but did not create a hierarchy of laws and did not discuss the relationship between the different types of law. Gratian did that in his first 20 distinctions. These distinctions stimulated later canonists to reflect upon law and its sources. Gratian began his *Decretum* with the sentence: 'The human race is ruled by two things, namely, natural law and usages' (*Human genus duobus regitur naturali videlicet iure et moribus*). On the basis of this introductory sentence the canonists grappled with the concept of natural law and its place in jurisprudence for centuries. Their commentaries resulted in an extraordinary rich jurisprudence on natural law and reflections on its relationship to canon and secular law. A text of the last great Latin Church Father, Isidore of Seville (†636), became key to the jurists' developing ideas about the foundations of natural law and its relationship to human law. Isidore took some of his notions of natural law from the Romans: It was a higher law and it had divine origins. Other elements of natural law were part of the Roman and the Christian traditions: Marriage, the raising of children, and the right of self-defense. Isidore fashioned two principles that had never been connected to natural law: The common possession of all things (*communis omnium possessio*) and an extraordinarily striking phrase, one liberty of all 'human beings' (*omnium una libertas*). The first principle led the jurists into a thicket of rights for the poor. The idea that the poor and the disadvantaged had property rights that trumped ownership rights has remained a fundamental principle in European criminal law until the present day (Tierney, 2014: 22–37 et passim). At first glance, the second should have led them to conclude that all human beings were equal and that slavery was evil. Slavery, however, was too entrenched in the structure of human society. The jurists creatively but lamentably constructed permissive natural law to explain how one human being could be owned by another. Although a chorus of jurists and theologians began to deplore slavery in the sixteenth century, it took a bloody American civil war in the nineteenth century before all Christian legal systems finally rejected the evils of slavery.

A distinguished historian has written that Gratian's *Decretum* was 'essentially a theological and political document, preparing the way – and intended to prepare the way – for the practical asserting of the supreme authority of the papacy as lawgiver of Christendom' (Southern, 1995: 286). This sentence might describe the purpose of Anselm of Lucca (and other canonists of the reform period) but not Gratian's plan for his work. If Gratian's goal for the *Decretum* were to be limited to one idea (a dubious idea) it would be that he wanted to describe the relationship of law to all human beings. Gratian's purpose is clearly revealed in the first distinctions in which he analyzed the different types of law, just as Anselm of Lucca's purpose is revealed at the beginning of his collection: The authority of the bishop of Rome.

After he discussed law in the first 20 distinctions, Gratian then turned to issues of ecclesiastical government and discipline. For example distinctions 31–36 treat the morals of the clergy; 60–63 ecclesiastical elections; 64 and 65 episcopal ordination; 77 and 78 the age of ordination; and 95 and 96 secular and ecclesiastical authority. In the *causae* Gratian discussed the problem of simony (*causa* 1); in *causae* 2–7 he treated procedural matters; 16–20 monks; 23 war; and 27 to 36 marriage. One important part of the *Decretum* was added later. At the end of the book a long tract on sacraments (*De consecratione*) was added later. Gratian's teaching and his *Decretum* established canon law as a partner to Roman law first in Bologna and then all over Europe. He also prepared the way for a sophisticated canonical jurisprudence.

Gratian had a near contemporary in Constantinople who was a key figure for the Christian legal tradition's development in Eastern Europe. Theodore Balsamon was the most important canonist in Byzantium during the twelfth century. He was born in the early decades of the century and died sometime after 1195. Gratian may have eventually become a bishop, but Theodore Balsamon joined the ranks of the clergy quite early and was a high-ranking member of the ruling elite in Constantinople. He was ordained a deacon of Hagia Sophia, the most important church in Constantinople. Afterwards he assumed the positions of *nomophylax* and *chartophylax* as well as that of *protos* of the Church. A *nomophylax* meant 'guardian of the law' and was a prestigious post at the imperial court. He was the president of the school of law and was given senatorial rank. In the 1170s the Emperor Manuel I and the Patriarch of Constantinople, Michael, commissioned him to revise the *Nomokanon of XIV Titles* (ca. 612–625). Balsamon carried out this task and also wrote a commentary on the *Nomokanon*. The work has given him a reputation and a position in Greek Orthodox canon law similar to Gratian in Western canon law. But there the similarity ends. The emperor commissioned Balsamon to revise canon law. Gratian worked well outside the circles of secular and ecclesiastical power. Balsamon revised an earlier work that had become the authoritative book of canon law in the East. Gratian fashioned a collection of canon law that was different from any prior collection. Balsamon continued the Byzantine tradition of melding secular law with canon law. He compared all the imperial law in the *Nomokanon* with those in the *Basilika* (τὰ Βασιλικα), a collection of imperial laws from the late ninth or early tenth century. Those secular laws in the *Nomokanon* that were not in the *Basilika* were considered abrogated. For the ecclesiastical canons in the collection, Balsamon explained their place in the canonical tradition when he discussed them in his commentary. He noted any that had been abrogated or derogated by subsequent legislation. Gratian used Roman law but took many of his texts from earlier canonical collections. He 'canonized' Roman law.

Balsamon continued to work on his commentary on the *Nomokanon* for a long time, possibly until he died. He took later imperial and ecclesiastical legislation into account. The last novella that he mentioned was issued by Isaac II after April 1193 (Troianos, 2012b: 180–184, 200–205 et passim).

A comparison of Gratian's and Balsamon's ecclesiology is revealing. Gratian described a church that was centered in Rome and that had jurisdictional independence from secular rulers. Although he did not emphasize papal authority to the same degree that the compilers of eleventh-century canonical collections had, he included all the fundamental papal decretals from Pseudo-Isidore as well as genuine papal decretals that established papal jurisdictional primacy. In contrast Balsamon's church was not independent. The emperor had the authority to establish, derogate, and abrogate canonical norms. Balsamon insisted that the emperor should exercise this power with caution and only in exceptional cases. He did not, however, grant the emperor authority in dogmatic questions (Gallagher, 2002: 153–184).

Balsamon's significance was central in the Byzantine canonical tradition. During both the late Byzantine as well as post-Byzantine periods, canonists cited and used excerpts from his commentary. He also influenced Slavic canonical literature. His works were translated or were transmitted by later canonists. For the Christian legal tradition, Balsamon's conception how the Christian Church and the state influenced and informed Eastern, Greek, and Slavic Christian traditions remained a touchstone of the Orthodox Christian tradition.

Although it was not a highly polished or well-organized text, Gratian's *Decretum* quickly became the standard textbook of medieval canon law in the Italian and transmontane schools. Its disorganization was not a major problem, and its other flaws were minor. Gratian left repetitions and seams in his text that betrayed its long period of gestation. The revisions of his work sometimes introduced confusion and ambiguity, but the canonists were only sometimes dismayed by his conclusions, comments, or organization.

In the formative age of canon law after Gratian when the study of canon law and Roman law became the primary disciplines in the schools in Italy, Southern France, and Spain, the jurists began to fashion the first tools to construct a legal system that met the needs of twelfth-century society. Gratian's *Decretum* surveyed the entire terrain of canon law, but his book was only an introduction to the law of the past. Although it provided a starting point for providing solutions, it did not answer many contemporary problems directly. The four most pressing areas in which the jurists used the new jurisprudence to transform or to define institutions were procedure, marriage law, norms governing elections, and the structure of ecclesiastical government. In the first half century after Gratian, the jurists concentrated on these problems, and their teachings and writings vividly reflect these concerns (Pennington, 2008: 214–227).

Many reasons compelled the papacy to take notice of the law school at Bologna. The Church had become much more juridical during the course of the twelfth century. St. Bernard of Clairvaux's famous lament in his letter to Pope Eugenius III (1153) that the papal palace is filled with those who speak of the law of Justinian confirms what we can also detect in papal decretal letters. The new jurisprudence influenced the *arengae* and the doctrine of decretals. Canonists undoubtedly drafted these letters in the curia. The rush to bring legal disputes to Rome became headlong in the second half of the twelfth century. Litigants pressed the capacity of the curia to handle their numbers. Popes delegated many cases to judges-delegate, but the curia was still overburdened.

If he had seen the canon law curriculum at the Law School at Bologna ca. 1350, Gratian would have been pleased and surprised. He would have been pleased that his book still occupied a central place in the study of canon law. Every student of law studied the *Decretum*. He would have been surprised that Dante Aligheri placed him in *Paradiso* (Canto 10 lines 97–99 and 103–105). Not many poets have bestowed honors on jurists. He would not have anticipated the triumph of the papal decretal. Gratian understood canon law as being based on many different kinds of authoritative texts. By the end of the twelfth century, however, the canonists were transfixed by papal appellate decisions that the papal curia rendered on cases that had been appealed to Rome from every corner of Christendom.

These appellate decisions were the result of a very sophisticated ecclesiastical court system. One of the most important consequences of the Gregorian Reform Movement in the second half of the eleventh century was to define the role of ecclesiastical courts in Christian society. Fundamental principles were established that delineated the boundaries of secular and ecclesiastical courts. The first and most important was that no member of the clergy could be tried in a secular court. It took a century before this principle was accepted by the secular courts throughout Europe. The assassination of Archbishop Thomas Becket (†1170) was the singular event that persuaded Christian secular rulers to concede that clerics were not under their jurisdiction (Duggan, 2004).

The establishment of ecclesiastical courts as a powerful and universal institution in Christian society began in the early twelfth century. The first necessary step was to create a structure and a jurisprudence that would guide the courts when they exercised their authority. The papal chancery was the first court to seek guidance on legal procedure. Haimeric, the Papal Chancellor, turned to Bologna and to the leading teacher of Roman law in the 1130s, Bulgarus, for instruction on how to conduct a court case and what the norms of procedure were. Bulgarus responded with a treatise that drew exclusively on the Roman law procedure that he knew in Justinian's *Codex* and *Digest*. Haimeric's request was inevitable. Ecclesiastical courts and secular courts needed theoretical and practical information on how courts should function. Haimeric did not ask Bulgarus for an academic treatise; he asked him for solutions to the practical needs of the papal curia (Pennington, 2016b: 126–131).

Gratian taught with Bulgarus in Bologna and added much Roman law on procedure to the last version of his *Decretum*. He raised a series of questions about the rules of procedure that were central for resolving cases in twelfth-century society: Must a plaintiff be restored to his property before a trial? Can witnesses be drawn from the household of defendants? May someone younger than 14 testify in court? Must a defendant prove his innocence if his accusers' proofs failed?

The jurists called this procedure the *ordo iudiciarius*. The procedural rules that governed the *ordo* were adopted by ecclesiastical courts and secular courts during the twelfth and thirteenth centuries. Based on Roman law norms but leavened by Christian theological doctrines, the *ordo iudiciarius* governed the courtrooms of ecclesiastical courts in every corner of Christendom and the secular courts of the continent. Only the English common law courts were immune to its authority, but they too were influenced by it to a limited degree (Pennington, 2016b: 132–134). For the Christian legal tradition this pan-European court system created a powerful dynamic. As we shall see later in the discussion of the evolution of due process, when the jurists of the *Ius commune* debated the norms of procedure, they approached each issue equipped with a common understanding of the law that was forged by having been educated with the same set of texts of Roman and canon law. Perhaps even more remarkably, the ecclesiastical courts functioned for centuries alongside secular courts. Each had their jurisdictional boundaries – which sometimes gave rise to disputes between the Church and rulers – but for the most part exercised their 'divided sovereignty' without difficulty or dispute. Ecclesiastical courts heard cases that involved clerics, both criminal and civil, and any case in which an ecclesiastical institution, like a monastery, was embroiled. They also heard matters that pertained to marriage, divorce, and, depending on the issues, cases dealing with wills, contracts, and certain criminal offences. Ecclesiastical courts had the same coercive jurisdiction as secular courts. They could not, however, render any 'blood' decision that would impose the death penalty or any other mutilation of a person's body. They did, however, develop the practice of handing over persons who had been convicted of crimes' deserving harsh punishments to secular authorities, especially in cases of heresy.

At the end of the fourteenth century Gratian would have noticed an even more remarkable development in the jurisprudence of the *Ius commune*. Canon and Roman law had been the main material in every European law school curriculum for two and a half centuries, but now it was beginning to be difficult to tell the difference between a canonist and a Romanist. Since the beginning of the twelfth century canonists had understood that discipline could not exist without Roman law jurisprudence. By the middle of the twelfth century Gratian incorporated Irnerius's *authenticae* and many texts from Justinian's codification into his *Decretum*. The first glossators of the *Decretum* cited many texts from Roman law. The twelfth-century glossators of Justinian's codification also referred to Gratian. The teachers of Roman and canon law not only taught together but shared the same texts and problems. This cross-fertilization increased in the thirteenth century and can be seen in many areas of jurisprudence.

Christianity infused the *Ius commune* with fundamental ideas that shaped its jurisprudence: Natural law, biblical texts, and the dignity and rights of the human person. The centrality of natural law in the legal system was supported by Roman law. Christian theological traditions were also important sources for Christian jurisprudence. Further, the jurists who interpreted and taught Justinian's codification were influenced by the same sources as the canonists. This created a close relationship between the two laws of the *Ius commune*. An example of this symbiotic relationship of the two laws, as well as the importance of religious norms for the evolution of European legal thought, can be seen in the development of procedural norms and principles of due process in the thirteenth century, one of the most significant accomplishments of Christian jurisprudence (Pennington, 1998: 9–47).

The evolution of a sturdy doctrine of due process began in the middle of the twelfth century on a biblical source: the story of Adam and Eve in Genesis chapter 3. Two canonists concluded that God himself foreshadowed the *ordo iudiciarius* by confronting Adam and Eve in Paradise and demanding that they explain their actions. On the basis of this biblical example the jurists constructed an argument that retained its power and authority until the seventeenth century. No individual jurist rethought the juridical basis of due process; rather a number of them struggled with these issues over the next 50 years. It was not a development only within canonical jurisprudence. Pope Innocent IV had argued that a defendant's right to a trial could not be taken away. In the second half of the thirteenth century, the canonists and the Romanists (civilians) discussed the issue intensively. These jurists created an intricate and fruitful dialectic that eventually resulted in the first clear statement of a defendant's right to a trial in the history of jurisprudence.

In the 1250s and 1260s, a number of jurists explored the question of whether the prince could deny anyone a trial. A civilian, Odofredus de Denariis, discussed the prince's authority to deny his subject's the right of a hearing in court. The emperor can, he argued, deny an action for the recovery of a right that is derived from natural, civil, or pretorian law. Another civilian, Guido of Suzzara (†1293), picked up some of the threads in Odofredus' *Commentary*. Like Odofredus, he focused on the connection between a right protected by natural law and a person's right to pursue his case in court. Guido noted that the emperor cannot take away an action depriving a person of ownership because property rights were grounded in natural law.

The jurists after Guido quickly made the connection that Odofredus and Guido anticipated. An anonymous glossator of the *Digest* may have been the first to write that the right to a trial is derived from the law of nations, which had almost equal authority to natural law in the jurisprudence of the *Ius commune*. Significantly, he did not specify whether all actions are derived from the law of nations or only those actions based on the law of contract. The jurists had long concluded that natural law had established contracts.

At the end of the thirteenth century the jurists moved, slowly, toward the realization that in cases involving contracts a defendant had a fundamental right to a hearing, a trial, and to a defense. Since this right was founded on natural law, the prince could not unilaterally deprive a subject of it. Although these ideas did not immediately sweep the field – one can find examples of jurists steadfastly maintaining that actions were a part of civil law – they did become firmly entrenched in the literature.

The most sophisticated and complete summing up of juristic thinking about due process in the late thirteenth and early fourteenth centuries is found in the work of a canonist, Johannes Monachus. He was a French canonist who studied in Paris, became bishop of Meaux, and an advisor to Philip the Fair. He died in 1313. While glossing a *decretalis extravagans* of Boniface VIII (*Rem non novam*), he commented extensively on the rights of a defendant. He began by asking the question: Could the pope, on the basis of this decretal, proceed against a person if he had not cited him? Johannes concluded that the pope was not bound by positive law, but he could not violate natural law. Since a summons had been established by natural law, the pope could not omit it. He argued that no judge, even the pope, could come to a just decision unless the defendant was present in court. When a crime is notorious, the judge may proceed in a summary fashion in some parts of the process, but the summons and judgment must be preserved. A summons to court (*citatio*) and a judgment (*sententia*) were integral parts of the judicial process because an Old Testament text, Genesis 3.12, proved that both were necessary. Johannes referred to the history of the judicial process first told by the canonists Paucapalea and Stephen of Tournai and given final form by Guilielmus Durantis in the Prologue of his *Speculum iudiciale*. Even God was bound to summon Adam to render a defense. Perhaps persuaded by the inner logic of God's judgment of Adam and Eve, Johannes took medieval conceptions of due process one step further: Everyone is presumed innocent unless they are proven culpable; the law is more inclined to absolve than to condemn. Another canonist, Guilielmus Durantis, stretched this norm to its ultimate extreme: Even the devil should have his case heard in court.

An argument might be made that the pope or some other judge could know the truth about a case from secret sources and not learn them from the courtroom, but Johannes Monachus did not think that this objection was valid. A judge is not a private person and does not judge as one. He is a public person, and he should learn the truth publicly. Although the prince's will has the force of law if it is regulated by reason, his will without reason is not, according to Aristotle, 'a secure rule'. When the prince judges without a discussion and examination of a case, his will is not informed by reason. Finally, Johannes cited Aristotle again. There are two types of principalities: Despotic and politic. The first is similar to the relations between a slave and his master. The slave has no right to resist. The second is a polity of free men, who have the right of resistance. A free polity governs the Church; it is not a despotism.

Johannes's gloss is a remarkable defense of due process in law. Nothing in his gloss, however, is without antecedents, but no jurist before him had written such a thorough analysis of a defendant's right to a public and proper trial. His long commentary on *Rem non novam* was incorporated into the *Ius commune* and was read by thousands of jurists during the next three centuries. It is a splendid example of how the fusion of ancient Roman jurisprudence and canonical jurisprudence formed basic norms and principles of European legal systems.

The courts that investigated heresy, called the inquisitorial courts, were not one of the happy chapters in the Christian legal tradition and its court procedure. The courts were called 'inquisitorial' because an *inquisitio* or investigation was one of the standard methods, modes of proof, that had evolved in ecclesiastical procedure to investigate crimes in the second half of the twelfth century (Pennington, 2016a: 8–29). Pope Innocent III established norms for the procedure at the Fourth Lateran Council in 1215, and the jurists quickly expanded on the rules. By the end of the thirteenth century an *inquisitio* had gained equality with the older accusatorial mode of proof in both ecclesiastical and secular courts.

Pope Gregory IX was the first to appoint inquisitors whose sole purpose was to root out heresy in the 1230s. The mode of proof that the first judges used was inquisitorial that swiftly led to violating the basic rules of fairness that were enshrined in the jurisprudence governing court procedure. Pope Innocent III had equated heresy with treason. In Roman law, an accusation of treason deprived defendants of a number of procedural rights. Treason was the worst possible crime that a person could commit in the secular sphere. During the thirteenth century heretics and their followers were viewed as a horrific threat to the Church, Christian institutions, and society. Judges used these Roman law exceptions to due process as justifications for eliminating the procedural rights of defendants.

Although the 'Inquisitorial Courts of Heretical Depravity' generally followed the norms of procedure, as the thirteenth century progressed, their violations of defendants' rights became more prevalent. The Dominican and Franciscan orders provided many of the judges to inquisitorial courts. They sometimes brought zealotry and outrage to the courtroom. Key norms of the judicial process were altered, derogating the rights of defendants. The most important were that the witnesses were not identified and defendants were not permitted to have legal assistance.

The most important violation of canonical procedural norms was the use of torture. Pope Innocent IV opened the door to torture for the prosecution of heretics in 1252. The pope promulgated a set of constitutions that were instructions to secular judges in Lombardy on how they should prosecute heresy. Innocent compared heretics to bandits, murders, and thieves, and commanded that they should be interrogated in the same way but without damaging their bodies or putting them in danger of death. The unfortunate result of this papal mandate was that heresy became a crime for which torture could be employed by the inquisitorial courts with some regularity (Kelly, 2015: 773–777). Although torture was used sparingly by those courts, judges used torture to arrive at the truth well into the seventeenth century – if only rarely (Black, 2009: 81–88). Torture was a glaring exception to the centuries-old Christian legal tradition that blood should never be shed in the ecclesiastical courtroom. Societies, however, when faced with dangers the elites consider especially threatening, often revert to barbaric measures.

Another significant part of Christian jurisprudence after Gratian was its radical departure from Roman law's treatment of women in marriage law and procedure. The norms of marriage law the jurists found in Justinian's codification focused on consent of the parents as being the key element in a valid marriage. Pope Alexander III's (1159–1181) appellate court decisions were crucial for abolishing parental power over their children's marriage. As a result of these decretals that were immediately incorporated into canonical jurisprudence, the free consent of the woman and the man, not their parents, became the touchstone of a marriage's validity until the sixteenth century. An unintended result of this change was the proliferation of clandestine marriages. In the sixteenth century, the Catholic Church promulgated the decree *Tametsi* at the Council of Trent (1563) to deal with the problem. *Tametsi* required that a marriage was not valid unless it was publicly proclaimed and presided over by a priest, i.e., *in facie ecclesiae*. The consent of the Church replaced parental consent. Protestant churches re-established parental consent at the same time (Witte, 2006: 580–605). In any case, during the medieval and early modern periods, women were given equality to men in marriage law.

Roman law limited women's legal rights in many ways. Beginning in the twelfth century, the jurists of the *Ius commune* rejected many of those limitations. Consequently, by the beginning of the thirteenth century, as the most distinguished scholar who has studied the procedural rights of women in ecclesiastical courts has written: 'Before an ecclesiastical judge, indeed, a woman was then (i.e., in the early thirteenth century) completely equal to a man. She could, as he could, have the right to bring a court case (ius accusandi)' (Minnucci, 1994: 279).

The institutionalization of legal studies in European law schools meant that not only did their jurisprudence merge but also the jurists' self-image. By the end of the fourteenth century many jurists would have been puzzled by the question 'are you a civilian or a canonist?' Religious law and ancient Roman law had become perfectly fused together. Baldus de Ubaldis (†1400) is an example (Pennington, 1997: 35–61). He wrote commentaries on Roman, canon, and feudal law texts. He also taught all three laws. Most significantly, he wrote thousands of *consilia* (legal opinions) for judges and litigants in which he dealt with canonical and secular problems. He could be considered a model jurist for the late medieval *Ius commune*.

The Protestant Reformation rebelled against papal authority but did not destroy the importance of canonical jurisprudence and the *Ius commune*. All the Reformers, to a lesser or greater extent, incorporated the medieval *Ius commune*, shaped by canonical, Roman, and feudal jurisprudence, into their legislation and legal thought. Protestant jurists were aware of the debt owed to Roman canon law. Conrad Lagus (†1546) had warned his Protestant colleagues that the canonists' jurisprudence on procedure, the *ordo iudiciarius*, was essential for the functioning of the law courts:

> At the same time I warn you not to reject the *Ius canonicum* and its judicial norms. They preserve the customs of common usage. Since these rights are now observed everywhere in the courts, they expedite cases when conducting trials.

The Protestant jurists who taught medieval canon law at the reformed universities limited their teaching and publishing to certain books and subjects, especially marriage and procedure (Pennington, 2015).

The jurisprudence of canon law had been intricately entwined with secular law and norms for centuries. While the reformers could easily disentangle Catholic theological thought and traditions from their more pristine set of beliefs, they could not just as easily reject Catholic jurisprudence and norms embedded in the teachings of canon law and return to a purified set of legal norms. Luther had studied law. He and other law students had absorbed the doctrines, norms, and institutions of the *Ius commune* from the past four centuries. As we have seen, every law school in Europe had a curriculum in which students studied canon law, Roman law in its medieval guise, and feudal law. The *libri legales* were not balkanized into different disciplines but integrated into a set of common texts.

There was another avenue for Christian jurisprudence's influence on the world of law. With the settlement of the New World in the sixteenth century, Portugal and Spain ruled over Central and South America. Those powers had not yet replaced the institutions of the *Ius commune*, and the *Ius commune* followed in the footsteps of the conquistadors. In North America where English common law and Protestant jurisprudence held sway, the broad jurisprudence of the *Ius commune* had very little influence. The rights and equality of human beings had become a key feature of Christian jurisprudence supported by natural law. Historians have often noted that Spain was the only colonial power in which questions about just titles, ownership of human beings, and just sovereignty of native peoples arose. The other colonial powers at this time, especially the English and the Dutch, never were compelled to consider the rights of the natives.

The Iberian jurists who lived in the New World brought their law books with them. They recognized injustice when they saw it and were dismayed. Bartolomé de las Casas (†1566), Diego de Avendaño (†1688–1698?), and others condemned the enslavement of natives and objected to the Spanish mistreatment of them. They questioned the legitimacy of the conquests and had more than a little success in Spanish courts. The sources that Las Casas used suggest a reason for this. Because of the conflicts with Muslims during the medieval period, the *Ius commune* was forced to develop theories that were preliminary to a nascent international law. It was still a powerful force and tool in Catholic lands in the early modern period. In contrast, when the Reformation came to England and the Low Countries, much of the jurisprudence of 'popish' law was destroyed – except in the areas that we have noted – or at least rendered ineffectual. Protestant jurists, Hugo Grotius (†1645), often called the Father of International law, and Samuel von Pufendorf (†1694) incorporated the ideas of Las Casas and the Spanish jurists into their works, but their texts and sources did not have the same authority in the courtrooms of the Northern colonial powers. Consequently, even if there would have been someone, a Las Casas in England or Holland, he would not have had authoritative sources with which to support his arguments. The plight of the native North American Indians in the past and today may, in some measure, be traced to the destruction of three centuries of legal philosophizing and more importantly the abandonment of 500 years of basic, authoritative legal texts in the sixteenth-century Northern European law schools (Pennington, 2018).

There is one last ironic twist in the story of canon law's influence on European legal systems. The direct influence of the *Ius commune*, Roman and canon law, ended in the seventeenth and eighteenth centuries with the emergence of the nation state and with the *iura propria*'s becoming main material for teaching law. However, the influence of canon law began to wane much earlier. At the Fifth Lateran Council and at the Council of Trent in the sixteenth century, the popes mandated that the canons of the councils could not be interpreted outside the Roman curia. That meant they could not be commented on or taught in the classroom. This led to diminishing the importance of canonistic teaching and scholarship as a source of law. The papacy was keenly aware that the writings and opinions of the canonists had for centuries shaped the law of the Church (Sinisi 2016: 209–229). By the early sixteenth century Rome wanted to have one source of law in the Church: Rome. Roman centralization in the first half of the sixteenth century was the first step in the secularization of European law and the separation of religious law from it. Roman canon law became isolated from secular law and exercised much less influence on it.

Christian religious law from the seventeenth to the twentieth centuries is the story of fragmentation and in some cases a return to the antinomianism of early Christians. A few of the Protestant sects maintained much more continuity with earlier traditions than others. English canon law kept much of Roman canon law intact but substituted the English monarch for the pope. With the centralization of legislation and of interpretation in Rome, the jurists who taught canon law in the schools lost much of their importance. It is not by chance that the last massive commentaries on the books of the *Corpus iuris canonici* were written in the early seventeenth centuries. The canonists turned to another type of literature: Encyclopedic historical coverage of all aspects of canonical jurisprudence. They produced large multi-volume works arranged according to the structure of the *Corpus iuris canonici*. Two forces destroyed the importance of canon law in the law schools of the *Ius commune*: The papacy and the growing importance of the various *iura propria*, the national legal systems, in the seventeenth century. Of course, the *iura propria* led to the demise of the study of Roman law too.

Within the Catholic tradition, it is ironic that when the Catholic Church promulgated the *Codex iuris canonici* of 1917 that replaced the *Corpus iuris canonici*, it abandoned in large part its jurisprudential tradition. Until 1917 Roman Catholic canon law was based on conciliar legislation, papal mandates, and papal appellate decisions. It was a 'case law' tradition. Instead of building upon that tradition, the compilers of the *Codex* turned to the secular codifications of the eighteenth and nineteenth centuries for a model. In turn, these codifications were arranged according to the principles of ancient Roman law, especially the organization of Justinian's *Institutes*. This model broke significantly from the historical roots of secular and religious law. Its format has plagued Catholic canon law ever since 1917. Legal systems that are based on codes have one great disadvantage: They are inert. In the 1990s, Manlio Bellomo argued that rigid codes of laws are outdated, cannot respond to changes in society, and must be replaced by a more flexible source of law (Bellomo, 1994: 29–33). The new *Codex iuris canonici* of 1983 and the 1990 Code of canons of the Oriental Churches changed the content and internal structure of the 1917 *Codex*, abandoning the model of Justinian's *Institutes* and adopting a systematic centered around the theological notion of 'people of God'. However, they did not depart from the codification model.

The Christian religious legal tradition's central characteristics have triumphed and penetrated every secular legal system in spite of its fragmentation in early modern Europe. Its norms are reflected in all the major Western legal attempts to formulate a set of basic principles that should be respected. The French 'Declaration of the Rights of Man and the Citizen' of 1789 embodied many of the principles that had evolved as part of the *Ius commune*. Men 'and women' are born free and equal. The common good must regulate society. Men 'and women' have natural rights, and every man 'and woman' is presumed innocent. These same principles have been repeated again and again until they were codified in the Universal Declaration of Human Rights in 1948. While contemplating the unusual emphasis in the Western legal traditions on human rights, Brian Tierney summed up the significance of the Christian legal tradition with this observation: 'Western Europe in the twelfth century, the interactions of religion and society did in fact form a new kind of Christian culture, a sort of seedbed in which theories of human rights and civil rights could take root and flourish' (Tierney, 1987: 164). Tierney was aware that the Christian tradition could also produce lamentable intolerance, but in the end the rights of human beings prevailed. The French revolutionary motto could be considered a shorthand definition of the entire Christian legal tradition: *Liberté, égalité, fraternité*.

Further reading

Hess, H. 2002. *The Early Development of Canon Law and the Council of Serdica*. Oxford University Press.
Jasper, D. 2001. 'The Beginning of the Decretal Tradition' in W. Hartmann and K. Pennington (eds) *Papal Letters in the Early Middle Ages*. The Catholic University of America Press. 3.
Pennington, K. 2016a. 'Introduction' in W. Hartmann and K. Pennington (eds) *The History of Courts and Procedure in Medieval Canon Law*. The Catholic University of America Press. 3 ff.

References

Bellomo, M. 1994. *The Common Legal Past of Europe, 1000–1800*. Translated by L. G. Cochrane. The Catholic University of American Press.
Black. C. F. 2009. *The Italian Inquisition*. Yale University Press.
Blumenthal, U.-R. 1988. *The Investiture Controversy: Church and Monarchy from the Ninth to the Twelfth Century*. University of Pennsylvania Press.
Blumenthal, U.-R. 2001. *Gregor VII.: Papst zwischen Canossa un Kirchenreform*. Primus Verlag.
Duggan, A. 2004. *Thomas Becket*. Arnold.
Gallagher, C. 2002. *Church Law and Church Order in Rome and Byzantium: A Comparative Study*. Ashgate.
Hartmann, W. 1993. 'Der Investiturstreit' in *Enzyklopädie deutscher Geschichte*. Vol. 21. R. Oldenbourg. 149.
Helmholz, R. H. 1996. *The Spirit of Classical Canon Law*. University of Georgia Press.
Kelly, H. A. 2015. 'Judicial Torture in Canon Law and Church Tribunals: From Gratian to Galileo'. 101 *The Catholic Historical Review*. 754.
Lange, H. 1997. *Römisches Recht im Mittelalter, 1. Die Glossatoren*. C. H. Beck.
Minnucci, G. 1994. *La capacità processuale della donna nel pensiero canonistico classico, 2: Dalle scuole d'oltralpe a S. Raimondo di Pennaforte*. Quaderni di 'Studi senesi' 79. Milano: A. Giuffrè.
Pennington, K. 1997. 'Baldus de Ubaldis'. 8 *Rivista internazionale di diritto commune*. 35.
Pennington, K. 1998. 'Due Process, Community, and the Prince in the Evolution of the Ordo iudiciarius'. 9 *Rivista internazionale di diritto commune*. 9.
Pennington, K. 2004. 'Natural Law' in *Dictionary of the Middle Ages: Supplement 1*. Thomson-Gale. 417.
Pennington, K. 2007. 'The Growth of Church Law' in F. Norris and A. Casiday (eds) *The Cambridge History of Christianity, 2: Constantine to c. 600*. Cambridge University Press. 386.
Pennington, K. 2008. 'The Decretalists 1190–1234' in W. Hartmann and K. Pennington (eds) *The History of Canon Law in the Classical Period, 114–1234: From Gratian to the Decretals of Pope Gregory IX*. The Catholic University of America Press. 211.
Pennington, K. 2010. 'Caesaropapism' in *The New Catholic Encyclopedia: Supplement 2010*. Gale. 1183.
Pennington, K. 2011. 'Lex naturalis and Ius naturale' in S. E. Young (ed.) *Crossing Boundaries at Medieval Universities*. Brill. 227.
Pennington, K. 2012. 'The Beginning of Roman Law Jurisprudence and Teaching in the Twelfth Century: The *Authenticae*'. 22 *Rivista internazionale di diritto commune*. 35.
Pennington, K. 2014. 'La biografia di Graziano, il Padre del diritto canonico'. 25 *Rivista internazionale di diritto comune*. 25.
Pennington, K. 2015. Protestant Ecclesiastical Law and the Ius commune. *Rivista internazionale di diritto comune* 26. 9.
Pennington, K. 2016b. 'The Jurisprudence of Procedure' in W. Hartmann and K. Pennington (eds) *The History of Courts and Procedure in Medieval Canon Law*. The Catholic University of America Press. 126 ff.
Pennington, K. 2018. 'Bartolomé de las Casas' in R. Domingo and J. Martínez-Torrón (eds) *Great Christian Jurists in Spanish History*. Cambridge University Press. 98.
Radding, C.M. and Ciaralli, A. 2007. *The Corpus iuris civilis in the Middle Ages: Manuscripts and Transmission from the Sixth Century to the Juristic Revival*. Brill.
Sinisi, L. 2016. 'The Commentaries on the Tridentine Decrees in the Sixteenth and Seventeenth Centuries: The First Remarks on a Category of "Prohibited" Works"'. *Bulletin of Medieval Canon Law* 33. 209.
Southern, R. W. 1995. *Scholastic Humanism and the Unification of Europe*, 1: *Foundations*. Oxford University Press.
Tanner, N. 1990. *Decrees of the Ecumenical Councils*, 1: *Nicaea I-Lateran V*, 2: *Trent-Vatican II*. 2 Vols. Georgetown University Press.
Tierney, B. 1987. 'Religion and Rights: A Medieval Perspective'. 5 *Journal of Law and Religion*. 163.
Tierney, B. 1988. *The Crisis of Church and State 1050–1300*. University of Toronto Press.

Tierney, B. 2014. *Liberty & Law: The Idea of Permissive Natural Law, 1100–1800*. The Catholic University Press of America.
Troianos, S. 2012a. 'Byzantine Canon Law to 1100' in W. Hartmann and K. Pennington (eds) *The History of Byzantine and Eastern Canon Law to 1500*. The Catholic University Press of America, 115.
Troianos, S. 2012b. 'Byzantine Canon Law from the Twelfth to the Fifteenth Centuries' in W. Hartmann and K. Pennington (eds) *The History of Byzantine and Eastern Canon Law to 1500*. The Catholic University Press of America, 170.
Vinogradoff, P. G. 1909. *Roman Law in Medieval Europe*. Harpers.
Wessel, S. 2012. 'The Formation of Ecclesiastical Law in the Early Church' in W. Hartmann and K. Pennington (eds) *The History of Byzantine and Eastern Canon Law to 1500*. The Catholic University Press of America, 1.
Witte, J. 2006. 'Honor Thy Father and Thy Mother? Child Marriage and Parental Consent in John Calvin's Geneva'. 8 *Journal of Religion*. 580.

3

The Islamic tradition

A history

Knut S. Vikør

The historiography of the early development of Islamic law, the *Sharī'a*, is highly contentious both among Muslims and secular historians. Thus, it is impossible to provide a single history that all will agree to. There is, however, general agreement that the sources of revelation only formed the raw material for the law of Islam and that its formulation is the result of human endeavour by fallible scholars. Thus, the history of this human endeavour can be an object of research.

For the believer, God revealed what He chose to reveal to the Prophet Muḥammad (ca. 570–632 CE), through His direct speech in the Qur'ān and through His guidance of the Prophet. Muḥammad's acts and sayings are known as his *Sunna* and are expressed in a body of individual narratives called the *ḥadīth*. Most Muslim scholars accept that the statements in the Qur'ān and Sunna must be explained and systematized before they can become an applicable set of rules. The process of formulating rules of conduct on the basis of revelation is known as *ijtihād*, and it is the formative part of the scholarly pursuit of jurisprudence, *fiqh* (Schacht, 1964; Kamali, 1991; Vikør, 2005; Hallaq, 2009). The latter term literally means 'understanding' and is thus the human element of the formation of the law, but Muslim scholars insist that as what they do is to uncover the divine will, it is not law-making, only elucidation of what God has decided, according to the ability of the scholar. A just Muslim society must have knowledge of this Sharī'a and apply it.

Origins

For the believer, the question of *why* the early Muslims immediately began a process of defining rules of conduct does not pose itself: it was God's will and intention. The historian, however, will link the genesis of this process to the unrolling of events in the early years. Muḥammad began his proselytization in the polytheist town of Mecca. Having gained a following of younger Meccans, he was increasingly seen as a threat by the leading circles in Mecca and was forced to emigrate to the rival town Yathrīb, or Medina as it became known (Watt, 1956).

On arrival, Muḥammad signed an agreement with the tribes of Medina, which established his position there. However, his group of supporters in Mecca had come with him. In the stateless society of the Arabian town, the only way to exist socially or politically was as a member of a tribe. The emigrants were of course still members of their tribes and families in Mecca, but these were now their enemies and could not provide them with protection. To attach them to local Medinan tribes as 'clients' was clearly not seen as an option, Muḥammad himself would then also have to be a subservient client. Thus, the only logical solution was that the emigrants became a separate community with Muḥammad as their leader. But as this community could not be based on tribal affiliation, nor one of kingdom, some other definition of them had to be found. The logical one was what they had in common: religion. So, the original group of believers coming from Mecca became a political entity under Muḥammad because that was the only way to provide an existential framework for the emigrants. And the community then needed rules of authority, which Islam had to provide.

As the Muslim community rapidly expanded to become an empire in the first two generations after the Prophet, the need for a more elaborate legal framework became even more pressing. Not so much for the conquered peoples, Christians in majority, as they were allowed to maintain the social and legal system from before the conquest. But the Muslim armies and later settlers found themselves in new and unfamiliar surroundings that raised new problems that required answers. As the empire grew, the issue of standardization also rose: the various conquered provinces had a widely varied background and history. Should these regional differences prevail, or should a unified law for the Muslim empire be established?

There were three main possible sources for a new legal system. One was the tribal law of the Arabic peninsula, which the new rulers were familiar with (Nallino, 1940; Schacht, 1950; Vikør, 2014). Another was the existing legal systems of the conquered provinces, Roman law in Syria and Persian law in Iraq – in practice, the 'provincial' Roman law was the main contender for influence here (Goldziher, 1904; Crone, 1987). The third was a new legal and ethical system based on the religious precepts of Islam, as it developed in the first decades after the Prophet's death (al-Azami, 1985; Hallaq, 1990, 2002, 2009). Historians have conflicted sharply over the relevant weight of these three systems in the early period, from those who claim the first caliphs simply adopted Roman law and gave it an Islamic cover, to those who insist the caliphs to the best of their ability emulated the example of the Prophet in Medina with no regard for other worldly sources. One intriguing alternative theory has been put forward by the historians Patricia Crone and Martin Hinds (Crone and Hinds, 1986). They claim that the very first caliphs saw themselves as equals to the Prophet. Cosmic time was divided into two by the Prophet's death. Until then, God spoke to mankind through recurring prophets and messengers. With the Qur'ān, this period of revelation came to an end and ushered in the second era, that of the caliphs. They were now God's representative on earth (in Arabic, *khalīfat Allāh*), and religious authority sprang from them.

If the early caliphs thought in this way, their caliphal arrogance only lasted a generation or less. They came instead to be seen as *khalīfat rasūl Allāh*, the representative or successor of Muḥammad, not God, and clearly not a successor in his capacity as prophet, but as the worldly leader of the community of believers, *amīr al-mu'minīn*. But it is more than likely that legal authority in this early period still sprang from the caliph and his governors in regulating the affairs of Muslim garrisons and communities in their newly acquired territories. To help the governor to administer the local Muslims, they appointed aides called *qāḍīs* that could make decisions on the governor's behalf (Tillier, 2009). This term *qāḍī* was then later transmuted into the judge of the Sharīʿa courts when such developed.

We have few indications of how these earliest institutions judged and thus how far their decisions were based on religious morality, tribal ethics or borrowings from Roman law. Some historians would however want to reduce the importance of the difference between the three elements. The nomadic Arabic tribes had been in continuous contact with Syria and Iraq, and their practices were already influenced by the moral and legal thinking there, while the Roman law had taken on a local colour from the same region (Hallaq, 1990). Thus, the differences between these three sources for early Muslim law may not be as formidable as sometimes assumed.

The traditional Muslim historiography of *fiqh* does not, however, focus particularly on this 'practised' caliphal law, but rather on the development of groups of religious scholars who were particularly concerned with the law. In a traditional categorization of the early scholars (plural *ʿulamāʾ*), two types are often identified. One is those interested in collecting and transmitting *ḥadīth* narratives about the Prophet. Such scholars met in gatherings called *mudhākarāt* (rememberings) where they exchanged *ḥadīth* (Melchert, 1997: 1–31). The purpose was to excel in knowing as many *ḥadīth* as possible, with little or no critical appreciation. The scholar who could recite the largest number of *ḥadīth* was the most prominent whether these narratives contradicted each other or not. The method was thus cumulative, to add to your store of Prophetic traditions.

The other type of scholars was those who sought to find answers to problems that might arise. These also met and exchanged views, but the purpose here was to arrive at one solution which was correct and the others incorrect. These contests were called *munāẓarāt* (investigations) and were thus not cumulative but competitive. The method was logical and discursive. We are not sure how this logic developed, as the views we have reported from them may have been adjusted later to what then became established methodology. A common assumption, however, is that their basis for decision was *sunna*, practice, in an earlier meaning: the established practice in the Muslim community *here* (Schacht, 1964: 28–33; Hallaq, 2001). That is, that there was one *sunna* in Damascus in Syria, which should be followed there, and another in Kufa in Iraq. Those who lived in Medina gave their own local *sunna* a special authority, since that was the original centre of the Muslim community where the Prophet had resided, and thus was most likely where the earliest and most authoritative practice was maintained (Dutton, 1999; Brockopp, 2000). However, the actual practice of the Prophet himself was not given decisive authority in this first period. As late as the end of the eighth century, the prominent scholar Mālik ibn Anas (d. 795) could state that the Prophet had given such and such an answer, but the established practice in Medina had come to be so and so, and that was then the correct answer.

From this, the two main approaches of these earliest generation of scholars came to be known as the Madinan school of thought and the Iraqi or Kufan school (Kufa being the dominant city in Iraq at this time). However, these geographic terms are probably misleading, as there was no unanimity in Kufa and certainly not in Iraq as a whole, and the earlier groupings of scholars, such as they were, were probably much looser and cut across geography than the term 'schools' would indicate.

It is also not clear how distinct these budding legal discussions, or 'living traditions' as they were called (Schacht, 1964: 29), were from the legal practices of the state. Muslim historiographers tend to emphasize that the caliphs (or at least good and pious caliphs) did their best to implement the Sharīʿa on the Prophet's example and listened to the scholars. Still, it is probably best to consider the law of the governors and the legal discussions of the independent scholars as analytically distinct in these first centuries, although it must be assumed that each was informed by the other to a larger or smaller degree. One indication of this is the exacerbated musings of Ibn al-Muqaffāʿ (d. 757), the secretary of the first caliph in Baghdad, Manṣūr. He said that all these different opposing views of the scholars were confusing and difficult to practise (Opwis, 2010: 14–15). The new caliph should collect them all and then on his own authority decide which version of each rule was the law to be applied. However, this first lonely voice for a codified law of Islam had no consequence.

A more serious attempt by the caliph to assert religious authority was the conflict called the *Mihna*, although that concerned a theological and not a legal issue: whether the Qur'ān was created in time or was an eternal aspect of God (Watt, 1998: 178–250). The caliph Ma'mūn (d. 833) tried to impose the former view as an official theology but was met with strong resistance by the scholars, and the policy of a 'state Islam' was abandoned after about twenty years. From this moment on, then, the *'ulamā'* were able to establish their control over doctrinal matters, including the development of law, and deny the caliph any position of 'pope'.

In spite of these conflicts, historians agree that the injunctions that are unequivocally stated in the Qur'ān were from the beginning recognized and followed by caliphs and by scholars. The issue to be settled was the authority of the Prophetic *ḥadīth* versus established pre-Islamic practices and/or the caliph's own opinions in the first century or two of Islam, and how to derive legal rules from the sources of revelation.

As mentioned, the early scholars should rather be seen as independent than as members of any of the 'schools' that appeared later and which they were retroactively linked to. But some of these legal scholars came to be remembered as particularly influential. Four of them are today remembered as the 'founders of the four schools of law', or the 'four *imāms*' of Sunnī Islam. They all lived in the late eighth and early ninth centuries: Abū Ḥanīfa (d. 767), Mālik ibn Anas (d. 795), Muḥmmmad ibn Idrīs al-Shāfi'ī (d. 820) and Aḥmad ibn Ḥanbal (d. 855). There were however many other scholars of comparative status. Thus Muḥammad al-Shaybānī (d. 804) and Abū Yūsuf (d. 798) are today considered the two foremost followers of Abū Ḥanīfa but were most likely seen as independent and influential scholars in their own time.

The development of the *madhhabs*

As the new state solidified, in particular after the rise of the Abbasid dynasty and the move to Baghdad in the mid-eighth century, the problem of relying on 'our practice here' became more evident. A homogenization of the law to promote the unity of the empire was required. Thus, legal discussions began to look for a shared source of authority. Slowly, this began to be seen as the practice of Muḥammad and the earliest community of Medina. Thus, the *mudhākarāt* transmissions of the original *ḥadīth* transmitters and the *munāẓarāt* of the legal scholars both became important, in that the stories of the Prophet's statements and actions came to be seen as the major authority for the legal rules (besides the Qur'ān). This development did not happen without conflict, however. The legal scholars were divided between those who would put the main emphasis on the Prophet's example, the *ahl al-ḥadīth*, and those who held on to established practices and logical discourse, the *ahl al-ra'y*. Eventually, however, *ra'y*, originally meaning 'the correct view, our *sunna* here', became an expression of abuse, 'personal whim without Prophetic authority', and *sunna* came to mean the Prophet's practice only, not the local practices of the various Muslim regions.

The transition from *ra'y* to *ḥadīth* as the basis for law is normally credited to the most famous scholar of legal methodology, Muḥammad ibn Idrīs al-Shāfi'ī (Schacht, 1950: 11–20; Hallaq, 1997: 21–35). However, for *ḥadīth* to be usable as a source of law, the uncritical accumulation of all stories about the Prophet had to be abandoned, and a methodology for sifting the *ḥadīth* was developed. This process will be discussed in Chapter 8, on the sources of revelation. Suffice it here to state that the process of '*ḥadīth* studies' began in the late eighth or ninth century and has never really ended. Al-Shāfi'ī died in 820, but his Prophet-centred methodology was probably only universally adopted about a century after his death (Hallaq, 1993). He is also credited with founding one of the four *madhhabs*, but his methodology has influenced all four schools, with variations.

The individual efforts of legal scholars then also began to be institutionalized. The major scholars had of course always had students who transmitted their statements and defended their views against rivals. It was however only from the tenth century that we see these students organize themselves with a generally accepted leadership in each town, recognized centres of learning and a fixation of legal views into a clear body of opinion. In this process, the amorphous groups of scholars began to coalesce into structured groups. One way to date this development is to look at the biographies of the legal scholars. The early scholars can be described as following the opinion of such and such an authority, but different biographers may disagree about which authority he followed, or we find that he disagrees with his 'master' as much as he agrees. However, for scholars living from the eleventh century on, there is no such wavering in the biographies. At that time, structures had been established with a basic set of opinions according to a methodology specific to them and set out in a shared literature (Melchert, 1997: 54–67). Eventually, the aspiring scholar was bound to follow one and only one such set of methods and opinions, disregarding those of other groups. Thus, they had become 'schools of law', *madhhabs* (literally, 'methods'). These shared a common legal basis but were both methodologically and in their legal rules (*aḥkām*) separate, so rather than one Islamic law, we can for the classical period rather speak of four Islamic laws within Sunnism, with noticeable differences of opinion within each *madhhab*.

Clearly, this did not happen overnight. Today, we speak of four and only four schools in the majority Sunnism, while the various branches of Shīʿī Islam each have their own *madhhab*. For the latter, law schools follow theological divisions, but the four Sunnī schools are only marginally linked to theological diversity. It is better to see them as the final, imperfect, attempt at reaching a consensus in law in the absence of a fixed authority that could determine one authoritative opinion for all of Sunnī Islam. (For reasons of brevity, we will focus on Sunnī law here, but much of Shīʿī legal history is parallel but separate.)

We should thus see the formation of the four Sunnī schools of law as a process in retrospect. The foundational authority of the Qurʾān was always there, but the authority of the prophet Muḥammad as a legal source grew over the first two or three centuries. When the traditional Muslim historiography says that the early Muslims immediately after the Prophet's death saw his example as the touchstone for correct behaviour, a more critical historical interpretation would suggest that this is, at least in part, a projection backwards of a view that came to be dominant much later, in the same way that the status of the four 'founders' of the schools of law were elevated to unassailable authorities only centuries after their deaths (Vikør, 2005: 89–113). They were in their lifetime prominent scholars but not necessarily in law. Ibn Ḥanbal was a *ḥadīth* scholar who appears to have been suspicious of the very nature of *fiqh* as a human legal endeavour (Melchert, 1997: 13–18). But later his opinions were collected and formed the basis for the *madhhab* that bears his name.

Neither were they the only 'founders'; a number of other scholars were also credited with having formed schools of law, although they themselves were probably equally unaware that they had done so. Notable among these was al-Awzāʿī (d. 774), who represented the *sunna* of Damascus and Syria (as opposed to the Iraqi views of his contemporary Abū Ḥanīfa), but who fell out of favour partly because Damascus became a backwater when the capital was moved to Baghdad in the Abbasid revolution of 750 (Schacht, 1950: 119, 288–289). Ṣufyān al-Thawrī (d. 778) and Jarīr al-Ṭabarī (d. 930) had legal scholars who followed them probably until the eleventh or twelfth century but eventually merged with the four dominant schools (Schacht, 1964: 60; Melchert, 1997: 3–6, 191–197). One particular current that may or may not have been a school, was the Ẓāhirīs whom we really only hear about through the denunciations by their opponents. They are named from their consistent, but impractical view that the texts of revelation must be practised literally (*ẓāhirī*) rather than through human interpretation (Goldziher, 1971 [1884]; Osman, 2014). Thus, they made a useful polemical contrast to whatever point other legal authors wanted to explain. Only in the eleventh century, in far-off Andalus, do we find a positive exposition of a Ẓāhirī set of rules by the brilliant scholar Ibn Ḥazm (d. 1065). His opinions, which he sought to anchor directly in the sources rather than through legal discourse, was however not followed outside of his time.

Thus the Sunnī world settled on the four schools of Ḥanafīs, Mālikīs, Shāfiʿīs and Ḥanbalīs. Although they were all formed in the central lands of Islam, they began from about the thirteenth to fourteenth centuries to be distributed geographically. North Africa west of Egypt and later West Africa follows the Mālikī school; the Shāfiʿīs dominate the Indian Ocean from East Africa over South Arabia to South-East Asia, as well as being strong in Egypt and Syria; and the Ḥanafī school dominates wherever Turks or Mongols have held sway, from Anatolia over Central Asia to India. The fourth school, the Ḥanbalīs, was the youngest and did not have a geographical basis before the Wahhābī movement adopted it in what was to become Saudi Arabia in the eighteenth century. But it was always present among scholars in the major centres of learning.

The 'orthodox' view was that, while a commoner need not choose a particular *madhhab* (although geography may not have given them much choice), a legal scholar had to stay within the jurisprudence of his own school and could not pick and choose opinions between them. Nevertheless, the schools were generally tolerant towards each other under the principle of *ikhtilāf*, divergence. God had revealed his intent in the revelation, but the elaboration of legal rules on this basis was by necessity a fallible human activity, and no scholar could arrogate for himself the authority to speak on behalf of God. Thus, it was the duty of the scholar to work as hard as possible to discover what God's intention was, but ultimately, he could be wrong and an opposite view, equally based in work on the Revealed texts, correct. This is expressed in the final sentence of any legal text and opinion, '*wa'llāhu aʿlam*', 'but God knows best'. A commonly held *ḥadīth* says that any scholar who does his utmost to provide a legal opinion and discovers God's intent, will receive two rewards in Heaven, one for the effort and one for being correct. The one who does his utmost but is wrong, will receive a single reward, for his effort (al-Bukhārī, 'Iʿtiṣām' 20–1, in Vikør, 2005: 73n). It must be noted, however, that this tolerant view was challenged by the opposing one that rejected the corresponding expression '*kull mujtahid muṣīb*' (every scholar who does his utmost in finding an answer, is correct). God has only one opinion which is the correct one and must be found, in accordance with the alternative statement of the Prophet that 'My community will split into 72 sects, and 71 of them will end up in Hell' (al-Tirmidhī, 'Imān' 18, in Vikør, 2005: 73n). The more tolerant view has however prevailed in most of Muslim history.

In practical terms, this meant that in the regions where a single school was dominant, such as North Africa, there was only one court, practising the *madhhab* of that region. But in much of the Middle East, several schools overlapped, and in the largest cities like Cairo and Damascus all four schools were present (Escovitz, 1984; Rappaport, 2003). There, various types of accommodation were found over time, be it a separate court for each *madhhab*, or that judges from different schools could be attached to the same court. Either way, each judge should rule according to his own school's opinion only. But once a judge had ruled in a case, his decision was respected by the other judges in that town, even though their school would have ruled differently. Thus, a disgruntled plaintiff could not go from one court to the other to seek a better solution. In theory, it was the defendant who had the right to select which judge or court a conflict should be settled in, but this may not have worked out easily, as most court cases consisted of claims and counter-claims, and it was part of the judge's job to decide who was the actual plaintiff and who the defendant.

The basis for the law

The area of competence of the Sharīʿa stretches beyond what we would call law and encompasses all acts for which God has a plan for human behaviour. Muslim scholars recognized this distinction by dividing the area of the Sharīʿa into two: on the one hand, man's relations to God, called *ʿibadāt*, worship; and on the other, man's relations with man, *muʿāmalāt*, 'works' or 'interrelations'.

The distinction between *ʿibadāt* and *muʿāmalāt* may seem to correlate with what we respectively would say was outside and inside the field of law. It must be emphasized that the methodology and sources of the Sharīʿa made no distinction between the two, only that it was the latter category of conflicts that would appear in court. But some acts which we definitely would call legally relevant, and brutally so, were considered to be part of *ʿibādāt*. Those were the *ḥudūd* rules, five or six criminal acts that were given specific and brutal punishments: stoning for adultery, amputation for theft, whipping for drunkenness (Vikør, 2005: 282–287). They are singled out because scholars consider that in these, not only the transgression but also the punishment was spelled out in the Qurʾān (albeit with some problems for the stoning penalty, see Chapter 8, this volume). Thus, God set up those five penalties as His borders, *ḥudūd*, for behaviour and the believer cannot therefore question them but must follow them simply because God said so, like the rules for prayer and fasting.

This view did not, however, deter later scholars from fencing in the *ḥudūd* with conditions and requirements that made them hard or sometimes impossible to actually apply. They could do this because in the fifth *ḥudūd* rule, the Qurʾān says that anyone who accuses another of adultery without providing exceptional proof (four witnesses instead of two) should himself be whipped. This was taken as a general indication that for the *ḥudūd* to be applied, particularly stringent requirements of proof must be filled.

The law, the scholars and the state

After the episode of the *mihna*, the division of labour in the legal field was fairly straightforward, at least in the view of the scholars. The competent scholars of law, the *fuqahāʾ*, formulated the law, and the *sulṭān*, the ruler, put it into practice. This was exemplified in stories of the great caliphs sitting at the feet of the great scholars and adopting their decisions (Vikør, 1996: 51). The reality was probably somewhat different. On the one hand, it may be seen as something of an anomaly that a state power should so easily abandon control over what is sometimes seen as the definition of the state: the legitimate use of coercion. The scholars should be financially independent from the state. They were not appointed to scholarship by the ruler, neither did they take orders from him. Indeed, to refuse the sultan's money which by default was illegitimate – as all rulers went beyond the strict rules of tax collection set up by the Sharīʿa – was seen as a mark of piety by the scholars.

But there was of course a point of interaction between the intellectual and the political power, and that was the courtroom (Vikør, 2005: 168–184; Tillier, 2009). As mentioned earlier, the early *qāḍīs* were probably mainly administrative aides to the governors of the first Arab garrison towns. Eventually, however, they came to be seen as religious scholars who presided over Sharīʿa courts and should follow the strict procedures and rules developed in *fiqh*. In this capacity, the *qāḍī*-judge was appointed by the sultan (or his local representative), and the state power ensured the effectuation of any decision, in particular punitive, that the *qāḍī* made. In pristine theory, the judge should not receive payment from the ruler, only gifts from the plaintiffs or others who sought his advice, but of course the position did from the outset come with certain financial remunerations. The sultan, having appointed the judge, could also remove and replace him, and often did. Thus, there were at times a running tug of war between the judge and the governor over how much freedom the judge had in issues of political significance. The population of the town could also petition to the sultan – or riot – to have an unpopular judge removed, and this was also a not infrequent occurrence.

As the scholars claimed independence from the state, there came also the problem of how to authorize the law in cases of doubt. The judges were religious scholars who had training in law and could use their own competence to determine the correct rule to apply. However, they could also seek the advice of independent counsel. This was all the more important, as the Sharīʿa court system did not know any formal system of appeal; a decision of the *qāḍī* was immediately effective and could be re-examined only by indirect means (such as the removal of the *qāḍī*) (Powers, 1992). Instead, the judge, as well as all parties to a case, could go to another instance, which could be seen as the 'living law book' of the Sharīʿa: the *muftī*.

The *muftī* was not a member of the court and had no knowledge of individual cases, nor any authority to decide in them (Tyan, 1960: 219–229; Masud et al., 1996). He was a source of legal reference and opinion only. Any party could approach a *muftī* with a legal question (*istiftā'*), which was couched in the hypothetical: '*If* a man ʿAmr does such and such to a man Zayd, under those and those circumstances, what is then the legal rule for this?' to which the *muftī* would answer (always in writing) on the basis of his knowledge of *fiqh*, 'In such a case, the law is like this'. This legal opinion is a *fatwā*, and the person who asked could present it to the court in support of his view. But opposing parties could provide contradictory *fatwās* from different *muftīs*, for example by phrasing the circumstances of the question differently. The *qāḍī* thus had the freedom and task to decide which, or indeed any, of the submitted *fatwās* were relevant to the case in hand. The *fatwā* was not a judgment in the case. But he could not oppose the actual content of the *fatwā*, only its relevance.

This gave the *muftī* a certain competence for legal elaboration and interpretation. However, after the great period of legal formulation was deemed to be over by the twelfth or thirteenth century or so, this competence was considered to be very limited. The *muftī* must of course stay within his particular school of law (the same as the *qāḍī* who referred to him), and he must base his opinion, explicitly or implicitly, on the established 'majority opinion' (*maʿrūf*, or similar) among the scholars. While he could in theory be a *mujtahid*, a scholar who had the capacity for legal interpretation within his school, that leeway was limited (Calder, 1996). Actual development, which of course always took place, was most often framed in such a way as to indicate that this new view was in reality what the early scholars had intended all along (Jackson, 1996). Thus, once formed, the law of the *madhhabs* were meant to be stable over time.

Unlike the *qāḍī*, the *muftī* did not have any formal position or appointment either by the state authorities or any other body. Like other scholarly posts, accession to the rank of *muftī* was informal and based on the acceptance by his peers and those who sought his advice. Scholars received their learning literally at the feet of established scholars, be it in study circles in the mosques, or in other venues. Once an aspiring student had reached the level his teacher considered adequate, he was given a written certificate, an *ijāza*, that authorized him to go out and teach either a particular book or a more general subject. Later on, he could then again issue his own *ijāzas* to his students. Thus, the class of *ʿulamā'* was self-recruiting. If a scholar who had specialized in legal studies reached such a renown locally or regionally that applicants started coming to him with questions and accepting his answers, then he was a *muftī*. This was therefore also an authority based on personal merit and coming from below, not (like the *qāḍī*) from above.

Again, this was the theory, and it probably worked this way in particular in smaller localities and towns. A legal scholar could also move from the status of *qāḍī* to *muftī* and back again in the course of his career, depending on merit and situation, filling other positions that also required learning, such as teacher and market inspector, and so on in between. However, in the middle period, from the Mamlūk period (1250–1500) on, the rulers of the land were already seeing the benefit of having their own circle of religious advisers (Tyan, 1960: 224). They gathered groups of prominent *muftīs* into an advisory council in the capital and requested their opinions on major issues of policy, such as the correctness of starting a war or similar. Thus, the *muftīs* began to be drawn into the state structures, while the ruler could gain religious legitimation for policies or acts that might otherwise have been challenged by opponents.

In contradiction to the general theory, *muftīs* could also in some cases sit in court and become part of the regular proceedings, although it was still the task of the *qāḍī* to pass judgment (Brunschvig, 1965). But in the most severe and important cases, it became customary to request a *fatwā* from the *muftī* on the correctness of the legal basis for the judgment. This was particularly so in cases that involved capital punishment, which often came to be regularly submitted to a *muftī* before the verdict could be final. Beyond that, the ruler or city governor would also have to sign off on any conviction to death, although it might vary to what degree the governor could oppose a clear verdict by the judge confirmed by a *muftī*. Nevertheless, it may be said that the ultimate legal power of life and death was one that the ruler never willingly accepted to pass from his hand, however formalistically, and that on this level, the Sharīʿa courts had to accept the superiority of state power.

The ruler also had additional ways to control legal matters in his state, because the Sharīʿa courts were not necessarily the only courts of the land. Each state and century could have its own structure of courts in addition to the formal Sharīʿa courts. In general, one can group such courts into three categories, the *maẓālim*, the *muhtasib* and the police courts. All of these were recognized under the umbrella of the Sharīʿa and were completely legitimate according to Islamic law, but they still functioned in parallel to the Sharīʿa courts.

The *maẓālim* court was known as the sultan's court, although the sultan himself would probably preside over it only rarely, delegating this power to the local governor or even to a *qāḍī* who here functioned as the sultan's representative (Tyan, 1960: 433–536). Its stated objective was to right wrongs (*maẓālim*) that the Sharīʿa courts could not address. The main reason for this failing was the very strict rules of procedure of the Sharīʿa system. Conviction required, for example, two identical eye witnesses of unquestionable morality or a confession expressed to the judge in court, while material or circumstantial evidence had at best limited or indirect effect. In all, the many restrictions could make it very hard or impossible to get a conviction even when the defendant's guilt appeared to be obvious. Judges may of course in historical reality have bent these rules, but indications are that they were actually most often followed fairly stringently. Thus the Sharīʿa courts can be said to have been better adapted to be a forum for settling disputes between 'civil' parties than as a tool to sanction crimes, even though both functions were certainly within the court's stated objectives.

This opened space for a separate court to which an injured party could turn. The *maẓālim* was clearly meant to follow the same Sharīʿa rules as the courts but could dispense with its procedures. Unlike the Sharīʿa courts, there was no contestation between plaintiff and defendant, instead the injured party raised a case to the sultan or governor, who could if he so chose rule on it without even hearing the accused party. He could accept any evidence he saw fit and in general make his decision with no regard for the strict rules of the Sharīʿa courts. It was thus fully the ruler's court. Nevertheless, a *maẓālim* court would often have one or more regular *qāḍīs* present to advise the sultan. Thus, the two systems should be seen as complementary rather than in conflict. It must also be noted that the freedom of the *maẓālim* could of course strike both ways. A claimant to the sultan could also risk the decision going against him, perhaps more so than in the more predictable Sharīʿa court.

The police court was a more everyday venue for minor matters, but was, like the *maẓālim*, assumed to follow the Sharīʿa rules, but not its procedures (Tyan, 1960: 567–615). Public drunkenness should in a Sharīʿa court when properly proven lead to a conviction of 40 lashes; in the police court, the drunk could be thrown in jail for a day or two, perhaps after a round with the stick. Confessions extracted by beatings were not acceptable in the Sharīʿa court but were more than common in the police courts.

The market inspector, or *muḥtasib*, was a court closer to the Sharīʿa system and was always presided over by a legal expert, perhaps on a career path to judgeship (Tyan, 1960: 616–650; Müller, 1999: 247–322). Its formal area of competence was wide; it should guard the 'balance' (*ḥisba*) of society and could thus rule on moral issues that influenced public morality. However, in practical terms, its focus was more limited to what we may call municipal matters. Thus, the *muḥtasib* should ensure for example that public roads were navigable and could order the destruction of building extensions that hindered passage on the roads. Mostly, however, as the title indicates, his job was to oversee the markets and guarantee the fairness of commerce, the truthfulness of weights and measures, and similar practical matters.

A major shift in the relationship between the state and civil society occurred when the Ottoman empire rose in the early sixteenth century to control most of the Middle East from Algeria to Iraq. The Ottoman empire was a more modern state structure with a well-developed bureaucracy, and it represented a clear centralization of power into that state and away from the autonomous religious establishment – at least in the central lands of the empire. This could be seen in two new features of law: the *kanun* and the *shaykh al-islām*.

The *kanun* was series of lawbooks (*kanun-name*) formulated by the sultan and based on his authority alone (Repp, 1988). Originally, each new sultan issued his own *kanun-name*, but they soon began to directly adopt their predecessor's book, so the *kanun* became a permanent set of rules. In theory, it was, like the *maẓālim* court earlier, meant only to supplement the Sharīʿa in the areas where the law was unspecific, a clarification of how it should be understood in the empire. However, in reality the *kanun* soon became the primary source of law and the *fiqh* of the Sharīʿa secondary, thus the Ottoman judges were told to look first to the *kanun*, and only if no answer was found there, to search the *fiqh* literature. It must be noted, however, that the *kanun* only covered certain areas of law, in particular penal, administrative and economic issues, and in most cases the *kanun* did not contradict the established opinions of *fiqh*, so the practitioners may not have felt any great conflict between the two.

The sultan could also to a much wider degree than before instruct the judges in the courts, 'there is a brigand in your region: Find him and sentence him'. Thus, the need for a separate sultan's *maẓālim* court was reduced, and these become rarer or disappeared in the central regions of the empire, while similar bodies remained in some provinces, sometimes under the name of the governor's *majlis*, council.

Through this development the state asserted its power over what had been an independent judiciary. The same could be seen in the status of the *muftī*, where the top echelons had already begun to be enmeshed with the state. The Ottoman sultans institutionalized that by appointing a state *muftī* over the empire in an office they called the *shaykh al-islām*, the 'leader of Islam', with a bureaucratic apparatus around him (Heyd, 1969; Imber, 1997). The *shaykh al-islām* had the authority to issue *fatwās* that the courts were bound to follow and he should base them both on the Sharīʿa and on *kanun*. The *fatwās* became more formalistic rather than the argued judicial discussion of earlier *fatwās*. Those of the *shaykh al-islām* became ritualized statements often limited to 'yes' and 'no', confirming established law and judgments. This institutionalization of the *muftī* office was, again, most effective at the top level and in Anatolia, as local *muftīs* often maintained the traditional informal role, and the provinces to a larger degree had their own structures.

One important difference between Istanbul on the one hand and Ottoman Damascus and Cairo on the other, was the status of the *madhhab*. Like the earlier Mamlūks, the Ottomans followed the Ḥanafī school, and they formalized this as the state *madhhab* to be applied in court. This was not an issue in Anatolia, which was predominantly Ḥanafī already. However, in Syria and Egypt, as well as more distant regions, the majority population followed the Shāfiʿī or Mālikī schools. The Mamlūks had put the four schools on an equal footing in both Cairo and Damascus, letting each school have its own chief judge (*qāḍī al-quḍāt*) whose main task was to appoint judges to its Sharīʿa courts. When the Ottomans replaced the Mamlūks, the Ḥanafī court became the official court, but judges from the other schools were still tolerated (Brunschvig, 1965). In some cases, they were integrated into the state court and could fill in for a Ḥanafī judge when required, or separate courts for dispute settlement could co-exist.

The function of this multiplicity can be illustrated in a difficult situation of family law (Tucker, 1998: 84–85). The four *madhhabs*, while sharing a common basis of rules, also differ in many issues. One of these is judicial divorce (a divorce performed by a judge in the absence of, or against the wishes of the husband, who otherwise has full freedom to divorce his wife). In Mālikī law, the judge had a wide authority to perform such a divorce at his own discretion. In Ḥanafī law that option is virtually non-existent, unless the original marriage contract contained formal flaws that made it void, and the presence and acceptance of the husband was mandatory. It was commonly recognized that the latter rule caused grave problems for abandoned wives, as in the case where a husband travelling abroad had disappeared and not left his wife with any means of survival. Under Ḥanafī law she could not dissolve her marriage to contract a new one for her support. If such a case was brought to trial, the Ḥanafī judge might then excuse himself from the sitting and leave the room to his Shāfiʿī colleague, who performed the divorce according to Shāfiʿī rules, which did allow the judge to stand in for an absent husband. The Ḥanafī judge, on his return, would then accept the ruling under the principle that each judge's verdict was final, even when it was against his own *madhhab*.

The modern period

With the nineteenth century, a new era opened with the influence of Western models in law as in other social areas. The change was however gradual and varied according to circumstance. In the Ottoman empire, a process of reform called the *tanzimāt* began from the 1830s onwards and involved a number of new laws that came to replace the classical Sharīʿa (Vikør, 2005: 222–239). As we have seen, the Ottoman legal system was already a modernizing modification of the classical model with state encroachment into the religious field, but the basis of the earlier Ottoman state law was still the Sharīʿa. The new laws that came into effect in the *tanzimāt* were to a much larger degree influenced from a fully non-religious, European model. The *khaṭṭ-i sharīf* of 1839 abolished the distinction between Muslims and non-Muslims in areas of law, and the criminal code of 1858 was a Turkification of the French law and abolished the *ḥudūd*. The courts were also modernized with the introduction of three levels of appeal courts. In 1873, some of these new rules were organized into a more ambitious set of laws called the *Mecelle*, primarily covering areas of economic law.

In some ways, this system represented a continuity of the older legal systems. The Mecelle, for example, was still largely based on rules taken from Ḥanafī law, although with modifications.

Also, the traditional dual system of a Sharīʿa court and a sultan's or state court reappeared, only now the state courts were not *maẓālim* following Sharīʿa principles, but civil courts practising the new westernized or modernized laws. Throughout the century, however, the plaintiffs could still, as in the older system, choose whether to go to the Sharīʿa courts or the civil courts (Peters, 2005: 69–102). For example, in cases of murder or bodily harm, it might be more difficult to achieve a verdict in the Sharīʿa court following classical procedures, but if the plaintiff won, he could gain considerable financial compensation (*diyā*, 'blood money') from the miscreant. If he took the case to the civil courts following modern procedures, it would be easier to win a conviction, but the civil court did not hand out any *diyā*, which is unknown to Western penal law.

The main methodological difference between the classical and the modern was codification, however. There are elements of classical Sharīʿa that can be seen as moving towards the establishment of a set of fixed rules, such as the 'prevailing opinion within the *madhhab*', and the Ottoman *kanun* clearly is a significant step towards codification. Nevertheless, in the field of *fiqh*, the law has a basic indeterminacy where a qualified legal scholar can discuss a legal issue and challenge the majority opinion, or, rather, challenge the majority opinion of what the majority opinion was – he would generally claim that his own was the *actual* majority opinion of his school. This was not only theory; there were clearly variations both regional and individual within the four schools, and it was the scholars themselves, not any state body, that ultimately was the authority over what the law was.

From the nineteenth and particularly the twentieth centuries, this authority was transferred to the legislature of the new states, and the law was codified in a fixed form. The new code could, and often did, reiterate the majority opinions of the prevailing *madhhab*, but the state body was now the final decision maker and could introduce the amendments it wanted and which it believed would be accepted by the public (Peters, 2002). The legal scholars of the *ʿulamāʾ* could be consulted, or they could be ignored, depending on political whim.

Another major difference was that the law now became territorial, limited by the geographical boundaries of the new states. This was not the case of the classical *madhhabs*. As they were not linked to any state structure, they were also 'international', spanning the Muslim world, even though the legal elements of the Sharīʿa did depend on there being *a* Muslim ruler. Outside the *dār al-Islām*, however, many rules did not have legal validity. The Ottoman system changed this to some extent, as we have seen, giving the Ḥanafī school the status of state approval. But Ḥanafī law was also practised outside the Ottoman world and did not there depend on the Ottoman state authority for defining its law. Any regional differences that could be discerned between how the rules were practised were informal and outside the realm of the state. This all changed with the nation states; the law of Pakistan could be based on, e.g. Ḥanafī law, but once it was formulated by the Pakistani legislature, it became Pakistani law, not Ḥanafī law, and could thus differ from any Sharīʿa-based law of other states also following the Ḥanafī school.

The competence of the Sharīʿa was now mostly restricted to one domain alone: family and personal status law. The penal code, as well as financial, administrative, economic and other matters, were in most countries placed under new laws inspired by European models, the French codes being a particular favourite. The main exception was the Gulf area, where Saudi Arabia is the only country that officially still practises not just the laws of the Sharīʿa in all fields but also its court system, the state (the king) having no influence on legal formulation (Vogel, 2000). In theory, the Wahhābī current that dominates Saudi Arabia does not recognize any *madhhab* and allows each judge to establish the law from his knowledge of the revelation ('judicial *ijtihād*') and moral judgment. In practice, however, the rulings tend to follow the Ḥanbalī *madhhab*, which in this way for the first time acquired a territorial basis. Saudi Arabia allows the king to issue decrees in areas not covered by the Sharīʿa. These resemble laws and are enforced by special courts. They are not considered 'laws' in Saudi terminology, however, that being restricted to the divine and *fiqh*-based Sharī'a. Also, other shaykhdoms in the Gulf allow the classical *fiqh* a wider range of competence beyond family law, but in a more mixed and traditional form than the ideology-driven Saudi system (Ballantyne, 1990, 2000).

The clearest step in the opposite direction was made by Turkey under Atatürk (d. 1938) who abolished the Sharī'a completely and fully Europeanized the republic's legal system. In the Arab world, Tunisia has also restricted the influence of the Sharī'a considerably, and only minor influences of classical law can be discerned in some areas such as inheritance.

The other Arab countries have a hybrid system of old and new, where the Sharī'a rules form the basis for a codified family law, and in some countries the judges may refer to classical *fiqh* as a subsidiary legal source in the absence of a code (thus particularly in the Gulf). In virtually all countries, however, the modern states have sought to modify the Sharī'a rules to bring it more in conformity with modernized thinking. Mostly such changes go in the direction of improving the position of women in areas of marriage and divorce. Almost all Muslim countries have introduced some form of minimum marriage age, which was unknown to the classical Sharī'a, although the Sharī'a did recognize the difference between the marriage *contract*, which could be concluded from birth, and the time of marital *cohabitation*, which would normally be at or around the age of puberty. How high this minimum age is now set, depends on the states' ambition to reform. It could be 15, which is basically an assumption of puberty, or raised to 16, 18 or even 20 (and normally higher for boys than girls) (an-Na'im, 2002; Otto, 2010).

An important aim in setting a minimum age concerns the freedom to choose, or at least influence the choice of partner. The Sharī'a requires the acceptance, passive or active, by the bride and groom, and thus does not accept forced marriage. However, when a binding contract has been established at birth or any time before the 'age of discernment' by the father, such an acceptance becomes moot (this right of the father to contract marriage is called *ijbār*). It is in particular Mālikī law that accepts a binding *ijbār*, while the Ḥanafīs allow such a child marriage to be dissolved if the girl rejects it on reaching majority. By raising the minimum age of marriage to puberty or another age when the parties are able to make an informed choice, the issue of *ijbār* should disappear. Nevertheless, most countries of Mālikī dominance have also introduced laws specifically banning *ijbār*. This, of course, indicates that the practice still persists. In the same way, most states have introduced elements to limit the husband's absolute right to divorce (*ṭalāq*) and strengthen the wife's access to judicial divorce.

Interestingly, this is most often done in such a way as not to openly challenge the concepts of the Sharī'a. Instead, legislators play on the differences between the *madhhabs*. As can be seen, the Ḥanafīs have very strict rules on divorce but are more lenient in marriage, while the Mālikīs are the opposite, stricter in marriage and lenient on divorce. So, the legislators try to pick the Mālikī rules for divorce and Ḥanafī rules for marriage. Such a combination of rules from different *madhhabs* is known to classical *fiqh* under the name of *talfīq*, but was, as indicated, considered unacceptable for long periods (Carroll, 1996; Krawietz, 2002). Today, however, it becomes a way for the codifying state to change the Sharī'a-based rules without appearing to go against the divine law. Also, it is possible, like Morocco and Egypt, to change the content of the Sharī'a rule while maintaining its name. In the current Moroccan family law, *ṭalāq* – the husband's unilateral right to divorce his wife – is affirmed in law, but is now open to both husband and wife and must be presented to court (Buskens, 2003).

On closer scrutiny, however, it can often be seen that efforts that appear to be in favour of women can be less so in practice. The reason is that what stands out in most of these reforms is that power is transferred from the private sphere to the courts. While the settlement of a divorce was probably often a negotiation between husband and wife and their families, it is now the judge who determines the economic consequences by deciding who is 'at fault' for the dissolution of the marriage. This may not always be to the benefit of the wife, as the economic burden in an outright repudiation was under the Sharīʿa always on the husband alone. So, modernity moves legal authority from civil society (here, the private sphere) to the state.

Reintroduction of 'the Sharīʿa'

In the twentieth century, and in particular from the 1970s, the 'reintroduction of the Sharīʿa' has become a rallying call for various brands of political Islam. The Sharīʿa has of course never been 'gone'; it was always operative in the ritual and moral sense as guidelines for Muslims. Many Muslim countries also mention the Sharīʿa as a 'source' for their laws, and for many believers, the concept of Sharīʿa does not refer to a particular set of rules but to the divine will of welfare and justice, which can be well served by the modern laws. Indeed, even some moderate Islamists have said the same thing. Any law that provides morality, justice and welfare, is 'Sharīʿa' as far as they are concerned (Wickham, 2015: 187). But this is not consistent or clear, and expanding the role of traditional Sharīʿa rules in one way or another is definitely an important rhetorical element for many Islamist groups. While those groups that are far from the corridors of power have tended to be fairly vague about what they actually mean, we have clearly seen a resurgence of Sharīʿa-based laws in many countries.

This may take the form of reversing modernizations done in the area of family law. Thus, Iran, which had in 1967 raised the minimum marriage age to 18 for girls, after the revolution again opened up the possibility of marriage from the age of 9 with the court's consent (Mir-Hosseini, 2010: 353). In the economic field, this takes the form of the growth of an 'Islamic banking system', which avoids giving and taking interest on loans, as is forbidden in the Sharīʿa. Such institutions may be provided on a voluntary basis, or in some countries become compulsory.

However, the major area for the 'reintroduction' of the Sharīʿa refers to penal law, and in particular the symbolically charged *ḥudūd* rules against fornication, drunkenness, theft and 'highway robbery', *ḥirāba*. The latter is then often expanded to mean 'revolt' and can so be interpreted rather liberally to cover any violent opposition to the state. It is particularly Islamist currents of the *jihādī* variety that argue that these *ḥudūd* rules must be the core of the Sharīʿa, since it is they that have the clearest basis in the revelation, the *ḥudūd* being defined, as we recall, as being the rules where the sanction itself is considered to be stated in the Qurʾān directly. Often, these *jihādists* scoff at the limiting rules that earlier *fiqh* used to restrict the application of the *ḥudūd*, as a human intervention to limit the divine will. So, the *jihādists* may want to apply the *ḥudūd* directly and to a much higher degree than in the classical, 'medieval' system. The more established groups such as the Islamic State does, however, surprisingly, actually often adopt a classical *fiqh* discourse, perhaps to bolster their image as a 'serious Islamic' current.

The increased use of Sharīʿa penal law is not restricted to the *jihādists*, which have (besides the possible IS experiment) never achieved actual statehood. A number of established Muslim states have, under Islamist influence, adopted Sharīʿa penal codes. These include Iran, Sudan, Pakistan (at recurring occasions), Afghanistan and a number of Muslim federal states in Northern Nigeria (Layish and Warburg, 2002; Peters, 2006; Lau, 2014). This was in some cases done through changes in the codified laws (thus Sudan and Nigeria), or by simply stating that the courts should apply *fiqh* (Iran immediately after the 1979 revolution). In many cases, the reality then is a combination of or balance between codified law applied by lawyers trained in modern law and *fiqh* applied by religious scholars. This makes the issue of education and competence of the lawyers often a crucial, but unresolved issue, as this is a very politically sensitive issue that is in considerable flux.

References

al-Azami, M. M. 1985. *On Schacht's Origins of Muhammadan Jurisprudence*. Islamic Texts Society.

Ballantyne, W. 1990. 'A Reassertion of the Sharī'ah: The Jurisprudence in Gulf States', in N. Heer (ed.) *Islamic Law and Jurisprudence*. University of Washington Press. 149.

Ballantyne, W. M. 2000. *Essays and Addresses on Arab Laws*. Curzon.

Brockopp, J. E. 2000. *Early Mālikī Law: Ibn 'Abd al-Ḥakam and his Major Compendium of Jurisprudence*. Brill.

Brunschvig, R. 1965. 'Justice religieuse et justice laïque dans la Tunisie des Deys et des Beys jusq'au milieu du xixe siècle'. 23 *Studia Islamica*. 27.

al-Bukhārī, M. b. I. 1982. *Ṣaḥīḥ al-Bukhārī*. 'Alam al-kutub.

Buskens, L. 2003. 'Recent Debates on Family Law Reform in Morocco: Islamic Law as Politics in an Emerging Public Sphere'. 10(1) *Islamic Law and Society*. 70.

Calder, N. 1996. 'Al-Nawawi's Typology of *muftīs* and its Significance for a General Theory of Islamic Law'. 3(2) *Islamic Law and Society*. 137.

Carroll, L. 1996. 'Qur'ān 2:229: "A Charter Granted to Wife"? Judicial khul' in Pakistan'. 3(1) *Islamic Law and Society*. 91.

Crone, P. 1987. *Roman, Provincial and Islamic Law: The Origins of the Islamic Patronate*. Cambridge University Press.

Crone, P. and Hinds, M. 1986. *God's Caliph: Religious Authority in the First Centuries of Islam*. Cambridge University Press.

Dutton, Y. 1999. *The Origins of Islamic Law: The Qur'an, the Muwaṭṭa' and Madinan 'amal*. Curzon.

Escovitz, J. H. 1984. *The Office of* qâḍî al-quḍât *in Cairo under the Baḥrî Mamlûks*. Klaus Schwarz Verlag.

Goldziher, I. 1904. 'The Principles of Law in Islam' in H. Williams (ed.) *The Historians' History of the World*. Vol. 8. Hooper & Jackson. 294.

Goldziher, I. 1971 [1884]. *The Ẓāhirīs: Their Doctrine and their History*. Brill.

Hallaq, W. B. 1990. 'The Use and Abuse of Evidence: The Question of Provincial and Roman Influences on Early Islamic Law'. 110(1) *Journal of the American Oriental Society*. 79.

Hallaq, W. B. 1993. 'Was al-Shafi'ī the Master Architecht of Islamic Jurisprudence?' 25(4) *International Journal of Middle Eastern Studies*. 587.

Hallaq, W. B. 1997. *A History of Islamic Legal Theories: An Introduction to Sunnī uṣūl al-fiqh*. Cambridge University Press.

Hallaq, W. B. 2001. 'From Regional to Personal Schools of Law? A Reevaluation'. 8(1) *Islamic Law and Society*. 1.

Hallaq, W. B. 2002. 'The Quest for Origins or Doctrine? Islamic Legal Studies as Colonial Discourse'. 2 *UCLA Journal of Islamic and Near Eastern Law*. 1.

Hallaq, W. B. 2009. *Sharī'a. Theory, Practice, Transformations*. Cambridge University Press.

Heyd, U. 1969. 'Some Aspects of the Ottoman fetvā'. 32(1) *Bulletin of the School of Oriental and African Studies*. 35.

Imber, C. 1997. *Ebu's-Su'ud: The Islamic Legal Tradition*. Edinburgh University Press.

Jackson, S. A. 1996. 'Taqlid, Legal Scaffolding and the Scope of Legal Injunctions in Post-formative Theory: *muṭlaq* and *'āmm* in Jurisprudence of Shihāb al-Dīn al-Qarāfī'. 3(2) *Islamic Law and Society*. 165.

Kamali, M. H. 1991. *Principles of Islamic Jurisprudence*. Islamic Texts Society.

Krawietz, B. 2002. 'Cut and Paste in Legal Rules: Designing Islamic Norms with *talfīq*'. 42(1) *Die Welt des Islams*. 3.

Lau, M. 2014. 'The Re-Islamization of Legal Systems' in R. Peters and P. Bearman (eds) *The Ashgate Research Companion to Islamic Law*. Ashgate. 235.

Layish, A. and Warburg. G. R. 2002. *The Reinstatement of Islamic Law in the Sudan under Numayrī: An Evaluation of a Legal Experiment in the Light of its Historical Context, Methodology and Repercussions*. Brill.

Masud, M. K., Messick, B. and Powers, D. S. (eds). 1996. *Islamic Legal Interpretation: Muftis and their Fatwas*. Harvard University Press.

Melchert, C. 1997. *The Formation of the Sunni Schools of Law: 9th–10th Centuries C.E.* Brill.

Mir-Hosseini, Z. 2010. 'Sharia and National Law in Iran' in J. M. Otto (ed.) *Sharia Incorporated: A Comparative Overview of the Legal Systems of Twelve Muslim Countries in Past and Present*. Brill. 319.

Müller, C. 1999. *Gerichtspraxis im Stadtstaat Córdoba: Zum Recht der Gesellschaft in einer mālikitisch-islamischen Rechtstradition des 5./11. Jahrhunderts*. Brill.

an-Na'im, A. (ed). 2002. *Islamic Family Law in a Changing World: A Global Resource Book*. Zed Books.

Nallino, C. 1940. 'Considerazioni sui rapporti fra diritto romano e diritto musulmano', in *Raccolta di scritti, editi e inediti*. Istituto per l'Oriente 1940–42, IV, 85–94.
Opwis, F. 2010. *Maṣlaḥa and the Purpose of the law: Islamic Discourse on Legal Change from the 4th/10th to 8th/14th Century*. Brill.
Osman, A. 2014. *The Ẓāhirī Madhhab (3rd/9th–10th/16th Century): A Textualist Theory of Islamic Law*. Brill.
Otto, J.M. (ed). 2010. *Sharia Incorporated: A Comparative Overview of the Legal Systems of Twelve Muslim Countries in Past and Present*. Brill.
Peters, R. 2002. 'From Jurists' Law to Statute Law or What Happens when the Shari'a is Codified'. 7(4) *Mediterranean Politics*. 82.
Peters, R. 2005. *Crime and Punishment in Islamic Law: Theory and Practice from the Sixteenth to the Twenty-First Century*. Cambridge University Press.
Peters, R. 2006. 'The Re-Islamization of Criminal Law in Northern Nigeria and the Judiciary: The Safiyyatu Hussaini Case', in M. K. Masud, B. Messick and D. S. Powers (eds) *Dispensing Justice in Islam: Qadis and their Judgments*. Brill. 219.
Powers, D. S. 1992. 'On Judicial Review in Islamic Law'. 26(2) *Law & Society Review*. 315.
Rappaport, Y. 2003. 'Legal Diversity in the Age of *taqlīd*: The Four Chief *qāḍīs* under the Mamluks'. 10(2) *Islamic Law and Society*. 210.
Repp, R. C. 1988. 'Qānūn and Sharīʿa in the Ottoman Context', in A. al-Azmeh (ed.) *Islamic Law. Social and Historical Contexts*. Routledge. 124.
Schacht, J. 1950. *The Origins of Muhammadan Jurisprudence*. Oxford University Press.
Schacht, J. 1964. *An Introduction to Islamic Law*. Oxford University Press.
Tillier, M. 2009. *Les cadis d'Iraq et l'état abbasside (132/750–334/945)*. IFPO.
al-Tirmidhī, M. b. ʿĪ. 1962. *al-Jāmiʿ al-ṣaḥīḥ: wa-huwa Sunan al-Tirmidhī*. Maktabat Muṣṭafā al-Bābī al-Ḥalabī.
Tucker, J. E. 1998. *In the House of the Law: Gender and Islamic Law in Ottoman Syria and Palestine*. University of California Press.
Tyan, É. 1960. *Histoire de l'organisation judiciaire en pays d'islam*. Brill.
Vikør, K. S. 1996. *Sources for Sanūsī Studies*. Centre for Middle Eastern Studies.
Vikør, K. S. 2005. *Between God and the Sultan: A History of Islamic Law*. Hurst.
Vikør, K. S. 2014. 'The Origins of the Sharia', in R. Peters and P. Bearman (eds) *The Ashgate Research Companion to Islamic Law*. Ashgate. 13.
Vogel, F. E. 2000. *Islamic Law and Legal Systems: Studies of Saudi Arabia*. Brill.
Watt, W. M. 1956. *Muhammad at Medina*. Clarendon Press.
Watt, W. M. 1998. *The Formative Period of Islamic Thought*. Oneworld.
Wickham, C. R. 2015. *The Muslim Brotherhood: Evolution of an Islamist Movement*. Princeton University Press.

4

The Hindu tradition

A history

Domenico Francavilla

Introduction

Considering that Hindu law, although in new forms, is still existing law, it can be said (Derrett, 1998) that the Hindu legal tradition is the one that can claim to be of the greatest antiquity among those that still have relevance in the contemporary world.

In order to provide a preliminary overall picture of the origin and evolution of the Hindu legal tradition, we can distinguish some great epochs that mark main passages. A first epoch, spanning many centuries, may be seen as the epoch of the development of traditional Hindu law and can be divided into the following phases: the Vedic period (c. 1500 BC–c. 500 BC), the classical period (c. 500 BC–c. AD 200) and the late-classical period (AD 200–1100). In this long period, the Hindu tradition elaborated fundamental legal concepts, rules and institutions. It is worth remembering that Hindu law has never been the sole legal tradition in South Asia, and it developed in interaction with other South Asian traditions, particularly Buddhism. From c. 1100, a post-classical period of Hindu law starts and merges with what we can call, looking at general Indian history, the epoch of Muslim domination. This epoch is marked by the growth of the presence of Islam in South Asia, which had already begun in the previous centuries, and its political importance with Islamic kingdoms. During this epoch, however, not much change occurred in Hindu law as such, while the Islamic tradition deeply influenced the Indian legal tradition considered as a whole. In the colonial epoch, which started in the 1600s and ended with the independence of India in 1947, a new phase began, characterized by significant changes in Hindu law. A final epoch of the development of Hindu law may be identified as starting with Independence and the birth of the Republic of India, which has its founding document in the 1949 (1950) Constitution. In this last phase, Hindu law acquires its current form in India as religious law evolving in close interaction with state law.[1] The choices made in the first decade after Independence have remained firm, but Hindu law has continued its evolution along paths that in part are still to be fully understood.

Hindu law is clearly a South Asian law, and its historical evolution is closely connected with Indian history. Unlike, for example, Buddhist or Islamic law, it has not massively spread in areas of the world other than the one in which it originated. Nevertheless, Hindu law in ancient times also spread in Southeast Asia (Huxley, 1995), and today there are autonomous manifestations of Hindu law in Nepal, Pakistan and Bangladesh which differ from Indian Hindu law in some ways due to different contexts and to the political history of these countries.[2] Furthermore, there are significant manifestations of Hindu law related to the phenomenon of the Hindu diaspora outside the Indian subcontinent, for example in east Africa, the Caribbean, Canada, the United States and European countries. In Europe, the presence of Hindu communities, particularly in the United Kingdom, may be at the origin of new manifestations of Hindu law, that is to say, European Hindu laws. Some scholars believe that it is possible to speak of an *angrezi dharma*, an English *dharma*, and thus of a particular Hindu law in England, in the same way as, on the other hand, one could speak of an *angrezi shariat*.[3] Hindu law, once transplanted into a new environment as personal law that Hindus continue to observe, retains its capacity for autonomous development, regardless of whether the new country recognizes it. Indeed, interaction with a completely new environment necessarily influences the form that Hindu law assumes in Europe and other parts of the world.

Hindu law, as personal law, 'follows' Hindus. In fact, Hindus observe it as members of a particular religious and cultural community, and not as residents in a particular territory or subject to a particular political entity. In its simplest but still useful meaning, Hindu law is the law of Hindus. It is the set of rules of behaviour, institutions and related concepts developed within the various religious and cultural traditions that are considered part of Hinduism.[4]

Since Hindu law concerns, except for some exceptions, Hindus alone, it is important to determine what it means to belong to Hinduism (Knott, 1998; Michaels, 2004; Chapter 24, this volume). Defining who Hindus are is highly problematic for a variety of reasons. It should first be noted that the modern concept of Hindu is linked to a cultural process of building Hinduism as a unitary religion that occurred in a relatively recent period, that is to say in the nineteenth century. Western orientalists mainly conducted this process, but eventually the category of Hinduism became part of a commonly accepted way of defining their own identity by Hindus themselves. Yet they always have a much more specific and articulated sense of belonging.

In recent Indological studies, the entire category of Hinduism as a religion has been questioned. It has been observed that it would be more correct to talk about a bundle of religions that recognize each other, or a socio-cultural unity (Sontheimer and Kulke, 1989; Michaels, 2004; Chapter 14, this volume). In other words, the label 'Hinduism' includes several autonomous religious traditions, and its pluralistic character is paradigmatic. The different traditions within it share some concepts and practices but can be radically different in decisive aspects. In such a jagged picture, the existence of an orthodoxy on which to measure some variations as more or less heterodox, is problematic. The attempts that have been made to define the core of Hinduism usually focus on three aspects: the recognition of the authority of the sacred texts of the Vedas, the acceptance of the law of *karman* and hence belief in the cycle of rebirths, and acceptance/membership of the caste system. If these three elements are central to Hinduism, one can observe that there are communities in which they are all present but also communities where their importance is less or their specific meanings diverge from mainstream views, and nonetheless these communities consider themselves and are seen as part of Hinduism (Flood, 2004).

It should also be remembered that the term *hindū* originally referred to the populations living in the north-western part of the Indian subcontinent, around the Indus river. These populations certainly had different religious beliefs, but being Hindu meant to belong, not to a certain religion, but to an ethnic-cultural complex within which different faiths and different views of the world could coexist. The term *hindū* was later used mainly to define inclusively the people of the Indian subcontinent not belonging to Islam or to other religions clearly differentiated from those of Hindus.

The issues concerning the definition of 'Hindu' raise several problems in describing the history of Hindu law, because this category is a retrospective one. What we call Hindu law is the legal manifestation of a complex of religions, philosophies and practices elaborated in very different contexts and that necessarily reflects this plurality, Under the label 'Hindu law' a series of ancient and modern laws may be included. To what extent are they part of a single legal tradition? To what extent can we consider them collectively as religious law? Can we assume that this legal tradition has developed since Vedic times until now in an uninterrupted way? The answers to these questions depend on our expectations about what a single legal tradition should look like, about the possibility of clearly separating religion from other factors producing law in context, and about what counts as continuity and disruption in a tradition.

The Hindu legal tradition has gone through historical events and has interacted with other laws, becoming more and more complex and transforming itself. Since various laws originated in the Indian subcontinent and others were imported in different historical periods, the Hindu legal experience can be understood only considering the coexistence and interaction of a variety of models, indigenous and received. They gave rise to different concrete manifestations of law depending on the relationship between different elements in a variety of historical contexts and in different parts of India and elsewhere. Ultimately, there are many Hindu laws which, nevertheless, share some rules, institutions and values.

The concept of legal tradition serves to identify continuity over time, the passing on from one generation to another of a set of concepts and rules of behaviour. The idea of the origin of tradition in a past that is still present and authoritative is crucial (Glenn, 2004). It has been emphasized that traditions may be invented (Hobsbawm and Ranger, 1983). However, particularly in the legal field, the invention of tradition is part of the process of legitimation and cultural elaboration of law and, therefore, is a factor that concretely influences the making of law.

A second important point is that in analysing the Hindu tradition there is always the risk of considering it more cohesive than it actually was and, even more so, of identifying the part with the whole, thus falling into an involuntary form of Orientalism. More precisely, in the study of Hindu law, the ever-present risk is to overestimate the role played by Brahmanical thought on *dharma*. This depends on the fact that the sources available to scholars to understand Hindu law in its formative phase are Sanskrit sources incorporating Brahmanical thought.

This Brahmanical model assumed a particular relevance in the historical development of Hindu law. It is a model elaborated by a cultural élite, entitled to the study and teaching of the *dharma*, which finds its most complete formulation in the texts of the *dharmaśāstra* and of the Mīmāṃsā school, which collectively elaborated Hindu jurisprudence (Francavilla, 2006; Jha, 1964). This manifestation of Hinduism, even if it cannot be representative of all the forms assumed by Hindu tradition, represents a paradigmatic model through which tradition has progressively been defined in its variety, by adhesion or by contrast (Halbfass, 1990a, 1990b).[5]

There have always been in India, as everywhere, conflicting philosophies and conceptions deriving from different cultural traditions and sub-traditions. Therefore, Hindu jurisprudence reflects the history of intellectual interactions, which is often a history of integration and further elaboration of originally competing views. Secondly, learned elaborations do not set aside the importance of implicit or non-verbalized knowledge systems, which were and are common in many areas of Indian society. As a result, one must be aware of the fact that the internal variety of Hinduism has meant that there has been a plurality of models of law within it and that the diffusion and penetration of the Brahmanical model into practice has not been homogenous in different Hindu contexts.[6]

Provided that we are aware of the complexity of the label 'Hindu law', as concerns both the term 'Hindu' and the term 'law', the study of the Hindu legal tradition, in my view, offers the possibility of observing a multi-millennial legal evolution. In the following sections, we will see the main aspects of this history, starting from the difficult issue of the origins of this law until its contemporary application in India as a part of the official legal system in matters relating to family and succession, and we will try to define some basic characteristics emerging from this historical evolution.

Origins of Hindu law

The assumption of c. 1500 BC as the beginning of the Hindu legal tradition is largely conventional. This dating adopts as a criterion the presumed period of composition of the first Vedic texts. There are, however, many theories according to which the Vedic corpus has much older origins. Secondly, the same criterion may be called into question, considering that the date of the composition of the first Vedic texts may not be decisive for determining the beginning of the Hindu legal tradition.

Hinduism, differently from other religions, does not have a distinctive point of departure, and this could be a further argument against its definition as a unitary religion. According to a common, although controversial, traditional view, in a period between 2500 and 1500 BC some Indo-European populations moved from central Asia to the Indian subcontinent, coming into contact with the populations living in the Indus valley. The Hindu tradition, in this view, originated in the formation of a new culture deriving from the interaction of different populations and from the prevalence of the culture of people of Indo-European origin, with their language and their cultural universe based on sacred knowledge (Veda), only partly expressed in the existing Vedic texts (Vedas).

The origins of Hindu law can be identified in the thought and institutionalized practices that developed in the Vedic world. Concepts and ancestral rules were constructed within the symbolic and philosophical universe expressed by the texts of the Vedas (Miller, 1985). In the Vedic period, a first concept of order that is relevant for law was elaborated. It is the concept of *ṛta*, the cosmic order that manifests itself in the regularity of the cycles of nature, in the alternation of day and night, in the elements perceived as constant in the manifestation of the world. As is typical of ancient civilizations, the social order was conceptualized in the same way, based on belief in the existence of a natural order of things.

The Hindu concept of social order was therefore built around the original perception of the existence of a network of relations between macrocosm and microcosm (Menski, 2003). The cosmic order and the human order are seen as inextricably interlinked and influence each other, according to the magical mentality that is also typical of ancient civilizations. Human beings' action is considered holistically as part of a whole. In its formative phase, Hindu law is based on a mythical cosmology in which the universe spread out as the differentiation of an eternal divine principle. From this differentiation comes the visible world that is destined to be reabsorbed into a non-differentiated state following a cyclical process. In this conception, disorder consists in the progressive cleavage of the connections that unite the parts of the world, both at the cosmic level and at the social and individual level.

The idea that order must be continuously maintained by the action of human beings characterizes Vedic thought. The paradigm of 'making order' is the ritual action through which, given the interconnection of macrocosm and microcosm, human beings can influence the course of things and participate in the conservation of the world. At the same time, the idea is affirmed that even social activities have both macrocosmic and microcosmic effects.

The concept of *dharma*, which is central in the elaboration of the law in the Hindu tradition, is rooted in the Vedic world. *Dharma* was initially conceived as a ritual quality of things and actions. Dharmic action is the action to which super-sensory effects are reconnected and which produces order. As a result, the concept of *dharma* is also referred to the result of action, and then to order itself and to the set of duties aimed at maintaining order.

An understanding of the origin and development of science and learning is the proper context for an understanding of law as a part of this culture. People in very ancient communities, very different from modern ones as concerns their size and features, elaborated their vision of life and developed a system of sciences, organizing their knowledge on different aspects of human activities.

The entire system of sciences of this civilization was developed through or around the Vedas. The ritual conception of life and cosmos embodied in the Vedas is central to the elaboration of Hindu culture at its origin (Malamoud, 1998). Every science was developed in connection to ritual, trying to provide the appropriate knowledge for the correct accomplishment of rites, which affect the relations of human beings at every level in an interconnected whole. In this context, grammatical science, etymology, logic and also other sciences, such as mathematics, astronomy or the science of building are conceived, explicitly or implicitly, as auxiliary sciences of the Vedas.[7] For instance, the origin of Indian theories of meaning and interpretation may be seen as closely linked to the necessity of an appropriate understanding of Vedic texts. Hymns, rituals, philosophies, arts and social practices formed an integrated system of beliefs and actions in which this culture expressed and progressively defined itself.

Within the context of the birth and development of Hindu culture and system of sciences in the Vedic period, a science regarding *dharma* gradually arose, and in the classical period it became the core of Hindu jurisprudence. In this regard, it is worth remembering that, according to many authors, the role of the Vedas in Hindu culture has been widely overstated, because it represents a cultural construct with limited reach in reality. Specifically, as regards law and the question of the antiquity of Hindu law, two prominent comparative law scholars, Zweigert and Kötz (1998: 315–316), have highlighted that Vedic texts are not legal texts and, thus, cannot be assumed as evidence of the beginning of a legal tradition. In this view, we could speak properly of a legal tradition only starting with the much later appearance of *dharmasūtras*, doctrinal texts on *dharma*. In addition, Zweigert and Kötz (1998: 315) make reference to the little impact of Vedic texts on law arguing a very common view:

> Although the Hindus regard the Veda as a divine revelation and as the source of their religion and law, its practical influence on the spiritual life of the Hindu population has been very slight for many centuries; it cannot be said that the Veda has had much impact on the development of Hindu law, especially as it contains very little material with a specific legal content.

However, a periodization of Hindu legal history based on the particular features of texts expressed by the tradition is provided with an internal logic but at the same time is not sufficient. In fact, following this criterion, the very same appearance of *dharmasūtras*, whose legal character is debated, would not provide a firm basis to envisage the beginning of a legal tradition. Secondly, and more significantly, the identification of law with the existence of legal texts could lead to the negation of the existence of law in certain societies. Therefore, the question is: assuming that Vedic texts are not legal texts, what law was the law of the Vedic period?

The peculiarity of law in the Vedic period should be understood considering that it was grounded on customs and chthonic concepts.[8] Menski (2003: 86 ff.) has pointed out that the Veda does not contain norms but is an expression of a complex cultural system, concepts and myths, at the root of this ancient legal system. In this sense, there was a law that could be said to be Vedic, even if it was not verbalized in Vedic texts as we know them. Therefore, even if Brahmanism carried out the *cultural operation* to put the Veda at the apex of the normative system, as it is in the theories of our concern, nonetheless in the Vedic period a set of beliefs, practices, rules and institutions formed what we can call Vedic law. The Vedas-as-texts were part of this cultural complex, even though they were not meant to be legal texts as we would understand them. In other words, the term 'Vedic' may well refer to Vedic culture as a whole rather than to Vedic texts.

Historical evolution

The classical period is the period of maximum development of the theoretical elaboration of Hindu law. In this period, a science of *dharma* developed, the theory of sources was completely formulated and the basic principles of Hindu social organization were organically built. The subsequent late-classical period and the post-classical period represent a less innovative phase. On the cultural level, there emerges a more complex theorization of the role of the sovereign as protector of *dharma* (Menski, 2003).

The elaboration of the concept of *dharma* and of dharmic rules reaches its peak in the classical period (Lingat, 1998). Given its centrality, this concept has received various philosophical elaborations within what we call the Hindu tradition. Moreover, it is a pan-Indian concept, fundamental in Hinduism as well as in Buddhism and Jainism, and Hindu elaborations of *dharma* interacted with competing views. From this, an even greater complexity of meanings of this very general term was derived.

The two sciences dealing specifically with *dharma*, even if with different aims and roles, were *dharmaśāstra* and Mīmāṃsā (Davis, 2010a). This scholarly tradition represents the core of Hindu jurisprudence. The Sanskrit term *śāstra* may be meant as a science and a teaching. Olivelle (2005: 41) explains:

> The term *śāstra* . . . may refer to a system or tradition of expert knowledge in a particular field, that is, to a science. It refers especially, however, to the textualized form of that science, that is, to an authoritative compendium of knowledge signaling a breakthrough achievement within the history of that tradition and serving as a point of reference to subsequent investigations within that tradition . . . A *śāstra* may present new material and present the material in new ways; but essentially it is a crystallization of a long tradition of accumulated knowledge.

Dharma-śāstra, in its wider sense, is the science and teaching of *dharma*, dealing with questions concerning behaviour that one should adopt and, thus, the way to lead one's life (Derrett, 1973). In a stricter sense, *dharmaśāstra* is a specific class of normative texts.

The Mīmāṃsā is closely linked to the *dharmaśāstra*, and their origins should be searched for in the same context of learning (Kane, 1962–1975).[9] If *dharmaśāstra* is the part of the *śāstra* dealing specifically with *dharma*, Mīmāṃsā is the philosophy whose particular subject of investigation is *dharma*. Mīmāṃsā's experts carried out an extensive elaboration of *dharma* developing a theory of interpretation and describing in an organized way the rules of *dharma*. Their extent and role, however, are different, and while *dharmaśāstra* is meant to describe dharmic rules, the Mīmāṃsā, as a more theoretical science, is concerned with the epistemological investigation into the nature of *dharma* and the ways to know it. In this sense, one can argue that Hindu jurisprudence, which in this context may be meant as the science of *dharma*, is made up of a theoretical and a practical jurisprudence.[10]

The works composing the *dharmaśāstra* are made up of rules of behaviour and represent a practical jurisprudence that directly addresses the appropriate way to behave in different contexts. In a legal experience that is not based on sovereign rule-making, a prominent place is played by the authoritative opinions of experts of *dharma*, who may claim to be and actually are perceived as the recipients of an authoritative tradition. On the other hand, those who adhere to the legal-cosmological framework of *dharma* will naturally search for a source of guidance in the expert opinion of subjects who are qualified because of being good and learned. However, the experts of *dharma* are themselves part of society and, in this sense, they cope with what they have before their eyes. Ultimately, their role in living laws depended on acceptance in social contexts.

Therefore, the process of ascertaining *dharma* cannot be restricted to the opinions of learned interpreters. This science of *dharma*, taken by itself, appears as a coherent and self-sufficient body of knowledge that was developed through centuries, but it is only a part, albeit indeed a fundamental one, of the complex phenomenon that is labelled as 'Hindu law'.

From texts different normative systems were derived through the work of interpreters (Lingat, 1998), whose works could be more or less authoritative in different local areas and parts of Hinduism. Furthermore, doctrinal law needed to deal with local customs and political power, and local legal systems developed as a combination of different factors. Nonetheless, it is worth highlighting that the doctrinal elaboration of *dharma* legitimized differences within the tradition. Different normative systems were elaborated in a unitary way, due to the theoretical foundation they found in the work of interpreters. In this regard, certainly Hindu jurisprudence was able to elaborate a conceptual approach that was capable of combining unity and diversity.

Hindu law continued to develop during the Islamic period (Menski, 2003). In the first place, one can observe that Islamic law and Hindu law, although presenting many differences, are both largely independent from state law. Secondly, the Muslim rulers, partly for reasons of political expediency, partly for reasons of real openness to Indian cultural pluralism, did not aim at deeply changing the law followed by their Hindu subjects. Therefore, medieval Hindu law could continue its evolution in continuity with the previous period.

However, during the Muslim period, Hindu law underwent transformations, due to the interaction with new practices and doctrines. In some respects, because Hindu communities could essentially continue to live according to their personal law, also thanks to the existence of traditional systems of dispute settlement, there was a somewhat self-defensive strengthening of the Hindu tradition. For example, in this period, the literature on *dharma* sees the flourishing of the *nibandhas*, that is to say, of digests of dharmic rules that served as repositories of solutions for interpreters. In addition, an interaction occurred as regards certain institutions such as polygamy, which is typical of Islam but which had important manifestations also in some Hindu communities, even though the ideal Hindu marriage is monogamous (Menski, 2003). Criminal law and other important public law matters were deeply Islamized in this period, but Islamic law became one of the components of the Indian legal tradition without eliminating the relevance of Hindu laws, confirming the typical pluralistic legal framework under which different communities can live according to their own particular law.

It is with the arrival of the Europeans, and therefore with the penetration in India of western laws, that Hindu law underwent considerable changes. One of the first needs felt by the colonial administration was to introduce a system of criminal and civil justice for the colonizers themselves, but the crucial problem that the British faced was to decide how to administer the laws of the local populations and, in particular, to what extent to apply English law to them. In this complicated story, a fundamental moment occurred in 1772 when the Warren Hastings's Regulation introduced the system of listed subjects, according to which Hindu law and Islamic law were to be applied to Hindus and Muslims, mainly in matters related to personal status, particularly marriage and successions.[11]

At the same time, the British began to intervene massively in other areas of the legal system, using also the instrument of the code, inspired by the codification processes in continental Europe, which had not found space in England. The political need for codification was to achieve greater uniformity and to reform some aspects of pre-existing laws developed in India. In this respect the most important work is probably the Indian Penal Code (1860), modelled directly on the English law of the time. In the same period there were other important legislative acts destined to have a deep influence on the Indian legal system, for example in the field of contract law and commercial law. These reforms also affected Hindu law, since the penal code, which has a territorial character, contains rules that also affect the institutions of Hindu law, and classical Hindu law had its own rules for contracts, which were then set aside, at least at the official level. More generally, in some cases the colonial administration intervened also in matters falling within personal status, trying to reform some aspects of personal laws considered less acceptable from the western point of view, such as the legal status of widows.

In the colonial period, one of the most particular events of the history of Hindu law occurred as a consequence of the system of listed subjects, namely the formation of Anglo-Hindu law, just as there was Anglo-Muslim law, which resulted from the application of Hindu law in the colonial courts. The judges who found themselves having to apply Hindu law had considerable difficulty. Above all, at the beginning, they diminished the role of customs by thinking that the texts of *dharmaśāstra* could be considered the equivalents of western codes and, therefore, they sought to apply the rules contained in them. To do this, they decided to resort to the aid of *pandits*, experts of Sanskrit and particularly of the texts on *dharma*, who were charged with identifying in that immense literature the rules of law applicable to the concrete case. This experiment did not succeed and, detached from the traditional interplay of sources, the Hindu law applied in the courts became one that actually existed only in the mind of the colonial judge (Derrett, 1976–1978: vol. 3).

In a later period, the role of customs was re-evaluated, but the criteria set for their recognition were so rigid that many customs were not applied, and this led to a certain extent to the disappearance of some customary norms. Furthermore, judges were often called upon to judge according to equity, justice and good conscience, and thus applied Hindu law according to their legal and moral sensitivity. It should be noted, however, that recourse to the colonial courts was not the rule and that Hindu law continued to be followed largely at an informal level, being independent of the intervention of a colonial sovereign power, just as in part it could be separated from the intervention of a Hindu sovereign power. Therefore, the Anglo-Hindu law applied in the courts, all considered, had a limited effect on the evolution of Hindu law as a whole, since disputes were rarely resolved by making recourse to those courts.

After Independence, the steps to take in order to reform the system of personal laws that had come into the modern age from the past were widely debated. The Constituent Assembly found itself faced with a particularly complex situation as regards the application of personal laws. Many believed that a uniform civil law would be the best embodiment of the principle of Indian secularism, clearly marking the separation of law from religion. On the other hand, proceeding to the drafting of a uniform civil code at the beginning of the existence of the Republic of India certainly represented a very demanding and very dangerous test, given the risk of increasing social conflict. For this reason, the project was abandoned, and only a constitutional provision of a programmatic nature was introduced, in the part dedicated to the Directive Principles of

State Policy, namely article 44, according to which: 'The State shall endeavour to secure for the citizens a uniform civil code throughout the territory of India'.

If the goal of uniformity for all Indian citizens of law in matters of personal status – in other subjects uniformity already existed – appeared too ambitious, a goal that seemed feasible and was chosen to pursue was that of simplifying Hindu law, which, even individually considered, was characterized by considerable complexity and lack of uniformity. The reform of Hindu law was accomplished with four legislative acts that are also collectively listed, albeit rather improperly, as the Hindu code. In 1955 the Hindu Marriage Act was promulgated, and in 1956 the Hindu Minority and Guardianship Act, the Hindu Adoptions and Maintenance Act, and the Hindu Succession Act. These laws represented an attempt to amend and codify the rules of Hindu law in force.

These legislative reforms were based on pre-existing Hindu law, but they also introduced new rules or generalized rules that were followed only by a part of the Hindu population, as in the case of the prohibition of bigamy and the introduction of divorce. Despite the reformist intent, an in-depth analysis of these laws shows how the problem of uniformity/diversity was dealt with, leaving intact a framework of substantial legal pluralism. In fact, the Indian legislator avoided regulating the matter in all its aspects and gave great space to customary law, through a series of rules that officially recognized local and group customs in the presence of a series of conditions.

The mid-1950s reforms can be seen as the point in which Hindu law acquires its form in independent India: they are the outcome of an Indian, non-colonial policy. Clearly, the evolution of Hindu law did not stop in the 1950s. Other legislative reforms focusing on some specific issues were introduced later. Among these, we can mention the Marriage (Amendment) Act of 1974 and the Prohibition of Child Marriage Act of 2006. These legislative interventions have aimed to impact on aspects of traditional Hindu law that were not fully addressed in the 1950s. In addition to legislation, the work of the Courts has been very significant for the evolution of Hindu law; the courts have demonstrated in most cases a remarkable ability to move between tradition and modernity in search of effective solutions to the problems of protection in particular of women and members of disadvantaged social groups (Menski, 2003).

It would be simplistic to consider the evolution of Hindu law in Independent India by referring only to official Hindu law, that is to say, to Hindu law as a part of the Indian legal system applied by state courts (Chiba, 1986). In fact, Hindu law is relatively autonomous from state law, and traditional institutions can resist modernizing attempts by the state and be followed as unofficial law by some Hindu communities, both in terms of substantive and institutional rules. The ineffectiveness of state legislation derives in some cases from this fact.

Therefore, from Independence onwards, Hindu law did not remain immobile and developed above all in the sense of modernizing, but not in a linear way. In the contrast between traditionalists and reformists, a new phase of Hindu law, the postmodern one, characterized by overcoming the logic of the contrast between tradition and modernity, has developed according to Menski's convincing opinion (Menski, 2003).

Central characteristics

The Hindu legal tradition finds in the concept of *dharma* its most important normative concept. The term *dharma* has considerable semantic scope and can be translated, depending on the context, as 'religion', 'law', 'justice', 'duty', 'prerogative' (Doniger et al., 1991) As noted by Olivelle (1999: xxi):

> The term *dharma* may be translated as law if we do not limit ourselves to its narrow modern definition as civil and criminal statutes but take it to include all the rules of behaviour, including moral and religious behaviour, that a community recognizes as binding for its members.

Dharma embraces all the duties that the individual must observe in order to have correct behaviour. No clear distinctions are drawn between different kinds of duty and, therefore, the distinction between ethical, social and legal norms does not have a real purpose in the elaboration of *dharma*. In the texts on *dharma* one can find together rules concerning the correct performance of rites, and rules concerning land ownership and the settlement of disputes. There are internal distinctions, such as the one between *dharma* related to penance (*prāyaścittadharma*) and *dharma* related to the settlement of disputes (*vyavahāradharma*), but in all cases where *dharma* is involved there is a qualification of action as a duty on a plurality of levels. In other words, the observance of dharmic rules will have a positive effect as regards religious merit of the individual and, at the same time, as regards the preservation of social and cosmic order.

The semantic core of the term *dharma*, which derives from the Indo-European root *dhṛ*, expresses the action of sustaining. *Dharma* is therefore in its most general meaning what sustains the world and the social order. *Dharma* has a prescriptive meaning but also a descriptive one as the nature of things (Francavilla, 2006). The concept of *dharma* is therefore a concept of order, a culture-specific elaboration of the idea of the existence of norms that regulate the course of nature and social life.

Reflection on *dharma* was conducted from the Vedic period in close connection with reflection on *karman*, also stemming from the ritual context. The theory of *karman*, which characterizes most of the philosophies of Hinduism, can be seen as a retributive theory of the consequences of actions. *Karman* is the action seen from the perspective of the consequences that it produces and identifies itself at the beginning with ritual action, to then become any action that has supersensory effects. A certain action can produce spiritual merit or demerit, and the term *karman* is usually referred to as this effect of the action. The link between *dharma* and *karman* lies in the fact that positive *karman* derives from *dharma*-compliant action, whereas negative effects on the spiritual level derive from action contrary to *dharma*. In most Hindu philosophies, the quality of rebirth depends on the quality of *karman*, according to the fundamentally cyclical conception of existence as a series of successive rebirths.

Dharma can therefore be defined as what must be done to sustain the cosmos and the social order, and to acquire spiritual merit so as to bring benefit in this life or in a subsequent life. The system of thought in which the concept of *dharma* is developed is characterized by a cosmology and a soteriology. Beyond the differences between specific philosophical and religious elaborations, to establish that an action is *dharma* means nothing more than to affirm its value and therefore its normativity and its dutifulness.

It is this concept that has provided the Hindu tradition with an ideal model of society through which to evaluate emerging forms of life in the different social contexts of Hinduism, institutionalizing some within the tradition as approved forms and excluding others. The role of *dharma* as a value standard in the construction of the laws of the Hindus also implies that its relevance goes beyond a single manifestation of Hindu religiousness and may even be compatible with the lack of an authentic religiosity. In other words, the concept of *dharma* has represented in the Hindu tradition an equivalent of the concept of justice in the west. Regardless of a specific philosophical elaboration, it has been able to orientate the structures of the communities and the lives of individuals, penetrating the Hindu tradition in all its variety.

The idea of justice that is incorporated in the concept of *dharma* is not based on an abstract concept of moral good but on the idea of appropriateness or correctness. In other words, dharmic action is the appropriate action for a particular person in a given context. Based on a cosmology for which every individual has a place in the world and a specific duty to perform, what counts on the dharmic level is that everyone does what corresponds to his or her nature. In this way, everyone takes part in the process of preserving order, gaining for himself or herself a spiritual merit.

Dharma, being based on the idea of the appropriateness of actions, is structured as a set of duties that are differentiated according to different spaces and times, to the personal condition of who acts and who is the addressee of the action, as well as to the features specific to the context. This to some extent always applies to law, but in Hindu law the dependence of the dharmic rule on the specific context is taken to the extreme and explicitly conceptualized (Doniger et al., 1991).

Hindu law therefore develops as a set of rules of behaviour differentiated according to social class (*varṇa*) and caste of belonging (*jāti*), as well as, albeit of less practical importance, stage of life (*āśrama*).[12] These rules are progressively institutionalized from the Vedic period to the classical period and find their main formulation in the texts on *dharma*. It must however be considered that Hindu law has always been widely customary and that these texts in many cases consolidate already observed rules at a customary level.

Varṇa and *āśrama* together constitute the *varṇāśramadharma*. In the Brahmanical elaboration, this category provides a first level of differentiation of duties and is used in the texts on *dharma* as a general scheme to describe the duties falling upon each person, adopting as paradigmatic the model of Brahmins (Olivelle, 2005). These duties are further differentiated on the basis of the belonging to a caste (*jāti*), which is connected to *varṇa* and is further divided into sub-castes (*upajāti*).[13] What has to be pointed out is that the rules of behaviour are different because of belonging to one or the other class. In fact, a given behaviour may be prohibited for a certain person in a specific context and, on the contrary, be permitted if the agent or the addressee changes.

These categories relate to the distinction between common *dharma* (*sāmānya-* or *sādhāraṇa-dharma*) and particular *dharma* (*viśeṣa-dharma*). The first one includes a series of behaviours that are held as common to all people and may be reduced to a list of general virtues such as non-violence, forgiving, compassion and inner discipline, while the second one is the complex network of duties defined from the *varṇāśramadharma* and from belonging to a certain caste. The relationship between the two levels of *dharma* is such that the general *dharma* represents a residual category, rather than a set of basic principles from which one should derive the rules to regulate one's own behaviour. Only if a specific norm of behaviour based on one's own peculiar *dharma* cannot be found, should one act according to those principles.

This model presented in *dharmaśāstra* actually remains at a certain distance from practical life. Caste is one of the more complex issues in Hinduism and Hindu law. While the Brahmanical elaboration of caste we find in Sanskrit literature is an extensive and coherent one, it is worth remembering that the phenomenon of caste is much more complex and diversified.

Dharma is by nature very flexible. Given that it can vary widely depending on the circumstances, personal and local contexts, it can be seen to some extent as indefinite or open as regards content. Some rules are institutionalized in certain contexts, others, even opposite, in others. Since the law must guarantee a stable reference for action, the law of a specific community may be more or less rigid, but, in principle, the *dharma* is always modifiable. The character of eternity is referred to *dharma* as an ordering principle, which may have, without contradiction, different historical manifestations.

Hindu pluralism is not just a question of fact. It is legitimized starting from the same structure of Vedic revelation. As highlighted by Menski (2002), considering that Vedic revelation is not considered an expression of the will of a personal god and is received by an indeterminate number of savants who are at the origin of the different traditions of Hinduism, from the outset a stable core, a creed that provides the premises for a single law is missing.

The paths of Hinduism that emerge in the post-Vedic periods, from devotional *bhakti* movements to the more recent ones, find in tradition considered as a whole concepts and texts to which can be attributed a central role in their specific elaboration of Hindu religiosity. However, if it can be assumed that the religious and devotional life of Hindus increasingly differs, the normative core of Hinduism, which is the basis of the various Hindu laws, remains strongly marked by this ancient elaboration of *dharma*. Hinduism is considered as an orthopraxis more than an orthodoxy, and different beliefs can coexist with common practices.

Historically, Hindu law has been a complete law, with norms regarding family relationships as well as other areas of law. In other words, within the framework of the Hindu tradition, rules and institutions have been developed for the various fields of human activity, from ritual to trial, from marriage to property. In many cases, the strictly religious layer of Hindu law, centred on the concept of *dharma*, with the associated cosmology and soteriology, has functioned as a criterion for assessing the conformity of some rules, having their origin elsewhere, with the standard of behaviour required of a Hindu.

The individual historical systems that have developed in the Indian subcontinent have always realized to some extent integration between norms having different origins. In the transition to modernity, the scope of relevance of Hindu law has shrunk or has changed. Large parts of law have completely detached themselves from Hindu law and have been replaced by rules of western origin. In fact, as we have seen, from the colonial period, Hindu law has been officially in force in India only in matters of personal status and in a few other matters. Moreover, in these matters, Hindu law has been simplified through some reform attempts made by the state.

The introduction of state sources of Hindu law partly changes the nature of this law as a religious law, since the Indian Republic is secular and a law that regulates family relations between Hindus cannot be considered a religious law, even though it intervenes on a complex of socio-religious practices. State intervention on Hindu law, however, is not such as to constitute a complete break with tradition, given that large parts of traditional law are recognized and applied by the state bodies themselves. Secondly – and this is probably the most important point – official Hindu law does not exclude the relevance of traditional Hindu law at the unofficial level. This unofficial Hindu law is the law that is not recognized by the state (Chiba, 1986), but it is no less important in the life of Hindus and it does not lack legality in their view.

Unofficial Hindu law can be opposed to official Hindu law or it may exist in separate areas. As for the first aspect, the classic example is the persistent diffusion of institutions such as the marriage of children in some areas of Hinduism despite its prohibition in official law. As regards the second aspect, in the law of classical India, the part relating to ritual and the whole set of rules that regulate the life of Hindu social groups in the most minute aspects were conceived in a unitary way with family law and with the other parts of the law in a common dharmic horizon. These rules certainly have not disappeared but, at least from the point of view of the state, they are separate rules and are no longer legal.

Conclusion

As we have seen, Hindu law has a long and complex history. It has the strength of a tradition, that is to say, of a set of rules and concepts transmitted from one generation to another. Moreover, it may be considered religious law, because, even considering the controversy regarding Hinduism as a religion, it has developed in close connection with a concept of the sacred, a cosmology and a soteriology. This character does not require an understanding of Hindu law as a sort of purely religious law. It is rather a living law where religious concepts and rules play an important role, not unlike other religious and even non-religious laws, and these concepts and rules may be legitimized in religious terms to different extents depending on the context.

These two aspects, tradition and religion, lead many to consider it a backward law, a legacy of the past, which should progressively disappear from contemporary India and other parts of the world. In this negative perception, certain institutions of traditional Hindu law certainly play a role. In particular, castes, child marriages, the condition of women, dowry-related violence, the status of widows and so on, are seen as true symbols of injustice to be fought. Moreover, Hindu law tends to be 'essentialized', not unlike what happens with other religious or traditional laws, and is therefore considered an immutable law, devoid of rationality and incapable of evolving by adapting itself to the needs of a modern society (Menski, 2003).

India's modernizing intervention on Hindu law, a law that is now connected to the constitutional framework and reformed in some aspects, does not change the particularly controversial role of Hindu law in Indian law. Hindu law is the oldest legal layer of Indian tradition and is now an official component of the legal system of the Republic of India. In this transition, it has undergone significant changes but always within a framework in which the legal diversity of Hindus is recognized.

The alternative model is a uniform and completely secular law, based on citizenship and not on religious and community affiliation. In principle, the adoption of a uniform civil code in India, which, as we have seen, is provided for in the Constitution, would represent 'the end of Hindu law' as such, or at least of its history as an official personal law in Indian experience. The debate on the adoption of the uniform civil code has never ceased in India. However, more than sixty years after the Constitution, the system of personal laws still resists, and Hindu law is evolving along complex paths in interaction with constitutional principles.[14]

State intervention on Hindu law poses general problems regarding the characteristics of this law. Menski (2003) pointed out that immediately after Independence there was a phenomenon of reconstruction of Hindu law according to the model of modern western laws. In the colonial period, the western discovery of Hindu law had already posed numerous problems arising from cultural difference, which, intertwined with the needs of the colonial administration, had led to a substantial misunderstanding of the cultural postulates and practical operation of Hindu law (Menski, 2003). The Indians themselves, even after Independence, have corroborated an image of Hindu law as a structurally modern law, endowed with written norms and therefore easily reformable in its contents through state intervention. From these reconstructions one could derive the impression that Hindu law is nothing other than a part of the legal system of the Republic of India that *ratione materiae* applies to certain citizens. Actually, Hindu law is a much more complex reality. The identification of Hindu law with state regulation of Hindu family and succession matters provides a reductive image. In fact, on the one hand, Hindu concepts of law and specific rules may be still operative in matters not included in personal status, relating for instance to the limits of the role of the state (Menski, 2003); and, on the other, not all Hindu family and succession law has been expressed as legislation.

Analysis of both historical evolution and contemporary reality shows that Hindu law is a living reality in continuous transformation, which manifests itself in an informal way more than in state black letter law. It would therefore be simplistic to think that, if the Indian legislator decided to abolish the system of personal laws, Hindu law as such would disappear, or that new legislation on Hindu law in a framework of greater simplification could supplant traditional Hindu law.

Hindu law has its own identity and particular characteristics. It is worth highlighting that it governs the lives of millions of people and its importance is underestimated due to historical and cultural factors. As a conclusion, Hindu law is still vital in the contemporary world and continues its evolution both in interaction with state laws and following the internal logic of tradition.

Notes

1 This periodization of Hindu law, which is slightly different from that used by Menski (2006), is of course very fluid. Many other periodizations are possible based, for instance, on a more analytical consideration of the historical development of Hindu religions or on Indian political history.

2 Local differences are important even as far as Indian Hindu law is concerned. For example, Hindu laws of South India are significantly different from the laws of the North – and North and South are still certainly very broad categories. Differences within Hindu law based on countries may depend on other factors. For instance, Hindu law in Pakistan and Bangladesh is the law of a minority of the population in a largely Islamic context. On the contrary, Nepalese Hindu law has enjoyed a privileged position deriving from the fact that, at least until 2008, Nepal was the last Hindu kingdom.

3 On this perspective, see Menski (1987), Ballard (1994) and Shah (2005).

4 Not all rules of conduct are also legal rules. However, as we will see, in the Hindu context no clear distinctions are drawn between different normative spheres. Therefore, the discourse on Hindu law, both from the point of view of scholars and from the internal point of view of tradition, tends to be inclusive. The delimitation of a properly legal sphere according to a paradigm based on modern and western conceptions of law is meaningful mainly as far as modern Hindu law is concerned.

5 'Brahmanism' is a term denoting a main component of the history of Hinduism, which is closely linked to Vedic knowledge and culture. On the various phases of Hinduism, see Flood (2004). Hinduism has become in the course of time an increasingly complex reality, but even if the so-called Neo-Hinduism movements, mainly *bhakti* movements, are now the most widespread, Brahmanism is still one of the basic cultural components of Hinduism.

6 In this chapter, I will mostly consider Hindu law through the lens of the learned tradition of Hindu jurisprudence. An overview of the historical development of Hindu law based on rulers, corporate groups, temples and other social agents may be read in Davis (2010b). A more stringent historical analysis of the development of Hindu law would require focus on specific contexts. An attempt in this direction with reference to Kerala may be read in Davis (2004).

7 Some sciences are significantly named 'limbs of the Veda' (*vedāṅga*). For an introduction, see Flood (2004).

8 On the importance and characters of chthonic traditions, see Glenn (2004).

9 The oldest treatise is the collection of *sūtras* attributed to Jaimini, the *Pūrvamīmāṃsāsūtra*. There is no doubt that Jaimini himself is the compiler and arranger of a system of thought previously developed. According to Verpoorten (1987), the work of Jaimini should be dated around 450–400 BC.

10 Concerning the relation between *dharmaśāstra* and Mīmāṃsā, it is possible to see a broad correspondence with the relationship between *usul-al-fiqh* and *furu-al-fiqh* in Islamic law. In this perspective, the Mīmāṃsā, meant as theoretical jurisprudence, seems closer to the *usul-al-fiqh*, while the *dharmaśāstra*, more concerned with rules, would be the *furu-al-fiqh*.

11 For a description of colonial law, see Jain (1981) and Menski (2003).

12 For details on the *āśramas*, see Olivelle (1993).

13 For a brief discussion of several theories related to the origins of castes and a description of legal rules based on castes in classical Hindu law, see Lingat (1998: 29–45).

14 For a review of different opinions on the uniform civil code, see Dhagamwar (1989) and Menski (2008).

References

Ballard, R. (ed.). 1994. *Desh Pardesh. The South Asian Presence in Britain*. Hurst & Co.
Chiba, M. (ed.). 1986. *Asian Indigenous Law in Interaction with Received Law*. KPI.

Davis, D. R. Jr. 2004. *The Boundaries of Hindu Law: Tradition, Custom and Politics in Medieval Kerala*. Corpus Iuris Sanscriticum et fontes iuris Asiae Meridianae et Centralis.
Davis, D. R. Jr. 2010a. *The Spirit of Hindu Law*. Cambridge University Press.
Davis, D. R. Jr. 2010b. 'A Historical Overview of Hindu Law' in T. Lubin, D. R Davis Jr. and J. K. Krishnan (eds) *Hinduism and Law: An Introduction*. Cambridge University Press. 17.
Derrett, J. D. M. 1973. *Dharmaśāstra and Juridical Literature*. Otto Harrassowitz.
Derrett, J. D. M. 1976–1978. *Essays in Classical and Modern Hindu Law*. Vols. 1–4. Brill.
Derrett, J. D. M. 1998. 'Introduction' in R. Lingat, *The Classical Law of India*. Oxford University Press.
Dhagamwar, V. 1989. *Towards the Uniform Civil Code*. N.M. Tripathi.
Doniger, W. et al. 1991. *The Laws of Manu*. Penguin.
Flood, G. 2004. *An Introduction to Hinduism*. Cambridge University Press.
Francavilla, D. 2006. *The Roots of Hindu Jurisprudence. Sources of Dharma and Interpretation in Mīmāṃsā and Dharmaśāstra*. Corpus Iuris Sanscriticum et fontes iuris Asiae Meridianae et Centralis.
Glenn, H. P. 2004. *Legal Traditions of the World. Sustainable Diversity in Law*. Oxford University Press.
Halbfass, W. 1990a. *India and Europe: An Essay in Philosophical Understanding*. Motilal Banarsidass.
Halbfass, W. 1990b. *Tradition and Reflection: Explorations in Indian Thought*. State University of New York Press.
Hobsbawm, E. and Ranger, T. (eds). 1983. *The Invention of Tradition*. Cambridge University Press.
Huxley, A. 1995. 'Buddhism and Law: The View From Mandalay'. 18(1) *Journal of the International Association of Buddhist Studies*. 47.
Jain M. P. 1981. *Outlines of Indian Legal History*, fourth edition. N. M. Tripathi.
Jha, G. 1964. *Pūrva Mīmāṃsā in its Sources*. Banaras Hindu University.
Kane, P. V. 1962–1975. *History of Dharmaśāstra*. Vols 1–5. Bhandarkar Oriental Research Institute.
Knott, K. 1998. *Hinduism. A Very Short Introduction*. Oxford University Press.
Lingat, R. 1998. *The Classical Law of India*. Oxford University Press.
Malamoud, C. 1998. *Cooking the World. Ritual and Thought in Ancient India*. Oxford University Press.
Menski, W. F. 1987. 'Legal Pluralism in the Hindu Marriage' in R. Burghart (ed.) *Hinduism in Great Britain*. Tavistock. 180.
Menski, W. F. 2002. 'Hindu Law as a "Religious" System', in A. Huxley (ed.) *Religion, Law and Tradition: Comparative Studies in Religious Law*. RoutledgeCurzon. 108.
Menski, W. F. 2003. *Hindu Law. Beyond Tradition and Modernity*. Oxford University Press.
Menski, W. F. 2006. *Comparative Law in a Global Context: The Legal Systems of Asia and Africa*. 2nd edn. Cambridge University Press.
Menski, W. F. 2008. 'The Uniform Civil Code Debate in Indian Law: New Developments and Changing Agenda'. 9(3) *German Law Journal*. 211.
Michaels, A. 2004. *Hinduism Past and Present*. Orient Longman.
Miller, J. 1985. *The Vision of Cosmic Order in the Vedas*. Routledge & Kegan Paul.
Olivelle, P. 1993. *The Āśrama System: The History and Hermeneutics of a Religious Institution*. Oxford University Press.
Olivelle, P. (ed.). 1999. *Dharmasūtras: The Law Codes of Āpastamba, Gautama, Baudhāyana and Vasiṣṭa*. Oxford University Press.
Olivelle, P. (ed.). 2005. *Manu's Code of Law*. Oxford University Press.
Shah, P. 2005. *Legal Pluralism in Conflict. Coping with Cultural Diversity in Law*. Glass House Press.
Sontheimer, G.-D. and Kulke, H. (eds). 1989. *Hinduism Reconsidered*. Munshiram Manoharlal.
Verpoorten, J. M. 1987. *Mīmāṃsā literature*. Otto Harrassowitz.
Zweigert, K. and Kötz, H. 1998. *An Introduction to Comparative Law*. 3rd edn. Clarendon Press.

5

Comparative remarks

A history of religious laws

John Tolan

'I've gotta use words when I talk to you' says Sweeny in T. S. Elliot's *Sweeny Agonistes*, and this sums up nicely what many social scientists feel when they try to transport their conceptual baggage across cultural and historical frontiers. How can one suppose that one's concepts will be able to apply to or elucidate cultures distant in space or time? Yet without those concepts, how can we possibly compare human societies across time and space? The four authors of this first, historical section of this *Handbook on Religious Laws* have been given the formidable task of briefly describing the origins, historical evolution and central characteristics of Jewish, Christian, Muslim and Hindu legal traditions. Each chapter had to span multiple centuries and huge geographical areas.

These four traditions all base their legal systems to a certain extent on sacred texts: the Sanskrit Vedas, composed in the second millennium BCE; the Torah, compiled over the sixth and fifth centuries BCE; the New Testament, written during the first and second centuries CE; and the Qur'ān, written down in the seventh century CE. Yet these various texts have complex histories of authorship (and of debates about their divine or human origins). While they are often seen as an important (or primary) source of norms and rules for the societies that revere them, there are other, rival sources with implicit or explicit validity. Moreover, in each of these traditions, sacred texts were filtered through a rich, varied and often conflicting body of exegesis (on this 'exegetical impulse', see Fowden, 2014).

The basic concepts of religion and law (in English and other languages) are of course products of long and rich historical evolution. The structure of this *Handbook* is based on the idea that Judaism, Christianity, Islam and Hinduism are distinct 'religions', indeed 'world religions'. This idea may seem self-evident, but as Tomoko Masauzawa reminds us, it is an invention of the nineteenth century, when 'religious studies' (as opposed to earlier disciplines such as theology, canon law, *fiqh* or Talmudic studies) emerged as a distinct discipline. Each religion had its sacred texts, its theology, its rites and its history. Religious studies permitted scholars to examine these religious objectively and comparatively, in theory without partisan bias (Masuzawa, 2005). In many ways this was a significant intellectual achievement. Yet it comports a real danger of essentialization of these 'religions', downplaying both the overlap and interconnectedness between them and the great diversity and divergence within each of them. It is hence worthwhile to take a brief look at the history of the concept.

Religio, in ancient Latin, refers both to an attitude of reverence, respect and fear of the gods and to the devotion shown towards them. The term is almost never used in the plural in classical Latin: *religio* is a general attitude and behaviour that can be adopted towards one or many gods. While each god/goddess has his/her own specific cult and rituals, in no sense do these amount to different 'religions'. Hence an ancient Roman would not understand the question 'what religion are you?' Cults in the ancient Mediterranean were often (though by no means always) associated with civic governance. Thus for an Athenian, the festivals associated with Athena were civic, political, social and religious events of major importance: these different elements were inextricable. For Romans, the same is true for the cult of Vesta or Capitoline Jupiter – and, later, for the cult of the deified emperors. Refusal to participate would indicate lack of civic duty as well as religious duty. Jews were early on granted exemptions from taking part in traditional Roman cults, but these privileges were given to Jews as a people or *ethnos*, not a 'religion'. The Romans had many accords with different nations (*gentes* or *ethnoi*), recognizing their rights to maintain traditional social, legal and at times, cultic practices. Roman accords with the Jews were thus nothing exceptional, even if certain stipulations were unique to the Jews (not bringing imperial insignia into the city of Jerusalem, exempting Jews from participating in cults of Roman deities, not summoning them to court on the Sabbath, etc.).

Things changed with the advent of Christianity and its adoption by the elite of the Roman Empire. In 325, Constantine called the council of Nicaea, the First Ecumenical Council of the Church, which established the credo (or Nicene Creed): the basic statement of faith to which every Christian was supposed to adhere. It also established the primacy of four bishops, those of Jerusalem, Alexandria, Antioch and Rome (Constantinople would later be added to the list), patriarchs who in theory exercised authority over lesser bishops. Arguably, Nicaea represents the invention of Christianity as the first 'religion' in the modern, commonly accepted sense of the term: a 'faith' to which its members must adhere (the Creed) and a 'Church' structured along hierarchical lines. There was never a 'credo' defining what Jews had to believe, neither of course was there ever one for the adepts of Jupiter, Athena or Isis.

Can we conceive of ancient Judaism as a religion? Daniel Boyarin speaks of a process of 'Christian invention of Judaism' in the fourth and fifth centuries, as Christian writers define orthodoxy over and against those outside that orthodoxy: Jews, 'Hellenes' (i.e. pagans) and heretics. The Roman state plays a key role in the institutionalization of the Christian Church, as we see notably through the *Theodosian Code*, promulgated in 438 by Theodosius II, which brings together laws of Christian emperors from Constantine I to Theodosius II. These laws characterize Judaism as a 'sect' (*secta* CTh 16.8.2, 8.8, 8.9), sometimes adding for good measure qualifiers such as 'beastly' or 'nefarious' (*feralem sectam* 16.8.1; *nefariam sectam* 16.8.1). Some laws refer to Jewish 'perversity' or 'incredulity' (*perversitatem iudaicam* 16.8.19; *incredulitate judaica* 16.8.19). Yet other laws present Judaism as a *religio* alongside Christianity. A hierarchy of Jewish officials was recognized and given, quite explicitly, the same privileges as the high officials of the Christian Church, creating what Amnon Linder has called a 'Jewish Church' (Linder, 2006: 157). In other words, imperial officials and bishops recognized 'Judaism' as a religion at the same time that they sought to keep it distinct and separate from Christianity and the Christian Church. At the same time, a rabbinical elite that had succeeded in obtaining social and intellectual dominance within the Jewish community not only accepted these developments but actively embraced them. In other words, emerging Jewish and Christian religious elites defined the new Jewish and Christian 'religions' and 'churches' and strove to erect a firm and watertight barrier between the two (Boyarin, 2004).

Our concept of 'religion' was in short created by and for Christianity and applied with ambiguity to rivals such as Judaism. Islam, in its different forms, seems to correspond well to the concept of religion, as it is also faith-centred, with the *shahada* serving as credo. Yet in many of its manifestations, it lacks the hierarchical clergy essential to the Christian concept of religion. Further afield, our concept of religion becomes increasingly problematic. Witness, for example, the debates, from seventeenth-century Jesuits to twenty-first-century scholars, as to whether Confucianism qualifies as a 'religion'. 'Hinduism', as Domenico Francavilla notes, in fact brings together a constellation of different sacred texts, beliefs and rituals and is perhaps best considered a 'bundle of religions'. It is in confrontation with Islam and Christianity that Hinduism is defined (from the outside, and subsequently from within) as a 'religion'.

The term 'law' also poses questions. Each of the four authors presents different terms in various languages which can render 'law' in the four religious traditions. Even within European tradition, as Kenneth Pennington reminds us, there are diverse concepts, in particular the Latin terms *ius* (which more or less corresponds to the Spanish *derecho*, the Italian *diritto*, the German *Recht* or the French *droit*) and *lex* (with the equivalent terms *ley, legge, Gesetz* and *loi*). This fundamental distinction for most European languages is, in English, lost in translation. The difficulty is more acute when one goes further afield to non-European languages. We have seen that 'law' can be translated (imperfectly) by terms such as *halakha, sharī'a, fiqh, dharma*, and a host of others. The problem is not simply an academic one. As Domenico Francavilla relates, British colonial administrators attempted to apply and enforce 'Hindu law', which they understood as a series of rules recorded in ancient Sanskrit 'law books': 'detached from the traditional interplay of sources, the Hindu law applied in the courts became one that actually existed only in the mind of the colonial judge'.

Each of the four authors has addressed the question of sources of law, often a complex mix of sacred texts, glosses to those texts, other legal traditions (royal, civic, imperial) and legal precedence based on the decisions of judges. Historians of Indian law distinguish the 'pre-classical' period of the composition of the Vedas (or Śruti), the 'classical period' of composition of Smṛti (oral tradition recorded in writing during the first millennium BCE and the first several centuries of the first millennium CE, and constantly revised), and the post-classical period of exegetical and legal commentary to this legal corpus (roughly fifth to seventeenth centuries CE). While Brahamanic legal scholars frequently referred to the Vedic texts as authoritative, the diversity and ambiguity of these texts gave them large leeway for creative adaptation to changing circumstances. Several medieval scholars argued that an edict issued by a king was by definition in accordance with *dharma* and hence inherently legitimate (Mathur, 2007: 7–8). Various medieval Hindu scholars affirmed that *nyaya* (reason) was at least as important as *agama* (written authority) in establishing law and in adjudicating. This gave a wide berth to authorities to adopt legal practice to changing local circumstances. This does not mean of course that the ancient text could be spurned. On the contrary, as Mathur notes (2007: 30), evocation of textual authority was an essential part of the legal practice of kings and the Brahmans in their entourage 'by claiming to be great followers and patrons of dharma, the rulers furthered their own right to rule'.

Comparisons can be made between the complex web of sources that form the basis for Jewish and Muslim 'law'. The Torah and the Qur'ān are both normative texts, containing specific, detailed rules concerning what it is permissible to eat, sexuality and marriage, inheritance, rules of conduct in war, etc. (in comparison, the Vedas have relatively few specific rules of comportment). Yet these texts do not offer rules on everything, and even when they do offer clear strictures, these are not always respected. Oral tradition (the 'oral Torah' or Talmud for Jews; Hadiths for Muslims, roughly comparable to the Hindu Smṛti), subsequently given written form, is an important complement (and at times corrective) to the legal strictures of scripture. These traditions were complex, diverse and not accepted by all: the Karaites rejected the Talmud, affirming that only the Torah bore legal and religious authority. In other communities, the Talmud became authoritative, though as Talya Fishman has shown, the adoption of the Babylonian Talmud by European Jewish communities was much more gradual than has often been assumed (Fishman, 2011). The Talmud itself affirms *dina de-malkhuta dina*, Aramaic for 'the law of the kingdom is the law', recognizing the validity of law of other (gentile) provenance (Washofsky, 1989: 293). This means that Jews are obliged to respect the legal restrictions imposed upon them by their (non-Jewish) rulers, but it also has broader implications, as it pleads for a flexibility of Jewish law across diverse societies. Against those rabbis who purported to derive legal strictures from their exegeses of Torah and Talmud, others countered that the consensus and accepted traditions were the ultimate guarantors of legality, and thus varied in function of time and place. Indeed a common phrase found at the conclusion of many rabbinic responsa is 'this is the *halakhah* and this is the custom' – in other words, legal decisions should ideally correspond both to the textual basis of Jewish law and to established (and sometimes quite local) custom. For Hayya Gaon (active in tenth-century Iraq), consensus of the Jews is the ultimate source of legal practice: 'go out and see what the people do' he says; only subsequently should textual authority be sought to bolster legal practice (Fishman, 2017: 36–38). Jewish 'law' is a corpus of texts (Torah, *halakhah*, responsa), authoritative and interpretive, but it is also a process, a constant dialogue.

The same issues were discussed among Muslim jurists. In the eighth century, debates raged between the *ahl al-ra'y* (advocates of 'common sense' or 'rational discretion') and the *ahl al-hadith* (partisans of the Hadith) (Hennigan, 2009). The differences between the two parties were perhaps not as pronounced as often portrayed: the partisans of *ra'y* would at times cite Hadith to bolster their arguments while the corpus of Hadith, compiled and written down principally in the ninth century, bore the imprint of the multiple judicial traditions of the caliphates' predecessors. As Knut Vikør remarks, while in theory there were three separate sources for Islamicate legal traditions (pre-Islamic Arab tribal law, law of the conquered empires and religious precepts), in fact 'the differences between these three sources for early Muslim law may not be so formidable as sometimes assumed'. Arabs of the peninsula had been in contact with the Roman and Persian empires well before Muhammad, and the ninth-century compilations of Hadiths allowed the post-facto islamization of Persian, Roman and other legal traditions. *Sunna* (tradition or practice) in early Islam varied from place to place.

A striking similarity between Jewish and Muslim legal cultures is the practice of judicial consultation: *responsa* in Jewish tradition (i.e. *She'elot u-Teshuvot*, 'questions and answers'), and *fatāwā* (singular *fatwā*) in Islam. An individual writes to a learned legal scholar (rabbi or mufti) posing a specific legal question. The rabbi or mufti responds, giving his answer to the question, providing citations of texts from scripture and especially the opinions of previous scholars. The author places himself firmly in a legal tradition (Maliki muftis, for example, cite above all Maliki legal authorities), at the same time often noting divergent opinions. The *responsum* or *fatwā* is thus neither a 'law', as it is not binding, nor is it a judicial decision, as it is not issued by a judge to adjudicate a specific case. It is rather a learned opinion, at times directly solicited by rulers or judges, to be taken into account (or not) in judging analogous cases – and to be cited and discussed in subsequent *responsa* or *fatāwā*. This practice of constant reflection on and interpretation of legal issues gives a certain flexibility to these legal systems, allowing evolution over time and diversity across different geographic regions, or with different traditions locally (for example, different *madhhabs*). If God is the ultimate source of Law (*halakha* or *sharī'a*), that Law is filtered through a rich and complex web of commentaries and interpretations.

Hence a 'law code' as such is a concept foreign to Jewish and Muslim traditions (and to Hinduism as well). Indeed, as Joseph E. David remarks, already ancient Mesopotamian law 'was understood in terms of divine authorship and heavenly origins. Thus in principle Mesopotamian law was not legislated, but revealed and given – not promulgated, but commanded'. Hence in theory a Muslim or Jew could not *legislate*, could not author new law, but could only interpret the law of God. The idea of divine origin of law exists of course in other ancient societies, including Greece and Rome: the nymph Egeria supposedly dictated to King Numa Pompilius laws for Rome. Yet this did not prevent the Senate and subsequently emperors from affirming their legislative authority – just as the divine authority of the Vedas did not prevent Hindu kings from making law.

Christianity emerges among Jews living under Roman law, and we find from the beginning a tension between these two sources of law. We see this in two key passages of the Gospel of Matthew. 'Do not think that I have come to abolish the Law or the Prophets; I have not come to abolish them but to fulfil them' (5:17). While the first Christians were Jews who followed Jewish Law (concerning dietary restrictions, circumcision, etc.), Paul and other preachers opened the community to Gentile converts who were not obliged to follow Jewish law. For some exegetes, this passage from Matthew indicates that Jesus scrupulously respected Jewish law and brought out its true meaning, hence transforming it. In any case, by the third century for Christians these issues belonged to the realm of exegesis, not legal practice. Jesus also asserted, according to Matthew, 'Render unto Caesar the things that are Caesar's, and unto God the things that are God's' (22:21). This suggests, to some commentators, separate legal spheres, the Empire and the Church, each legitimate in its own realm.

It is of course impossible here to address the rich variety of legal responses to these issues across Christian communities. Armenia and Ethiopia were the first kingdoms to become Christian, in the fourth century, and remained independent kingdoms throughout most of the Middle Ages. In many Muslim-ruled territories Christians remained a numerical majority (elsewhere a significant minority) for centuries after the Muslim conquest. The various Christian communities enjoyed considerable legal autonomy, and their religious leaders (bishops, in particular) were often recognized by Muslim rulers as de facto heads of their communities, often acting as judges in disputes between members of their communities. Like Jews in Muslim and Christian lands, they had to try to accommodate both the legal traditions of their own religious communities and the strictures imposed by the law of the dominant culture (Simonsohn, 2011).

Kenneth Pennington examines one manifestation of Christian tradition, that of Latin Europe in the Middle Ages. He shows how the eleventh and twelfth centuries were particularly important in the development and interpenetration of two traditions, Roman law and canon law. The European medieval ruler is also a legislator: a source of law, as well as an enforcer of legal tradition. This is not a negation of the divine character of law, but often an incarnation of it: the ancient emperors were deified, and medieval European monarchs claimed to be king *Dei gratia*, through the grace of God. The relationship between king and Church varies widely during the Middle Ages and is often a source of conflict or negotiation.

The Roman practice of *codification* had a significant impact on the emergence and evolution of Christian law within and outside of the empire. Christian emperors such as Theodosius II in 438, Justinian (529–534), or Leo VI (896–912) had their jurists compile, organize and edit collections of laws that were in each case meant to become definitive law codes to be used in law schools and by judges and administrators. The process involves a respect for legal tradition (as it brings together laws promulgated by different emperors, up to and including the current one), a desire to harmonize and unify the law, and a recourse to the authority of the emperor as the promulgator of the new code. Yet the *leges* (laws) brought together in the code were authoritative only in so far as they were seen to reflect *ius*: an unjust law could be contested, or ignored by a judge.

As Pennington notes, there is no clear distinction between 'lay' and 'religious' law here: the Roman state legislates on the privileges of bishops, the abolition of pagan rituals, the rights of Jews to have synagogues and respect the Sabbath, etc. What is more, the emperors, from Constantine I (306–337) to Constantine XI (1449–1453), exercised control over the Church, calling ecumenical councils and influencing the choice of bishops, in particular the patriarch of Constantinople.

In the Latin West, local and regional Church councils legislated independently of Constantinople, often (but not always) under the tutelage of local rulers. Many of the kings of the new kingdoms in Europe issued their own law codes: the Salic Law of the Franks (issued by Clovis c. 500), the Burgundian Law (Gundobad, 473–516), the Law of Æthelberht for the Anglo-Saxons (Æthelberht of Kent, 589–618), the *Edict of Rothari* (by the Lombard King Rothari in 643), various Wisigothic law codes and other texts issued by other rulers. Many of these codes provided not a replacement but a complement to Roman law codes. They were *ethnic* laws, meaning that they applied to a group defined as Frankish, Burgundian, Lombard, or simply 'barbarian' (as opposed to Roman). Thus within the same kingdom, different laws applied to different people, according to their status as 'Romans' or 'barbarians', as slave or free, as lay or cleric, woman or man, etc. In these law codes, as in Roman law, there is no distinction between 'religious' and 'secular' law: we find texts on the inviolability of sacred space, the privileges of bishops, etc.

The bishops of Rome, or popes, gradually asserted their independence from Constantinople and their ascendance over other bishops in Western Europe. But they were to fall under the control of other rulers, in particularly the Ottonian Emperors in the tenth to eleventh centuries. The struggle between emperors and popes for control of Church offices (known to historians as the 'investiture controversy'), took place at the same time as the renaissance of the study of Roman law in Europe, particularly in Bologna. Popes and emperors hired legal scholars to wage, on their behalf, what historians have dubbed a 'Zitatenkampf', a war of citations (Fuhrmann, 1982), mining Roman law texts and other legal documents to prove the ascendency of their respective champions. Other rulers followed suit: kings, dukes, counts, municipal councils of the emerging cities. All hired lawyers trained in Bologna and elsewhere to help them codify their legal traditions and assert their legitimacy.

The judicial map of Europe was thus a patchwork of overlapping and at times rival jurisdictions. During the twelfth and thirteenth centuries, kings of France, England and other kingdoms gradually affirmed their ascendency over their vassals. The right to adjudicate conflicts was of course an important and jealously guarded prerogative of sovereignty; it was also an important source of income. Kings of England and France increasingly positioned their royal courts as appellate jurisdictions superior to the seigneurial courts. They also developed a system of royal courts which was soon reputed to be quicker, more efficient and fairer than the seigneurial courts. The biographers of Saint Louis depict him sitting under an oak tree outside his castle at Vincennes, patiently receiving the legal complaints of his humblest subjects. Under Louis IX, as Jacques Le Goff explained, 'l'état s'avance masqué, sous le masque de la sainteté' (Le Goff, 1996: 701).

Royal judges were in rivalry and conflict not only with the seigneurial and municipal jurisdictions but also with clerical courts. The immunity of clerics from lay judicial systems, their right to be judged solely in Church courts, was one of the main issues of the papal reform movement that provoked the investiture controversy. In England, it provoked a conflict between King Henry II and Thomas Becket, Archbishop of Canterbury, which led to the latter's murder. Despite attempts at compromise and resolution, it remained a bone of contention throughout the Middle Ages and beyond.

A vivid image of this jurisdictional checkerboard is found in an illumination in a manuscript (c. 1300) of the *Sachsenspiegel* (Mirror of the Saxons). The *Sachsenspiegel* was a code of laws written first in Latin (in the first quarter of the thirteenth century) and translated into German. It proved to be a real medieval bestseller, as its over 300 extant German manuscripts attest. The *Sachsenspiegel* had a profound impact on the study and practice of law in the German-speaking Europe from the fourteenth to the sixteenth century, and to an extent even until the nineteenth (Kümper, 2004).

In Figure 5.1 we get a glimpse of the complexity and multiplicity of medieval judicial venues, but they are placed in a clear hierarchy, from top to bottom. In the highest register, Christ gives two swords to the pope and the emperor, both of whom are kneeling before him. This parallelism might suggest the equality of ecclesiastical and lay justice, though it is important to note that the pope is at Christ's right hand (the same side which the blessed occupy in the last judgement scenes): this suggests the pre-eminence of the pope over the emperor. To drive this hierarchy home, on the next level down, the emperor plays the role of squire to the pope, showing his subordination. The four bottom images all depict judgement scenes with a judge on the right meting out justice to those before him. The first of these scenes portrays the court of the bishop, the next the court of the cathedral provost, then the court of the count acting under royal authority of the king, and finally the Schultheiss (more or less equivalent of mayor), who exercises justice at the municipal level.

While this illumination of the *Sachsenspiegel* depicts the justice system as an idealized hierarchy, with a clear clerical bias (as ecclesiastical justice occupies the higher registers), the reality of course was more complex: the struggle between judges and jurisdiction, and a lack of clarity in many cases of who should judge whom in what circumstances. This left considerable leeway, in many cases, for the practice of forum shopping in medieval societies: between royal, ducal,

Figure 5.1 Der Sachsenspiegel

Source: Bibliothek Herzog August, Wolfenbüttel, Ms Aug 3.1 (early 14th c.), f. 10 (http://dbs.hab.de/mss/). © Herzog August Bibliothek Wolfenbüttel

comital and seigniorial jurisdictions; between different ecclesiastical authorities (abbots, bishops, archbishops, pope); between lay and ecclesiastical jurisdictions; and finally between 'minority' jurisdictions (rabbis, bishops, qādīs) and 'majority' jurisdictions (on this, see Tolan, 2015). In contrast to the idealized hierarchy of the *Sachsenspiegel*, in fact there are many grey areas and areas of conflict.

Perhaps somewhat paradoxically, as Pennington shows, this plethora of *leges* did not prevent the *Ius commune*, the study of law fusing Roman and canon traditions, from shaping the legal education and legal culture of jurists throughout the Middle Ages and beyond. Protestant legal scholars continued to rely on it heavily in the early modern period, even if some elements of canon law (including of course everything relating to the papacy and the Church hierarchy) they rejected. Over the course of the sixteenth and seventeenth centuries, Rome increasingly tried to exercise the monopoly over the teaching and transmission of canon law, at the same time as the princes of Europe gradually imposed a text-based national legal framework into which the churches (Catholic or Protestant) were subjected to national laws and to the jurisdiction of secular courts.

The gradual imposition, in most European countries, and then in their former colonies, of a system of law based on written constitutions and written codes of laws, has fundamentally changed traditional practice of legal study and of adjudication. This tradition in many cases is largely forgotten, which is one of the factors that explains the incomprehension that many European colonial administrators demonstrated towards the traditional legal systems of their colonies. A telling example, as we have seen, is the attitude of British colonial judges who sought written 'laws' in what they perceived as canonical Hindu texts.

The richness and complexity of these legal/religious traditions is important not only for historians or antiquarians: it resonates with current issues concerning the nature of religious law and its place in society. Fundamentalists within each of the four traditions practise what Francavilla (following Eric Hobsbawm) refers to as the 'invention of tradition'. This often involves the idealization of a lost 'golden age': the era of the Rabbinic sages, the age of the Apostles, the time of Muhammad or the rule of the *Rashidun* ('rightly guided' caliphs), a Hindu golden age before the arrival of Buddhism, Islam and Christianity. And associated with this vision of the golden age was, more often than not, the obedience towards a canonical text that was a clear and unequivocal guide to belief and practice.

In the vision of Hindu tradition promoted by the Bharatiya Janata Party, the 'invention of tradition' simplifies and unifies a rich and complex web of legal and religious traditions, with a decidedly nationalist agenda. Some politicians and polemicists use this invented tradition to call into question the 'Indianness' of non-Hindus, be they Muslims, Christians, Buddhists or Sikhs. For this reason, scholars who counter this essentialized narrative of an invented Hindu tradition and attempt to show the diversity and complexity of Hindu tradition (as Francavilla does in these pages) become targets for denigration and lawsuits. The most infamous case is that of University of Chicago professor Wendy Doniger, whose *The Hindus: An Alternative History* was attacked by fundamentalists as a heretical work by an orientalist infidel, creating a polemical tempest that finally led Penguin India to withdraw the title from publication (Doniger, 2009).

The perils inherent in such simplified views of legal/religious history are evident in Islamist conceptions of *sharīʿa*, as Vikør shows: imagining *sharīʿa* as a simple code of law based on Qurʾān and Hadith is to ignore the long and rich history of Islamic legal culture, based on constant discussion and reinterpretation, and on a multitude of textual and practical elements. A prime example, as we have seen, is the question of *ḥudūd*: Qurʾānic punishments for specific crimes, often involving amputation or death. Jihadists and other Islamic purist reject centuries of legal discussion, the tradition of *fiqh*, as un-Islamic, imagining that the Qur'ān provided the principal legal structure to the first generation of Muslims – when, on the contrary, 'Muslim' law along with 'Islam' itself as a distinct legal/religious category, emerged gradually over the first several centuries following the *hijra* (Donner, 2012). This fundamentalist concept of *sharī'a* as derived solely from Qur'ān and Hadith is first found in the Wahabite sect in eighteenth-century Arabia, which gradually spread through opposition (often violent) to more traditional forms of Islam. Fundamentalist conceptions within and beyond Wahabism were strongly influenced by Protestant Christian fundamentalism, adopting similar strategies of unfiltered literalist readings of sacred texts (Redissi, 2007).

A clear conception of the richness and complexity of Hindu, Muslim, Christian and Jewish conceptions of law, in their long history of composition and exegesis of fundamental texts, is an antidote to simplistic, fundamentalist conception of law.

References

Boyarin, D. 2004. 'The Christian Invention of Judaism: The Theodosian Empire and the Rabbinic Refusal of Religion'. 85 *Representations*. 21.

Doniger, W. 2009. *The Hindus: An Alternative History*. Penguin.

Donner, F. 2012. *Muhammad and the Believers: At the Origins of Islam*. Harvard University Press.

Fishman, T. 2011. *Becoming the People of the Talmud: Oral Torah as Written Tradition in Medieval Jewish Cultures*. University of Pennsylvania Press.

Fishman, T. 2017. 'The Relative Authorities of Text and Tradition in Medieval Jewish Jurisprudence: Geonic Exceptionalism in its Islamic Context' in J. Tolan et al. (eds) *Religious Minorities in Christian, Jewish and Muslim Law (5th–15th Centuries)*. Brepols. 27.

Fowden, G. 2014. *Before and After Muhammad: The First Millennium Refocused*. Princeton University Press.

Fuhrmann H. 1982. 'Pseudoisidor, Otto von Ostia (Urban II.) und der Zitatenkampf von Gerstungen (1085)'. 68 *Zeitschrift Der Savigny-Stiftung Für Rechtsgeschichte: Kanonistische Abteilung*. 59.

Hennigan, P. 2009. 'Ahl al-ra'y' in K. Fleet et al. (eds) *Encyclopaedia of Islam*. Brill. Online version at http://dx.doi.org/10.1163/1573–3912_ei3_COM_22177.

Kümper, H. 2004. *Sachsenspiegel: Eine Bibliographie – Mit einer Einleitung zu Überlieferung, Wirkung und Forschung*. T. Bautz.

Le Goff, J. 1996. *Saint Louis*. Gallimard.

Linder, A. 2006. 'The Legal Status of the Jews in the Roman Empire' in S. Katz (ed.) *The Cambridge History of Judaism. Vol. IV. The Late Roman-Rabbinic Period*. Cambridge University Press. 128.

Masuzawa, T. 2005. *The Invention of World Religions, or, How European Universalism was Preserved in the Language of Pluralism*. University of Chicago Press.

Mathur, A. 2007. *Medieval Hindu Law: A Study of Post-Smrti Changes in Hindu Law*. Oxford University Press.

Redissi, H. 2007. *Le Pacte de Nadjd. Comment l'islam sectaire est devenu l'islam*. Seuil.

Simonsohn, U. 2011. *A Common Justice: The Legal Allegiances of Christians and Jews Under Early Islam*. University of Pennsylvania Press.

Tolan, J. 2015. 'The Infidel Before the Judge: Navigating Justice Systems in Multiconfessional Medieval Europe' in D. Weltecke, U. Gotter and U. Rüdiger (eds) *Religiöse Vielfalt und der Umgang mit Minderheiten: vergangene und gegenwärtige Erfahrungen*. UVK-Verl.-Ges. 57.

Tolan, J. et al. (eds). 2017. *Religious Minorities in Christian, Jewish and Muslim Law (5th–15th centuries)*. Brepols.

Washofsky, M. 1989. 'Halakhah and Political Theory: A Study in Jewish Legal Response to Modernity'. 9 *Modern Judaism*. 289.

Part II
Sources of law

6

Jewish law

The sources

Joseph E. David

Traditionally, the concept of a legal source was considered crucial for any understanding of the essential aspects of law, whether origin, validity, or operation, and thus was assumed to be an indispensable part of any general theory of the concept of law.[1] However, although many scholars have noted a consensus among legal theorists that the problem of the sources of law is a pivotal one, analysis of the subject has been severely neglected. Legal sources were rarely a commonly discussed topic in the traditional literature of Jewish law. At first glance it seems almost an impossible task to create a comprehensive account of Jewish legal sources, not only because of the variety of ways that law is conceived but also due to the lack of a vocabulary to define them.

Nevertheless, the nature of the sources of Jewish law and the manner in which they function and construct the body of that law and its operation appear to be integral to any depiction of Jewish law. Although its sources rarely were discussed straightforwardly in traditional literature as a discrete subject, articulated ideas and perspectives concerning them may be identified by analyzing the assumptions underlying deliberations that touch on them.

More than anything else, the question of the sources of Jewish law is impacted by the theocentric–anthropocentric predicament. Namely, there is a tension between the two polar opposites that characterize divine law, because it is of heavenly origin, yet subject to human application and manipulation. In the following discussion, we shall outline the major themes and attitudes towards the sources of Jewish law and their nature against the backdrop of the theocentric–anthropocentric predicament. As a methodological matter, I propose that we understand the various attitudes towards the legal sources of Jewish law through a conceptual analysis focused on two parameters: the variety of meanings ascribed to the concept of legal sources, and the different notions of what is entailed in being a source for legal matters.

Variations of meaning and function

An elucidation of the different meanings and ideas that underlie the term 'legal sources' is needed on the conceptual level, but has operative importance as well. To borrow Hart's terminology, legal sources are principles of a 'second order' in regard to the law and so function as 'power-conferring rules' that recognize, create, terminate, and alter the existing law.[2] Yet common usages of the term 'legal sources' are inattentive to the different ways such sources operate in the argumentative discourses of law. Recognizing the variety of meanings ascribed to 'legal sources' is instrumental for both the theory and the practice of law, but even more so for the comparative study of legal systems.

Legal sources have been given various definitions and concept-based classifications. For the present purpose, we shall consider three different meanings *qua* usages that define three types of legal sources:[3]

1) *Material sources* provide the substantive content of law. They include sources that are recognized as obligatory and authoritative (e.g., legal codes, customs, and conventions) as well as inspirational materials (e.g., legal scholarship, notably that of comparative law).
2) *Normative sources* determine the normative status and value of a certain behavior or state of affairs (whether one demanded, permitted, or prohibited under the law[4]). They institutionalize, validate, or legalize certain expectations and transform them into legal norms or rules.
3) *Epistemological sources* serve as standards of legal knowledge and certainty. In the absence of clear knowledge about requirements and applications of the law, an epistemological source provides instruction and leads to correct legal answers.

Many common usages of the term 'legal source' are indifferent to this classification. At times, such indifference may be reasonable: in some cases, a single 'source', such as a constitution, sovereign will, or Scripture, encompasses all three meanings by at once providing legal content, validating it, and supplying means of obtaining accurate knowledge of it. Notwithstanding, there is no justification for broadly disregarding the separate senses of 'legal sources'. As we shall demonstrate below, segregating these different senses is a potent tool in mapping major trends and attitudes towards the legal sources of Jewish law, because each of the approaches to this challenge presents a different variation on the three meanings. Segregation of the meanings of 'legal sources' thus is also a conceptual device for dealing with the theocentric–anthropocentric predicament.

'Source' and 'resource'

Another conceptual elucidation will help to address the very concept of a 'source' for adjudication or interpretation within the law. Legal sources usually are imagined and conceptualized as either *source qua origin* or *source qua constituent*, two distinct notions that imply different types of relationship between source and law.

Source qua origin accentuates the causes of the law, its foundations, its beginnings, and the process of its derivation. This notion is based on an emanatory, usually Neoplatonist, logic[5] according to which the body of the law stems from a metaphorical spring or fountain – hence the common term *fons legis*. Interestingly, this notion of legal sources is shared by multiple incompatible jurisprudential accounts that presume the law to be a preexisting entity independent of interpretation, application, and actualization.[6] Under this notion, the source and the law are in effect identical – the latter actualizes the former. This concept of a legal source normally corresponds to a discovery model in which adjudication is essentially about discovering or identifying existing rules and norms.

Meanwhile, the notion of *source qua constituent* embraces a different view of the essence of law and adjudication. It does not assume that the law and its source necessarily are identical. Rather, legal sources are the building blocks or ingredients of law. This notion interchanges 'source' with 'resource' and corresponds to the realist view and the constitutive model, according to which legal sources are simply components or means by which the law is imposed, legislated, or applied.[7]

As realist theorists have noted, the emanatory model is inclined to reduce or deny human agency in the law and to treat that agency as redundant. Conversely, endeavors to enlarge and empower human agency within the law tend to embrace the constitutive notion of legal sources or sourcing.[8]

To this distinction as well, traditional legal theories are inattentive, although as we shall see, the choice between positing these two notions as alternates or combining them is pivotal for some attitudes to the question of the sources of Jewish law.[9] We are led to realize that some discussions about these legal sources refer to different objects and that the confrontation with the theocentric–anthropocentric predicament looks different through the lenses of the different notions.

The biblical paradigm: strong epiphanism

Historical discourses about the sources of Jewish law are typified by a struggle with a biblical paradigm in which epiphany is the ultimate source of law. Against this classical background, later accounts of the sources of Jewish law can be seen as reactionary attitudes harking back to an archetypal model that inherently associates the sources of the law with the epiphany of the divine word. Clearly, the biblical model raises questions about the role and the weight of human agency in the law and its operation, and thus the various understandings of the sources of Jewish law can be examined through the margin between epiphany and human prudence.

The core of the biblical legal metanarrative and the primary source of Jewish law is epiphany, defined as the appearance or manifestation of the 'word of God'. More precisely, epiphany in the biblical framework is the ultimate and the exclusive legal source in its three above meanings or functions: the content of the law and its normative status derive from their being the word of God. Likewise, legal knowledge is dependent on the transmissibility of the law through epiphany and particularly prophecy. I suggest the term 'epiphanism' for the view that the word of God is the primary source of law, and 'strong epiphanism' to denote the view that the divine word is the sole source of law.

Strong epiphanism, the dominant perspective in the Old Testament regarding the sources of the law, is consistent as a perspective on the law and its sources with the covenantal framework of the law and the conception of divine commandment. The perspective has several expressions in the Pentateuch, chiefly the substance and function of YHWH's commandments revealed to the Israelites, whether directly or through the mediation of Moses as the spokesman of God.[10] The normative status of these commandments as law stems from their epiphanic context, as described in Moses's last speech:[11]

> The LORD said unto me, 'Gather Me the people together, and I will make them hear My words' . . . And the LORD spoke unto you . . . And He declared unto you His covenant, which He commanded you to perform – the ten commandments; and He wrote them upon two tables of stone; And the LORD commanded me at that time to teach you statutes and judgments.

Epiphany, according to this perspective, also provides legal answers in cases of factual uncertainty or lack of knowledge. Suspicion of adultery is resolved by divine judgment (*judicium dei*) in the ordeal of bitter water.[12] In cases where the law is unknown, YHWH is consulted directly,[13] through designated mediators[14] or by means of divination or cleromancy.[15]

Historically speaking, strong epiphanism did not remain a dominant or vibrant perspective after the close of the biblical epoch. The Second Temple Period brought with it the introduction of human prudence as a necessary element in the conception of law and legal sources, and this major change gave rise to conflicting perspectives on the nature of the laws and their operation. This development in turn produced different ideas and articulations. Some of these reassessed the weight and function of human prudence relative to epiphany, either pretending to maintain the biblical perspective of strong epiphanism or else reducing or even refuting it altogether.[16]

Grappling with the biblical model in Late Antiquity

Epiphany was not a vibrant perspective or a central pillar of the Jewish *Weltanschauung* in Late Antiquity. It instead was a historical phenomenon, part of the glorified past of biblical times. While late-ancient Judaism hardly could be content with strong epiphanism, the biblical paradigm could not be simply ignored, and so attitudes in Late Antiquity towards the problem of the sources of Jewish law are characterized by efforts to account for the relevancy and applicability of strong epiphanism in post-epiphanic times. The challenge of grappling with the biblical paradigm was to account for the role and meaning of human agency in relation to the idea of a divine law.

In the discussion to follow, we shall outline the major attitudes towards the sources of the law that developed in late-ancient Judaism. Each of these offers a different resolution to the theocentric–anthropocentric predicament in which it reworks the conceptual content of 'legal sources'.

Judeo-Hellenic parallelism

The Judeo-Hellenic perspective on the sources of divine law is essentially compatible with that of the Hebrew Bible. It is well known that the intellectual agenda of Hellenic Jews beginning in the second century BCE was to reconcile and harmonize biblical narratives and other content with the philosophical worldview of the Greeks, following from the presumption that these two seemingly alien perspectives were in fact parallel representations of a single transcendent truth. Mosaic laws were taken to be a divine *nomos* reflecting the cosmic order and the eternal laws of nature (Reinhartz, 1986; Martens, 2003). Hebrew scripture and Greek metaphysics were accordingly understood as parallel expressions of the same truth with the same view of the dependency of the divine law (*nomos*) on divine wisdom (*logos*) and the derivation of the former from the latter. The difference between the two traditions was reduced to the instrumental: they represent parallel media by which divine law is known to human beings.

The Judeo-Hellenic perspective on the question of legal sources, crystallized through Middle Platonism, should be understood in light of the above. It subscribed to an emanatory model, embraced the notion of *source qua origin*, and with regard to the separable senses of 'legal sources', relied on the possibility of segregating the material and normative meanings, considered to be determined by transcendent divinity, and the epistemological meaning, a role that might be given to human prudence. Thus, in addition to epiphany, the epistemological source of the law includes human contemplation as a means for acquiring and applying knowledge of the law.

Philo is perhaps the most prominent and elaborative representative of Judeo-Hellenic parallelism concerning the legal sources of Jewish law. Following the Stoics' formulations and terminology, he associates the biblical God, *logos*, and the description of the order of nature as the 'right reason' (ορθος λογος). The 'right reason' – the divine order of nature itself – manifests as the law of nature. Therefore, to follow the *logos* of nature is to follow the *nomos* of nature.

Philo consequently views the Ten Commandments as given according to nature,[17] the biblical ordinances as consistent with nature,[18] and the world itself, described as a 'megapolis'

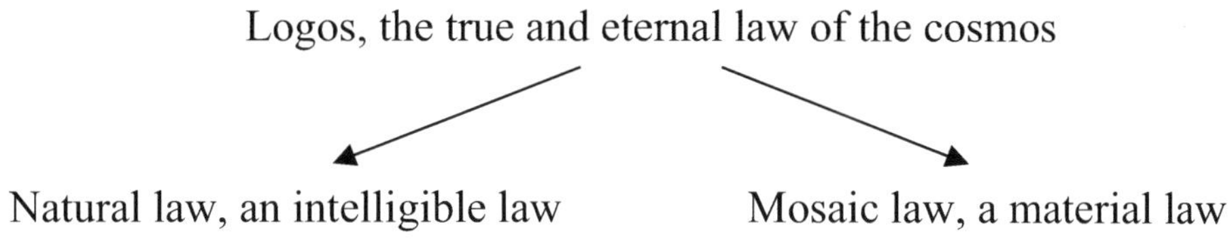

Figure 6.1 Logos, the true and eternal law of the cosmos

governed by a single law, as the *logos* of nature.[19] He stresses epiphany as a legal source, in the material and the normative sense, by describing the biblical God as the Lawgiver[20] and the Mosaic law as given by the 'voice of God'[21] or an outcome of the 'oracles of God'.[22] Yet Philo claims that since both God and the 'eternal law'[23] are intelligible, they can be apprehended through either epiphany or contemplation (see Figure 6.1).

The Judeo-Hellenic perspective apparently afforded some legitimacy to human prudence as an epistemological legal source. However, this was not a radical move away from strong epiphanism, but only a slight breach. In the Judeo-Hellenic model, as in that of Scripture, the epiphany of the divine word is the sole legal source in the material and the normative sense. Human prudence, to be sure, is a legitimate epistemological source of law, but only as a secondary alternative to epiphanic revelation. Moreover, the legitimacy of human prudence under this model excludes any active role. The overall dynamic of the law and its sources thus remains theocentric.

Rabbinic ambivalence: the human source celebrated and denied

Biblical strong epiphanism was less easy to reconcile with the rabbis' scholastic values and active legal engagement. Their scholasticism was first and foremost about acknowledging their own active role in generating, construing, and shaping the law, and strong epiphanism seemed to demonstrate a contrast between their self-perception and the conception of the law as a jurists' law. The biblical model seemed to trouble the rabbis much more than it challenged Hellenic Jews, because in the rabbinic mind, the theocentricity of the biblical paradigm appeared to leave no room for an active human role within the law.

In practice, the rabbis' confrontation with the strong epiphanism of the Bible produced two opposing attitudes. One expressed an aspiration to preserve the biblical model of strong epiphanism, even at the expense of repudiating the active legal involvement of rabbis, but because it did not truly solve the fundamental theocentric–anthropocentric tension and was inconsistent with the scholastic conception of *halakhah*, it fomented a cognitive dissonance around the rabbis' active legal role. The second attitude approached the theocentric–anthropocentric predicament differently, by justifying legal anthropocentrism as a supplement or replacement of strong epiphanism. Where the first attitude dimmed or downplayed human jurisprudence, the second authorized and empowered such involvement. Still, the rabbis' discomfort with the biblical model frequently is noticeable in traditions voicing both attitudes, and the theocentric–anthropocentric predicament seems never to stop aggravating rabbinic discourse about the sources of the law. In the meantime, the rabbis' wrestling with the strong epiphanism of Scripture introduced various ideas about how the rabbis engaged with the divine law and was the source of an elaborate conceptual vocabulary for describing their activities in connection with it, vocabulary that came to predominate in rabbinic literature and later shaped rabbinical discourse about the legal sources.

In the following sub-sections, we shall outline the two rabbinic attitudes towards the biblical paradigm, which dominate talmudic literature and were embraced by post-talmudic legal thinkers and jurists. Each of the attitudes approaches the theocentric–anthropocentric predicament by emphasizing additional perspectives and *ethea* concerning the nature of the law, its content, and its concatenation over time.

Fantastic law

Motivated by the aim of preserving the biblical paradigm, some rabbis presumed to minimize their own juristic role in generating and developing law. Without claiming the continuation of prophecy beyond biblical times to their own, they took the view that the revealed law was not a body of rules but a miraculous container of infinite laws and rulings waiting to be discovered.

This attitude stretches the Sinaitic epiphany of the revealed law beyond the historical setting of the bible by means of the idea of continuous revelation. It posits that revealed law is composed not of fixed and stable content but of undefined content whose revelation is endless. The rabbis' juristic expertise is correspondingly scaled down, reduced to reliable transmission of the continuously revealed law and discovery of existing legal content.

This attitude embraces the ethos of an uninterrupted chain of transmission directly connected to the epiphanic events of the Bible. It is an ethos based on an amplification of biblical narrative in which the two tablets handed down to Moses ('written with the finger of God . . . on them was written according to all the words'[24]) were not limited to the Decalogue, but miraculously encapsulated infinite legal content, including rulings and norms that would be developed in the future:[25]

> *And on them . . . according to all the words* – [viz.] Scripture, Mishnah, Talmud, and Aggadah. Even what the advanced student of the future is destined to say before his teacher already was said to Moses at Sinai.[26]

In this depiction, the source of the law remains epiphanic in the three above senses – materially, epistemologically, and normatively. Legal expertise is flattened, and the core activity of the rabbis as jurists is truncated like that of channels and expositors of a law established long ago. The narrative alters the biblical narrative of the Sinaitic revelation by giving the law a mystical dimension and assuming continuous revelation. Critically, it denies any possibility of legal change, development, or extension: the only possible involvement of human prudence in this model is through discovery. Officially, there can be room for neither constitution nor legislation.[27]

Official majoritarianism

For all intents and purposes, the rabbis' creation of *halakhah* and their conception of the law as a jurists' law presumed active human agency within the law. Many rabbis of Late Antiquity were uncomfortable with the mystical attitude described earlier, because their self-perception as active generators of the law contrasted with the naïve description of their project as passive transmission and occasional discovery of preexisting content. Further complicating the issue, the geist of rabbinic scholasticism and anthropocentric legalism seemed a direct contradiction to the presuppositions of strong epiphanism.

For these rabbis, coping with the biblical paradigm required that they justify a retreat from the biblical model and advocate active human jurisprudence. This endeavor was the source of carefully defined attitudes defining the human character of the legal sources of the law. The anthropocentric attitudes of this model were based on exegetical methods that gave novel descriptions to the nature of the revealed law and its sources.

Both attitudes celebrate majoritarian procedure as a valid legal source that supplements, or even replaces, epiphany as the ultimate source of law. Rabbinic legitimization of human jurisprudence thus reflects a momentous shift in some of the most significant aspects of the law – from divine to institutional authority, from substance to form, from content to procedure, from fixed law to open-ended law. Yet as demonstrated later, the different attitudes are at odds regarding the proper designation of the human component of legal sources. One attitude claims that the Mosaic law essentially included an assemblage of multiple rationales, rather than a holistic collection of positive rules and legal norms. This view proclaims both the intelligibility of the revealed law and its indeterminacy:[28]

> The words of the Torah were not given clear-cut. Rather, on each and every matter that God expressed to Moses, He gave forty-nine aspects [i.e., reasons] for purifying and forty-nine aspects for impurifying. He [i.e., Moses] said before Him, 'How long will it take us to clearly understand *halakhah*?' He said to him, '*After the majority to incline*[29] – If a majority [of jurists] would impurify, [then it is] impure; if a majority [of jurists] would purify, [then it is] pure'.

This depiction deviates from the biblical account, and in fact from the very biblical conception of the law as divine commandment, by portraying revelation as divine reasoning or resources for use in human decision making and determination of law.

From a conceptual point of view, this account introduces two intriguing points. First, it departs from the common notion of *source qua origin* and instead subscribes to *source qua constituent*. The revealed law essentially is a raw material in the hands of jurists. Second, this account expresses attentiveness to the different meanings and functions of legal sources and differentiates the material and normative meanings: while the former is epiphanic, the latter is human. In other words, the account advocates a conception of divine law that consolidates the theocentric and anthropocentric aspects, the primal matter of the law being epiphanic and its final shape a human construction.

The second rabbinic account suggests that the tension between the biblical paradigm and the rabbis' world is soluble by giving unambiguous priority to the anthropocentric perspective, a view that took on the slogan 'it is not in heaven'. The rabbis decontextualized this phrase[30] and rendered it as a principle terminating the biblical paradigm of strong epiphanism. In the rabbinic reading, the words denoted not the accessibility of the law but the inconsequence of epiphany in legal decisions:[31]

> What does 'it is not in heaven' mean? Rabbi Yirmeyah said, '[It means that] we do not heed a heavenly voice [Hebrew: *bat qol*], since You [i.e., God] already wrote in the *torah* given at Sinai, "after the majority to incline"'.[32]

In the above homily, the rabbis argue for the irrelevance of epiphany in legal determinations and adjudication: 'we do not heed a heavenly voice'. This view of the sources of divine law indeed is radical – perhaps it seems scandalous – in its explicit legitimization of majoritarian procedure as a legitimate legal source replacing epiphany. More generally, conceptual segregation here legitimizes human jurisprudence. Epiphany is an acknowledged legal source only in its fundamental meaning, in that its legal content is of heavenly, or divine, origin.

The normative and epistemological senses of the legal source are human things – the rabbis' opinions and majoritarian procedure.

This rabbinic attitude can be summarized as a systematic and conscious retreat from strong epiphanism and its replacement or supplementation by the institutionalized procedure of majoritarian rule. The departure from the biblical paradigm and legitimization of human prudence are achieved by *ethea* (namely, approval of the law's indeterminacy or the termination of epiphany) and conceptual segregation between the different senses of legal sources. Nevertheless, human prudence in the rabbinic perspective notably is an institution that empowers rabbis as officials of the law regardless of their human faculties. Only in post-talmudic settings was human prudence in law identified with rationality and reasoning independent of official status.

Medieval Judaism: traditionalism and human reason

As in Late Antiquity, Jewish attitudes during the Middle Ages were polarized between those who repudiated human involvement in the law and others who celebrated human prudence. Nevertheless, it would be unfortunate to view these medieval trends as a mere continuation of talmudic attitudes. A closer look discloses that these patterns in medieval Jewish thought mirrored concurrent trends in Muslim intellectual circles where traditionalism competed against rationalism[33] and competing views of the nature of legal sources were part of a comprehensive religious consciousness and sensibility that involved not only scriptural exegesis but also rival religious ethics informed by the dichotomy of *taqlid* and *ijtihad*.[34]

Perfect transmission

Repudiation of human prudence as a legal source was a typical position of traditionalist medieval Jews, and consistent with the traditionalist view in which tradition was considered not only a trustworthy channel of information but the sole and sufficient source of knowledge. Compared to talmudic attitudes, medieval repudiations of human prudence as a legal source took broad perspectives and made strong claims about the epistemological value of transmission and the feasibility of uninterrupted transmission of the entire body of revealed law. Medieval repudiation of human prudence as a legal source was associated with traditionalist morality that included the requirement to investigate and affirm the credibility of chains of transmitters (Arabic: *isnad*) and established the demand for compliance with tradition (*taqlid*).

Historiosophic expressions of such a traditionalist geist are featured in literary writings from the eighth century onwards. Some of these express a strict loyalty to the transmitted law redacted in the Talmud as transmitted with no rabbinic interference.[35] Other expressions of the traditionalist ideology are evident in various detailed accounts of the continuous chain of transmission from the Sinaitic revelation to the Middle Ages (David, 2008).

Such attitudes were consciously expressed as systematic heuristics. A notable example is found in the writing of Judah ha-Levi (1075–1141), a prominent adversary of any human agency in religious matters. As a defender of traditionalist naiveté and blind compliance, ha-Levi reflected on Jewish law with a sophisticated version of strong epiphanism complemented by a concept of consecutive tradition (Arabic: *khabar mutawatir*). His argument was that Jewish law revealed and constructed during the prophetic epoch had been passed down through numerous, congruent, uninterrupted, and sound chains of transmission (*isnad*) and left no room for active human involvement whatsoever. Nevertheless, many medieval Jewish attitudes embraced the opposite position and to varying degrees legitimized human prudence as a legal source.

Reasoning and rationality

Medieval approaches to the legitimacy of human prudence as a legal source differ from their talmudic counterparts in two key ways: the nature of the human involvement at stake and the nature of the sought-after legitimacy.

Unlike the positions of Late Antiquity, medieval approval of human jurisprudence focused on reason and rational faculties rather than institutionalized procedures. While for the talmudic rabbis epiphanism was set against formal majoritarianism, for medieval jurists the alternative to epiphanism was human reasoning and rationality, irrespective of number.

Talmudic and post-talmudic stances further differed in the style of justification needed for the approval of human prudence as a valid legal source. As explained earlier, the supremacy of majoritarian rule as a normative source rested on scriptural instruction ('after the majority to incline'). In this respect, legitimization of human prudence in the talmudic model remains dependent on epiphanic ordinance. In the medieval model, however, the validity of human prudence as legal source was not reliant on scriptural verse but was considered a self-evident truth.

Here, too, Jewish approval of human prudence as a legal source ought to be understood in light of Islamic jurisprudential thought. We presently shall outline two medieval approaches endorsing intellectual activity as a source of Jewish law that differ with regard to the nature of the intellectual activity approved and its value with respect to those parts of the law that were revealed through epiphany. Each of the two approaches is based on a doctrinal distinction that demonstrates the basic structure of the law and the relationship between its epiphanic and human elements.

The first view is based on a distinction between the categories of revealed law, known through epiphany, and derivative law, which is derivable from the former by certain modes of reasoning, including intellectual exertion (*ijtihad*) and judicial analogy (*qiyas*). This model presumes that the revealed law of God was in principle incomplete, limited, and in inherent need of completion and extension by deduction and inference; the human source of the law in this model is identified with derivative reasoning. An example of such an account of Jewish law can be found in Maimonides's introduction to his *Commentary on the Mishnah*:[36]

> After Moses . . . died, having bequeathed to Joshua the explanations that had been given to him, Joshua and the people of his generation studied them . . . And that which he [i.e., Joshua] did not hear directly from the prophet . . . required discussion and deliberation; he derived (אסתכרג' אלחכם) . . . by means of analogical reasoning (באלקיאס באלקואנין) . . . and with these derived laws . . . when such difference of opinion occurred, they followed the ruling of the majority, as the Lord said: 'after the majority to incline'. Know that prophecy is not effective in investigating and commenting on the Torah or in the study of the derived laws through the thirteen [exegetical] principles.

Understanding the import of the above requires an awareness of its conceptual nuances. Maimonides takes the legal source as resource, based on the notion of *source qua constituent*. Divine law is conceived as comprised of a core of revealed law that is the resource for development of further laws by jurists. The segregation of the senses of the legal source here serves as a mechanism that resolves the theocentric–anthropocentric predicament: epiphany is a legal source only in its material meaning. In normative and epistemological terms, the source of the divine law is human derivative reasoning. Ultimately, this view approaches the Sunni legal theory based on the botanic metaphor, in which the law is compared to a flourishing vegetative organism, comprised of 'roots' and 'branches' whose 'cultivator' is the jurist.

Epiphany → Derivative reasoning → Majoritarian procedure

Figure 6.2 The tri-stratum structure of sources and functions of law

The above excerpt and similar expositions illustrate the gap between late-ancient and medieval advocacy of human jurisprudence. While for the talmudic rabbis the human alternative to epiphany was represented by the power of a formal procedure, post-talmudic thinkers emphasized rational capacities as a unique aspect of human jurisprudence. For the latter scholars, majoritarian procedure was not an essential human prudence but an instrumental default to achieve practical decisions in the absence of agreement among jurists.

The medieval approach thus suggested a tri-stratum structure of the different sources and functions of law. Epiphany is the origin and core material of the law. Later comes derivative reasoning, which extends the existing law to new circumstances or cases in doubt. Only in the final stage is formal procedure introduced as an arbitrary device for choosing among legitimized plausible answers (Figure 6.2).

Alongside the tri-stratum model and legitimization of derivative reasoning, an additional trend among medieval Jewish rationalist thinkers acknowledged rationality as the legitimized expression of human jurisprudence and, heavily inspired by Greek philosophies, took rationality as the basic principle of reality at large (Figure 6.2). The fact that derivative reasoning and rationality have much in common, including terminology, is the reason for the blurring of differences between them in many historical accounts. However, derivative reasoning, like human inferential capacity, is not identical to rationality, a divine capacity that human beings share with God. Rationalism did much more than legitimize human involvement in applying and extending revealed law. It equivalized, to some extent, rationality and epiphany, making human prudence in divine law not only supplementary to epiphany but comparable to it.

Rational legal thinkers among both the Rabbanites and the Karaites, walking in the footsteps of the Mu'tazilites,[37] adopted the typology of a divine law based upon a distinction between laws known only through revelation (*sam'iyyāt*) and rational laws acquired through intuitional faculties (*'aqliyyāt*).[38] The exact definition of the two categories and the legitimacy to extend each were subject to debate. While some jurists (e.g., Se'adya b. Yosef al-Fayumi, 882–942) limited the extension of the law by derivative reasoning (*qiyas*) to rational laws, others (e.g., Abu Yusuf Yaqub al-Qirqisani, first half of the tenth century) argued that even 'revelational laws' were extensible by derivative reasoning (David, 2010; Ravitsky, 2016).

Since rationality, as a feature of the divine that is shared by humans, is a source of law, the rationalist outlook essentially escaped the theocentric–anthropocentric predicament. As a result,

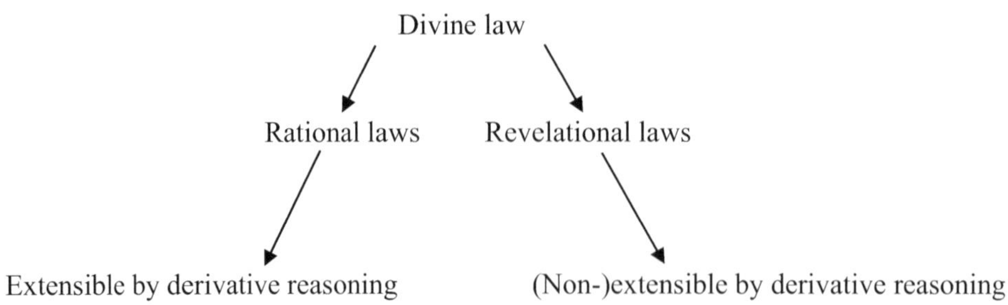

Figure 6.3 Divine law

human action was not only a normative and epistemological legal source but also a material source of the divine law. Here we can observe differences between the Judeo-Hellenic and the Judeo-Arabic struggle with the biblical paradigm of strong epiphanism. While the Judeo-Hellenic model insists on the unity of the law and suggests parallel epistemologies for the same singular divine law, Judeo-Arabic rationalism acknowledges the possibility that the material source of divine law is human (Figure 6.3).

To conclude, the leitmotif of the various attitudes towards the question of the sources of Jewish law is the grappling with the innermost dualism of the very idea of divine law, originated in heaven and applied in the human domain by human beings. It is part of the general aim of a revelation-based religion to balance between the epiphanic and the human measures and to allocate each against the other. It is a story of bridging a gap between glorified past and an imperfect present; between imaginations of an intimate divinity and human contingent reality.

Notes

1 The general obsession with the sources of law may be related to the nontrivial and unsolved issue of the relationship between normativity and factuality. I suspect that the quest for legal sources is related to the extensive efforts to objectify the standing body of law by anchoring it in factual grounds. Legal sources provide a sort of factual gravity to the abstract format of the law, so that the quest for legal sources becomes a proclamation of the law's factual foundation. 'A law has a source if its contents and existence can be determined without using moral arguments . . . The sources of a law are those facts by virtue of which it is valid, and which identify its content' (Raz, 1979: 47–48).

2 From such a perspective, 'source' is a problematic metaphor, because it mistakenly invites us to imagine immanency. 'Law is not something that "flows" from a "source"; rather, it is a form of language and argumentation that carries with it a certain amount of persuasiveness when one man or group of men is trying to get another man or group of men to behave in a certain manner . . . Law does not "come from" a place. In a claim-oriented sense, one might say that a "source" of "law" is any argument used to claim that a given primary rule or norm is in fact a rule of law. Such arguments, when they become structured through countless repetitions, become "secondary rules"' (D'Amato, 1971: 264–265).

3 Modern accounts of the conceptual analysis of 'legal sources' have been inspired by various imagery. Austin (1863), inspired by literary imagery, pointed out three denotations of 'legal sources': authorship of the law (i.e., the sovereign); documents that inform the law; and motivating causes of the law. Under the inspiration of Aristotelian logic, the dichotomy of form and matter led Salmond (1924: 117) to differentiate between the 'formal' source and the 'material' source of law. Antonino Rotolo (2005) presents a triple division of some similarity to ours. Roscoe Pound (1946) argues that 'no less than five senses are to be found in the books'.

4 In Islamic law there are five modi or normative qualification (*al-aḥkām al-khamsa*) of a given act – *wajeb* or *fardh* (required, obligatory), *mandoob* (recommended), *mubah* (permitted but morally indifferent), *makrooh* (discouraged or abominable), *haram* (forbidden or prohibited). Talmudic law also acknowledges multiplicity of normative degrees. In the Middle Ages, against the Islamic influences, the 'five qualifications' were also adopted by Jewish jurists (Kraemer, 1996).

5 See Manzin (2003). Medieval scholastics further developed the Neoplatonic logic of the law and thus portrayed the law as 'divine offspring' born to the 'womb of the eternal wisdom' (*sapientiae seu utero*): 'In eternal wisdom, it is the reason of fertility (*fecunditatis*) that conceives, nourishes, and gives birth to every universal law. All of the exemplary reasons are in fact conceived from eternity in the womb of eternal wisdom' (Bonaventure, *BonHe* 1891, 426, XX.5); 'The *iura* come forth due to a divine suggestion. They draw their origin from heaven and are promulgated by the mouth of the princes. The most just laws and the sacred canons proceeded from a single womb or divine source (*ex uno utero vel fonte divino*)' (Baldus de Ubaldis, *QBS*, 118ra, n. 3).

6 The fact that naturalists and positivists share this notion of 'sources' may explain the lack of theoretical accounts of it.

7 This nonidealist insight underlies John Gray's monumental work in which he articulated the foundations of the realist approach to legal theory and legislation (Gray, 1909: 152–309). In some sense, clarification of the distinction between the law and its sources facilitates the realist view that 'all law is judge-made law' and 'the court is the sole legislative organ in the state'.

8 The difference between a legal source and the act of sourcing is more than mere verbification. It can represent different attitudes towards the legal source – passive subordination or dynamic manipulation – but mainly marks different logical orders, either the derivation of conclusions from a given source or, alternatively, the grounding of given stances in recognized sources.

9 A salient example is the Sunni theory of Islamic legal sources (*usul al-fiqh*), whose basis is a botanic metaphor that views the body of the law (*shariah*) as a growing tree that is manipulated to some extent by the jurist (*mujtahid*), whom it depicts as the cultivator. The botanic metaphor preserves the emanatory aspect while providing room for the constructivist power of jurists: 'for the rules are fruits. Each fruit has a quality and a substance in itself, and each has a source of fruition, a cultivator, and a method of cultivation. The fruits are the rules . . . the person who imparts the results is the *mujtahid* [one who practices independent reasoning or *ijtihad*]' (Al-Ghazali, *al-Mustasfa min 'ilm al-usul*, 7:1)

10 Ex. 4:10–12.

11 Deut. 4:11–14.

12 Num. 5:11–31.

13 Moses consults God concerning the daughters of Zelophehad (Num. 27), Jethro's advice (Ex. 18).

14 'If there arise a matter too hard for thee in judgment . . . being matters of controversy within thy gates: then shalt thou arise, and get thee up into the place which the LORD thy God shall choose' (Deut. 17:8).

15 Notably through the *urim ve-tummim*. See: 1 Sam. 14:41.

16 It must be acknowledged that strong epiphanism never completely vanished as a perspective on the legal sources of Jewish law, and certain leading Judaic jurists in various historical contexts subscribed to this view as the accurate one in their projects. For example, R. Jacob, of Marvège (twelfth to thirteenth century) used to consult the 'heavenly voice' to resolve his legal dilemmas, later edited in a collection titled 'responsa from heaven' (She'elot u-Teshuvot Min ha-Shamayim). The great codifier, R. Joseph Qaro (1488–1575) recorded in a diary the consultations he had with his heavenly mentor on legal matters (Werblowsky, 1962). In modern times, epiphanism was revived among religious Zionists by R. David Cohen (1887–1972) who argued that the Zionist revival called for a change in the legal paradigm (Cohen, 1970).

17 *Det*. 52.

18 Abr. 5.

19 *Ios*. 28–31.

20 *Sacr*. 131; *Det*. 68; *Mos*. 2.48; *QE* 1.42; *Spec*. 2.129.

21 *Mos*. 2.34.

22 *Decal*. 15; *Legat*. 210.

23 The written Mosaic law is described as secondary to a higher law, namely, the law of nature, which is the highest manifestation of eternal law.

24 Deut. 9:10.

25 JT *Peah* 13a.

26 A parallel version appears in BT *Megillah* 19b: 'What is the meaning of *and on them was written according to all the words*? It teaches us that God showed Moses the minutiae of the *torah*, and the minutiae of the *scribes*, and the innovations that would be introduced by the *scribes*'.

27 The quoted homily sarcastically describes what might be termed legal innovation as in fact mere recovery of previously revealed content.

28 *Midrash Tehillim* 12.

29 Ex. 23:2

30 'It is not in heaven, that thou shouldest say, Who shall go up for us to heaven, and bring it unto us, that we may hear it, and do it? Neither is it beyond the sea, that thou shouldest say, Who shall go over the sea for us, and bring it unto us, that we may hear it, and do it?' (Deut. 30:12–13). In the Deuteronomic context, Moses's words of encouragement emphasize that God's instructions are accessible despite their heavenly origins. The prophet's aim is to persuade the Israelites to remain loyal to YHWH's commandments even in exile or in the absence of mediating leadership such as his own.

31 BT *Bava Metzia* 59b. The above translation is based on the Soncino edition (late fifteenth century), MS Munich 95 and MS Vatican 115a.

32 Ex. 23:2.

33 The debate over the authority of human reason divided the Islamic world into two camps: traditionalists (*ahl al-hadith*) and rationalists (*ahl al-ra'y*). Islamic legal historiographies often describe this rift as the background for the growth of jurisprudence as an autonomous discipline and the development of its

literary form, *usul al-fiqh*. Such a debate did not divide the contemporary Jewish intellectual world, although the conceptual apparatus shaped by Islamic jurists did underpin Jewish attitudes to the question of legal sources.

34 The term *taqlid* (تقليد) is used in legal, ethical, and theological contexts to denote imitation, blind obedience to the decisions of religious authorities, and adherence to one of the traditional schools. It is commonly contrasted with *ijtihad* (اجتهاد), a personal effort, which in the same contexts signifies independent reasoning as a source of validation. The tension between *taqlid* and *ijtihad* reflects the meta-legal perplexity in the Islamic legal world and was one of the subjects of contention between Shiite and Sunni jurisprudence.

35 Such a view is illustrated in a quote ascribed to Yehudai Gaon (mid-eighth century): 'I never instructed you anything other than matters that both were evidenced in the Talmud and I was instructed in by my rabbi, and he was instructed in by his rabbi, and so forth' (1928/1929: 557–559).

36 My translation based on Shilat, 1997: 28–29 (Heb.); 228–229 (Jud-Arb.).

37 On the rational–revelational typology of divine law in Mu'tazilite thought, see Hourani, 1960.

38 This distinction is a familiar one in the *Book of Beliefs and Opinions* (*Kitab al-Amanat wa-al-I'atiqadat*) of Se'adyah Gaon. Some scholars traced it to Se'adya's own endeavor to bridge the religious doctrines of rationalism (*mu'tazilah*) and authoritarianism (*ashari'a*), while others took it as a synthetic reading of the Aristotelian concept of belief coupled with the Stoic concept of consent (Wolfson, 1942). With the discovery of Mu'tazilite and Karaite writings over the years, it became clear that the distinction had preceded Se'adyah (Ben-Shammai, 1972).

References

Austin, J. 1863. 'Lecture XXVIII: On the Various Sources of Law' in *Lectures on Jurisprudence (The Province of Jurisprudence Determined)*. Vol. 2. J. Murray. 525

Ben-Shammai, H. 1972. 'The Division of the Commandments and the Concept of Wisdom in R. Sa'adya Gaon's Thought'. 41 *Tarbitz*. 170.

Cohen, R. D. 1970. *The Voice of Prophecy: The Hebrew Logic of Revelation* (in Hebrew). Mosad Harav Kook.

D'Amato, A. A. 1971. *The Concept of Custom in International Law*. Cornell University Press.

David, J. E. 2008. 'Critical Transmission in Early Medieval Rabbinic Thought' in A. Ravitzky and A. Roznak (eds) *New Streams in Philosophy Halakhah* (in Hebrew). Magnes Press. 345.

David, J. E. 2010. 'Legal Comparability and Cultural Identity: The Case of Legal Reasoning in Jewish and Islamic Traditions'. 14(1) *Electronic Journal of Comparative*. 1.

Gaon, Y. 1928/1929. *Ginzei Schechter*. Vol. 2. Jewish Theological Seminary of America.

Gray, J. C. 1909. *The Nature and Sources of the Law*. The Columbia University Press.

Hourani, G. F. 1960. 'Two Theories of Value in Medieval Islam'. 50(4) *The Muslim World*. 269.

Kraemer, L. 1996. 'The Influence of Islamic Law on Maimonides: The Case of the Five Qualifications'. 10 *Te'udah*. 225.

Manzin, M. 2003. 'From Order to System. The Neoplatonic Basis of Modern Legal Theory'. Paper Read at IVR 21st World Congress, Lund (Sweden), August 12–18.

Martens, J. W. 2003. *One God, One Law: Philo of Alexandria on the Mosaic and Greco-Roman Law*. Brill.

Pound, R. 1946. 'Sources and Forms of Law'. 21(4) *Notre Dame Law Review*. 247.

Ravitsky, A. 2016. 'Sa'adya Ga'on and Ya'qub al-Qirqisani on the Logical Structure of the Rational and Traditional Laws: Logic and Kalam in the Karaite-Rabbanite Controversy'. 84(1–2) *Tarbitz*. 159.

Raz, J. 1979. *The Authority of Law: Essays on Law and Morality*. Clarendon Press.

Reinhartz, A. 1986. 'The Meaning of Nomos in Philo's Exposition of the Law'. 15 *Studies in Religion/Sciences Religieuses*. 337.

Rotolo, A. 2005. 'Sources of Law in the Civil Law' in R. A. Shiner (ed.) *A Treatise of Legal Philosophy and General Jurisprudence*. Springer. 142.

Salmond, J. W. 1924. *Jurisprudence*. 7th edn. Stevens and Haynes.

Shilat, Y. (ed). 1997. *Maimonides' Introduction to His Commentary on the Mishnah*. Shilat Press.

Werblowsky, R. J. Z. 1962. *Joseph Karo: Lawyer and Mystic*. Oxford University Press.

Wolfson, H. A. 1942. 'The Double Faith Theory in Clement, Saadia, Averroes and St. Thomas, and Its Origin in Aristotle and the Stoics'. 33(2) *Jewish Quarterly Review*. 213.

7

Christian law

The sources

Burkhard J. Berkmann

Norman Doe quite ambitiously titled one of his popular books *Christian Law*, but admits nonetheless: 'There is no global system of Christian law . . . applicable to all of the followers of Jesus Christ. Each church or ecclesial community has its own laws or other regulating instruments consisting of binding norms' (Doe, 2013: 1). Therefore, an exposition of the Christian legal sources must distinguish between denominations and their respective understanding of law, while at the same time such a comparison reveals relations and common roots. An exposition limited to one chapter can only examine principles without considering every detail.

Various denominations and their legal concepts

Eastern Orthodox tradition

Eastern churches is the generic term for those churches which either originate from the eastern parts of the Roman Empire or its outskirts, or have been evangelised from there (Potz and Synek, 2014: 27). It is the common term for the Byzantine Orthodoxy, the Oriental (pre-chalcedonian[1]) Orthodoxy (see later), the Assyrian Church of the East and the Oriental Catholic churches (see later). However, only the churches of the Byzantine tradition are designated as Eastern Orthodox churches or simply as Orthodox churches in a strict sense (Bremer, 1998: 1144), so this section only refers to them.

Orthodox churches include autocephalous and autonomous churches. An autocephalous church is recognised as independent under its own head bishop (ancient Greek: κεφαλή = head) (Mori, 2007: 93f). Its most fundamental legal concept consists in the fact that it can elect its bishops, including the supreme leader, autonomously without the need for confirmation by a higher-ranking authority (Anapliotis, 2015: 56). This status is undisputedly bestowed upon 14 churches at this time. Besides them, there are further churches with an autonomous status. While these are widely independent as well, they are assigned to an autocephalous church as their mother church, which routinely reserves itself a right of confirmation, in one way or another, for the election of the daughter church's supreme leader (Potz and Synek, 2014: 418). An autocephalous church, depending on its size and historic significance, can be elevated to a Patriarchate. The nine Patriarchates are governed by a Patriarch. The other autocephalous churches have an archbishop or metropolitan as their head.

Oriental Orthodox tradition

The Oriental Orthodox churches are subsumed under the Eastern churches as well, but they need to be distinguished from the Eastern Orthodox churches of the Byzantine tradition. In the classical age, Christian communities expanded beyond the borders of the Roman Empire to Persia, Armenia, Georgia and Ethiopia. The christological controversies of the fifth and sixth century as well as political reasons led to the foundation of different churches, which continue to exist today (Kaufhold, 2012: 215).

The sources of canon law which originated before the separations constitute a common legal heritage. This predominantly concerns canons that are traced back to the Apostles or their successors and resolutions by the synods of the fourth century, namely the councils of Nicaea (325) and Constantinople (381) (Kaufhold, 2012: 216). The body of law of the individual churches was subsequently expanded by various means. Some of them held further synods, which entailed the creation of law. Besides that, mainly in the thirteenth century, private compilations of law emerged and evolved into a formative influence (Kaufhold, 2001: 1291).

Catholic tradition

The Catholic church includes 23 churches *sui iuris*, all of which recognise the primacy of the Roman Pontiff.[2] The Latin church, which is the largest of these churches by far, is governed immediately by the Pope and originated in the western part of the Roman Empire. Conversely, the origins of the 22 Oriental Catholic churches are in the eastern parts of the Empire or its outskirts. They are governed by their own heads (e.g. Patriarchs or major archbishops) and synods.

Old Catholic tradition

The Old Catholic communion of churches consists of certain Catholic churches not recognising the Roman primacy. They mostly originated from protest against the dogmas of the First Vatican Council (1869–1870) concerning the papal infallibility and have been united in the 'Union of Utrecht' since 1889 (Neuner, 1993: 469). The five Old Catholic bishops in the Netherlands, Germany and Switzerland proclaimed a corpus of three documents on 24 September 1889, which was occasionally labelled the 'Convention of Utrecht' (Arx, 2001: 3). Among these, the 'Declaration of Utrecht' is of particular importance since it contains the ecclesiastical principles by which the episcopal office is administered. The other two documents are the 'Utrecht Agreement' and the 'Utrecht Regulations', which were amended in 1952 and 1974 respectively (Arx, 2001: 3). In 2000, they were fundamentally revised and incorporated as 'Order' and 'Rules' into the newly created 'Statute of the Old Catholic Bishops United in the Union of Utrecht' (25 May 2000).[3]

Anglican tradition

The 'Anglican Communion' is a worldwide communion of churches dedicated to the tradition and theology of the English reformation. However, they do not consider their 'reformation' as a breakup with the pre-Reformation church, but rather as a necessary reform of the Catholic church on the British Isles. The fundament of its teaching consists of the '39 articles' and the *Book of Common Prayer*, which originated in the sixteenth century, mostly written by the Archbishop of Canterbury Thomas Cranmer. Within Anglican teaching, there is a wide range between the High Church (Anglo-Catholicism), which is akin to the Catholic church in liturgy and teaching, and the Low Church, which is closer to Protestantism, particularly Calvinism.

The Anglican Communion, with about 80 million faithful associated to it, consists of 38 independent national churches and provinces (Doe, 2003: 3). The most noted, but not the only one, is the Church of England, whose supreme governor is the British monarch. It is a state church (*established church*). Besides, there are churches which are not state churches anymore (*dis-established*) or have never been (*non-established*) (Doe, 2003: 12). Each church holds autonomy and the capacity to regulate and govern its matters independently (Cianitto, 2007: 155; Hill et al., 2006: 193).

Protestant tradition

The term 'Protestant' is used for those denominations which emerged from the Reformation (sixteenth century). There are two main traditions: the Lutheran tradition, going back to Martin Luther and based on the Augsburg Confession (*Confessio Augustana*, 1530), and the Reformed tradition, going back to Calvin and Zwingli and expressed in the Helvetic Confession (*Confessio Helvetica posterior*, 1566) (Kalb et al., 2003: 541). They do not see themselves as a separation from the Roman Catholic church, but as a recollection of the Gospel of Jesus Christ, according to which Christians are supposed to, and want to, live (Frieling, 1995: 1045).

The Protestant communities are predominantly organised on a regional level, namely as 'Landeskirchen' (national/regional churches). Churches of the episcopal-consistorial type are governed by a bishop and his consistory, which are opposed to the synod. Conversely, within churches of the synodal type the elected Regional Synod occupies the central role, while other councils and offices are derived from it. Because of the great diversity, the deliberations in this chapter must be limited to the Protestant home countries of Germany and Switzerland.

Traditions of free churches

'Free churches' is a collective term for various Christian communities which cannot be defined precisely. Originally, it meant such Protestant communities which were independent from states as opposed to the state churches. Within this broad array, different groups can be observed, especially Methodists, Baptists, Presbyterians and Congregationalists.

Differences exist in their constitutional structure, especially regarding the episcopal office. With the Methodists, some communities do have bishops, while others do not. Following the Calvinistic tradition, Presbyterians reject a separate grade of bishops. The Congregationalistic communities locate the ultimate authority on the local level (Doe, 2013: 7). An intermediate level to some extent between a centralised, hierarchical legal structure and independent congregations is occupied by the Baptist tradition, 'which locates authority on the local level but assigns some functions to national Unions and Conventions' (Goodliff, 2012: 5).

Legislation on the international, national and local level

Catholic tradition

In the Catholic church, three levels of legislation must be distinguished. The most important one is the universal church. On this level, legislative competence is held by the Pope (c. 332 § 1 CIC[4]) as well as the College of Bishops, e.g. if it convenes for an Ecumenical Council (c. 337 CIC). The papal power is immediate, meaning that it binds local ecclesiastical entities as well (c. 333 § 1 CIC). On the level of particular churches legislative competence is assigned to the diocesan bishops (c. 391 § 2 CIC). On the intermediate level, which usually comprises one nation, episcopal conferences (c. 455 CIC) and particular councils (c. 445 CIC) have legislative power. In the law of the Oriental Catholic churches, however, the synod of bishops of the respective patriarchal church is the legislative body par excellence (c. 110 CCEO[5]).

Legal acts of an administrative nature, subordinate to the law, cannot only be enacted by the legislative bodies but also by authorities with executive power. On the international level, these are most notably the departments of the Roman Curia, and on the diocesan level the Vicars General and Episcopal Vicars (c. 479 CIC).

Old Catholic tradition

The International Old Catholic Bishops' Conference with the Archbishop of Utrecht as its president[6] considers itself as a supreme entity, but it does not infringe upon the jurisdiction of its members in their local churches.[7] However, it ascertains whether a bishop has gravely harmed fundamental principles and determines whether he ought to be deprived of membership.[8] The communion is based on the concept of autonomous episcopal churches. The individual local churches have their own ecclesisastical constitution, canonical provisions, doctrinal and liturgical norms.[9]

Orthodox tradition

In the Orthodox sphere, legislative power is essentially designed in a synodal manner (Potz and Synek, 2014: 330). Norms enacted for the universal church are named 'general laws'. Such norms have been issued or adopted by an Ecumenical Council (Potz and Synek, 2014: 328). Norms enacted for local churches or other circumscriptions are named 'particular laws'. On the level of local churches, local synods are acting, in which clerics as well as laymen may participate, depending on the provisions in the respective statute (Potz and Synek, 2014: 331). On the intermediate level, there are Metropolitan bishops, who are of minor significance today, and the respective supreme leaders, especially the Patriarchs, with their synods alongside. The leaders of the autocephalous churches and their synods have judiciary, legislative and administrative competence in matters concerning the whole autocephalous church (Potz and Synek, 2014: 455). However, they have no capacity to interfere with internal matters of the eparchies.

After the last Ecumenical Council was held in 787 (Nicaea II), the idea to convene a pan-Orthodox council in the modern age became more and more worthwhile. Following decades of preparation, a 'Holy and Great Council' was held 18–26 June 2016 on the isle of Crete, whose eight final documents contain numerous legally relevant provisions (Vletsis, 2017: 161). Since four of the invited churches did not participate, it is now being discussed whether and for whom the resolutions are binding, or how they can be adopted in the entire Orthodox sphere (Synek, 2017: 117–121).

Anglican tradition

The Anglican churches are 'episcopally led and synodically governed' (Doe, 2003: 43). The legislative and executive powers are allocated to the various hierarchical levels. On the national or regional level there is a national or regional assembly, on the level of ecclesiastical provinces a provincial assembly and on the diocesan level a diocesan assembly (Doe, 2003: 43). The diocese is a territory under the spiritual leadership and oversight of a bishop (Doe, 2003: 58). Within the Church of England, there are different models of legislation on the various ecclesiastical levels, usually with participation of the clergy as well as the laity. Diocesan bishops do not have an explicit general legislative power (Doe, 1996: 88). While legislative power is largely concentrated at the national church in England, it was allocated to other levels of circumscription by different means in other provinces, thereby bestowing further legislative competence upon the dioceses (Doe, 2003: 38).

A more recent development is the emphasis of legal commonalities within the Anglican Communion. As a body, the Lambeth Conference was established and first convened in 1867. It is the assembly of all bishops of the Anglican church. Its resolutions 'only bind a church by its adoption of them, when they are incorporated in its own law' (Doe, 2003: 347). Furthermore, the Anglican Consultative Council was established in 1968–69. 'However, whilst no legislative competence is given by its written constitution, in the exercise of its advisory functions the Council often issues quasi-legislation – policy documents and other such instruments sometimes give rise to "expectations" of their adoption by member churches' (Doe, 2003: 350). Finally, the Primates' Meeting has gathered Primates and moderators from the 39 provinces of the Anglican Communion since 1978. The existence of an Anglican *ius commune*, which transcends individual churches, is regarded as facilitating ecumenical considerations (Doe, 2003: 350; Hill et al., 2006: 200).

Protestant tradition

Within the Protestant churches in Germany, legislation is focused on the level of the 'Landeskirchen', each of which has its own legal system. The synod, which usually is the legislative body, facilitates a broad participation of elected representatives from the ecclesiastical circumscriptions as well as other appointed persons contributing important qualifications (Anke, 2016: 191). In order not to endanger the denominational character of the normative content, instruments such as blocking minorities and rights of veto for bishops – according to their spiritual mission – are provided (Heckel, 2016: 480f; Tappenbeck, 2010: 184). Administrative acts are the responsibility of church governments and church administrations (Anke, 2016: 192).

The 'Evangelische Kirche in Deutschland' (EKD, Evangelical Church in Germany) exists on the national level and is formed by 20 Lutheran, United and Reformed churches. During the last decades, it accomplished a harmonisation of law regarding important subject matters (Anke, 2016: 175). Nevertheless, it does not have a native legislative competence, but only one deferred by its individual member churches (Anke, 2016: 176).

In Switzerland, particular importance can be ascribed to the legal documents by the 'Schweizerischer Evangelischer Kirchenbund' (SEK, Federation of Swiss Protestant Churches) (Tappenbeck, 2017: 35). The member churches can subject themselves to its resolutions by way of their constitution (Tappenbeck, 2017: 115).

On the international level, there are several church unions, but they do not have legislative competence with immediate effect to the participating churches. Their resolutions must rather be adopted into the law of the respective member churches (Anke, 2016: 178). Furthermore, there are bilateral and multilateral treaties between churches.

Summary

In conclusion, it can be noted that the three levels – international, national and local – can be found in all legal traditions covered. The significance ascribed to them, however, differs greatly. In the Catholic church, the most important level is the one of the universal church, while the national level is of minor relevance. In the Orthodox sphere, the level of the universal church could be of major importance in theory, while in practice the Ecumenical Council essentially fails as a legislative body. In the Anglican and Protestant traditions, the international level is the least developed one. It only consists of unions without immediate legislative competence. In these traditions, the centre of legislative activities is mostly on the local or regional level; in the Church of England, however, it is on the national one.

Instruments of regulation

Catholic tradition

The major part of Catholic canon law is codified. The 'Code of Canon Law' (CIC), dating from 1983,[10] applies to the Latin church, while the 'Code of Canons of Oriental churches' (CCEO), dating from 1990, applies to the Oriental Catholic churches. These two codes of law comprise the core of the church's body of law. In many areas, however, they only constitute a legal framework which needs to be specified further. This is accomplished by a number of other laws, by General Executory Decrees (c. 31 CIC) and Instructions (c. 34 CIC). In a formal sense, however, the church does not have a constitutional law as superior to simple statute law. A further source of ecclesiastical as well as secular law are concordats (c. 3 CIC), i.e. treaties entered into by the Holy See with other subjects of international law to regulate matters concerning the church.

Hence, written law is of the greatest importance among the sources of law. In comparison, customary law only plays a minor role (c. 23–28 CIC; c. 1506–1509 CCEO). Court decisions and individual administrative acts are only binding for the specific case in which they were issued. Autonomous subjects, such as religious orders, associations and universities, have their own statutes.

Orthodox tradition

Since the Orthodox tradition preserved its early sources in the most uncompromised fashion, a chronological exposition of the legal instruments seems obvious. The earliest sources include documents on church organisation from early Christianity such as the pastoral letters, the *Didache*, writings of Ignatius of Antioch, the *Didascalia*, the *Traditio Apostolica* and the Apostolic Constitutions (Potz and Synek, 2014: 296; cf. Anapliotis, 2009: 7). Added to this are the writings of the church fathers (Potz and Synek, 2014: 298). The resolutions of the synods of the first millennium, including ecumenical councils as well as local synods, are at the centre of the canon law still valid today (Potz and Synek, 2014: 300). The Trullan Council (Quinisextum, 691–692) was the first synod to declare a compilation of canons to be binding law.[11] The closer affiliation of Orthodox churches with the state becomes apparent when considering that laws of the Roman Emperors concerning the church were included in the systematic compilations of Byzantine canon law (Potz and Synek, 2014: 302). These compilations are named 'Nomocanons', *nomos* referring to the civil and *canon* to the ecclesiastical regulations. The Nomocanon in 14 titles (seventh century) was long held in esteem, but it was gradually supplanted by Nomocanon of Patriarch Photios I of Constantinople (883) (Mori, 2007: 86f).

As complementary sources of law, there are monastic canons, monastery statutes (Typica), penitential books and Nomocanons, Patriarchal decrees and synodal resolutions, which were not included in the compilations of canons (Potz and Synek, 2014: 304). Several private compilations, most notably the *Pedalion*,[12] attained quasi-official status through their approval by the official church, but this does not entail completely equal status (Potz and

Synek, 2014: 304). Given the lack of a codification, customary law is of particular significance (Potz and Synek, 2014: 346).

Since the nineteenth century, church constitutions, also called 'statutes', began to appear next to the early sources. They are the organisational fundament of modern Orthodox churches, while certain matters such as the organisation of courts or the order of elections are frequently outsourced into special laws (Potz and Synek, 2014: 321). In former communist countries, new statutes were created after the revolutions of 1989.[13]

Anglican tradition

Due to the autonomy of the individual Anglican churches, each of them has its own legal system different from the others (Doe, 2003: 1). Nevertheless, there are models, traditions and principles common to all, thus achieving unity and affinity to a certain extent (Hill et al., 2006: 194f). Hence, one needs to distinguish between *canon law* as the legal system of a specific church and *anglican canon law* as the *ius commune* of the entire Anglican Communion (Doe, 2003: 5f).

Almost every church within the Anglican Communion – with the exception of England and Scotland – has a constitution in the formal sense. Besides, there are further species of law whose precise designations vary (Doe, 2003: 21). Types of legal sources present in the Church of England are:[14]

- *Pre-Reformation canon law*: the classical canon law, unless abrogated by more recent law
- *Book of Common Prayer* (1661) and the *Thirty-nine Articles of Religion* (1562–1571): doctrinal and liturgical regulations
- *Statute Law*: enacted by the Church of England or the Parliament
- *Measures*: since the *Enabling Act*, they were enacted by the Church Assembly at first, later in the same manner by the General Synod, and required parliament's assent from the outset until the present day
- *Canons*: enacted until 1969 by the *Convocations* of *Canterbury* and *York*, later by the *General Synod*. They require *Royal Assent*

'Alongside these species of formal laws exist less formal and sometimes unwritten sources: customs or traditions, the decisions of church courts, the "Principles of canon law"' (Doe, 2003: 22) as well as 'quasi-legislation, informal administrative rules . . . "directions", "guidelines", "codes of practice" or "policy documents"' (Doe, 2003: 23).

Protestant tradition

The current Protestant church law in Germany closely resembles secular law in its typology. The constitution of a 'Landeskirche', sometimes also called 'church order' or 'fundamental order', has priority (Anke, 2016: 189). The church law derived from the constitution consists of the laws enacted by the synods as legislative bodies. Church governments and church administrations, however, issue directions and guidelines. Since the synods are not convening permanently, an instrument named 'ordinance in lieu of a law' is provided (Anke, 2016: 192). Ecclesiastical bodies are enacting their internal statutes within the scope of their self-governance (Anke, 2016: 192f). State-church-treaties, mostly between national churches and federal states, come in addition. Particular types of legal sources are the 'Lebensordnungen' ('orders of life'). As orders of ecclesiastical life and Christian practice, they predominantly concern liturgy and church ministries (Anke, 2016: 194).

In Switzerland, the particular conception of state-church-law in most cantons must be taken into consideration. Where the evangelical-reformed churches are awarded the privileged status as statutory corporations, the canton usually reserves a right of approval for decrees on ecclesiastical organisation in order to verify the democratic and constitutional requirements which this status entails (Tappenbeck, 2017: 27). Therefore, national churches split the subject matters to be regulated into two types of legal sources. Church constitutions, which are subject to cantonal approval, contain the fundamental regulations regarding church organisation. Conversely, such provisions concerning the internal life of the church, which are closely linked to its teaching, are compiled in church orders not requiring approval (Tappenbeck, 2017: 28). Customary law and case law are of minor significance in the Protestant sphere (Anke, 2016: 195; Tappenbeck, 2017: 34).

Traditions of free churches

Between the various free churches, similarities and differences regarding sources of law become apparent. Methodists label their corpora of law 'Methodist Law', 'Church Law', 'Laws of the Church', 'legislation', etc. The 'General Rules of the Society of the People called Methodists' (1743) originate from the founder of the Methodist movement, John Wesley (Doe, 2013: 26). Individual churches normally have a constitution, which may be contained in a 'Book ofDiscipline', a 'Manual of Law' or 'Code'; in addition, there are bylaws (Doe, 2013: 26). Furthermore, adherence is often required to customs, usages, judicial decisions and articles of religion (Doe, 2013: 26).

Presbyterians employ, for example, a 'System of Law', 'Code' or 'Book of Church Order' (Doe, 2013: 27). 'These instruments may in turn contain a constitution, bylaws and normative doctrinal texts' (Doe, 2013: 27). Furthermore, the church may provide a model constitution for a local church (Doe, 2013: 27). A particular position among the Presbyterian communities can be ascribed to the Church of Scotland ('Scots Kirk'), which, since 1921, is no longer state church, but 'national church' of Scotland. Theologically, it justifies the existence of its laws mainly with reference to the Old Testament and Romans 13 (Weatherhead, 1997: 1f). Ranking immediately after the Bible, there are the *Declaratory Articles*, amendments to which are subject to strict limitations, followed by other legislative acts (Weatherhead, 1997: 2).

'A national Baptist Union or Convention normally has a constitution, the provisions of which may be classified as "laws" and, sometimes as "bylaws"' (Doe, 2013: 28). A regional association of churches and a local church may have their own constitutions (Doe, 2013: 28). A particularity in Baptist congregations is the concept of the 'covenant', by which the faithful assume obligations towards God as well as their congregation. Typical subjects concern ecclesiastical discipline, membership, worship service, spiritual guidance and ministers (Deweese, 1990: 205). Its theological fundament is the covenant, into which God and the faithful entered at baptism and which is remembered at the Lord's Supper (Deweese, 1990: 207f).

Subject matters

The central subject matters governed by Christian laws concern ecclesiastical life: the organisational structure of the respective community, proclamation of the faith and acts of worship, especially the sacraments. The organisational structure includes membership as well as the different offices and hierarchical levels. In addition, there are regulations on church property and finance as well as penal – or at least disciplinary – provisions concerning the case that the faithful grossly offend against the Christian community. Procedural norms ensure the application and execution of material law.

The emphasis, however, can certainly differ between the individual denominations. While courts in the Catholic church predominantly handle marriage cases, their Orthodox counterparts focus on penal cases. Depending on the state-church-relations, law of church assets can include a church tax law or employment law. The law of marriage is part of the law of liturgical acts. In the Protestant sphere, it is limited to the act of wedding as such, while in the Catholic sphere, it mainly concerns the requirements for entering into a valid marriage. Beyond that, there are only occasional norms on family law, and they do not include matrimonial property law, maintenance law and inheritance law. A general law of contract is not a subject of Christian legal traditions.

Interpretation

The methods of interpretation in the Catholic,[15] Orthodox (Potz and Synek, 2014: 344) and Protestant (Tappenbeck, 2017: 26) tradition are essentially the same as those well known from the continental-European jurisprudence. At the same time, theological particularities such as the salvation of souls and individual justice, as well as the nature and mission of the church, must be borne in mind. Since the Orthodox tradition lacks a systematisation of the legal sources, the Holy Canons are frequently invoked in a selective manner, in the sense of a topical jurisprudence (Potz and Synek, 2014: 281). The fundamental criterion of interpretation does not consist in the aim to develop a positive legal system, but rather in helping the faithful to live duly according to the mystery of the church (Mori, 2007: 90).

Role of theology

The New Testament shows scepticism and criticism towards the law in several passages.[16] Hence, the relationship between Christianity and legal norms is characterised by ambivalence. By no means is salvation expected from obedience to the law. The existence of an internal church law, different from state law, is deemed in need of justification. For this purpose, theological justifications are researched in particular. More specifically, however, differences between denominations become apparent once again.

Theological justification of church law

In Orthodoxy, with reference to the Gospel according to St. Matthew, the theological reason for law in the church is seen in the fact that Jesus Christ did not come to abolish the law, but to fulfill it (Matthew 5:17) (Potz and Synek, 2014: 275f). In addition, Orthodox theology links the dogma of the divine and human nature of Jesus Christ to the foundation of church law. Neither the divine nature nor the historic contingency of the canons alone must be emphasised in a biased fashion (Potz and Synek, 2014: 276).

In a similar way, the existence of canon law in Catholicism is justified by the principle of incarnation. As Jesus Christ is true God and true man at the same time, the divine and the human element are merging into a single, complex reality within the church.[17] Therefore, the church is not only a spiritual community withdrawn from any legal regulation but also a visible assembly, which requires a legal system like any other human society.

In Protestantism, however, the contrast between faith and law, which is set up in the Letter to the Romans, is escalated. A human being attains salvation 'by faith alone' – not because of his or her good works. However, if faith alone and not the behaviour of the faithful is relevant, then law, which tries to stimulate a certain behaviour, cannot be of major significance.

The Protestant understanding of the church is based on Luther's two kingdoms doctrine, i.e. the separation of spiritual and temporal matters (cf. De Wall and Muckel, 2014: 245). The pure invisible church of the heavenly kingdom is distinguished from the sin-tainted visible church of the earthly kingdom (Witte, 2009: 70f). Hence, while Roman Catholic teaching emphasises the unity of both elements, their distinction is central in Protestantism. According to Protestant teachings, 'unlike the invisible Church, the visible Church uses law together with the Gospel to govern its members' relationships with God and with fellow believers' (Witte, 2009: 71). Since church law, in consequence, can only concern the temporal part of the church, its drafting could be left to the secular authorities for a long time in church history. This stance, however, was challenged by the negative experiences with Nazi and communist authorities, leading to the development of new theories for a justification of church law in the twentieth century. Today it is stressed on the one hand, that church law must be tied to the church's mandate of proclamation (Munsonius, 2015: 19) and is even part of the church's missionary testimony (Tappenbeck, 2010: 163). On the other hand, considerable leeway is conceded to legal creativity, where considerations of functionality play an important role (Munsonius, 2015: 19). Protestant tradition particularly emphasises that the function of church law is not to convey salvation but to serve the church (Kalb et al., 2003: 541).

Bible and doctrine of faith as legal sources?

In Orthodoxy, the Bible itself is considered a source of law (Mori, 2007: 85). This does not only apply to the commandments of Jesus Christ and the directions of the Apostles, which are included in the New Testament, but also to many provisions of the Torah like the prohibition of interest (Potz and Synek, 2014: 291). However, it must be taken into account that the Bible, particularly the New Testament, contains only a few passages which can be immediately adopted as legal norms.

In the Catholic and Protestant sphere, the prevailing notion is that the Bible does not contain legal norms, which are applicable immediately, but the immutable values and principles based on which legal norms must be developed. The special significance ascribed to the Bible by Protestantism becomes apparent in the fact that an awareness of a church law strictly derived from the Bible has been partially preserved in the Reformed sphere (Tappenbeck, 2010: 162).

Another question is the relationship between doctrine of faith and legal norms. Doctrines are not legal norms, but the norms are based on the doctrine and must not contradict it. The resolutions of the early councils already distinguished between dogma and canons. Protestant Confessions are not commonly considered to be law, but they are legally relevant inasmuch as they constitute the fundament of the legal system (De Wall, 2016: 40–45; Tappenbeck, 2017: 37–40). In many current documents of the Catholic church, the passage from theological statements to legal norms is fluent. Nevertheless, a fundamental distinction between ethical and legal norms is made. The so-called 'liturgical law' constitutes a special category.

Natural law and divine law

Regarding the concepts of natural law and divine law, there are major differences between Christian denominations.

The Catholic codes obviously take the notion of a natural law and a divine law for granted by using these terms. The antonym is human law, which is also designated as 'merely ecclesiastical law' in the sphere of the church. Divine law is the law which has a divine origin. According to traditional doctrine, it is subdivided into natural law and positive divine law. Natural law is based on human nature and was provided by God as part of his creation, so it can be considered as included in the order of creation. It can be discovered by the natural light of reason – and therefore by every human being – and is binding for everyone. Conversely, positive divine law has been positively implemented by God through relevation. It is predominantly based upon Biblical precepts. Both forms of divine law are considered immutable. More recent approaches in canon law challenge whether divine law itself can be considered as legal norms. It is rather considered to only provide immutable principles, values and rights, which require substantiation in human language, which itself is mutable (Pree, 1995: 134; 1997: 38).

Orthodox theology never presented a systematic doctrine on natural law (Mantzaridēs, 1998: 80). It does not distinguish between natural and supernatural revelation since natural revelation can only be realised by the light of supernatural revelation (Mantzaridēs, 1998: 80). Besides positive law, the existence of natural law, which is deemed to derive from the natural ethical norm originating from human conscience, is acknowledged (Mantzaridēs, 1998: 75).

Lutheran tradition challenges natural law as well as positive divine law. It is held against natural law that human reason suffers from the effects of sin in the post-lapsarian world such that it cannot recognise what is right by itself, but only through grace (Stonebraker and Irving, 2015: 425). The notion of a positive divine law included in the revelation is criticised because the actual content of the revelation is not the law but justification by grace alone (Pirson, 2002: 328). A greater receptiveness for divine law becomes apparent in Calvinist theology, which strives for a Biblical foundation in its reorganisation of congregational institutions (Pirson, 2002: 328). More recent approaches show that there is a Protestant tradition of reasoning which accepts natural law and can even provide elements to reinforce it, which is of increasing significance in a globalised world (Stonebraker and Irving, 2015: 435).

In the Anglican tradition, the relationship between canon law and revelation is assessed differently. According to Doe, the concept of divine law in the Church of England is predominantly used in two senses: as a fundamental source of the church law created by humans, and as a criterion of validity for laws developed by the state as well as the church (Doe, 2007: 39). For canonists, canon law attains its fundamental value out of Christ's will, which is revealed as expressed in Scripture (Doe, 2007: 39). In the eyes of Stevick, 'Church law does not come by divine revelation, but from the church's concrete historic experience' (Stevick, 2000: 131). 'It comes from the church, which in turn comes from the redemptive work of God. Law in the church always arises out of pre-legal realities and serves meta-legal ends' (Stevick, 2000: 132).

Mechanisms of legal change

The law of Christian communities is mostly enacted by legislative bodies. Therefore, it can be amended by the same authorities rather easily. Even the codification in the Catholic church did not cause a petrification, since the 1917 code has been replaced by the 1983 code, which in turn has already been amended five times, with continuously decreasing intervals between the individual amendments.[18] Divine law is withdrawn from any alteration, but as discussed earlier, there are different perceptions of divine law.

The extent to which the faithful can participate in amending the law differs greatly. It is highest in those Protestant communities where legislation is accomplished in a quasi-democratic manner. In the Catholic church, there are possibilities of participation by way of synods, which advise the legislative authorities. The diocesan synod on the local level must include priests, members of religious orders and laymen as its members, while the synod of bishops on the universal level may call in these faithful as consultants. Besides, customary law can develop in the community of the faithful, which can even rescind contradicting positive law under certain circumstances.

In Orthodoxy, amendments to the law on the level of the universal church prove most difficult, since the required legislative body would be a pan-Orthodox council, which, however, rarely convenes for historical reasons. In light of this situation, principles like *Achresia* and *Oikonomia* accomplish a certain compensation. *Achresia* means that an ecclesisastical law can be rescinded by lack of application (Anapliotis, 2009: 20). The principle of *Oikonomia*, however, means a deviation from the strict wording of canons for pastoral reasons. It is exercised by the ecclesiastical authority, which is competent for the respective subject matter. Therefore, it provides a high degree of flexibility in the practical application of aged law under fundamentally changed historic conditions (Potz and Synek, 2014: 336). If certain canons are regularly suspended by way of *Oikonomia*, this may lead to a de facto abrogation (Potz and Synek, 2014: 336f), but *Oikonomia* is not a mechanism to amend the law. It rather remains an instrument to be applied on an individual case, without creating customary law of a certain kind. Nonetheless, customary law is of major significance in Orthodoxy, be it complementary or contradictory to positive law (Potz and Synek, 2014: 346). The distinction between immutable and mutable canons is accomplished by determining whether they are dogmatically rooted or merely of disciplinary character; according to a number of dissenting opinions, however, all canons are considered immutable (Potz and Synek, 2014: 279).

Considering the dominant role of the legislative entity in most Christian denominations, the role of courts and legal scholars is a minor one. For example, c. 19 CIC grants them only secondary priority when filling gaps in the law. Nevertheless, there are examples to the contrary. Under the rule of the 1917 code, the court of the Roman Rota established a case law regarding reasons for nullity of marriage based on psychological grounds, for which only scattered starting points could be found in the 1917 code, but which was eventually adopted into the 1983 code.

Conclusions

Although there is no uniform legal system in Christianity, many similarities between those of the individual denominations become apparent, which distinguish them from other religious laws at the same time. The kinship of the legal sources can be explained by the fact that all Christian denominations originate from the same ancestral tree. The common roots of all legal traditions are the New Testament and the early councils. In Orthodoxy, the canons of the early church are still in force today. In the Catholic sphere, they were part of medieval compilations of law, especially the *Corpus iuris canonici*. This *Corpus* remained in force until it was substituted by the first codification in 1917, which, however, adopted a significant part of its contents. It was a leading principle for the drafting of the CCEO that it should incorporate the Oriental sources. The Church of England deems pre-Reformation canon law as a valid legal source today, unless it has been overturned by more recent law. A more severe break happened in Protestantism, particularly as Luther burned the *Corpus* in 1520 in Wittenberg (Witte, 2009: 53). In fact, however, early Protestant law was based on the early sources as well (Witte, 2009: 72). A comparison of different Christian laws can be of significant ecumenical merit by bringing to light common principles from a legal rather than a dogmatic scope, and even facilitate legal convergence.[19]

Translation by Fr. Augustinus Fries

Notes

1 So called since these churches separated from the Roman imperial church after the council of Ephesos (431) or after the council of Chalcedon (451).
2 Cf. Annuario Pontificio, 2017: 3–10.
3 Text in 91 *Beiheft zu Internationale Kirchliche Zeitschrift*, 28–42.
4 Code of Canon Law.
5 Code of Canons of the Eastern Churches.
6 Art. 1 lit. c Rules.
7 Art. 2 Order.
8 Art. 3 lit. g Order.
9 Cf. Art. 12 Order.
10 Its predecessor, the first code in the history of the Catholic Church, was enacted in 1917.
11 Mori, 2007: 86. By adopting resolutions of earlier particular councils and writings by church fathers, this council bestowed pan-orthodox significance on them. Ohme (2006: 32) calls it a 'first synodal codification'.
12 Greek πηδάλιον, Russian кормчая книга, English 'rudder': a compilation of Orthodox church law by Nicodemus of the Holy Mountain (1749–1809).
13 Regarding the statute of the Russian Orthodox Church of 2013, cf. Anapliotis, 2015: 19.
14 Regarding this enumeration cf. Cianitto, 2007: 144.
15 C. 17f. CIC, c. 1499 CCEO.
16 E.g. Mark 2:27; John 1:17; Romans 6:14 and 10,4; Galatians 3:13.
17 Art. 8 sec. 1 LG.
18 Codex Iuris Canonici (25 January 1983), Acta Apostolicae Sedis 75 II (1983), 1–317, amended by Motu Proprio Ad tuendam fidem (18 May 1998), Acta Apostolicae Sedis 90 (1998), 457–461, by Motu Proprio Omnium in mentem (15 December 2009), Acta Apostolica Sedis 102 (2010), 8–10, by Motu Proprio Mitis iudex (15 August 2015), by De concordia inter Codices (31st May 2016), Osservatore Romano of 16 September 2016, 4 and by Motu Proprio Magnum Principium (3 September 2017), Osservatore Romano of 10 September 2017, 4.
19 Cf. Doe, 2015: 169: 'While dogmas may divide churches, profound similarities between their norms of conduct produce juridical convergence. This reveals that the juridical norms of the faithful, whatever their various denominational affiliations, link Christians through their stimulation of common forms of action . . . This must count for something in the ecumenical enterprise'. Doe, 2013: 384: 'A comparison of the juridical instruments of churches, in a global compass, reveals profound similarities between the Christian traditions in their treatment, as to both internal and external relations, of church ministry, governance, doctrine, worship, ritual, ecumenism, property and public activity in the State and wider society. From these similarities emerge principles of Christian law common to the churches studied'.

References

Anapliotis, A. 2009. 'Die so genannten "Apostolischen Kanones". Eine Einführung' in A. Anapliotis (ed.) *Ἱεροὶ Κανόνες τῶν ἁγίων καὶ πανσέπτων Ἀποστόλων. Heilige Kanones der heiligen und hochverehrten Apostel*. EOS-Verlag. 5.

Anapliotis, A. 2015. 'Einleitung' in A. Anapliotis (ed.) *Die Statuten der Russischen Orthodoxen Kirche (2013), der Russischen Orthodoxen Kirche im Ausland und der Deutschen Diozese der ROKA*. Kloster des Hl. Hiob von Počaev. 11.

Anke, H. U. 2016. 'Rechtsquellen und kirchliche Gesetzgebung' in H. U. Anke, H. de Wall and H. M. Heinig (eds) *Handbuch des evangelischen Kirchenrechts*. Mohr Siebeck. 162.

Arx, U. von. 2001. 'Vorwort'. 91 *Beiheft zu Internationale Kirchliche Zeitschrift*. 3.

Bremer, T. 1998. 'Orthodoxe Kirchen' in *Lexikon für Theologie und Kirche*. 3rd edn. Vol. 7. Herder. 1144.

Cianitto, C. 2007. 'Il diritto della Chiesa d'Inghilterra' in S. Ferrari and A. Neri (eds) *Introduzione al diritto comparato delle religioni*. Eupress. 135.

De Wall, H. 2016. 'Grundfragen des evangelischen Kirchenrechts' in H. U. Anke, H. de Wall and H. M. Heinig (eds) *Handbuch des evangelischen Kirchenrechts*. Mohr Siebeck. 5.

De Wall, H. and Muckel, S. 2014. *Kirchenrecht. Ein Studienbuch*. 4th edn. C. H. Beck.

Deweese, C. W. 1990. *Baptist Church Covenants*. Baptist Sunday School Board.

Doe, N. 1996. *The Legal Framework of the Church of England. A Critical Study in a Comparative Context*. Oxford University Press.

Doe, N. 2003. *Canon Law in the Anglican Communion. A Worldwide Perspective*. Clarendon Press.
Doe, N. 2007. 'Aspects de la réglementation de l'Église d'Angleterre'. 57 *Revue de droit canonique*. 29.
Doe, N. 2013. *Christian Law. Contemporary Principles*. Cambridge University Press.
Doe, N. 2015. 'The Ecumenical Value of Comparative Church Law: Towards the Category of Christian Law'. 17 *Ecclesiastical Law Journal*. 135.
Frieling, R. 1995. 'Evangelische Kirchen und Gemeinschaften' in *Lexikon für Theologie und Kirche*. 3rd edn. Vol. 3. Herder. 1044.
Goodliff, P. 2012. 'Baptist Church Polity and Practice'. 159 *Law and Justice*. 5.
Heckel, C. 2016. 'Die Verfassung der evangelischen Landeskirchen' in H. U. Anke, H. de Wall and H. M. Heinig (eds) *Handbuch des evangelischen Kirchenrechts*. Mohr Siebeck. 437.
Hill, M., Doe, N. and Sandberg, R. 2006. 'The Canon Law of the Anglican Communion. An Emerging Reality'. 53 *Österreichisches Archiv für Recht & Religion*. 193.
Kalb, H., Potz, R. and Schinkele, B. 2003. *Religionsrecht*. WUV Universitätsverlag.
Kaufhold, H. 2001. 'Altorientalisches Kirchenrecht' in *Religion in Geschichte und Gegenwart*. 4th edn. Vol. 4. Mohr Siebeck. 1290.
Kaufhold, H. 2012. 'Sources of Canon Law in the Eastern Churches' in W. Hartmann and K. Pennington (eds) *The History of Byzantine and Eastern Canon Law to 1500*. The Catholic University Press of America. 215.
Mantzaridēs, G. I. 1998. *Grundlinien christlicher Ethik*. EOS-Verlag.
Mori, G. 2007. 'Il diritto delle Chiese ortodosse' in S. Ferrari and A. Neri (eds) *Introduzione al diritto comparato delle religioni*. Eupress. 83.
Munsonius, H. 2015. *Evangelisches Kirchenrecht. Grundlagen und Grundzüge*. Mohr Siebeck.
Neuner, P. 1993. 'Altkatholische Kirchen' in *Lexikon für Theologie und Kirche*. 3rd edn. Vol. 1. Herder. 468.
Ohme, H. 2006. 'Einleitung' in H. Ohme (ed.) *Das Konzil Quinisextum. Griechisch-deutsch*. Brepols. 11.
Pirson, D. 2002. 'Ius divinum' in *Lexikon för Kirchen- und Staatskirchenrecht*. Vol. 2. Schöningh. 328.
Potz, R. and Synek, E. 2014. *Orthodoxes Kirchenrecht. Eine Einführung*. 2nd edn. Plöchl Druck.
Pree, H. 1995. 'Zur Wandelbarkeit und Unwandelbarkeit des Ius Divinum' in H. Reinhardt (ed.) *Theologia et jus canonicum. Festgabe für Heribert Heinemann zur Vollendung seines 70. Lebensjahres*. Ludgerus-Verlag. 111.
Pree, H. 1997. 'The divine and the human of the ius divinum' in R. Torfs (ed.) *In diversitate unitas. Monsignor W. Onclin Chair 1997*. Peeters. 23.
Stevick, D. 2000. 'Canon Law in Anglicanism'. 60 *Jurist*. 124.
Stonebraker, J. and Irving, S. 2015. 'Natural Law and Protestantism: A Historical Reassessment and its Contemporary Significance'. 4(3) *Oxford Journal of Law and Religion*. 421.
Synek, E. 2017. *Das 'Heilige und Große Konzil' von Kreta*, Verlag Plöchl.
Tappenbeck, C. 2010. 'Evangelisches Kirchenrecht. Insbesondere in seiner reformierten Prägung' in R. Pahud de Mortanges et al. (eds) *Religionsrecht. Eine Einführung in das jüdische, christliche und islamische Recht*. Schulthess. 155.
Tappenbeck, C. 2017. *Das evangelische Kirchenrecht reformierter Prägung: Eine Einführung*. Theologischer Verlag Zürich.
Vletsis, A. 2017. 'Das Ende oder der Beginn des synodalen Lebens in der Orthodoxie?' 31 *Orthodoxes Forum*. 153.
Weatherhead, J. (ed). 1997. *The Constitution and Laws of the Church of Scotland*. Board of Practice and Procedure, Church of Scotland.
Witte, J. Jr. 2009. *Law and Protestantism: The Legal Teachings of the Lutheran Reformation*. Cambridge University Press.

8

Islamic law

The sources

Knut S. Vikør

While the classical jurisprudence (*fiqh*) of Islamic law speaks of 'four sources' to the Sharīʿa, there are actually only two that refer directly to divine revelation: the Qurʾān which was revealed to the prophet Muḥammad, and the Prophet's statements and acts, his *sunna*, collected and transmitted in a body of normative stories and anecdotes called the *ḥadīth*, or 'Prophetic traditions' (Kamali, 1991: 14–228; Vikør, 2005: 31–88). The Prophet had no supernatural attributes according to standard theology (the Sufi mystics would disagree), so there is an issue why his statements beyond those that transmit the Qurʾān also represent a divine revelation. One explanation is to claim that the Prophet, being the exemplary human, is infallible: he cannot say anything that is not correct. However, most views of the Prophet would restrict his attribute to being free of sin (*maʿṣūm*), which preserves him from a conscious lie but not from being honestly mistaken. Many *ḥadīth* stress his human side, providing statements of the type, 'when I speak as a Prophet, you must follow my example, but I have my own likes and dislikes as a man, and you need not follow me in that' (Muslim, 'Ṣaid', 7). Clearly, such stories are responses to claims that everything the Prophet said and did was indeed normative and represented divine will. A more pragmatic explanation is that divine revelation was continuous throughout the Prophet's life. So, if the Prophet had inadvertently made a mistake, God would correct him in a later revelation. In the absence of such a correction, the Prophet's statement must thus reflect God's will.

However, neither the Qurʾān nor the *ḥadīth* are limpid sources but in contrasting ways. The text of the Qurʾān is not disputed by Muslims but is not always directly understandable, and only a small fraction of its verses refer to what may be considered legal matters, perhaps around 350 of the 6,200 verses (Kamali, 1991: 19–20). Thus, human intellectual intervention is required to bring out the legal content or actual rules in many of the Qurʾānic verses. Some, however, like some rules of marriage, or the 'Qurʾānic shares' of inheritance, are direct and practical.

The *ḥadīth* are generally more directly applicable: a story will tell of an issue or a problem being presented to the Prophet, and he will answer: This is the rule. The problem here is that, unlike the Qurʾān, the *ḥadīth* literature has no clear boundary (Brown, 2009: 1–123). The *ḥadīth* can represent divine revelation if it is true, that is if it represents an actual statement or act of the Prophet, but clearly not if it is untrue and a later falsification. The *ḥadīth* were narrated orally from the individual who observed the Prophet's action to one or many listeners, who then repeated the story to their audiences, and so on in a chain of at least three or four links before the story was written down from the late eighth century onwards, that is at least 150 or 200 years after the events they related. Over this time, the number of claimed *ḥadith* had grown to an impossible mass of hundreds of thousands of quite contradictory stories. So, the *ḥadīth* collectors had to devise means to sift this body of texts to discover the authentic example of the Prophet. Various methods were used, mostly focusing on the transmitters rather than the content of the stories. In this way, the collectors could structure their works according to probable level of authenticity from 'sound' (*ṣaḥīḥ*) through several levels of 'probable' to 'weak'. However, as the collectors themselves were individual scholars without any corporate authority to back them, many alternative collections appeared, differing in which *ḥadīth* they included as 'sound'. Later on, a selection of six to nine works were granted the stamp of 'orthodoxy', but in particular two, the 'two sounds' of al-Bukhārī (d. 870) and Muslim ibn al-Ḥajjāj (d. 875), were given special status, and it was difficult to argue against a *ḥadīth* that was included in both of these. Beyond them, however, legal discussion would to a large degree consist of debates about which *ḥadīth* outranked the others in authenticity.

The collectors included *ḥadīth* in principle solely on the basis of authenticity, and they were therefore cumulative in content. Thus, several variants of the same story could be included in the same collection if they were all given credit as 'sound' in transmission. In particular, a *ḥadīth* could relate an event of the Prophet's life and his rule with the context in which he stated it, juxtaposed to a version that gave just the statement of the rule without the context. This could clearly be the basis of later legal debates about whether the rule depended on the context or was meant to be universally applied. The *ḥadīth* collectors left those decisions to the legal specialists, as their object was not to formulate the law but just to collect what the Prophet and his companions had said or done.

Formulation of the law from the sources

The two other 'sources' (*uṣūl*) in the classical theory of law were called *ijmāʿ* and *qiyās*. The former, 'consensus', is often legitimized by a *ḥadīth* from the Prophet: 'My community will not agree on error' (Ibn Māja, 'Fitan', 8 and al-Tirmidhī, 'Fitan', 7 in Vikør, 2005: 76–77), meaning that if there was full consensus on an issue in the Muslim community, divine will had to be at work (Rahman, 1962; Hasan, 1992). Therefore, a view reaching this level of concurrence must in itself be a third form of divine revelation and did not need further basis in the Qur'ān or Sunna. However, this *ḥadīth* was considered weak, and the argument contained some logical problems. For example, what was meant by 'my community' or by 'consensus': was it the acceptance by the totality of Muslims in the world, learned as well as unschooled? Or only those who had competence in law, the scholars? How many Muslims would have to disagree for a consensus not to be reached; was a single dissenting voice enough? If so, would a sinful Muslim count as the voice that broke the consensus? And further, how could one know that a consensus was reached, was a positive statement of agreement required, or only the absence of stated disagreement? If the latter, how could it be known that there was no such dissenting voice anywhere? How long had the community to wait to make sure a dissenter did not appear? Some said one generation without dissent after an opinion was made public was sufficient, but in that case, why was this generation more important and decisive than the following one?

In short, the principle of consensus, while generally accepted, could not be very productive in legal formulation. The theoretician al-Shāfiʿī summed up that consensus as an independent principle was only valid as a way to give a legal basis for self-evident truths, such that it was necessary to breathe or that the Muslims had to pray (Calder, 1983). Otherwise, consensus was only formed around statements and acts reported from the Prophet's early community, and these then already had legitimacy in *ḥadīth*, which for al-Shāfiʿī was the most important source alongside the Qurʾān.

In practical reality, consensus came to play a completely different role, not as a 'source' for the law alongside and independent from Qurʾān and Sunna, but as a way to select which legal rule among several alternatives was to become a 'positive' rule, that is, the one to be applied. Thus, it came after the procedure of formulating rules based on the two recognized sources. This process of rule formulation was called *ijtihād*, 'effort'. It became known as a 'fourth source' of Islamic law under the name of its most widespread process, *qiyās*, or analogical reasoning (Kamali, 1991: 197–228; Hasan, 1994; Vikør, 2005: 54–74). It involved taking a specific statement or act from the Qurʾān or Sunna and expanding it into a general rule by discovering the 'effective cause' (*ʿilla*) of the original rule.

The classical example of this process is a Qurʾānic verse that a particular beverage, *khamr*, is the 'devil's work' (Qurʾān, 5:90–1). From this Qurʾānic statement, the act of drinking *khamr* was classified in the category 'forbidden'. *Khamr* was a common type of wine, but not the only type. So were other similar beverages like *nabīdh* also forbidden? In order to avoid saying vaguely that 'the one is similar to the other', the jurists developed a methodology to discover, not *why* God had forbidden *khamr*, as that may be unknowable, but what it was about *khamr* that *caused* God to forbid it. In this case, the context of the Qurʾānic verse was telling: the verse followed statements on other dissolute behaviour like gambling, from which it must be deduced that the cause must be the intoxicating nature of *khamr* which made men act irresponsibly. This could then be transferred to other items that had the same effect, and from the original statement that *khamr* is of the devil, we get a general rule that it is forbidden to consume any substance that causes intoxication, *nabīdh* included.

Not all jurists approved of these procedures, which clearly brought a strong element of human intellect into the fashioning of the divine law. The key to the process was determining the *ʿilla* of the source rule, and that was seldom expressed directly in the verse or *ḥadīth*. Many jurists considered that going too far in basing the *ʿilla*, and thus the generalized rule on scholarly deductions weakened its basis on the divine will. To accommodate such reservations, limits were placed on the *qiyās* methodologies. Thus, one could for example not build one analogy on another; any analogy must be based directly on a text of revelation. Still, many scholars who preferred a stricter and more direct connection to the revelation would if possible discard *qiyās* and similar human methodologies altogether. Instead, they lowered the level of probability for accepting *ḥadīth*. Thus, in the case of wine, there was a Prophetic saying that stated simply, *kull muskir khamr*, 'everything that intoxicates is wine' (Muslim, 'Ashriba', 73; Vikør, 2000). Even if that *ḥadīth* was considered weak, less likely to be the Prophet's expression, a weak *ḥadīth* was preferable to human *qiyās*. It should be noticed that most often there was agreement on the actual rule: drinking all kinds of alcohol was forbidden. The disagreement was about how to establish this rule in law.

Analogy and the discovery of *ʿilla* was the most productive form of *ijtihād*. There were however others, sometimes known as the 'subsidiary sources of law'. The most important of these were *istiḥsān* and *istiṣlāḥ*, both of which meant to avoid a general rule in circumstances where it would lead to unjust and unacceptable hardship for the believers, under the general Qurʾānic statement, 'God wants ease for you and not hardship' (Qurʾān, 2:185). Evidently, these rules of exception were also specified and delimited in strict methodologies, so as not to give general access to dispense with any legal rule one wanted. Other concepts are *istiḥṣāb*, the principle that in case of indeterminacy from other rules, the preferred result is not to change an existing situation, and *ʿurf*, 'custom', a term used in different ways (Kamali, 1991: 283–309). Here it generally means that the rule should be specified by local circumstances, the law could, e.g. require 'fair rent', but local custom would decide what 'fair rent' was in any particular place and time. Such leeway was of course necessary if the law was to be practicable in a civilization that spanned centuries and in so widely diverse societies as the Muslim empire soon came to be. In fact, while some rules are very detailed (such as those of inheritance), others, including much of the penal law, were quite vague as to sanctions and left that to the judge's discretion (*taʿzīr*), which again allowed for easy adaptation to changing social conditions.

Another process which clearly introduced an element of human reason in determining the content of the divine revelation, was the concept of 'abrogation' (*naskh*). The issue here was cases where the sources of revelation appear to contradict each other. Wine, *khamr*, is not only mentioned in the verse about it being 'the devil's work' but also as a 'delight' (Qurʾān, 47:15). Many similar conflicts occur, and the scholars had to try to resolve them. One method was to consider each verse to refer to a different context, or other ways to 'unify' their legal import. But a common solution was to say that a later revelation abrogates an earlier one: God revealed His intention in steps suitable to the ability of the early believers to follow it. The latest rule is His final will. Unfortunately, the Qurʾān is not organized chronologically, so it was up to the scholars to determine the order of revelation and thus of priority in such internal contradictions. A complex set of concepts of abrogation was established, and there were cases where the 'rule is abrogated, but not the text' (that is, we can still see the earlier, invalid, text in the Qurʾān) and cases where the 'text is abrogated, but not the rule' (God has effaced from our memory the text of His latest, valid rule, and only the earlier, invalid one remains visible). The latter, which seems fairly counter-intuitive, was used to explain why the *ḥudūd* rule of stoning an adulterer is not mentioned in the Qurʾān, while the arguably far milder – but legally invalid – punishment of temporary house arrest is expressly stated (Qurʾān, 4:15–16). As, according to al-Shāfiʿī, only the Qurʾān can abrogate the Qurʾān, there must have been a later Qurʾānic verse that abrogates 4:15, and when we cannot find any such now, then it is because God for reasons of His own has removed this verse from our memory (Burton, 1990: 122–164).

In all, these methodologies of developing a law from the sources of revelation was known as the science of *uṣūl al-fiqh*, the 'roots of jurisprudence' as opposed to the work on the actual rules, the *furūʿ*, 'branches'. However, as this process was unmistakeably a human scholarly endeavour and evidently contested by rival scholars every step of the way, it could not become actual law (or even non-legal rules of behaviour) without a further step of sifting all the various interpretations, analogical deductions and claims of *ḥadīth* authenticity. As the scholars had been successful in denying the caliph and state any say in matters of religious science, including that of *fiqh*, they could not look for a caliphal deciding voice; neither did Sunnī Islam establish any formal internal religious authority of the type of pope or patriarch. Some Shīʿī variants did have such an authority in a living *imām* (thus most of the Ismāʿīlī and Zaydī branches), but even the majority Shīʿī groups, the Imāmīs of Iran, Iraq and Lebanon, actually dispensed with that as they believe that last *imām* went into seclusion in the year 874. For the Sunnīs, this is a matter of theology; all humans whatever their religious station stand on the same level in relation to God after the disappearance of the Prophet. So, no Muslim however schooled can speak in the name of God, except by citing His revelation – but not for the interpretation of it when contested by other similarly schooled scholars.

Thus, with no external and no internal fixed authority, the scholars had to settle for the principle of consensus – not here the universal *ijmāʿ* consensus that was a divine gift, but the more limited pragmatic consensus of 'the majority opinion'. They were not able to achieve such a full uniformity even within Sunnism, but arrived a part of the way towards it in forming four *madhhabs*, schools of law, each of which was supposed to form a consensus within them. To anchor the consensual opinions of the schools, they were as far as possible attributed to the eponymous early founders of each school: Abū Ḥanifa, Mālik, al-Shāfiʿī and Ibn Ḥanbal: 'This is what Mālik said is the most correct' (see Chapter 3, this volume). But clearly Mālik did not pronounce on every issue that was to be settled, so further concepts such as *maʿrūf*, the 'known' or the *arjaḥ*, 'the most prevalent, best' solution came to be ways to define the opinion that scholars within the school were supposed to follow.

The legal literature

Which opinions and rules were to be applied in this way, was a matter for the recognized scholars of law, the *fuqahāʾ*, to decide. Initially an open field where aspiring students flocked around a locally renowned scholar, the transmission of knowledge and its authorization came to be focused in colleges, *madrasas*, where students could live off benevolent donations (the same that most scholars depended on) and memorize the words of the teacher (Makdisi, 1981; Chamberlain, 1997).

Such transmission from teacher to student was in the first centuries only oral; the student made notes of what the teacher said and memorized it. Thus, the works of these early scholars tend to exist in different recensions, *riwāyāt*, stemming from the original notes of different students who varied in what they had written down (Muranyi, 1997; Melchert, 1997). From the middle of the tenth century, we begin to see greater homogeneity in the transmitted texts, which indicates that teachers now began to hand over written texts to their students, leaving less room for individual variations in transmission (Schoeler, 2006). The legal discourse was however still open; legal works would normally introduce an issue and then present all the different views of different scholars on it, maybe with a note of which was preferred by such and such authoritative scholar (indicating it was the author's view). Once these conclusions began to be framed in recognized words like 'the preferred view', it was clear that they constituted what the practitioners of the school were supposed to follow. But it was still open to opposing scholars within the school to challenge these views if they felt that the discussion in the school provided them with arguments.

The assumption in the early literature was that those who put the laws into practice, the judges, as well as the muftis who framed legal opinions for individual cases, were themselves scholars and could navigate the discursive literature to find what was the correct conclusion within their *madhhab*: they were *mujtahids*, qualified to define the law within the methodologies of the schools and the sources of revelation. From the thirteenth and fourteenth centuries onwards, it appears to have been recognized that this expectation of scholarly competence was not realistic. Thus, we begin to see a different type of legal literature in the schools, 'abbreviations' (*mukhtaṣar*) that summed up the school's view (Fadel, 1996). In these works, a topic was raised and the solution given without any argumentation or discussion of variant opinions: in such and such a situation, the opinion of our school is that the rule is so and so. Some see these *mukhtaṣars* as the beginning of codification, in the sense of establishing one simple and authorized set of rules to be applied. They may indeed be a step on that way, but it should be noted that no-one had authorized these scholars to write a *mukhtaṣar*, there could be different such works in circulation for each school, and the judge who considered himself competent could freely ignore it for a different opinion in the school – and often did so (Fadel, 1996: 233). Nevertheless, the development of the *mukhtaṣar* literature did certainly lead to greater uniformity and homogeneity of the law within each of the four schools.

These simplified works were supplemented by other *genres*, which could also lead to authorization and homogenization. The muftis had, within the limits of their scholarly competence, the task to provide legal opinions on disputed questions. Originally relevant only for the individual case for which it was issued – *fiqh* does not recognize precedence as a principle – the written opinions (*fatwās*) of famous muftis would be collected and the contextual specificities removed to focus on the legal discussion involved (Hallaq, 1996). After two or three rounds of increasing abstraction, these *fatwā* collections would then take the shape of a legal commentary of a general nature, which later muftis or other scholars could use in legal arguments. Still, the authority of these works resided only in the competence and scholarly quality of the mufti who had originally written it, and how that was appreciated by the later scholars.

Natural law, human law and divine law in the Sharīʿa

The scholars of Islamic law clearly recognized that the formulation of the practiced law had a human as well as a divine element. There has however been a discussion about how to conceptualize that, in particular what exactly is meant by the terms Sharīʿa and *fiqh*. Briefly, two views can be seen: on the one hand, that the Sharīʿa is the divine law that resides with God and only He can truly know: it is God's rules and opinions, which he has for every issue. He has made as much as He wants of His Sharīʿa clear to the humans through the revelation. But for humans to understand the revelation and practise the divine Sharīʿa, we must use our intellect. That human effort, as well as its result, is *fiqh*. Thus, the Sharīʿa is strictly speaking a body of rules that only God can know, and what we have in the mundane world is only *fiqh*, merely an imperfect reflection of the divine Sharīʿa.

Most often, however, the term Sharīʿa is used for the body of rules that we can see and which are practised in this world, while the term *fiqh* refers to the efforts to develop and discuss the law, a science of law, divided into the two fields of legal theory, *uṣūl*, and elaboration of the various branches of the law, *furūʿ* (Vikør, 2005: 2). It would seem that the former view, which reserves the term Sharīʿa for the divine element of the law, ultimately ungraspable by humans in its totality, is a way to protect the term Sharīʿa from the imperfections of the law as hammered out through fallible human scholarship, but is also a way to justify an opening for change and modernization of the law: what we then change is not the actual divine Sharʿīa but merely the human *fiqh*, which could represent or not represent God's authentically intended rules, since God is silent after the death of His last Prophet Muḥammad and has not sanctioned any interpretation over another. So, contesting *fiqh* is less dangerous than contesting the Sharīʿa would be.

A variant of this view, however, is to delimit the Sharīʿa in another way: There are some elements of the law where we do have absolute certainty about the divine will: those that directly apply the rules of the Qurʾān. In addition to some elements of inheritance rules (the *farāʾid*, or 'Qurʾānic shares') and similar, they are specifically the *ḥudūd* laws against theft, marital infidelity, intoxication and robbery or rebellion. These then constitute the core of the actually divine Sharīʿa, or even *are* the Sharīʿa. This view has been promoted by some *jihādī* groups as arguments for focusing on the *ḥudud* in their campaigns to 'reintroduce' the Sharīʿa. However, this view is clearly blind to the fact that even those rules were developed through *fiqh*, and are not at all stated unequivocally in the Qurʾān. It was only the *fuqahāʾ* who, after logical discussions, established that these penalties must be thus extrapolated from the Qurʾānic text. They are not incontestable; in fact there is not even a full agreement about which rules are included among the *ḥudūd* (some scholars would, e.g. add *radd*, apostasy, while others would exclude intoxication from the *ḥudūd*).

In the legal development, the focus was thus on the texts of the revelation, which grounded the law in the divine will. An issue of some discussion in the *uṣūl al-fiqh* literature of legal theory, was how to combine this with the human intellectual endeavours to formulate a law. In particular, whether human reason could provide a separate source or a legal authority beyond direct references to the revelation and God's expressed or indirectly discovered will. That is, whether there is an element of natural law in Islamic law.

Many historians of Islamic law reject this possibility, at least as far as the established legal schools are concerned, and state that there is no component of natural law in the Sharīʿa. God was the only authority for any legal rule and the only one who could determine what was right or wrong, permitted or forbidden. Without revelation, there would be no morality or law (Crone, 2005: 264).

However, more recent studies have challenged this view and believe that there can be found elements that may be linked to natural law, giving reason a role as an authority independent of revelation when thinking about the law (Emon, 2005, 2010). They link this to the discussion in Islamic theology and legal theory around God's intention with the Sharīʿa (His *maqāṣid*) and the connected answer that this purpose is clearly stated to be the welfare (*maṣlaḥa*) of the individual or society (Opwis, 2010). The issue is what this welfare is grounded in. In simplified terms: everyone agrees that what God ordains is good. But is it good because God has ordained it – and if he had ordained the opposite, then that would also have been good – or is it good because God is good and just, and always does what is best for mankind? In other words, does the concept 'good' have a meaning outside of (or 'before') revelation, a logical meaning that can be comprehended by man?

One element of this discussion is the more theological issue of whether God, in the latter case, does good because of His nature, that He as a just god is compelled to do the good. This position, promoted by the early current known as the Muʿtazila, was rejected by what later became the standard Sunni theology, as it put a restriction on God's omnipotence (Watt, 1998: 180–250). God is indeed good, the later critics said, but only because He chose to be so, He could have chosen to be otherwise. This line of discussion is of lesser importance to the legal debate, as revelation is what it is (and is uniformly good). However, the issue of the *maqāṣid* of the law was very relevant in the field of theory of law, *uṣūl al-fiqh*.

The issue can be raised in two contexts. One is *inside* the legal methodologies to discover the legal consequence of a source text, that is within the process of *qiyās*, 'analogy'. There are myriad ways to establish the 'effective cause' (*ʿilla*, or *ratio legis*) of a rule expressed in the Qurʾān or *ḥadīth*, some more speculative than others. Could an evaluation of the common good, *maṣlaḥa*, be used here to establish what the *ʿilla* might be? One example given by al-Juwaynī (d. 1085) is a marriage contract, details of which may or may not be regulated in analogy with commercial contracts (Opwis, 2010: 47). However, he says, since a marriage is different from a commercial relation, the jurist should instead of direct correspondence with commercial contracts, look at the *maṣlaḥa* result of his answer, which promotes the intention of marriage. In other words, social welfare could be a factor in formulating the legal rules within the *qiyās* system.

Another question is whether *maṣlaḥa* can be the source for a legal rule when there is no text of revelation at all on which to base it, that is in a totally unprecedented case outside the *qiyās* process. That is known as *maṣlaḥa mursala*, an independent *maṣlaḥa*. This was more controversial. A fairly restrictive use of it was that of Abū Ḥamīd al-Ghazālī (d. 1111), who was an important scholar in what became a standard theology in Sunnism. He recognized *maṣlaḥa* as an independent principle, if the result without doubt promoted God's purposes with the Sharīʿa, which he defined as five: the protection of religion, life, intellect, family and property (Opwis, 2010: 67). However, he also structured these into four levels: necessity (*ḍarūra*), need (*ḥāja*), improvements and preference. Independent *maṣlaḥa* may only be used in the first of these cases. For example, it is the duty of a father or guardian to provide his children with appropriate marriage partners. That is thus a need, but it is not a necessity like the duty to provide food and clothing for them. Only the latter is a *ḍarūra*, necessity that qualifies for *maṣlaḥa mursala*.

Ghazālī added further restrictions which made this concept less important for him. Another theoretician that expanded more on *maṣlaḥa* was Ibrāhīm al-Shāṭibī (d. 1388). For him, *maṣlaḥa* is not restricted to one aspect of legal development alone; it is the overall underlying principle of the Sharīʿa, its meaning, *maʿnā* (Masud, 1995; Opwis, 2010: 251). Thus, we must understand that particular rules that may not be relevant in each case are still valid because they serve a universal principle of welfare: a Muslim may shorten his obligatory prayer when he is on travel. This is so even if the travel does not cause any particular hardship for him, because the universal rule of shortening the prayer does provide ease for travellers in general (Opwis, 2010: 254). Further, al-Shāṭibī accepts that legal rules can be based directly on *maṣlaḥa mursala*, under certain conditions (e.g. that it is necessary to have a rule) and that the *mujtahid* in that case has to consider the outcome of the rule (Opwis, 2010: 315).

This connects to the question of rights and obligations, which in the *uṣūl al-fiqh* are conceived in two forms: the *ḥuqūq al-ʿibād*, the rights of man (the worshipper) and the *ḥuqūq Allāh*, the rights of God. Read literally, this seems to be a distinction between 'human rights' and obligations towards God, but here the language can obfuscate the real meaning. There were of course no concepts of individual 'human rights' in the pre-modern or medieval thinking of Islamic law. All humans belonged to categories, and their rights and duties depended on these categories, primarily those of Muslim versus unbeliever, man versus woman, and free versus slave. All these had rights (the heathen unbeliever possibly excepted), but different rights. More to the point, God did not have 'rights', because as the creator He had no need of them – God does not enter into any contractual relation with His own creation.

Instead, the concept of God's rights, *ḥuqūq Allāh*, must be understood as the obligation to fulfil God's intentions, which was *maṣlaḥa*, welfare. Thus, God here represents God's will, and *ḥuqūq Allāh* must be understood as a legal obligation to promote public welfare. An interesting aspect of this is that the sultan or other ruler is also subservient to this God's intention, and the idea of *ḥuqūq Allāh* could be used against a sultan who transgressed against the interests of public welfare. The *ḥuqūq al-ʿibād*, on the other hand, represents the individual rights of each person. It was a matter of contention which of these rights, those of God, the society at large, or those of the individual, would prevail if they came into conflict, but one view was that since God has no personal interest in his 'rights', He can forgo them, and the rights of the individual for redress should therefore trump the public interest if the two were opposed (Emon, 2005: 379–390).

Opening the gates of *ijtihād*

One effect of grounding the authority of the *madhhab* rules in the opinions of the four founders, 'this is what Abū Ḥanīfa said' (whether or not he actually said it), was a basic conservatism in the law. As indicated, legal development never stopped in reality, but it was made to appear as if it had stopped with the founders, and that any further changes merely filled in gaps left open, in a way they would have originally been settled had the founders pronounced on them. This was formulated in the expression that the 'gates to *ijtihād* are closed'. While this term is often quoted as an incontestable fact by modern historians of Islamic law, it was in fact disputed, and many later scholars claimed both that legal development could never stop ('no age can be without a *mujtahid*', a scholar capable of performing *ijtihād*) and that they themselves had the ability to perform *ijtihād* (Hallaq, 1984). However, there were several levels of *ijtihād*. Most Muslim scholars agreed that no new schools of law beyond the four Sunni ones could be created in this later age. That is what is meant by 'completely free *ijtihād*', and those gates were closed. But it was possible in later times to perform various levels of rule formulation *within* the *madhhab*, using the established methodology of the *madhhab* on new situations to create a new rule (a high level of *ijtihād*) or a new modification of an existing rule (Calder, 1996).

In spite of this opening, and also because many *madhhab* scholars would try to restrict even such limited legal development as much as possible, voices began to be heard from the eighteenth century onward for a wider opening, the 'gates to *ijtihād* can never be closed'. Interestingly, such voices for legal reform often came from the peripheries of the Islamic world, starting perhaps with Shah Walī Allāh of India (d. 1762), followed by Muḥammad ibn 'Alī al-Shawkānī of Yemen (d. 1839), Aḥmad ibn Idrīs (d. 1837) and his student Muḥammad ibn 'Alī al-Sanūsī (d. 1859) of Morocco, Yemen and Libya, and others (Peters, 1980). The main argument of these scholars was that the Sharīʿa must be based on the sources of revelation and not on the views of the school founders or later scholars.

As the most productive sources for legal discussions were the *ḥadīth*, they thus promoted *ḥadīth* studies and insisted that a new critical evaluation of *ḥadīth* could bring forth knowledge that had either been lost or was unavailable to the earlier scholars. At that time, many orthodox scholars abstained from addressing the *ḥadīth* critically and insisted that only the established *fiqh* of the early authorities was now a fit object of study. Thus, the reformers argued for a return to the original sources of revelation. They also tended to be critical of the subsidiary methods of *qiyās*, human analogical reasoning, the importance of which they would reduce to the benefit of studies directly on the sources of revelation (Vikør, 2000).

The term *ijtihād* has in our time become a mantra for 'modernizing' the Sharīʿa. The pre-modern scholars who argued for an 'opening of the gates' certainly implied reform but not in the sense of freely adapting the revealed law to contemporary conditions in a free-for-all fashion. On the contrary, they strongly rejected *ra'y*, personal opinion, and indeed considered any legal opinion not properly based on a source of revelation as 'whims', be that the whims of the early founders or of contemporary scholars. Their object was to work on the sources in the same classical manner as the early scholars had. What they claimed was that the early scholars, including the founding authorities, could not have any precedence over studies done later on the same type of sources with the same methodology. The early scholars could be wrong, or they could have been unaware of sound *ḥadīth* that had come to light later. Thus, they repeated hagiographical stories for each of the four school founders saying, in essence: 'If you find a *ḥadīth* that is in opposition to what I have said, then leave my opinion and follow the *ḥadīth*'.

Thus, these nineteenth-century reformers have been termed *la-madhhabī*, 'non-school'. Indeed some, like Ibn Idrīs mentioned earlier, did express views that would indicate that anyone who follows one of the schools is performing *shirk*, idolatry, since he is putting the (human) jurists of the school above God (that is, above any *ḥadīth* that might oppose their school's view) (Ibn Idrīs, 2000: 47–130). However, in most cases, these reformers did generally identify with a school but insisted that a scholar must have the right to look above the fences between the schools and see if a scholar in another school had found and used a *ḥadīth* that was more sound than one's own. Thus, what they opposed was *ta'aṣṣub al-madhhab*, '*madhhab*-fanaticism', the total rejection of any opinion presented by schools other than their own.

Modernity and the sources of revelation

The idea of combining views from different schools, *talfīq*, was not totally unheard of earlier either, but did become an important tool for the next generation of reformist scholars, who unlike the eighteenth- and early nineteenth-century reformists, worked under the challenge of new legal ideas from Europe. New laws were enacted, some codifying rules based on the Sharīʿa, but without its methodology, others borrowed more or less wholesale from European laws (see Chapter 3, this volume). In the nineteenth century, the former was most common, but the education of new generations of legal experts in the ways of European law led to western-inspired legal thinking becoming dominant, even when they worked on those areas of the law that were retained as a 'reservation' for Sharīʿa rule, such as family and personal status law.

While lawyers in the Muslim world would still receive some training in *fiqh*, the methodology of how to refer to the sources, how to evaluate various views of *fiqh* against each other, and so on, remained generally foreign to the training and thinking of twentieth-century lawyers. Thus, modern law makers and lawyers would most often refer to the Qurʾān and Sunna either by mimicking traditional texts, or eclecticly quote bits from the Qurʾān and Sunna in support of whichever legal view they had developed by their own methodology. The development of the law was thus removed from the traditional muftis to state legislative bodies. Egypt did introduce the office of state mufti in 1895 (the first being the famous modernist Muḥammad ʿAbduh), but it soon lost any influence over the legal developments (Skovgaard-Petersen, 1997). Thus shorn of their legal competence, the muftis instead became private councillors for individual Muslims in matters of ritual or everyday adaptation to the rapidly changing technical and social circumstances of the country.

The new legislators tended to see the gates of *ijtihād* as wide open, without the strict methodology of *ḥadīth* criticism that had prevailed a century earlier, but primarily as a way to adapt the law to the current times. Indeed, the plural, *ijtihādāt*, has come to mean 'legal development' in general, while the two terms for legislation, *tashrīʿ* (from the same root as Sharīʿa) and *taqnīn* (from Kanun, the Ottoman state law) has come to be used more or less interchangeably, although the latter more specifically means codification.

With the rise of Islamism and political Islam, in particular from the 1970s, such modernity was challenged by political forces that called for the 'restoration of the Sharīʿa'. They, like the modernists, favoured a renewed *ijtihād*, but here in the meaning of discarding the impurities that later tradition had falsely introduced and returning to the pure Sharīʿa of the Prophet's own time, either as an ethic found in God's intentions of *maṣlaḥa*, or, alternatively by adopting literally any practice of the Prophet, in large or small matters, that they believed to be attested in the Sunna (the latter trend was known as 'Salafism'). However, for many, this call for *ijtihād* was more a slogan that should free them from the authority of the traditional scholars, than a project of actual legal reform. In most cases, the Islamists focused more on either resisting the moral liberalism of modern society, or for the more radical, to reinstate the *ḥudūd* laws as a symbol of 'pure Sharīʿa'. In neither case did these Islamists tend to go deeply into a scholarly discussion of an internal development of the Sharīʿa and most often sought scholarly legitimation in citing traditional *fiqh*, if they at all referred to scholarly debates.

An exemplary case of how these references to Sharīʿa and the sources of revelation could be played out in practice, is the story of the Egyptian constitution after 1970. Until that time, the law only said that 'Islam is the religion of the state' (§3, from 1956). In 1971, under president Sadat, the phrase 'and the principles of the Islamic Sharīʿa is a main source for legislation' was added (now §2). In 1980, this was strengthened to say that the Sharīʿa was *the* main source, but still only its 'principles'. This caused considerable controversy, but the decision of what these 'principles' were and how they were to be applied, was given to the new Constitutional Court, manned by professional lawyers with a secular training (Lombardi, 2006). They did test a number of new laws against §2 but decided that these principles of the Sharīʿa could be either some fixed and undisputed rules, or the *maqāṣid*, the goals of the Sharīʿa. The former, they decided, were quite few, while the latter was the *maṣlaḥa*, public welfare. So, any law that promoted the general welfare of the Egyptian people without expressly contravening the few rules they found to be fixed would be acceptable under §2, and in the years of its existence, the court only overturned one minor law on this ground.

After the Arab Spring revolution in 2011, a new constitution was again to be made, and a constitutional assembly was established with a strong element of Islamists, the majority from the ruling Muslim Brotherhood, and a smaller but vocal group by the emerging and more conservative Salafi parties (Vikør, 2016). The liberal and secular currents successively withdrew from the assembly, leaving it to the Islamists. The Salafi groups first attacked §2, which clearly had not worked to strengthen the Sharīʿa in actual legal practice. They suggested replacing the word 'principles' of the Sharīʿa with the 'rules' of the Sharīʿa. This was however rejected by the Brotherhood, which did not disagree strongly with the prevailing opinion that §2 referred to the *maṣlaḥa* general welfare of Egypt. They did not want to rock this particular boat, so §2 remained unchanged.

Instead, the assembly introduced two new paragraphs, both of which were fairly ambivalent. One was §4, saying that the religious authorities of al-Azhar, the central seat of Islamic learning in Egypt, should 'be consulted' in matters of the Sharīʿa. It was not clear what this was to mean or whether the intention was to move the authority of interpretation from the judiciary to the religious scholars. Even more impenetrable was §219, which described how the interpretation was to be done. The published English translation did not provide much insight: 'The principles of Islamic Sharia include general evidence, foundational rules, rules of jurisprudence, and credible sources accepted in Sunni doctrines and by the larger community'. Some deconstruction of the Arabic text may however indicate how a new law was to be tested against the Sharīʿa. First, the law should be seen against the undisputed text of the Qurʾān and *ḥadīth* (general rule texts). Then, against the 'methodologies and basics' of Islamic jurisprudence (*uṣūl al-fiqh*), and finally against the established rules of the four schools of law. It was still not clear how this process was intended to work, but it seems to indicate that a fair amount of *ijtihād* was to be allowed, and that new laws of Egypt should be tested directly against the Qurʾān and Sunna, not just against the rules of the established schools.

This was never put to the test, as the military deposed the Islamist government soon afterwards and abolished the constitution. The new constitution they promulgated soon after retained §2 and allowed al-Azhar a smaller role in questions of religion, but not particularly of law. The complicated §219 was removed. Thus, Egypt returned to the situation it had been before the revolution in 2011. In all its complexity, the exercise indicated one manner in which an attempt was made to integrate a traditional religious authority (al-Azhar), new Islamist sensibilities and a codified constitution into one text.

The example from the revolutionary process of Egypt shows how the sources of revelation remain relevant, not just as a remote historical text but as a living basis for potential legal development. However, since the meaning of these texts has always been, and remains, contested, the issue of authority over the sources and over what methods of inquiry could be used on them, became central. After the early attempts by the caliphs to arrogate this authority to themselves were defeated, the religious scholars could dominate the field as the *wuratha al-anbiyāʾ*, the heirs to the prophets. But today they are challenged both by would-be scholars without classical training from the independent Islamist circles, and by modernizing state authorities who rely as much on western-trained legal experts as on the traditional religious scholars, who nevertheless still persist in their promotions of the classical sciences of theology and Sharīʿa.

References

Brown, J. A.C. 2009. *Hadith: Muhammad's Legacy in the Medieval and Modern World.* Oneworld.
Burton, J. 1990. *The Sources of Islamic Law. Islamic Theories of Abrogation.* Edinburgh University Press.
Calder, N. 1983. 'Ikhtilâf and ijmâʿ in Shâfiʿî's Risâla'. 58 *Studia Islamica.* 55.

Calder, N. 1996. 'Al-Nawawi's Typology of *muftīs* and its Significance for a General Theory of Islamic Law'. 3(2) *Islamic Law and Society*. 137.
Chamberlain, M. 1997. 'The Production of Knowledge and the Reproduction of the A'yan in Medieval Damascus' in N. Grandin (ed.) *Madrasa: La transmission du savoir dans le monde musulman*. Arguments. 28.
Crone, P. 2005. *Medieval Islamic Political Thought*. Edinburgh University Press.
Emon, A. M. 2005. 'Natural law and natural rights in Islamic Law'. 20 *Journal of Law and Religion*. 351.
Emon, A. M. 2010. *Islamic Natural Law Theories*. Oxford University Press.
Fadel, M. H. 1996. 'The Social Logic of *taqlīd* and the Rise of *mukhataṣar*'. 3(2) *Islamic Law and Society*. 193.
Hallaq, W. B. 1984. 'Was the Gate of *ijtihād* Closed?'. 16(1) *International Journal of Middle Eastern Studies*. 3.
Hallaq, W. B. 1996. 'Ifta' and ijtihad in Sunni Legal Theory: A Develomental Account' in M. K. Masud, B. Messick and D. S. Powers (eds) *Islamic Legal Interpretation: Muftis and their Fatwas*. Harvard University Press. 35.
Hasan, A. 1992. *The Doctrine of ijmāʿ in Islam: A Study of the Juridical Principle of Consensus*. Kitab Bhavan.
Hasan, A. 1994. *Analogical Reasoning in Islamic Jurisprudence: A Study of the Juridical Principle of Qiyas*. Adam Publishers.
Ibn Idrīs, A. 2000. *The Exoteric Aḥmad Ibn Idrīs. A Sufi's Critique of the Madhāhib and the Wahhābīs*. Edited and translated by B. Radtke et al. Brill.
Ibn Māja, M. b. Y. n.d. *Sunan*. Dār al-fikr ʿarabī.
Kamali, M. H. 1991. *Principles of Islamic Jurisprudence*. Islamic Texts Society.
Lombardi, C. B. 2006. *State Law as Islamic Law in Modern Egypt: The Incorporation of the Sharīʿa into Egyptian Constitutional Law*. Brill.
Makdisi, G. 1981. *The Rise of Colleges: Institutions of Learning in Islam and the West*. Edinburgh University Press.
Masud, M. K. (ed). 1995. *Shāṭibī's Philosophy of Islamic Law*. Islamic Research Institute.
Melchert, C. 1997. *The Formation of the Sunni Schools of Law: 9th–10th Centuries C.E.* Brill.
Muranyi, M. 1997. 'Die frühe Rechtsliteratur zwischen Quellenanalyse und Fiktion'. 4 *Islamic Law and Society*. 224.
Muslim ibn al-Ḥajjāj. n.d. *Ṣaḥīḥ Muslim*. Maṭbaʿat ʿĪsā al-Bābī al-Ḥalabī.
Opwis, F. 2010. *Maṣlaḥa and the Purpose of the Law: Islamic Discourse on Legal Change from the 4th/10th to 8th/14th century*. Brill.
Peters, R. 1980. '*Idjtihād* and *taqlīd* in 18th and 19th Century Islam'. 20(3–4) *Die Welt des Islams*. 131.
Rahman, F. 1962. 'Concepts sunnah, ijtihād and ijmāʾ in the Early Period'. 1 *Islamic Studies*. 5.
Schoeler, G. 2006. *The Oral and the Written in Early Islam*. Routledge.
Skovgaard-Petersen, J. 1997. *Defining Islam for the Egyptian State: Muftis and Fatwas of the Dār al-iftā*. Brill.
al-Tirmidhī, M b. ʿĪ. 1962. *al-Jāmiʿ al-ṣaḥīḥ: wa-huwa Sunan al-Tirmidhī*. Maktabat Muṣṭafā al-Bābī al-Ḥalabī.
Vikør, K. S. 2000. '"To Follow a madhhab is Shirk": Anti-madhhabism in a Nineteenth-Century Tradition'. Paper, Third Conference on Islamic Law, Harvard.
Vikør, K. S. 2005. *Between God and the Sultan: A History of Islamic Law*. Hurst.
Vikør, K. S. 2016. 'Islamic Law in the Modern World: States, Laws and Constitutions' in L. Buskens and A. van Sandwijk (eds) *Islamic Studies in the Twenty-First Century. Transformations and Continuities*. Amsterdam University Press. 205.
Watt, W. M. 1998. *The Formative Period of Islamic Thought*. Oneworld.

9

Hindu law

The sources

Domenico Francavilla

Complexity of sources in Hindu law

The history of Hindu law spans many centuries. As a result, theories and practices of sources of Hindu law should be considered in a plurality of contexts, bearing in mind that, although there have been profound transformations, these mainly concern interaction between the traditional sources of Hindu law and new sources in the colonial period and in contemporary India.

In fact, over the centuries new sources have been introduced, without completely replacing older ones. Since the colonial period, sources imported from western legal culture, and confirmed in independent India, interacted in complex ways with traditional sources of Hindu law. The colonial period thus represents a watershed in the history of Hindu law sources, marking a distinction between classical, or traditional sources, and modern sources, and has become a common topic in studies on Hindu law. This does not mean that before the encounter with western models of law, the Hindu tradition was static as regards sources. In fact, the development of traditional Hindu law has known different theories of sources from the Vedic period to the post-classical period, even though coherence exists, at least in Brahmanism. In this regard, it is worth remembering that one of the main differences between Brahmanism and Buddhism is the very authority of the Vedas. Furthermore, the introduction of modern state sources does not completely set aside the autonomous evolution of traditional sources, although this phenomenon is very difficult to investigate, given its place at the margins of official law.

A second preliminary remark is that sources of Hindu law can be analysed under two different, although connected, perspectives: as a theory of sources developed in Hindu jurisprudence, and as sources in practice in different local contexts. Although we can reach a detailed understanding of theories of sources, developed in Sanskrit literature available to us, knowledge about sources in practice in the ancient Hindu context is more scattered and uncertain.

The theoretical system of sources of Hindu law found its most complete formulation in the classical period, but Hindu interpreters always expressed questions about the authority to recognize the various sources acknowledged in practice. Their basis of authority and their relationships have been subject to very complex investigation, based on philosophical and theological understanding (Davis, 2010).[1] This theoretical construction provides instruments for legitimizing, within tradition, rules that had their origin elsewhere and allowed Hindu law to evolve over time, adapting to different social contexts and at different times, while maintaining a remarkable cultural unity.

Thanks to this theory of sources, interpreters were able to lay the foundations of the laws that have governed the lives of Hindu communities in different parts of the Indian subcontinent. However, as we will see, Hindu law in practice is the outcome of interaction between an expert tradition (Olivelle, 2005) and local customary rules. The relevance of traditional sources for modern Hindu law is therefore mainly in the fact that they were crucial to form the basic institutes of Hindu law and they provided a legal structure that guided interpreters in solving practical problems. Moreover, traditional sources are still considered sources of modern Hindu law. Handbooks on Hindu law (Diwan, 2004) include a description of traditional sources, and the judge in a secular court in contemporary India may refer to them. Even though the introduction of modern sources has not altogether eliminated traditional sources, it has diminished their scope and importance in official Hindu law. However, since Hindus may follow their law beside state law, official recognition is not strictly necessary, and traditional sources may operate at the non-official level. From the point of view of a Hindu, if not from a state perspective, several kinds of sources interact with each other in different spheres of life.

This chapter will first consider the traditional system of sources of law, aiming at describing both its theoretical foundation and how it works in practice. Then it will analyse modern sources of Hindu law and interaction with pre-existing sources in order to provide an account of the development of tradition and the current state of affairs in contemporary India.

The classical theory of sources

The roots of dharma

The sources of traditional Hindu law identify themselves with the sources of *dharma*, although some interpreters recognize non-dharmic sources as subordinate. The Sanskrit term used to indicate the source of *dharma* is *dharmamūlas*, which literally means 'roots of dharma'. *Dharma* exists independently from an act of human or even divine authority, and therefore the term 'root' or 'source' must be understood as a means of knowledge of *dharma*, as what makes *dharma* known, following the interpretation given by medieval commentators.[2] The sources acknowledged as having authority for knowledge of *dharma* are four: *śruti, smṛti, sadācāra* and *ātmanastuṣṭi*. In Hindu texts, there are some variants, mainly concerning the fourth source, which, as we will see, is more controversial.[3]

The *śruti* identifies itself with the Vedas, the sacred texts of Hindu tradition. The term *śruti* literally means hearing, what was heard, and in this context refers to the hearing of the Vedic word by inspired savants, *ṛṣis*. Therefore, the form of revelation in Hinduism is oral. The Vedic texts were written down very late, and their transmission has taken place and continues to take place in oral form through the Vedic schools, which have developed particular mnemonic techniques to guarantee the accuracy of transmission. 'Veda' means the totality of valid knowledge and, more specifically, four texts recognized as endowed with authority by tradition: *Ṛgveda, Sāmaveda, Yajurveda* and *Atharvaveda*. These are composite texts, made up of hymns, songs, formulas, and ritualistic and philosophical treatises. For each of these collections there are several versions. As a result, the Vedic revelation from the outset is considered as multiform, being received by a plurality of subjects. The existence of a plurality of texts and traditions is allowed (Menski, 2002).

The second source of *dharma* is the *smṛti*. The term literally means memory, what is remembered, and can broadly correspond to the category of 'tradition'. *Smṛti*, as a category, includes different kinds of texts. The most important in terms of law are *dharmaśāstras* and *dharmasūtras*.[4] These texts have been considered equivalent to western codes, but they are in fact works of a doctrinal nature, interpretive texts, where an author elaborates and systematizes dharmic rules, taking into account the other sources and often proposing original solutions.[5]

The *dharmaśāstras* were in turn the object of interpretation, giving rise to two other types of works: commentaries (*bhāṣya*) and digests (*nibandha*). A commentary is an exegetical work on a specific *dharmaśāstra*. *Nibandhas* are organized following a subject-based criterion and collect different normative texts under different titles. The commentaries ended up with incorporating the commented text, and the most authoritative ones acquired the same authority of the commented text.[6] *Nibandhas* are mainly tools for interpreters: reference works that provide the main rules and opinions on a specific topic.

The *sadācāras*, also called *śiṣṭa-ācāras*, are the practices of virtuous men, that is to say those who are learned in the Vedas and who act in accordance with them. Therefore, these are essentially models of behaviour considered normative by virtue of the quality of the people who put them into practice. These qualified practices should not be understood as what is normally done by most people, that is customs (*caritras*) that do not have a dharmic character but are still important in the making of Hindu law in social reality. *Sadācāras* can be considered as a form of transmission of the knowledge of *dharma*, even though non-textual (Francavilla, 2007). The fundamental difference with written texts included in *smṛti* is that in *sadācāras* one can find the rules of correct behaviour for potentially endless situations, while only a part of these rules can be consolidated in written texts.

Ātmanastuṣṭi consists in the sense of inner satisfaction resulting from behaving appropriately, that is to say, according to *dharma*, in a given context. Of course, considering the sense of inner satisfaction a source of *dharma* does not mean that everyone can behave in the way he or she chooses. A subjective qualification is required. In fact, only the approval of people learned in the Vedas and who normally behave in accordance with them can amount to a source of *dharma*. This fourth source of *dharma*, given its particular features, is a controversial one for both Hindu interpreters and western scholars.[7]

Epistemological foundations and the theory of lost Veda

The Vedas are considered eternal and without author. In Hinduism, there are theistic and non-theistic schools, and therefore different views can be found on this point. According to the doctrine of Mīmāṃsā, however, broadly understood as the school of Hindu hermeneutics, Vedic statements are not only not human work but are not even divine work. In this context, the authority of the revealed text is not based on the divinity and infallibility of a personal God but on the divinity of the Vedic word (Jha, 1964).

Dharma can only be known through Vedic revelation. In fact, it belongs to the sphere of *ought*: human beings cannot know it through perception or other means of knowledge based on perception, nor, unlike in Buddhism, is it believed that it can be known by intuition. From an epistemological point of view, the Veda, which is knowledge obtained through the word (*śabdapramāṇa*), is the only possible source of knowledge of *dharma*. However, considering the sources of knowledge of *dharma* from the point of view of the practical ascertainment of dharmic rules, the other three sources, which theoretically have subordinate authority to that of the Vedas, are certainly more important at the practical level (Menski, 2003).

This epistemological approach requires interpreters to develop a theory of Vedic foundation for all sources. The works that fall within *smṛti* do not have independent authority, since, as the authors are human beings, they may contain faults or opinions that are entirely personal and not based on a true knowledge of *dharma*. Consequently, their authority must be connected to the Vedas, by ascertaining or at least reasonably assuming the existence of a link between the two sources. In general, the rules contained in this source are considered to be a simple transmission of rules already contained in the Veda. In reality, the correspondence between Vedic texts and *smṛti* texts is very small, and therefore the interpreters, in order to assert the existence of a Vedic foundation, make use of a particular hermeneutical strategy. Put in simple terms, their reasoning is that, if it is not possible to identify an explicit Vedic text that provides a basis for a *smṛti* text, one can assume that the former has been lost. In other words, it is believed that a rule contained in a text of the *smṛti* was originally contained in a part of the Veda which has subsequently disappeared due to, for example, an interruption in the transmission of the text. It may also be assumed that that particular text is actually present in the Vedas but that it is difficult to identify it because it is implied or because it is the result of an interpretive work carried out on elements dispersed in different versions. On the other hand, the specific function of *dharmaśāstra* is precisely to extract, organize and transmit the knowledge of *dharma* by resorting to various sources, including the Vedas. This is clearly an interpretive fiction, but it has a sound basis and can be used for recognizing, on a theoretical level, a Vedic foundation for texts that were recognized as authoritative in practice, which is a key indicator of their being part of the Vedic tradition.

Connection with the Vedas is also required for the authority of *sadācāras* and *ātmanastuṣṭi*. The same line of reasoning as we have seen in the case of the *smṛti* is followed, and therefore it is believed that they are based on existing or assumed Vedic texts. In the latter case, it is believed that a certain practice has been formed on the basis of a Vedic text that has subsequently disappeared, while the practice has continued to be observed. In addition, *sadācāras* are qualified behaviours, behaviours of authoritative people, and this guarantees a subjective connection with the Vedas. The subjective criterion is the crucial one to establish the authority of the *ātmanastuṣṭi*, since the sense of personal satisfaction of people considered to be learned in the Vedas and hence virtuous is deemed to be normative. The underlying theory is that the ethical expertise gained in assessing the correctness of human actions in a dharmic perspective leads these individuals almost naturally to the knowledge of *dharma* and correct behaviour.

In conclusion, all sources recognized by tradition have authority to the extent they are grounded on the Vedas. It is important to emphasize that this is a strategy of legitimizing new rules that are not in Vedic texts. As Olivelle (1999: xli) observes, 'the theory of lost Veda is used as a hermeneutical strategy for theoretically deriving the whole dharma from the Vedas, while in practice other sources are taken into account'. In this way, the theory of the Vedic foundation of all sources also makes it possible to ensure the evolution of tradition and its differentiation from competing traditions that do not recognize the authority of the Vedas, such as, for example, the Buddhist tradition.

Vedas, from an epistemological point of view, are thus the sole means of knowing *dharma*, which is considered as an order that exists irrespective of divine or human law-making. *Dharmamūlas* have to be understood as sources of knowledge, for *dharma* is recognized and not posited, and this points to a transcultural idea of natural law. However, Olivelle (1999: xxxix) notes that the theological definition of *dharma*, which makes of *dharma* the content of Vedic injunctions, 'clearly defines it as positive, albeit revealed, law, rather than a cosmic or natural order which can be gathered through investigation, introspection or deductive inferences'.

In fact, natural law theories, especially modern theories, normally involve the view according to which law may be known through reason. At least in the classical Hindu view, one cannot know *dharma* through reason but only through revelation. Furthermore, in Sanskrit literature we find opinions leading to a sort of Hindu positivism. In a commentary on the *dharmaśāstra* of Manu,[8] it is argued that what makes something dharmic is Veda, and thus if the Veda states that to kill is *dharma* in a specific context, this cannot be criticized stating that to kill is clearly adharmic, that is to say, that its adharmic nature may be known independently from the Veda.

The problem of the possibility of knowing *dharma* through reason is linked to another important issue, that is, the view of a normative system as a rational system that makes it possible to derive rules from other rules and in which a prominent role is played by general principles. Concerning *dharma*, there are no general principles from which it is possible to derive rules. In reality, general principles that can provide a foundation for other rules may be found in the common or general *dharma* (*sādhāraṇadharma*), which includes for instance *ahiṃsā* (non-violence). However, in the Hindu conception, *sādhāraṇadharma* is not usually meant in this way. Ramanujan (1989: 48) notes that:

> [e]ach addition is really a subtraction from any universal law. There is not much left of an absolute or common (*sādhāraṇa*) *dharma* which the texts speak of, if at all, as a last and not as a first resort. They seem to say, if you fit no contexts or conditions, which is unlikely, fall back on the universal.

As a conclusion, even though *dharma* may be seen as a natural order that is not posited by Vedic revelation, which is a means of knowing *dharma*, from an epistemological point of view, the conception according to which *dharma* can be known only through revelation is firm and, in this sense, the category of natural law seems less appropriate.

Interpretation and sources in practice

The role of interpreters is crucial in the evolution of Hindu law. As noted by Lingat (1998), they seek to derive the rule of *dharma* that they consider appropriate from the set of authoritative texts. If the texts could give rise to different interpretations, the one that best suited the needs of the time and was closer to customs was preferred. In this dynamic between textual and non-textual elements, interpreters carried on a process of evolution of the dharmic system, in accordance with the particular needs of the social context they addressed.

From the theory of the Vedic foundation of all sources, important consequences arise for Hindu hermeneutics. In general, cases of conflict (*virodha*) between sources of different authority are decided on the basis of a hierarchical criterion for which, between Veda, *smṛti, sadācāra* and *ātmanastuṣṭi*, the preceding source has greater authority than the following one. If the conflict occurs between two sources having equal authority, in particular between two Vedic texts, it is believed that both patterns of behaviour are valid and one can choose between them. This option (*vikalpa*) is considered a last resort when interpreters have tried to solve antinomies using various hermeneutic techniques.[9] However, the Vedic legitimacy of all sources means that in all cases of conflict it becomes possible to frame the issue as a case of conflict between Vedic texts. For example, one can consider a case of conflict between Vedas and *smṛti* as a case of conflict between an existing Vedic text and a lost Vedic text on which the text of the *smṛti* is based. This means that from a dharmic point of view, one can consider conflicting rules equally valid. In fact, the Hindu legal tradition does not envisage the possibility of abrogation of Vedic texts, while it assumes that the authority of a Vedic text may be only compressed by a conflicting Vedic text.

This particular theoretical construction makes it possible to clarify some of the features of the Hindu normative system that give it great flexibility and have permitted the continuity and unity of Hinduism, even in the presence of enormous differences within it. The normative system retains its unity through the theory of common origin in the Vedas of contradictory injunctions and acceptance of the fact that the same Veda is internally varied. In other words, the inner variety of *dharma* corresponds to the inner variety of the Vedas (Halbfass, 1990a, 1990b).

The dharmic system thus presents itself as a very comprehensive set of behavioural patterns all considered valid regardless of the authority of the source prescribing them. This is an extremely undefined system, which needs further definition based on the context, through the work of interpreters and confirmation of practice, giving rise to different normative systems. From the point of view of Hindu interpreters, these normative systems find their authority in the same set of texts and are parts, or rather different forms, of a whole perceived as one. From an external point of view, the plurality of normative systems is actually the starting point on which interpreters then construct a theory that allows them to integrate these different systems into a culturally unitary order through the fiction of Vedic legitimation.

It should also be noted that the hierarchical principle would require that the appropriate rule of behaviour for a given situation be searched for first in the Vedas and then in the other sources. On the contrary, as Menski (2006: 216) remarks, the order of the sources in the process of determining *dharma* is reversed:

> These statements establish an obvious hierarchy of sources, down from the divinely inspired, 'revealed' Veda to individual, intuitive discretion of the 'reasonable Hindu'. However, this hierarchy of sources does not make sense in real daily practice. Hindus would not ascertain their *dharma* first by looking up rules in Vedic texts, they would certainly start the other way round and examine their conscience first . . . In social reality, the sequence of sources of *dharma* is completely reversed. To find the actual sources of classical Hindu law, we must read this hierarchy in reverse order. Thus, individual satisfaction about 'doing the right thing in the right way at the right time', collectively and individually experienced, is chronologically and factually the first source of *dharma*.[10]

The underestimation of non-textual elements of Hindu law and the simultaneous overestimation of *smṛti* texts seems to be the result of a disregard for a Hindu conception of law, which, assimilated to western legal experience, is interpreted by giving prominence to its formal aspects and limiting the role of individuals in the process of ascertaining *dharma*. Instead, according to Menski (2006: 217): 'Leaving the decision first of all to the individual gives primary importance to individual perceptions of right and wrong. Classical *dharma*, thus, relies on the individual's self-controlled ability to discern appropriate action, almost by intuition'.

It should be noted that the texts in which subjective requirements are determined for a pattern of behaviour or personal approval to be considered normative are the work of Brahmins and are addressed, first, to Brahmins, that is to say, to the priestly class. In this regard, it can be assumed that the behavioural model of *śiṣṭas*, the people learned in Veda, is easily understood in a Brahmin context. However, a general principle seems to emerge, that is to say to find sources of guidance in rules accepted by one's own community and particularly by esteemed and authoritative people belonging to it.

Vedas are the primary source of *dharma* because they serve to provide a foundation for the whole system of sources. However, from the point of view of the actual operation of Hindu law, Vedas have little relevance and the crucial level is in the rules contained in the lower sources, in particular *sadācāras*, namely behaviour patterns and customary rules.

Dharmic law as elaborated by interpreters has interacted with originally non-dharmic laws. The role of *dharma* in the making of Hindu law as a whole has been much debated. According to Lingat (1998), *dharma* represents ideal law that enters into history through coming into contact with customs, the mediation of interpreters and the intervention of sovereign power.

In the Hindu institutional framework, the sovereign, who embodies political power, is only one among many decision makers, and his power is not exclusive. As Flood observes, in the classical view the sovereign was part of an integrated community and primarily guaranteed a sacred unity (Flood, 2004: 67 ff.). The theory of sovereignty is elaborated with reference to *dharma*. The king, like everyone, has his specific duties, his *rāja-dharma*. His primary duty is to protect subjects from external and internal dangers. Secondly, he must allow his subjects to live according to their *dharma* and he is in this sense the guardian of *dharma*. In Hindu political theology, the king, who is divine, is a point of contact between the cosmic order and the social order (Flood, 2004). *Dharma* is beyond the reach of sovereign power. This means not only that the order of *dharma* cannot be altered by historical acts of the sovereign but also that the sovereign cannot claim to be the depositary of the truth of *dharma*. In general, the Hindu model is devoid of the idea of a centralized definition of what *dharma* is (Menski, 2003). That is why Hindu law does not rely on the idea of obedience to the will of a sovereign who establishes what is right and wrong for everyone, but rather on the idea of adherence to a cosmic order in which the sovereign takes part. Hindus conceive order as locally controlled (Menski, 2003): specific individuals and communities are entitled to define the set of duties that they consider binding in social life. The role of the king, who has the power of punishment (*daṇḍa*, stick), is to enforce these duties. This role becomes culturally more important, especially in late-classical elaborations, based on a vision of human decadence, according to which human beings, who originally adapted spontaneously to *dharma*, are increasingly corrupt and weak, so that only an external power can force them not to break this order.

The king holds the power to promulgate decrees (*rājaśāsana*), which are important as sources of law, but he operates in the non-dharmic realm of the organization of the state or commerce. One of the most important roles of the sovereign is the administration of justice. In the Hindu tradition, the sovereign has the eminent, but not exclusive, task of resolving disputes. Alongside royal courts, courts related to caste, family and other social groups exist, with more or less informal features. In the texts on *dharma, vyavahāra* is the part devoted to settlement of disputes. Prominent figures in the royal courts were the Brahmin experts of *dharma*, who provided the king or royal officers with their opinion based on knowledge of the normative corpus. Colonial courts also referred to these *pandits*, learned experts of dharmic literature, but this experience was soon considered a failure.

There is some debate as to whether this model, found in the texts of tradition, is a realistic model. In this regard, it may be noted that, although not having general normative power, the sovereign has the power to rule his kingdom and that in dharmic questions the sovereign could intervene, albeit in a limited way, as he himself is an interpreter of *dharma*. In this sense, one should not underestimate the role of the king in the sources of Hindu law.

In the elaboration of traditional law, great importance was given to the establishment of the *pariṣad*, that is to say, a council of experts of *dharma* and the Vedic sciences, who had the task of deciding on difficult hermeneutic issues. The *dharmaśāstras* contain many of these decisions. The *pañcāyat* is also very important: an institutionalized council at caste and village level that can resolve disputes and make decisions concerning the community.

Modern sources

As regards modern sources of Hindu law in India, it should be emphasized that these are sources having state origin and therefore stand at a different level from those of traditional law.

The listed subjects system provided for the application of Hindu law with its traditional sources to Hindus on a personal basis in colonial courts, in matters relating to family and succession. Nonetheless, new sources of Hindu law were introduced, namely judicial precedents, 'equity, justice and good conscience' and legislation. This system was confirmed after Independence, as Hindu law is still applied on a personal basis in family and succession law. In 1955–56 four Acts were passed: the Hindu Marriage Act (1955), the Hindu Adoptions and Maintenance Act (1956), the Hindu Minority and Guardianship Act (1956) and the Hindu Succession Act (1956). In the following years other statutes had an impact on Hindu law, among which, for instance, the Prohibition of Child Marriage Act (2006).

Modern sources introduced profound changes. Indeed, even though it is possible to trace rough equivalents of modern sources in traditional Hindu law, legislation, equity and precedents are not sources that have exact correspondences in the Hindu model (Lingat, 1998; Davis, 2007b).

Starting with justice, equity and good conscience, one can observe that traditional Hindu jurisprudence does not lack references to the equity of a decision, so that even a rule of *dharma* contained in an authoritative *dharmaśāstra* can be disregarded in a concrete case if it leads to injustice. However, in a technical sense, we are here faced with a common law principle introduced in the application of Hindu law. If the English judge who had to apply Hindu law did not find the solution to a case, he had to judge following equity, justice and good conscience. In fact, this applied not only in the case of a complete gap but also in the absence of a principle approved by the judge, which is another kind of lacuna, an ideological lacuna. Therefore, the application of this criterion ended up coinciding with the application of the principles of English law, known by judges and approved by them, with some adjustments due to the need to adapt to the specificities of the Indian situation. Many colonial judgments, however, stated that the solutions should not be contrary to the general principles of Hindu law, which was recognized as culturally autonomous. In other words, Hindu law was considered a jurisprudence on its own terms, containing in itself principles and rules suitable for solving any given case (Diwan, 2004: 52).

Legislation and judicial precedent are the two fundamental modern sources for Hindu law in India. In the classical model, there was no room for a general law-making power of the king or of any assembly. In particular, the idea that political power could decide authoritatively what was *dharma* was alien to Hindu views, both because the sovereign was seen as being subject himself to *dharma* and because the definition of *dharma* was considered to be the task of individual communities. In other words, every community, if not every individual, was entitled to define the set of duties which should be complied with.

Legislation became a source of Hindu law in the colonial period. However this source, although important, was never intended to replace the other sources. In particular, legislative efforts never claimed to codify Hindu law entirely, and even the reform laws passed immediately after Independence, regardless of claims, were in fact limited in scale. As Menski (2003) observes, legislation represents in India today a written source in interaction with the complex of Hindu customs, as in classical India Hindu law developed through an interaction of those same local norms with the learned law of *dharmaśāstra*, which it is worth remembering had a doctrinal and non-legislative character (Menski, 2003).

The Constitution of India 1949 (1950) is a modern source of Hindu law in the sense that courts applying Hindu law can only interpret it in the light of constitutional principles. The same principles inspire modernizing legislative action. In particular, constitutional principles are a filter for Hindu rules related to untouchability, caste and gender differences.

As for judicial precedents, the Hindu tradition holds very few traces of judgments pronounced in the courts in the classical period. The point is that it was believed there was no need to preserve contingent decisions that, unlike doctrinal treatises on *dharma*, did not aspire to describe an eternal *dharma*. The principle of binding precedent was introduced in the colonial period for all Indian law and therefore for Hindu law, and is still a crucial part of the application of Hindu law in state courts. As Diwan observes, there are two important aspects of the doctrine of binding precedent in Hindu law. The first is that:

> [p]ractically all the important principles and rules of Hindu law have now been embodied in case law. In such cases, recourse to original sources is not necessary. Reference to leading decision is enough. In this sense, precedent or case law is the source, by and large, of most of the rules and precedents of Hindu law.
>
> *(Diwan, 2004: 52)*

From the colonial period precedents tend to limit recourse to traditional texts and their complicated exegesis. Even more significantly, in the course of time, courts take knowledge of customs mainly through previous judgments. A second aspect highlighted by Diwan is that:

> [p]recedent is a source of law in the sense that by the process of judicial interpretation, doctrines, principles and rules of law have been introduced in the body of Hindu law. For these principles, doctrines and rules, the source of authority is precedent.
>
> *(Diwan, 2004: 52)*

Another interesting aspect of the modern system of sources relates to customs. The widespread recognition of customs in Hindu law is tempered by the legal definition of customs, which limits their applicability. Article 3 of the Hindu Marriage Act (1955) provides:

> In this Act unless the context otherwise requires: (a) the expressions 'custom' and 'usage' signify any rule which, having been continuously and uniformly observed for a long time, has obtained the force of law among Hindus in any local area, tribe, community, group or family; provided that the rule is certain and not unreasonable or opposed to public policy; and provided further that in the case of a rule applicable only to a family it has not been discontinued by the family.

Assessment of the antiquity of custom can vary, but it is not required that a customary norm has an immemorial origin. Secondly, custom has to be uninterrupted and certain. Furthermore, it should not be unreasonable, immoral, or contrary to the principles of public policy.[11] The burden of proof of the existence of custom falls on the subject who intends to use it. It is significant that customs can be local and therefore have a territorial scope, or personal and referred to tribe, community, groups and families. This shows firstly the extent of recognition of customary norms and, secondly, recalls a principle of classical Hindu law, according to which the sovereign, when ruling on a dispute, firstly had to ascertain the largely customary rules that the parties recognized as their law.

Considering the problem of inner variety of Hinduism, it can be observed that official recognition of local and particular norms allows different communities to have their particular traditional law applied by the courts, at least in some cases, for instance as regards marriage solemnization, even though within a state regulatory framework.

Conclusion

Hindu law today is an official component of Indian law, even though large parts of it are not state derived. In fact, in many cases, legislation has simply incorporated norms that were already present in traditional law, both doctrinal and customary law. In other cases, applied norms are customary norms, which by definition are spontaneous rules from below not involving production by the state. Hindu law provides important indications on possible interactions between state law and religious law, as it embodies a model for which state law is the framework of a series of norms of different origin.

In independent India, official Hindu law does not have a truly religious nature, because Hindu laws are passed or enforced by organs of a secular state, even though they will affect the lives of Hindus. It is interesting to note that official Hindu law can be applied by judges who may not be Hindu, but, for example, Muslim or Catholic, and in any case their religious beliefs are not relevant for the exercise of their duties as judges.

At the same time, customs and, even though in rare cases, the views of the experts of *dharma*, still play a role in the system of sources of Hindu law, which also continues to evolve independently of state law. In this perspective, one could argue that the legal framework has changed and is now a mixed one: on the one hand, traditional Hindu law with its legitimacy in a dharmic framework and, on the other, state norms, which are independent of *dharma*. The latter in some cases may not prevent Hindus from adhering to norms which are legal in dharmic terms, when this is not in conflict with constitutional values, while in other cases they may be more or less in opposition to unofficial Hindu law.

In fact, alongside official Hindu law, there is unofficial Hindu law, that is, law followed by Hindus on a traditional basis, irrespective of state recognition. The differences between official and unofficial Hindu law should not be overestimated. Between the two there is a dynamic relationship according to which an originally unofficial rule can become official and vice versa. The interweaving of these systems (traditional/modern; official/unofficial) can give rise to unexpected combinations. For example, a Hindu doctrinal rule in conflict with a Hindu customary rule can become the content of an Indian Act on Hindu law. Even more generally, the conflict between traditional Hindu law and state Hindu law can certainly stand on the level of the content of specific rules, but it can also operate at the more fundamental level of the view of the role of the state in defining rules that must be followed. In Chiba's terms (1986), a conflict may involve legal postulates rather than the content of rules.

One can thus understand Hindu law by distinguishing between the law produced by Hindus and the law applied to Hindus. The two aspects, which normally coincide, tend to be distinct in modern Hindu law in India, but Hindu law remains a unitary phenomenon and, in this perspective, may be defined as the law observed by Hindus, composed of rules produced within the tradition and rules of external origin insofar as they succeed in entering Hindu living law. Real law stems from the interaction and combination of multiple types of laws.

Notes

1 This underlying understanding gives a specific identity to Hindu law. In fact, if, on the one hand, the sources of Hindu law may have some correspondence with sources accepted by other law, for instance Muslim law, their theoretical construction is conceivable only within the framework of beliefs and philosophies elaborated in Hinduism.
2 See, for instance, the commentary of Medhātithi on *Manusmṛti* II.6 (Jha, 1999: 180): '"*Root*", here means *cause*. The *Veda* and *Smriti* can be a "cause" only in the sense that they serve to *make known* – not in that of *producing*, nor in that *helping to stand*, which are the two senses in which the "*root*" is the *cause* of the Tree'.
3 The best known verses including a list of sources of *dharma* are *Manusmṛti* (II.6, II.12) and *Yājñavalkyasmṛti* (I.7). For a detailed analysis of sources of *dharma*, see Lingat (1998), Menski (2003), Francavilla (2006) and Davis (2010).
4 Lingat (1998) remarks that the two kinds of work differentiate themselves on the basis of a series of elements, among which, from a formal point of view, the fact that *dharmasūtras* are written in prose while *dharmaśāstra* are written in metric verses. *Dharmaśāstras* are also later works, more universalistic in character.
5 Also included are categories of texts of very different types such as *Itihāsas* and *Purāṇas* (Flood, 2004).
6 Remarkably, different interpretations of the same text, as found in different commentaries, can be the basis of different rules adopted in different parts of India. For example, different opinions contained in two commentaries, *Dāyabhāga* and *Mitākṣarā*, are at the origin of some differences in the law of succession in Bengal, where the authority of the first text prevails, and in other areas of India where the second prevails (Rocher, 2002)
7 According to Lingat (1998), personal satisfaction, having no outside authority for man, should not be considered a genuine source. On the role of this source, see Menski (2003), Francavilla (2006) and, from a different perspective, Davis (2007c).
8 See the commentary of Medhātithi on *Manusmṛti* II.6 (Jha, 1999: 186 ff.) and Francavilla (2006: 99–100).
9 See in detail Francavilla (2006). In reconciling seemingly contradictory texts, the distinction between *vidhi* and *arthavāda* plays an important role. The *vidhis* are injunctions while the *arthavādas* are texts that contain the mere description of a fact and have the function of commending the fulfilment of the prescribed act or completing the prescriptive content of a *vidhi*. Given that a real conflict exists only between two injunctions prescribing two alternative actions, one of the ways to resolve a seeming conflict, conciliating the two texts, is to consider one of them a *vidhi* and the other a simple *arthavāda*. Interpreters frequently resort to this kind of argument.
10 This point is strongly criticized by Davis (2007c), because it supersedes knowledge emerging from original Sanskit texts.
11 The judicial interpretation of these requirements is difficult and often controversial. See, for instance, Bhaurao Shankar Lokhande v State of Maharashtra, AIR 1965 SC 1564, and Bhimashya & Ors. v Smt. Janabi @ Janawwa, 2006 (13) SCC 627.

References

Chiba, M. (ed.). 1986. *Asian Indigenous Law in Interaction with Received Law*. KPI.

Davis, D. R. Jr. 2007b. 'Maxims & Precedent in Classical Hindu Law'. 33 *Indologica Taurinensia*. 33.

Davis, D. R. Jr. 2007c. 'On Ātmatuṣṭi as a Source of Dharma'. 127(3) *Journal of the American Oriental Society*. 279.

Davis, D. R. Jr. 2010. *The Spirit of Hindu Law*. Cambridge University Press.

Diwan, P. 2004. *Modern Hindu Law*. 13th edn. Allahabad Law Agency.

Flood, G. 2004. *An Introduction to Hinduism*. Cambridge University Press.

Francavilla, D. 2006. *The Roots of Hindu Jurisprudence. Sources of Dharma and Interpretation in Mīmāṃsā and Dharmaśāstra*. Corpus Iuris Sanscriticum et fontes iuris Asiae Meridianae et Centralis.

Francavilla, D. 2007. 'Through Words and Practices: The Transmission of the Knowledge of *Dharma* in the Hindu Legal Tradition'. 33 *Indologica Taurinensia*. 57.

Halbfass, W. 1990a. *India and Europe: An Essay in Philosophical Understanding*. Motilal Banarsidass.

Halbfass, W. 1990b. *Tradition and Reflection: Explorations in Indian Thought*. State University of New York Press.

Jha, G. 1964. *Pūrva Mīmāṃsā in its Sources*. Banaras Hindu University.
Jha, G. 1999. *Manusmṛti with the Manubhāṣya of Medhātithi*. Vol. 3. Motilal Banarsidass.
Lingat, R. 1998. *The Classical Law of India*. Oxford University Press.
Menski, W. F. 2002. 'Hindu Law as a "Religious" System' in A. Huxley (ed.) *Religion, Law and Tradition: Comparative Studies in Religious Law*. RoutledgeCurzon. 108.
Menski, W. F. 2003. *Hindu Law. Beyond Tradition and Modernity*. Oxford University Press.
Menski, W. F. 2006. *Comparative Law in a Global Context: The Legal Systems of Asia and Africa*. 2nd edn. Cambridge University Press.
Olivelle, P. (ed.). 1999. *Dharmasūtras: The Law Codes of Āpastamba, Gautama, Baudhāyana and Vasiṣṭa*. Oxford University Press.
Olivelle, P. (ed.). 2005. *Manu's Code of Law*. Oxford University Press.
Ramanujan, A. K. 1989. 'Is There an Indian Way of Thinking? An Informal Essay'. 23(1) *Contributions to Indian Sociology*. 45.
Rocher, L. (ed.). 2002. *Jīmūtavāhana's Dāyabhāga: The Hindu Law of Inheritance in Bengal*. Oxford University Press.

10

Comparative remarks

The sources of religious laws

Gary F. Bell

Introduction

A discussion of the sources of religious laws is always complex and sometimes sensitive. It raises many issues, including first and foremost the extent to which a religious law is influenced or even formulated by human agents. No matter how revealed, divine or sacred the highest sources of a religious law may be held by the believers, the reality is that, at least in this world, it is not God (or Gods) who apply the law, but human beings. The question becomes: to what extent does a given religious law include human elaboration and maybe even innovation, and are these human contributions considered part of the religious law or just applications of it? In order to preserve the divine, revealed or sacred character of their law, it would seem, to an outsider at least, that some movements within the traditions go to great lengths to avoid recognising the human origin of some of the religious law, or when they recognise human agency, go to some length to limit its theoretical importance. In fact, going back to the purest divine, revealed or sacred sources and rejecting human and particularly institutional elaborations, has been the leitmotiv of many radical reformist movements – for example the Protestant Reformation (*Sola Scriptura*) or Wahhabism and Salafism.[1] Therefore, the role of human agency is one of the main issues that arises when discussing the sources of religious laws, and this comparative exercise will therefore address this issue.

The other issue is how the religious legal tradition relates to State law or even how it survives modern and often colonial State law. In some traditions, the question was asked early on (the political leaders in Islam being under the Sharīʿa, the Dharma of the Raja in Hindu Law, giving to Caesar what belongs to Caesar and to God what belongs to God in Christianity), but a more radical challenge comes from the advent of the modern Westphalian State and of colonialism, and their claim to be the source of all laws (religious laws being occasionally authorised by State law as a limited, alternative source of law – sometimes State-enforced and legislated as legal pluralism in personal matters).

But before looking at the influence of human agency and of the State on the sources of religious laws, we should first explain why the chapter on Christian laws stands out from all the others when it comes to sources of law. The reader will have noticed that the chapter on the sources of Christian laws is very different from the chapters on Hindu, Jewish and Islamic laws. In comparison to these other chapters, the one on Christian laws seems focused on a much narrower concept of religious law and seems much less concerned with the divine or revealed nature of that law. This could be explained in large part by the different approaches taken by the authors – some more theoretical, some more positivist. However, this could also be explained by a comparison of the sources of law in Christianity and in other religions, which will be the first comparison that will be discussed here.

Comparing Christian sources and other religious sources

All the other chapters started with divine, revealed or sacred sources of law and moved slowly down a hierarchy of sources of law, keeping in mind the issue of whether lower sources of law are divine, revealed or sacred or are human elaborations, innovations and even changes to the religious law. In Jewish and Islamic law, the hierarchy is in principle very strong, and the text of the most revealed sources cannot be contradicted or undone by lower sources (although internal contradictions within the same hierarchical level may sometimes have to be resolved). In Hindu law the hierarchy is there but less conclusive on the validity or invalidity of lower sources – local customs for example may prevail over the Vedas at least in practice, and in any event the Vedas are often rather vague. However, the chapter on Christian sources did not concern itself first (and not even mostly) with a hierarchy of sources – not that it does not exist (it is indeed mentioned in the chapter), but it did not seem to matter very much in the limited fields that Christian law governs today and especially since a lot of the Christian law being described seems to be man-made, even legislated by Church authorities. How come so much of that law seem to be man-made and almost independent of the revelation?

A second major point of difference is an understandable assumption mentioned later in that chapter: whereas the other religious laws aim at regulating all human relationships and the relationship to God(s) – including for example the law of contract law, of torts, (of obligations), of crime, of property, of successions, of marriage, and also of prayer, of fasting, etc., the Christian religious law is much narrower in scope, limited, as mentioned in the chapter, to ecclesiastical life, that is mainly the organisational structure of the community, proclamation of the faith and acts of worship, especially the sacraments. Christianity, very early on, made two fundamental choices that reduced the role of its religious law to a minimum: (a) it freed Christians from having to follow Jewish law (the Old Testament was no longer a source of strict law – Christ gave Christians a new law[2]) – salvation comes from faith rather than from following the law; and (b) it increasingly recognised that Christians do not have or need a religious law on most matters as they were instructed to submit to State law,[3] and therefore most of their law is concerned with the internal affairs of the Church rather than with regulating society as a whole.[4] In the past, when Christianity was an official religion, canon law did regulate or heavily influence some fields of law that are today perceived as secular either through jurisdictional claims (over the clergy for example) or an extension of influence (over some contractual matters for example). But for a few centuries now the law of the Church has played a much more limited role – the line between Church law and State law has now been drawn differently. This is a fundamental difference with the other three religious laws – there is no longer a Christian law of contract, the way there is an Islamic law of contract and even an Islamic law of sale for example. These differences are worth explaining.

Christians and the Torah, and even the New Testament

Jesus was a Jew and the vast majority of his early disciples were also Jews who felt bound by the Torah. Jesus claimed that he did not come to abolish the law and the Prophets but to fulfil them.[5] As more Gentiles converted to Christianity, many questions were raised: do they have to eat kosher, do they have to be circumcised, i.e. do they have to follow the law? What did Jesus mean by him fulfilling (πληρῶσαι – *plērōsai*) the law?

There are examples in the Gospel where Jesus seems critical of the ritualistic requirements of the Torah. For example, he seemed to have rejected the dietary requirements of Jewish law.[6] In the case if the adulteress, he confronted those who wanted to stone her according to the law[7] and cleverly found a way of avoiding such punishment.[8]

The early Church concluded that the Torah does not strictly apply to Christians. In one of his epistles (part of the New Testament) Paul teaches that men and women are saved not by the work of the law but by means of faith.[9] He wrote:

> [k]now that a person is not justified by the works of the law, but by faith in Jesus Christ. So, we, too, have put our faith in Christ Jesus that we may be justified by faith in Christ and not by the works of the law, because by the works of the law no one will be justified.[10]

Finally, when asked whether the Gentiles converting to Christianity should eat kosher and be circumcised, the Council of Jerusalem decided as follows as reported in Acts 15:28–29:

> It has been decided by the Holy Spirit and by ourselves not to impose on you any burden beyond these essentials: you are to abstain from food sacrificed to idols, from blood, from the meat of strangled animals and from illicit marriages. Avoid these, and you will do what is right. Farewell.[11]

So, no circumcision, but we should eat kosher meat ('abstain from blood'). Surprisingly, however, even that rule which is part of the New Testament is no longer followed by Christians – is no longer law – we do not eat kosher, so even the New Testament is not followed literally as law.[12]

The Bible therefore has an important, but limited role to play in Christian law. The Christian law mentioned in the chapter on Christian law is mainly about the management of the Church's affairs – it is basically Church discipline and organisation. In Christianity, the law does not play the fundamental role it plays in Judaism and Islam. Protestant Churches are even more reluctant to recognise a role for the law than the Catholic Church is – Luther repeated that 'Juristen, böse Christen' – 'Lawyers are bad Christians'.

Christians and Caesar: Church law and State law

As mentioned earlier, Christian law does not govern society in general, and Christians accept the laws of the civil authorities as applying to them. When asked whether one should pay a tax imposed by Rome, Jesus replied:

> 'Show me the money you pay the tax with'. They handed him a denarius and he said, 'Whose portrait is this? Whose title?' They replied, 'Caesar's'. Then he said to them, 'Very well, pay Caesar what belongs to Caesar – and God what belongs to God'.[13]

Jesus also said: 'Mine is not a kingdom of this world'.[14] When Pilate reminded him that he had life and death power over him, Jesus said: 'You would have no power over me at all if it had not been given you from above'.[15] Secular powers come from above and Christians therefore recognise the powers of constituted authorities.[16] The separation of Church and State is recognised and the law is mainly a matter for the State, not for the Church. In the past, the separation of Church law and State law was not always as clear as it is today: there were papal states, the canon law governed (and Church courts had jurisdiction over) many matters that would be considered secular matters today, and the influence of Christianity and canon law on secular law has been great (see Berman, 1983). It remains that today, canon law does not attempt to regulate most matters.

What then are the sources of Christian law?

The above discussions explain why the chapter on Christian law is so different from the others. The author rightly started by explaining the diversity of churches and since Christian law is really essentially Church law, each Church will have its own authorities and its own way of legislating. The chapter therefore starts with the human sources of law – the human authorities within the churches that can adopt the laws. That is correct as most of Church law is human law. It is only later in the chapter that the role of interpretation and higher sources, such as the Bible and theology are discussed. It is not that they are not important and superior, but when one reads for example the Code of Canon Law of the Latin Catholic Church, it does not read like the Bible – theological references, although more frequent in the 1983 Code (after Vatican II) than in the 1917 Code, are not very frequent.

Human agency and the sources of religious laws

Given that all four religious traditions have divine, revealed or sacred sources of law, and given that the law is interpreted, applied and sometimes completed by humans,[17] one must ask: where does the divine end and the human start? And are the human contributions part of the religious law in question – do they get authority and legitimacy as sources of religious law notwithstanding their human nature? Another way to ask the questions is to ask what the role of human reasoning is in a given religious tradition, or, yet in another more extreme way, whether there is a place in the religious tradition for a concept of natural law, i.e. for finding law through human reason from sources other than the divine, revealed or sacred text.

The more legally detailed a divine, revealed or sacred source is, the less of a need for human agency there should be. However, as is clear from all the chapters, these sources tend to be vague and incomplete and require human agency.

In Islamic law, even though some parts of the *Qur'ān* are very detailed (successions for example), 'only a small fraction of its verses refer to what may be considered legal matters, perhaps around 350 of the 6,200 verses' (Chapter 8, this volume). It is clearly insufficient in its details to govern all aspects of life – it has only very general principles on contract law, for example (e.g. keeping one's word). The *Sunna* (made up of the *ḥadīth*), also part of the revelation, is a necessary complement, but, although the *ḥadīth* are more detailed and practical, they have no clear boundaries, and human agency is needed even to determine their very authenticity. The *matn* or chain of transmission of the *ḥadīth* is a list of men (human agency) who transmitted the story from generation to generation and it is for other men, scholars, to judge whether the *matn* makes this *ḥadīth* sound, probable or weak. So, the very revealed source is subject to human agency in determining its boundaries.[18] The presence of human agency is even clearer in the lower sources of Islamic law. The *ijmāʿ* is the consensus of human agents (scholars or the whole community – that is debated) possibly independently of the revelation (though never against it), and the *ijtihād* is a human effort at interpreting and extending by analogy or reasoning (the extent and even availability of *ijtihād* being a matter of debate).

In Jewish law, the *Torah* is more detailed in its law than the *Qur'ān*, yet it needed elaboration to govern the Jewish community over the centuries. The chapter on Jewish law focuses on the 'theocentric-anthropocentric predicament', another way of asking what the role of human agency is and whether it is recognised openly. The chapter explains how the tradition has attempted to define the proper role of transcendent divinity and of human prudence and agency. Strong epiphanism – only the word of God is law – was eventually abandoned in favour of a weak epiphanism which recognises the role of human agency. It established the law, for example in one early form, through an institutional procedural majority of rabbis or eventually even through the recognition of human reasoning as a source of derivative laws. Inspired by the Greeks, some went as far as to assume a divine law above the revealed law from which a separate branch of law based on reason rather than revelation could be elaborated – one gets close to the western concept of natural law.

In Hindu law, the highest source is the *śruti*, which 'identifies itself with the Vedas, the sacred texts of Hindu tradition'. 'The Vedas are considered eternal and without author' (Chapter 9, this volume). Since in principle, 'the Veda . . . is the only possible source of knowledge of *dharma*' (Chapter 9, this volume), it leaves in theory very little space for human agency, but this is not the end of the story. The three other sources of Hindu law, *smṛti, sadācāra* and *ātmanastuṣṭi*, all of which are by human agents, and which 'theoretically have subordinate authority to that of the Vedas, are certainly more important at the practical level' (Chapter 9, this volume). They must all be based on the Vedas, but an outsider would be forgiven for concluding that the links to the Vedas are often quite weak and are often simply assumed through a peculiar hermeneutical strategy. The *smṛti* for example include *dharmaśāstras* and *dharmasūtras*, which are doctrinal texts (human agency). These texts must be based on the Vedas, but when there is no text in the Vedas that support them, one may be assumed:

> Put in simple terms, their reasoning is that, if it is not possible to identify an explicit Vedic text that provides a basis for a *smṛti* text, one can assume that the former has been lost. In other words, it is believed that a rule contained in a text of the *smṛti* was originally contained in a part of the Veda which has subsequently disappeared due to, for example, an interruption in the transmission of the text. It may also be assumed that that particular text is actually present in the Vedas but that it is difficult to identify it because it is implied or because it is the result of an interpretive work carried out on elements dispersed in different versions.
>
> *(Chapter 9, this volume)*

The *sadācāra* (the practice of virtuous men) and the *ātmanastuṣṭi* (the sense of inner satisfaction resulting from behaving appropriately) are even more clearly human than the *smṛti*, and although the *ātmanastuṣṭi* is more controversial as a source of law, it is clear that there is a lot of space for human agency in the Hindu tradition. It should be said however that, although human reason, no doubt, plays a role in all the actions of the human agents within Hindu law, this legal tradition does not specifically see human reason as a source of law and classically held that one cannot know the law through reason.

The chapter on Christian law started with human agency and thus seemed to assume that most Christian law today (or, as I prefer to call it given its limited ambit, 'Church law') is the product of human agents, which are the different authorities of each church described at the beginning of that chapter. These authorities adopt the different types of legislation described in the chapter. But what of divine agency, of God's law?

As explained earlier, most Christian denominations do not take literally what looks like legal texts in the Bible. The relationship of Christians to the Torah is very different from that of most of the Jewish people. As explained, it is not that the Old Testament cannot inspire our laws occasionally, but it mainly inspires our morals – we do believe that 'thou shalt not kill' but the Church is not (or no longer) in the business of adopting or implementing general criminal law – we leave that to civil authorities, which in Christian lands, at least in the past, may have inspired themselves from Christian values.

As to the legal-sounding texts of the New Testament, we also sometimes take some liberty with them – as mentioned, the obligation to eat kosher meat[19] is now ignored.[20] But sometimes some rules of the New Testament are observed more strictly than others. For example, the Catholic Church, known for its opposition to divorce,[21] will nonetheless allow a Christian to divorce and to remarry in one circumstance: when both spouses were not Christian at the time of the marriage and one converts to Christianity, but the other does not. The reason why this is allowed is simply because Paul said so in 1 Corinthians 7:10–15.[22] This is called the Pauline Privilege and is implemented by specific legislation in the form of canon law[23] – again, interestingly, the Church sees the need to legislate to implement the text of the New Testament – as if the Bible was the inspiration for the law but not the law itself.

All this to say that the revealed texts do not play a major role in Church law and human agency seems to be the main factor, even though in some instances (Pauline Privilege) the biblical command is more directly implemented and seen as unavoidable. To put it differently, the Bible is seen as the source of the theological reasons why the law should be legislated by the Church in a certain way. The Bible itself is rarely implemented as a binding source of law without further human elaboration.

Could Christian law be elaborated without reference to the revelation? What is the place of natural law? The Catholic tradition accepts the notion of natural law, that is the notion that law could be deducted by reason from nature. Since God is the creator of nature and of man's reason, what is rightly deduced by reason from principles of nature could indeed be God's will, and since God is one, natural law and the revelation could never contradict one another. It may well be that the original sin makes it difficult for men to understand that natural law (hence the need for revelation and grace), but that natural law objectively exists. Most Protestant Churches, however, because they insist on *Sola Scriptura*, and because they see nature and reason as thoroughly and irretrievably corrupted by sin, reject the notion of natural law as a source of law.

Religious laws and the State

Let us start this part with Christian law, since the concept of a Westphalian secular State independent of religion (separation of Church and State) and claiming a monopoly on law is a product of the Christian insistence on the separation of Church and State – 'to Caesar what belongs to Caesar'.

As mentioned earlier, the Christians have early on, at least in principle,[24] accepted a separation between Church and State. They, through colonisation, exported and imposed the concept of secular modern State throughout the world. This concept of the State, which is compatible with Christianity (the Church does not seek to be the source of most law), has wreaked havoc among many religious and customary laws around the world, and this has a lot to do with sources of law.

Legislation by the secular State has been accepted as a valid and the main source of law by Christianity, and therefore the relationship with State law is not mentioned in the chapter on Christian law. In fact, the churches themselves have often adopted State-like legislation along with its corresponding methodology (interpretation of legislation) as their main form of law.

However, in classical Hindu, Islamic and Jewish laws, State legislation was never an important source of law, and it was seen as either outside, or subsidiary to, religious law. And then came colonisation.[25]

With western colonisers in power in most of the world, State law often replaced religious sources of law except for so-called personal laws (family and successions essentially), and even in these fields where the religious law was allowed to survive, the State often legislated away the traditional sources of laws.

The clearest example of this is Hindu law in India, so much so that the chapter on the sources of Hindu law is in two parts: the classical theory of sources (see earlier description) and modern theory of sources (essentially Anglo-Hindu legislation and case law which later were modified and adopted as Indian legislation). The modern sources, although they implement rules inspired by classical sources, are completely different and bring in a completely different methodology – that of the English common law. These modern sources are limited to personal laws – in other fields of law, the Hindu law (contracts, etc.) has been completely replaced by the common law and by State legislation that do not even attempt to reflect Hindu law. The State-legislated personal laws also import the supremacy of reason over religion – a western way of thinking of the relationship between reason and religion – when State law allows Hindu customs to be applied, it does so only if they are 'not unreasonable'.

The chapter on Islamic law also reflects the drastic changes brought about to the sources of law by the advent of the modern State. The first part of the chapter describes the traditional sources of Islamic law, and the second part of the chapter discusses 'modernity and the sources of the revelation'.

That part describes the first attempts at legislating the *Sharīʿa à l'européenne* and how this led to a radical change in method – the *fiqh* became 'generally foreign to the training and thinking of twentieth-century lawyers' (Chapter 8, this volume). This led to calls in the 1970s for a restauration of the *Sharīʿa*, but such calls for purity also meant a rejection of traditional scholarship in favour of a return to the original sources. The author then gives us the case of Egypt as a case study of how debates on the sources of law took the shape of debates about the text of the constitution of the State of Egypt. The relationship between traditional sources of Islamic law and the State as a source of law is an unresolved problem and a source of debate and political battles in many if not most Muslim-majority countries. The resurgence of a desire by Muslims to be governed by Islamic law raises questions as to what role the State should play. This is an open unresolved question.

The chapter on *Jewish law* does not address the issue of the relationship between Jewish law and the modern State. Maybe, having been in the minority in the diaspora for centuries, the Jewish law has become used to working separately from the State and without having any formal relationship with it. One wonders however whether the sources of Jewish law have needed to somehow interact with the sources of State law in Israel.

Conclusion

The issues faced by many of these traditions are very similar – what is the role of human agency in religious laws and how do the traditional sources of religious law survive the advent of the modern State and its claim to legislate on everything? The latter is the real challenge religious laws face today, especially in the parts of the world that are less and less religious or even less and less tolerant of religions. The authors were able to describe the approaches of each tradition, often reflecting a diversity of approaches within the same tradition.

Notes

1 Protestantism, at least Lutheranism and Calvinism, as they exist today have nothing in common with the radicalism of today's Salafism, but this is because, after a few centuries, we tend to forget how truly radical the Protestant Reformation was, how it was in large part the rejection of certain sources of law and doctrine the Catholic Church had accumulated over centuries, and how it was unfortunately accompanied by violence (from both sides).

2 'A new commandment I give to you, that you love one another: just as I have loved you, you also are to love one another' (John 13:34).

3 'Then Jesus said to them, "Give back to Caesar what is Caesar's and to God what is God's"' (Mark 12:17).

4 For a fuller explanation of these fundamental shift of early Christianity, see Bell (2012).

5 'Do not imagine that I have come to abolish the Law or the Prophets. I have come not to abolish but to complete them. In truth I tell you, till heaven and earth disappear, not one dot, not one little stroke, is to disappear from the Law until all its purpose is achieved' (Matthew 5:17–18).

6 '"Nothing that goes into someone from outside can make that person unclean; it is the things that come out of someone that make that person unclean" . . . When he had gone into the house, away from the crowd, his disciples questioned him about the parable. He said to them, "Even you – don't you understand? Can't you see that nothing that goes into someone from outside can make that person unclean, because it goes not into the heart but into the stomach and passes into the sewer?" And he went on, "It is what comes out of someone that makes that person unclean. For it is from within, from the heart, that evil intentions emerge: fornication, theft, murder, adultery, avarice, malice, deceit, indecency, envy, slander, pride, folly. All these evil things come from within and make a person unclean"' (Mark 7:15, 7:17–23).

7 'If a young woman who is a virgin is betrothed to a husband, and a man finds her in the city and lies with her, then you shall bring them both out to the gate of that city, and you shall stone them to death with stones, the young woman because she did not cry out in the city, and the man because he humbled his neighbour's wife; so you shall put away the evil from among you' (Deuteronomy 22:23–24).

8 '"Teacher", they said to Jesus, "this woman was caught in the act of adultery. The law of Moses says to stone her. What do you say?" . . . He said, "All right, but let the one who has never sinned throw the first stone!" When the accusers heard this, they slipped away one by one, beginning with the oldest, until only Jesus was left in the middle of the crowd with the woman' (John 8:4–5, 8.7, 8.9).

9 'For we maintain that a person is justified by faith apart from the works of the law' (Romans 3:28).

10 Galatians 2:16. See also: 'The entire law is fulfilled in keeping this one command: "Love your neighbour as yourself"' (Galatians 5:14).

11 See also Galatians 2:1–10.

12 Although this might be a case of two contradictory passage of the New Testament. See what Paul wrote: 'Eat anything that is sold in butchers' shops; there is no need to ask questions for conscience's sake, since to the Lord belong the earth and all it contains' (I Corinthians 10:25–26).

13 Matthew 22:19–21.

14 John 18:36.

15 John 19:11.

16 See Romans 13:1–7.

17 Although this is not the object of this book, it should be mentioned that over the centuries and still today, the role of human agency in interpreting, completing and applying the law has been overwhelmingly and continues to be overwhelmingly played by men rather than women. In this chapter I hesitate to use the term 'men' as there are some, but very few, historical exceptions and more recent exceptions – particularly in Protestant Christianity but also in some Islamic majority countries, women have started to play a role in the application and even the elaboration of the law, but this remains exceptional.

18 We tend to forget this, but the same is true in Christianity. Who decided which books would be part of the Bible, i.e. the biblical canon? The Church did, i.e. human agents determined which books were revealed and reflected the faith of the Church and which were not. Protestants and Catholics do not agree on which books are part of the Bible – Luther removed seven books from the Old Testament because they were in Greek rather than Hebrew and thus perceived as not original – even though early Christians in fact were using the Greek rather than the Hebrew version of the Old Testament. In the New Testament, Luther also questioned the canonicity of, but failed to remove, the Books of Hebrews, of James, of Jude and of Revelation, in part, it seems, because these books did not sit well with the

Protestant tenets he was proposing, particularly James' insistence that without works, faith is dead. See Bruce (1988: Kindle Locations 2379–2389).

19 Acts 15:28–29.

20 Although the Seventh-Day Adventists do follow kosher rules.

21 Based on Matthew 5:32, with parallels in Matthew 19:9, Luke 16:18 and Mark 10:11.

22 'To the married I give charge, not I but the Lord, that the wife should not separate from her husband . . . and that the husband should not divorce his wife. To the rest I say, not the Lord . . . But if the unbelieving partner desires to separate, let it be so; in such a case the brother or sister is not bound. For God has called us to peace'.

23 For the Latin Church of the Catholic Church, see the *Code of Canon Law*, canons 1143–1147; for the Eastern Catholic Churches, see the *Code of Canons of the Eastern Churches*, canons 854–858.

24 It is impossible to review here the history of the relationships between Church and State and the many instances when the separation was not maintained, often because the State infringed on the Church independence but also vice versa. However, since the Investiture Controversy (eleventh and twelfth centuries), the Catholic Church has asserted its independence in Church matters, but again nothing is black and white in history and one has to try to explain the Papal States.

25 Colonisation is not the only way in which State law may have pushed away traditional sources of religious laws. For example, the Mecelle (or Majalla) of the late Ottoman Empire was inspired by western codifications but without colonisation.

References

Bell, G. F. 2012. 'Religious Legal Pluralism Revisited: The Status of the Roman Catholic Church and Her Canon Law in Singapore'. 7 *Asian Journal of Comparative Law*. 49.

Berman, H. J. 1983. *Law and Revolution, The Formation of the Western Legal Tradition*. Harvard University Press.

Bruce, F. F. 1988. *The Canon of Scripture*. Intervasity Press [Kindle Edition].

Part III

Dynamics of belonging and status

11

Jewish law

Dynamics of belonging and status

Suzanne Last Stone[1]

Introduction

The first issue this chapter addresses is the boundaries of the religious community. Phrasing the inquiry in terms of conversion into the religion and conversion out to another religion, as this volume does, already glosses over one of the most central features of Judaism: the historic unity of Judaism as a religion and national entity. Thus, a Jew from birth who has no religious commitments or even one who converts to another religion is still a Jew in the eyes of the religious legal tradition (B. Sanhedrin 44a; *Shulhan Arukh, Even Haezer* 44:9). True, converts to Judaism must evidence religious commitment, but there is today a serious debate within the religious legal sources whether a desire to join the Jewish people, even in the absence of sincere religious commitments, may suffice for conversion. Before the Jewish emancipation, when Jews lived largely segregated lives within communities structured around Jewish religious practices, there was little need to resolve the theoretical question because religious identity and national identity were one and the same. Today, the questions 'who is a Jew?' and 'who is a convert?' are one of the most intractable questions dividing the Jewish community, most especially in the modern state of Israel, where criteria of belonging have profound state legal consequences. The struggle to preserve the historic unity of religion and nation in the face of increased calls to split them apart is a central dynamic of the religious legal tradition's approach to questions of belonging.

The second issue this chapter addresses is the differential obligations and privileges of the members of the Jewish community. Judaism is an intricate system of incumbent obligations that touch on nearly all facets of life, public and private, the family, the market, and political institutions. Obligations create a hierarchy of personhood and status. Thus, Jews have more obligations than non-Jews, and Jewish men have more obligations than Jewish women. Traditionally, not only are women exempt from many of the obligations incumbent on men (B. Kiddushin 29a, 34a), but women do not have equal access to many of the privileges conferred by the religious law, such as composing a quorum for public prayer,[2] testifying in the religious court (b.Nid.49b), assuming positions of public authority in the Jewish community (B. Yevamot 54b; Maimonides, Laws of Kings 1:5), and deciding religious legal questions.[3] In short, women's place is in the private sphere (the family and, in Jewish tradition, the marketplace) and not the public sphere (the study halls, religious courts, and political institutions). Today, women's religious role is one of the key markers dividing the various denominations within Judaism. Even Orthodox Judaism is divided within itself over this issue.

In what follows, I will be reporting the perspective of the religious legal tradition, the *halakha*. The status of the *halakha* as a normative, binding legal system, was challenged in different ways by the advent of denominationalism in Judaism in the nineteenth century. Reform Judaism originally strove to modernize the *halakha* but, over time, largely abandoned it as an ongoing legal project. Instead, Reform Judaism approaches the traditional sources as resources for religious ethics. While I will note significant *halakhic* innovations within Reform Judaism, the discussion that follows primarily emphasizes legal sources produced within classical and contemporary streams where the *halakha* continues to be viewed as an ongoing, binding legal project.

Entering the religion

A Jew is a member of the 'people of Israel', which is described in the Hebrew Bible as a distinctive nation, set apart from other nations (Numbers 23:8). The ambiguity of Judaism as a religious commitment or a national identity already appears in the Bible. The Bible begins with the account of a family that grew into a people to whom, generations later, God revealed his laws, the oral and written Torah, at Sinai. The giving of the Torah is the moment of election or 'chosenness'. From then on, Israel must serve as a 'holy nation of priests' (Exodus 19:6) and an exemplar to the world (Isaiah 42:6, 49:6, 60:3). The biblical account thus could be read to affirm the existence of a national community that is prior to and distinct from the religious community that later received the Torah at Sinai. Yet, most traditional commentators read the biblical description of the Sinai revelation as the moment of origin of the 'people of Israel', akin to the birth of a new national entity. That nation consists of all those who stood at Sinai and those as yet unborn (Deuteronomy 29:4). Indeed, Maimonides depicts Sinai as essentially a moment of mass conversion (Maimonides, Laws of Forbidden Relations 13:1–3). In this reading, it is the Torah, and adherence to its commands, that create and define the people of Israel. Thus, this reading puts in question the possibility of a national identity that is separate and distinct from a religious identity. These two contrasting understandings of the import of Sinai and the giving of the law underlie many of the current controversies over 'Who is a Jew?'

The biblical texts do not speak in terms of conversion. In the Bible, Israel is a nation with a practical political existence in addition to a spiritual mission. The biblical polity is composed of Israelites, resident aliens (*ger toshav*), and sojourners ('*ger*'). There was 'marrying in', however, in that strangers living among the Israelites assimilated into the nation through marriage. The biblical book of Ruth offers a glimpse of this social reality, where the bonds of love and loyalty propel Ruth to join the Israelite people. After sovereignty was lost, the biblical heritage was refashioned for life in exile. The Talmudic rabbis re-read the biblical description of the *ger* as referring to converts attracted to the Torah and the way of life shaped by the commandments, and so they described the biblical Ruth. The Talmudic rabbis also set more clearly defined membership rules in general. A Jew, according to the Talmudic rabbis, is a matter of birth and determined by matrilineal descent (Deuteronomy 7:3–4; *Pesikta Rabati ad loc.*; B. Yevamot 23a; B. Kiddushin 68b). (Today, the Reform denomination of Judaism has expanded membership to include patrilineal descent.)[4] The Talmud also describes the procedure for accepting converts who must declare, before a formal institution, their 'acceptance of the commandments', and, in addition, must undergo circumcision (if male) and ritual immersion (B. Yevamot 47a; Maimonides, Laws of Forbidden Relations 13–14; Edrei, 2015). The ritual marks an irrevocable change in status. 'Once he [has been immersed] and comes up, he is like an Israelite for all matters' (Shulhan Arukh, Yoreh Deah 268:3).

The Talmudic discussion of who is an acceptable convert combines the biblical legacy emphasizing the wish to join a people with the characteristically rabbinic emphasis on the spiritual: the wish to form a relationship to God through acceptance of the authority of the Torah and individual observance of the commandments. For example, the court must inform the potential convert about some (though not all) of the religious laws. But the court also must inform the potential convert of the oppressed condition of the Jews so that the potential convert can make an informed choice whether to join a downtrodden community (B. Yevamot 47a; Maimonides, Laws of Forbidden Relations 14). This inextricable mix of national and spiritual elements is continued in the later codes and responsa literature, and the degree of emphasis on absolute religious sincerity is often a function of the decisor's assessment of the social realia or his philosophical or theological commitments. Thus, Maimonides, the rationalist philosopher, who describes Judaism as a religion of principles, a philosophical religious faith or community of ideas, de-emphasizes the national elements and rules out conversion for 'ulterior' motives such as love of a Jew (Maimonides, Laws of Forbidden Relations 13:14).

Until modernity, these two meanings of conversion – joining a people and commitment to a religious idea and regime – had minor practical import. Jews lived in cohesive, traditional communities in which observance of the religious commandments was the way of life for community members. The historical-national community and the religious community were essentially one (Howe, 1976: 11). Rabbinic decisions on conversion were rendered in light of the background assumption that a convert who joined the Jewish community would naturally observe a Jewish religious way of life. The rise of the civil state and the emancipation of the Jews ruptured this connection by making it possible to live as a Jew outside the traditional community. By the nineteenth century in Europe, all the familiar aspects of modern Jewish life today – assimilation, the rise of denominations within Judaism and, most especially, intermarriage – led to increasingly sharp controversies about relaxing the requirements for conversion (Walzer et al., 2003: 283–285, 290–294).

From a legal standpoint, the debate centers on the technical meaning of 'accepting the commandments'. Already in the medieval period, commentators split over the question whether acceptance implies observance of the commandments as part of the formal conversion process or, rather, merely 'a condition for continuation of the process', in which case, the conversion would still stand even if the convert failed later to observe the commandments (Maimonides, Laws of Forbidden Relations 13:17). In the modern period, the mainstream responsa literature seeks to balance the traditional legal norms stressing religious observance with broad-based policy considerations: Should converts for the sake of marriage be accepted by the Orthodox lest they join, instead, the Reform denomination? Will insincere conversion nonetheless increase the chances that the children of the marriage will remain within the community? The Reform eventually moved to patrilineal descent in addition to matrilineal descent to address the predicament of children of intermarriage (CCAR, American Reform Responsa 550). Even some decisors from within the Orthodox denomination insisted that the idea of Judaism as a shared peoplehood obligated the court to accept converts even though 'we know they will not observe all the commandments' (Edrei, 2015: 117).

In the diaspora, Jewish communities and denominations are largely decentralized, each setting their own standards for admission to Judaism. The consequences of different criteria of admission are largely cultural and personal, not legal. In the state of Israel, however, admission to Judaism has significant legal consequences. For example, Israel's Law of Return states that 'every Jew has the right to come to Israel' and acquire immediate citizenship (Law of Return 5710–1950. S. H. 5710, 159; 4 L.S.I. 114). In addition, Israel follows the *millet* system, and thus matters of personal status (marriage, divorce, and conversion) are delegated to religious courts of the various religious subgroups in Israel. The Jewish religious courts are all Orthodox, which is the established denomination in Israel.

In order for state officials to decide whether individuals are or are not Jewish, they need, as Ruth Gavison put it, an 'operational criterion' (2004: 95). At present, there is no agreement among the Israeli populace about what this criteria should be. The religious segment of the population, and even segments of the secular Zionist population concerned with preserving national unity, want the criterion to be the traditional religious one, acceptable to all groups; that is, a person born of a Jewish mother or who has converted in accordance with the religious law. Others advocate decoupling a national Jewish identity from the religious identity and adopting a secular national definition. Already Ben Gurion, Israel's first Prime Minister, had argued, citing the Book of Ruth, that there should be a conversion route to Judaism that complemented the reality of modern Jewish national identity in the state of Israel (Edrei, 2015: 109–111).

Debates among religious legal decisors in Israel take place against this fraught backdrop and against the social realia of new waves of immigration to Israel. Thus, a crisis was precipitated by the absorption of a large number of individuals from the former Soviet Union, who self-identified as Jews and met the criterion of the Law of Return (to which a secular definition of Jewishness was added in 1970) but who did not meet the Orthodox religious criterion of matrilineal descent and thus were not deemed 'Jews' by the religious establishment for purposes of burial in a Jewish cemetery or the marriage laws. The obvious remedy is conversion, yet most of these individuals are secular and do not wish nor intend to practice the religious commandments. Contemporary rabbinic responses to this crisis split over how much weight may be given to the convert's desire to ally themselves with the fate of the historical community of Jews, serving in its army and participating in its civic life. Orthodox rabbis who embrace Zionism and thus recognize a Jewish national identity that is separate from a Jewish religious identity, are struggling to read the traditional precedents anew and debating how far the traditional criterion of full commitment to observe the religious law as a precondition to conversion can be relaxed (Goren, 1983: 149–150; Unterman, 1974: 13–20; Walzer et al., 2003: 283–285, 290–294). More traditionalist rabbis, however, currently dominate the religious courts charged with matters of personal status. They are philosophically opposed to Zionism as a new form of Jewish secular national identity and object to the very idea of a national, secular Jewish identity that is separated from the religious identity. In reaction to the pressure brought to bear by the religious Zionist stream and most especially by the Reform denomination to relax the standards for conversion, the ultra-traditionalists have, instead, insisted on meticulous observance of religious law and ritual as the sole criterion of conversion. Indeed, their policing of conversions has become increasingly stringent to the point of annulling conversions post facto, in itself an innovation in the *halakha*.

Leaving the religion

Rashi's famous maxim 'Even though he has sinned, [still] he remains a Jew', summarizes the majority position of the Jewish religious law (Rashi, *Responsa Rashi*, no. 171, 173–175). Although the Jewish religious law recognizes conversion from other religions to Judaism, the majority view is that it simply is not possible to cease being a Jew. Apostasy is neither lawful nor legally effective. Jewishness is a status that carries with it both obligations and privileges, however. The obligations incumbent on the Jew – to fulfill the commandments – do not cease even if an individual leaves the religion for another religion. Privileges accorded to a Jew in good standing, such as the right to be the recipient of social welfare and acts of loving-kindness, will be denied to the apostate, however, because he is a 'sinner'. A 'sinner' is a legal category encompassing apostates, heretics, and 'rebellious sinners' (Morell, 1969: 448–457). The common element is rebellion against the authority of the religious law, either by publicly denying its validity or transgressing core precepts such as Sabbath observance in public. Such 'sinners' no longer enjoy rights of association with covenantal members. Social contact with them is forbidden, they are neither mourned nor eulogized, and intermarriage with them is forbidden (Stone, 2006: 17). 'Sinners' are Jews, but they lose their status as covenantal 'fellows', a category that turns on conduct and not ascription. Thus, one may be a Jew for the purposes of incurring an obligation to God to observe the law, yet not a Jew for the purposes of asserting rights of fellowship.

The sole traditional commentator to recognize conversion to another religion as a quasi-legitimate option is the thirteenth-century Talmudist and philosopher, Menahem Ha-Me'iri. His view is a logical outgrowth of his attitude toward Christianity as a legitimate religion. Ha-Me'iri, like other rationalist philosophers of his era such as Maimonides before him, understood religion as both a matter of correct beliefs and also as functional: Creating good social order by stipulating moral standards that constrain behavior. The Talmudic rabbis already paved the way for the quasi-legitimation of other religions by distinguishing between idolaters and nations that obeyed the Noahide commandments, the seven laws rabbinic tradition identifies as the content of God's revelation to humanity (refraining from idolatry, blasphemy, murder, theft, sexual immorality, eating a limb torn from a live animal, and establishing courts). Noahides merit 'the world to come' (Maimonides, Laws of Kings 8:11). By contrast, idolatry, in the biblical presentation and in rabbinic tradition, is not only false but is associated with moral corruption (Stone, 2006: 13–16). The Talmud treats the Noahide as a status that is no longer legally available for technical reasons, however.[5] Ha-Me'iri's innovation was to create a new category – nations constrained by the ways of [a moral-fostering] religion – which he applied to Christianity.[6] (Concomitantly, he ruled that Christianity was not idolatrous. Before him, Maimonides had similarly ruled that Islam was monotheistic [Blidstein, 2004: 237–247].) Thus, Ha-Me'iri grants these two religions a certain legitimacy, and Jews who convert to Christianity and Islam have successfully exited the Jewish religion. Yet, even for Ha-Me'iri, this exit is only partial. The offspring of a Jewish mother who converted to another religion would not need to convert to Judaism if they desired to return to Judaism.

The willingness to recognize the offspring of those who converted to another religion as still Jewish is also a function of the Jewish historical experience. Periodically, the community was beset by waves of coerced conversions. While, in theory, Jews were commanded to martyr themselves in these circumstances – and many did – the rabbis treated the failure to martyr oneself with great lenity. Those who were forced to convert, and their offspring no matter how many generations later, do not need to convert to Judaism to regain their place in the Jewish community. This general attitude spilled over to the treatment of willing converts, as well. Though they were sinners, they could regain their full status as Jews, including privileges and not only obligations, upon their 'return' (Goldin, 2014: 222–231).

Despite the near-unanimity of *halakhic* opinion (in itself a rarity), treating a Jew who converts to another religion as nonetheless still a Jew, the Israeli Supreme Court, in the famous case of *Oswald Rufeisen v. The Minister of the Interior* (Landau, 1971; HCJ 72/62 Rufeisen v. Minister of the Interior, 16 PD 2428 [1962]), refused to allow a Jew who converted to Christianity to invoke the Law of Return, and this ruling is now enshrined in the latest version of the Israeli legislation. The *Rufeisen* case is another illustration of the sharp debate over whether *halakhic* norms ought to be the exclusive criterion for defining Jewishness in the modern state of Israel. The facts were exceptional: Oswald Rufeisen, also known as Brother Daniel, was born in Poland before the Holocaust into an Orthodox Jewish family. He was hidden with Christians during the war and converted to Catholicism. He was also an active member of the Resistance, helping to save many fellow Jews from destruction. Brother Daniel wished to gain automatic citizenship in Israel under the Law of Return, arguing that although his faith was Catholic, he belonged to the Jewish people. The Court conceded that Brother Daniel met the *halakhic* definition of a Jew. But it ruled that Jewishness under the Law of Return, a secular law, should follow the popular meaning or 'common parlance'; that is, the present consensus of world Jewry. In the eyes of the common Jewish people, the Court surmised, 'a Jew who has embraced another religion has withdrawn himself from the Jewish nation and has no place in the Jewish community' (Landau, 1971; HCJ 72/62 Rufeisen v. Minister of the Interior, 16 PD 2428 [1962] 32).

The borders of the Jewish community were also policed through the excommunication of heretics. Unlike apostates, heretics wish to stay in the community 'but only on their own, deviant, terms' (Walzer et al., 2003: 317). Heresy is part of the drama of sectarianism and schism and, for all the historical scholarship delving into sectarian splits, it remains something of a mystery why certain deviant groups continue to be tolerated while other deviant groups were eventually ousted. Originally followers of Jesus were Jewish Christians within the larger Jewish community and then excluded. The Karaites were once a Jewish sect and then excluded. Because Judaism by and large does not have a single set of correct opinions, heresy is often a function of deviant practice rather than beliefs. It is the attitude to the law and legal practice that generally leads to schism. Thus, Jewish Christians eventually rejected Jewish religious legal practices, and the Karaites accepted the authority of the Bible but not of the rabbis and rejected the rabbinic interpretation and elaboration of the law.

The drama of sectarian schism – the splitting of the Jewish religion into different religions – that accompanied much of Jewish history through the medieval period, was replaced in modernity with denominationalism. Reform Judaism was the first successful challenge to legal practice to remain within the Jewish religious fold. Denominationalism also includes secular Jews, and this marks another important turning point in the definitional battles over Judaism as religion and national identity. In an age of secularism, R. Abraham Karelitz (2005; the *Hazon Ish*) writes that a secular Jew who does not practice the commandments cannot be deemed a heretic.[7] In this specific context, even ultra-traditional rabbis recognize Judaism as a national identity distinct from a religious commitment.

Rights and obligations of adherents

With the Emancipation, the dissolution of both ghettos segregating Jews from the rest of society, and Jewish governmental structures (the legally recognized *kehillot*) that enforced the unity of Jewish society through the use of sanctions, including the *herem* [excommunication], Judaism has come to resemble a private religion in outward form. Yet, many of the religious obligations incumbent on adherents still must be performed in a communal setting. Thus, even in the contemporary period, Judaism maintains something akin to a 'state within a state' structure. In the traditional *halakhic* conception, the unity of Jewish society derives from the subjection of all its constituent parts – political organs, the family, and the individual – to the exclusive authority of the religious law. All aspects of life are governed by the law, including private individual conduct, private family relations, social relations, and market activity. These laws are not only cultic, such as circumcision, kosher dietary rules, Sabbath and holiday observance, and ritual purity laws. They include the obligations of fathers to educate their children, the obligation of children to care for parents, economic restrictions on maximizing profits designed to protect weaker parties and redistribute resources in light of need, unfair competition laws, restrictions on slander and gossip, tort and criminal law rules, and the like.

Covenantal obligations are imposed on the individual as a member of the collective. The law imposes a duty on adherents to associate with one another. It is not only that many legal obligations, from the cultic to the mundane, can be performed only in a group setting. Rather, as Maimonides summarizes, 'one who diverges from communal paths, even if he commits no transgression but merely separates himself from the congregation of Israel, and does not participate in its sorrows, loses his share in the world to come' (Maimonides, Laws of Repentance 3:11). The social solidarity that the law stipulates must be extended to all covenantal fellows. The biblical injunction to 'love one's neighbor as oneself' (Leviticus 19:18), is interpreted restrictively in the classical religious sources. One's neighbor is a fellow Jew (excluding those mentioned earlier – the rebellious sinner, heretic, or apostate – who lose the privileges of 'fellowship'). The rabbinic tradition is less concerned with the problem of commanding emotions as it is concerned with concretizing the biblical principle in specific acts: Visiting the sick, comforting mourners, extending interest-free loans, redeeming captives, sabbatical cancellation of debts, and special forms of charity. Such a system may, and does, respect individual rights of personhood and property, but it cannot confer on its members the kind of freedom or autonomy presupposed by liberal society (Stone, 2006: 16).

While the precept 'love one's neighbor', is interpreted restrictively to apply only to fellow Jews, other biblical verses and rabbinic traditions extend the circle to whom duties of social solidarity and concrete acts of benevolence are owed. The Bible also enjoins Israelites to 'love the stranger as oneself' (Leviticus 19:33–34) and to provide the stranger with food, clothing, and agricultural charity (Leviticus 23:22; Deuteronomy 24:19). In its original biblical setting, the stranger is an individual of non-Jewish birth living in the land in close proximity with Jews who accepts Jewish political authority. The social solidarity that Israelites owe to the stranger is ascribed specifically to the stranger's material and political dependence. The stranger does not have an allotted portion of the land and is therefore associated with the Levite, the widow, and the orphan (Deuteronomy 10:17–18). The rabbinic tradition equates the biblical stranger with the resident stranger, which it identifies as a non-Jew who accepts the Noahide laws (B. Avodah Zarah 69b; Maimonides, Laws of Kings 8:10). The Talmud extends this line of thought even to pagans who live in close proximity to Jews, because it is a duty to 'pursue paths of peace' in social life (B. Gittin 61a). So, shared ethnic and religious ties, shared moral commitments, and shared political space give rise to varying levels of social solidarity obligations (Stone, 2006: 17–19).

Responsibility for performing the law and providing for the well-being of oneself and others rests on each individual community member. The social organization of Judaism, which includes extensive education of children and adults in Talmudic legal reasoning and the details of the law as well as weekly public recitations of the Torah, is designed to promote self-governance, to enable persons to perform the law themselves. Rabbinic culture from the Talmudic period onward, exalted study of the law as a form of religious worship and even debated whether it was a higher form of worship than the actual fulfillment of the commandments (M. Peah 1:1; B. Moed Kattan 9a–b; B. Kiddushin 40b). With the spread of print and popular Talmudic commentaries such as that of the eleventh-century exegete, Rashi, the ideal of Torah and Talmud study spread to lay members (Walzer et al., 2003: 580–581).

Both the strong bonds of fellowship reciprocally owed among community members and the religious value assigned to the study and mastery of the law by lay members, and not only a clerical elite, tends to reduce the force of social hierarchies but does not eliminate them entirely. Hierarchies of various sorts are set out in the biblical texts. The most prominent religious hierarchy is that of the priesthood, which is hereditary. The priests, who are genealogical descendants of Aaron, have a special role in the Temple service. They are mediators between God and the people and, as such, endowed with a certain measure of holiness. During the Second Temple period, the priests were a ruling class. After the destruction of the Temple, the rabbinic class, who were interpreters, judges, and scholars of the law, emerged. Mastery of the law became the religious ideal and the primary avenue to achieve closeness to God. In place of a priestly aristocracy, a meritocracy emerged. The crucial social hierarchy that emerges in the Talmudic period is between the learned and the ignorant. Yet, anyone can be a scholar, and stories about former peasants, converts, brigands, and illiterates becoming great Torah scholars abound in the Talmud (Walzer et al., 2003: 108–124).

When it comes to women, however, this meritocratic spirit is absent. Although the Bible and Talmud are replete with portraits of strong women – from the matriarchs to Deborah the judge to Beruriah the scholar (B. Berakhot 10a; B. Avodah Zarah 18a) – the Talmud treats them as the exception rather than the rule. The classical legal texts exclude women from performing public religious roles, such as leading prayer, counting in the prayer quorum, chanting the Torah portion in synagogue, and holding positions of political authority in the Jewish community. The usurpation of men's public role by women is cited in the Talmud as a breach of the 'honor of the community' (B. Megillah 23a). Concomitantly, the verse in Psalms: 'the honor of the daughter of the king is inward [hidden]' (Psalms 45:14) is often cited as an allusion to women's private role (Maimonides, Laws of Marriage 13:11). The Talmud also devotes much discussion to clarifying the disparate obligations incumbent on men and women – women are exempt from performing a variety of (time-bound) positive commandments (B. Kiddushin 29a) – and the variety of 'citizenship' roles women may not perform: They are not counted in the ritual quorum for public prayer, they may not give formal testimony, they may not become masters of the law, and they cannot assume positions of political authority (see earlier). In a religious culture in which performance of commandments and knowledge of the law endow persons with status, exemption from performing certain commandments and exclusion from the study hall and courts of law inevitably means a constriction of religious personhood and reduction in status.

It is unclear from the Talmudic discussion whether the restriction on women's role is sociological or due to an ontological conception of gender. The Talmud refers to women as 'light-headed' (B. Kiddushin 80b) – implying both a spiritual and moral deficiency and a deficiency in legal reasoning abilities – even as it extols the legal acumen of the exceptional Beruriah (B. Avodah Zarah 18a). By the medieval period, women's exemption from various positive commandments was attributed to their distinctive role as mothers and caregivers (Abudraham, 1877: 10). Yet, women worked in the market and, indeed, a well-known poem about women's virtue, traditionally sung at the Sabbath table, extols the 'woman of valor' who conducts business for the family (Proverbs 31:23–24). This model of marital roles – in which the woman works in the general marketplace while the man devotes his time to Talmud study – has only intensified in contemporary ultra-traditionalist religious circles. Additionally, the Talmud assumes that married women will cover their hair, as was the practice in the surrounding Near Eastern cultures, and details other forms of requisite coverage of body parts and restrictions on women singing in public, lest men be enticed to lewd thoughts (B. Berakhot 24a). Ultra-traditionalists in the modern period have also intensified these regulations. Today, the different forms (or lack of) head-coverings are visible markers of differing group allegiances within the larger stream of orthodoxy.

The struggle for women's equality within the religion and access to public religious leadership roles is a key issue across the denominational streams. Both the Reform and Conservative denominations have issued legal responsa authorizing female rabbis, and gender equality is now the norm (Graetz, 1994: 17–19; Greenberg, 1988). Within the Orthodox Jewish community, gender equality is disputed and, indeed, this issue is a critical marker of divisions within orthodoxy. Paradoxically, the struggle for women's rights within the religion first manifested itself within traditionalist circles. Sara Shnirrer founded the Bet Ya'akov schools, which revolutionized women's education among Eastern European Orthodox Jews. These schools provide girls with a substantial religious education, though they do not teach the Talmud or mastery of religious legal materials. She successfully persuaded the regnant halakhic authority of her day, Isaac HaKohen (the *Hafetz Hayyim*), that, in conditions of modern fragmentation, women's education was a vital element in preserving the tradition (*Likkutei Halakhot, Sotah* 11b). While the study of the Talmud still is reserved for men in ultra-traditional circles, Talmud mastery has become an acceptable feature of women's religious education in more modern streams of orthodoxy. Instead, the battle has moved to the ordination of women (Fox, n.d.; Orthodox Union, 2017) and women's public prayer (Feinstein, 1959–present, *Igrot Moshe*: Orakh Hayim 4:49, Yoreh Deah 1:101; Frimmer and Frimmer, 2013; Sperber, n.d.).

Women also suffer a great disadvantage in the arena of divorce.[8] Pursuant to Jewish divorce laws, both parties to the marriage must freely consent to divorce.[9] Gender inequities are due to the consequences that ensue when consent is withheld. Without a Jewish divorce, the woman is unable to remarry, and the child of a union between a woman who has not secured a Jewish divorce and a new partner has the status of a *mamzer*. These children are permitted to marry only other illegitimate Jews or converts (Shulhan Arukh, Even Haezer 4). Pursuant to biblical law, however, a man may have more than one wife. Because it is not a violation of biblical law for a man to have relations with another unmarried woman,[10] the children of such a union suffer no stigma. Because men's lives will not be seriously disadvantaged under Jewish law if they do not obtain a formal Jewish divorce from their wives, men sometimes withhold the Jewish divorce out of spite or as a bargaining chip, seeking to trade the Jewish divorce bill for money. Solutions to the plight of the 'chained woman' have proved far too elusive, most especially in the modern period. When rabbinic courts had civil enforcement powers, they were able to order the man to give a divorce and back these orders with social, economic, and religious sanctions. Famously, Maimonides held that, in cases where the woman is entitled to a judicially ordered divorce, the Jewish court may use physical coercion to 'force the man until he proclaims "I wish [to grant the divorce]"' (Maimonides, Laws of Divorce 2:20). Rabbinic courts no longer have enforcement powers, except in the state of Israel (see later). A variety of solutions have been pursued, such as clauses in pre-nuptial contracts,[11] annulments (Rackman, 1989: 187–188), communal pressure, and actions in the courts of the civil state, but the problem still persists.

The interweaving of religion and state in Israel greatly complicates the question of women's rights in Judaism. From the very beginning days of the state, women's equality was an intense subject of dispute between the secular and religious segments of Israeli society. Social equality was part and parcel of the ideology of the founding generation, and the original political compromise agreement between the secular and religious parties secured women's right to vote in exchange for other concessions to the religious parties (Rabinovich and Reinharz, 2008: 57). At the same time, however, the founders had decided to retain the millet system in the region since Ottoman rule. According to the millet system, as noted earlier, the state delegates matters of personal status to state-funded religious courts, which are under the state's jurisdiction and which decide those matters pursuant to the religious laws of the various religions comprising Israeli society. The Basic Laws of Israel guarantee equal rights to women but contain an exception for laws relating to marriage and divorce (Rabbinical Courts Jurisdiction (Marriage and Divorce), 5713–1953, §§ 1–2; Sefer Hahukim [SH] No. 134 p. 165). Religious discrimination against women in matters of divorce is thus perpetuated at the civil level. At the same time, the rabbinic courts in Israel have enforcement powers. Theoretically, the rabbinic courts in Israel, unlike their diaspora counterparts, are empowered to exercise these powers to aid women to obtain a Jewish divorce. Increasingly, however, the religious courts are locked in a power struggle with the civil system over their independence and jurisdictional reach, and women have been caught in the middle (High Court of Justice 6929/10 Jane Doe v. the Great Rabbinical Court (March 20, 2013); High Court of Justice 6866/03 Vaknin v. the Netanya Regional Rabbinical Court (2003)).

Yet, religious women have also been at the forefront of social change in Israel, and they use the state's legal system to effect change within religious society. The Shakdiel case is a telling example. The state of Israel established local councils that allocate funds for religious services. Leah Shakdiel, a religious woman, wished to serve on her local council, but the rabbi of the locality contended that this violated religious legal strictures on women holding public positions relating to religious affairs. The Supreme Court of Israel upheld her right to serve in an opinion written by Justice Menahem Elon, a justice with expertise in Jewish religious law. Elon rested his opinion partly on secular grounds but also partly on religious legal grounds, arguing that the sources, when reinterpreted in light of the changed condition of life in a modern Jewish state, permitted women to serve (*Leah Shakdiel v. Minister of Religious Affairs et al.* HCJ 153/57). Quite recently, *haredi* (ultra-traditional) women have petitioned the civil courts for the right to form their own religious parties, despite rabbinic objections. And the High Court is now considering the question of women's public prayer services at the site of the Western Wall (Women of the Wall). In the diaspora, these debates are private, but in the state of Israel, given religion-state entanglement, they are public. And changes in state norms inevitably penetrate into religious life and eventually into the religious law.

Further reading

Batnitzky, L. F. 2013. *How Judaism Became a Religion: An Introduction to Modern Jewish Thought*. Princeton University Press.

Ferziger, A. 2015. 'Beyond Bais Ya'akov: Orthodox Outreach and the Emergence of Haredi Women as Religious Leaders'. *Journal of Modern Jewish Studies*. 140.

Notes

1 I wish to thank my research assistant, Tzvi Benoff, for his meticulous attention to detail.

2 Many medieval rabbinic authorities were of the view that the Talmud did not address women's ability to compose a quorum for prayer. Instead, they argued that public prayer is an example of 'holy utterances', a class of public religious activities that legally require a quorum of ten adult males (Maimonides, Laws of Prayer 12:3).

3 Religious decisors generally act in one of two capacities: as a judge or a community rabbi. The traditionalist argument is that women's disqualification from serving as a religious judge follows from their disqualification from serving as a judicial witness, because someone who may not testify in court is forbidden to judge (Shulhan Arukh, Hoshen Mishpat 7:4; *Sma ad loc.*). Traditionalists argue further that serving as a community rabbi falls under the category of assuming a position of public authority.

4 The Central Conference of American Rabbis (the Reform rabbinic organization in America) also requires that the child is raised to adhere only to the Jewish faith and is taught to fulfill certain commandments (CCAR, American Reform Responsa 550).

5 This may have been due to the fact that they were considered idolaters, or simply a reflection of mutual alienation (Halbertal, 2000: 84).

6 The term is mentioned and applied many times throughout his commentary on the tractate Avodah Zarah of the Babylonian Talmud.

7 Karelitz argues that such a person has the status of a *tinok shenishbah*, a child captured and raised by gentiles and therefore cannot be held accountable for failing to fulfill religious commandments. Kariletz extended this principle to encompass anyone raised in a secular society (Kariletz, Shulhan Arukh, Yoreh Deah 2:11).

8 The divorce procedure in Jewish law requires the husband to write (or commission a scribe to write) a divorce bill (*get*) and give it to his wife of his own free will (Maimonides, Laws of Divorce 1:1).
9 Talmudic law permitted a man to forcibly divorce his wife. In the tenth century, the German rabbinic authority, Rabbi Gershom, issued a ban forbidding divorce that did not have the consent of both parties (Shulhan Arukh, Even Haezer 178:9).
10 Though this is the position of most authorities, Maimonides held to the contrary (Maimonides, Laws of Marriage 1:4).
11 There have been a number of iterations of such contracts, each with their particular nuances, endorsements, and detractors. The earliest indication of an Orthodox pre-nuptial document can be traced to Morocco in the 1953 (Amar, 1986: 359–375, 468; Levmore, 2009: 29–49).

References

Abudraham, D. 1877. *Abudraham*. Schriftgisser.
Amar, S. 1986. *Sefer HaTakkanot HaMishpat HaIvri BeKehillot Morocco, vol. I*. Jerusalem.
Blidstein, G. ed. 2004. 'The Status of Islam in Maimonidean Halakhah,' in *Studies in Aggadic and Halakhic Thought*. Ben Gurion University Press. 237–247.
CCAR. 1983. 'Report of the Committee on Patrilineal Descent on the Status of Children of Mixed Marriages,' *CCAR Yearbook*, vol. 94.
Edrei, A. 2015. 'Identity, Politics, and Halakhah in Modern Israel'. 14 *Journal of Modern Jewish Studies*. 109.
Feinstein, M. 1959–present. *Igrot Moshe*. Rav Moshe Feinstein Foundation Inc.
Fox, J. n.d. 'Can Orthodox Women Receive Semikah?' Available at https://static1.squarespace.com/static/5348363de4b0531dce75bc53/t/56f98a945f43a661a42076f4/1459194516989/160328_Women+and+Semikha.pdf.
Frimmer, A. and Frimmer, D. 2013. 'Women, Keriat Hatorah, and Aliyyot'. 46(4) *Tradition*. 67.
Gavison, R. 2004. 'Can Israel be Both Democratic and Jewish?' Available at https://ruthgavison.files.wordpress.com/2015/10/can-israel-be-both-jewish-and-democratic-full-book.pdf.
Goldin, S. 2014. 'Jewish Self-Definition Against Christianization' in I. Katznelson and M. Rubin (eds) *Religious Conversion: History, Experience, and Meaning*. Routledge. 222–231.
Goren, S. 1983. 'Denouncing the People of Israel in Matters of Conversion'. *Shanah BeShanah*. 149.
Graetz, M. 1994. 'Responsum Regarding the Ordination of Women as Rabbis' (in Hebrew) in D. Golinkin (ed.) *Responsa of the Vaad Halakha of the Rabbinical Assembly of Israel*. Masorti Movement. 17.
Greenberg, S. (ed). 1988. *The Ordination of Women as Rabbis: Studies and Responsa*. JTS Press.
HaKohen, I. M. 1922. *Likkutei Halakhot*. Piamant.
Halbertal, M. 2000. *Between Torah and Wisdom* (in Hebrew). Magnes Press.
Howe, I. 1976. *World of Our Fathers*. New York University Press. 11–13.
Karelitz, A. I. 2005. *Hazon Ish: Yoreh Deah*. B'nei Braq.
Landau, A. F. (ed.). 1971. 'HCJ 72/62 Rufeisen v. Minister of the Interior, 16 PD 2428'. *Selected Judgements of the Supreme Court of Israel, Special Volume*. 1.
Levmore, R. 2009. 'Rabbinic Responses in Favor of Prenuptial Agreements'. 42(1) *Tradition*. 29.
Morell, S. 1969. 'The Halachic Status of Non-Halachic Jews'. 18(4) *Judaism*. 448.
Orthodox Union, 2017. 'Responses of Rabbinic Panel'. Available at www.ou.org/assets/Responses-of-Rabbinic-Panel.pdf.
Rabinovich, I. and Reinharz, J. (eds). 2008. *Israel in the Middle East*. 2nd edn. Brandeis University Press.
Rackman, E. 1989. 'The Problems of the Jewish Woman in this Generation and the Ways to Solve Them' (in Hebrew) in *HaPeninah: Sefer Zikaron LePeninah Refel*. Jerusalem. 187.
Sperber, D. n.d. 'Partnership Minaynim'. Available at www.yeshivatmaharat.org/ordination/.
Stone, S. L. 2006. 'Judaism and Civil Society' in M. Walzer (ed.) *Law, Politics, and Morality in Judaism*. Princeton University Press. 12.
Unterman, I. Y. 1974. 'The Laws of Conversion and their Implementation' (in Hebrew) in *Torah SheBa'al Peh*. Mosad Harav Kook. 13–20.
Walzer, M. et al. (eds). 2003. *The Jewish Political Tradition vol. 2*. Yale University Press.

12

Christian law

Dynamics of belonging and status

Norman Doe

The World Council of Churches' Faith and Order Commission paper, *The Church: Towards a Common Vision* (2013), which took twenty years to prepare, represents 'an extraordinary ecumenical achievement' in ecclesiology.[1] One of the subjects it addresses is the Christian faithful. For *Common Vision*, the Church (universal) consists of Christ's followers (the people of God), with 'obligations of responsibility', all of whom are 'interrelated'; and each institutional church has its own 'membership', for which faith in Christ is essential, their discipleship sustained by the Holy Spirit.[2] The faithful share 'communion' (*koinonia*), a key concept embracing 'participation, fellowship, [and] sharing' – 'As a divinely established communion, the Church belongs to God and does not exist for itself', but is 'missionary', called and sent 'to witness to that communion which God intends for all humanity' (para. 13); and the Holy Spirit 'equips the Church with its essential gifts, qualities and order' (para. 16). The purpose of this chapter is to explore the legal systems of various Christian traditions worldwide, and how they reflect, but indicate substantially deeper agreement beyond, these *Common Vision* propositions about the faithful and the communion they share. While 'communion' is a theological category (central to *Common Vision*), it also has normative-juridical aspects, particularly apposite in light of the *Common Vision* focus on communion as shared action and order – as spiritual communion is about relationships, so juridical systems seek to facilitate and order the communion of the faithful associated together in a church.[3]

The people of God

The Christian traditions studied here distinguish between the laity and the ordained ministers of the church who together constitute 'the people of God'. The canon law of the Roman Catholic Church provides that Christ's faithful (*christifideles*) are 'incorporated into the Church of Christ through baptism'. The faithful constitute the 'people of God'; each of them 'participates in their own way in the priestly, prophetic and kingly office of Christ'; and each is called according to his/her own condition 'to exercise the mission which God entrusted to the Church to fulfil in the world'.[4] However, by 'divine institution, among Christ's faithful there are in the Church sacred ministers, who are in law also called clerics; the others are called lay people'.[5] Nevertheless, by virtue of baptism, all Christ's faithful (lay and ordained) enjoy within the church 'a genuine equality of dignity and action' to contribute 'each according to his or her own condition and office, to the building up of the Body of Christ'.[6]

Orthodox canon law contains the same distinction. Some jurists define the church (*ekklesia*) as 'the new people of God living in hierarchical order for the purpose of realizing the Kingdom of God on earth': 'It is composed of all who correctly believe in Christ as God and Saviour of the world and are united organically by the same Orthodox faith and the same sacraments'; and it is 'distinguished into clergy who are consecrated through the sacrament of the priesthood, and the laity' (Patsavos, 1975: 5–6). However, there is a basic equality between clergy and laity:

> Church organization consists of two parts, of the order of the clergy and that of the laity. The distinction does not carry the sense of division or opposition between the faithful, nor that of the formation of privileged classes, in the sense of greater rights or fewer responsibilities, nor that of a difference in worth or quality being created amongst the faithful.

Nevertheless, 'the laity does not have the special property of the priesthood, even though they participate through baptism in the triple office of the Lord. Everyone, however, clergy and laity, partakes of one and the same Spirit'. Importantly, the distinction 'is external and in no way eliminates the fundamental principle of the equality of all the faithful toward the gifts of the grace of the Spirit'; indeed: 'The order of the laity also has by divine law the duty and right to be governed by the clergy' (Rodopoulos, 2007: 117). Anglican laws are similar: 'the *laos* is the whole people of God, but for the purposes of law, a lay person is a person who is not in holy orders'.[7] Yet, all persons are 'equal in dignity before God' and 'as human beings created in the image and likeness of God [are] called to salvation through Jesus Christ'; moreover, a church should provide for 'the affirmation and development of the ministry of all the baptized and should have, at the appropriate level, a commission or other body to promote these'.[8]

There is a high degree of juridical unity between these Catholic, Orthodox and Anglican approaches and churches of the Protestant tradition. In Lutheranism, the 'people of God' embraces the priesthood of all believers,[9] which includes the lay and ordained faithful: lay persons are those other than ordained ministers and pastors;[10] for example, the Evangelical Lutheran Church of America speaks of the baptised 'people of God' and 'the universal priesthood of all of its baptised members' to whom it has the duty to equip and support in their ministries in the church and the world.[11] Methodist laws too, recognise the common ministry of Christian service through baptism and the priesthood of all believers,[12] distinguish lay and ordained persons,[13] and embrace the equality of the faithful; for instance, for the Methodist Church in Ireland:

> [e]very member of the Church is equal in spiritual privilege, has the same access to God through Christ, and is charged with the duty of establishing His Kingdom upon earth. The acknowledgment of this spiritual equality in the Methodist Church has led to the recognition of laypersons as being of an equal status with ministers in all the Courts of the Church.[14]

Much the same applies in the Reformed churches. For the United Reformed Church in Great Britain: 'The Lord Jesus Christ continues his ministry in and through the Church, the whole people of God called and committed to his service and equipped for it'.[15] Presbyterian churches also recognise the ministry of all the believers,[16] and they distinguish between lay and ordained persons.[17] By way of contrast, while the juridical instruments of a local Baptist church present the congregation as a manifestation of the Body of Christ, for some, the congregation is composed of 'members' and 'ministers', and for others it is composed of 'members' and 'ordained ministers'; but these instruments do not yield a full juridical treatment of the equality of each category of ecclesiastical person.[18] From these shared rules emerges the principle that the church is the 'people of God' composed of both lay people and ordained ministers who share a fundamental equality of dignity and mission.

The concept of church membership

All the Christian traditions studied here present in their legal instruments an understanding of what constitutes belonging to the institutional church by means of rules on admission and the use and maintenance of rolls or other registers of church membership to enable, e.g. the pastoral care of members. Admission to an institutional church is effected through and administered within the local church rather than at regional, national or international levels.

Roman Catholic canon law does not have a precise concept of membership of the institutional church; rather, the fundamental category is that of 'Christ's faithful' who together constitute the people of God.[19] Baptised persons 'are in full communion with the catholic Church here on earth who are joined with Christ in his visible body, through the bonds of profession of faith, the sacraments and ecclesiastical governance'.[20] At the local level, a parish, for example, is a 'community of Christ's faithful established within a particular church'.[21] Nevertheless, catechumens, who are not yet admitted into full communion with the Catholic Church, are 'linked with the Church in a special way since, moved by the Holy Spirit, they are expressing an explicit desire to be incorporated in the Church'.[22] The Roman Catholic Church also records in registers the names of those incorporated into the church by baptism. The parish priest of the place in which the baptism was conferred must carefully and without delay record in the register of baptism the names of baptised persons, the date and place of their birth, and the date and place of the baptism; there are also confirmation registers.[23]

Orthodox churches have a range of legal styles applicable to the laity, including the 'faithful', 'members' and 'parishioners'.[24]The latter category is very common. Various definitions are employed: parishioners are 'persons of the Orthodox confession, who maintain living contacts with their parish';[25] or else: 'Every person who is baptized and chrismated according to the rites of the Orthodox Church is a parishioner';[26] and again: 'Parishioners are those who, by virtue of their Baptism and Chrismation, are members of the Body of Christ and strive to live in accordance with their high calling (Ephesians 4.1) as Orthodox Christians'.[27] Some Orthodox churches also require a parish to maintain a roll of its parishioners.[28]

By way of contrast, Anglican churches' laws use the concept of a church 'member'. While each church 'should serve all who seek its ministry, membership in a church' may be based on any or all of the following: baptism; baptism and confirmation; and baptism, confirmation and communicant status, or regular attendance at public worship. In turn, there are various classes of church member. A communicant is a person who has received Holy Communion at such frequency and on such occasions as may be prescribed by law; and a communicant in good standing is a communicant who for a prescribed period has been faithful in worship and has supported the work and mission of the church. Names may be entered on a parish roll or other register, subject to such conditions as may be prescribed by law, enabling eligibility for selection to participate in governance and other functions and offices; but names may be removed from the roll in accordance with the law, justice and equity. Membership implicitly involves profession of the faith; acceptance of its doctrine, government, law and discipline; and the enjoyment of the fundamental and other rights and duties of the faithful.[29]

Lutheran legal instruments also define the membership of a church and the conditions for it, and they prescribe for the inclusion of the names of members on a church roll. The Evangelical

Lutheran Church in America is typical. Members of a congregation are those baptised persons on the roll of the congregation, namely: baptised members, those who have been received by baptism or baptised persons received by transfer from another Lutheran congregation; confirmed members, baptised persons confirmed in the congregation (or transferred to it); voting members, that is, confirmed members; and associate members, who hold membership in another congregation but desire to participate in the life of the congregation in which they enrolled.[30] There is little to distinguish Lutheran and Methodist laws on these subjects. Methodists also define membership and the conditions for it, and they require entry of names on a roll or register. By way of illustration, the law of the Methodist Church in Great Britain provides that: 'All those who confess Jesus Christ as Lord and Saviour and accept the obligation to serve him in the life of the Church and the world are welcome as members of the Methodist Church'. A candidate must be approved by the Church Council and publicly received (and baptised and confirmed if not already baptised and confirmed) at a service which includes the Lord's Supper. The Church Council must maintain various registers of the church members.[31] However, the members of the Methodist Church in Ireland are:

> [t]hose who, desiring to be saved from their sins through faith in our Lord Jesus Christ, and to associate themselves with the people of God in Christian fellowship, have been received into full membership in accordance with the Rules and Regulations of the Conference.[32]

The church welcomes those who have committed their lives to Christ, show evidence of that commitment in life, conduct and service, and formally accept the discipline of the church and obligations of membership. Such persons, after training under the oversight of a suitable leader, and approval of the Church Council, may be admitted into the privileges and obligations of membership and their names placed on the Membership Register.[33]

Churches of the Presbyterian tradition, within the context of the church as the people of God, also define membership of the institutional church, impose conditions for admission to it and provide for membership rolls. The Presbyterian Church of Wales is typical: 'The meaning and standards of membership are based on our doctrine regarding the nature and purpose of the Church of God on earth'. Accordingly, the admission of a new member is 'a responsible act on the part of all members of a local church under the guidance of the Minister and/or the Elders'. In turn: 'Membership is open to any individual interested in promoting the Objects who is accepted as a new member of the [Presbyterian Church of Wales] according to the Rules [or] is a member transferring from another Denomination according to the discretion of the Trustees'; the Trustees 'must keep a register of the names and addresses of members which must be made available to any Member upon request'. To be admitted as a member, a person must make 'a profession of faith in God and belief in Christ, and vows to be loyal to them and faithful to all the ordinances of the church'.[34] In Presbyterian law, the name of a member may be removed from the Membership Register on the occasion of for instance death, transfer or failure to comply with the responsibilities of membership.[35] Much the same approach is used in local Baptist churches. Typically, membership is open to individuals who provide evidence to the satisfaction of the local church of their personal experience of salvation by Christ and make 'a public profession of faith in Jesus Christ as Saviour and have undergone believer's baptism by immersion' and are in agreement with the church's Statement of Faith and Covenant. The names of those admitted are recorded on a register of church members,[36] and provision exists for removal of names on the occasion of, e.g. death, withdrawal, transfer or breach of the church covenant by way of failure to fulfil the obligations of church membership.[37]

The duties and rights of the faithful

The dynamics of church membership are defined in the juridical instruments of churches in all of the Christian traditions studied here by means of provisions on the functions of the faithful as terms, as it were, of their belonging. In some churches, instruments present duties and rights applicable to all the faithful whether lay or ordained, but in others they spell out duties, and more rarely rights, applicable specifically to the laity of the institutional church.[38]

Roman Catholic canon law distinguishes the duties and rights of all the faithful, lay and ordained, as well as those specifically applicable to the laity. When incorporated by baptism into the Church of Christ, and constituted as a person within it, each one of the faithful has 'such duties and rights which, in accordance with each one's status, are proper to Christians, in so far as they are in ecclesiastical communion and unless a lawfully issued sanction intervenes'.[39] The duties of all the faithful include: to preserve their communion with the church; to lead a holy life; to show Christian obedience to what sacred pastors (who represent Christ) declare as teachers of the faith and rulers of the church; to provide for the needs of the church; and to promote social justice and help the poor. Their rights include: to make known their need and wishes to the pastors; to be assisted by their pastors; to worship God; to establish and direct associations (for e.g. charitable purposes); to have access to a Christian education; and to vindicate and defend their rights.[40] The laity has specific obligations and rights: to strive so that the divine message may be known throughout the world; to permeate the temporal order with the spirit of the gospel; to build up the people of God through marriage and the family; and to acquire knowledge of and proclaim Christian teaching. They are also capable of admission to ecclesiastical offices open to them and of acting as experts and advisers.[41] These duties and rights derive from the fundamental dignity of the individual as a human person and as such are inalienable and inviolable.[42] Moreover, 'in exercising their rights, [the] faithful, both individually and in association, must take account of the common good of the church, as well as the rights of others and their own duties to others'. The appropriate ecclesiastical authority is entitled 'to regulate, in view of the common good, the exercise of rights which are proper to Christ's faithful'.[43] All the faithful are subject to church discipline, but there is no provision for formal defection from the Catholic Church.[44]

In Orthodox canon law, parishioners are bearers of prescribed duties and rights.[45] For example, in the Russian Orthodox Church all parishioners are:

> [o]bliged to take part in the divine services, make Confession and take holy Communion regularly, observe the canons and church prescriptions, carry out deeds of faith, strive for religious and moral perfection and contribute to the well-being of the parish . . . [and] . . . the material maintenance of the clergy and the church building.

As to rights, parishioners may participate in the Parish Meeting provided they regularly join in parish liturgical life, are over eighteen and have sufficient moral standing and experience of life. They are also subject to discipline and may be removed from the Parish Meeting.[46] By way of contrast, in Anglicanism, the principles of canon law common to the churches of the Anglican Communion do not specify duties and rights applicable only to lay persons. Rather, all the faithful, lay and ordained, by virtue of baptism, are responsible for church life and witness, and should: (a) regularly attend public worship, especially at Holy Communion; (b) practise daily devotion, private prayer, Bible reading, and self-discipline; (c) bring the teaching and example of Christ into every-day life; (d) uphold Christian values; (e) be of personal service to church and community; and (f) assist the church financially in its work and mission.[47] Two types of right are envisioned by the principles of canon law: inherent rights, and acquired rights. As to the former:

> [a]ll persons, equal in dignity before God, have inherent rights and duties inseparable from their dignity as human beings created in the image and likeness of God and called to salvation through Jesus Christ; however, baptism is the foundation of Christian rights and duties, and a church should respect both sets of rights and duties.[48]

All the faithful, ordained and lay, enjoy such rights to government, ministry, teaching, worship, sacraments, rites and property as may flow from their human dignity, baptism, the duties of others and law of that church. Indeed, in a church there is to be no unlawful denial of equal rights, status or access to the life, membership, government, ministry, worship, rites and property of that church on grounds of race, colour, ethnic, tribal or national origin, marital status, sex, sexual orientation, disability or age.[49]

Whereas Catholic, Orthodox and Anglican laws begin with duties and move to rights, in the Protestant traditions the reverse is often the case, and sometimes the two juridical categories are conflated. In the Evangelical Lutheran Church in Canada, the focus is on responsibilities:

> [t]he members of this church are to be constant in worship and in the study of the Holy Scriptures, regularly nourishing their life in Christ in the Sacrament of the Altar, presenting their children for Holy Baptism and providing for their Christian instruction.

They are 'called by the Spirit to lead godly lives, to promote the unity and welfare of the church in the bond of peace, to proclaim the gospel and to renounce the evil one'. The commitment of each baptised member to this call is 'to be expressed through this church, its synods and its congregations by a life of repentance, faith, prayer and the sharing of resources'.[50] By way of contrast, Methodists generally provide for the 'privileges and obligations of membership' (particularly holy living and participation in the sacraments and worship), and enable discipline and termination of membership. For instance, the Methodist Church of Ireland is once again typical: 'Every member shall have their name recorded in the Membership Register and should receive pastoral support and encouragement in their discipleship from the local minister and lay leaders'. But only those whose names are recorded in the Membership Register are entitled to be members of the Church Council, Circuit Executive, District Synod or Conference. As to the obligations of membership:

> All members are expected to (a) attend the means of grace, especially the ministry of the Word, united prayer, and the Sacrament of the Lord's Supper, (b) join with others in Christian fellowship, (c) engage in some form of Christian service, [and] (d) financially support the ongoing work and mission of the church through regular giving, so far as can reasonably be expected.

These rules are designed on the classical Methodist principle that the faithful are 'helpers one of another', a system which clearly expresses the dynamic interdependence inherent in the exercise of right and duties. Moreover:

> [a] member, who in the judgment of the Church Council, has persistently failed to fulfil the Obligations of Membership, despite being reminded of those obligations, shall be regarded as having withdrawn from membership of the church and their name shall be removed from the Membership Register.

The dual membership of different Circuits (and each Circuit is a unit of one or more local churches, namely the primary unit in which local churches express and experience their inter-connectedness in the Body of Christ) in the church is forbidden, but there is provision for the transfer of members from one Circuit to another, and for those who no longer accept the privileges and obligations of membership.[51]

In turn, churches of the Reformed tradition speak of the 'rights and privileges' and 'privileges and responsibilities' of church membership.[52] Presbyterian churches have particularly well-developed compendia of the rights and duties of church members. The Presbyterian Church in New Zealand is typical: (a) as to recognition of membership status, a member of the congregation has 'rights and privileges' to have the church council record their name on the roll of members, to receive baptism for their children, and to receive a certificate recording their own or child's baptism; (b) as to the sacraments, to participate in communion, and to have any child participate in communion; (c) as to governance, members have the right to attend, participate and vote at any meeting of the congregation on any matter brought before it, to stand for election to congregational office, to present a proposal to the church council or through the church council to the presbytery on matters affecting his or her interests or those of the congregation, and to receive, on leaving a congregation, a letter of introduction to another congregation. The responsibilities of members are: to lead a life consistent with their profession of the Christian faith; as far as able, to join in the worship, life and mission of the congregation, and to accept the spiritual oversight and discipline of the church; the Church Council has a duty to secure the implementation of these personal rights.[53] The instruments of Baptist Unions and local Baptist churches also provide for the 'privileges and obligations of membership'. For example: 'it is the duty of every Disciple to bear personal witness to the Gospel of Jesus Christ, in Family and Public Worship, in the observance of the ordinance of Baptism and the Lord's Supper, in conduct and in the Evangelisation of the world'.[54]

The regulatory instruments of churches do not contain compendia of general norms on the position of women in ecclesial life, though there are norms dispersed throughout legal texts which, for example, either allow or forbid the ordination of women, and rules which enable the admission of women to prescribed lay ministries.[55] The rules of some churches, however, deal expressly with female associations within the church.[56] Needless to say, some traditions also make provision for the religious life in communities. In the Roman Catholic Church women (and men) may be admitted to: institutes of consecrated life, societies of apostolic life and associations of the faithful.[57] Monasticism is also an important feature of Orthodox Christianity. This life is open to both women (nuns) and men (monks).[58] Rules typically provide for the admission, vows, transfer and withdrawal of men and women,[59] and, for example, in the Russian Orthodox Church a monastery is defined as 'a community of men or women, consisting of Orthodox Christians, who voluntarily have chosen the monastic way of life for spiritual and moral perfection and the common confession of the Orthodox faith'.[60] Anglicanism also enables the faithful (women or men) to associate in a religious order or other society which enjoys autonomy to establish and administer for its life in the community its own rules, statutes or other constitution. The relationship between an order or society and a church is governed by the mutual acceptance of their respective regulatory systems.[61]

The ordained ministers of the church

Suitable, qualified persons may be called to or otherwise 'set apart' for ministry which is understood (across the traditions studied here) to be of divine institution. By way of illustration, Roman Catholic law provides that: 'By divine institution some among Christ's faithful are, through the sacrament of order, marked with an indelible character and are thus constituted sacred ministers': deacons, priests and bishops.[62] Lutheran and Methodist ordained ministers engage in 'holy ministry', which is 'the gift of Christ to the church' and 'the church does not create the office of the public ministry, but it does call and ordain persons into that office' who are 'qualified by personal qualities, gifts and training'. 'God instituted the office of the ordained ministry', namely, 'a separated and ordained ministry'.[63] In the Reformed tradition too, ordained ministry is conceived as instituted by Christ, and ministers, elders and deacons 'represent Christ' (be they men or women);[64] and for Presbyterians, typically, Christ, 'for the edification of the visible Church . . . has appointed officers not only to preach the Gospel and administer the Sacraments, but also to exercise discipline for the preservation both of truth and duty'.[65] In turn, some Baptists practise 'ordination', others do not, but they have 'ministers'.[66] The Baptist Union of Great Britain sees ordination as the norm for ministry, especially where full-time ministry is in mind. Lay pastors are appointed where, for example, a small congregation is unable to afford full-time ordained ministry. Those who are ordained will normally be: called by God; trained at a recognised college; called by a church congregation; and ordained and inducted. At a service of ordination it is usual for the history of the call to be outlined with the call recognised through a resolution of the Church Meeting: 'In ordination a person's call from God to the pastoral ministry of Word and Sacrament is given public recognition as he or she is set apart to serve and to lead'.[67]

Ordination itself is the process by which the vocation of individuals to serve as ministers is recognised and by which persons are 'set apart' for ministry. Like the Roman Catholic Church, the Orthodox Church ordains clergy by way of the laying-on of hands. Ordination cannot be repeated – and candidates must be of the Orthodox faith, male, of sufficient age. Married persons may be ordained, but unmarried clergy cannot marry.[68] In Lutheranism, typically, 'By the rite of ordination the church sets a person apart' for ministry, and in Methodism a:

> Minister is constituted by the Call of God, the consent of the members of the Church, the election of the Conference, and the ordination to the office and work of a Minister in the Church of God by prayer and the laying on of hands.[69]

Similarly, in Presbyterianism, candidates must have an 'unimpeachable character', 'a deep experience of the truth of the Gospel', 'the calling of God by the Spirit, through the inward testimony of a good conscience, the manifest approbation of God's people, and the concurring judgment of a lawful court of the Church'. 'A minister at . . . ordination is set apart'.[70] Churches also have norms on appointment/election to ministerial posts, tenure and termination of their ministry (Doe, 2013: 86–93).[71]

Norms of churches also address the authority, functions and lifestyle of ordained ministers. For instance, an Orthodox priest is 'the spiritual father of his parish' and must 'treat his parishioners as his parochial family', deliver homilies, provide liturgy, instruct the faithful, visit parishioners, direct parish life and reside in the parish.[72] Roman Catholic clerics must 'seek holiness in their lives', refrain from associations inconsistent with the clerical state and lead a simple life avoiding worldliness.[73] In Lutheranism, 'Leaders in this church should demonstrate that they are servants by their words, life-style, and manner of leadership', recognising 'their accountability to the Triune God, to the whole Church, to each other, and the [church] . . . in which they serve'.[74] Likewise, for Methodism, 'Christ's Ministers in the Church [are] Stewards in the Household of God and Shepherds of His Flock'.[75] Within Presbyterianism, 'A minister at his/her ordination is set apart by the Church to lead it in . . . preaching the Word, the administering of the Sacraments, the pastoral care of members and their instruction in the Christian faith'.[76] It is also a principle of law that ministers are accountable for the exercise of their ministry to competent authority as prescribed by law (Doe, 2013: 93–101).

Oversight is addressed in the laws of all churches studied here and is exercised principally by an ordained minister, usually in collaboration with others (who may have a determinative or consultative voice).[77] Norms provide for numerous personal ministries of oversight at regional and/or national level, but the scope of their jurisdictions differs as between traditions – such as Catholic, Orthodox and Anglican bishops in their dioceses and beyond them archbishops, Methodist district superintendents and presidents of national Conference, and Presbyterian regional Presbyteries and moderators of General Assemblies (Doe, 2013: 102–113). Some allow global jurisdiction. Like the Catholic Pontiff with global teaching, sanctifying and governing authority over all the faithful, Orthodox Patriarchs enjoy an international jurisdiction (such as the Ecumenical Patriarch of Constantinople with authority over Greek Orthodox churches worldwide).[78] However, in Anglicanism, the Archbishop of Canterbury has no general jurisdiction over the autonomous churches of the Anglican Communion, but has 'primacy of honour' as 'focus of unity'; laws may provide otherwise.[79] Similarly, the Presidents of the Lutheran World Federation, World Communion of Reformed Churches and Baptist World Alliance exercise general oversight within these global bodies but not coercive jurisdiction (Doe, 2013: chapter 2).

Ecclesiastical offences and sanctions

There is remarkable juridical unity between the Christian traditions studied here as to the ecclesiastical offences and sanctions which lie at the heart of church discipline (see Doe, 2013: chapter 5). Prohibitions against the commission of ecclesiastical offences may apply to both ordained and lay people. Churches are in general agreement about the nature of an ecclesiastical offence, the definitional elements of the offence and the classes within the church to which offences apply. However, there is diversity in terms of the defences available to excuse an offender or justify their conduct. In the Roman Catholic Church, offences include apostasy, heresy, schism, blasphemy, perjury and harm to public morals.[80] Among Orthodox churches offences include: 'infringing the church discipline and teaching';[81] the violation of 'the doctrinal, canonical or moral norms of the Orthodox Church';[82] 'unorthodox belief, [and] breaches of canonical or moral discipline';[83] the violation of moral standards and the commission of more specified actions.[84] In Anglicanism, clergy and (in some churches) the laity may be tried for various offences such as: the commission of a crime under State law; immorality; teaching doctrines contrary to those of the church; violation of the law of the church or of ordination vows; habitual or wilful neglect of duty; conduct unbecoming the office and work of an ordained minister; and disobedience to the lawful directions of a bishop.[85]

These are mirrored, broadly, in Protestant churches. For example, Lutheran pastors may be disciplined for: preaching or teaching contrary to the faith confessed by the church; conduct incompatible with the character of ministerial office; wilful disregard or violation of church law; unlawful disclosure of confidential communications; and sexual misconduct.[86] Moreover, the lay faithful may be disciplined for prescribed ecclesiastical offences to the extent authorised by law.[87] In the Presbyterian Church in America an 'offence' is 'anything in the doctrines or practice of a Church member professing faith in Christ which is contrary to the Word of God'. Their commission is a ground for discipline; personal offences are violations of divine law involving wrongs to particular individuals; and public offences are heresies or immoralities.[88] Similarly, offences in Methodist churches may include: neglect of the vows of the baptismal covenant and regular absence from the worship without valid reason; immorality; practices declared incompatible with Christian teachings (such as being a self-avowed practising homosexual); crime; failure to perform the work of the ministry; disobedience to the order and discipline of the church; dissemination of doctrines contrary to those of the church; or racial or gender discrimination.[89] Disciplinary process may also be undertaken in Baptist churches for misconduct,[90] such as when a member becomes 'an offence to the church and to its good name by reason of immoral or unchristian conduct, or by persistent breach of covenant vows, or non-support of the church',[91] or: 'If any member is absent from services of the Church and/ or neglects to comply with any of the privileges and obligations of membership for a prolonged period without apparent good reason'.[92]

In turn, the churches make provision for the imposition of sanctions, including exclusion from the spiritual benefits of church membership. In the Roman Catholic Church, the penalty of excommunication may be imposed on those who obstinately persist in manifest grave sin; these are not to be admitted to Holy Communion.[93] Apostasy, heresy and schism incur automatic excommunication.[94] Similarly, in the Orthodox tradition, penalties include major excommunication (or *anathema*), total expulsion from the church,[95] and in Anglicanism excommunication may be imposed on both clergy and laity.[96] Similarly in the Evangelical Lutheran Church in Southern Africa, if 'a brotherly consultation' with the minister fails, the church committee may require the person to render an account and if this is unsatisfactory the congregation may deny 'some or all church rights' (such as deprivation of admission to office, rights to vote, or church burial, and denial of the Lord's Supper).[97] In Presbyterianism, for instance, in the United Free Church of Scotland: 'censures are not in the nature of penance or satisfaction . . . [nor] punishments or the exercise of retributive justice' but are 'the means of grace used for the recovery of the erring from sin and peril, for the protection of Christ's people from occasions of stumbling, and for the edification of the Church'. The church should seek to manifest 'a forgiving spirit in its own community'; moreover, sins or offences not publicly known may be addressed by private admonition, counsel and reproof, and the public censures are admonition, rebuke, suspension, deposition from office and excommunication.[98] Likewise, in the Presbyterian Church in America, excommunication is the excision of an offender from the communion of the church for 'gross crime or heresy'. Provision also exists for the removal of censures.[99] Admonition, reproof, suspension, excommunication and removal from membership or office are also found in instruments of Methodist churches[100] and Baptist Unions and Conventions.[101]

Conclusion

A Christian Law Panel of Experts[102] meeting in Rome from 2013 to 2016[103] has recently produced *A Statement of Principles of Christian Law* based on examination of regulatory instruments of churches within the traditions studied here. The Panel of Experts found that: (1) there are principles of church law and church order common to these churches and their existence can be factually established by empirical observation and comparison; (2) the churches of each Christian tradition contribute through their own regulatory instruments to this store of principles; (3) the principles have a strong theological content and weight and are fundamental to the self-understanding of Christianity; (4) they have a living force and contain within themselves the possibility of further development and articulation; and (5) these principles demonstrate a degree of unity between the churches, stimulate common Christian actions, and should be fed into the ecumenical enterprise to enhance fuller visible unity.[104]

A section in the *Statement of Principles* is devoted to the faithful, which recognises that: 'Some churches expressly use in their regulatory instruments the category "member", others do not. However, each church has an identifiable group of the faithful associated with it. For the purposes of this section, the word membership denotes both juridical categories'. First, as to the People of God, the Christian faithful constitute the people of God; all the faithful should be equal in dignity; baptism generates duties and rights for the faithful; and: the faithful includes lay and ordained people.[105] Second, as to Church Membership and Others Forms of Belonging, a church is made up of those incorporated into it in accordance with its proper laws and customs; a church should serve, in appropriate ways, all who seek its ministry regardless of membership; membership in a church, for the purposes of participation in its government, may be based on any or all of: baptism; baptism and confirmation or other mature demonstration of faith; and such other conditions as may be prescribed by law. The names of persons belonging to a church may be entered on one or more rolls or other registers of membership subject to such conditions as may be prescribed by law, and names may be removed from such rolls and registers in accordance with the law.[106] Third, as to the functions of the laity, the law of a church should generally set out the basic rights and duties of all its members; the laity should promote the mission of the church and bear witness to the Christian faith through their lives in the world; a lay person should engage in the collective ecclesial life, in proclaiming the Word of God, participating in worship, and receiving the sacraments; lay persons should maintain such Christian standards in their private lives as are prescribed by law; and lay persons are encouraged to practise daily devotion, private prayer, Bible reading and self-discipline, bringing the teaching and example of Christ into every-day life, upholding Christian values and being of service to the church and wider community.[107] There are also principles on lay public ministry.[108]

In turn, in the Section on Ordained Ministry:

> The churches set apart persons for ministry in a special rite, for most called ordination. The following principles apply to ordained ministry and also address ecclesiastical offices which, depending on the church concerned, may be held by either ordained or lay persons.

It goes on to state, first, as to ordination, ordained ministry is divine in origin and persons are set apart for it; a church may distinguish between different types of ordained minister; candidates for ordination must be called by God and by the church to ordained ministry; vocation to and suitability for ordained ministry are tested by the church through a process of selection, examination and training by competent authority; persons are generally admitted to ordained ministry through ordination; and ordination is administered by competent authority by means of the laying-on of hands and invocation of the Holy Spirit.[109] Second, on Ecclesiastical Offices, an ecclesiastical office is a position constituted by law; an ecclesiastical office exists independently of the person who occupies it; an ecclesiastical office enables the discharge of functions of the particular ministry attaching to it; an ecclesiastical office may be held by a person or persons with such qualifications as are prescribed by law; an ecclesiastical office is filled by a variety of means, often by appointment or election; the jurisdiction or other authority which attaches to an office is determined by or under the law; authority attaching to an office may be delegated to the extent provided by law; and the authority to exercise ecclesiastical office ceases upon lawful dissolution of the office, expiration of the stated term of office, attainment of the prescribed age limit, or the death, resignation, transfer, retirement or removal of the office holder.[110] Third, as to the Functions of Ordained Ministers, ordained ministers must be duly authorised by their church to exercise ministry; ministers are to preach the Word of God, teach the faith, administer the sacraments and provide pastoral care; ministers should fashion their ministry after the example of Jesus Christ; ministers must lead their private lives in a manner which befits their sacred calling; ministers may engage in such other occupations, including offices held beyond the local church, as are not forbidden by church law or competent authority; and ministers are accountable for the exercise of their ministry to the competent authority in the manner prescribed by law.[111] As to the Exercise of Oversight, oversight is an essential of ecclesial order; oversight is exercised by such authority as is designated by law; a church may have a system of international oversight or leadership; a minister has such international functions of oversight or leadership as are permitted by law; international church offices include those of pope, patriarch, primate, president, moderator, or general secretary; those who exercise international oversight or leadership are appointed or elected to that office by competent ecclesial authority; and a church may assign to such an office a coercive jurisdiction or a moral or persuasive authority.[112] Finally, sanctions should be lawful and just. They may include admonition, rebuke, removal from office and excommunication; they may be applied to the laity, clergy and office-holders to the extent provided by law; their effect is withdrawal from some of the benefits of ecclesial life; sanctions are remedial or medicinal; and a church may enable the removal of sanctions.[113] It is these principles of Christian law, common to the churches examined by the Panel of Experts, which define juridically the status and dynamics of belonging for Christians in the context of their place within an institutional church of particular ecclesial traditions.

Notes

1 Paper No. 214 of 2013: *The Church: Towards a Common Vision* (WCC Publications 2013), Preface, viii.
2 *Common Vision*, paras 7, 12, 14, 16, 18, 19, 21, 23, 27.
3 Much of the following material is derived from Doe (2013).
4 Code of Canon Law 1983 (hereafter CIC), cc. 204, 96: 'By baptism one is incorporated into the Church of Christ and constituted a person in it'.
5 CIC, c. 207: 'Their state, although it does not belong to the hierarchical structure of the Church, does pertain to its life and holiness'; see also cc. 96–112 for the canonical status of physical persons.
6 CIC, c. 208.
7 *The Principles of Canon Law Common to the Churches of the Anglican Communion*, Anglican Communion Legal Advisers' Network (Anglican Communion Office, London, 2008) (hereafter PCLCCAC), Principle 25.1.
8 PCLCCAC, Principle 26.
9 Lutheran Church of Australia (hereafter LCA): The Ministry of the People of God and the Public Ministry, 1992 (edited 2001) 1: Introduction; for the category 'Christian'.
10 LCA: Constitution, Interpretation: 'lay member' any 'any member ... other than a pastor'; Theses on the Church, 2 (citing e.g. Col. 1.13): 'The Church is the communion of believers ... those who ... have been led to faith in Jesus Christ ... The Church therefore comprises only believers and all believers at all times and places'.
11 ELCA: Const., ch. 7.10–11; see also 5.01 for the principle of inclusivity in terms, e.g. of colour.
12 Methodist Church in Great Britain (hereafter MCGB): Constitutional Practice and Discipline, Deed of Union, 4: the church holds 'the doctrine of the priesthood of all believers and ... believes that no priesthood exists which belongs exclusively to a particular order or class ... but [for] corporate life and worship special qualifications for ... special duties are required' for ordained ministry.
13 Ibid. 1: 'lay' means 'a person who is neither a minister nor a deacon'; Methodist Church of New Zealand (hereafter MCNZ): Laws and Regulations, Nature of New Zealand Methodism: ordained presbyters and deacons.
14 MCI: Constitution, s. 1.
15 URC: Manual, A.16 and A.19: 'This service is given by worship, prayer, proclamation of the gospel, and Christian witness; by mutual and outgoing care and responsibility; and by obedient discipleship in the whole of daily life, according to the gifts and opportunities given to each one. The preparation and strengthening of its members for such ministry and discipleship shall always be a major concern of the United Reformed Church'.
16 Presbyterian Church of Aotearoa New Zealand (PCANZ): Book of Order, 1.4: 'members' and 'ministers'.
17 Presbyterian Church in America (PCA): Book of Church Order, Preface, II.3.
18 See e.g. Baptist Union of Southern Africa (BUSA): Model Constitution for Local Churches, Art. 4.2; Bethel Baptist Church (Choctaw): Constitution, Art. III: 'professing members'; IV: 'ordained officers'.

19 See, however, CIC, c. 111: 'Through the reception of baptism a child becomes a member of the Latin Church if the parents belong to that Church'; the word 'member' (*sodalis*) is often used but with a narrow signification, such as being a member of a religious institute.
20 CIC, c. 205.
21 CIC, c. 515.
22 CIC, c. 206; for admission to the catechumenate by liturgical rite, see c. 788.
23 CIC, c. 877; see also c. 895: those baptised persons who have been confirmed are to be recorded in the confirmation register of the diocesan curia or when prescribed by the (national) Bishops' Conference.
24 Orthodox Church in America (OCIA): Guidelines for Clergy: 'Membership in the Body of Christ, His Holy Church, is defined by participation in the Holy Eucharist' and is incumbent on 'parishioners'.
25 Russian Orthodox Church (ROC): Statute, XI.3.
26 Greek Orthodox Archdiocese of America (GOAA): Regulations, Art. 18.1.
27 Ukrainian Orthodox Church in America (UOCIA): Statutes, Art. XI.5.
28 GOAA: Regulations, Art. 18.7: e.g. name, occupation, and date of baptism and/or chrismation and marriage.
29 PCLCCAC, Principle 27.
30 ELCA: Model Constitution for Congregations, ch. 8.01–02; see also 6.01.
31 MCGB: Constitutional Practice and Discipline, Deed of Union 8 and 9; Standing Orders 050 and 054: the Membership Roll is kept by the Pastoral Committee of the Church Council; the Community Roll lists non-members under pastoral care.
32 MCI: Constitution, s. 3: baptised children of members are 'junior members' and 'it is their duty and privilege when they reach the age of discretion to enter into full membership'; Regulations, Discipline and Government, 1.01: 'Membership ... is not conditional upon the acceptance of any theological tests, nor dependent upon any traditional authority or ecclesiastical ritual'; and: 'the spirit and practice of Christian love is the supreme test of membership'.
33 MCI: Regulations, Discipline and Government, 2.03–2.07: the register is reviewed annually.
34 PCW: Handbook of Rules, II: Membership and Model Constitution, Art. 4.
35 PCANZ: Book of Order, 4.4–4.10; 4.10: the council must give notice and an opportunity to be heard.
36 Riverside Baptist Church (Baltimore): Byelaws, Art. I: candidates must publicly request membership at a service, complete a class, be recommended by pastor and deacons and be accepted by majority vote at a meeting.
37 Central Baptist Church (Pretoria): Constitution, Art. 7.
38 For discipline, see Doe (2013: chapter 5).
39 CIC, c. 96; each physical person has duties and rights: as well as the laity (cc. 224–231), there are those attaching to, e.g. clergy (cc. 273–289), religious (cc. 662–672), married couples and parents (cc. 1135–1136).
40 CIC, cc. 208–223: 'obligations and rights of all the faithful'.
41 CIC, cc. 224–231: the 'obligations and rights of the lay members of Christ's faithful'.
42 CIC, c. 208.
43 CIC, c. 223.
44 CIC, c. 11: canon law binds those baptised or received into the church who enjoy the sufficient use of reason and have completed 7 years of age; for discipline, see cc. 1311, 1321–1323 and 1341.
45 Romanian Orthodox Church (ROMOC): Statutes, Art. 45: 'the faithful ... have rights to [e.g.] charitable assistance, to elect and be elected in the parochial bodies ... and duties ... to sustain, strengthen and witness the faith of the Orthodox Church; to live according to [its] teaching ... to participate in religious services; to have the Holy Sacraments; to fulfil acts of Christian mercy; [and] to maintain and to help the Church and her servants'.
46 ROC: Statutes, XI.3.
47 PCLCCAC, Principle 26.6.
48 PCLCCAC, Principle 26.1–3; 4: a church should respect rights and duties founded on the dignity of the human person and on baptism and those afforded by ecclesiastical authority; 5: the church is concerned with the welfare of people in all its aspects, physical, mental and spiritual, and should as far as possible respond to the needs of all.
49 PCLCCAC, Principle 26.7–8; and 26.10: 'All the faithful should recognise the unique status and needs of children and young people ... and a church should make such provision ... to ensure their special protection. Mistreatment of children, especially their sexual abuse, offends their humanity and the teaching of Christ'.

50 ELCIC: Constitution, Art. V.
51 MCI: Regulations, Discipline and Government, 2.04–2.07, 2.10–2.14.
52 E.g. URC: Manual, A.19: Christian service implies 'mutual and outgoing care and responsibility', worship, prayer, proclamation of the gospel, witness, and 'obedient discipleship in the whole of daily life'.
53 PCANZ: Book of Order, 4.4–4.10; see also 1.4: 'the responsibility . . . to study the Scriptures'.
54 Jamaica Baptist Union (JBU): Constitution, Art. III: 'it is the duty of every Disciple to bear personal witness to the Gospel of Jesus Christ, in Family and Public Worship, in the observance of the ordinance of baptism and the Lord's Supper, in conduct and in the Evangelisation of the world'.
55 See Doe, 2013: 62–71: lay ministries; 77–86: ordination, see e.g. CIC, c. 1024: only a man may be ordained; PCA: BCO 1.4 and 7.2: only a man may be appointed as elder; compare RCA: BCO, ch. I, Pt. I, Art. I: 'Ministers are . . . men and women . . . inducted to that office by ordination'.
56 ELCIC: Const., Art. XVII.1 and ABL, XVII: the Evangelical Lutheran Women of the ELCIC is 'an official women's organization' and a composite of congregational organizations; it has 'authority, in conformity with the personnel policies of this church, to employ an executive staff person and additional staff as needed to carry out its purpose'; it is responsible for its own financial affairs and is 'an integral part of this church'; MCI: RDG 17: Methodist Women in Ireland: this is an 'organizing body' to enable fellowship and mission; CLCS: 132: the Woman's Guild has a national structure but its congregational branch is subject to the 'spiritual supervision' of the Kirk Session of the local Presbyterian church.
57 CIC, c. 573–661; see e.g. 609: nuns; and 611: monks.
58 OOCL: 115, 129.
59 SOCA: Const., Art. 132: the vows are 'celibacy (chastity), obedience and voluntary poverty'; 133: candidates must be of 'good conduct and reputation'; 134: no-one under 20 'shall wear the monastic habit'.
60 ROC: Statute, XII.1–10: a monastery may be registered as a legal entity under State law; any monastic who withdraws has no claim on monastic property; a monastery may be represented in the assemblies of the church.
61 PCLCCAC, Principle 26.
62 CIC, cc. 1008–1009.
63 LCA: *The Ministry of the People and Public Ministry*, 1992: citing e.g. Acts 6.4.
64 Reformed Church in America (RCA): Book of Church Order, C. I, Pt. I, Art. 1: 'Ministers are . . . men and women . . . inducted . . . by ordination'.
65 PCW: Handbook, 4.1–2: 'A minister at . . . ordination is set apart'.
66 Bethel Baptist Church (Choctaw): Constitution, Art. IV; Riverside Baptist Church (Baltimore): BL, Art. II.
67 Baptist Union of Great Britain: Patterns and Prayers for Christian Worship (1991) 170.
68 CIC, e.g. cc. 1024–1033. For the Orthodox, see e.g. Patsavos (1975: 66–74).
69 MCI: Constitution, s. 4. For Lutheranism, see e.g. ELCA, Constitution, ch. 7.31.
70 PCW: Handbook, 4: qualities; PCA, Book of Church Order, 16: vocation etc.
71 Doe (2013: 86–93).
72 OCIA: Guidelines for Clergy, Priests and Deacons, 1–19; this cites e.g. Luke 22.27.
73 CIC, cc. 276–287: holiness; continence; celibacy; study; common life; simple life; residence; dress.
74 ELCA : Constitution, ch. 5.
75 MCI : Constitution, s. 1.
76 PCW: Handbook, 4.
77 This is often formalised through assemblies such as a presbytery, consistory, classis, regional or general synod.
78 CIC, c. 331: the Pontiff has 'supreme, full, immediate and universal ordinary power'; Rodopoulos, 2007: 213–221: Constantinople; see also ROC, *Statute*, 1: the Patriarch of Moscow and All Russia.
79 PCLCCAC, Principle 11.4.
80 CIC, cc. 1364–1399.
81 ROMOC: Statutes, Art. 14; see also Arts. 148–160: doctrinal, moral and canonical offences.
82 ROC: Statute, X.35: if the members of the Diocesan Council 'violate the doctrinal, canonical or moral norms of the Orthodox Church and if they stand trial in the ecclesiastical court or are under investigation, they shall be dismissed from their office by the decision of the Diocesan Bishop'.
83 Ukrainian Orthodox Church in America (UOCA): Statutes, Art. XII.
84 UOCA: Statutes, Art. VIII.

85 See e.g. West Africa: Const., Art. XXII.6: crime; Ireland: Const. VIII.53: immorality; West Indies: Can. 25: doctrine; Wales: Const., XI.18: disobedience to law; Canada: Can. XVIII.8: neglect of duty; Scotland: Can. 54.2: conduct unbecoming; New Zealand: Can. D.II.4: disobedience of lawful Episcopal directions.

86 See e.g. LCA: Const., Art. X.1.

87 Evangelical Lutheran Church in America (ELCA): Const., Ch. 20.21: all members may be disciplined for, e.g. denial of the faith, 'conduct grossly unbecoming a member of the Church of Christ', 'persistent trouble-making' and wilful disregard of the constitution and bylaws; ELCSA: G., 5: 'brotherly discipline' applies if 'a person publicly despises or insults the Christian faith, by word and deed, if he continually and consciously trespasses God's commandments or if he defames the glory of God'.

88 PCA: BCO, 29.1–4; see also 36: infliction of censures.

89 United Methodist Church in Northern Europe and Eurasia (UMCNEAE): BOD, para. 228(b) and para. 2702. See also MCI: RDG, 5.15: complaints may be made as to, e.g. the 'moral and religious character' of a minister, failure to believe and preach church doctrine, and failure to fulfil 'the duties of ministerial office'; Church of the Nazarene (COTN): Man., Part VI.I: e.g. 'violence to the Covenant of Christian Character or the Covenant of Christian Conduct' and wilful and continuous violation of membership vows.

90 JBU: Const., Art. V: disciplinary action may follow if members act 'in contravention of the Rules and Regulations of the Union' and 'in a manner injurious or calculated to be injurious to its interests'.

91 Riverside Baptist Church (Baltimore): BL Art. I. See also Bethel Baptist Church (Choctaw): Const., 'moral offence against the Lord and the church', 'doctrinal offence' and 'personal offence against another member'.

92 Baptist Union of Southern Africa: Model Const., Arts. 9 and 25.

93 CIC cc. 915, 916: any person conscious of grave sin may not receive Holy Communion without previously having been to sacramental confession.

94 CIC, c. 1364.

95 OOCL: 176–178; MOCL: 112: this cites, e.g. Mt 12.31–32 and 1 Cor 5.1–5; denial of burial is imposed on those under major excommunication, those who have died in a duel (or from wounds as a result) and suicides.

96 PCLCCAC, Principle 69.

97 ELCSA: G., 5; ELCA: Const., Ch. 20; ELCIC: Const., Art. 7: expulsion by a parish council.

98 UFCS: MPP, V.II: censures generally; VI: private reproof etc.

99 PCA: BCO, 30.1–5; 36: infliction of censures; 37: removal of censures. See also PCI: Code, para. 133: admonition, rebuke, suspension from rights and privileges of church membership, suspension and deposition from office.

100 MCI: RDG, 5.03–05; MCNZ: LAR, s. 2.29: suspension and expulsion of ministers; UMCNEAE: BOD, para. 361: interim suspension.

101 National Baptist Convention USA: Const., Art. IV: removal from office or expulsion from the Convention; Canadian National Baptist Convention (CNBC): BL 10–16: if a church ceases to cooperate with the Convention or becomes corrupt in doctrine or practice it is no longer in fellowship with the Convention; Riverside Baptist Church (Baltimore): BL Art. I: membership may be terminated by 80% vote 'but only after due notice and hearing, and after faithful efforts have been made to bring such member to repentance and amendment'.

102 The participants attended in their personal capacities not as representatives of their denomination, but they were selected for their expertise in the church law, church order or church polity, of particular Christian churches, namely: Anglican, Baptist, Catholic, Lutheran, Methodist, Orthodox, Presbyterian and Reformed.

103 At its first meeting in 2013, the Panel tested the hypothesis that it is possible to postulate and articulate principles of Christian law induced from the similarities of their regulatory instruments as proposed by Doe (2013).

104 A Statement of Principles of Christian Law Common to the Component Churches, Christian Law Panel of Experts, Rome 2016 ('Principles'). For the Panel: 'A principle of law common to the churches of the Christian traditions studied here is a foundational proposition or maxim of general applicability which has substance, is induced from the similarities of the regulatory systems of churches, derives from their juridical tradition or the practices of the church universal, expresses a basic theological truth or ethical value, and is implicit in, or underlies, the juridical systems of the churches'.

105 Principles II.1.

106 Principles II.2.
107 Principles II.3.
108 Principles II.4: Public Ministry Exercised by Lay Persons: Public ministry, a gift of God, is the fulfilment of a function assigned formally in a church to an office or other position exercised under authority on behalf of that church in the service of its mission and witness to the Gospel; the law should enable the laity to exercise public ministry in those offices and other positions lawfully open to them; lay persons may be admitted to such offices and positions provided they are suitable, qualified, selected and admitted by competent ecclesial authority for such term as is prescribed by law; lay ministers and officers exercise such public and representative ministry within and on behalf of a church and perform such functions as may be prescribed and permitted by its law; and the authority to discipline, dismiss or reappoint a lay minister or officer depends on, and its exercise must comply with, the law of the church.
109 Principles III.1.
110 Principles III.2.
111 Principles III.3.
112 Principles III.4.
113 Principles V.5.4–5.

References

Doe, N. 2013. *Christian Law: Contemporary Principles*. Cambridge University Press.
Patsavos, L. J. 1975. *Manual for the Course in Orthodox Canon Law*. Hellenic College, Holy Cross Orthodox School of Theology.
Rodopoulos, P. 2007. *An Overview of Orthodox Canon Law*. Orthodox Research Institute.

13

Islamic law

Dynamics of belonging and status

Anver M. Emon

What does it mean to 'be Muslim', or to adhere to the Islamic religion? The idea of who the Muslim is has taken on special significance since 11 September 2001, when being Muslim became a proxy for a whole host of concerns about security, terrorism, and the law-abiding citizen. There is a certain irony in writing a chapter on the Islamic legal approach to belonging (i.e. being Muslim) when that very legal tradition is invoked in a politics of fear (e.g. 'Shari'a creep'), and informs exclusionary policies of policing in North America and Europe. Yet indulging that irony and interrogating it for what it reveals – not only about Islamic law but also about the way the 'Islamic' is cast by policy makers – reveals the subversive potential of the comparative project that animates this volume.

This chapter will explore the premodern legal doctrine and more contemporary approaches, on entry and exit from the community denoted by 'Islam'. This analysis will centre on the implications of entry, belonging, and exit on one's status under Islamic law. It will also address the status of women and other subordinated Muslim groups under the law. In all cases, it should be understood that the doctrinal analysis below applies to individuals living within an Islamic regime, which premodern Muslim jurists generally understood in imperial terms. In other words, the 'jurisdiction' of the legal analysis extended to the borders of Islamic suzerainty. Outside those borders, there was considerable debate about whether and to what extent Islamic law could be applied extra-territorially (see Chapter 23, this volume).

Entering the religion and religious community

There are two ways Muslim jurists understood how one is deemed to be Muslim, namely birth and conversion. When one is born to a father who is Muslim, jurists presumed that the children were also Muslim. A child's faith follows the father's, not the mother's (Tucker, 1998: 117). To understand the gendered operation of this rule requires examining certain marital rules and restrictions. Generally, Muslim men are legally permitted to marry non-Muslim women who belong to the so-called Abrahamic communities (i.e. Jews and Christians), collectively referred to as the People of the Book (*ahl al-kitab*). Muslim women, however, are prohibited as a matter of law from marrying a man who is not Muslim (Esposito, 2001: 19). Consequently, to the extent a Muslim man's marriage to a non-Muslim woman was legally recognized, so too was the Muslim identity of their children. But given the exceptional and illicit situation of a Muslim woman marrying a non-Muslim man, their offspring were not deemed to be within the community of Muslims.

The second path of entry is conversion. There are different views of what is necessary for conversion. For some, a potential convert must take some time to understand the religion and accept the unity of God. But the *sine qua non* of conversion is the declaration of faith, namely the *shahada*: 'There is no god, but God and Muhammad is his Prophet' (*la ilaha illa Allah, wa Muhammad rasul Allah*). One's conversion to Islam is effected by this declaration. But given that ritual performances have socio-political implications (Freidenreich, 2011), it is necessary to emphasize that political inclusion in the community of Muslims requires that the *shahada* be made in front of witnesses (Alavi, 2007: 9).

Making this declaration of faith has a range of implications for the new Muslim. For instance, pronunciation of this declaration implies immediate conversion, with all the benefits and obligations that being Muslim entails. So for instance, in a *hadith* ascribed to the Prophet Muhammad, we encounter a hypothetical about an enemy soldier on the field of battle fighting against a Muslim soldier who is on the verge of striking a death blow to the fallen enemy soldier. If that fallen enemy pronounces the declaration of faith, we are told that his life should be spared.[1] Whether or not this is what happened historically, the significance of the hypothetical lies in its rhetorical emphasis on the radical effect of pronouncing the *shahada*.

Of course, when one converts to Islam, the question that often arises is whether and to what extent is that person obligated to the full scope of Islamic law, in particular the ritual rules of worship such as prayer and fasting, as well as the dietary restrictions around what one can and cannot eat. It may be that a lot depends on whether the history of revelation and obligation remains relevant for today's convert. For instance, suppose a set of rules (e.g. prohibition of alcohol consumption) evolved gradually before becoming finalized in a general prohibition or obligation. Is the modern day convert held to the final rule in an all-or-nothing fashion, or can the modern convert benefit from the gradual process of revelation, as if the process itself is part of the normative system of obligation? The prevailing position will depend, in part, upon how one understands the history of the Prophetic message, and whether that history itself has normative implications for future members of the faith. In the case of alcohol consumption, there are three verses in the Qur'an that address the consumption of alcohol, which were reportedly revealed to the Prophet Muhammad on three separate occasions in the following historical order:

> Q. 4:43: O those who believe, do not come to prayer in a state of intoxication until you can understand what you say [in prayer].
>
> Q. 2:219: They ask you [the Prophet] about wine and gambling. Say [to them] 'In them is much evil and bounty for people, but their evil is greater than their good'.
>
> Q. 5:90–91: O those who believe, indeed wine, gambling, idolatry, and fortune telling using arrows are an evil from Satan. Avoid [this] evil so that you may succeed. Satan wants enmity and hatred to exist among you by means of wine and gambling. He [wants] to keep you from remembering God and from prayer. Will you not abstain?

Each subsequent verse negated (or abrogated) the former, leaving only the third in force. If the historical process of revelation is of no legal significance, then today's convert is held to the general prohibition against alcohol consumption. But if the historical process of revelation is itself part of the normative content of the verses, the convert's legal obligation cannot be reduced to a narrow positivist command, and instead is situated in a contextual process of gradually coming to the faith tradition. On this reading, the verses are read as having been addressed to a nascent community of recent converts, where the gradual scaling up of prohibition is itself part of the normative framework of obligations upon the new Muslim today. A third reading may read the verses not merely as positivist statements of law, or as part of a normative historical process, but rather in the context of Muhammad's changing political role. When Muhammad was preaching in Mecca, the Prophetic mission was one of preaching, conversion, and faith-based commitment. But once he migrated to Medina in 622 and assumed political leadership, the rules of ritual worship were no longer merely private matters of conscience but assumed political content associated with the formation of a new community of subjects. On this reading, anyone entering the faith of Islam was also entering a political community, where membership involved compliance with the full scope of ritual requirements. The third approach and the first approach result in the same outcome, but for different reasons. These three approaches to reading the alcohol prohibition verses, reflect ongoing contests over how we come to know what Islamic law is or requires.

In modern Muslim communities today, conversion intersects with a range of other considerations that affect notions of inclusion and exclusion. In the United States, for instance, conversion among African Americans has generated considerable scholarly interest (Curtis, 2002). However, African American Muslims often note that their 'status' as full fledged members (and especially as leaders) of the US Muslim community is beset by an already toxic history of racism in the United States. At the same time, Muslim Americans of various backgrounds nonetheless perform (if not co-opt) certain cultural, artistic, or musical forms and expressions of Blackness to situate their identity at a time in American history in which the Muslim is marginalized, securitized, and rendered alien if not a threat (Khabeer, 2016). Consequently, we see a lively discourse that distinguishes between white and black converts to Islam, and the problematic space of immigrant Muslims in this US racial binary (Jackson, 2005; see also, Grewal, 2014; Galonnier, 2015). Of particular interest is a controversy concerning the white convert cleric Hamza Yusuf, who in December 2016 made public statements against the Black Lives Matter movement.[2] Black Lives Matter is a social movement in the United States that has protested vigilante violence as well as police brutality and killings of black Americans. Concerned allies and critics considered Yusuf's remarks to be uninformed, a reflection of white privilege, or both.[3] Muslims in the United States of all backgrounds voiced opinions about Yusuf's comments, which were particularly poignant after a year of police shootings of unarmed black men, and the rise of a white supremacist 'Alt-Right' movement that informed a presidential campaign in which the image of the 'Muslim' was contested as either friendly neighbour or threatening spectre.

Leaving the religion and the religious community

Leaving Islam is a more complicated matter, depending on whether and to what extent religion is conceived as purely personal and private, or also and at the same time, highly communal and thereby political. Suppose a Muslim quietly stopped practicing the core rituals of faith (e.g. prayer, fasting, charity, pilgrimage) and no longer believed in the unity of God or the prophecy of Muhammad. If that person lived as a hermit, or in a community of non-Muslims, or simply enjoyed a high degree of privacy and anonymity from those around him, this kind of departure may hardly be noticed by anyone other than the person who believes no more. He may still be an apostate, but only in the eyes of God, and thus occasions no worldly consequences. Indeed, this view is present in various Qur'anic verses that stipulate that the punishment for apostasy is not in this world, but in the hereafter. As Qur'an 16:106 states: 'Whoever disbelieves in God after having believed – not those who are compelled despite their heart being sated in faith, but rather those who open their hearts to disbelief – shall suffer the wrath of God and a great torment'.

But for premodern Muslims the implications of leaving the faith were not purely personal or a matter of conscience; they were also and at the same time communal and political. The relevant political project is the Muslim community, modeled after what has historically been represented as the universal aspiration and ambition of the Islamic message, which took political effect in the lives of people through expansion, conquest, and imperialism (see generally Emon, 2012). The universality of the Islamic message and its political effect through conquest collapsed the idea of the Muslim as believer with the Muslim as political and legal subject. On this approach, apostasy (*irtidad*) is more analogous to relinquishing one's citizenship. At worst, it is an act of treason. It matters little whether one converts from Islam to another religion, or simply leaves the Islamic tradition without adopting another. The point is that the Muslim has left the Islamic faith and, as such, has left the community of believers-cum-citizens. For this reason, it is not surprising that jurists considered apostasy to violate what they called a 'right of God', which the Hanafis defined as aimed at ridding the world of evil. To commit apostasy was to bring evil or corruption into the world, and thereby adversely affect the public weal (Heffening, 2012).[4]

The legal consequences for apostasy are punitive and can be severe. There is a conflict in the early literature (e.g. *akhbar* and *athar*) about whether the apostate must be given a chance to repent. Some early traditions indicate that the apostate must be executed immediately when apprehended. Others grant the apostate a period during which he may be counselled to recant his apostasy and return to the fold of Islam. But in the *fiqh* tradition, which represents a later stage of doctrinal development, there is unanimity that the male apostate must be executed as long as he has reached the age of majority, has his full mental capacities, and has not committed apostasy under duress. The *fiqh* on female apostates features more disagreement between the early jurists. Hanafi and Shi'a jurists required that a female apostate be imprisoned until she recants her apostasy, whereas the Shafi'is, Malikis, and Hanbalis demanded that she be executed.[5]

In addition to the punitive sanction against the apostate, there are a range of ancillary legal effects on the body and interests of the apostate. An apostate who has been executed shall not be buried along with other Muslims or enjoy the Muslim burial rites. According to some jurists, any property the apostate owned in Muslim-ruled lands shall be confiscated by the governing authorities, whereas other jurists allocate the property to the apostate's heirs.

Today, many debate whether apostasy remains part of the Islamic legal tradition, and in particular whether and to what extent it should inform Muslim majority state legal systems. In the 1990s in Egypt, a group of conservative religious authorities initiated a legal proceeding to divorce Nasr Hamid Abu Zayd from his wife on the grounds that his academic writing on the Qur'an effectively rendered him an apostate (Berger, 2003; Olsson, 2008). In 2006, Afghanistan prosecuted one of its citizens for committing apostasy. More recently, Morocco's religious establishment reversed its earlier position and declared apostasy should no longer be subject to capital punishment, and redefined the crime as approximating high treason.[6] For some, the ongoing legal salience of apostasy in some Muslim majority states' legal systems runs contrary to the various human rights conventions and treaties that these countries have signed and ratified (see, for example, Barry, 2009). It flies in the face of the Universal Declaration of Human Rights, in which religion is understood as personal, private, and a matter of conscience. But such critiques fail to appreciate the political work that apostasy does in making the state possible. As Abdullah Saeed (2011) suggests, apostasy provisions in Islam coincide with the imperial project of Islam, and it had the effect of silencing dissenters.

For modern critics, the legal consequences of apostasy conflict directly with more contemporary human rights' approaches to religious freedom. But from a different, ironic, angle, this presumed contrast between apostasy in Islam and religious freedom in human rights today becomes a comparison. I compare apostasy in Islam to religious freedom in the language of human rights, because in both cases, what we are calling 'religion' is also intimately tied to a political project of community or the state. Winnifred Sullivan (2007) has expertly shown how the claim of a universal, absolutist commitment to religious freedom in the shadow of the regulatory state is hubris at best, impossible at worst. As recent decisions from the European Court of Human Rights suggest, when we litigate religious freedom claims in a modern constitutional state legal system, we often confront the fact that the freedoms of belief and conscience are not absolute (Bhuta, 2012). They are subject to regulation in large part because of the political implications of observing religious rituals that intersect with (if not interfere with) a public space subject to an avowedly secular governmental approach. For instance, when the European Court of Human Rights held in *Sahin v Turkey* that Leyla Sahin could not attend a Turkish medical school wearing the headscarf, it was in part because the symbolic space of the university was designed to signal certain core values of the Turkish state, in this case secularism and democracy.[7] In *Dahlab v. Switzerland*, when Ms. Dahlab learned she did not enjoy the religious freedom to teach in a Swiss primary school wearing the headscarf, the school became a public space whose symbolic content both informed and was informed by the secular state project of Switzerland.[8] In other words, these cases reveal the way in which regulating religion is intimately tied to a political project of the secular state.

These examples from the European Court of Human Rights suggest that when apostasy is critiqued from the vantage point of human rights, what goes unidentified or unaddressed is the work of 'secularism' in fashioning what counts as religion, law, and the state. Secularism, on this critical reading, aims to de-politicize the religious and thereby render it to the margins of political life. But, as others have shown, apostasy rules serve the interests of the Muslim majority state by operating as a litmus test for evaluating the state's legitimacy as a political project, in this case Islamic, worthy of the Muslim citizen's compliance (Agrama, 2012; Mahmood, 2015).

Rights and obligations of adherents

Muslims who believe in God and consider themselves members of the Muslim community are considered to be obligated to the ritual obligations and laws of Islam, known in Arabic as Shari'a. Shari'a can mean different things. Lexically, it means the path to the watering hole. In a theological vein, it refers to the law of God, or more specifically the law in the mind of God. On this second reading, Shari'a is epistemically out of reach of human interpreters, given the theological perfection and omniscience of God and the infallibility of humanity (Emon, 2012: 7–12). Consequently, many would argue that the relevant body of Islamic law is contained in treatises of *fiqh*.

Fiqh is a curious term of art, let alone genre of literature, in Islamic legal history. In the *Encyclopedia of Islam* (second edition), *fiqh* is initially defined as 'understanding, knowledge, intelligence', but is later specified for its technical legal use to mean 'jurisprudence', specifically the legal doctrinal jurisprudence of Islamic law. Its scope is wide:

> [i]n addition to the laws regulating ritual and religious observances (*'ibādāt*), containing orders and prohibitions, it includes the whole field of family law, the law of inheritance, of property and contracts and obligations, in a word provisions for all the legal questions that arise in social life (*mu'āmalāt*); it also includes criminal law and procedure, and finally constitutional law and laws regulating the administration of the state and the conduct of war.
>
> *(Schacht and Goldziher, 2012)*

Often the terms *fiqh* and *furu*ʿ (branches) are used to refer to the same doctrinal corpus. In fact, the *Encyclopedia of Islam* entry for *furu*ʿ directs the reader to the entry for '*fikh*'. *Fiqh* as a genre of legal literature reflects such a wide scope of subject matter that this is not the appropriate place to discuss what it is or its scope of application to Muslims in different contexts.

Within that genre, however, jurists recognized that different substantive rules had different implications for the interests of litigants. Premodern Muslim jurists distinguished between two types of rules. The first they called the *huquq Allah* or the 'rights of God'. These were not so much 'rights' that inhered in God, but rather a set of rules that had important implications for public policy or public order. Within this category fell rules on criminal law and punishment, for instance. Premodern jurists recognized that criminal law and punishment had both retributive and deterrent effects, and so must be understood as not being simply about a personal, individual injury to a particular victim, but rather as posing a more general, systemic injury to society. The second type of rule fell into the category they called *huquq al-ʿibad* or *huquq al-nas*, which has been translated as rights of individuals or even human rights. These might include substantive rules on property, contract, and personal injury. It may also be that some substantive rules have a mix of both individual interests as captured by the *huquq al-ʿibad* category, as well as a public order dimension as reflected in the *huquq Allah*. Jurists argued that the criminal punishment for sexual slander (*qadhf*) is one such mixed right (Emon, 2006).

It is tempting to infer from the *huquq Allah* and *huquq al-ʿibad* distinction a premodern conception of 'right'. A more conceptually appealing approach is reflected in Wesley Newcombe Hohfeld's taxonomy of jural composites that, in the aggregate, help explain rights debates and analyses (Hohfeld, 1920). For instance, Hohfeld held that rights and duties are mutually constitutive and correlated with each other, but that not every claim or interest is easily understood in the abstract sense of 'right'. A Hohfeldian approach to rights, claims, and legal reasoning help inform how different rules that, for example, fall within the *huquq Allah* (e.g. sexual slander (*qadfh*), theft (*sariqa*), and other *ḥudud* penalties) reflect the sometimes competing interests between individuals (whether claimant or wrongdoer), and between individuals and the ruling authority (e.g. deterrence, retribution, compensation, social standing, and reputation). For instance, the Maliki school of law granted standing to witnesses of *qadfh* to file a claim with the authorities. If *qadhf* were merely a private right or claim interest, only the victim should have standing. But because the Malikis understood *qadhf* as a mixed right, they created procedural rules that reflected a public commitment to combat certain social ills, even if doing so also subjected the victim's reputation to public scrutiny against the victim's personal preference. As another example, Shafiʿis and Hanbalis granted a theft victim to seek compensation (*ḥaqq al-ʿibad*) *and* permitted the ruling authority to amputate the thief's hand (*ḥaqq Allāh*). Ḥanafīs, however, only permitted one or the other, while the Maliki's only allowed for both depending on the financial ability of the thief to pay compensation. These different approaches reflected different legal balances between the interests of victims, defendants, and the ruling authority in service of a presumed public order. The juristic distinction between *huquq Allah* and *huquq al-ʿibad* offers a compelling legal heuristic to address the complex dynamics that underlie the operation of what modern legal scholars would call 'rights'.

More contemporary debate on Islam and Islamic law, however, does not focus on this premodern distinction. Rather, and perhaps more pertinent for this volume, a discussion of rights and Islamic law requires that we unpack questions about whether and to what extent one's commitment to Islam (and presumably to Islamic law) poses a challenge or conflict with the Muslim's obedience to and compliance with specifically the law of modern states, especially in countries where Muslims live as minorities. This presumed challenge assumes a particularly poignant place in our contemporary legal landscape, as security agencies, public safety departments, and justice departments around the world utilize the case of the Muslim extremist as the paradigm for assessing the efficacy of domestic and international anti-terrorism policies. In a notorious report, security analysts in the United States claim that Shari'a is the next great threat to the United States. They propose using Muslim Americans' adherence to Shari'a as a litmus test for the threat they pose to the republic. The report relies on a range of assumptions that posit the 'Muslim' as somehow distinct from any other religious community (Center for Security Policy, 2010). But as M. Steven Fish (2011) has shown through a fascinating analysis of polling data around the world, Muslims are not distinctively religious, nor distinctively committed to abiding by religious requirements, compared to any other religious community. They are no less capable than any other religiously identifiable group of self-interested, profit-maximizing, and rational behaviour when weighing faith commitments against the pragmatic demands of their situation.

The presumption that someone who self-identifies as a Muslim must somehow be committed to Shari'a in an all-or-nothing fashion implicitly views the individual through the lens of a single aspect of their identity in order to distinguish them from others.[9] The reality is that Muslims make choices every day that cannot be reduced to their religious pedigree. They make choices that may even pose challenges to their tradition as they navigate a complex world. Moreover, unless they live in a Muslim majority state with legislation that implements an aspect of the historical Islamic legal tradition, 'Islam' does not make a claim upon Muslims in the same formal way that the state, with its monopoly over coercive institutions, makes a claim upon them as citizens or legal subjects. Muslim compliance with Shari'a is a product of informal modes of coercion and persuasion that exist alongside a range of factors, including but not limited to cultural mores, economic incentives, and the formal legal system of the state.

Agency in a pluralist normative context begs the question of whether and to what extent informal norms of Islamic law may or may not affect the scope to which the Muslim subject can partake of the full range of formal legal entitlements, rights, and freedoms in a liberal and democratic society. This, it seems, is the heart of the current state of angst on Islam and Muslims within topics like multiculturalism, militant democracy, immigration and citizenship, and so on (see, for instance, Emon, 2009). The answer to this question demands not only that we inquire into what Islamic law says or requires but also how Islamic law gets invoked, framed, and represented within the state in which Muslims live.

For example, suppose a Muslim man and woman living in New York wish to marry. Under Islamic law, marriage is solemnized through a contract (*'aqd al-nikah*). A valid contract is formed when three elements are met: offer, acceptance, and an exchange of a *mahr* or dowry (Esposito, 2001: 16, 23). The *mahr* is either a financial sum or property given by the husband to the wife in anticipation of marriage. A Muslim couple may consecrate their marriage with this form of Islamic contract and also register their marriage with the state registrar of marriages. This approach, which blends the informal and the formal, represents a parallel approach to solemnizing marriage that conforms with both Islamic law and state law. Now suppose that same husband and wife begin divorce proceedings. Prior to the distribution of the marital estate, the wife asks the court to first allocate to her the full amount of the *mahr*, and only thereafter dissolve the estate pursuant to the state's guidelines for marital estate distribution upon divorce. Will the court enforce the *mahr* provision? As Natasha Bakht (2015) has shown, courts in the United States and Canada are inconsistent on this matter. For some, the *mahr* is a religious provision that a secular court cannot enforce. For others, the *mahr* is akin to a prenuptial agreement and enforceable on domestic contract law grounds (Bakht, 2015). Moreover, one cannot discount policy considerations in community property jurisdictions, in which the marital estate is deemed, for public policy reasons of gender equality, to be split in half between the two parties. To enforce the *mahr* would privilege one party over the other despite the public policy of community property regimes to ensure an even split of the estate between the two parties. In this context, what is a Muslim to do? In jurisdictions that enforce the *mahr*, there is little problem in pursuing a parallel approach to consecrating a marriage. But in a jurisdiction that does not enforce the *mahr*, either the Muslim couple forgoes the Islamic marriage contract, or they form the Islamic contract for symbolic purposes. Even then, if the parties are aware that the *mahr* payment will not be enforced, including it in the Islamic marriage contract constitutes an illusory promise. Arguably, Muslims living in that jurisdiction must contend with this legal problem as a matter of *de novo* reflection on what Islamic law is and what it can be in the context of that specific jurisdiction. This hypothetical, in other words, reveals how the interaction between both legal traditions (one formal, the other informal) is neither a one-way street nor a zero-sum game, but rather demands critical analysis by those who operate in both traditions.

Part of the needed critical analysis requires an assessment by and for Muslims about the nature, content, and aspiration of Islamic law for Muslim minorities living in liberal democratic polities. So much of the historic tradition of Islamic law was framed for a polity in which Muslims were both rulers and the demographic majority. But today's Muslims living as a minority must contend with the implications for Islamic law of a post-colonial context in which European ideas have penetrated the Muslim majority world, and a globalized world in which Muslims have migrated for education, employment, and a safe place to raise their families. Legal lacuna in the historical tradition make themselves felt across a range of issues. Indeed, contemporary Muslims debate these lacunae when they invoke the novel category of *fiqh al-waqi*ʿ (the law for the situation). This Arabic phrase is a terminological placeholder for the absence of *fiqh* in a context that is radically different from the reality of premodern Muslim jurists (Judy, 2004). A subcategory of this concern with *fiqh* as lacuna is the vibrant topic of the *fiqh* of Muslim minorities (*fiqh al-mustaqilla*). This is a more recent development that scholars have addressed given both conversion to Islam in Europe and North America, and immigration to these regions in the latter half of the 20th century (March, 2006; Caeiro, 2010). Both topics provide conceptual sites for compelling debates on orthopraxy for and in Muslim communities in the modern world where (a) the speed of technological development (e.g. transportation, internet, etc.) has changed the experience of living in and moving around the world, and (b) Muslims are dispersed across borders, living in varying political, economic, and social circumstances as minorities or majorities in different nation-states. The approach to this new *fiqh* of Muslim minorities offers a range of approaches for Muslims living in, for example, Europe who must enact their agency in the context of formal law posited by the state, and the informal norms of an Islamic legal tradition that may not have the relevant content to guide action in fundamentally altered political, cultural, and social contexts.

Among various issues that this new *fiqh* for minorities addresses are basic economic issues such as commercial banking, mortgages, and interest. Advocates of Islamic financing use historical contract doctrines to inform a range of financial products that presumably comply with Qur'anic principles against interest and overt speculation. Critics of this Islamic finance regime, such as Mahmoud El-Gamal, argue that Islamic financing does not, in practice, achieve an equitable distribution of risk and equity. Rather, as El-Gamal (2006: xi, 178) argues, 'Islamic finance has placed excessive emphasis on contract forms, thus becoming a primary target for rent-seeking legal arbitrageurs' chasing the conventional financial market'. Timur Kuran (2004: 33) draws on the neo-classical economics of F. Hayek to suggest that the telos of an Islamic economics as a just distribution of equity, risk, or resources is little more than a 'false conceit'. The most common critique, however, is that the various techniques to facilitate an interest-free banking or financial regime do not, in fact, avoid interest. The *murabaha* contract is often singled out for this critique. Advocates of Islamic finance would call *murabaha* a contractually based sale with a price markup. But this is only possible because of the two contracts involved in the transaction. In the case of a home mortgage formalized under a *murabaha* contract, the bank purchases a home from the seller for $100,000. It then turns around and sells that same home to the buyer for $120,000 in monthly instalments paid over the course of a set of years. Technically, each contract is valid on its own terms. But taken together, it is hard not to see the price-markup as equivalent to interest-based financing. While one can argue that the bank assumes the full risk of home ownership pursuant to the first contract, that equity interest may be illusory where the two contracts are formed within seconds of each other to facilitate the sale of the house by the seller to the buyer. Despite this critique, Islamic finance continues to grow, expanding its reach to Muslim communities in North America and Europe. It chases the returns on conventional financial products while sanctifying various financial products with the brand of 'halal'.

The limited scope of this critique of Islamic finance stands in stark contrast to the numerous critiques directed at Islamic law on gender grounds. From feminist scholars to human rights advocates, all take aim at the overt patriarchy across a range of issues in Islamic law (e.g. marriage, divorce, inheritance, child custody). The sheer volume of critique over such a long period of time makes this point uninteresting and hardly novel. What remains interesting, though, are the unstated assumptions underlying such critiques. For some critics of Islamic patriarchy, one way forward is through secular notions of equality, as articulated in contemporary constitutional documents and human rights declarations. But this embrace of secular equality ignores the hegemonic dynamics that make 'secular' equality seem obvious if not commonsensical. For instance, Ziba Mir-Hosseini (2003) argues that the feminist and human rights critiques remain embedded within a colonialist, hegemonic paradigm that re-instantiates the primacy of the 'West' at the cost of any effective agency internal to the Islamic tradition. For her, Islamic law must be reformed from within by incorporating gender as a mainstream mode of analysis. Consequently we find a contest among reformers of Islamic law about the way forward. For instance, among feminist critiques some are committed to a more secular form of equality. Others who adhere to an 'Islamic feminism' problematize the project of secularism while pursuing a critique that they consider more rooted in the values, ethics, and traditions that emanate from the Islamic tradition.[10]

Notes

1 Bukhari, www.hadithcollection.com/sahihbukhari/116-Sahih%20Bukhari%20Book%2083.%20Blood%20Money%20(Ad-Diyat)/6535-sahih-bukhari-volume-009-book-083-hadith-number-005.html.
2 For a recording of his initial remarks, see NOW, 2016, www.youtube.com/watch?v=uxpKFzskVds.
3 See, for example, Muhammad, 2016, at www.patheos.com/blogs/truthtopower/2016/12/imam-hamza-yusuf-compound-ignorance-white-supremacy/.
4 On the meaning of 'rights of God' generally, see Emon, 2006.
5 For an overview of the various positions, see Heffening, 2012.
6 Jabrane, E. 'Morocco's High Religious Committee Says Apostates Should Not Be Killed'. *Morocco World News*. 6 February 2017. Available at www.moroccoworldnews.com/2017/02/207505/moroccos-high-religious-committee-says-apostates-should-not-be-killed/.

7 *Sahin v. Turkey*. Application no. 44774/98. European Court of Human Rights. 10 November 2005.
8 *Dahlab v. Switzerland*. Application no. 42393/98. European Court of Human Rights. 15 February 2001.
9 On this phenomenon, particularly as it relates to government policy toward Muslim minority groups, see Davidson, 2012; Sen, 2007.
10 For a range of feminist perspectives on Islamic legal reform of patriarchy, see generally, *Islam and Feminism*, Issue 1 of *Contestations: Dialogues on Women's Empowerment*, available at: www.contestations.net/wp-content/uploads/2011/01/contestations1.pdf.

References

Agrama, H. 2012. *Questioning Secularism: Islam, Sovereignty and the Rule of Law in Modern Egypt*. University of Chicago Press.

Alavi, K. 2007. 'Pillars of Religion and Faith' in V. Cornell (ed.) *Voices of Islam, Volume 1 Voices of Tradition*. Praeger. 5.

Bakht, N. 2015. 'The Incorporation of Shari'a in North America: Enforcing the Mahr to Combat Women's Poverty Post-relationship Dissolution' in A. Emon and R. Ahmed (eds) *Oxford Handbook on Islamic Law*. Oxford University Press.

Barry, J. 2009. 'Apostasy, Marriage, and Jurisdiction in Lina Joy: Where was CEDAW?' 41 *New York University Journal of International Law and Politics*. 407.

Berger, M. 2003. 'Apostasy and Public Policy in Contemporary Egypt: An Evaluation of Recent Cases from Egypt's Highest Courts'. 25 *Human Rights Quarterly*. 720.

Bhuta, N. 2012. 'Rethinking the Universality of Human Rights: A Comparative Historical Proposal for the Idea of "Common Ground" with Other Moral Traditions' in A. Emon, M. Ellis and B. Glahn (eds) *Islamic Law and International Human Rights Law: Searching for Common Ground?* Oxford Univesity Press. 123.

Caeiro, A. 2010. 'The Power of European Fatwas: The Minority Fiqh Project and the Making of an Islamic Counterpublic'. 42 *International Journal of Middle East Studies*. 435.

Center for Security Policy. 2010. *Shariah: The Threat to America*. Center for Security Policy.

Curtis, E. 2002. *Islam in Black America: Identity, Liberation, and Difference in African American Islamic Thought*. SUNY Press.

Davidson, N. 2012. *Only Muslim: Embodying Islam in Twentieth-Century France*. Cornell University Press.

El-Gamal, M. 2006. *Islamic Finance: Law, Economics and Practice*. Cambridge University Press.

Emon, A. M. 2006. 'Huquq Allah and Huquq al-'Ibad: A Legal Heuristic for a Natural Rights Regime'. 13 *Islamic Law and Society*. 325.

Emon, A. M. 2009. 'Islamic Law and the Canadian Mosaic: Politics, Jurisprudence, and Multicultural Accommodation'. 87 *Canadian Bar Review*. 391.

Emon, A. M. 2012. *Religious Pluralism and Islamic Law: Dhimmis and Others in the Empire of Law*. Oxford University Press.

Esposito, J, with DeLong-Bas, N. 2001. *Women in Muslim Family Law*. 2nd edn. Syracuse University Press.

Fish, M. S. 2011. *Are Muslims Distinctive? A Look at the Evidence*. Oxford University Press.

Freidenreich, D. 2011. *Foreigners and Their Food: Constructing Otherness in Jewish, Christian and Islamic Law*. University of California Press.

Galonnier, J. 2015. 'The Racialization of Muslims in France and the United States: Some Insights from White Converts to Islam'. 62 *Social Compass*. 570.

Grewal, Z. 2014. *Islam is a Foreign Country: American Muslims and the Global Crisis of Authority*. New York University Press.

Heffening, W. 2012. 'Murtadd' in P. Bearman et al. (eds) *Encylopaedia of Islam*. 2nd edn. Brill.

Hohfeld, W. N. 1920. *Fundamental Legal Conceptions as Applied in Judicial Reasoning, and Other Legal Essay*. Yale University Press.

Jackson, S. 2005. *Islam and the Blackamerican: Looking Toward the Third Resurrection*. Oxford University Press.

Judy, R. 2004. 'Sayyd Qutb's fiqh al-waqii, or New Realist Science'. 31(2) *Boundary*. 113.

Khabeer, S. A. 2016. *Muslim Cool: Race, Religion, and Hip Hop in the United States*. New York University Press.

Kuran, T. 2004. *Islam & Mammon*. Princeton University Press.

Mahmood, S. 2015. *Religious Difference in a Secular Age: A Minority Report*. Princeton University Press.

March, A. 2006. 'Liberal Citizenship and the Search for an Overlapping Consensus: The Case of Muslim Minorities'. 34 *Philosophy and Public Affairs*. 373.
Mir-Hosseini, Z. 2003. 'The Construction of Gender in Islamic Legal Thought and Strategies for Reform'. 1 *Hawwa*. 1.
Olsson, S. 2008. 'Apostasy in Egypt: Contemporary Cases of Ḥisba'. 98 *The Muslim World*. 95.
Saeed, A. 2011. 'Ambiguities of Apostaasy and the Repression of Muslim Dissent'. 9 *The Review of Faith and International Affairs*. 31.
Schacht, J. and Goldziher, I. 2012. 'Fikh' in P. Bearman et al. (eds) *Encylopaedia of Islam*. 2nd edn. Brill.
Sen, A. 2007. *Identity and Violence: The Illusion of Destiny*. W.W. Norton.
Sullivan, W. 2007. *The Impossibility of Religious Freedom*. Princeton University Press.
Tucker, J. 1998. *In the House of the Law: Gender and Islamic Law in Ottoman Syria and Palestine*. University of California Press.

14

Hindu law

Dynamics of belonging and status

Werner Menski and Kalindi Kokal

Introduction

The dynamics of belonging and of status for and among Hindus involve much awareness, in theory and practice, about pluralities and their navigation at all levels. As Flood (2003: 1) highlights, 'questions concerning the relation of Hinduism to state and global politics, to the individual, and to the politics of identity are of great relevance to Hindus everywhere'. Our main aim here is first to describe and explain how adherents enter and leave the religious traditions of Hinduism, what social and legal frameworks exist, what associated religious rites one may need to be aware of, and what tensions may arise. Regarding the rights and obligations that membership entails, we address limitations of rights and entitlements for adherents under various types of law, especially in relation to different forms of discrimination. That topic relates closely to current rights-focused national and international law debates. Since these have tended to be remarkably hostile about Hinduism-related issues, this has not only put Hindus on the defensive and contributes to what is widely perceived as 'Hindu nationalism', often equated with *hindutva* ('Hinduness') ideologies. It also hinders constructive understanding of 'the Hindu other', complicated by various essentialising tendencies in discussing the internally defined key concerns of community members, who are themselves today, as ever, divided in their views. Flood (2003: 1) notes in this regard:

> Secularists in India would wish to see the complete erosion of religion in the public sphere of governance and its relegation to the private realm, while many religious nationalists would wish to see even more growth in the influence of religion in the political and public arena.

Part of this contested use of modernity, then, a concept which involves privileging of 'rationalization, the autonomous individual, capitalism and the nation state' (Smith, 2003: viii), relates more generally to principled opposition towards any form of organised religion, not only Hinduism. It also rejects 'traditional' basic principles of connectedness in concerted efforts to privilege individual autonomy. Further, presuming (rather innocently) that regulation of people's lives through state-centric laws should be strengthened to empower individuals, it cultivates 'modern' visions of human development which seem to dream of enlightened autonomous individual action as the driving engine. On the other hand, much traditional thinking, frequently subsumed today under 'Hindu nationalist' labels, would favour the religiously infused socio-cultural identity of individuals as integral parts of groups, allowing patterns of self-controlled ordering at various levels that leave both individuals and communities more leeway and discretion for all kinds of day-to-day actions, with less direct state involvement. Continuing to perceive modern state law as a somewhat inferior mechanism and tool for maintaining some higher order than state-centric law, this can still fall under broad 'rule of law' structures, but has not lost sight of deeper roots and patterns of connectivity, which modern Enlightenment thinking has sought to break. In what ways this struggle, at various levels, is post-modern, and/or to what extent it feeds from certain 'traditional' and 'religious' value-based judgements and perceptions that privilege social and ethical norms over more strictly legal spheres and rules, remains to be seen from case to case.

Entering the religion

While as a philosopher and insider, Sharma (1996: 61) simply states that 'the pluralistic nature of Hinduism is well known', Derrett (1968: 330) in a historically informed legal analysis observed:

> The Congress Party, in its pre-Independence manoeuvres, established the theory that all 'Hindus' form one community. In the sphere of religion this was more than questionable, but in the field of law it was patently false. Not only had several 'schools' of Hindu law developed from the ancient texts and the judicial interpretation of their rules, but various High Courts interpreted the law differently. Customs at variance with the book law were widespread and irreconcilably diverse, yet they were in some parts of India predominant, and in the rest of India were enormously important.

While the general thrust of scholarship goes against making assertions about a unified Hinduism stretching into the ancient past (Flood, 2003: 10), there are also scholarly claims, not just about the centrality of textual traditions and their exegesis (Flood, 2003: 10) but more pertinently here about essentialising understandings and usage of core conceptual elements from within 'Hindu' traditions and religion that cannot be just brushed aside or declared politically incorrect. Sharma (2004: 36) clearly confirms that the Hindu view of human rights 'starts out not with the individual but from the cosmos'. This starting point concerns above all ancient, effectively global, visions of macrocosmic and microcosmic ordering, specifically the *rita/satya* and *dharma* complexes (Miller, 1985; Menski, 2003: 86–93, 2006: 204–209), which underpin what became later known as 'Hinduism' and 'Hindu law'. They incorporate all aspects of creation into a web of interconnectivity, in which every individual entity plays a role and has a place. We further explore the practical effects of this basic essentialising at various points later, accepting in principle that this ambivalently instrumentalised essentialism (especially in light of recent abuses of *Hindutva* ideology and also earlier patterns of systematic discriminations based on caste and gender, among others), seems to be an important part of Hinduism (see also Smith, 2003: viii).

Surely, critical caution seems advisable, especially regarding scholarly methodology, practice and politics. While assessing any Hindu concepts, philological methods assume particular relevance, given the – albeit elitist – foundational structure of ancient texts. Yet these indological methodologies, too, remain highly contested and are under review (Flood, 2003: 11). Here, too, major problems arise through scholarly and popular essentialisations of the deep internal pluralities within all key concepts related to Hindu culture and Hinduism. While even the basic core notions and implications of *rita/satya* and *dharma* are extremely dynamic and context-sensitive, however, any specific sub-concepts used in Sanskrit and various other related languages can clearly mean many different things.[1] Sanskrit, an ancient language of utmost sophistication, allowed skilful hiding of pluralising evidence in all spheres, often related to earlier developments in traditional societies that scholars struggle to rediscover today.[2] Presumptions that certain textual elements, even down to the level of individual syllables, may be more authoritative or 'correct' than others, will always need to be scrutinised. They could be clerical errors, so to say, but changed wordings may reflect complex ritual changes, internal processes of differentiation that could lead to exclusionary mechanisms for certain individuals or groups that failed to follow such innovations. Western presumptions about stagnation in 'traditional' societies, thus, form potential mental blocks, even today, for deeper understanding of the intricate connections between textual detail, socio-ritual normativity, and patterns of internal flexibility and change within Hindu cultures.

Given such complexities regarding entry to the primary textual sources, it is instructive to start the present discussion about 'that nebulous abstraction' (Flood, 2003: 1) called Hinduism with what is published in major dictionary entries. Hinnells (1995: 211) begins with a somewhat circular definition for Hinduism, 'the name given to the highly diverse religious tradition that has evolved in India over the last 3,000 years and is today represented by the beliefs and practices of well over 500 million Hindus'. While counting numbers can quickly lead to highly politicised discussions, sparking much disagreement over who actually belongs and who not,[3] helpfully, this entry immediately goes on to explain that:

> [d]iversity is the key to understanding the religious life of Hindus since Hinduism is not a unity, having no 'founder', no single creed, no single universally accepted scripture, no single moral code or theological system, nor a single concept of god central to it.
>
> *(Hinnells, 1995: 211)*

Further, as the same source continues:

> It is rather a tradition that embraces a wide variety of religious positions, incorporating both small local cults that may be known to only a few villages, to major sects like Vaishnavism, Shaivism and Shaktism that have millions of adherents, rich mythologies, temples, iconographies and theologies, each of which could be considered a 'religion' in its own right.

In other strands of secondary literature, this immense diversity is colourfully depicted through numerous images. For example, Lipner (1998: xv) argues that understanding the living realities of India's major religious system certainly requires awareness of the deep Hindu roots of this huge polycentric banyan tree. Flood (2003: 2) pinpoints that from a Hindu nationalist perspective, 'Hinduism has an essence manifested in multiple forms', while Michaels (2004: 12) reports on widespread doubts whether there was ever something that one could label 'Hindu'. Going down that route, however, would throw the baby out with the bathwater, for it is undeniable that something, however diffuse, confused and confusing, does exist and may be called 'Hinduism'. Flood (2003: 8) confirms that despite much scepticism among scholars about the category 'Hinduism' and even 'Hindu', 'both terms are here to stay and indeed can be meaningfully used'.

Given the close connection of anything 'Hindu' with identity, Hindu law cannot neatly segregate 'religion', 'culture' and 'law' (Menski, 2012). As 'belonging' means many different things to people in various contexts, a plurality-conscious methodology, strongly reflected in lived practice, involves complex amalgamations at all levels, connecting various forms of belief, practice and understanding or consciousness. This affects every Hindu community, clan, family and individual, all inevitably enmeshed in this complex global superstructure with many glocal manifestations which outsiders struggle to unravel.

Hindu internal diversity is prominently depicted in academic literature. Lipner (1998: 5) asserts that the huge banyan tree of Hinduism could never be cut down by legal intervention and will always grow new shoots. Such images also convey that Hinduism as a family of culturally similar traditions is marked by unity-in-diversity (Lipner, 1998: 6), a phrase also widely used by lawyers (see Derrett, 1968: 330–338). Since Hinduism is 'not a homogenous religion at all, but is rather a potpourri of religions, doctrines and attitudes towards life, rites and cults, moral and social norms' (Michaels, 2004: 3), it seems more like a collection of ways of life rather than a religion. Such assertions also identify the existence of internal boundaries that may then only be crossed at certain costs.

An earlier dictionary of Hinduism (Stutley and Stutley, 1977: xvii) states that it 'is now generally used as a term to summarize the aspirations – both unsophisticated and intellectual – of the majority of the Indian people. But any simple definition of it is difficult, perhaps impossible'. Again, this reflects clear-cut realisation that Hinduism is a rather different kind of religion than Christianity or Islam. An entity of such massive and quite diffuse dimensions will always have had many entry and exit points of religious and ritual relevance, also since it never existed in a closed space. From earliest times, people who were not fully committed Hindus (if one could even define what that means) would encounter its emerging elements as something to either embrace or reject, or to merely adopt partially. Complex local processes of incomplete and gradual Hinduisation resulted in confusingly rich varieties of 'traditions'. This generates practical predicaments even today, when an individual may claim conversion to Hinduism, only to be faced with credibility challenges.[4] In India itself, the recent controversy over reconversions (*ghar wapsi*) organised by Rashtriya Swayamsevak Sangh (RSS) outfits, encouraging Muslims and Christians to 'reconvert' to Hinduism, raised several such questions. These RSS outfits believed that people they encouraged to 'reconvert' were forced to become Muslims and Christians, first during the time of Moghul rulers and then under British colonial rule.

While there may be no real barriers, any Hindu individual may at certain moments be asked to enter or leave a specific local or sectarian community even within Hinduism, given that there are so many internal boundaries, especially in today's modern *guru*-focused cults. Simple rituals of incorporation might provide a remedy, sometimes on the spot. Given the importance of rituals and purity in daily life cycles, individuals may need to undergo certain rites of purification to be allowed to enter a certain ritual space or arena. But at other times there seems to be complete openness.

Recent huge controversies in India, including court cases, about the rights of Hindu women who might be polluted by menstruation to enter certain major temples reflect such boundary struggles.[5] Blood-related pollution, an ancient source of anxiety, picked up today for political purposes, relates historically also to temple entry barriers for low caste persons or formerly perceived 'untouchables'. Today such controversies tend to be exploited by rights-focused activists, especially those who hate 'religion' per se and wish to impose rules of secularised equality on all domains of the public space. The term 'Hindu', Flood (2003: 8–9) observes, 'has notably become charged with cultural and political meaning and arouses strong feelings when its integrity is apparently threatened, as, for example, by the controversial claim that Hindus have been beef eaters at times in their history'.[6]

While there is strong evidence of Hindu majoritarian political essentialism, there are clearly many dissenting voices of Dalits and other low caste Hindus (Flood, 2003: 9). Subsumed under various forms of so-called Adi movements (Gundimeda, 2016), they tend to claim that non-mainstream voices and practices have equal if not older rights to recognition of various entitlements, not only regarding the modern nation state and its formal constitutional guarantees but also respect for their culture (Jangam, 2016; Singh, 2016). The intense politicisation of anything to do with caste, Hindu nationalism and Hindu identity generally has given rise to a huge literature full of claims and counter-claims about belonging or not belonging to 'Hinduism' (see Flood, 2003: 9).

Globalising Hindu essentialism forms an invisible backdrop in such contests. Since ancient times, the largest possible picture with regard to belonging can be drawn really widely, in that some Hindus may argue (as actually many Muslims do for their faith, too) that everyone is really a Hindu, people are just not aware of this. Such views are not necessarily 'fundamentalist' in a negatively aggressive way. Feeding on ancient concepts of connectivity, they might merely reflect the strong underlying macrocosmic, and hence almost totalitarian, reach of the foundational concept of interconnectedness, linking not only every human but all other elements of creation into one huge network of relationships. In its Hindu manifestations, this perception as an initially macrocosmic vision, based on Nature (Miller, 1985; Menski, 2003: 86–93), does not discriminate between people of different religions and perceives everyone and everything as exposed to the same risks arising from the potentially destructive forces of Nature, against which some form of insurance, ritual or otherwise, may then be sought by seeking refuge in 'religion'. Later developments of what may be called 'classical' Hindu conceptualisations, oscillating around microcosmic *dharma*, still quite radically privilege total inequality-cum-interconnectedness, arguing in principle that all individuals are entities in their own right, at any moment of time, but remain at the same time inextricably connected to everything else around them, too. As a direct result, it seems, many Hindus prefer vegetarian diets, as they would not wish to eat another living being, given the possibility of humans being reborn as animals, provided of course one believes in this principle of rebirth itself. Such perceptions of connectedness cause grave concern to more extremist protagonists of non-violence, including monks, nuns and various forms of 'renouncers', who would even worry about eating dry nuts and seeds, which still contain some form of life. Various extremes of theoretical possibilities would, thus, need to be matched with the practicalities of life.

It remains thus possible to argue rationally that one is simply born a Hindu and can never really, as discussed further later, leave the religion, even if one adopted another faith. At the same time, it is common to find enormously varying perceptions and practices of socially coloured rituals of incorporation and inclusion for new-born children and, later, marking entry to the stage of pupilhood (*brahmacarya*), the so-called thread-ceremonies. Given the tensions between preferences for 'right belief', 'right thought' and 'right action', however, Hindus have no agreed guidance, policy or practice for any of this either. Certainly, Hinduism as a whole does not know or demand a formal ritual of baptism to mark an individual's allegiance to the faith,[7] again reinforcing silent presumptions that one is already born a Hindu anyway.

An important early study on the various ritual elements (*samskāras*) of a Hindu's life from conception to death, while significantly not carrying an index entry on 'baptism', includes several ritual stages from birth ceremonies to the piercing of the baby's ears (Pandey, 1969: 70–105). This richly illustrates how deeply concerned various Hindu societies became over time to develop certain rituals of incorporation that would gradually involve a young person more visibly into the respective family and/or wider community. Flood (2003: 6) observes:

> Traditionally, ritual has constrained a Hindu's life from birth through marriage to death in the life-cycle rites (*samskāras*) and ritual orders social relationships and relationships with

> divine, embodied beings, the gods of temple and shrine. Ritual is passed through the generations from teacher to student and from mother to child, and while ritual changes, it does so at a much slower rate than other social forms. The relationship between ritual and social history is difficult to assess.

The rich textual sources examined by Pandey (1969) confirm that the liminal phase of child birth, with all its wonders about the miracles of conception and birth, and its risks for young babies and their mothers, reflects grave apprehensions of dangers, giving rise to various taboos and increasingly complex rituals. Pandey (1969: 70) argues that birth ceremonies were developed over time to protect especially the mother and the child. Such ceremonies took on many local socio-cultural features and were not purely 'religious' rituals of entry into a faith community.

Birth rituals immediately connect the new-born to the line of ancestors (Pandey, 1969: 73–74) and are as important for the whole family as for the new-born child, especially males. Rituals to enhance the child's intellectual well-being form part of the ceremonies (Pandey, 1969: 74), as do ritual elements, with plenty of magic, that stress longevity and good health (Pandey, 1969: 75–76). Naming rituals are covered next, as 'the Hindus very early realized the importance of naming persons and converted the system of naming into a religious ceremony' (Pandey, 1969: 78). In the various dimensions and aspects of naming, too, Hinduisation processes may be identified. Indeed Pandey (1969: 79) suggests that name-giving 'was more a custom than a ceremony in the beginning', as reflected in various layers of ritual literature. Here we also find suggestions that auspicious name-giving distinguished the Aryans from 'the non-Aryan peoples with whom the Aryans were not willing to form matrimonial relations' (Pandey, 1969: 81). Further, caste-related differentiation patterns of naming are identified as important, as the idea of caste was deep-rooted in the Hindu mind (Pandey, 1969: 81). Yet there will always have been disagreement over whether birth in a particular family really made a child's future a foregone conclusion. Notably, at this point, Pandey (1969: 81) adds a comparative comment, claiming that the caste complex was not peculiar to ancient Hindus alone and was still prevalent also among other Indo-European peoples.

Naming practices, linked mainly to the early days of a child's life, utilised complex strategies to reflect the multiple interconnectedness of new-born persons with everything around them, the lunar constellation, the time of the month, the family deity, and they also provided an individual popular name (Pandey, 1969: 82–84). Meticulous attention to detail reflected awareness that this individual's identity and ideal positioning would be largely reflected through this name-giving. Hence it is often possible, even today, to identify instantly from a person's name what kind of Hindu s/he may be. In some specific cases, though, unusual or awkward names may have been chosen for certain ritual reasons.

Later in a Hindu baby's life, cutting the young child's hair has both pollution-related as well as religious motivations, probably since Vedic times, basically connected to hopes for good health and long life (Pandey, 1969: 94–101). Overall, Pandey's important study clearly identifies these early life cycle rituals as dramatic ritualisations of the intense connectedness of individuals to everything around them. They 'were the expression of human beliefs, sentiments, aspirations, hopes and fears, and they catered for human needs' (Pandey, 1969: 280). Even in advanced modernity, the 'origin of life, its constituents and their combinations are still puzzling the human mind, and there does not seem to be any possibility of solving the central problem of life satisfactorily' (Pandey, 1969: 281). Pandey (1969: 281) even cited Albert Einstein at the very end of his book to reinforce an underlying feeling of true religiousness as a matter of highly intelligent coping with the reality of connectedness. At the same time it is made very clear that there is no uniformity of Hindu life cycle ritualisations, as much depends on the respective sociocultural context. Hinnells (1995: 213) similarly concludes his above-quoted entry, claiming that:

> Hinduism as a single religious universe is affirmed whenever a Hindu accepts as a fellow Hindu someone with beliefs and practices that differs substantially from his or her own, and it is this self-identity, rather than a community of doctrine and practice, that gives Hinduism the cohesion and coalescence of a great world religion.

Hindus are therefore extremely aware of difference and can be extremely discriminatory among themselves, mainly based on caste (*varna* or *jati*), particularly also relating to perceived or actual pollution of 'the other'. One sees here, again, glimpses of the underlying sense of macrocosmic and microcosmic order (Menski, 2003), suggesting fundamental idealised obligations of pluralist management of diversity of religions and laws, perceived in theory, managed in practice and executed in a conscious manner, as a constant necessity to avoid chaos. Latent fears of grave disorder and hence chaos seem widespread among Hindus even today (Naipaul, 2011: 15). Earlier apprehensions are strongly reflected in old Hindu notions of *kaliyuga*, a well-known term for the ongoing age of confusion and chaos. Another ancient concept depicts the potentially grave harm of ultimately self-destructive *mātsyanyāya*, 'rule of fish' (Sen, 2009: 20) or rather more drastically 'shark rule' (Menski, 2016: 303). The duty of avoiding this kind of fatal chaos scenario implicates all human actions and agency in self-interested concern about the sustainable (as we tend to call it today) future of the world. This does not suggest a completely fatalistic Hindu perspective which grants humans no agency. In fact, it demands exactly the opposite. The ancient key concept of *karma*, the basic principle that all action results in consequences, so that any non-action also becomes a form of action, is crucial here. It justifies various forms of Hindu ritualisation and constantly takes Hindus as a collective body back to the very basics of 'religion' as a back-up insurance mechanism, often in theistic form, given the rather vague recognition of 'something you think of who's controlling the world' (Naipaul, 2011: 13). This big 'It', which for Hindus does not have to be a superhuman He, but is a conceptual supreme force (*brahman*) rather than a supreme divine God-like entity (*Brahma*), underpins the very many sectarian orientations of Hindus worldwide. The birth rituals, as shown, and any later rituals of inclusion that Hindus may have devised, assiduously seek to connect the included individual properly to the entire cosmos. All the rest depends on the fluidity of 'being Hindu' in one's own, very practical, day-to-day way. That different ways of 'being Hindu' contain the potential for denigration of any Hindu 'other' is thus absolutely clear, but should be softened by the latent, humanising awareness of everyone being connected. We know of course that such idealised awareness of liquidity and connectedness was constantly overridden and often cruelly exploited by horrific discriminatory practices among Hindus.

Leaving the religion

In light of the previous section we can be quite brief now, given that direct links to the theme of leaving Hinduism are provided by an important recent historical study of the biopolitics of gender and caste. Gupta (2016: 166–207) presents persuasive evidence that many Hindus saw conversion as an escape route from often gruesome discriminations.[8] Gupta (2016: 166) notes that 'religious conversion has been one of the common expedients resorted to by those at the bottom of caste hierarchies in India, to improve their position, reject stratification, reconfigure social boundaries, and register protest as well as social assertion'. But the act of leaving Hinduism also generated further fuzziness and would rarely constitute a complete break. Gupta (2016:

166–207) also provides amazingly instructive pictorial evidence from the 1920s and 1930s about how conversion led to changes of converts' dress codes, in particular, reflecting new-found status claims. Conversion did not mean complete disappearance from the social environment; it marked various dynamics of status negotiations.

Given the immense internal flexibility of Hindu forms of belief and practice, and the depth of awareness of human interconnectedness, first of all, in principle as well as practice, the policing of exit boundaries would be much more difficult for Hindus than for other religions. The notion of apostasy does not bite here as strongly as it would for other religions. If members of different communities, not only in religiously plural Kerala, customarily used to attend each other's holy places, how could one draw any neat boundaries? Intricate puzzles for lawyers were thus posed, since Christians, and not only famous singers or filmstars, could legally claim to be 'Hindus also' (Derrett, 1978: 212). Complex litigations resulted in famous Supreme Court cases about freedom of religion as a fundamental right under Articles 25–28 of the Indian Constitution.[9]

It would have been impractical and deeply damaging in social and economic terms to draw firm boundaries, and indeed this is mostly not what happened. In religiously highly plural places, like Kerala, and certainly not only there, mixed forms of Hindu Christians and Christian Hindus continue to exist. Unsurprisingly, therefore, recent intensive field studies, too, confirm that religious identity among Indians remains often remarkably liquid (Solanki, 2011). In practice, latent awareness of global interconnectedness in its Hindu *avatar* would mean that any failure to comply with specific accepted religious and ritual norms and standards will be noticed by others, but continuing social and economic relations meant, for example, that Hindus would now buy meat (and probably also leather footwear and other goods) from Muslims, demonstrating that complete excommunication and rigid cutting off of all people who converted to Christianity or Islam would be virtually impossible.

Perceptions of complete loss of social esteem from a Hindu majoritarian perspective may arise, affecting ritual and social status of an individual or family, often depicted as a sinking into 'hell', an image which looks suspiciously like a borrowing from other religions. This negative impact would probably be much stronger for high-caste converts, given that low-caste Hindus already suffered status deprivation. The complexity of potential consequences, in conditions where latent perceptions of connectedness in some form persist, even if one desperately seeks to disconnect, also explains to a large extent why 'caste' statuses did not get fully erased after conversion to Christianity.[10] In this context, it seems that gruesome caste-based discriminations imposed on low caste people in the early decades of the twentieth century led not only to revolts (see Sheeju, 2015; Gupta, 2016: 181) but also created a 'language of sympathy' (Gupta, 2016: 84), with multiple agendas, including the realisation that such basically inhuman practices, however motivated, amounted ultimately to self-harm to the body of Hindus as a community. While the threat of mass conversions caused fears, anxieties and violence (Gupta, 2016: 12, 36, 168), such realisations did not mean that caste-based discrimination ceased. Rather, it probably took different, often more subtle forms. There is now increasing evidence of how low caste communities have been fighting back and also today vigorously oppose the various forms of discrimination to reassert their own perspectives and status (Jangam, 2016; Singh, 2016).

The many millions of Hindus who abandoned Hinduism, however, were largely lost in terms of personal law. This, too, has given rise to most intriguing and highly politicised litigation, for example about the effects of conversions by married Hindu men on their rights to polygamy.[11] The new religious minorities formed their own socio-legal groups, largely governed now by the respective personal laws of Muslims or Christians.[12] Current efforts to re-convert people into Hindus and virtually 'bring them home' (*ghar vapsi*) indicate highly politicised repercussions of a resurgent Hindu nationalism. This also reflects nervousness that Hindu majoritarian claims have come under challenge even in India, today or may do so in the future. Since modern India, as the world's largest democracy, remains influenced by Hindu domination and displays concerted national efforts to develop a culture-specific legal system not found anywhere else on the globe, it seems that this, too, adds some acerbic spice to how Indian governance is being assessed worldwide, by outsiders and insiders alike, when it comes to matters of 'religion'. In this context, matters of exit from Hinduism remain relevant but are not really central given that other human rights concerns have acquired more prominence.

Rights and obligations of adherents

The heavily politicised discourses related to Hinduism and Hindu law and their role in India today are not merely a matter of Hindu nationalist projects and ongoing struggles over the universality of human rights.[13] They arise also in relation to superiority claims of international legal concepts, structures and institutions, connected to rights-based assertions in the name of human rights. Traditionally, similar kinds of challenge generated much political heat and ideological irritations over the allegedly 'false religion' of Hinduism (Shah, 2015: 4), referred to as 'monster tradition' (Oddie, 2006: 46), especially in specialist missionary literature on India. Scholars asserting the inherent political incorrectness and modern irrelevance of Hinduism and Hindu law conveniently forget that modern, secular traditions are rooted in specific Western-dominated local, cultural and religious moments and traditions. Against this, the Foreword in Shah (2015: vii) identifies 'a wider political project of evangelists and the Left with regard to Hindu society', in clear text, a nasty conspiracy, meaning that even in Britain today, legislative efforts to criminalise discriminatory aspects of Hinduism are being employed and, so it is feared, misused, as part of global battles in the market of souls.

In the context of the Indian Republic since 1947, considering the rights and obligations placed upon adherents to Hinduism, one sees first of all significant legal trends to equalise the status of different types of Hindus. This is a sign of official recognition of the different rights and obligations of the hugely diverse communities all over the country that may be covered by the collective label 'Hindu', including also Sikhs, Jainas and Buddhists. In other words, it is also an acknowledgement of the continuing central role of socio-cultural normativities and specific customary patterns of life, not only in relation to the personal law system. By itself, this recognition reflects of course also a democratic structure in which all individual citizens are deemed to be equal before the law, as guaranteed under Article 14 of the Indian Constitution of 1950. Most radically, Article 17 abolished untouchability and outlawed its practice, further laying down that the enforcement of any disability arising from untouchability shall be an offence. This shows that the post-colonial Indian state was not afraid to use legislation to reform some of the more questionable and – in today's world – intolerable forms of discrimination among Hindus and those they are dealing with on a daily basis. While this strategy matches the leading constitutional *Grundnorm* of equality before the law in Article 14, that Article itself (and more so those immediately following it) would explicitly permit reasonable classification. It thus seems to be that under this provision, rather than under the less clear-cut Article 13, which has been widely criticised by lawyers, the ongoing formal recognition of Hindu personal laws continues to be permitted. That this has not been openly debated by constitutional lawyers is a telling sign that 'unity in diversity' means little to them, or rather, is sought to be sidelined or even abolished. Indeed, significant discomfort about the constant need for diversity management feeds into the still ongoing debates over a Uniform Civil Code for India, with an agenda to have one law for all Indians, thus abolishing the personal law systems for different communities. In light of what we have written in the two previous sections, it would be clear that there is no clearly defined set of generally applicable rights and obligations for all Hindus, given the overwhelming strength of customary law and the internal flexibility, subtleness and situation-specificity of the Hindu key concept of *dharma*. While turning the plurality-conscious Hindu personal law system into a uniform state-made law is a rather overambitious and unrealistic form of asking for the moon,[14] the persistence of such debates discloses several layers of deep discomfort about how Indian laws today should manage formal and informal inequality, not only in relation to internal differences among Hindus of various kinds but also in relation to the co-existence of different, also internally diverse, other religious communities, mainly Muslims, Christians, Parsis and Jews.

Since the academic assessment of anything to do with Hinduism in today's world seems to experience major ideological problems with the basic principle of interconnectedness, prominent irritations persist among protagonists of individual rights, opposing group rights. The Enlightenment principle of absolute autonomy of the individual seems also implicated here, rather than problems over how to manage diversity and inequality. The other aspect of modernity, state-centric control of laws, generates further heartburn. Yet when we find that so many individuals in Indian society today continue to engage in informal dispute settlement processes, we see reasonably, increasingly, and quite clear-cut reflections of various diversifications of individual status and roles, with ritual as well as other socio-economic, cultural and legal dimensions. In other words, it remains a hallmark of the Hindu way of life in India today that different kinds of Hindus, as individuals and as members of various kinds of communities or social groups, mainly connected by descent or locality, are engaged in living forms of Hinduism and Hindu law. These may be conceptually more or less vaguely connected through the *rita/dharma* context, as explained earlier, but this actually results in the exercise of considerable agency by Hindus as individuals and groups to construct and 'live' their religion as they see fit. It would, thus, be conceptually misguided to see this as evidence that Hindus are even today subject to some kind of rigid 'religious' authority that determines their rights and obligations. Rather, as explained earlier regarding the methods of working out one's *dharma* in a very practical day-to-day sense, this is a complex hybrid of religious and secular normativities and considerations.

Given that many aspects of Hindu law are – as they have always been – secular in nature rather than purely religious (Menski, 2003), it remains thus a huge but unfortunately rather common conceptual mistake to treat everything 'Hindu' or 'Muslim' merely as religious. This suggests that also in a postmodern setting, legal recognition of cultural pluralism, which includes value pluralism, can facilitate desirable aims such as achieving better gender equality (Solanki, 2011: xxii). India, so much is clear, is not Europe. It does not divide or seek to segregate law and religion, separating the secular and the religious, but treats them as intertwined and inevitably connected, with multiple differentiating effects in terms of the persons involved and ever-present situation-specificity.

There is thus, above all, no viable case for complete eradication of 'religion' from the various aspects of governance in post-colonial India. In Europe, too, religion has come back into the public space rather than being evicted. As long as the right to freedom of religion, freedom of expression and the right not to be discriminated against on grounds merely of religion are protected by India's strong Constitution, there is little cause for ringing alarm bells about the fact that 'religion' seems to remain so strong in India. Moreover, in constitutional terms, the Republic of India is quite simply not allowed to turn into a Hindu state (*rashtra*). The avowedly secular Indian Constitution of 1950 guarantees and seeks to achieve equidistance of the state law to all religions, in a basic condition of Hindu domination, thus expecting non-discrimination of the non-Hindu 'other' as a basic principle. As the Holy Book of this intensely plural nation, this modern-looking Constitution clearly represents, and seeks to safeguard, a higher form of law than merely state-made laws. Unsurprisingly, thus, Indian law and India's handling of Hindu law continue to rely on various ancient principles of self-controlled ordering, and there is a marked continuity (Menski, 2003; Williams, 2006). This reflects a demographic reality, which is unlikely to change, even if the share of non-Hindus in India is gradually going up.

The warning examples of two major Muslim-dominated states next door, Pakistan and Bangladesh, clearly suggest, moreover, that in comparison with these two countries, India has been doing much better in finding the right balance in relation to religious diversity and senses of 'belonging'. The challenge to navigate the expectations of majoritarian Hindu domination, modernist claims for constraints on its 'traditional' structures including the multiplicity of 'religions' and the consequent personal laws, and the plurality-conscious acknowledgement of its own deep-rooted diversities, can even be faced with considerable success – though obviously never with complete perfection – by a Hindu nationalist government. Such a popularly chosen democratic government seems to be as aware of the demands and expectations of the international community as its own commitment to the country's pluralist religious and cultural identity. It is this scenario of plurality-conscious sensitivity that forms the bedrock of India's surprisingly successful democracy today, keeping 'shark rule' at bay through skilful diversity management at all levels. Given the sheer size of the country, this is inevitably a mammoth challenge, always leaving much work to be done and generating a never-ending panorama of conflict scenarios. Politicising 'religion' for ulterior motives, from that perspective, too, then, becomes a potentially harmful unconstructive activity that is politically dangerous, ideologically suspect, and simply not in line with Hindu identity postulates, both traditional and modern. Simply expecting Hindus or Hindu-dominated India to shed their socio-cultural identity elements in favour of some imagined secular global value structure effectly asks several hundred million people to disown their very highly diffuse identity and to follow a uniform pattern for the sake of 'modernity'. That this antagonises many Indians and generates a sense of defensiveness has become increasingly obvious (Sarkar, 2001: 36). This partly explains why supposedly universal idioms of modernity are deeply mistrusted in India as hidden claims of Western superiority, even while we observe that many Indians appear busy copying elements of modernity. While in India, too, upper class elites dominate public discourses and the production of published knowledge (Sarkar, 2001: 53), this does not mean that Hinduism and Hindu law could just be extinguished by encouragement to abandon Hinduism, or to adopt modernist secular reforms. A shared sense of belonging to a kind of rainbow nation, in religiously extremely plural manifestations, too, is a matter of pride for many Indians, rather than shame or a sense of lack of progress and development. While many modernist scholars clearly do not trust the central Hindu concept of righteousness (*dharma*), which is indeed rather idealistically expecting that everyone should be doing the right thing at any moment of their life, for the benefit of the greater public good, the fact that India survives as a viable democracy, despite its size and complexities, speaks for itself and adds to the oddly hybrid status of this Hindu-dominated nation that cannot be a Hindu state. And if one must speak in terms of 'rights' and 'obligations', this is probably the only 'obligation' that every Hindu has. However, since this obligation has no prescribed expression or form, how it is met depends entirely on individuals' assessment of a situation and their willingness to 'risk' the karmic consequences of their action or inaction.

In the final analysis, it appears that the vastly differentiated perceptions of Hindu rights and obligations are perceived as everyone's unique and individual contribution to an imagined sense of macrocosmic order that is in principle much higher than the legal order of any nation state and/or the various social orders that individuals and groups live in on a daily basis. From a Hindu perspective, there is no inherent contradiction between being an individual actor and agent, as well as at the same time a member of various social groups, an equal citizen of a nation state and also a global citizen. The need to balance these competing expectations and role models, at any moment of one's life, is exactly captured by the never-ending diversities of *dharma* and *karma* in the lived experience of Hindus of all kinds. They may not be aware of this, at all moments of their life, but they are joined together by this shared, hazy imagination of karmic risk and precariousness, which is precisely one of the ancient hallmarks of being a 'good' Hindu. Since right belief or orthodoxy is an impossible and in practice immensely plural challenge for Hindus as a global collectivity, situation-specific right action as liquid orthopraxis but also equally liquid awareness of one's actions and constantly changing positionality, seem to be the key markers of what it actually means to be a Hindu and to belong.

Notes

1 A pertinent example is *vyavahāra*, widely translated as 'judicial proceedings', but actually including all types of formal and informal dispute settlement, even invisible mental processes of making up one's own mind (Menski, 2007).

2 An example from the Vedic body of texts on marriage rituals demonstrated this conclusively (Menski, 1984: 319). In Rigveda 10.85.38, the Sanskrit text reads *punah*, while in the otherwise identical slightly later verse at Atharvaveda 14.2.1, the alternative reading is *sanah*. This minute textual modification was found to introduce a momentous ritual sophistication in secretive magical priestly involvement at this crucial moment.

3 Flood (2003: 2) refers to approximately 700 million people classed as Hindu by the Census in India. There are hundreds of millions more now.

4 A highly significant example was a recent asylum case in the UK of a Pakistani Muslim who claimed to have abandoned Islam and embraced Hinduism, as he was attracted by its atheist principles and its capacity for critical thought, rather than blind belief in any male authority figure. The utterly ridiculous manner in which this thoughtful individual was virtually tortured by Home Office officials challenging his clearly stated beliefs led, on revision, to the granting of the asylum claim and even a new identity.

5 Two public interest litigation cases attracted particular attention. W.P. (Civil) 373 of 2016 was filed by the Indian Young Lawyers' Association in 2006 to seek entry of women into the famous Sabarimala temple in Kerala. That case is still pending. Civil Appelate Jurisdiction PIL 55 of 2016, filed by activists seeking women's entry to the shrine area at the Shani Shingnapur temple in Ahmednagar district in Maharashtra, was decided on 31 March 2016. The Court directed that women be allowed entry into the said area of the temple.

6 For recent politicised agitations over such issues, see Pathania (2016).

7 Sampath (1991: 323, n. 16), one of India's leading Hindu law experts, however, pointed out that the Hindu birth rituals (*jātakarma*) are very close to Christian baptism.

8 For an example from the 1930s, regarding diet rules, see Pathania (2016: 261–262).

9 See Derrett (1968; 1978: 211–212).

10 On this theme, see with further references, Doss (2013).

11 In this regard, *Sarla Mudgal v. Union of India*, AIR 1995 SC 1531 seems most prominent, also in terms of political misuse of such issues by scholars, not to speak of the judge who decided this case.

12 Disquiet over continuation of Hindu customs among Muslim converts is, for example, reflected in the promulgation of the Muslim Personal Law (Shariat) Application Act of 1937.

13 Struggles now arise also regarding caste discrimination in Britain (Shah, 2015).

14 On Indian diversity management in various spheres, see now the Special Issue of *Verfassung und Recht in Übersee* 49.2 (2016).

References

Derrett, J. D. M. 1968. *Religion, Law and the State in India*. Faber & Faber.

Derrett, J. D. M. (ed.). 1978. *Essays in Classical and Modern Hindu Law*. Vol. 4. Brill.

Doss, M. Christhu 2013. 'Missionary Insurgency and Marginality of Modernity in Colonial South India'. 33(3) *South Asia Research*. 223.

Flood, G. (ed.). 2003. *Hinduism*. Blackwell.

Gundimeda, S. 2016. 'Dalit Activism in Telugu Country, 1917–30'. 36(3) *South Asia Research*. 322.

Gupta, C. 2016. *The Gender of Caste*. University of Washington Press.
Hinnells, J. R. (ed.). 1995. *A New Dictionary of Religions*. Blackwell.
Jangam, C. 2016. 'Caste from Below: Memory and Subversion of Caste in Chindu Yakshaganam'. 36(3) *South Asia Research*. 343.
Lipner, J. 1998. *Hindus. Their Religious Beliefs and Practices*. Routledge.
Menski, W. 1984. *Role and Ritual in the Hindu Marriage*. London: SOAS. Unpublished PhD thesis.
Menski, W. 2003. *Hindu Law. Beyond Tradition and Modernity*. Oxford University Press.
Menski, W. 2006. *Comparative Law in a Global Context*. Cambridge University Press.
Menski, W. 2007. 'On Vyavahāra'. 33 *Indologica Taurinensia*. 123.
Menski, W. 2012. 'Plural Worlds of Law and the Search for Living Law' in W. Gephart (ed.) *Rechtsanalyse als Kulturforschung*. Vittorio Klostermann. 71.
Menski, W. 2016. 'Justice, Epistemic Violence in South Asian Studies and the Nebulous Entity of Caste in Our Age of Chaos'. 36(3) *South Asia Research*. 299.
Michaels, A. 2004. *Hinduism Past and Present*. Orient Longman.
Miller, J. 1985. *The Vision of Cosmic Order in the Vedas*. Routledge.
Naipaul, V. S. 2011. *India: A Million Mutinies Now*. Vintage International.
Oddie, G. A., 2006. *Imagined Hinduism*. Sage.
Pandey, R. B. 1969. *Hindu Samskaras*. Motilal Banarsidass.
Pathania, G. J. 2016. 'Food Politics and Counter-Hegemonic Assertion in Indian University Campuses'. 36(2) *South Asia Research*. 261.
Sampath, B. N. 1991. 'Hindu Marriage as a Samskara: A Resolvable Conundrum'. 33(3) *Journal of the Indian Law Institute*. 319.
Sarkar, T. 2001. *Hindu Wife, Hindu Nation. Community, Religion, and Cultural Nationalism*. Hurst & Company.
Sen, A. 2009. *The Idea of Justice*. Penguin.
Shah, P. 2015. *Against Caste in British Law*. Palgrave Macmillan.
Sharma, A. 1996. *Hinduism for Our Times*. Oxford University Press.
Sharma, A. 2004. *Hinduism and Human Rights. A Conceptual Approach*. Oxford University Press.
Sheeju, N. V. 2015. 'The Shanar Revolts, 1822–99: Towards a Figural Cartography of the Pretender'. 35(3) *South Asia Research*. 298.
Singh, S. 2016. 'Dalits in Punjab: Cultural Assertion and Heritage Reconstruction'. 36(3) *South Asia Research*. 356.
Smith, D. 2003. *Hinduism and Modernity*. Blackwell.
Solanki, G. 2011. *Adjudication in Religious Family Laws*. Cambridge University Press.
Stutley, M. and Stutley, J. 1977. *A Dictionary of Hinduism*. Routledge.
Williams, R. V. 2006. *Postcolonial Politics and Personal Laws*. Oxford University Press.

15

Comparative remarks

Religious laws and dynamics of belonging and status

Francis Messner

Methods of religious affiliation and the procedures for entering and exiting a religion, together with the rights and duties assigned to their members, constitute an excellent reference point, which reflects not only the functioning and doctrines of religions but also the state of societies and the institutional organisation of the nations concerned. At a time of communitarian tensions and forms of religious radicalism going hand-in-hand with a progressive secularisation of societies, the issue of jointly belonging or being affiliated to a nation and a religion, the procedures for entering into and exiting from a religion, and the rights and duties of members of these groups, are of very particular sensitivity. They help us to understand the dissimilarities and elements common to different religions (Christianity, Hinduism, Islam, Judaism) and to assess the extent to which they collide with state laws.[1]

Towards a separation of belonging?

For centuries, belonging jointly to a religion and a nation, with differing conditions according to the religion, constituted a whole that at first glance was indissociable. The idea behind this fusion/confusion was to maintain the homogeneity of a group, to consolidate political power, to cement the nation and to establish, especially in the West with the rise of regalism, a centralised state. This principle of *cujus regio ejus religio* (such the religion of the prince, such that of the country), gradually came to an end in Europe following the initial effects of the Reformation (leading to relative religious tolerance), then of the French Revolution from the late 18th century. In France, for example, the Declaration of the Rights of Man and of the Citizen marked a clear break from the *Ancien Régime*. Since the Revolution, religion has been an opinion and not a body that merges with the nation. Currently, the distinction between religious affiliation and citizenship is one of the principles recognised by Western states. Indeed, a person's religious affiliation is a private matter reflecting relations between individuals and is, as such, protected against any attempts by public authorities to advertise it. The obligation to declare one's religious convictions or affiliation to a religious confession is explicitly prohibited by almost the entirety of constitutions in European states. Article 140 of the Basic Law of the Federal Republic of Germany states that 'No person shall be required to disclose his religious convictions', while the Spanish (Article 16 § 2) and Polish (Article 57 § 7) constitutions specify that no-one could be obliged to declare their ideology, religion or beliefs to the public authorities. A reference to religion linked to a person's identity is no longer included in population census records, even if the latter may include anonymised data on religious belonging. In Austria, Estonia, Finland, Lithuania, the Czech Republic, the Netherlands, Portugal and Slovenia, official statistics provide evidence of religious and/or ethnic belonging, while respecting the anonymity of individuals.

This distinction between citizenship and religious affiliation, which has established itself as a normal part of life in Western society, is often ignored in the rest of the world or more often religious affiliation and citizenship are linked socially and/or normatively. To cite just one example of this, the Constitution of the Kingdom of Morocco proclaims in its preamble that:

> A sovereign Muslim State, attached to its national unity and to its territorial integrity, the Kingdom of Morocco intends to preserve, in its plentitude and its diversity, its one and indivisible national identity. Its unity is forged by the convergence of its Arab-Islamist, Berber and Saharan-Hassanic components, nourished and enriched by its African, Andalusian, Hebraic and Mediterranean influences. The preeminence accorded to the Muslim religion in the national reference is consistent with the attachment of the Moroccan people to the values of openness, of moderation, of tolerance and of dialog for mutual understanding between all the cultures and the civilizations of the world.[2]

In addition, Article 3 stipulates that Islam is the state religion which guarantees the free exercise of faiths. In Qatar, citizenship is granted only to women who marry a Qatari, with few exceptions. But even in this case, it is not automatically granted to non-Muslim women whose children will necessarily become Muslim.

This 'separatist' distinction attached to fundamental rights is now accepted by Christianity, but it is still necessary to differentiate and underline the important historical differences between the Protestant – particularly Lutheran – churches, the Orthodox churches and the Catholic Church. The latter has defended its autonomy with regard to the French State in a structured and well-argued manner from the 16th–17th centuries onwards. Indeed, German Catholic canonists – anxious to defend the prerogatives of the Roman Church – developed the theory of the church as an unequal society. It is unequal because – like the state – it holds sovereignty, unlike the colleges and corporations existing within the state, which are equal among themselves. The theory of unequal society cultivated in pontifical universities became *societas perfecta* (a perfect society), then later a complete society. This separatist notion of the church being autonomous with respect to the state can be found implicit in the Code of Canon Law of 1983, despite a change of vocabulary which does not create a fundamental break from the Code of 1917, even if the vocabulary does undergo a theological shift. A Catholic is above all a member of a religion of universal character, even if forms of a Catholic confessional state existed into the 1960s and 1970s. In contrast, in the Nordic countries of Lutheran tradition, citizenship was linked to belonging to the state church. Swedes, for example, were obliged to be part of the Evangelical Lutheran Church until 1860, when the right for a Swedish citizen to leave the church was recognised, subject, however, to joining another Christian church. It was not until 1951 that a Swede could leave the national church freely and unconditionally. Such is not the case for Judaism in Israel, Hinduism in India and Islam in Muslim states, where the link between nation and religion – far from being merely symbolic, as can still be the case in some Western states – is enshrined in texts and jurisprudence. Being Jewish therefore enshrines belonging not only to a religion but also to a nation, combining a political existence with a spiritual mission. This stance is far from theoretical in Israel, where the Supreme Court can decide as needed who is part of the Jewish community (Chapter 11, this volume). It appears that the principle of jointly belonging to a nation and a religion occurs at some point in history in all religious traditions. The separation that seems inevitable in the light of current changes in societies is not always taking place easily and quickly. Some religions are in fact less adapted in the present state of their doctrine to initiate this process, which can also be slowed down by political powers anxious to maintain a foundation of common values based on religious ideas.

Entering into the religion

The affiliation of the descendants of Jewish and Muslim parents, i.e. their entry into the community, is quasi automatic, even if the rules are not the same in both cases. There are no formal religious rites enshrining affiliation.

When the father is Muslim, the children are presumed to belong to the Muslim religion (Chapter 13, this volume). Sometimes to signify this affiliation, the father 'whispers' the call to prayer into the ear of the new-born child. Assuming strict observance of the precepts of this religion, all the children are Muslim. Indeed, a Muslim man may marry a non-Muslim woman, which is not the case for a Muslim woman who can only marry a co-religionist.

The acquisition of Judaism (also linked to descent) is subject to more complex rules (Chapter 11, this volume). It is handed down by a Jewish mother descended from two Jewish spouses who celebrated their marriage under Jewish law in the presence of a rabbi considered to be legitimate by the community concerned.

The issue of religious affiliation must be understood in Hinduism in the light of pluralism, which is to some extent institutionalised within this very religion, as well as in the light of state intervention within the context of a policy of national identity. Being Hindu means above all being integrated into a social framework split into castes and into a normative framework with which religious rites are associated. But Hindu law and its interpretation – like the diversity of the streams constituting it – are also plural, even if it is possible to find common foundations. In reality, the divergence from the other internal laws of religions is important. The concepts and representations are not the same. Thus, for Hinduism, human rights come from the cosmos – where each entity has its role to play – and not from the individual as such. The interdependence between all beings plays a fundamental role, whereas in the West the emphasis is placed on the individual. Adhering to Hinduism means first and foremost adhering to a constituent sect of Hinduism within the framework of the discriminatory caste system, the constraints of which tend to favour a system that facilitates multiple belonging (Chapter 14, this volume).

Christianity is out of step with Islam, Judaism and Hinduism in terms of formalising the affiliation of children born to Christian couples. The religious dimension clearly supplants the community dimension, and links with the public authorities in this field are very weak, if not non-existent. Affiliation to the various Christian churches is clearly egalitarian in character. Everyone is part of God's people by virtue of being baptised, without a fundamental difference between men and women being created or, moreover, between laypeople and ordained ministers. Entry into the Christian religion is always subordinated to a religious act termed 'sacramental' (Chapter 12, this volume): baptism. Note that the emphasis on commitment combined with acceptance of the democratic model by the historical Protestant churches and Anglicanism has led to the creation of several forms of religious affiliation. The first, purely sacramental, is attached to reception of a sacrament of baptism, while the second is often achieved by the existence of a register comprising active members actually dedicated to the administration and activities, including those of a religious nature, of the parish or local community. Many Protestant churches distinguish between baptised members, voting members and even associates. The latter are members of other Christian communities, yet participate in parish life. This differentiation in religious involvement is illustrated by the representations and definitions of what the community of believers – the church – ought to represent for each of us. It is either a People's Church/*Volkskirche* or a Church of Confessors. The former accepts regular worshippers, occasional ones, but also Cultural Christians, while the latter accepts only devout members professing their faith, which is the case of evangelical communities. The status of affiliation differs from one church to another. Religious affiliation in the historical Protestant churches is characterised by the theological figure of the invisible church, which is related to a broad or multitudinist notion of belonging to the visible church. This notion was equally widespread in the Catholic Church, with specific characteristics linked to territories. With the lukewarm reaction of the multitudinist institutions, however, the masters of the faith met in conventicles, movements, associations of the faithful and brotherhoods.

Conversion is, after the family setting, the second entrance door to a religion. In Islam, the conversion procedure is in principle limited to the recitation of a formula summarising the profession of faith (*shahada*) before witnesses. This minimalist approach is linked to the nature of the religious community, which is often also seen as a political community that needs to be strengthened (Chapter 13, this volume). It must be noted that the time spent preparing for and learning about Islam is in this specific case – which is not shared by all Muslim communities – incidental. Its absence before the convert enters into the religion does not facilitate a reasoned learning of the rules governing the individual and collective life of the Muslim believer. This observation must, however, be tempered by the fact that training sessions are now being organised for converts by certain federations of Muslim groups, particularly in Western countries. But this is less a preparation for conversion than a catechism of perseverance. In addition, some movements have set up training courses for those applying for conversion.

Judaism is, like Islam, a religion and a people that has made a covenant with God, but with the conviction shared by its members of its oppression throughout history. Conversion thus takes on a particular meaning by integrating the difficulties linked to the very existence of this community. As a rule, the conversion procedure is long and demanding. It includes learning and knowledge about the rules and doctrines specific to this religion. But in some cases, the argument of the urgency of sustaining the Jewish people is facilitating acceptance of converts who are non-believers (Chapter 11, this volume). The Jewish religion comprises several streams (Orthodox, liberal, conservative) and is based on a decentralised organisation that leaves it to the local communities to set the criteria for conversion. Elements common to Islam and Judaism, including the links between religion and nation or belonging to a community, do not entail the creation of similar procedures as regards conversion.

In Hinduism, one is born in principle as a Hindu and no longer leaves one's religion, but this affirmation, which also applies to other religions, is contradicted by the existence of a ritual of incorporation. It is therefore possible to become Hindu when one is not a native of this religion. This ritual, or rather these rituals, are indicators of the difficulties of entering into this community, which is at the same time a religion, belonging to a caste, a family, a nation, but which supposes, moreover, an integration into the cosmos where each element is interdependent (Chapter 14, this volume). It is difficult to compare this procedure with other religions and more particularly with Christian churches which emphasise equality between believers, as well as a distinct separation between citizenship and religious affiliation.

In the Christian religions, conversion is generally preceded by a substantial period of preparation (Chapter 12, this volume); so, in the Catholic Church, candidates for baptism are required to follow a progressive preparation made up of several stages. It is determined by universal and specific Catholic ecclesial law. The candidate for conversion is first welcomed by the person in charge of the parish's catechumenal group. On this occasion, they become pre-catechumen.

This first meeting aims to clarify the motivations of the person and to inform them of the content and duration – about two years – of the suggested pathway. At the end of this first contact, the person in charge appoints someone to accompany the individual throughout the preparation (Canon 788, Code of Canon Law). At the end of the preparation period, the pre-catechumen enters into the Christian community where he or she receives the name 'catechumen'. They then take both spiritual and intellectual training. Upon entering the catechumenate, the candidate for baptism becomes a member of the Catholic Church with a special status. Even without yet being baptised, they have the right, for example, to a church wedding or a religious funeral. The procedure is roughly the same in the different Christian churches, which furthermore mutually recognise the First Sacrament of Baptism. Such is the case for Catholic, Orthodox, Anglican, Reformed and Lutheran churches. Some evangelical communities like the Baptists refuse these agreements and re-baptise adults using immersion.

Exiting from the religion

Religious affiliation is enshrined in the West in societies marked by multiple belonging that is often considered equivalent. Moreover, members of different religions or people without religious affiliation – whether indifferent, atheistic or agnostic – live together within the same territory. This is not without consequences for life in society. The current notion of non-restrictive religious affiliation is also put into perspective in that it refers to one affiliation among others – trade union, associative, political, cultural – and that multiple belonging and spiritualities are developing without being formally attached to a religious institution. Moreover, if we take the European example, it must be noted that the right to change religion is not only enshrined in morals but also in law and, in particular, European human rights law: 'Everyone has the right to freedom of thought, conscience and religion; this right includes freedom to change his religion or belief' (Article 9 ECHR).

The situation is distinctly different, at least in other latitudes, for Islam and Hinduism. If belonging to Hinduism is presented as immutable, an arranged exit from this religion is considered by some as a means to escape discrimination generated especially by the caste system. But conversion does not result in a total break from Hinduism, but rather negotiation of a status within the context of double belonging, such is the difficulty of leaving a religion with multiple deep roots. Moreover, leaving Hinduism, especially in the high castes, leads to the loss of an envied social position and the exit from Hindu personal status (Chapter 14, this volume). A communitarian notion of affiliation is to be found, but in a sharper and non-negotiable manner, among Muslims for whom religion and nation are one in their representation of the model of pre-modern Islam (Chapter 13, this volume). Exiting from Islam does not only have consequences for spiritual life; it especially affects the common good. Under Muslim law, an apostate man who is of adult age and has not acted under duress is punished by the death penalty. Women are entitled to preferential treatment. They are sentenced to prison terms. Many Muslim states (such as Somalia and Saudi Arabia) still punish apostasy today by the death penalty or by imposing prison sentences, including for those involved in conversions accused of proselytism. The commitment to the principle of not changing religion is implicit in the Declaration of Human Rights in Islam, adopted in Cairo on 5 August 1990 by the Organisation of Islamic Cooperation. It represents an adaptation of the Universal Declaration of Human Rights to the demands of Muslim countries. Fifty-seven states have ratified it. It limits the freedom to choose and change one's religion, freedom of expression and confirms the inequality of rights between men and women. These stances are now unacceptable to contemporary liberal and democratic states. It should be noted, however, that the authorities of Muslim communities most often accept the rules laid down by democratic states, integrate them and even undertake to promote them. It is thus explicitly stated in the preambles to the conventions agreed with the State of the Grand Duchy of Luxembourg that the signatory religions guarantee 'respect for constitutional rights and freedoms, public order and democratic values, the promotion of human rights and equal treatment and equality between men and women'.[3] Religious communities undertake 'to remove from the organisation of the community any member who acts or calls for action in violation of these principles'.[4] Similarly, the agreement between the City-State of Hamburg and the Muslim communities represented by the *Ditib* and *Schura* in Hamburg[5] guarantees in Article 1 the right to distance oneself from representations of one's own religion – in short, to leave one's religion. Moreover, both partners undertake to combat all forms of discrimination based on origin, gender, sexual orientation, various religious convictions – including changing one's religion – and political beliefs (Agreement between the City-State of Hamburg and Muslim Communities, Article 2).[6] Similarly, the charter of the values and principles of Muslims in France (formerly the UOIF, close to the Muslim Brotherhood), published in March 2017, 'condemns coercion in religion and guarantees everyone the free choice of his beliefs as well as that of the expression of his thoughts and opinions',[7] which constitutes an evolution in relation to previous stances that are distinctly more rigid. Leaving Islam is certainly condemned by the founding texts of this religion but without entailing penal sanctions, at least in the West where the armed civilian wing is absent.

Like Hinduism and Islam, exiting from the Jewish religion is complicated. In principle, one remains Jewish all one's life: even the one who has sinned remains Jewish (Chapter 11, this volume). The historical experience of forced conversions illustrates the limitations of this approach. Jewishness cannot be erased. Apostasy is simply not recognised by Jewish law. It has no effect and whoever leaves their religion continues to be subject to Hebrew law. But then they are, as a sinner, inflicted with a kind of excommunication that confines them to the margins of the community.

The issue is raised differently in Christianity (Chapter 12, this volume). Thus, for the historical Protestant churches, with the exception of certain periods of tension in the 19th century, the term apostate is no longer used. Moreover, the transition to another Christian church which shares the same confession of faith does not pose any particular problems:

> The United Protestant Church of France (EPUdF) – Lutheran and Reformed Communion – professes that no one church can claim to demarcate the Church of Jesus Christ, for God alone knows those who belong to Him. Its *raison d'être* is to proclaim the Gospel to the world. It is therefore open to everyone whom it calls to believe in Jesus Christ, to deepen their faith by reading the Bible and listening to preaching, to receive baptism if it has not already been given to them and to partake of the Lord's Supper.[8]

The United Protestant Church of France has a constitution without Protestant penal law that determines a catalogue of sanctions for members who leave one of its communities. It is above all a personal decision arising from freedom of conscience. On the other hand, some Protestant churches envisage, but only in cases of notable unworthiness, striking off a member from the electoral register, which does not exclude them from the church but deprives them of the ability to influence the governance of the local community. On the other hand, the stances of the evangelical churches are more rigid.

Exiting from the Catholic Church is not without consequence. Canon law cites three causes: apostasy, which is the total rejection of the Catholic faith; heresy, which according to the texts is obstinate denial, after receiving baptism, of a truth of divine, Catholic faith which must be believed, or else obstinately doubting this truth; and, finally, schism or refusing to submit to the Supreme Pontiff or to take communion with members of the Church who submit to him. Conversion to another religion, as well as the request for removal from the baptismal register, entails a number of consequences for the former member, such as prohibition from receiving the sacraments and more particularly the Eucharist, inability to perform the roles of godparents at baptism and confirmation, and renouncing Catholic Church funerals. The German Bishops' Conference goes further.[9] It considers that administrative membership of a public law corporation representing the Catholic Church as established by German religious law/*Staatskirchenrecht* mechanically merges with religious/canonical affiliation, which obliges the faithful to fund the Church so that it is able to carry out its mission (Canon 222) and to maintain communion with it (Canon 209). Initiating a procedure with the civil administration to leave the Church with a view to no longer paying Church Tax is interpreted as the desire to distance oneself from this community. The penalty in this case is severe. It entails the end of the right to receive sacraments, to sit on church bodies, to hold canonical office, to belong to a Catholic association and to have a religious burial. A member who leaves the Church undergoes the same sanctions as an excommunicated person without the excommunication being pronounced. But leaving the Catholic Church never erases the sacramental character of baptism. According to Catholic doctrine, it imparts an indelible character that obstructs any debaptism procedure. Exiting from the Church is mentioned in the baptismal register, but the baptism entry in the register cannot be deleted.

Rights and duties of members

In Muslim law (Chapter 13, this volume), the rights and duties of members go beyond the religious sphere as envisaged in the West, where temporal and spiritual are, subject to national variations, distinctly separated. Muslim law not only concerns worship but also applies to the recognition of a status of religion in life in society and to relations between individuals. It tends to govern the totality of existence of believers and sometimes non-believers in Muslim society. In this respect, the confessional state constitutes an ideal framework to facilitate achievement of these objectives, insofar as it does not distinguish the spiritual from the temporal. The minority character of Islam within a country marked by the neutrality of the state and religious pluralism does not fail to provoke a collision between state law and religious norms, or at least a misunderstanding within the recently settled populations. Their strict application could encourage the creation of communities with strong normative autonomy. Islam is in principle a complete civilisational act based on the Qur'an, proclaiming a single and exclusive God, a single law and a community of believers whose aim it is to achieve unity (*Umma*) and where every act, whether individual, collective or societal, is valued in the light of these norms. But secularisation and religious pluralism have forced Islam to adapt and develop forms of normative regulation compatible with life in society in Europe. Books devoted to the *Fiqh* of Muslim minorities have been written in order to answer Muslims' questions. If the confessional state constitutes a favourable framework for the almost automatic implementation of the rights and duties of members of Muslim communities, the neutral state, on the other hand, encourages religious authorities' inventiveness in finding a suitable fit between religious norm and the secular legal system.

In the Jewish religion, Hebrew law also plays a decisive role. Its jurisdiction does not stop at the synagogues; far from it. It extends to all areas of existence and, in a way, the whole of existence falls under religious law. Moreover, the Jewish religion is above all experienced collectively, societally one could say. This reality is illustrated by the imperative obligation to gather at least ten male persons for Sabbath worship. The hierarchy within the Jewish community does not have a sacred nature. It essentially boils down to a hierarchy of knowledge (Chapter 11, this volume). Knowledge of the founding texts constitutes an obligation for all members of the Jewish community and is not reserved for a clerical elite. The religious reorganisation following the destruction of the Temple of Jerusalem replaced the hereditary priesthood with a learned meritocracy capable of interpreting the texts. It is the distinction between scholar and ignoramus that produces the religious hierarchy, but with the exclusion of women from religious functions of a public nature. This division of tasks where the man studies the Torah and the woman works and runs the house is not accepted by all streams of Judaism. Thus, liberal Judaism trains and appoints female rabbis. This notion can also be corrected by state law when worship is organised by the state. In France, therefore, for the *départements* of the Rhine and Moselle, the consistories and the chief rabbis, after much procrastination, admitted that women could vote in the consistories in 1990 (Messner, 2008). On the other hand, the eligibility of women to participate in consistories was imposed by the administrative court in 2006 on the grounds that local law texts must be interpreted in the light of notions prevailing today.[10]

Rights and obligations in Hindu law (Chapter 14, this volume) are difficult to define because of the multiplicity of rules laid down by each 'sect'. Certainly, personal status exists, but it emerges from secular law on the basis of an attempt to unify characteristics, rather than from religious law. In fact, Hindu law – which does not exclude multiple belonging – is applied in a flexible fashion.

Developments regarding rights and duties in Islam and Judaism concern, on the one hand, the interpenetration of state law and religious norms and, on the other, the distinct role of women and men in these religious groups and more broadly in society. They are characterised by an absence of clerical hierarchy. This is not the case for Christianity, where the emphasis is on the organisation and internal workings of religious groups. The separation between temporal and spiritual is perfectly integrated by Christian religions, even if differences remain between Protestantism, Catholicism, Orthodoxy and Anglicanism. Moreover, Western states have established a legal system that is barely favourable to legal pluralism. The forms of normative regulation of religions are not legal orders producing, with few exceptions, law recognised by the state or binding on the state. When the judge is confronted with religious norms, they are considered as a religious phenomenon, which in this case means a social or individual reality, not a legal one.

In Christianity, the distinction between cleric or minister of religion and the layperson is recurrent within the topic of rights and duties, even if the terminology used requires clarification and explanation. Indeed, there is *stricto sensu* no cleric in Protestantism. The Reformation swept away this distinction rooted in Catholicism. The pastor is above all a theologian-preacher-doctor exercising a relationship-based profession that involves leading, listening and accompanying people. In the Protestant churches, the ecclesiastical state differentiating the cleric from the layperson has been abolished. Specific roles are certainly necessary for the correct functioning of the community, but all laypeople – the faithful – are priests and all ministers of worship, i.e. pastors, are laypeople. In the words of Jean-Paul Willaime, the priesthood of the faithful leads to the secularisation of ministers of worship in Protestantism (Willaime, 2016). Likewise in the Catholic Church, the emphasis is now placed on all the faithful of Christ/*Christifideles* incorporated into the Church by baptism and who are part of the people of God:

> For this reason, made sharers in their own way in Christ's priestly, prophetic, and royal function, they are called to exercise the mission which God has entrusted to the Church to fulfil in the world, in accord with the condition proper to each.
>
> *(Canon 204)*[11]

Canon 207, however, later reminds us that distinctions exist between the faithful, who can be clerics, laypeople or else devoted to God by means of vows.

Christian – and more particularly Protestant religions – often make an additional distinction, which is not without consequence for the rights and duties of the persons concerned, between members who entered the community by baptism and those baptised who are actually involved in the life of the local or parish community by the regularity of their participation in worship and by their involvement in parish activities or in the administrative affairs of the parish. In this regard, those recorded in a parish register separate from the baptismal register and still called the Christianity register have specific rights. If the latter have the right to receive a certificate of baptism and to participate in the sacraments, the former have the right to participate or at least to elect those called to participate in the deliberative assemblies and the executive of the confession.

Conclusion

The comparison of the internal laws of the Christian, Muslim, Jewish and Hindu religions in terms of affiliation reveals a very heterogeneous picture with, however, a double fault line between Hindu law and other religious laws and between Muslim and Jewish laws and Christian laws. Very complex Hindu law applies with specific features to a multitude of groups and subgroups, 'sects' in a caste system with a special definition of the individual related to the cosmos, where each living being has a role to play in the context of an interdependence of the living. Islam and Judaism are characterised by their inclusive character and by a fusional notion of religion and nation. In the absence of a confessional state, such a posture presupposes doctrinal changes, which is indeed the case for these communities in the West. Christianity, religion of the exit from religion according to Gauchet (1999), has in most cases integrated and assimilated the separation between the temporal and the spiritual. Protestantism and Catholicism have forged a religion with a universal message less and less constrained by ethnic, national or local characteristics. These different notions are not without repercussions for life in society and in particular for the foundation of common values strongly marked by religious ideas for Islam, Judaism and Hinduism in countries where these religions are in the majority. These religious ideas are less perceptible in the West where this foundation of common values is attached to fundamental rights, sometimes in contradiction with the former.

It should be emphasised that the internal laws or disciplines of each religion are diverse. Protestantism is very diversified in this respect, and Lutheran church law does not cover the same provisions as the regulation of a Baptist or Pentecostal community. Even within Catholicism, there are differences between Latin canon law, the Code of Canons of the Eastern Churches and especially the canon law of the Lefebvristes.[12] With the exception of the canons of the first millennia, Orthodox canon law also shows diversity linked to national situations. Similarly, Hebrew and Muslim laws are interpreted according to the plurality of streams which cut across these religions. It is therefore important to retain the main distinctive principles to which these religions are attached and their ability to evolve.

Entering into and exiting from a religion therefore take on a very particular dimension according to these different notions. To leave or enter into Islam or Judaism equally consists in joining or leaving an ethnic group or nation, thereby risking isolation and marginality. This fusional model remains prevalent even for a newly settled Islam, whereas Jewish communities have succeeded over the very long term in forging mechanisms facilitating the balance between doctrinal requirements and temporal realities. Similarly, in Hinduism, the links between religion and nation are important. But adaptations tolerating multiple belonging do, however, soften the effects of conversions. This dichotomy is barely discernible in Christianity, except for residual forms in Orthodoxy where religion and nation are more firmly bound. For entry into Christianity, particular emphasis is placed on the progressiveness of the approach, on spiritual preparation and intellectual training. A similar approach exists in Judaism and is gradually being adopted by certain streams of Islam, particularly in Europe. While exiting from a religion has consequences in all religions, it must be noted that the sanctions are not the same and that the principle of the death penalty for apostasy in Islam arouses controversy.

The theme of the rights and duties of members of the Christian, Muslim, Jewish and Hindu religions essentially revolves around women's rights, the levels of commitment of members and the distinction between clerics/ministers and laypeople. Religious rules determine the place and role of women in the religious community and sometimes in public. Women cannot perform the role of priests in the Catholic Church, nor leadership and preaching roles in Islam and Judaism in which, moreover, they are not recommended to study the founding texts. Likewise, in Hinduism, as a rule the woman must take a back seat behind the man. Only historical forms of Protestantism have put an end to this distinction. Women can have access to all positions without discrimination. A distinction between clergy and layperson remains in Catholicism and Orthodoxy, while, in other religions, knowledge of the founding texts and theological knowledge prevail.

However, the rules are not immutable in their interpretation. The arrangements concerning the place of women are real in Judaism, in which certain streams train rabbinic women, and in Islam, where women hold positions in mosques. The Catholic Church has not been left behind. More and more women hold positions of responsibility locally, regionally in dioceses and even in Roman dicasteries.

If religious laws have always been evolving, globalisation and the inclusion of the religious phenomenon within plurality have accentuated an irreversible process that highlights the porosity between the different models of internal law of religions on the one hand, as well as between them and the foundation of common values, on the other.

Notes

1 The choice of the expression 'religious affiliation' resulted from observing a tendency to mobility in religious membership and to the individualisation of convictions in the contemporary world. The idea of 'affiliation', even if it refers etymologically to 'filiation' – to a religion handed down by the family – can also be interpreted in connection with a proactive notion of religious choice – one becomes affiliated with a religion – whereas the notion of belonging does not suggest this personal approach.

2 www.constituteproject.org/constitution/Morocco_2011.pdf.

3 Convention between the State of the Grand Duchy of Luxembourg and religious communities established in Luxembourg, 26 January 2015, preamble.

4 *Ibid.*, Article 2.

5 Contract between the Free and Hanseatic City of Hamburg, the DITIB Regional Association in Hamburg, SCHURA – the Council of Islamic Communities in Hamburg and the Association of Islamic Cultural Centres, 13 November 2012, Hamburg Parliament, 20th term, Official Record 20/5830 of 13.11.2012.

6 *Ibid.*

7 Musulmans de France. Charte des valeurs and principes, 15 April 2017, in www.uoif-online.com/wp-content/uploads/2017/04/CHARTE-MUSULMANS.

8 United Protestant Church of France. Lutheran and Reformed Communion. Part 1, Constitution, Article 1, www.eglise-protestante-unie.fr/organisation/references-et-documents-administratifs-6.

9 Allgemeines Dekret der Deutschen Bischofskonferenz zum Kirchenaustritt, 20 September 2012, www.bistum-trier.de/no_cache/bistum-bischof.

10 Administrative Court of Strasbourg, order of 29 September 2006 (*Mme Jeanine Elkouby/Consistoire israélite du Bas-Rhin*).

11 In www.vatican.va/archive/ENG1104/_PT.HTM.
12 Referring to traditional Catholics who refused the mainly liturgical developments decreed by the Second Vatican Council.

References

Gauchet, M. 1999. *The Disenchantment of the World. A Political History of Religion*. Princeton University Press.

Messner, F. 2008. 'Régime des cultes. Organisation et institutions des cultes statutaires et non statutaires et congrégations'. *Jurisclasseur Alsace-Moselle*. Fasc. 231.

Willaime, J.-P. 2016. 'Le statut des ministres du culte musulman en France dans une perspective comparative', paper presented at the International Symposium *Le statut des pasteurs protestants*, 16 and 17 November.

Part IV
Marriage

16

Jewish law

Marriage

Elimelech Westreich and Avishalom Westreich[1]

Introduction

In this chapter we introduce basic Jewish law (*halakhic*) regulations and doctrines regarding key legal institutions related to marriage.[2] One way of understanding legal institutions is to shed light on turning points in their development or in times of change. We focus mainly on changes that have taken place over time in Jewish law concerning marriage and divorce, primarily on those that are relevant to the status of the wife within this regime. This includes the following topics:[3] the formation of marriage, which affects the conditions under which the partners enter into the marriage contract; bigamy, which affects both the marriage contract and the course of the marriage; mutually agreed and coerced divorce, which affects the end of the marriage; and levirate marriage, which affects both the beginning and the end of the marriage.

The legal corpus in question took form in the Mishna[4] and the Talmud[5] in the first half of the first millennium, in the Land of Israel and in Babylon. The Mishnah and the Talmud are the basis for the regulation of marriage and divorce in Jewish law, although they have been creatively interpreted, and at times entirely changed, by various Jewish traditions throughout the Middle Ages and into the modern era.

The Babylonian Geonim, who lived and worked within an Islamic empire, spread the Talmud and its rules throughout the Diaspora. The Geonim adopted in principle the Talmudic rules in matters of marriage but introduced significant changes regarding the wife's right to a unilateral, no-fault divorce, against her husband's will, and to her financial rights in this type of divorce (Westreich, 2002a).

The Talmudic arrangements concerning these topics were generally followed without significant changes by Eastern (Mizrachi) communities, mainly in Iraq, Iran, and Yemen, until their emigration to the State of Israel, in the middle of the 20th century. A different stream of Judaism, the Sephardic, with strong connections to the Mizrachi stream, evolved in Spain at the end of the first millennium and spread to the Mediterranean basin after the expulsion in 1492. This stream modified the Talmudic arrangements in matters of bigamy and forcible divorce of the wife, using contractual tools. Their main aim was to protect the wives against cruel behavior of the husbands. In Central and Western Europe, at the turn of the second millennium, a new stream emerged, the Ashkenazi, which revolutionized the fundamental issues concerning marriage and the wife's status, and upgraded the legal and social status of wives. Their measures spread to Poland and Eastern Europe at the beginning of the modern period, and immigrants brought these to the New World and to the Land of Israel.

The formation of marriage

Engagement (Shiduchin)

Shiduchin (engagement) is the pre-marriage stage in which the families of the groom and bride bargain and agree about the marriage, its date and place, and the economic duties and obligations of each of the parties. There is no formal requirement for *shiduchin* as part of the marriage. Talmudic sages, however, strongly recommended beginning the marriage process with *shiduchin* because of matters of modesty, but skipping it has no effect on the validity of the marriage (Maimonides, Ishut 3:22). In the Ashkenazi community, it was common to sign a detailed contract, called the *shetar tenaim* (a deed of clauses or an engagement contract). The *shiduchin* agreement was merely a civil contract, without any matrimonial results, although in the pre-modern era, in some Ashkenazi communities, both sides took an oath that added a religious aspect to the contract, strengthening the obligation of the parties and preventing easy breach. Today, however, it does not commonly serve as a civil contract proper, but rather, in some traditional communities, as a ritual act.[6]

Betrothal and marriage (Kiddushin and Nissuin)

According to Talmudic law, marriage can be performed only between a man and an unmarried woman, both Jewish, without close blood relations or relative connections, and generally both adults. A married woman has no capacity to marry before she divorces (Maimonides, Ishut 1:3), unlike a married man, who can be married bigamously.[7] Marriages of minors below the age of 12 for girls and 13 for boys are void, except in special circumstances (Maimonides, Ishut 3:12, 4:7.). A Jewish man or woman has no capacity to marry a gentile, and such marriage is considered void. The list of relatives whom one cannot marry is given in the Torah (Leviticus 20: 10–26), and marriage involving such relatives is considered void (Maimonides, Ishut 1:5). Talmudic sages added other relations, and marriage in such cases is considered voidable (Maimonides, Ishut 1:6).

Usually, the consent of both spouses to the marriage is mandatory (Maimonides, Ishut 4:1). In two exceptional cases, the consent of the wife is not required: that of a girl under the age of 12 who is considered a minor and may be married by her father (Maimonides, Ishut, 3:11), and that of a widow whose husband has died without descendants (levirate marriage) (Maimonides, Ibum VaHalitsa 1:1–2). These exceptions were practiced to different extents in various Jewish traditions. At present, in the State of Israel, marriage of minor girls under the age of 18 is prohibited by state law[8] and by the ordinance of the Chief Rabbinate of Israel (the Jerusalem Ban), enacted shortly after the establishment of the State of Israel (Shershevsky, 1993: 452). Ashkenazi traditions have cancelled levirate marriages and ruled that the ritual act of *halitsa*, which severed the levirate ties between the widow and her brother-in-law, was obligatory. In Sephardic and Mizrachi communities, levirate marriage was common, based on some opinions in the Talmud, and the widow was often forced to enter the levirate marriage.[9] The Chief Rabbinate of Israel intervened in this issue as well and prohibited levirate marriage, obligating the brother-in-law (*yavam*) to release the widow by performing *halitsa*.

Marriage includes two separate stages: *kiddushin* (betrothal) and *nissuin* (the actual marriage). *Kiddushin* connects the couple in a matrimonial bond that affects mainly the woman. From the moment of the *kiddushin* onward, she is considered 'the wife of a man' and cannot marry another man unless the groom releases her by a bill of divorce (a *get*) or upon his death. No economic or conjugal obligations, however, are established at this stage, and the couple cannot yet live together as husband and wife. The *nissuin*, which is associated with the groom taking the bride into his home (today, by the ritual process of standing under the canopy), completes the marriage and finalizes the complete set of mutual legal rights and obligations.

Kiddushin was originally a private act that contained two dimensions, a contractual and a ritual one. The man conducts the ceremony by himself or by proxy, in the presence of two witnesses, who are constitutive, not merely declarative. During the ceremony, the man gives the woman a sum of money, commonly in the form of a ring, and says to her 'you are betrothed (*mekudeshet*) to me according to the law of Moses and Israel'. The *kiddushin* can also be performed by the granting of a deed of *kiddushin* or by sexual intercourse (rather than by the giving of money), although the latter was severely condemned by the sages (Maimonides, Ishut 3:21). In all cases, there is a demand to say the phrase 'you are betrothed' to the woman, although no single formula exists, and the *kiddushin* may be valid even if the saying is omitted altogether.[10] Because of the contractual nature of the *kiddushin*, the rules of Jewish contract law are implied. For example, a condition may be added allowing the *kiddushin* to be cancelled if the condition is not met (Maimonides, Ishut 6:1).[11]

The private nature of the *kiddushin* caused many difficulties. For example, a man could argue that he had betrothed a woman although she had not given her consent (or was forced to give her consent). Similarly, the time elapsed between *kidushin* and *nissuin* could cause many problems (Freiman, 1945: 2–5). In the long history of Jewish law, different solutions were offered, but unlike the decrees of the Catholic Church on marriage at the Council of Trent, they were not unequivocal enough to entirely overcome all the obstacles. The last amendment intended to minimize complications was that of the Chief Rabbinate of Israel. In the Jerusalem Ban, the Rabbinate enacted the following requirements: advance registration of the bride and groom at the offices of the Rabbinate; ceremony performed by an official rabbi of the Rabbinate; public ceremony in the presence of at least ten men; betrothal and marriage performed at the same time (Shershevsky, 1993: 452–453). Circumventing these requirements may result in a defect in the marriage, not only from the religious but also from the civil point of view, because in Israel marriage and divorce are recognized only if performed according to religious law.[12]

In the past, the second stage, *nissuin*, was usually performed after about 12 months. The rite was centered on the *hupah*, the marriage canopy, which symbolizes the entrance of the bride into the house of the groom and the beginning of communal life. Nowadays, all Jewish ethnic groups perform both the *kiddushin* and *nissuin* under the *hupah*, so that the two elements are united. As part of the same ceremony, the husband gives his new wife the *ketubbah*, which is the marriage contract. The *ketubbah* contains various obligations of the husband, mainly economic, but additional clauses as well. In the Sephardic *ketubbah*, for example, there may be a monogamy clause, and occasionally a clause against forcible divorce of the wife, discussed later. The ceremony is rich in religious activity, such as the 'seven blessings', the breaking of a glass in remembrance of the destruction of the Temple in Jerusalem, and a declaration by the groom not to forget Jerusalem.

The marriage crystalizes the mutual obligations of the husband and wife. Sexual relations are now permitted, and both sides are obligated to them. The mutual economic obligations of the couple also come into effect at this time. According to Maimonides, when a man marries a woman, he is obligated in ten matters (mainly to support his wife), and derives benefits in four matters (Maimonides, Ishut 12:2–3). A regime of separation of property is in effect during the marriage, although the husband has the right to the income of his wife's property and has the obligation to manage it, and the wife is restricted in making transactions in her property. Unlike the wife, the husband is not restricted, but a mortgage is imposed on all his property in order to secure his wife's *ketubbah*. The husband also has an obligation to pay maintenance to his wife, but if she works, she must hand over her income to her husband. Alternatively, she can keep her income from work but is no longer entitled to maintenance. This system was not necessarily unfavorable to the wife in the pre-modern era, but at present, because of radical socio-economic changes, it has become discriminatory against wives. In recent years, in Israel, rabbinical courts, which have some jurisdiction in matters of economic relations, responded to this challenge with great hesitation. Only after the intervention of the Israeli legislature and the Supreme Court did rabbinical courts adopt a modern equal property system (see Westreich, 2019).

The nature of marriage

The objective of marriage is reflected in one of the most important codes of Jewish law, the *Arba'ah turim* (often referred to simply as the *Tur*) of R. Jacob ben Asher. In the opening lines of the part devoted to family matters, *Even ha'ezer*, R. Jacob ben Asher writes:

> May the name of the Holy One, blessed be He, be blessed for His desiring the good of His creations. For He knew that 'It is not good for man to be alone' [Gen. 2:18], and he therefore made a helpmate for him. Furthermore, man was created for the purpose of being fruitful and multiplying, and this is impossible without the helpmate.

The association between man and woman has two aims: partnership with a 'helpmate" (Genesis 2:18) and procreation (to 'be fruitful and multiply') (Genesis 1:28). Jewish marriage includes both aspects, at times in a tense relationship, at other times in concert. Relationships between husband and wife in Jewish law are not always equal or mutual, and intensive research is devoted to these issues when it comes to divorce.[13] Nevertheless, the role of cooperation or partnership in Jewish law and Jewish marriage cannot be disregarded. In the words of the prophet, 'she is your friend and your covenant wife' (Malachi, 2:14). Focusing on the partnership aspect of Jewish marriage can lead to greater equality between men and women.

Some argue that the main characteristic of traditional Jewish marriage is the husband's control over his wife and view the relationships between them as an acquisition. Admittedly, acquisition is found in Talmudic sources with regard to marriage (the Hebrew term is *kinyan*; see Mishnah, Kiddushin, 1:1). We prefer to define marriage, however, from a Jewish legal perspective, as a contractual relationship rather than an acquisition. In other words, *kinyan*, the term used for contracting marriage, does not necessarily imply appropriation or acquisition, but rather affects *in personam* relationships, as shown later.

Two issues are raised to prove that Jewish marriage has an acquisitional aspect: the sexual control, which according to this view the husband exercises over his wife, and the inferior legal status of the wife in matters of divorce, especially as reflected in the laws of the rebellious wife. (Matters of divorce, including the changes in the course of the history of Jewish law regarding the law of the rebellious wife, are discussed later.) According to the Talmud and the medieval codes, the wife has a basic *right* to a sexual life (the commandment of *'onah*), which the husband is *obligated* to fulfill, rather than being entitled to it. Rape within marriage is strictly forbidden, as stated in *Tur* and *Shulchan Aruch*: 'rape is prohibited, even if it is his wife'.[14] The husband is obligated to live a normal marital life with his wife, in addition to his monetary and social obligations. Although there are unequal elements in this relationship, as described earlier regarding the financial aspects of marriage, the legal construct, despite the literal use of the acquisitional language, is better understood in modern terms as a contractual relationship (see Westreich, 2015).

Because procreation is considered to be one of the important objectives of marriage, it greatly influences the legal aspects of marriage. Infertility can be a ground for bigamy and forcible divorce. After the death of the husband, infertility creates a levirate bond if the deceased husband is survived by a brother. The levirate bond binds the widow, without her consent, to her brother-in-law, in a matrimonial relation similar to betrothal. To sever the bond, a ritual procedure called *halitsa*, which functions similarly to divorce, is required.[15] The levirate bond can also serve as a ground for bigamy of the brother-in-law if he is married. Throughout the history of Jewish law, all these issues have greatly affected the marital status of the wife. Today, in Israel and in other Western countries, their practical use and legal relevance (i.e., infertility as a ground for divorce, or the obligation to consummate the levirate marriage) have greatly diminished, and their practical effect on the character of marriage is often only theoretical.[16]

The structure of marriage: monogamy v. polygamy

Talmudic roots and Eastern tradition

This section traces the development of various trends in Jewish law concerning polygamy and monogamy among the Mizrachi, Sephardic, and Ashkenazi ethnic groups in the Middle Ages.[17] The Bible imposes no limitations on polygamy (Friedman, 1981, 1986: 7–11). Important figures in the Bible, both before and after the Torah was given, had more than one wife. Neither the Bible nor the Mishnah express any reservations against polygamy and impose no limitations on the marriage agreement. Indeed, the Mishnah has many provisions that are more applicable to a polygamous than to a monogamous society.

The first halakhic stand against polygamy can be found in the Babylonian Talmud, which provides the woman with legal means of protection against a man taking multiple wives. A difference of opinion between Rava and Rabbi Ammi is recorded in Tractate *Yevamot*, with R. Ammi, taking the position that 'a man who takes another wife must divorce his first wife and give her her *ketubbah*'. Rava disagreed, maintaining that 'if a man takes another wife, this is permissible on condition that he provides for her needs'.[18] According to Rava, unbridled polygamy is allowed, the only limitation being the man's ability to fulfill his legal obligations to his wives. Rabbi Ammi's position found expression in the tradition of the Land of Israel. On the basis of other sources from the Land of Israel, found in the *genizah*, Mordechai A. Friedman has shown that from the time of the Jerusalem Talmud (3rd and 4th centuries) onward, actual practice followed Rabbi Ammi in the Land of Israel and in areas under its influence, first and foremost Egypt, until the 9th century (Friedman, 1986: 16–23). Rava's position was reflected in the Babylonian tradition and was followed in all the important halakhic codes of the post-Talmudic period, which were produced mainly in the Sephardic environment.[19]

Sephardic tradition in the Mediterranean: curbing the husband's power

Sephardic Jews originate from the Iberian Peninsula. Their approach to the protection of the woman's matrimonial bond, especially the curbing of polygamy, was shaped during the Middle Ages. The fundamental tenet was the position of Rava, but the Sephardic tradition developed a legal barrier to polygamy using the contractual tool of the monogamy clause.

Monogamy clauses spread throughout Spain in the Middle Ages, and from there to places where the Spanish exiles settled. These provisos included all or part of the following undertakings: (a) not to marry another woman; (b) issue a writ of divorce in case of breach of the clause; (c) pay the *ketubbah* in case of breach; and (d) pay compensation in addition to the sum of the *ketubbah*. Occasionally, an explicit condition was added, stating that the husband was released from his obligation if his wife did not give birth within a specific period, usually ten years.

Another tool used to restrict polygamy was the monogamy oath, intended to add a proscriptive dimension to the contractual obligation, giving greater force to the monogamy clause and closing any existing legal loopholes. One difficulty concerning the validity of a commitment to grant a divorce has to do with a fundamental uncertainty in Jewish law regarding whether a man can be obligated to divorce his wife following an undertaking of a contractual nature. It is difficult to say how common this oath was in Spain, but among the Spanish exiles in the Mediterranean basin in the 16th century, it was widespread and went hand in hand with the monogamy clause (Westreich, 2002b: 282–288).

In some places, the prohibition against polygamy was based entirely on custom and was obligatory as an implied condition, because it was considered that the woman 'married on this assumption', in the words of Rabbi Al-Ashbili (Westreich, 2002b: 162–163). The laws of the Christian kingdoms, perhaps more than any other legal factor, greatly strengthened the protection of Jewish women's marital relationship. As the Reconquista marched on in Spain in the 12th century, Moslem territory gradually came under Christian control and cultural influence. As a result, the legal system began intervening in matters of Jewish family law, and laws that were passed in various kingdoms imposed prohibitions against polygamy and forcible divorce among Jews (Baron, 1957: 136–139, 393–394). Even in cases in which the husband had just cause according to the Sephardic tradition, such as fulfilling the fertility or the levirate commandment, the legal barriers were not always removed by the Christian rulers.

Following the expulsion from Spain, the Sephardic community spread mainly to the Ottoman Empire and the Maghreb, which were Muslim territories. Although the monogamy clause had by then become common practice and was implemented in every *ketubbah*, fully recognized by halakhic authorities, the Muslim rulers tolerated unlimited polygamy. As a result, Jewish women were deprived of the highly effective protection against bigamy granted to them earlier in the Christian kingdoms of the Iberian Peninsula. In sum, the protection of women's marital status weakened, especially when the husband could show just cause for changing the marital relationship, most notably in cases of infertility and levirate marriage.

Legal doctrines concerning fertility played a key role in Jewish family law and had many practical consequences in cases of polygamy and forcible divorce. Infertility was common in the past, and so were many situations that gave rise to a levirate bond if the husband died childless and was survived by a brother. These phenomena were important causes for changing the marital relations between spouses and contributed to the creation of polygamous families. Because Sephardic communities lived in a Muslim environment, where polygamy, levirate marriage, and forcible divorce were allowed, there were no impediments to them. The Mizrachi tradition, which differed from the Sephardic one, provided even less protection to wives.

Ashkenazi tradition: strict defense of women

The ban of Rabbenu Gershom: a revolutionary change

According to prevailing tradition, in the 11th century Rabbenu Gershom Meor Ha-Golah[20] enacted the two famous regulations (*takkanot*) prohibiting polygamy and forcible divorce.[21]

The formulation of the regulation against polygamy, as it appears in an important source, is as follows:

> A ban of Rabbenu Gershom Meor ha-Golah, issued as a regulation in the communities, prohibiting bigamy; it may only be waived in the presence of one hundred men from three lands and three communities, nor may they consent unless they see clear reason for waiver, and the woman's *ketubbah* must be deposited in trustworthy hands in the form of cash or pledges.[22]

We believe that the Ban of Rabbenu Gershom was originally limited in scope and judicial force (for more detail, cf. Westreich, 2002b: 70–74). By the mid-12th century, primarily in the wake of internal halakhic developments, a stronger regulation was required to protect the women's interests, which in the past had been protected by existing halakhic principles, such as the rule of the rebellious wife instituted by the *Geonim*, according to which the wife had the right to a unilateral no-fault divorce on demand, together with some financial rights (Westreich, 2002a). Any possible influence of the surrounding Christian society cannot be ruled out, but this influence was indirect. Christian society affected Jewish society, which in turn affected Jewish law (Westreich, 2002b: 69). Clear expression of this can be found in Ravyah's decision not to waive the Ban on the grounds of infertility, which he based on a societal norm, commenting: 'How many sickly and barren women are there [among Jews], yet no one says a thing about it' (Westreich, 2002b: 113).

The Ban brought about a revolutionary change in the legal status of women, and it differs from all other legal sources that protected women. The comments of medieval halakhic authorities reveal an exceptional attitude toward this legislation. Rabbenu Asher (Rosh) said that Ashkenazi Jews related to the Ban as if it had been decreed in Sinai (*Resp. Rosh*, ch. 43, sec. 8), and in one case he stressed that Rabbenu Gershom intended to equate the status of women with that of men, but not to grant women preference over men (Resp. Rosh, ch. 42, sec.1). Sages viewed the Ban as extremely powerful legislation, which in the words of Ravyah, was 'something in which we are not the masters, empowered to waive it' (Westreich, 2002b: 116). It was cogent legislation on the level of public law and denied any possibility of adding conditional clauses, making the protection of women's marital relationship a matter of public interest in every respect.

The Ban and infertility

The main test of the force of the Ban lies in the causes for which it can be waived. In contrast with Sephardic tradition, the Ashkenazi attitude was that the Ban extended beyond the limited interest of protecting women against the whims of their husbands, and was intended to bring about a change in family structure and to make the woman's marital status closer to that of the man. This approach made it possible to reject various claims for waivers based on objective factors, even if they were firmly grounded in Talmudic law. The most prominent example concerns failure to fulfill the fertility commandment, one of the most important precepts in the teachings of the sages. Infertility, the root cause of failure to fulfill the commandment, was one of the main reasons for men taking several wives in areas where polygamy was practiced (Friedman, 1986: 8). Ashkenazi legal tradition and social practice in the Middle Ages flatly rejected the fertility commandment as a cause for waiving the Ban (Westreich, 2002b: 111–119). Since the 13th century, in the entire extensive body of rulings from Western and Central Europe, we cannot find a single case in which a man sued to divorce his wife or marry a second woman exclusively on the grounds that his wife was barren. This stands in contrast to the situation in Spain during the same period, or in the Ottoman Empire in the 16th century, where such suits were commonplace. Several factors, legal as well as extra-legal, made it possible to reject the fertility commandment as a just cause for waiving the Ban.

The commandment of levirate marriage fell into the same category: a situation that arises objectively, without the behavior of either party causing it. In the early stages of the development of the Ban, the commandment superseded it, but in time, the Ban took precedence over the commandment (Westreich, 2002b: 127–136). Only in cases that originated in the woman's behavior, as when the woman severely transgressed against the faith or was rebellious, was the Ban set aside. Even in these cases, however, a procedure for waiving the Ban was required, as opposed to just ruling that it did not apply, which would have given the legal system control over the policy of waiving the Ban (Westreich, 2002b: 154–155).

Remedies and defenses

Another area in which the Ban was unique and markedly different from all other defenses protecting women's marital relationship throughout Jewish history was that of the remedies and procedures necessary to waive the Ban (Westreich, 2002b: 155–157). First, it is important to stress that a violation of the Ban was a matter of public law, therefore the public was a party to the claims and could institute legal proceedings in cases of violation, alongside the woman who was affected and independently of her. The first remedy, chronologically speaking, was an injunction that could be obtained in advance, before the man had violated the Ban. Flagrant violation of the Ban by a man taking a second wife without permission was rare.

The main legal redress offered by the public was a ban, a punishment for criminal offenses whose main thrust was to ostracize a person from Jewish society, isolating him and preventing him from having any religious, social, or communal relationship with his fellow Jews. In a small, closed religious society, such as Jewish society in the Middle Ages, this was a severe punishment, and it would not be an exaggeration to say it was even more severe than imprisonment, common today. The woman could take her husband to court for violation of the Ban, and was also offered the direct remedy of suing to force her husband to divorce his second wife. To avoid criminal and civil sanctions that could be imposed on the man for violating the Ban, he had to receive a special waiver. In this respect, Ashkenazi tradition introduced a unique method of supervision and control, the waiver by 100 rabbis from 3 countries. A ruling permitting a man to marry another woman (or to divorce his wife against her will) could be issued only if 100 rabbis from 3 countries consented, after duly considering and examining the case. This unique procedure can be described as the horizontal, as opposed to the vertical appeal. Given the conditions of life in the Middle Ages, this was a difficult and costly undertaking, greatly reducing the number of cases in which the Ban was waived.

Restricting polygamy for all Jewish ethnic groups in the State of Israel

Since the 19th century, the Land of Israel was the meeting place of various Jewish ethnic groups that had different traditions regarding polygamy. In general, each ethnic group persisted in its heritage, with few changes in the patterns that had been followed for many generations, as described earlier. The first attempt to restrict polygamy took place in 1936, when the British rulers in Palestine prohibited bigamy and imposed a five-year prison sentence on offenders.[23]

One of the elements of the crime was that the second marriage had to be void from the religious point of view.[24] As far as the Jews were concerned, there was a huge loophole in the law because the second marriage was not void for any of the Jewish communities. Mizrachi Jews had no limitations on bigamous marriage; Sephardic Jews were restricted by contract, but the second marriage was valid; and even for Ashkenazi Jews, the second marriage was merely voidable, but not void. As a result, no Jew could be indicted according to this law.

The two Chief Rabbis, Herzog (Ashkenazi) and Uziel (Sephardic), exhorted the British Mandatory authorities to change the penal code and declare all instances of bigamy by Jews a criminal offense, whatever their ethnic origin (Westreich, 2003). Toward the end of Mandatory rule, in 1947, the British legislators changed the law and established a rule that is still in effect today, with some modifications. Soon after the establishment of the State of Israel, in 1950, the Chief Rabbinate of Israel, headed by Rabbis Herzog and Uziel, changed the religious rules by an enactment that prohibited all men and women from being part of a bigamous marriage 'except with a marriage permit issued under the signatures of the Chief Rabbis of Israel' (the Jerusalem Ban) (Shershevsky, 1993: 431).

This enactment was intended to prohibit polygamy for all Jewish ethnic groups, whatever their tradition, and to enact a uniform Jewish law and custom concerning the family structure by making it monogamous. There is no unanimity among the religious judges (*dayanim*) in the official rabbinical courts about the nature and effectiveness of the Jerusalem Ban. Some believe that the Jerusalem Ban was intended to extend the norms set by the Ban of Rabbenu Gershom to all Jews, so that all Jewish women would enjoy equal protection.[25] Others argue that the Jerusalem Ban made Mizrachi wives equal to Sephardic ones, who are protected by the monogamy clause. Others yet do not accept the Jerusalem Ban at all, holding that nothing has changed. Nevertheless, even the latter agree that there is a custom in the State of Israel not to marry two women, and that this custom has the force of a legal norm applicable to all.[26] In any case, in matters of polygamy, all Jews (and non-Jews) in Israel, irrespective of ethnic origin, are subject to the criminal law of the State of Israel, which carries a five-year sentence for 'a married man who marries another woman' (The Criminal Code, section 176).

To evade criminal penalties, a man wishing to marry a second wife must obtain from a rabbinical court a ruling that allows him to marry another woman, approved by the President of the Great Rabbinical Court (The Criminal Code, section 179). Even after such a ruling has been secured, the man still can be prevented from obtaining a marriage license to marry a second wife by means of an appeal to the High Court of Justice, which supervises the President of the Great Rabbinical Court in this matter.

When does the rabbinical court allow a man to marry another woman? The answer varies in the different ethnic traditions. According to the Ashkenazi tradition, a man is never allowed actual bigamy, which is living with two women simultaneously. The purpose of the permission to marry a second woman is to force a woman to accept divorce (a *get*) in case she refuses or is not qualified to do so, when there are sufficient grounds for divorce. In practice, even rabbis belonging to Eastern or Sephardic ethnic traditions usually refrain from issuing marriage licenses that would result in situations of practical bigamy. But in the Biton case, Rabbi Ovadia Yosef, the Sephardic Chief Rabbi, permitted a man from the Moroccan community to be married simultaneously to two women,[27] the first wife agreeing to the marriage because she was barren. But the High Court of Justice rejected his position and accepted the view of Rabbi Goren, the Ashkenazi Chief Rabbi, according to whom bigamist marriages were unacceptable in Israel. At present, all requests for a license to marry a second woman in Israel are in practice divorce claims, and if a rabbinical court allows a man to marry a second woman it demands that he first deposit with the court a *get* and the *ketubbah* for his first wife's benefit.

Nevertheless, Eastern and Sephardic judges (*dayanim*) require far fewer and lighter elements in support of a suit to marry a second woman than do Ashkenazi judges. Ashkenazi judges would reject without hesitation a request from a man to divorce a woman who had given birth to one or more daughters, or alternatively to be allowed to marry a second woman, whereas Eastern judges might accept such a request.[28]

In all cases, however, attitudes toward fertility have been affected by modern medicine, which can determine with certainty which spouse is responsible for the couple's inability to conceive, and offers both treatment for infertility and artificial alternatives. Modern medicine has also undermined the scientific views accepted by the Talmud and *Halakha*. As cases of infertility and the death of young men have declined, far fewer levirate bonds have formed. Levirate marriage was challenged after the establishment of the State of Israel and the encounter of the Sephardic and Mizrachi communities with Ashkenazi Jews (Westreich, 2003–2004). It was also challenged by the spirit of equality that penetrated the Jewish communities throughout the Middle East and the Maghreb, as the women of Morocco stated around 1950, 'we do not want to be like prisoners of war' (Westreich, 2009–2010).

At the end of the 20th century, bigamy appears to have been almost eradicated from all ethnic groups of Jewish society. But in the 21st century, we detect contradictory signs: one legal, the other social. The first is a verdict of a district rabbinical court, issued on June 30, 2011, with the agreement of the R. Shlomo Amar, the former Sephardic Chief Rabbi and President of the Great Rabbinical court.[29] The rabbinical judges allowed a man of Yemenite origin to live with two wives because the first one could not give birth in 26 years of marriage and despite many medical treatments. The wife, who is of Tunisian origin, agreed to the bigamous marriage. Furthermore, in recent years, a few social organizations have been active in the social arena in favor of polygamous marriage, usually by encouraging men and women to wed in private, in other words, enter into a marriage that may be religiously recognized, but without civil permission and without registration.

On December 5, 2016, R. Yitzhak Yosef, the current Sephardic Chief Rabbi and President of the High Rabbinical Court of Appeal, published a public indictment against practicing bigamy by celebrating the second marriage privately, without obtaining the authorization of the official rabbinical institutions. In his opening words, he attacked:

> [a]n organization that is supported by people who call themselves 'rabbis,' religious judges, mystics. These people interpret wrongfully the Torah and the Halakha, especially the ruling of my father, R. Ovadia Yosef. They spread the false idea that nowadays there is no restriction on bigamy, and that on the contrary, it is a *mitzvah* to marry a second wife.[30]

Does this mean that polygamy, which has provoked strong opposition, is making a comeback, together with private marriages, which have caused much distress to Jewish society? Only time will tell.

Dissolution of marriage

Divorce: general overview

When discussing divorce in Jewish law, we need to distinguish 'between the right to demand a divorce or initiate divorce proceedings, and the right or power to perform the formalities necessary . . . to dissolve an existing marriage' (Brody, 1999: 230). Typically, divorce in Jewish law, as unanimously accepted by Talmudic and post-Talmudic sources, is executed by a writ of divorce (*get*) delivered by the husband to his wife. Like marriage, the divorce is a private act between the two spouses. In practice, however, especially today, it requires the judicial decision of a rabbinical court, and it is carried out under the strict supervision of the court. Rabbinical courts may compel the spouses to go through this process, although the execution of the divorce is still by means of a *get* given by the husband to his wife. We find rare cases in which divorce is executed by a constitutive act of annulment on the part of a rabbinical court, and there are cases (or at least a halakhic possibility) in which a terminative condition may retroactively annul the marriage (Westreich, 2012: chs 4 and 7). The *divorce* procedure, however, rather than marriage annulment, is always executed by a *get* given by the husband.

Divorce requires the consent of both spouses: the husband's agreement is fundamentally mandated by the Mishnah and Talmudic law, and that of the wife is required according to the Ban of Rabbenu Gershom, as noted earlier.[31] The Mishnah lists several cases in which the husband is coerced to divorce his wife. Several others are added by the Talmud and by post-Talmudic authorities, usually cases of faults, blemishes, and so on, which support the wife's entitlement to a divorce.[32] Similarly, there are cases in which the husband is entitled to divorce. According to Talmudic law, before the Ban of Rabbenu Gershom, the husband usually had the right to unilaterally divorce his wife, with or without a basis in fault and with or without her consent. The effect of a fault or blemish in such cases was therefore mainly financial (i.e., the wife would not receive payment of her *ketubbah*). After Rabbenu Gershom's Ban, consent for divorce, or fault or blemish on the part of the wife became necessary to establish the husband's right to divorce, not only to support his financial claims.

Throughout the history of Jewish law, there have been traditions that expanded the right of the wife to initiate divorce, up to a complete right to unilateral divorce on demand.[33] Generally, however, these traditions have not been accepted, although in recent years there is some revival of views that support no-fault divorce, although in a qualified way, as discussed later.

When a divorce suit is justified, the other spouse is ordered to divorce, which in some cases justifies imposing sanctions on him or her. In countries other than Israel, the only possible implication of a decision by the rabbinical court to divorce may be social pressure on the recalcitrant spouse. In Israel, however, religious courts have jurisdiction in matters of marriage and divorce.[34] Regarding Jewish couples, the law provides rabbinical courts with the unique authority to impose sanctions on recalcitrant spouses. These include indirect measures, such as social sanctions, the denial of a driver's license, or a ban on leaving the country, and in rare cases, may result in the imprisonment of the recalcitrant spouse (usually the husband).[35]

According to the Rabbinical Courts Jurisdiction Act, rabbinical courts have exclusive jurisdiction in matters of marriage and divorce (section 1), and these matters should be adjudicated according to Jewish law (section 2). Similar legal arrangements are in force with regard to other religious denominations.[36] Therefore, decisions regarding marital status in Israel are made by the religious tribunals of the state, and their decisions are recognized by the civil authorities.[37] Matters of property distribution related to divorce are under the jurisdiction of rabbinical courts when one party binds this issue to his or her divorce suit (section 3), and should be adjudicated according to civil law.[38]

Forcible divorce

One of the most significant discrepancies between Jewish law and modern civil divorce law is the legitimization of no-fault divorce. Although there is ground in Jewish law for unilateral no-fault divorce, as noted earlier, this approach is not accepted by all. Even when divorce is justified by a rabbinical court, it is not always possible to coerce the recalcitrant spouse to agree to the divorce, especially when it requires the cooperation of a recalcitrant husband. The other spouse, often the wife, remains 'chained' to an unwanted or practically dead marriage, without a legal way of remarrying. This is known as the *agunah* problem (plural: *agunot*, chained wives), a situation in which the husband cannot or refuses to divorce. Since the Ban of Rabbenu Gershom, a man whose wife refuses to accept divorce may also be considered a chained spouse, but for internal halakhic reasons, the problem of chained husbands is less acute. Extensive scholarly writing has been devoted to proposing solutions to this problem, both from within Jewish law and from a civil perspective. In the unique Israeli situation, rabbinical courts have legal power to coerce divorce, but some have argued that they do not use it sufficiently.[39]

Coerced divorce in Jewish law begins with the husband's right to unilaterally divorce his wife. The Mishna contains a dispute between Beth Shamai, Beth Hillel, and R. Akiva regarding the husband's right to divorce.[40] Beth Shamai claim that only adultery is a ground for divorcing one's wife. Beth Hillel disagree and hold that the range of grounds is much broader, and even if the wife 'burned his food', it is enough to justify divorce. R. Akiva took the extreme position, arguing that there is no need for any ground, and a husband may divorce his wife even if he finds another one that is better looking. The Talmud does not decide the dispute, although the common rule is that a wife may be divorced even without her consent, whereas the man may not be coerced to deliver a *get* against his will (but see later).[41] The Babylonian Talmud adds, however, some restrictions: it is immoral to divorce one's first wife because in this case, according to some sages, 'even the altar sheds tears over the divorce'.[42] This Talmudic passage was later used by rabbinical courts as an argument against arbitrary divorce.[43]

There is great similarity between the development of the law of bigamy and the law of forcible divorce in the three ethnic groups.[44] The Mizrachi group follows the arrangement of the Talmud, that is, the husband has the power to divorce his wife without any ground, although according to some opinions this is immoral. At the opposite extreme is the Ashkenazi tradition, which rejects forcible divorce entirely. The legal source is the Ban of Rabbenu Gershom, which is considered almost similar to the ban against bigamy in most aspects, as, for example, the grounds for waiving the Ban, the sanctions for violating it, and the procedure for lifting it. Some sages adopted an extreme position and regarded a *get* given without the consent of the wife as void. The regulation not to divorce a woman against her will was formulated in the above source as follows: 'A regulation not to give a woman a writ of divorce (*get*) against her will, and the *get* is as nothing'.[45] Both aspects of the Ban gave Ashkenazi wives solid protection and upgraded their marital status, bringing it quite close to that of the husband.

When the situation called for waiving one of the two regulations of Rabbenu Gershom, the ban on polygamy or the ban on forcible divorce, the former was waived. If it was not practically feasible to divorce a woman, bigamy was permitted. This was purely formal, however, because in practice the man was required to deposit a writ of divorce and the *ketubbah*, thereby severing his marital relationship.[46] This preference shows how deeply internalized the idea of monogamous family structure had become in the social and legal tradition unique to Ashkenazi Jewry in the Middle Ages.

Occupying the middle position between the Mizrachi and the Ashkenazi groups is the Sephardic tradition. Its attitude is a complicated one, and there are different sub-streams. In principle, the Sephardic tradition accepted the rule of the Talmud that a husband can divorce his wife without her consent, and the Ban of R. Gershom did not spread to Spain, but R. Nissim of Girona, an important Sephardic sage of the 14th century, ruled that the ban was accepted in Spain. After the 1492 expulsion from Spain, only a minority of Sephardic communities accepted the Ban, but we find a rather common practice among Sephardic Jewry of adding a clause to the *ketubbah* that forbids forcible divorce (Segal, 2010: 132–179). This clause was strengthened by an oath that was held in high regard. Among the Sephardic community in Israel, in the 20th century, this clause is not common, but the criminal code of the State of Israel closed the gap by punishing forcible divorce by five years of imprisonment.[47]

Another obstacle that stood before the Sephardic wife regarding forcible divorce was the rule of R. Eliahu Mizrachi, which permitted a husband to deposit a *get* and the sum of the *ketubbah* in court and be released from 'bed and bread', even if forcible divorce as such is not permitted by law. The majority of Sephardic Jews seem to have accepted this rule, more or less. Only a minority, headed by the Sephardic Chief Rabbi Uziel, insisted on rejecting the rule, arguing that only if the husband has a good reason may the court use Rabbi Mizrachi's ruling, but not arbitrarily (Westreich, 2005).

The wife's right to unilateral no-fault divorce

The basic rule in Jewish law regarding the ability of the wife to divorce is that it requires the husband's consent, unless there is a good reason recognized by law.[48] Throughout the history of Jewish law, however, some traditions expanded the right of the wife to initiate divorce, even without the husband's consent. One important way of circumventing the requirement for the husband's consent was the law of the rebellious wife. The origins of this law and its use for unilateral divorce by the wife are found in the Talmud (Westreich, 2010a), from where it expanded and spread at the beginning of the Geonic period (Westreich, 2002a). According to this law, a man must divorce his wife if she refuses to have conjugal relations with him and demands a divorce, arguing that her husband is 'loathsome to me', even if she cannot claim one of the classic grounds for divorce. This ruling was incorporated into early legal codes, such as those of R. Alfasi[49] and Maimonides,[50] and was in force in Spain until the beginning of the 14th century. In the 13th century, this ruling began to be challenged, apparently under the influence of Ashkenazi rulings from the school of Rabbenu Tam,[51] which were vigorously introduced in Spain at the beginning of the 14th century by R. Asher ben Jehiel (Westreich, 2002a: 207–218). Only the Yemenites continued to use the rebellious woman rule, following Maimonides, until their emigration to the State of Israel. In recent years, however, this law has seen a revival in a moderated form.

Solving the problem of the modern chained wife

In recent years, there has been a growing focus on the *agunah* problem, which is considered one of the most acute problems for Jewish law in modern life. It has been extensively discussed, and several religious and civil solutions have been proposed.[52]

Despite and perhaps because of harsh criticism of the rabbinical courts, especially in Israel, significant developments appear to be taking place within the rabbinical courts aimed at solving the problem of *agunot*. The process is not complete, but we believe that the direction is important. As a traditional legal system, it is quite natural for rabbinical courts to take small steps in adjusting to the needs of our time.

There is a long halakhic tradition of creative solutions for classic cases of *agunot*, whose husbands disappeared or were mentally or physically unable to grant a *get*. It is therefore not surprising to find similar attempts in our time as well. A famous case in Safed, in which a regional rabbinical court gave a wife a *get* in the name of a husband who was in a permanent vegetative state (May 2014), could have served as a good model for a solution.[53] Unfortunately, this was a highly exceptional decision, which faced severe objections from leading rabbinical judges and Jewish law scholars. Chief Rabbi Yitzhak Yosef even intended to convene the Great Rabbinical Court in a special tribunal to cancel this decision, but the High Court of Justice ruled that the Great Rabbinical Court had no authority to do so.[54]

Developments in this area are manifest elsewhere. A much lesser known case, but similar to the one in Safed, came before the Haifa rabbinical court a few months later, in December 2014.[55] The husband attempted suicide and failed, ending in a permanent vegetative state. His wife became an *agunah*. The regional rabbinical court of Haifa retroactively annulled the marriage on the grounds that it was a mistaken marriage because of the husband's original mental illness. The rabbinical court received the agreements of well-known rabbinical judges, including some of the more conservative ones, which were added to the verdict. In the Safed case, the court faced criticism. The Haifa court, however, distanced itself from the Safed case, probably correctly, because of the specific circumstances of the case. In the Haifa case, annulment could be based on halakhic precedents, such as those set by the widely accepted 20th-century American halakhic decisor, Rabbi Moshe Feinstein, who advocated the annulment of 'mistaken marriages'.[56] The Haifa case was the first instance in which an official Israeli rabbinical court explicitly adopted the annulment option for an *agunah* and received widespread support. Thus, a somewhat disputed halakhic construct for marriage annulment is now a legitimate tool for solving the *agunah* problem.

We can point to some progress even regarding the modern *agunah* whose husband refuses to grant a *get* (rather than not being able to do so). Certain sources in Jewish law support putting some pressure on recalcitrant spouses, both husbands and wives, despite the above-mentioned rejection of the law of the rebellious wife. One of these, Rabbenu Yerocham (Provence, France, and Toledo, Spain, first half of the 14th century), justified coerced divorce when both spouses agree not to be together anymore ('both rebel one against the other'), but one of them refuses to go through the divorce process. In modern terms, this would be called an irretrievable breakdown of marriage. A growing number of rabbinical courts accept this view today. The practical result is that in many cases of *get* refusal, when there is a marital breakdown but one spouse refuses to divorce, possibly to exact revenge or obtain a more favorable divorce settlement, the rabbinical court obligates the husband or the wife to grant or accept the *get*. This is the case even if there is no fault attached to either side, and no side has a legitimate and classic ground for divorce. Some rabbinical courts have therefore adopted the view of Rabbenu Yerocham (and of similar sources, which are not always in the mainstream), as the basis for their rulings aimed at solving problems of *get* refusal.[57]

Recent rabbinical verdicts have also shown some willingness to assign responsibility to relatives of the recalcitrant spouse, when it is clear that they have a negative influence on him. In one case, the Tel-Aviv regional court sent the father of the recalcitrant husband to jail for 30 days (March 2016).[58] This was an exceptional case, and the father appealed to the High Court of Justice. The High Court of Justice approved in principle the position of the rabbinical court and the appeal was dismissed, although it offered to impose on the father a fine of NIS 5,000 per day instead of sending the father to prison for 30 days (Misc. Crim. App. 2137/16; Misc. Crim. App. 6188/18). The important point is the willingness of the rabbinical court to impose sanctions on other family members to solve an *agunah* problem.

The process has not run its course yet, and in some respects, there is still a long way to go. Rabbenu Yerocham's view is not always accepted. Other important elements needed to solve the *agunah* problem are not yet accepted or not practiced widely enough by rabbinical courts in Israel, such as the use of prenuptial agreements, which could assist greatly in solving the *agunah* problem. Too many leading halakhic figures reject this practice, and the rabbinic establishment does not encourage it. The resistance may be due to internal halakhic reasons, such as the rejection of Rabbenu Yerocham's view; policy considerations, such as the rejection of general enactments that may affect what is considered to be the image of Jewish marriage (as opposed to adopting practical solutions); or political-institutional reasons, such as the fear of diminishing the authority of the rabbinical courts as a result of various solutions coming into widespread use.[59]

Despite the many obstacles, rabbinical courts have been taking important steps to solve individual cases involving *agunot*. These steps involve halakhic creativity and wise use of halakhic sources, in combination with the legal tools provided by Israeli law. Rabbinical courts recognize the problem and are willing to take creative steps to finding solutions. It is a gradual process, but one that is of great importance for modern Jewish law, in particular for enabling Jewish marriage and divorce law to be practiced in modern Jewish society.

Notes

1 This research was supported by the Israel Science Foundation (grant No. 922/16). We wish to thank also the David Berg Institute for Law and History, at the Buchmann Faculty of Law, Tel Aviv University, and the Hadassah-Brandeis Institute, Brandeis University, whose support was instrumental for this research.
2 Our method is historical. For a dogmatic description of Jewish marriage law, see Shershevsky (1993). Shershevsky wrote most of the topics in the entry on Family Law and Inheritance, Encyclopedia Judaica, which were collected in *The Principles of Jewish Law* (edited by M. Elon) Encyclopedia Judaica, Jerusalem (1968–1973).
3 Most of the topics were researched intensively by us, excluding the section on the formation of marriage, which was researched by Freiman (1945).
4 The Mishnah is the first Jewish code or compilation after the Bible. Its aim was to organize the written law and the oral law in a systematic way. It is the collective product of scholars who were active mainly in the first two centuries CE, and it was compiled by Rabbi Judah the Prince (Yehuda Hanassi) around the year 200 CE.
5 The Talmud is a compilation of the intellectual activity of Jewish scholars and academies (*Yeshivot*) from the beginning of the 3rd century to the end of the 5th century. It begins with the interpretation of the Mishna and it incorporates the Mishnah. Nevertheless, in many cases, the main discussions of the Talmud are independent of the Mishnah and unrelated to it. The legal reasoning of the Talmud and its way of thinking are a unique phenomenon in the Jewish tradition, and as far as we know, there is nothing similar in any other culture. Our discussion, however, refers mainly to the code of Maimonides, which is the best-known compilation of Talmudic law and an approachable text. The reader who is interested in the Talmudic text or in the other well-known post-Talmudic codes, like *Tur* or *Shulchan Aruch*, can do so with the aid of the common references to the code of Maimonides cited by the classic commentaries.
6 See in great detail Shershevsky (1993: 353–355). Shershevsky uses the term 'betrothal' for *shiduchin*, but we prefer the term 'engagement'. We use the term 'betrothal' later for *kiddushin*.
7 Although this was changed in a post-Talmudic enactment; see later.
8 Age of Marriage Law, 5710–1950, section 2.
9 Maimonides, Yibum VaHalitsa 1:2. Note that simultaneously with the Israeli enactment (around 1950), discussed *infra*, an official congregation of rabbis in Morocco, despite being part of the Sephardic and Mizrachi tradition, also prohibited levirate marriage unless the widow gave her full consent.
10 Maimonides, Ishut 3:8. For the basis of betrothal, see Mishnah, Kiddushin, 1:1.
11 The practice of adding conditions to betrothal agreements ceased from the early modern period onward. It remained in use, however, to prevent some problematic levirate connections, when there was a danger that the brother-in-law might refuse to perform the *halitsa* or be unable to do it. See Shulchan Aruch (Even HaEzer 157:4).
12 Regarding Jews, see the Rabbinical Courts Jurisdiction Act (Marriage and Divorce), 1953, and see also *infra* notes 36–38.
13 See references and discussion *infra*.
14 *Tur, 'Oraḥ ḥaim* 240, based on BT *Nedarim* 20b.
15 See Maimonides, Yibum VaHalitsa, 1:1–2.
16 Regarding levirate marriage, see *supra* note 9; Shershevsky (1993: 452). Regarding infertility, see the discussion later.
17 For a comprehensive discussion, see Westreich (2002b).

18 The disagreement with R. Ammi is discussed at length by Friedman (1986).
19 Sefer Halakhot of Rabbi Isaac b. Jacob Alfasi, *Yevamot* 65b; Maimonides, Mishneh Torah, *Ishut* 14:3. Rabbi Asher b. R. Jehiel, BT *Yevamot 65a*, sec. 17; *Tur, Even ha-Ezer*, ch. 1; Shulhan Arukh of Rabbi Joseph Caro, *Even ha-Ezer*, ch. 1.
20 According to Grossman (2001: 111), Rabbenu Gershom was born between 950–960 and died in 1028.
21 Henceforth these two regulations are referred to simply as the Ban.
22 *Resp. Maharam of Rothenburg* (Prague printing, Bloch ed., Budapest, 1895) sec. 865 (p. 159c). The formulation in other sources is quite similar and provides no further significant information on the *takkanah* against polygamy. Cf. Finkelstein (1964: 139–140).
23 Section 181 of the Penal Code, 1936, Palestine Gazette (Supp. 1) No. 652, p. 190. For details, see Radzyner (2010).
24 '181. Any person who, having a husband or wife living, marries in Palestine in any case in which such marriage is void by reason of its taking place during the life of such husband or wife, is guilty of a felony and is liable to imprisonment for five years. Such felony is termed bigamy'.
25 Rabbi Eliezer Shapira, Great Rabbinical Court of Appeal, Appeal/82/ 261, 272, in the appendix at the end of Rabbinical Court Decision 12, p. 378. For a broad discussion, see Westreich (1995: 251–253).
26 Westreich (1995); Judge Ben Shimon, Regional Rabbinical Court, File 7481/82, Rabbinical Court Decision 12, p. 226. This was recently affirmed by the present Sephardic Chief Rabbi, Yitzhak Yosef, 'A Responsum of Rishon Le-Zion, the Head of the High Rabbinical Court, as Regards the Prohibition against Marrying a Second Wife and the Prohibition against Private Marriage' (Rabbinical Courts Official Website, December 8, 2016, www.rbc.gov.il/Pages/Articles.aspx).
27 High Court of Justice 160/75 *Biton v. The Chief Rabbi of Israel Rabbi Goren*, P.D. 30(1), 309.
28 This approach enjoyed the complete agreement of Rabbi Ovadia Yosef, who discussed it in detail in a ruling he handed down in the Great Rabbinical Court. See Responsa Yabia Omer, Section 7, Even Ha'Ezer sec. 2. For a detailed discussion, see Westreich (1995: 272–273, 277–278).
29 File 1/765725 Rabbinical Court (Netanya), *Plonit and Ploni* (petitioners) (June 30, 2011).
30 Rabbi Yitzhak Yosef, *supra* note 26.
31 *Supra* notes 20–22; Westreich (2002a, 2002b: 69–74, 113, 116).
32 Mishnah, Ketubbot 7:10; Rabbi Moses Isserles (Rema), gloss to Shulhan Arukh, *Even Ha'ezer* 154:1. In these cases the wife receives her financial rights (the *ketubbah* payment, i.e., the husband's obligation to make the payment written in the marriage document, including the wife's dowry, her wife's prenuptial property, etc.).
33 The Geonic tradition adopted this view (ca. 7th–11th centuries CE) regarding the rule of the rebellious wife; see Westreich (2002a). Another old Jewish tradition, which was practiced in the first millennium in the Land of Israel, adopted a similar view based on a contractual agreement. See Westreich (2011).
34 Rabbinical Courts Jurisdiction Act (Marriage and Divorce), 1953.
35 Rabbinical courts derive their authority to apply these and other measures from the Rabbinical Courts Law (Enforcement of Divorce Decrees) 1995 (1994–95) (Isr.).
36 Concerning Christians and Muslims, see sections 52 and 54 to the King's Order in Council, 1922–1947. Concerning the Druze, see Druze Religious Courts Law, 1962.
37 There are some exceptions, including interfaith marriage or civil marriage performed abroad, which are beyond the scope of this discussion.
38 See Financial Relations between Spouses Law, 5773–1973; HCJ 1000/92, *Bavli v. High Rabbinical Court* 48(2) PD 221 (1994) (Isr.).
39 See Westreich (2012: chs 8–9). For an extensive discussion of the *agunah* problem and its solutions, including multiple references to classic sources and modern scholarly writings, see the 5-volume set and many working papers published by the *Agunah* Research Unit of the University of Manchester's members: Bernard S. Jackson, Yehudah Abel, Shoshana Knol, Nechama Hadari, and Avishalom Westreich: www.manchesterjewishstudies.org/publications/.
40 Mishnah Gitin 9:10.
41 Mishnah Yevamot 14:1.
42 BT, Gitin, 90:2.
43 Arba'ah Turim, Even Ha-Ezer, 119.
44 Regarding bigamy, see *supra*.
45 Responsa Maharam of Rothenburg (Prague printing, Bloch ed., Budapest, 1895), p. 159d. For other versions, cf. *Encyclopedia Talmudit*, Vol. 17, p. 390.
46 *Supra* note 22.

47 The Penal Law, 1977, section 181.
48 *Supra* notes 31–33.
49 Sefer Halakhot, Ketubbot 63b.
50 Mishneh Torah, Ishut, 14:8.
51 Sefer ha-Yashar, Responsa Section, 24.
52 *Supra* note 39.
53 See File No. 861974/2 Rabbinical Court (Safed), *Plonit v. Ploni* (May 20, 2014). In this case, the court quite innovatively carried out the divorce in which the husband did not (and could not) cooperate, by granting the *get* in his name, considering the court as his proxy.
54 See 'Entire Rabbinical Court to Rule on Comatose Husband Divorce Case', *Times of Israel*, November 18, 2016, www.timesofisrael.com/top-rabbinical-court-to-rule-on-controversial-divorce-case/. Because Yosef criticized the Safed decision, it is clear that the convention was intended to cancel it. The convention, however, did not take place because of a petition submitted to the Israeli High Court of Justice, which ruled that the Great Rabbinical Court had no authority to rule in the matter. See HCJ 9261/16, *Plonit v. Great Rabbinical Court*.
55 See File No. 870175/4 Rabbinical Court (Haifa), *Plonit v. Ploni* (December 29, 2014).
56 On using mistaken marriage as a possible solution for the *agunah* problem, including an analysis of R.M. Feinstein's view and some additional references, see Westreich (2010c).
57 On the debate about no-fault divorce in the case of a marital breakdown, see Westreich (2010b, 2014: 81–93).
58 See File No. 927170/1 Rabbinical Court (Tel-Aviv), *Plonit v. Ploni, Almoni and Almonit* (March 14, 2016).
59 See Radzyner (2018). For the influence of the political-institutional considerations on rabbinical courts, see Radzyner (2013).

References

Baron, S. W. 1957. A *Social and Religious History of the Jews*. 2nd edn. Vol. 5. Columbia University Press.
Brody, R. 1999. 'Evidence for Divorce by Jewish Women?' 50 *Journal of Jewish Studies*. 230.
Finkelstein, L. 1964. *Jewish Self-Government in the Middle Ages*. 2nd edn. P. Feldheim.
Freiman, A. H. 1945. *Seder Kidushin VeNisuin*. Jerusalem.
Friedman, M. A. 1981. 'Hilkhot Ishut be-Ikvot Ma'asim li-Vnei Eretz Israel'. 50 *Tarbiz*. 209.
Friedman, M. A. 1986. *Ribui nashim be-Yisrael: Mekorot hadashim me-Genizat Kahir [Jewish Polygyny in the Middle Ages: New Documents from the Cairo Geniza]*. The Bialik Institute.
Grossman, A. 2001. *Hakhmei Ashkenaz ha-Rishonim*. 3rd edn. Magnes Press.
Radzyner, A. 2010. 'Rabbis Drafting Criminal Legislation: The Shaping of the Prohibition against Bigamy for Jews in Mandatory Palestine' in E. Katvan, M. Shilo and R. Halperin-Kaddari (eds) *One Law for Man and Woman: Women, Rights and Law in Mandatory Palestine* (in Hebrew). Bar-Ilan University Press. 151.
Radzyner, A. 2013. 'Problematic Halakhic "Creativity" in Israeli Rabbinical Court Rulings'. *20 Jewish Law Annual*. 103.
Radzyner, A. 2018. 'Jewish Law, State, and Social Reality: Prenuptial Agreements for the Prevention of Divorce Refusal in Israel and the United States'. 33(1) *Journal of Law and Religion*. 61.
Segal, A. 2010. *Prenuptial Agreements in Jewish Law: Protecting Women in Their Marital and Postmarital Life*. Ramat Gan. PhD thesis.
Shershevsky, B. Z. 1993. *Family Law* (in Hebrew). Reuven Mas Publishing House.
Westreich, A. 2010a. 'Coercion of a *get* in a Case of *Moredet* in the Mishnah and Talmud' (in Hebrew). 25 *Bar-Ilan Law Studies*. 563.
Westreich, A. 2010b. 'The Right to Divorce in Jewish Law: Between Politics and Ideology'. 1 *International Journal of the Jurisprudence of the Family*. 177.
Westreich, A. 2010c. '"*Umdena*" as a Ground for Marriage Annulment: Between Mistaken Transaction (*Kiddushei Ta'ut*) and Terminative Condition'. 20 *Jewish Law Association Studies*. 330.
Westreich, A. 2011. 'Divorce on Demand: The History, Dogmatics, and Hermeneutics of the Wife's Right to Divorce in Jewish Law'. 62 *Journal of Jewish Studies*. 340.
Westreich, A. 2012. *Talmud-Based Solutions to the Problem of the Agunah*. Deborah Charles Publications.
Westreich, A. 2014. *No Fault Divorce in the Jewish Tradition* (in Hebrew). The Israel Democracy Institute.

Westreich, A. 2015. 'Book Review: Melanie Landau, Tradition and Equality in Jewish Marriage: Beyond the Sanctification of Subordination'. 28 *Nashim: A Journal of Jewish Women's Studies and Gender Issues*. 147.

Westreich, A. 2019. 'Accommodating Religious Law with a Civil Legal System: Lessons from the Jewish Law Experience in Financial Family Matters'. 33 *Journal of Law and Religion*. Forthcoming.

Westreich, E. 1995. 'Husband's Claims in Matters of Infertility in the Rabbinical Court of Israel' (in Hebrew). 25 *Mishpatim*. 241.

Westreich, E. 2002a. 'The Rise and Decline of the Law of the Rebellious Wife in Medieval Jewish Law'. 12 *Jewish Law Association Studies*. 207.

Westreich, E. 2002b. *Temurot Be-Maamad Ha-Isha Ba-Mishpat Ha-Ivri: Masa Bein Masorot [Transitions in the Legal Status of the Wife in Jewish Law: A Journey through Traditions]*. Magnes Press.

Westreich, E. 2003. 'The Legal Activities of the Chief Rabbis during the Period of the British Mandate: A Response to the Zionist Challenge' in A. Sagi and D. Schwartz (eds) *A Hundred Years of Religious Zionism* (in Hebrew). Vol. 2. Bar-Ilan University Press. 83.

Westreich, E. 2003–2004. 'Levirate Marriage in the State of Israel: Ethnic Encounter and the Challenge of a Jewish State'. 37 *Israel Law Review*. 426.

Westreich, E. 2005. 'Early Roots of Rabbi Uziel's Approach on Matters of Family Law' (in Hebrew). 4 *Netanya Academic College Law Review*. 793.

Westreich, E. 2009–2010. 'Jewish Family Law Meets the Challenge of Modernity: The Debate on Levirate Marriage among Moroccan Sages' (in Hebrew). 26–27 *Dinei Israel*. 163.

17
Christian law
Marriage

Agustín Motilla

The first obstacle to tackling the issue of marriage in Christian Churches is the difficulty of finding a common doctrine among the different Churches which make up Christianity and within each tradition. An exception is marriage doctrine in the Roman Catholic Church. The Latin Church and Oriental Church form a global community governed by the Holy See. Unity of the doctrine results in the two general laws or Codes, one for the Latin and the other for the Oriental Churches, both of which are approved by the Pope.

We can find some homogeneous doctrines on marriage in the various Orthodox Churches that split from Rome in the schism of 1054. Although there is no central power governing the Eastern Churches, and they are substantially independent and self-governed,[1] they commonly accepted the doctrine set down by the seven first ecumenical councils.

Problems in the search for a common doctrine multiply after the Western schism of the 16th century and the appearance of the Reform Churches. The differences in the understanding and practice of Christianity were evident from the very beginning. Nevertheless, some guiding principles are accepted in each tradition. For example, all Lutheran Churches are united by the common doctrine set down in the Augsburg Confession. Each of the component Churches of the Anglican is autonomous and juridically self-governing, but they are in communion with the See of Canterbury and each other. They are not part of a federation but held together by 'bonds of affection' through four 'instruments of unity' (Hill, 2018: 2.01–2.03).

The lack of a common doctrine or law does not rule out the presence of some common key principles, derived from the Bible or the Gospels. Therefore, there are similarities in those institutions. They share a moral and spiritual dimension in the way of salvation through Jesus (Doe, 2013: 1–2). One of them is marriage.

We can find common patterns in the various doctrines of Christian law regarding marriage, such as the acceptance of Saint Augustine's theory of the three benefits of marriage (in the broad sense).[2] There are also common elements in all Christian marriages, such as the requirement of mutual consent – without coercion, error or condition – of the couple; the inexistence of obstacles to marriage such as being underage, having a blood relationship, or being bound by a previous marriage that has not been dissolved; and the solemnization of marriage following a legal form (Witte, 2012: 326f.).

Despite these similarities, we can also find different models of Christian law regarding marriage because of the diverse interpretations of the Holy Scriptures: the Bible and the patristic tradition. These models are based on the different emphasis each Christian Church puts on the elements that conform with marriage in the biblical concept: Roman Catholics and Orthodox believers highlight the sacramental character; Calvinists its conventional nature; and Lutherans the natural and social significance.

Differences are especially remarkable when a marriage is to be dissolved (Doe, 2013: 265). Only the Roman Catholic, Orthodox and some Anglican Churches have rules regarding the causes and proceedings of nullity. Civil divorce is radically excluded by the Roman Catholic Church. The indissolubility of marriage is a main and constitutive principle in Catholic marriage, with only the Pope being able to grant dissolution and only in rare circumstances. Other Christian Churches are more open-minded regarding this issue. Orthodox and Anglican Churches, despite stating the indissolubility of marriages, tolerate divorce based on pastoral reasons: the salvation of believers' souls demands its recognition. Protestant Churches directly recognize civil divorce on some grounds. Therefore, all Christian Churches, except the Roman Catholic, permit re-marriage of divorcees within the church if certain conditions are met.

There are also different political aims behind the different Churches' doctrines (Witte, 2012: 325–326): the exclusive jurisdiction over marriage affirmed by the Roman Catholic Church or the will of Lutheran Churches to leave this issue in the hands of civil powers.

All in all, the differences between Churches cannot hide the weight of the Christian concept of marriage in secular jurisdiction and regulations (Witte, 2012: 326f.). Aspects such as the mutual consent of the parties, the obstacles to the formation of the union, the existence of a legal form to express personal consent, or the rules on cases of nullity and dissolution, all of these originated in Christian law but are now common in Western civil law. Since Roman Catholic Church marriage law was the fundamental base of other Christian laws, we will start with it.

Roman Catholic Church marriage law

Roman Catholic marriage canon law was mainly developed in the Middle Ages (12th until 15th centuries) by the doctrine set down by Universities scholars. These laws interpreted and systematized Pontifical Law (*decretals)* based on the Holy Scriptures and Roman law.[3]

The nature of canon law marriage

There are three essential elements in the Roman Catholic concept of marriage, as it is defined by the Code of Canon law:

- The consent of husband and wife. Mutual consent creates an indissoluble relationship if both parties are baptized in the Roman Catholic Church (canon 1057).
- The marriage between baptized spouses is a sacrament; that is, one of the seven outward signs through which divine grace is given. This justifies the Church's exclusive jurisdiction over marriages between baptized people (canons 1055.2 and 1059).
- Marriage's aims are the generation and education of children and the shared good of spouses. There can only be a marriage between one man and one woman, and the marital relationship lasts all the spouses' lives (if the marriage has not been consummated or if it has been concluded between non-baptized spouses the Pope can dissolve it) (canons 1055.1, 1056 and 1142).

The formation of marriage

If there is a lack of one the essential elements referred to previously, the marriage is void. Historically, canon law has established certain causes for marriage nullity, which may be classified into three different groups:

Obstacles to celebrating a valid marriage. Impediments (Fornes, 2008: 51–93) are established by the Pope when the Church considers that a person is incapable of entering the marriage relationship. In some circumstances, the obstacle can be removed by the Church hierarchy. Four groups of impediments to marriage have been established: physical incapacity (men who are under 16 years old, and women under 14 years old; impotence or the inability to complete the sexual act with the other partner); legal incapacity (being bound by a previous marriage not already dissolved; being a member of the clergy of the Roman Catholic Church; being a member of religious orders with a vow of chastity; and marriage with a non-baptized person); criminal offence (rape of a woman for the purpose of marriage; murder of the spouse in order to be free for another marriage); and family relationship (consanguineous, affinity or adoptive relationships) (canons 1083 to 1094).

As we said, mixed marriages – those between a baptized and a non-baptized person – are prohibited only when one of the parties has not been baptized in any of the Christian Churches. In that case, the Bishop can authorize the marriage if the Roman Catholic party promises to maintain his or her faith and to grant the Catholic education of the children, and the non-Catholic party is informed of these promises.

Lack of consent derived from incapacity. An error regarding the essential nature of Catholic marriage, or the identity of the spouse or his/her substantial qualities (especially if the error is provoked by his or her bad faith – *dolus*); simulation of consent; physical force or mental coercion; or consent with a condition on which the validity or the nullity of the marriage depends.

Lack of the marriage's legal form of consent. Consent must be expressed before two witnesses and a minister of the Roman Catholic Church, who must ascertain the couple's marriage intentions.

The dissolution of marriage

Only marriages concluded between two baptized parties and sexually consummated are, for the Roman Catholic Church, unable to be dissolved. Indissolubility means that only the death of the husband or the wife can break the union, allowing another marriage with a third person. On the other hand, the Roman Church allows the dissolution of marriages (López Alarcón and Navarro-Valls, 2001: 294–311) that have not been consummated when there is a just reason (the dissolution is reserved to the authority of the Pope), and of marriages between two non-baptized parties when one of them converts to the Catholic faith and wants to marry another Catholic person. The Church permits the dissolution of the first marriage because the need to safeguard the faith of the newly baptized is regarded as a principle of higher importance.

Marriage nullities are declared by the Roman Catholic courts if any of the previously explained causes exists. Following the procedure established by the recent reform adopted by the Pope, if the couple requests the nullity of their marriage, the Bishop decides in a definitive ruling.

In Spain, Italy, Portugal and in other countries the ecclesiastical rulings regarding marriage nullity can be recognized by the State. A civil court must ascertain that the ruling is not against the fundamental rights or other essential principles and values of the State domestic law. If so, the annulment also carries with it civil effects.

Orthodox Church marriage law

There is some unity in the faith, the worship and the law between the different Churches of Byzantine tradition, which split from Rome in the year 1054, although they are independent from each other. The principles of these Orthodox Churches are not far from those of the Roman Catholic Church (see Parlato, 2013: 135–136): they all share the doctrine stated by the seven first Ecumenical Councils.

These similarities also explain why the marriage discipline of the Orthodox Churches is the nearest to the Roman Catholic one. Generally speaking, it can be said that the differences in canon law are mostly based on ecclesiastical reasons. Orthodox Churches share with the Roman Church the faith in the sacramental nature of marriage: marriage is one of the seven sources through which God gives grace to men and women. That justifies the Churches' power to rule on this important institution.[4] However, differences arise as Orthodox Churches put the focus on the sacramental and spiritual basis of marriage and not, as the Roman Catholic Church, on the Latin concept of marriage as a legal contract between two parties.

The nature of marriage in the Orthodox Church

As we said, Orthodox marriage is one of the seven outward signs or sacraments. Through it, God gives spouses baptized in the Church spiritual grace. As an institution, marriage symbolizes the union between Christ and the Church.

Orthodox ecclesiology also coincides with that of the Roman Catholic Church in Saint Augustine's doctrine of marriage's benefits: the generation of children, unity, heterosexuality and indissolubility are the aims and properties of marriage, the essential content of the institution. Nevertheless, indissolubility takes on a much more flexible interpretation in the Orthodox doctrine: as we will see further on, for pastoral reasons (when harm or injury to one of the spouses could derive from the marriage) the Orthodox Churches allow its dissolution.

The formation of marriage

The valid formation of marriage depends on not breaching the essential content of this institution referred to before. Subjective conditions, such as a minimum age and the consent of both members of the couple, are also necessary. In addition, a specific legal form is required: the celebration must be held inside the Orthodox Church, following the canonical rituals, and must include the intervention of the priest.

Moreover, the Orthodox faith has rules about three different causes of nullity:

Lack of consent. This may be an error on the identity of one of the parties (*error in persona*), physical violence or mental coercion. As we can see, the nullity causes are noticeably reduced compared with those recognized by the Roman Catholic Church.

Obstacles to the celebration of a valid marriage. Male minors under 18 years of age and females under 14; those who are already bound by a valid marriage which has not legally been dissolved; members of religious orders bound by a vow of chastity; clergy members of the Orthodox Church already bound by a valid marriage (the second one is forbidden); family relationships (consanguineous, of affinity or adoptive); and mixed marriage between someone baptized in the Orthodox Church and a non-baptized person (if he or she is baptized in a Christian Church different from the Orthodox one, the marriage is only valid if it is celebrated in the Church and receives the blessing of the Orthodox priest). As we see again, the nullity causes and impediments are substantially reduced compared with the Roman Catholic ones.

Lack of marriage legal form (McGuckin, 2008: 309–323). The marriage must be celebrated inside an Orthodox Church, following the rituals prescribed by this faith and before the priest.

The Orthodox priest is not just a witness to the marriage (as he is in the Roman Catholic tradition[5]). He, as the person through whom divine grace is given, is an essential part of the validity of marriages.

The rituals are also important. They are carried out in consecutive ceremonies as prescribed by the sacred canons: the betrothals are symbolized by the exchange of rings; the marriage is celebrated with the expression of consent and the crowning of the spouses; and the final blessing is given by the priest.

The dissolution of marriage

The Orthodox Churches affirm, as one of the properties of marriage, the indissolubility of those celebrated before the Church between baptized spouses. Therefore, only the death of one of them can dissolve the ties and allow the marriage of the surviving spouse. Nevertheless, dissolution of the marriage (see Parlato, 2013: 140–143, 146–148) is tolerated if the principle of *oikonomia* is applied: if it is necessary to save the souls of the spouses, for pastoral reasons, or to avoid a scandal.

There are two different reasons that make dissolution permissible in the Orthodox Churches: justice (for instance the non-consummation of the marriage; or if one spouse wants to enter a monastery to be a monk, with the consent of the other one); or to avoid serious harm befalling to one of the spouses (cases of adultery by the other, abuse, alcoholism or drug addiction, etc.)

In these cases, the innocent party can ask the Bishop to dissolve his or her marriage. The Bishop tries to achieve a reconciliation of the spouses and, if it fails, accepts the civil divorce or dissolves the marriage himself. After that, the celebration of a new marriage according to the Church rites can be allowed. It should be noted that these ecclesiastical divorces are not recognized by the Roman Catholic Church. If the divorced Orthodox party wants to celebrate a canonical marriage with a baptized Roman Catholic, this marriage is not allowed by the Catholic Church, or, if the celebration takes place, it is void because of the previous marriage of the Orthodox party.

Like the Roman Catholic Church, Orthodox Churches do not recognize the validity of a previous civil marriage of a baptized member. Only when they celebrate marriage before an Orthodox priest and according to the Church rules and rites (before or after the civil marriage, if the State jurisdiction obliges them to have a civil ceremony), is the matrimony considered valid.

Reform Churches' marriage law

As we have seen, there are three elements on which the Roman Catholic Church built matrimony: it is a natural institution, directed to procreation and education of children; born of the free consent of the partners; and, between baptized partners, it is a sacrament through which divine grace is given. The Reform Churches which split from Rome in the 16th century agree, to some extent, with the two first statements: matrimony is a natural institution and its aims are procreation and raising of children, as well as the shared good of the spouses; and born of the mutual consent of the partners. However, they do not agree with the third one: it is not a sacrament. Although it has a spiritual nature, because God wants its existence in order to fulfil His will on earth, marriage is not one of the seven sacraments. It does not give Godly grace.

The consequences of this position are very important. First, Churches do not have exclusive jurisdiction in regulating marriage. Marriage is mostly a social institution and, therefore, it is the

State's competence to regulate it; however, civil regulation must take into account the theological basis of marriage drawn by the Churches as a spiritual institution.

Another dissenting point of the Reform Churches relates to the traditional ecclesiastical statement of the superiority of celibacy to married status. In the Reformers' point of view, all men are called to marriage as a remedy to sin. As a consequence, these Churches do not require the clergy's celibacy, or oblige members of religious orders to comply with a vow of chastity.

Beyond these common beliefs, there are indeed differences between the Reform Churches depending on the tradition they belong to. Some emphasize the natural and social character of marriage, some the contractual factor. We shall present three traditions, beginning with the one that is most distinct from the Council of Trent's concept of marriage, and proceed towards the one that is most similar.

Lutheran tradition

Lutheran tradition emphasizes the natural and social dimension of marriage. This concept determines every aspect of the Lutheran marriage doctrine.

The nature of marriage

All the Lutheran legal concepts regarding marriage derive from their theological principles (see Witte, 2012: 113f.). Denying its sacramental nature, the Reformers also deny the jurisdiction of the Church, of all Churches, over the institution. They consider it an historical usurpation, for political and economic reasons, of a civil competence.

Certainly, marriage is essentially a social institution in the earthly realm. Jurisdiction on marriage is a State business. Only the secular power must rule matters of capacity, celebration, nullity or dissolution of marriages and resolve legal conflicts about these issues before the courts. This perspective provides the foundation for civil law regarding marriage in countries like the Netherlands, Germany and Sweden.

Nevertheless, marriage is seen as a natural institution born of God's will for human beings. Churches should bless the unions which have already taken place before the civil authority. The couple must express before the Christian community their willingness to live their union according to natural and divine laws, thus sanctifying the civil tie. As marriage is a natural institution created for spiritual perfection of the spouses' souls, Reform pastors and theologians have the duty of advising the civil authorities how to fulfil this purpose; they must also explain to the community members how to follow God's divine plans for humankind through marriage.

Broadly speaking, the Lutheran Church accepts Saint Augustine's doctrine of the benefits of marriage, but partially diverges and holds a different order: the first benefit is the love and mutual support of the spouses; after this, the generation and education of the children; and, in third place, the couple's protection from sexual sins. As a remedy against sin, marriage is also a necessity for clergymen.

The formation of marriage

As was referred to before, civil authorities should establish and enforce the legal conditions for capacity and validity of marriages and, consequently, nullity and dissolution causes. Lutheran theologians and pastors must advise how marriage would also contribute to strengthen the faith of the spouses and fulfil God's plan. From this point of view, we can speak of the Lutheran doctrine on the validity, nullity and dissolution of marriages, though it is not as well systematized as the Roman Church's doctrine.

The Lutheran Church substantially diminishes the number of the Roman Church's impediments to marriage (Witte, 2012: 145–149). It rejects, of course, those based on priestly celibacy but also others like crime (murder of the spouse in order to be free for another marriage) or, in family relationships, affinity, public honesty (prohibition of marriage of one of a couple who is living together to someone who has consanguinity with the other partner), and adoption (the Reformers only consider consanguinity as an obstacle to marriage). The non-sacramental nature of Lutheran marriages allows the union between baptized and non-baptized partners, but the Lutheran Churches strongly advise against unions with people of other beliefs because of the moral and spiritual consequences that such a marriage could have. They do accept the impediments of a physical nature; that is to say, impotence and minority of age, and the ban on marriage of those already bound by a previous and valid matrimony.

As concerns consent, the Lutheran Church requires the free will of both partners. In early times, the Reformers asked also for the concurring consent of the parents or tutors, although few civil laws regarding marriage prescribed this condition for its validity and never when the couple had reached legal adulthood.

The blessing of the marriage by the pastor and its registration in the civil archives are highly recommended, but hold no relevance as far as the validity or nullity of the marriage is concerned.

The dissolution of marriage

The Lutheran Reform stating the stability of marriage, but as a social and non-sacramental institution, accepts its dissolution on certain grounds (see Doe, 2013: 263–264). Adultery by one spouse is definitely one of the causes for which divorce can be sought. Others have been admitted subsequently, such as abandonment, impotence, violence, refusal of sexual relations, etc. Overall, the Lutheran Church considers that it is the competence of civil authorities to rule on the causes and procedures of marriage dissolution.

Calvinist tradition

We can find the origins of this tradition in Geneva in 1536 under the influence of the exiled French theologian Jean Calvin. His ecclesiological and theological doctrine was a point of reference for many Christian movements and Churches: French Huguenots, Dutch Pietists, English and Scottish Presbyterian, New England Puritans, etc.

The nature of marriage

Calvinist tradition focused on marriage as a covenant between the parties or even between the parties and the community: spouses must confirm their union and their vows before the religious community; the pastor's blessing of the couple confirms the acceptance of God and the belief in the true faith. Civil authorities should safeguard the legality of the union and proceed to register it in the official archives.

Calvinists deny, as do Lutherans, the sacramental character of marriage, but they stress its spiritual and moral dimension. As an important means to the sanctification of men and women, the Church must regulate marriage's spiritual character, leaving civil law to regulate its social aspects. So, unlike Lutheran doctrine, Calvinist teachings affirm the Church's competence and jurisdiction regarding the moral and religious dimension of marriage, including its traditional goals and properties, especially procreation, monogamy and marriage as a remedy against concupiscence.

The formation of marriage

In contrast to Lutheran doctrine, Calvin and his followers did prescribe a specific marriage discipline. This was received and enforced in those countries where this branch of the Reformation had social and political presence.

For Calvinists, marriage is built on four fundamental pillars: the consent of the parties as expressed before the community; the consent of their parents or tutors; the presence of witnesses; and the blessing of the union given by the pastor. The absence of any of these elements is cause for nullity. As we said, civil authorities must implement the religious provisions and regulate the social and political matters.

Obstacles to the valid formation of marriage are those already described by the Reformers in the Lutheran tradition, with the addition of mental illness, lack of virginity of the woman when this has been presumed, a contagious illness and disparity of age between the man and the woman. As with Lutherans, mixed marriages are considered valid but highly discouraged because of the possible pernicious effects on the faith of the believer.

As we said, the marriage liturgy is, in the Calvinist tradition, an essential element of its valid constitution. Aspects of this are the manifestation of the consent of the couple before the community of faith, and the acceptance and blessing of the union by the pastor.

The dissolution of marriage

Calvinist tradition admits two causes for dissolution of marriage: adultery and unjustified desertion or abandonment by one of spouses. If either of these occurs, the innocent party can apply for a divorce before the civil court. After the civil ruling grants it, he or she can remarry in the church.

The Calvinist concept of marriage had a great influence on Geneva's Civil Ordinances of 1546 and on the laws of other countries where Calvin's followers were a majority.

Anglican tradition

Tied to the historical tradition in England, Anglican discipline has influenced the State law of certain Commonwealth countries.[6]

Historically, Anglican tradition is Catholic in origin and reformed in practice. Overall, it can be highlighted that transformations of medieval matrimonial canon law occurred more slowly in Anglican countries than in the Reformed ones. In general, Anglicans try to reach a situation of 'common good' where all the interests at play can come together: those of the couple, of the Church and of the State.

Adopting the Roman theological conception of marriage as a sacrament, Anglican tradition states the nature of marriage as an institution born of God's will to reach certain benefits, which are very important to the spiritual development of men and women, and to obtain stability and shared common good justifies the right of the Anglican Church to regulate it. The aims of marriage are the development of the personality, procreation and education of children, and the creation of a society of mutual help and a shared life.

The model of marriage in the Anglican tradition, as well as in the Roman Catholic and Orthodox Church, is life-long union, exclusively between a man and a woman, which symbolizes the mystical union of Christ and the Church.

The formation of marriage

The public consent of the partners is an essential element for the valid formation of marriage. Consent must be free, without fraud, error, coercion or mental conditioning. The acceptance of the union by parents was also required, but, nowadays, a lack of it does not affect the legal formation of the bond before the law.

Anglican tradition recognizes the impediments of consanguinity, impotence, a previous valid marriage (which has not been dissolved), crime and a minimum age of consent. At least one of the couple must be baptized and belong to the Anglican Communion.[7]

After the minister of the marriage instructs the couple about the nature, aims and requirements of marriage ruled by canon and civil law, and no impediment – civil or ecclesiastical – obstructs the marriage, he proceeds with the celebration. Before the priest and at least two witnesses, the parties give their free consent. This is a requirement for the valid formation of the union. Fulfilment of the civil law requirements established by the State is also necessary.

The dissolution of marriage

All the members of the Anglican Communion who are divorced or whose marriages have been annulled by the civil authorities may apply to the bishop or other ecclesiastical authority in order to obtain the nullity of the marriage (Doe, 2013: 262). The Church's procedure is governed by canon law. The grounds for an ecclesiastical declaration of nullity include absence of freely given and received consent, or of an intention to be married until death; lack of the required age to marry; or being within the prohibited degrees of relationship. After consultation with a person learned in the law, the bishop shall inform the applicant of his decision and issue a certificate of invalidity if the application is approved.

The 'common good' model was the justification for restricting the causes of dissolution of marriages. Civil divorce was only recognized by the Church on the grounds of adultery, abandonment, or abuse, or causes of equal importance.

Nowadays the Churches of the Anglican Communion agree that, while divorce is undesirable, it may be better than a destructive relationship (Doe, 1998: 284). Because of this, the Church, after working towards the reconciliation of the spouses, recognizes the legal effect of a civil law as terminating a sacramental marriage. The spouse is allowed to celebrate a new marriage according to Anglican rites, if the bishop authorizes it and the priest chooses not to take advantage of the conscience clause which permits refusal (see Hill, 2007: 309). Conditions to the Episcopal licence for a new marriage include: the impossibility of re-establishing a true marriage relationship between the partners of any former marriages; the person is repentant for the failure to keep marriage vows and considers himself able to make new vows; understands the Church doctrine and truly intends to enter such a marriage; and is prepared to fulfil his responsibilities, both moral and legal, with respect to any former marriage.

Further reading

Aznar Gil, F. 2008. 'Indisolubilidad del matrimonio y divorcio en las Iglesias ortodoxas'. 55 *Salmanticensis*. 441.

Bergendoff, C. 1967. *The Church in the Lutheran Reformation*. Concordia Publishing.

Bernárdez, A. 1998. *Compendio de Derecho matrimonial canónico*. 9th edn. Tecnos.

Bodensieck, J. (ed.). 1965. *The Encyclopedia of the Lutheran Church*. Augsburg Publishing.

Calvo Espiga, A. 2014. 'Análisis jurídico del art. 7 del Acuerdo de cooperación del Estado español con la Federación de Entidades Religiosas Evangélicas de España en la perspectiva de la doctrina y la liturgia protestantes del matrimonio'. 54 *Ius Canonicum*. 663.

Doe, N. 2002. *An Anglican Covenant: Theological and Legal Considerations for a Global Debate*. Canterbury Press.
Doe, N. (ed.). 2009. *Marriage in Anglican and Roman Catholic Canon Law*. Centre for Law and Religion.
Erickson, J. H. 1991. *The Challenge of Our Past: Studies in Orthodox Canon Law and Church History*. Crestwood.
Finocchiaro F. 2001. *Il Matrimonio nel diritto canonico*. Il Mulino.
Gassmann, G., and Meyer, H. 1983. *The Unity of the Church. Requirements and Structures*. LWF.
Gavin, F. 2009. 'An Outline of Marriage Preparation in Roman Catholic Discipline' in N. Doe (ed.) *Marriage in Anglican and Roman Catholic Canon Law*. Centre for Law and Religion. 27.
Hilbert, M. 2009. 'Dispensation for Non-Consummated Marriages: *de "processu super ratio"*' in N. Doe (ed.) *Marriage in Anglican and Roman Catholic Canon Law*. Centre for Law and Religion. 797.
Lo Castro, G. 2003. *Matrimonio, diritto e giustizia*. Giuffrè.
Marti Sánchez, J. M. 2015. *El matrimonio religioso y su transcendencia jurídica*. European Academic Press.
Moneta, P. 2007. *Il matrimonio nel nuovo diritto canonico*. ECIG.
Ombres, R. 2009. 'The Nature of Marriage and the Right to Marry in the Latin Code: Canons 1055–1062' in N. Doe (ed.) *Marriage in Anglican and Roman Catholic Canon Law*. Centre for Law and Religion. 17.
Örsy, L. 1992. *Theology and Canon Law: New Horizons for Legislation and Interpretation*. Collegeville.
Patsavos, L. J. 1975. *Manual for the Course in Orthodox Canon Law*. Hellenic College, Holy Cross Orthodox School of Theology.
Pospshil, V. J. 1996. *Eastern Catholic Church Law*. St. Martin.
Rhidian, J. 2000. *The Canon Law of the Roman Catholic Church and the Church of England: a Handbook*. T&T Clark.
Rodopoulos, P. 2007. *An Overview of Orthodox Canon Law*. Orthodox Research Institute.
Vadakumcherry, J. 1992. 'Marriage Laws in the Code of Canon Law and the Code of Canons of the Eastern Churches'. 26 *Studia Canonica*. 437.
Van Vliet, A. H. 1954. *Marriage and Canon Law*. Burns & Oates.
Vitale, E. and Berlingò, S. 2003. *Il matrimonio canonico*. Giuffrè.
Wamboldt, W. 1987. 'Canon Law on Indissolubility of Marriage in the Roman Catholic Church'. 21 *Studia Canonica*. 265.
Ware, T. 1963. *The Orthodox Church*. Penguin.
Witte, J. Jr. 2002. *Law and Protestantism: the Legal Teachings of the Protestant Reformation*. Cambridge University Press.

Notes

1 To the four old Patriarchs (Constantinople, Alexandria, Antiochus and Jerusalem) must be added the later ones of Russia, Serbia, Romania and Bulgaria. They congregate 300 million believers.
2 *Bonum prolis* or the proper generation and education of children; *bonum fidei* or the exclusion of relationships outside the couple; and *bonum sacramenti* or the indissolubility of the marriage.
3 For an overview of the history of Canon marriage law, see Amenta (2011).
4 The Orthodox Law is mainly contained in the *Nomocanones* adopted in the year 920, official in the Byzantine Church.
5 The role of the priest, since the Holy See 'Ne Temere' Decree, of 2 August 1917, is of an active witness: he must ask, in the name of the Church, for the consent of the couple (see canon 1114.2).
6 On the different ecclesiastical laws enacted by Churches belonging to the Anglican Communion, see Doe (1998).
7 Doe (2013: 257–258). Except in England where even two non-believers have a legally enforceable right to be married in their parish church according to the rites of the Church of England.

References

Amenta, P. 2011. *Administrative Procedures in Canonical Marriage Cases: History, Legislation and Praxis*. Wilson & Lafleur.
Cortés Diéguez, A. 2006. 'El matrimonio mixto en la Iglesia latina y en las Iglesias orientales católicas y ortodoxas. Aspectos teológicos y canónicos'. 63 *Revista Española de Derecho Canónico*. 655.
Doe, N. 1998. *Canon Law in the Anglican Communion. A Worldwide Perspective*. Clarendon Press.

Doe, N. 2013. *Christian Law. Contemporary Principles*. Cambridge University Press.
Fornes. J. 2008. *Derecho Matrimonial Canónico*. 5th edn. Tecnos.
Hill, M. 2007. *Ecclesiastical Law*. 3rd edn. Oxford University Press.
Hill, M. 2018. *Ecclesiastical Law*. 4th edn. Oxford University Press.
Lopez Alarcón, M. And Navarro-Valls, R. 2001. *Curso de Derecho matrimonial canónico y concordado*. 6th edn. Tecnos.
McGuckin, J. A. 2008. *The Ortodox Church. An Introduction to its History, Doctrine and Spiritual Culture*. Blackwell.
Parlato, V. 2013. 'Il matrimonio nelle Chiese ortodosse'. 64(1–2) *Studi Urbinati. Scienze giuridiche, politiche ed economiche*. 133.
Witte, J. Jr. 2012. *From Sacrament to Contract. Marriage, Religion and Law in the Western Tradition*. 2nd edn. Westminster John Knox Press.

18

Islamic law

Marriage

Roberta Aluffi

The nature of marriage

Islamic marriage is defined in very formal and essential terms by classical legal scholars (*fuqahā'*): it is the contract that makes sexual intercourse licit, or, to put it in a rather crude way, that makes the woman licit to the man. The very term for marriage, *nikāḥ*, means also sexual intercourse. Thus, *nikāḥ* excludes *zinà*, the illicit sexual intercourse, which amounts to a criminal offense (*ḥadd*) and is punishable with 100 lashes or, in the most serious cases, with stoning. Moreover, licit sexual intercourse is necessary to establish *nasab*, the patrilineal bond linking the child to his father and other agnates, who are the only relatives entitled to provide him with legal protection.

Marriage is dealt with from the moral viewpoint, too. As sexuality is part of human nature, its practice conforms to God's will, provided that it takes place within the legal framework of marriage.[1] Marriage is then considered by many as a *ʿibāda*, an act of obedience to God, a religious obligation enhancing the spiritual and physical wellbeing of individuals, fostering social harmony and ensuring the reproduction of the Islamic community.

Nevertheless, if a man is clearly disinclined towards marriage, or if he is not able to bear its costs, marriage is deemed reprehensible, or outrightly forbidden to him, not to cause prejudice to the wife. In this case, the interests of the women are taken into consideration, even if only indirectly. But, as a rule, the discourse on the nature, obligatory or recommended, of marriage is developed by scholars exclusively from the standpoint of men.

Beyond its strictly legal dimension as a contract (*ʿaqd*), marriage plays a major role in shaping the Islamic social order. After a *Qur'ānic* verse (IV, 21), it is hailed as a solemn pact (*mitāq*). At the conclusion of the contract, Muslims frequently highlight its importance by some rituals, as the reading of *Qur'ānic* verses, in particular the Opening Chapter (the *Fātiḥa*), or by the presence of religiously trained figures. Nonetheless, all these religiously flavoured elements are not necessary for the legal validity of the marriage, which rests on the consent of the contracting parties. They are simply ways to have the union blessed and to invoke the divine protection on it.

The social and moral implications of marriage induce contemporary legal scholars, as well as State legislators, to broaden the traditional scope of marriage. Apart from virtue (*iḥṣān*)[2] and chastity (*ʿafāf*), to be interpreted not as sexual abstention, but as an orderly practice of sexuality, the aims of the marriage are the foundation of an enduring conjugal life and the creation of a stable family. Alongside this shift in definition, a change in terminology takes place: the classical term *nikāḥ* is normally replaced by *zawāğ*, which evokes the idea of couple.[3]

The Islamic marriage is not simply the union of a man and a woman; it involves also an alliance between two family groups. This is apparent in the role played by the legal guardian (*walī*), the nearest male relative who represents the spouse at the conclusion of the contract, and at the same time embodies the interests of the family. *Fiqh* deals with a number of cases where the interests of the spouses and the families may come into conflict with each other. For instance, the marriage may be contracted by legal guardians before the puberty of one or both spouses:[4] as prepubescent children cannot consummate the marriage, they have no interest in it, at least temporarily; on the contrary, this kind of marriage may be of interest for their families. At their coming of age, at certain conditions, both spouses have the right of rescission. Moreover, the husband of age has the power to dissolve the marriage bond.

Another possible conflict of interest between the woman and her family arises when an adult woman contracts herself in marriage, doing so without her guardian. As any other woman's act or conduct, such a contract is susceptible to put the honour and the social status of her family at stake. Legal scholars disagree about the validity of this kind of contract. Those who admit it provide the guardian with the right of setting the marriage aside if it is not a suitable match because of the lack of *kafā'a*, that is to say if the husband is not the equal of the wife.

Finally, when the contract is entered into by the *walī* on behalf of the woman of age, her consent is presumed. If the legal guardian refuses to marry the woman to the man she likes, and who is her equal, the dispute is resolved by the judge.

The spouse choice

Equality (*kafā'a*) is a leading factor for the spouse choice; nevertheless, the lack of it does not *per se* entail the nullity of marriage.

Jurists' opinions about the criteria to properly assess *kafā'a* are diverse: descent, tribal affiliation, fortune, profession, or mere piety may be taken into consideration. The husband should be the equal of or superior to the wife, but not the reverse: it would be shameful for the woman, who is subject to the authority of the husband, to obey someone who is less than her. In other contexts, with a penchant for endogamy, husband and wife should be co-equals. By the formidable tool of *kafā'a*, the actual structures and hierarchies of different societies, as well as their changes, are perfectly integrated into the normative discourse, even if they conflict with the fundamental equality of Islam among all believers solemnly proclaimed by Islam.

The considerations regarding *kafā'a* may influence the selection of the spouses; but much more decisive for this choice are the stringent rules concerning blood relatives, relatives by marriage, and the religious affiliations of the spouses: they might end up in an outright prohibition of certain unions, entailing the nullity of the contract.

Qur'ān (IV, 23), as interpreted by *fuqahā'* defines the scope of incest by barring the man from marrying his mother and all female ascendants, his daughter and all female descendants, and his mother's and father's descendants. All these women are *maḥārim* (prohibited) to him. Cousins are not prohibited; rather, a specific kind of cousin, the patrilateral parallel cousin (the father's brother's daughter), is considered as a particularly appropriate bride. This kind of preferential mating corresponds to an Arab customary rule, and it is not prescribed by *šarīʿa*. Nevertheless, it has spread well beyond its original boundaries, with the Islamisation, and even more the Arabisation, of new converts.

Milk is equated to blood as a possible cause for marriage prohibition (*Qur'ān*, IV, 23). Fosterage may generate a relationship similar to the blood relationship, so that a man is prohibited from marrying his foster sister. Some jurists maintain that, more comprehensively, everything is prohibited by reason of fosterage which is so for reason of kindred. Fosterage is then a means to create a kind of artificial kinship.

Certain relatives by marriage, or affinity, are prohibited as well (*Qur'ān*, IV, 22–23). The man is barred from marrying any ascendant or descendant of his former wife, as well as any former wife of his ascendants and descendants.

Another crucial criterion for the choice of the spouses are their religious affiliations. Religion may be grounds for a marriage impediment. But, while impediments on grounds of consanguinity, fosterage, and affinity are permanent, so that they cannot be removed and the woman is prohibited to the man once and for all, the impediment on grounds of religion is temporary and can be overcome by an appropriate conversion.

A Muslim woman cannot marry but a Muslim man (*Qur'ān*, II, 221; LX, 10): she is prohibited to all non-Muslim males. On the contrary, a Muslim man may marry non-Muslim women, provided that they are *kitābiyyāt*, i.e. believers in a Sacred Book (*Qur'ān*, V, 5). This is indisputably the status of Jews and Christians, but also, according to some legal opinions, of Zoroastrians and Sabeans. All idolatrous women (*muškirāt*), instead, are prohibited to Muslim men (*Qur'ān*, III, 221).

This set of limitations on mixed marriages affects Muslim women and men differently: the admissible marriage partners are more numerous for men than for women. Given the hierarchical structure of the marriage, this gendered articulation of the ban on religiously mixed marriages ensures that a Muslim woman is never under the authority of a non-Muslim husband, whereas nothing shall prevent a Muslim man from exercising his authority on his Jewish or Christian wife. Moreover, as the child born of a Muslim father is Muslim, the allowed mixed marriages invariably give birth to Muslim offspring, at least from the point of view of the Islamic community.

As the prohibition to marry non-Muslims affects only women, it is a blatant violation of the principle of gender equality enshrined in the constitutions of many Muslim countries. At the same time, it resonates with deep feelings of aversion for this kind of union common in many societies. Thus, it may happen that statutes are accurately purged of this impediment, which nevertheless flourishes in circulars and regulations, and other minor sources are scrupulously applied.[5]

A way to overcome gender discrimination while maintaining the ban on interreligious marriages, is to extend the impediment to men: all Muslims, men and women, should be prohibited from marrying non-Muslims. The solution, put forward by some isolated *Sunni* scholar, corresponds to the mainstream opinion in *Shi'i* Islam.

Marriages between *Sunnis* and *Shi'as* are not prohibited on grounds of religion. Nevertheless, societies may show different degrees of aversion to this kind of union, and States' laws sometimes make them impossible, as in the case of Lebanon.

A last category deserves attention, as far as marriage impediments are concerned: that of apostates (*murtadd*). Persons having abandoned Islam are barred from marriage. So, if a Christian or Jewish woman is in fact a convert to her present faith from Islam, she is prohibited to all Muslim men.

Furthermore, apostasy (*irtidād*) after the conclusion of the contracts results in the automatic dissolution of the marriage, and a conviction for apostasy forces the condemned to separate from his wife/her husband.

The formation of marriage

The contract of marriage consists of the proposal and the acceptance, uttered by the two parties, in the presence of witnesses. The parties may be represented by duly appointed *wakīls* (proxies).

The statements may be made orally or in writing. What does matter is that they are definite and clear as to their meaning, since the marital status of two persons depends on them. Legal scholars deal at length with the expressions and formulas that may be used, either metaphorically or literally meaning marriage, and derived from the same roots as *nikāḥ* and *zawāǧ*. Scholars show their preference for the use of verbs in the past tense ('I offered you', 'I accepted'), as this unambiguously expresses the determination and commitment of the party. Acceptance may be replaced by silence, only when the context clearly indicates its meaning.

Both proposal and acceptance must be made in the same contractual session (*maǧlis*), that is to say before the parties separate, so as to exclude any uncertainty about the legal condition of the prospective spouses. Proposal and acceptance must be heard by the witnesses, two Muslim males or one male and two females. If the marriage is religiously mixed, one of the two witnesses may be Christian or Jewish.

The presence of the witnesses is required for the contract to be valid and at the same time ensures the publicity of the marriage. However, this kind of publicity is not adequate to meet the needs of contemporary complex and mobile societies: this is the reason why mandatory registration for marriages has been gradually introduced by legislatures, even if with different degrees of success. In certain countries, the lack of registration may involve criminal penalties. However, an unregistered marriage, even if difficult to prove, is considered as valid and may produce only in part the effects normally attached to marriage.

In Muslim countries, the conclusion of the marriage contract does not take place at the mosque, nor in a public office, but in a home. It represents a stage that is clearly distinct and separate from the wedding festivities and rituals, and is regulated by local customs which accompany the first sexual intercourse between the spouses (consummation) and involve as many people as possible. The marriage may be consummated years after its conclusion, and some of its effects are conditional on consummation.

The parties enjoy a wide scope of freedom in defining the content of the marriage contract; they may agree on various stipulations, normally aiming to improve the status of the woman, by curbing the husband's rights and reducing the wife's duties. The wife may stipulate that the husband will not take an additional wife (monogamy stipulation); the husband may delegate the wife the power to unilaterally dissolve the marriage by *ṭalāq* (delegated *ṭalāq*), so that the woman is on an equal footing with him as to marriage termination. Stipulations may concern the place of the conjugal dwelling and the spouses' rights to it, or fix in detail what the husband must pay as maintenance (*nafaqa*) to the wife. The husband may undertake to allow the wife to go out to work, or, conversely, not to force her to do so; he may promise not to prevent the wife from leaving the town or the country they're living in; the wife may promise to accompany the husband in his travels. Stipulations may be added to the contract at any moment as long as the marriage lasts.

The freedom of will of the parties is not without limits, though. Stipulations that are incompatible with the nature of marriage are void, but there is not a complete agreement on the implications of such a principle. For instance, Sunni *fuqahā'* unanimously reject the stipulation under which the marriage will last until the deadline agreed upon by the parties, while Shi'is allow temporary marriage (*nikāḥ al-mutʿa*). Stipulations effectly derogating the rigid separation of property regime between the spouses are considered void by all the *fuqahā'*, without exception.

Furthermore, the propensity of contracting parties to resort to stipulations varies widely between social environments, from country to country, and over time. The most frequent stipulations concern dower (*mahr* or *ṣadāq*): they quantify the sum to be paid by the husband to the wife and determine the schedule of payments. If the marriage contract includes no stipulation regarding the dower, the husband is liable to pay a fair or proper dower (*mahr al-mitl*), equal to the dower usually paid for a woman similar in social status to the bride. The stipulation which excludes the obligation to pay the dower is void and, according to certain scholars, renders the whole contract void.

Mahr belongs to the wife, who cannot be forced to spend it on household management, or the like. It is a sign of the husband's serious intentions and of the lawfulness of the union. It gives a measure of the bride's social status and, at the same time, of the groom's wealth. But fundamentally, it generates the asymmetry between husband and wife that characterises the entire structure of the marriage relationship from beginning to end. In fact, the right of the wife to *mahr* and the power of the husband to terminate the marriage by *ṭalāq* are interdependent (see later).

Mahr greatly varies in value, according to the country, the region, the social group. It may have a symbolic rather than actual value, or, at the other extreme, consist in a very substantial amount of money. In the latter case, *mahr* can effectively secure the financial interests of the woman in the event of widowhood or divorce; but, at the same time, it may represent a formidable obstacle to the marriage conclusion. To facilitate the conclusion of marriages, which is considered a socially and religiously desirable objective, some governments fix a ceiling for *mahr*.

Stipulations may specify the mode of payment of the *mahr*: the dower may be payable either immediately at the time of the contract (prompt dower, *mahr muʿağğal*), or, in whole or in part, on the dissolution of the marriage, for divorce or death (deferred dower, *mahr mu'ağğal*), when the woman is particularly vulnerable. If the contract does not specify whether the *mahr* is prompt or deferred, the presumption is normally in favour of prompt dower. The wife can refuse to consume the marriage, as long as the prompt dower has not been paid.

Polygamy

Polygamy, or, more precisely, polygyny, is allowed by *fuqahā'*, based on the *Qur'ān* (IV, 3). This principle is expressed as a temporary impediment, limiting an otherwise absolute faculty of the man: he may have up to four wives at the same time, but a fifth woman is prohibited to him.[6]

The *Qur'ānic* verse regulating polygyny requires the husband to treat all his wives fairly. The wife is entitled to a right to maintenance (*nafaqa*) *vis-à-vis* her husband. In case of polygyny, every wife is entitled to equal maintenance and a separate living accommodation: co-wives do not live together, unless they all agree to, renouncing their rights. The husband has to care for all his wives and spends his nights with each of them in turn.

While the relationship between the husband and his wives is regulated in every detail, the same cannot be said of the relations between the wives. Even if in some social contexts they are rather important, these relations are not legally relevant. There is no hierarchy among the wives, who are not entitled to reciprocal rights and obligations.

The exercise of polygyny has never been evenly spread throughout the Muslim world: it varies according to the period, the place, and the social background of the parties. Equally varied is the condition of the wives of a polygynist.

Polygyny became a contentious issue during the second half of the 19th century, within the framework of Western criticism of women's condition in Muslim societies.

Reformist scholars[7] put forward a new interpretation for the *Qur'ānic* verse (IV, 3) that requires the man to fairly treat his wives; they connected it with another verse (IV, 129), which states that men are not able to deal in fairness and justice between women, however much they wish. On this basis, they argue that the practice of polygyny is allowed subject to a condition that God himself declares out of reach for men, and conclude that it is virtually banned.

On the wave of this new interpretation of the *Qur'ānic* verses, new statutory measures were introduced in many States to the effect of limiting and controlling the exercise of polygyny. A married man has to apply for a special judicial authorisation if he wants to marry another woman. The court shall grant authorisation only in exceptional cases. The first wife must be notified of the new marriage, and the new wife of the existence of previous marriages. Moreover, the woman may include the monogamy stipulation in her marriage contract, so that, if her husband takes an additional wife, she can seek divorce and/or demand the payment of compensation. According to some statutes, even in the absence of a specific stipulation in the contract, polygyny constitutes a valid ground for divorce.

Rare are the countries, such as Turkey and Tunisia, where polygyny is prohibited outright and qualifies as a crime. Nevertheless, a gap may exist between black-letter law and practice, to the extent that authorities turn a blind eye to the phenomenon of non-registered marriages, concluded in a purely religious form.

The marriage relationship

The conjugal life is to be inspired by the love and mercy God has placed between the spouses (*Qur'ān*, XXX, 21). Husband and wife are urged to treat each other with respect, affection, patience, forgiveness, and mutual caring. But, apart from these general moral exhortations, the matrimonial relationship is regulated by a set of rather rigid rules, which, for the main part, concern the institution of *nafaqa*.

Nafaqa is the right of the wife, who is entitled to receive from her husband food, clothing, lodging, and, according to statute law, medical treatment. The obligation to pay *nafaqa* starts as soon as the wife moves into the conjugal dwelling, and lasts till the end of the *ʿidda*, the waiting period after the termination of marriage, during which the woman cannot marry another man. The *ʿidda* lasts three months, or three menstrual cycles; if the woman is pregnant, it lasts until childbirth. After the *ʿidda*, no alimony is due.

Nafaqa is due irrespective of the wife's needs. An affluent woman is entitled to maintenance, and the level of her maintenance must be in accordance with the standard of living to which she is accustomed. How to determine the *nafaqa* to be paid by a poor man to a rich woman is then a challenging question, thoroughly dissected by scholars, who reach different solutions. Normally, the level of the *nafaqa* is left to the parties who are free to define it by agreement. The important point is that *nafaqa* is a sign of respect towards the wife. It is her property and she manages it as she prefers.

If the husband fails to pay, many are the remedies available to the wife. She can sue for maintenance and have the judgement executed; she may be authorised by the court to borrow money in the husband's name or to collect *nafaqa* out of the husband's property, during his absence. She can bargain with her husband over divorce, or even seek it in court.

The wife is not required to contribute with *nafaqa* or any other property of hers to the costs of the household, nor to the support of her own children, even if her husband is unable to do so. The property of the spouses is strictly separate, and all the costs of the family are borne by the man.

In the discourse about women's rights in Islam, which is currently developed out of a polemical comparison with the UN documents, women's financial independence and *nafaqa* represent two particularly important issues. Unquestionably, Muslim women had their independence recognised long before European women. *Nafaqa*, on the other hand, is a more nuanced question. Ideally, the wife is not required to spend her money on household and family costs, nor to do housework, nor to care for the children. The husband will pay someone to do those services. But, if the man is unable to do so, or, if domestic help is not part of the *nafaqa*, because of the social status of the woman, the wife will do all the housework that is needed. This work will actually be an important contribution to alleviate the family burden that is placed on the man. Moreover, women working outside the home often contribute by their income to family expenses, deeming it necessary for the wellbeing of their beloved. The least that can be said, is that the rules regulating *nafaqa* are difficult to implement in their entirety.

Furthermore, the woman's right to *nafaqa* is not absolute, but it corresponds to her duty to obey her husband. This is the conclusion that, despite some terminological difficulties, interpreters unanimously draw from the *Qur'ān* (IV, 34): men have authority over women because they spend their property to support them.

As a consequence, the wife loses her right to *nafaqa* in case of disobedience or rebellion (*nušūz*). On the other hand, the most usual defence for a man summoned to appear in court on the grounds that he failed to pay *nafaqa*, is to accuse his wife of disobedience. To be considered obedient, the wife has to move to the conjugal dwelling, and not to leave it without the husband's consent or a legitimate reason. She has to fulfil her conjugal duties, and in particular not refuse sexual intercourse.[8] In general, she has to obey her husband, save where he orders her to perform an act which is religiously illicit.

In case of disobedience, the *Qur'ān* (IV, 34) allows the husband to warn his wife, then to refuse to sleep with her. As a measure of last resort, the man is permitted to use force against the wife and beat her. This *jus corrigendi* of the husband is a very contentious issue: the meaning traditionally attached to the *Qur'ānic* verse is refuted either on the basis of some subtle lexical arguments, or by reference to the general duty not to cause harm, or to the duty, specific to the spouses, to treat each other with affection and mercy (*Qur'ān*, XXX, 21).

In certain States, such as Egypt and Sudan, statutory law allowed the enforcement of obedience decrees through the assistance of the police. The wife was forced to return to the conjugal dwelling, to what was called *bayt al-ṭāʿa* (the house of obedience). This institution, not regulated by *fiqh*, was abolished in Egypt in 1967.

The relationship between husband and wife, shaped by the couple *nafaqa*/obedience, is deeply asymmetric and hierarchical, and characterised by the clear pre-eminence of the man over the woman.

Marriage dissolution

In Sunni Islam, marriage is contracted to last indefinitely, but it is not indissoluble.[9] The decision about its termination essentially lays in the hands of the husband. The wife is given a rather limited role: she may either persuade her husband to dissolve the marriage on the conditions they agree upon, or seek a judicial divorce against her husband's will.

According to *fiqh*, the husband puts an end to the marriage by *ṭalāq*, a unilateral act that takes place outside court. The presence of the wife is not necessary, neither is an express reason for the breakdown of the marriage required. *Ṭalāq* is valid even in the absence of witnesses. *Ṭalāq* is regulated in detail by the *Qur'ān* (II, 228.232), in a number of verses that restrain and limit a pre-Islamic form of marriage dissolution.

The husband has the power to pronounce *ṭalāq* three times. The first and the second *ṭalāqs* are revocable: the husband may take back his wife during the period of *ʿidda*, the three months, or more precisely the three menstrual cycles, following the *ṭalāq*. The revocation of *talāq* does not require the woman's consent. After the *ʿidda* period has expired, the husband may marry the woman again, by a new marriage contract and with a new *mahr*.

The third *ṭalāq* is instead irrevocable, and the husband is barred from remarrying the woman unless she undergoes an intermediate marriage: after the dissolution of this new marriage, the woman is permitted again to the first man.

The *Qur'ānic* verses plainly aim to make men aware of the serious effects of *ṭalāq* and discourage them from lightly pronouncing it, with the result of indirectly protecting women's interests. However, this form of protection for women is weakened by legal scholars, who allow the husband to pronounce all three *ṭalāq* at once, with the result that an irrevocable dissolution of the marriage is immediately operative, together with all its personal and financial effects. The triple *talāq* is considered a reprehensible innovation (*ṭalāq al-bidʿa*), but it is perfectly effective according to *fiqh*.

Ṭalāq may consist in explicit or metaphorical expressions: only in the latter case does the husband's intention to dissolve the marriage have to be proven. Otherwise, the marriage is terminated by the mere utterance of the expression containing the word *ṭalāq*, or other terms derived from the same root *ṭ-l-q*, as well as some archaic locutions as *īlā'* or *ẓihār*,[10] irrespective of the real capacity of the husband to make a sound judgement. An explicit *ṭalāq*, even if uttered by someone who is drunk, out of his senses, asleep, mentally deranged, under duress or overwhelmed, is perfectly valid and effective.

According to *fiqh*, the husband may also pronounce suspended *ṭalāqs*, in order to ensure the wife's compliance with his orders. For instance, he may swear that the marriage is to be considered dissolved by *ṭalāq* if the woman leaves the house. But such a weapon, intended to keep pressure on the woman, may easily backfire against the man if the woman leaves the house, taking advantage of the opportunity of securing her freedom from the marriage.

In fact, even in a legal environment that is, overall, unfavourable to them, women may find interstices to exercise their agency, possibly with the support of their families of origin. For instance, it is a good bargain for the woman if the husband confers his power of *ṭalāq* on her (*tafwīḍ*). The scope of the delegation may vary: an absolute delegation is normally inserted into the marriage contract and allows the wife to dissolve the marriage whenever she wants. On the other hand, a conditional delegation will take effect only under certain circumstances, normally if the husband does not keep to what he has promised. Such a delegation usually puts an end to a dispute between the spouses which arises in the course of the marriage. In any case, the delegated *ṭalāq* is irrevocable.

In fact, the delegated *ṭalāq*, if absolute, places the wife on an equal footing with the man as to the freedom to terminate the marriage; however, the unilateral power of *ṭalāq* still formally remains the privilege of the man, and the wife dissolves the marriage in his name. If the husband has not delegated his power to her, the wife who wishes to be freed from marriage may try to persuade the man to pronounce *ṭalāq* himself. The *ṭalāq* given by the husband for compensation paid by the wife is called *hulʿ*. *Fiqh* distinguishes two main cases: the wife either pays compensation (*ʿiwaḍ*), or renounces her rights (*ibrā'*). If the agreement involves the mutual waiving of any financial obligations between the spouses, it is called *mubāra'a*. Obviously, the waiver and the compensation may be combined together. The woman normally renounces the rights strictly connected with the marriage and its dissolution: the dower, or the part of it not yet paid; the maintenance for the *ʿidda*, the waiting period following the dissolution of the marriage; and the arrears payments for maintenance during the marriage. Quite often, the waiver concerns the children: the woman renounces her rights of custody (*ḥaḍāna*), or the wage she is entitled to as their *ḥāḍina*; more importantly, she may waive the children's right to be maintained (*nafaqa*) by their father. In general, any right claimed by the woman or her family against the man may be waived in exchange for *ṭalāq*. As to the compensation, it may consist of any asset; according to a prophetic tradition, it is the return of the sum paid as dower.[11]

However, the terms of the agreement are not always the successful outcome of the wife's initiative and agency; on the contrary, they may be the result of her extremely weak position, shamelessly exploited by the husband. The man enjoys an extraordinary bargaining power *vis-à-vis* his wife in negotiating the marriage dissolution by mutual consent. *Ṭalāq*, the key to the solution to the marriage breakdown, is his exclusive prerogative; moreover, he is never in desperate need to be free of a specific marriage in order to enter another one: polygyny allows him to indefinitely prolong the negotiations, while making the life unbearable for the wife. Eventually, she will be ready to pay a ransom for her freedom.

The woman's position is less miserable when a possibility exists for her to terminate the marriage irrespective of the husband's consent. Legal scholars, with the exception of the Hanafis, allow the wife to sue for divorce (*taṭlīq* or *tafrīq*) in the courts on a number of grounds: if the husband fails to pay maintenance (*ʿadam al-infāq*); if he is absent (*ġiyāba*); and if he causes harm (*ḍarar*) to her, i.e. if he treats her unjustly. A defect (*ʿayb*) or mental or physical disease are considered grounds for divorce for either spouse by all the scholars, including the Hanafis.

Divorce proceedings are long, they are held in public, and their result is uncertain. Nevertheless, they are a better option for women than other ways out of marriage: as mentioned earlier, during the 1930s Muslim women in India would renounce their faith to be rid of their undesirable marriages. Hanafi law, which was applied in the country, did not contemplate any form of judicial divorce, but, as with the other schools, it provided for the immediate termination of marriage in case of apostasy (*irtidād*) of one of the spouses. This practice created great turmoil in Muslim public opinion, and the *ʿulamāʾ* convinced the British government to pass an act, The Dissolution of Muslim Marriages Act (1939), allowing Muslim women to seek divorce.

This Act perfectly fits with the general trend that, at that time, started emerging in statutory interventions concerning family law across the Muslim world. To promote a more equitable balance between husband and wife in matters relating to marriage dissolution, legislatures tried to strengthen the wife's position and to limit the husband's powers. On the one hand, they generalised the judicial divorce and widened the grounds on which the woman can seek it. On the other, they transformed *ṭalāq* into a judicial procedure and made it more onerous to the man. Only in Tunisia were women and men granted perfect equality in their access to divorce proceedings.[12]

Current family codes expand the traditional list of grounds for divorce, so as to reduce the discretion of the court in assessing what constitutes harm and justifies the application for divorce lodged by the wife. Obviously, the breach of any clause inserted in the marriage contract is a valid ground for divorce. Polygamy, even in the absence of a specific clause to that effect, constitutes a ground for divorce according to certain statutes; the same happens in the case of extramarital relationships and same-sex activities. Other new grounds for divorce are gambling, drug addiction, and wine consumption, or behaviours that are contrary to the interests of the State (desertion or treason). However, the case-by-case evaluation by the court of the circumstances cannot be avoided, and it may prove particularly tricky when referring to episodes of ill-treatment of the wife.

For the sake of equality, access to divorce is sometimes open to the husband. This is not the case for *ṭalāq*, which retains its nature as a male privilege. However, some of its excesses are reined in: triple *ṭalāq* and suspended *ṭalāq* are abolished;[13] the actual intention on the part of the husband to terminate the marriage is required for the *ṭalāq* to be effective. What is more important, *ṭalāq* ceases to be a purely private act and is brought under judicial supervision: statutes normally provide that a court decree is needed to establish *ṭalāq*, or at least to authorise its drafting by the notary, and its registration. In some States, failure to register the *ṭalāq* within a set deadline involves criminal sanctions. Despite the efforts of the States to enhance the judicial supervision of *ṭalāq*, out-of-court *ṭalāqs* are still an important social phenomenon in many countries.

A private *ṭalāq* may concern a registered marriage. In this case, it is particularly detrimental to the wife: according to the law of the State, the woman is trapped in the marriage, whereas the man does not consider her as his wife anymore. For this reason, statutes often make the proof of the extra-judicial *ṭalāq* easier for women than for men. However, there are also cases where the out-of-court *ṭalāq* terminates a non-registered marriage. The man giving extra-judicial *ṭalāq* may have chosen informality as the only way of organising his conjugal life: he invariably omits to register the marriages he contracts,[14] because, faced with the cumbersome and bureaucratic procedures required, he cannot see the benefits of the registration. In fact, his preference for informality is normally shared by the social environment in which he lives. Conversely, a man may combine formality and informality, in such a way as to create a hierarchy between different conjugal unions. Alongside the main marriage, approved by the families and duly registered, he enters minor, non-registered marriages (*zawāğ ʿurfī, zawāğ al-misyar*): they are less demanding than 'official' marriages, but perfectly suitable to make sexual intercourse licit. Obviously, the position of a woman involved in an unofficial marriage is particularly vulnerable, and her rights are not protected upon dissolution.

As to judicial *ṭalāq*, the court is called upon to play an important role in attempting to reconcile the spouses and dissuade the husband from making use of his power to terminate the marriage. If mediation fails, the court ensures the rights of the woman: the deferred dower and the maintenance due for the waiting-period (*ʿidda*). In addition, current legislations provide for compensation in favour of the wife. The reform was introduced by reference to the 'gift of consolation' (*mutʿa*) that the *fuqahā'* recommended be given to the woman at the time of *ṭalāq*: what was recommended is now mandatory and regulated in different ways from country to country. Some statutory texts provide for *mutʿa* only in the case of arbitrary *ṭalāq*, pronounced without a reasonable cause; for others the arbitrary nature of *ṭalāq* is always presumed, and sometimes *mutʿa* is mandatory in types of judicial divorce other than *ṭalāq*. The wife's condition, the husband's financial situation, and the duration of the marriage are possible criteria to determine the sum to be paid as *mutʿa*. When courts award women substantial sums for *mutʿa* in case of *ṭalāq*, and especially when the husband has to deposit these sums prior to *ṭalāq*, men are encouraged to abandon their traditional prerogatives and to opt for other forms of dissolution, preferably on the basis of an agreement.

Statutes look with favour at *ḫulʿ*, the agreement on marriage termination: they try to strengthen the position of the wife in the bargaining, so as to protect her from being forced to adhere to unacceptable terms. They identify certain rights she cannot renounce in return for the *ṭalāq*, notably her right to custody (*ḥaḍāna*) and the maintenance of the children. Moreover, if the spouses agree on the principle of ending their conjugal relationship in exchange for compensation, but disagree on its amount, it is up to the court to fix it.

Ḫulʿ was transformed into a judicial divorce in Egypt (Law n. 1/2000). If the husband refuses the offers made by the wife to reach an agreement, she may apply for divorce, stating she is ready to return the dower and renounce all her outstanding rights. The wife does not need to provide grounds for her demand; neither is her culpability under discussion. The court will grant her divorce against the wishes of the husband. Similar procedures are available to women in other Arab countries.

Morocco introduced another way than *hulʿ* to empower women to terminate their marriage: the divorce for *šiqāq*, or discord. *Šiqāq* is an arbitral procedure regulated by the *Qur'ān* (IV, 35) and provided for by a number of statutory texts, as part of ordinary divorce procedures. But only the Moroccan code shapes it as a rapid, sure, and non-discriminatory way to dissolve the marriage. In case of disagreement making it impossible to continue married life, each of the spouses may petition for divorce. The court appoints two arbitrators to investigate the causes of the dispute between the spouses and attempt to reconcile them. If reconciliation proves impossible, the court grants the divorce and fixes the sums to be paid, taking into account each spouse's responsibility for the marriage breakdown. If the husband is to blame, the wife will be awarded her rights; otherwise, she will renounce the dower or return it.

Hulʿ and *šiqāq* show that a relation exists between the dower and the husband's exclusive power to determine the fate of the marriage by means of *ṭalāq*. As long as the wife is ready to waive her right to the dower, the husband cannot oppose her initiative to terminate the marriage.

Finally, mention must be made of *liʿān*, the oath taken by the husband in order to disavow the paternity of the child born from his wife. Besides this main function, *liʿān* entails marriage dissolution and creates a permanent impediment between the parties. The procedure is held in public, at the mosque, following the rules laid down by the *Qur'ān* (XXIV, 6–9). The husband accuses his wife four times of illicit sexual intercourse (*zinà*); then, in a fifth oath, he invokes the wrath of God upon himself if he is lying. The wife, in turn, swears four times that the husband is falsely accusing her; then in a fifth oath, she invokes the wrath of God if he is telling the truth. *Liʿān* is a very rare occurrence, even if in many countries it remains the sole means of rebutting the presumption of paternity.

The Islamic law of marriage, as summarily outlined, contributes to shaping the life of Muslim women, in interaction with statutes, case law, and customary law. It is the common reference for the supporters of radically different ideas, who animate the ongoing debate about the role of women in family and society throughout the Muslim world. It is sufficiently flexible to accommodate a wide range of solutions, even if not the most radical ones.

Further reading

Abu-Odeh, L. 2005. 'Modern Family Law, 1800–Present. Arab States'. 2 *Encyclopaedia of Women in Islamic Cultures*. 459.

Abu Zahra, M. 1957. *al-aḥwāl al-šahṣiya*. Cairo.

Agmon, I. 2006. *Family and Court. Legal Culture and Modernity in Late Ottoman Palestine*. Syracuse University Press.

Aluffi Beck-Peccoz, R. 1990. *La modernizzazione del diritto di famiglia nei paesi arabi*. Giuffré.

Anderson, N. 1976. *Law Reform in the Muslim World*. Athlone Press.

An-Nai'm, A. (ed.). 2002. *Islamic Family Law in a Changing World. A Global Resource Book*. Zed Books.

Beck, L. and Keddie, N. (eds). 1978. *Women in the Muslim World*. Harvard University Press.

Benkheira, M. H. 1997. *L'amour de la loi*. Presses Universitaires de France.

Benkheira, M. H., Giladi, A. and Sublet J. (eds). 2013. *La famille en islam d'après les sources arabes*. Les Indes Savantes.

Bernard-Maugiron, N. and Dupret. B. (eds). 2012. *Ordre public et droit musulman de la famille en Europe et en Afrique du Nord*. Bruylant.

Bianquis, T. 2005. *La famille arabe médiévale*. Editions Complexe.

Borrmans, M. 1977. *Statut Personnel et fammille au Maghreb de 1940 à nos jours*. Mouton.

Botiveau, B. 1993. *Loi islamique et droit dans les sociétés arabes*. Karthala.

Cuno, K. and Desai, M. 2009. *Family, Gender and Law in a Globalising Middle East and South Asia*. Syracuse University Press.

el-Alami, D. and Hinchcliffe, D. 1996. *Islamic Marriage and Divorce Laws of the Arab World*. Brill.
Esposito, J. L. 2001. *Women in Muslim Family Law*. Syracuse University Press.
Giunchi, E. (ed.). 2014. *Adjudicating Family Law in Muslim Courts*. Routledge.
Kandiyoti, D. (ed.). 1991. *Women, Islam and the State*. Temple University Press.
Layish, A. 1975. *Women and Islamic Law in a Non-Muslim State*. John Wiley & Sons.
Mahmood, T. 1995. *Statutes of Personal Law in Islamic Countries: History, Texts and Analysis*. Indian Islam Research Council.
Mir-Hosseini, Z. 1993. *Marriage on Trial. A Study of Islamic Family Law, Iran and Morocco Compared*. I. B. Tauris.
Nasir, J. J. 2009. *The Islamic Law of Personal Status*. Brill.
Pearl, D. and Menski, M. 1998. *Muslim Family Law*. 3rd edn. Sweet & Maxwell.
Rapoport, Y. 2005. *Marriage, Money and Divorce*. Cambridge: Cambridge University Press.
Shaham, R. 1997. *Family and the Courts in Modern Egypt. A Study Based on Decisions by the Sharīʿa Courts 1900–1955*. Brill.
Sonbol, A. E. A. (ed.). 1996. *Women, the Family, and Divorce Laws in Islamic History*. Syracuse University Press.
Tucker, J. 2000. *In the House of the Law. Gender and Islamic law in Ottoman Syria and Palestine*. University of California Press.
Tucker, J. 2008. *Women Family and Gender in Islamic Law*. Cambridge University Press.
Welchman, L. 2000. *Beyond the Code: Muslim Family Law and the Shar'i Judiciary in the Palestinian West Bank*. Kluwer Law International.
Welchman, L. (ed.). 2004. *Women's Rights and Islamic Family Law: Perspectives on Reform*. Zed Books.
Welchman, L. 2007. *Women and Muslim Family Laws in Arab States: A Comparative Overview of Textual Development and Advocacy*. Amsterdam University Press.

Notes

1 In classical law, the sexual intercourse between the master and his female slave is licit, too.
2 *Iḥṣān* is a very tricky legal term. While any person can be *ʿafīf*, the condition of *iḥṣān* is acquired only by marriage, or more precisely, by the consummation of the first marriage. Once a person becomes *muḥsan*, it is forever. Marriage protects the *muḥsin* person from illicit and immoral behaviours and at the same time transforms him/her into the guardian of the boundaries between sexes. His/her transgressions are then particularly grave and, in case of *zinà*, a *muḥsin* person deserves the most serious punishment of stoning, be he/she married at the time of the illicit sexual intercourse or not. From this point of view, marriage is like a rite of passage, allowing the definitive entrance of the individual in a new status.
3 *Qur'ān*, LI, 49.
4 At present, all Muslim countries forbid, or at least discourage, child marriage.
5 This was the case of Tunisia, where the circulars providing for the ban of marriages between Muslim women and non-Muslim men were repealed by a new circular in September 2017.
6 Another temporary impediment limits the man's free exercise of polygyny: the prohibition to contract marriage with any woman so related to his present wife that if one of them was a male, they couldn't marry because of their blood relationship.
7 V. in particular Qāsim Amīn, *al-Aʿmāl al-kāmila*, Beirut, 1976, t. 2, p. 93.
8 It is a matter of debate whether a right of the wife to sexual intercourse exists, too. The sexual deprivation of the wife may induce her to engage in an illicit sexual intercourse (*zinà*); that is the reason why some jurists consider the absence of the husband (*ġiyāba*), or his refusal to share the conjugal bed, as grounds for divorce (*hiğr*). The wife has less extensive rights than the husband, though, since she can seek divorce only if she has been deserted for a prolonged period of time (four months, in the case of *hiğr*). Anyway, the majority of the scholars maintain the husband's right to have sex cannot be transformed in the duty for him to be available for the sexual enjoyment of the wife.
9 Alongside the ordinary marriage, Shi'i law admits the temporary marriage (*nikāḥ al-mutʿa*), a contract entered into for the duration specified by the parties. This kind of marriage cannot be dissolved by the will of the spouses, but only by either death or the expiration of the time limit agreed upon. If the duration of the contract is longer than the expected life of the spouses, the *nikāḥ al-mutʿa* amounts to an indissoluble marriage.

10 *Īlā'* is the oath of the husband to abstain from sexual intercourse with the wife for four months; in the *ẓihār*, the husband swears that his wife is like 'the back (*ẓahr*) of my mother' to him. Both procedures are mentioned in the *Qur'ān*, respectively by II, 226–227 and LVIII, 2–4.

11 The tradition tells that the Prophet urged a man to pronounce *talāq* in exchange of the garden he had paid as *mahr*, as his wife was ready to return to him.

12 Equality at marriage dissolution is also ensured in other Muslim countries, such as Turkey, but by means of purely secular statutes, whereas the Tunisian code maintains the link with the legal tradition of Islam.

13 Recently, the practice of triple *ṭalāq* was banned by the Supreme Court of India, who declared it unconstitutional (Shayara Bano v. Union of India and others, 22 August 2017).

14 Women are often not in control of the marriage registration, and sometimes even ignore the administrative procedure and the benefits they could draw from it.

19

Hindu law

Marriage

Werner Menski and Gopika Solanki

For Hindus, marriage is also portrayed as a religious requirement, for a different reason than it tends to be argued for Muslims, who are asked to avoid *zina*, any form of extra-marital sexual relationship. Hindu marriage seems at first sight prominently a socio-cultural phenomenon. However, on deeper analysis Hindu marriage should also be seen as linked with macrocosmic *rita/satya* and *dharma* complexes (Menski, 2003: 86–93; 2006: 204–209), always connected to the *Grundnorm* that at any time Hindu individuals should remain aware of the idealised need to follow these broad, ultimately global patterns of expectations of macrocosmic Order/microcosmic ordering to the best of their abilities. The pressure of such expectations does not mean there is no individual discretion; quite the opposite. In this polyvalent Hinduism, the ideal of marriage between two souls, including gods, has also been interpreted as making space for sexual diversity in marriages.[1] Even the essentialised Hindu visions thus result not in rigid normative and ethnographic patterns but, in fact, quite the opposite, as happened in the totality of ethnographic evidence. Various expected forms of microcosmic ordering are expressed through many further, mostly idealised terms connected to *dharma*, such as *strīdharma*, the obligations of women; *patidharma*, a husband's duties; and so on.

This deeper context implies strong expectations that all Hindus should enter married life to reproduce.[2] We find this directly reflected in forthright claims by some Indian experts on Hindu marriage law. For example, Diwan (1988: 64) asserted: 'Marriage is one of the essential *samskaras* (sacraments) for every Hindu. Every Hindu must marry'. Such expectations are reinforced by the classical system of *varnāśramadharma*, the template-like set of obligations for every Hindu, always according to their stage of life and caste status. In this fourfold classification, preceded by childhood (*bālatva*), an initial period of study and preparation for married life, known in Sanskrit as *brahmacarya*, prominently involves celibacy. But after that, duly marked with often complex entry rituals, married life is the central stage of normal human existence, identified through the terms *grihastha* (householder) and *gārhasthya* (householdership).[3]

First, though, the Hindu child and young person should prepare for this central phase of life. This involves initially being looked after – even being pampered – by others, growing up, ritually and socio-economically protected as well as possible (Chapter 14, this volume). Then, for males, the ideal is undergoing the classical system of education, more specifically textual study, which could take many years. While this would not happen for the overwhelming majority of young Hindus, every Hindu, according to caste status and ability, should cultivate *svadharma*, the individual's potential or, as we might say today, aim to be 'the best you can be'.[4] One major purpose, for both young men and women, seems to be the preparation for the key stage of marriage and parenthood, combined with further acquisition and production of skills and knowledge (*jñāna*) and/or socio-economic assets (*artha*) for the comfort and sustenance of the family, the benefit of society and, ultimately, for upholding the universe.[5]

The highly diverse and often locally quite flexible caste-based structures of Hindu society suggest, therefore, that they are focused on practical secular issues, that young persons, prior to entering marriage, should acquire life skills and whatever else they may need later to survive decently. The manner and extent of preparations could also impact on potential choices of marriage partners. The skills acquired would largely be occupational, related to a specific community, learnt from parents and those around them. For most Hindus, this means some form of apprenticeship, probably often what today we would call 'child labour'. Hindu children, especially as they grow older and acquire more responsibilities, should share the burdens of daily life and participate as fully as possible in economic activities. Kakar (1978: 127) tellingly cites a North Indian proverb advising dutiful fathers how to lead their sons towards assuming full responsibility: 'Treat a son like a *raja* for the first five years, like a slave for the next ten and like a friend thereafter'. In lived reality, the effects of dreadful diseases and disasters often meant that even very young people might have to take on family responsibilities well before maturity (Menski, 1986: 205; Ross, 1973: 101).

Gendered structures were prevalent, as they still are largely today, with girls primarily expected to focus on acquiring household and caring skills, while boys would gradually be inducted into the respective activities of their family and community. Barring disasters and disruptions, the end of this phase of childhood, learning and focused preparation would be ritually marked, facilitating transition to the married stage of life through the sacrament (*samskara*) of the marriage rituals. In this way, the young male Hindu would be appropriately readied for entry into the next stage of life, marriage and householdership, while the young Hindu female would now be prepared for marriage and childbirth. In all of this, the vast internal pluralities of Hindu societies resulted in a multitude of diverse lived experiences (Derrett, 1968; Menski, 2003; Solanki, 2011); for example Nairs in Kerala practised matriliny and such arrangements also influenced gender roles.

The formation of marriage

Hindu marriage comprises various socio-cultural as well as ritual and religious dimensions. Later we discuss to what extent a Hindu marriage is a holy sacrament and/or may also be treated as a contract. As noted, many preparatory activities look secular and are informed by local cultural specificities rather than high Sanskritic culture. But this is never an either/or scenario. In dominant patterns of Hindu marriage regarding spouse selection, suitability and social standing of prospective marriage partners were not just determined by the individual characteristics of the young people but also the wider expectations of families, clans, communities and cosmic ideals. Much guidance, also of a textual nature, exists about due diligence processes of spouse selection and criteria for suitability. This often involves magic, importantly also looking at star signs, using horoscopes, charts and other devices to secure a fitting match. The prevalence of arranged marriage patterns with significant family involvement means that many arrangements might be made early, also in view of competition in the marriage market in a particular socio-cultural context.

Since Hindu marriage law applies to a wide variety of communities, the diversity of rules developed among Hindus about endogamy and exogamy is also reflected in the modern law.[6]

Traditional patterns have much continuing relevance, are extremely diverse and locally very specific. Endogamy that is too close, in particular village endogamy, reflects fears about incest, eugenic complications and sexual morality. Infringements of rules may in certain cases lead to 'honour killings', causing global headlines today.[7] While dominant patterns among Hindus, especially in northern and central parts of the subcontinent, remain patriarchal and patrilineal, some communities in India's southern states have followed more ambivalent patterns, including matrilineality, especially in Kerala.[8] There is a general tendency for Northern Indian perceptions and patterns to be more patriarchal and patrilineal, while some borderland groups and many Southern Indian communities retain notably female-focused variants of marital practices. A coherent overview is impossible, as there are basically no central ground rules binding all Hindus; everything is situation-specific and ultimately depends on 'customary traditions'.[9] These are themselves internally so diverse that it becomes important to highlight that any specific Hindu marriage ritual is ultimately a purpose-built ritual construct for that one occasion only, designed to achieve an ordered progression for both parties and their families, clans and communities – and finally the whole universe – to the fully married status of these two particular individuals at this particular moment (Menski, 2003: 298). We find therefore as much a solemn sacramental union with definite religious characteristics and a customary law contract with secular connotations, hence a hybrid, so typical of Hinduism. The paragraphs below provide further details on the nature of Hindu marriages.

Regarding the formation of a Hindu marriage, common sense and experience suggested since ancient times that genetic and eugenic considerations were crucial for achieving the larger cosmic objectives. The ultimate purpose of the highly sophisticated Vedic marriage rituals, under increasingly close priestly supervision, became the delivery of a ritually perfect bride to the husband's family (Menski, 1984). The strong focus on high quality progeny, clearly documented since Vedic times (c. 1500 BC), also materialised in many different rules about prohibited degrees of marital relationships. Such rules are too complex to be discussed here in depth.[10] In essence, eugenic concerns advised against marriage arrangements among spouses belonging to the same tribe, let alone the same clan or even family. Exogamy was therefore preferred, but posed its own risks. Apparently in Vedic times, inter-caste marriages were quite common (Diwan, 1988: 90), while caste-based discriminations later also impacted on marriage arrangements. Hindus became increasingly nervous about crossing too many boundaries, began to oppose inter-caste alliances and even curtailed inter-sub-caste marriages. However, opposition to such steps also continued, and, historically, social and religious reforms movements have promoted and advocated inter-caste and companionate marriage (Anandhi, 2008). These status-based differentiations were all abolished by the formal state law of India. Under section 5 of the Hindu Marriage Act of 1955, with very few remaining restrictions, any two Hindus of any caste or community background may marry (Diwan, 1988: 90). During the process of Hindu law codification during colonial rule, this came to mean one male and one female, as the idea of same-sex marriage runs against macrocosmic *Grundnorms* of the central importance of procreation.

Trends towards reducing status differentiations among Hindus on the basis of caste in relation to marriage have not, however, been replicated regarding the degree of prohibited relationships based on closeness of ancestors. In this respect, eugenic concerns seem to remain prominent. Great care is normally taken to ensure that prospective parties are not within the prohibited degrees of relationship, particularly in terms of clan (*gotra*). Related terms of *pravara* and *sapinda* are pertinent, too, both signifying closeness of more direct patrilineal relations. These would be easily identified since elaborate marriage rituals in the traditional joint family context also incorporate elements of ancestor worship, mainly through ritual recitation of the names of relevant males from earlier generations. Today, section 5 of the Hindu Marriage Act of 1955 contains among the conditions for a legally valid Hindu marriage that respectively 'the parties are not within the degrees of prohibited relationship unless the custom or usage governing each of them permits of a marriage between the two' (s.5 (iv)), and that 'the parties are not *sapindas* of each other, unless the custom or usage governing each of them permits of a marriage between the two' (s.5 (v)).

In practice, all of this means that a great variety of rather close family relations no longer form a legal bar to a marital union. For instance, Solanki (2011) found cross-cousin marriages among the Meghwals, a Dalit sub-group in Mumbai, with the children taking on the mothers' names before patriliny became standardised in state laws. Moreover, in several South Indian communities, particularly in Andhra Pradesh, marriage between a maternal uncle and his niece might be a preferred form of customary arrangement. Such family-centric considerations also seek to protect the young bride against the shock of marriage, a phenomenon observed by many writers that is still coming up in recent fieldwork.[11] Given that marriage is looked upon as 'her inevitable fate' (Ross, 1973: 268), marriage into a family that she already knows could be much easier for a girl than entering a community of total strangers. In this context, too, the certainly not-yet-abandoned, though formally illegal patterns of dowry transactions become relevant, as marriage among relatives may involve far less onerous expectations of bringing all kinds of material assets.[12]

A highly contested topic remains the age at marriage for Hindus (Menski, 2003: 322–373). Presently, the official minimum age under Indian law for all communities remains 21 years for males and 18 years for females. This provision, found also in s. 5(iii) of the Hindu Marriage Act of 1955, was amended in 1978 in line with the lead provisions under the colonial Child Marriage Restraint Act of 1929. This originally introduced a minimum age of 14 years for girls and 18 years for boys.[13] However, following ongoing activist and increasingly international pressure, India's most recent Act on this topic, the Prohibition of Child Marriage Act of 2006, now invalidates any forced marriage, but still does not automatically render all child marriages void, making them voidable instead. A subsequent 2008 Law Commission Report on Child Marriages sought to push for total nullification of all child marriages in India. Significantly, this has not been implemented, neither has India followed demands to adopt the international benchmark of an equalised minimum age of 18 years for both genders.

The reasons for this lie partly in national pride and strategic resistance to international pressure. But they also reflect 'traditional' socio-cultural concerns, including connection to the religious roots of Hindu marriage and protection of the young women involved, especially when they are happy with the arrangements made for them. As indicated, prudent concerns in navigating the marriage market may suggest that a family should look for possible partners early on, perhaps with a view to suitable family alliances, even while the prospective spouses are still children.[14] Families may then resort to engagements and other promises to marry, while everyone waits for the legally appropriate timing. However, such supposedly rational argumentations overlook important socio-economic facts. Hundreds of millions of Indians still suffer hunger and thirst on a daily basis today, both in urban and rural areas. An economically distressed family may indeed value the extra pair of hands of a teenaged daughter, particularly if she herself earns an income, however meagre. But a family may also seek to transfer the burden of looking after a young girl as early as possible, given that she cannot stay with her parents indefinitely. If a good match comes up, one may grab this chance, even if the girl is quite young. Some clues about balancing such competing expectations even come from ancient texts. Manusmriti 9.88–89 provides no blank cheque for child abuse and forced marriages. Clearly suggesting that the best interests of the bride should prevail, it advises:

88. To a distinguished, handsome suitor of equal caste should one give a daughter in accordance with proper custom (*vidhi*), even though she may not be of age.

89. A girl, though of marriageable age, should rather stay in the father's house until death than be given to a man devoid of good qualities.

Relevant guidance also comes from recent High Court cases on child marriage, showing that India's courts are not prepared to invalidate the marriage of a young girl, who may anyway be close to 18, especially when there is no evidence that the girl is unhappy.[15] High Court judges openly say that the state's laws are inconsistent and prefer to consider the circumstances of each case.[16]

The whole family will often be involved in making sure that suitable arrangements are made. Many males, not only among tribals (Dhar, 2014), feel obliged to seek work explicitly to facilitate a good marriage for a sister. Such economic motivations may reflect deeper concerns about 'religious' obligations, including concepts of 'debt' (*rna*). More importantly, though Indians do not like to discuss such matters, a common predicament is that young Indians, too, have increasingly become interested in 'romantic love' (Mody, 2008; Ross, 1973: 269–270). In such scenarios, a decision to arrange an early marriage for a young girl counters the risks of her being misled by a potentially unsuitable lover, again protecting the 'order'. Since many young people in India today are involved in their own match-making, experimenting with so-called 'love marriages', they might then present the parents with their own choice of partner. This is often elegantly redefined and dressed up as an 'arranged marriage' if there is parental agreement. The modern state, as Mody (2008) shows, remains unable to handle such patterns of social change with sufficient cultural competence.[17]

While child marriages have been formally outlawed in India, the thresholds remain rather high in international comparison.[18] In practice, current disparate trends include the frequently reported phenomenon that many Hindus marry rather late now. The most difficult problem remains therefore what one should do about 'infant marriages' rather than 'child marriage'. A forced marriage of a young child to another child, apart from the fact that cohabitation with a young child bride risks being a crime under state law, is manifestly not a good step forward, also in terms of *dharma*, if too early pregnancy results in potentially disastrous implications for mother and child. Here the 2006 Act has stepped in by instantly nullifying an infant marriage if the young spouse wants this to happen. This provision closely resembles the option of puberty in Muslim personal law. Since that was not the situation several decades ago,[19] we see significant positive developments in the interaction between state law and the various 'religious' personal laws of India.

A latently dangerous implication of partly deliberate non-discourse in such cases remains present, however. Following a religious customary Hindu marriage that violates the letter of the modern secular state law, the religiously coloured norms may prevail through appeals to the marriage's sacramental status. Provided the marital arrangement is endorsed by the young woman herself, however, the formally illegal marriage should be upheld, since otherwise the woman will suffer disproportionately. Such cases, where men might seek to exploit legal contradictions, raise difficult questions about the reality of consent given by young Hindu girls to their own marriages.

A broadly similar scenario persists in India today regarding polygyny among Hindus (Menski, 2003: 374–426). While the Hindu Marriage Act of 1955 abolished and criminalised the polygynous marriage of one man to a second or further woman, Hindu polygyny continues to exist, in various forms. Indian courts, including the Supreme Court, having become highly sensitised to the needs of women, may order a Hindu husband to pay maintenance to the 'wife', though the marriage is legally void.[20] Similarly, Solanki (2011: 198, 209) finds that the rhetorical criminalisation of Hindu polygyny is not implemented in practice and that women who are party to a polygynous Hindu marriage are entitled to maintenance payments. Such remarkable acceptance of social facts, based on recognition of the wife's socio-economic needs rather than religious tradition, applies also to the equitable principle of 'factum valet', which applies a presumption of marriage on the basis of observed, socio-religious facts. This principle remains very strong in Indian marriage law to protect Hindu wives and other Indian women (Menski, 2003: 287–318). The now widespread evidence of so-called 'unmarried cohabitation' in modern Western legal systems does not quite match this picture, since such relationships are often deliberately not registered with the state authorities.

In India, the state-based rules of marriage registration have long been a major political football. They illustrate most vividly the 'shared adjudication model' that Solanki (2011) elaborates on. That the legal validity of a Hindu marriage depends entirely on the performance of situation-specific customary marriage rituals (see later) is indicated when section 7 of the Hindu Marriage Act of 1955 provides:

> Section 7 – *Ceremonies for a Hindu marriage.*

(1) A Hindu marriage may be solemnized in accordance with the customary rites and ceremonies of either party thereto.
(2) Where such rites and ceremonies include the *saptapadi* (that is, the taking of seven steps by the bridegroom and the bride jointly before the sacred fire), the marriage becomes complete and binding when the seventh step is taken.

Subsection (1) clearly preserves the old customary position under Hindu law, whereby marriage solemnisation is achieved through performance of customary rituals. Since these vary enormously by locality, caste and family, and also from case to case, custom should always be interpreted flexibly. Hence it becomes important to be aware that India's postcolonial definition of custom, under section 3 of the 1955 Act, has actually been relaxed and expanded. It now signifies 'any rule which, having been continuously and uniformly observed for a long time, has obtained the force of law among Hindus in any local area, tribe, community, group or family' (Menski, 2003: 298). The phrase 'for a long time', rather than the much tighter earlier definition under Anglo-Hindu law, which demanded proof of custom followed 'since time immemorial', gives the game away. The reformed Hindu law of 1955 silently supported strong presumptions of the legal validity of all customary Hindu marriages, perhaps not so much to respect 'religious' tradition but reflecting socio-legal realism. However, this is often deliberately ignored by reform-focused activists and by many lawyers, too. In legal practice, this position, again a reflection of 'shared adjudication' (Solanki, 2011), is of utmost relevance for Hindus of all communities, including Brahmins.[21] Since the statutory law contains the same protective mechanisms for Hindu customary divorces, a provision skilfully hidden away in section 29 of the 1955 Act, the message of somewhat embarrassed, yet quite deliberate protection of Hindu religious and cultural norms becomes clearer.[22]

To complete the account of formation of marriage, it is necessary here to reiterate that a traditional Hindu marriage would be legally valid once all the rituals have been completed. This follows directly from the above-cited wording of section 7 in the 1955 Act. Recorded since ancient times,[23] there is much awareness that the precise point at which a marriage's legal validity comes into effect is difficult to determine. The key point is simply this: the socio-cultural and religious nature of a Hindu marriage already offers ample public registration, including a kind of 'cosmic registration' (normally with the holy fire as divine witness, even if it is only an oil lamp or candle). Any administrative state action can then be perceived as superfluous and somewhat redundant. This predicament is well-reflected by how the state law itself is drafted. Section 8 of the Hindu Marriage Act of 1955 covers registration of Hindu marriages. Several sub-sections then detail the provisions that ought to be made concerning registration of such marriages. However, section 8(5) tellingly concludes this section by providing: 'Notwithstanding anything contained in this section, the validity of any Hindu marriage shall in no way be affected by the omission to make the entry'.

In fact, the recent charades over Hindu marriage registration go much further when we consider various attempts at state level in federal India's by now 29 states. Following a much-cited Supreme Court judgment,[24] which directed the state to pass laws for compulsory registration of marriages, there was a flurry of legal activity (Solanki, 2014). Yet, there are several purportedly compulsory regulations for marriage registration, which sooner rather than later admit in one of the sections of the same Act or Rules that failure to register a Hindu marriage will actually not affect its legal validity.[25] What, then, is the point of all this agitation over marriage registration if we learn, ultimately, that a customarily solemnised marriage between a Hindu male and female is simply a legally valid Hindu marriage once the customary rituals are completed? The 'shared adjudication model' identified by Solanki (2011, 2014) brings out the continued co-existence of state law and socio-religious norms and ethics.

Hindus themselves will normally know who is married to whom, given the largely public nature of marriage rituals and the general openness of public spaces in India, which allows for much observation of what others are doing in their daily lives. So why are there such highly emotional discourses about Indian family laws regarding marriage registration? It seems that the legal provisions on Hindu marriage registration must be read in conjunction with the even more highly politicised debates over the proposed introduction of a Uniform Civil Code for the whole of India. Clearly, this would affect all Indians irrespective of religion. Allegedly, this reform would make India's personal law system redundant and legal administration would become much more efficient.[26] The relevant constitutional provision for this unifying ambition is found under Article 44 of the Constitution, a Directive Principle of State Policy rather than a Fundamental Rights clause. This, therefore, allowed the Indian state room for much leeway and non-implementation. Article 44 simply directs: 'The State shall endeavour to secure for the citizens a uniform civil code throughout the territory of India'.

While there have been frequent calls by modernists, activists and also many senior judges, even recently, for introducing such a Uniform Civil Code, this is not a matter that concerns only Hindu law. More importantly, given that India has by now more than 180 million Muslim citizens, the place of Muslim personal law under India's plurality-conscious legal system is the more critically pertinent battleground, overshadowing all other related discourses, conveniently hiding concurrent debates over Hindu marriage and divorce law and related matters. In such a chaotic situation, everyone's eyes are still on the world-famous *Shah Bano* case of 1985 and its much-misunderstood aftermath (Menski, 2003: 487–504).

In this case, Shah Bano, an old divorced Muslim wife, was granted the right to post-divorce maintenance by the Indian Supreme Court holding that there was no contradiction between India's Criminal Procedure Code, section 125 and the Quranic provision that a divorcing Muslim husband should be kind to the woman he divorces. This verdict led to riots by Muslim men, which made the government pass the Muslim Women (Protection of Rights on Divorce) Act of 1986 which continues to be wrongly presented by many writers as denying divorced

Muslim wives post-divorce maintenance. The Act was challenged as unconstitutional in *Danial Latifi v. Union of India*, AIR 2001 SC 3958, but it was held that the *Shah Bano* decision remained good law and was supported by the 1986 Act. Both Muslim and feminist scholars (and many press reports) have refused to report this highly contested legal scenario faithfully, while current focus on the Indian Muslim husband's right to divorce by a triple *talaq* continues to confuse and irritate many observers (Menski, 2012).

This has meant that more recent developments in relation to Indian family law have almost completely bypassed the radar of an agitatedly watching global scholarly community, which does not care to understand how Indian family laws work in daily reality and, moreover, is constantly exposed to a barrage of journalistically morphed opinions and much misinformation about the current state of Indian family laws. The effect has been an unholy alliance, mainly of modernists demanding more state-centric intervention and dominating the public arena in conjunction with an anti-Indian global press.

Widespread scholarly, journalistic and public assumptions that fundamental legal changes were brought about in Hindu law under British colonial rule appear thus, on closer scrutiny, rather underresearched. Historians of South Asia have tended to study only colonial archives and state law precedents and have paid scant attention to sources of religio-customary laws and practices on the ground. Several fieldwork-based studies on contemporary legal developments in India suggest that much of Hindu law in India remains based on internal self-regulation and continues to rely heavily on customary laws, sometimes intertwined with state laws, especially regarding marriage and divorce. Self-controlled ordering in family law remains an integral part of the lived experience of most Indians, supported through conditions in which multilocational justice remains prominent (Solanki, 2011: 60). There may well be some deeper conceptual and philosophical reasons for this, not just that the Indian legal system seems to be one of the messiest and most complex legal constructs ever produced in the world. As we gaze a little more intensely into the mirror to understand Hindu marriages, we may find some more answers, provided the person who does the gazing is prepared to keep an open mind about the huge internal diversities within understandings of what actually constitutes and creates Hindu marriages.

The nature of marriage

The conceptual nature of Hindu marriage as a connecting link between individuals, families, communities, societies and ultimately the cosmic whole indicates that it serves as a socio-cultural tool to strengthen stability and sustainability, expecting of all participants in this interconnected enterprise that they should contribute to the best of their ability. Hence, classical Hindu law has no conceptual problem with accepting the basic principle that men and women are complementary components in this cosmic chess game. Symbiotic interaction and multiple synergies are needed all along. The somewhat radical, global principle that everything is interconnected and thus to some extent composed of the same particles, and yet every manifestation of creation is a separate entity, underpins also the dominant Hindu conceptual understandings of marriage. Sharma (1996: 62–64) shows that this moral consciousness does not mean approval of all kinds of differentiation. The focus is not primarily on ideological constructs of gender equality but on empirical practice-focused observations (Sharma, 1996: 10) about gendered division of labour. That only women can give birth seems to have inordinately troubled ancient Hindu male priests. In those early pre-scientific times, when one could not work out how life begins and ends, the magic power of the female blood became a focus of priestly concern, arising during Vedic times and continued to the present (Menski, 1984).

The basic principle, that human action, embodied in the *karma* concept, is an essential motor for development and balancing, first focused on ritual action, later on every action in one's life, became contained within the *dharma* concept. A properly solemnised Hindu marriage is, thus, so to say, the major form of cosmic insurance policy that any Hindu couple is advised to purchase. Intriguingly, the complexity of the ritual challenges, already felt in those ancient times, results in the highly sophisticated priests themselves conceding ritual defeat at some crucial point (Menski, 1984: 372). They just could not handle the pollution of the bridal blood. As a result, later Hindu marriage rituals became less focused on the almost obsessive earlier concerns about the potentially polluting and destructive bridal blood. This matter is henceforth handled by women and lower caste functionaries, dramatised through customary sub-rituals. The major Hindu marriage rituals, as a complex process of ritual (and ultimately physical) amalgamation of husband and wife, became focused on ritual celebration of incorporation. A related major aim of such ritual performances is to bring about a crucial mental transformation of the two parties, so that consciousness of being married is being created. This is what the notion of *samskara* and its complex ritualisation, outlined in such minute detail by Pandey (1969), is ultimately concerned about.

We have already discussed the huge importance of customary diversity in the Hindu law of marriage and its lived reality. It makes sense to theorise Hindu marriages like a drama on stage, in which the respective actors, step by step, bring about the complete integration of bride and groom, transforming them ritually into husband and wife. There is indeed no point at which either spouse explicitly consents to this solemn process, a social contract which takes on high religious sacramental features, particularly in those forms of Hindu marriage that are elaborately ritualised by using many Sanskrit verses, with Vedic roots (Menski, 1984; Pandey, 1969). Detailed study of this highly sophisticated ritual material conveyed and confirmed that early Hindu (Vedic) priests got involved in an extended sequence of 'rites of passage' (van Gennep, 1960), with rituals of separation, extended risky liminal phases and many different rituals of incorporation. These involved family members and many others, but above all the two parties themselves and various priestly officiants. In their most elaborate manifestations, such marriages must have taken a long time to celebrate. There were also evidently numerous ritual changes over time. The major aim, all along, was to deliver ultimately to the husband and his family a perfectly endowed and ritually purified bride, ready to become a wife and, in due course ideally, a mother of many sons (Menski, 1984).

To presume, however, that all Hindu marriages have to follow this elaborate pattern would be a grave methodological error. The texts themselves tell us with abundant clarity that there are many ways of conducting these rituals. Even if some elements were left out, the basic expectation remains that the couple getting married is becoming a new entity within the macrocosmic system and should thereafter contribute to it. That is why even very simple Hindu marriage rituals, maybe just waving an oil lamp in front of the bride and groom, can solemnise a perfectly valid Hindu marriage (Holden, 2008). Consciousness can be created within seconds. As everything depends on the specific context of the couple's ritual status and socio-economic position, it may be even customary to perform no ritual at all, maybe just to distribute some sweets. A virtual zero ritual may be the appropriate custom, especially when the bride is a widow and/or it is a remarriage for both parties.[27] In principle, this is just as valuable and valid under Hindu law as the most elaborately Sanskritised sequence of rites conducted over several days.

This may sound extreme but is the logical consequence of Hindu custom being 'king', as situation-specificity determines the finer points of what is to be done, or not, as the case may be. Thus, even if one of the spouses is not a Hindu, provided some kind of Hindu ritual is performed, presumptions of a legally valid marriage may arise. Strictly speaking, this could not be a Hindu marriage under the Hindu Marriage Act of 1955. But there have been numerous cases where, for example, European men marrying Hindu women and following the customary instructions of the Hindu priest over several hours, have not been able to claim successfully later on that they were not legally married. Technically, in India, such a marriage ought to be registered under the secular Special Marriage Act of 1954, under which, like in European legal systems, the act of registration alone creates legal validity for the marriage. Yet where this did not happen, evidence that a Hindu marriage was solemnised might be sufficient proof to claim married status, especially when the rights of the wife and any children are at stake. In addition, the concept of inter-religious marriage is complicated by customary practices among Hindus as there is evidence of internal contradictions and heteroreligiosities on the ground, leading to hybrid practices that cross religious boundaries. For instance, Solanki (2011) studied marriage among the Meghwals, a Dalit group classified as Hindu and governed under Hindu law in state courts. However, the group worships Ramdev Pir, a Sufi saint, who is worshipped by both Hindus and Muslims, and group members belong to diverse religions such as Christianity, Islam, Buddhism and Hinduism. These caste members see themselves as Meghwals, inter-marry routinely and adjudicate marriage in their caste councils. As a result, marriages which may be perceived by the state as inter-religious are seen by the group as intra-caste marriage by the caste group, which does not contest its Hindu status granted by the state.

This confirms that after Indian independence in 1947, as Derrett (1968: 305) observed, 'the great chasm between custom and law remained'. Most formally unrecognised customs did not cease to exist in social reality, unless superseded or modified in their respective local context. Since custom is highly dynamic and constantly adjusts to new developments, India's Hindus could continue to rely on its inherent force. While acknowledging that local customs were important in Hindu law (Derrett, 1968: 320), most Indian lawyers remained remarkably ignorant of Hindu customary law (Kishwar, 1994: 2160). Since, as Derrett (1957: 3) observed, 'the private law of the Hindus is one of the most complicated in the world', the field was left to anthropologists, while lawyers concentrated on activist flag waving and numerous calls for reforms of the 'traditional law' of the Hindus. The dominant place of customary Hindu law in practice is confirmed by field observations, showing that only 5 per cent of cases ever reach the High Courts (Solanki, 2011: 32). Many millions of common Hindus would not even want any direct contact with the state (Derrett, 1968: 223). Observing, partly from his own personal experience, the fundamental incompatibility of *śāstric* training and busy legal practice, Derrett (1968: 304–305) noted that with few outstanding exceptions, 'Hindu judges have been undistinguished for learning in *dharmaśāstra*'.

In such complex conditions, we need to understand the concepts and nature of Hindu marriage law primarily through people's actual practice. A judge who might display such insights in today's secular environment would, however, face vigorous politicised challenges for adhering to Hindu nationalist trends (*hindutva*).[28] One major reason for such continuing ideological battles is scholarly politics, coupled with lack of appreciation about the close relationship of law, culture and religion, not only within the Indian legal system but in terms of theorising legal pluralism generally. While the Hindu legal system was not built on state-centric structures, it remains erroneous to declare it simply a 'religious' law, as it is actually a culture-specific natural law, based on ethics which are as much religious as secular (Menski, 2003). Failing to appreciate this, journalistic and academic discourses on Indian legal developments generally, and specifically on

Hindu law, which remains so strongly based on custom, have remained completely unable to understand the complex nature of Hindu marriage.

This then comes out in two kinds of debate over legal reforms. While the original ambitiously modernist plan of a comprehensive Hindu Code in the late 1940s had to be dropped because of public opposition, four separate Hindu law enactments, including the Hindu Marriage Act of 1955, were promulgated. As shown earlier, this skilfully built traditional Hindu concepts and customs into state law (Kishwar, 1994), serving as evidence of state-centric reconstruction (*Verstaatlichung* in German) of *dharma*, surely not the same as its complete removal or suppression, an agenda which remains as unrealistic today as in the 1940s. Concepts of marriage and divorce relate too closely to people's value systems, and hence their identity construction as Hindus of whatever kind, to be simply removed. Hence the legal validity of Hindu marriages in India remains primarily a culture-specific issue, depending even today on whether appropriate ceremonies were conducted in accordance with either party's custom. Marriage is not merely a matter of legal bureaucracy.

Overall, the selective reforms of Hindu law in the 1950s remained necessarily incomplete, respecting the perceived need to protect the basic nature of Hindu marriage. In today's democratic conditions, this puts important red light signals into the path of any government seeking to change people's laws. Significantly, though, many academic and legal commentators remain fiercely critical about India's reluctance to abolish personal laws, citing their various discriminatory effects (Parashar and Dhanda, 2008), as though state laws would automatically be gender-neutral and/or non-discriminatory. This view posits a false binary between state law as equalising and customary laws as anti-women and also goes against empirical evidence that customary laws can be gender-equal (Solanki, 2011, 2013). While much earlier for Derrett (1957: 271), it was still 'evident that Parliament has not legislated so far with the interests of the poor and illiterate citizens (i.e. the majority) in mind', and India's lawmakers might have known little about customary laws, yet they wisely allowed such laws to continue for people who could not afford access to potentially costly formal administrative and legal processes. When later Derrett (1978) pronounced classical Hindu law dead, he was issuing a wake-up call to modern India, showing that its secularising family law reforms had gone too far by creating new forms of precariousness for the very people one claimed to protect.

Today, activist emphasis on state intervention still puts much sustained pressure on the Indian state to intervene more aggressively in personal laws. The revised, refined strategy, however, hardly discussed so far, is not the abolition of Hindu personal law. While current rhetoric focuses on perceived and actual gender problems in operating Islamic laws in Hindu-dominated India, presently the instant 'triple *talaq*', what has largely been hidden from view is the gradual introduction of new general laws concerning the family, such as India's secular Domestic Violence Act of 2005. This kind of law applies to all citizens and is not interested in religion and local culture, but it strongly reflects international law principles and human rights expectations and the agenda of equality and non-discrimination. This emerging regime now conflicts head-on with some aspects of the existing personal laws of India and has already generated significant new case law which befuddles most academic analysts. Since this new scenario refuses open discussion about the deep plurality in the interface between Hindu and other religious and traditional ethics, people's normative practices, state law and international law coupled with human rights concepts, it prevents deeper insights into the continued relevance of Hindu marriage concepts, which are simply portrayed as an ideological enemy and manifestations of noxious Hindu nationalism. Hence proper legal analysis of the internal pluralities within Indian family laws remains contested.

The dissolution of marriage

Very briefly now, it is already evident that by analogy with Hindu marriage laws, India's Hindu divorce law, too, could not possibly be anything else today than deeply plural, much contested and again torn between more state involvement and continuing respect for customary patterns (see Holden, 2008; Menski, 2003: 427–483; Solanki, 2011).

Ideological debates about Hindu divorce have indeed been extensive and highly contested. On the one hand, writers have portrayed and protected the ideal of Hindu marriage as an indissoluble sacrament (Menski, 2003: 427, 430–438), an eternal bond (Lariviere, 1991: 37). That this is merely a pious ideal, however, becomes clear from the fact that Hindu customary law has always permitted divorce (Diwan, 1988: 162). Further, ancient Sanskrit texts suggested that in certain scenarios, mainly when the wife was defective, superseding her would be appropriate.[29] Other texts give similar rights to women, and the separation and remarriage of women, too, was certainly not unknown in ancient India (Lariviere, 1991: 42).

The many rules regarding termination, on the basis of various fault grounds, are discussed in all major textbooks on Hindu family law (Diwan, 1988; see Menski, 2001, 2003 with further references). There are only two major issues to debate here. Firstly, the rhetoric over the idealised position that Hindu marriage is an indissoluble sacrament, and thus Hindu divorce is not possible. That, we have already found, is clearly a pious ideal, as the social reality is very different. The Hindu Marriage Act of 1955 introduced in section 13 a large number of fault grounds, but also protected, hidden away in section 29 of the same Act (Holden, 2008; Menski, 2003: 428; Solanki, 2011), that under Hindu customary law divorces continue to be available, too.

The rest seems rhetoric, as gradually growing evidence of marital breakdown among Hindus in India has made it more and more prominent that divorce needs to be managed in terms of social policy as well as possible, since it cannot be prevented through legal intervention. Restrictive granting of divorces would cause havoc in society, but during the 1970s, granting divorces on the flimsiest pretexts caused much havoc as well (Derrett, 1978). After further liberalising divorce reforms in 1976, which introduced divorce by mutual consent for Hindus under section 13-B of the 1955 Act, the only major remaining issue seems to be now to what extent irretrievable breakdown of marriage should be recognised as a ground for divorce among Hindus. The real issue here is not actually the breakdown itself but the potential for its abuse through allowing unilateral repudiation of the marital tie by one spouse, while the other is keen to remain married, for whatever reason. Indian courts have thus faced enormous challenges of finding the right balance between freeing a spouse from the intolerable cruelty of a bad marital relationship, on the one hand, and concern for the decent survival of the rejected or abandoned spouse, if such permission to divorce was given (Menski, 2003: 429). Detailed case studies confirm that this is still a major issue today.

The continued recognition of Hindu customs and values confirms that 'the right law' for India remains today a culture-specific plural construct, a hybrid entity with Hindu elements, continuously challenged to prove that it is a 'good law'. The application of such laws is constantly subject to constitutionally motivated tests of justice and sustainability. Two competing trends of critique regarding the relationship of Indian law and Hindu religion may thus be observed. Firstly, we find continuing calls today for further legal intervention in 'religious' personal laws, often simplistically based on gender justice arguments and reference to principles of international law and human rights. Total ignorance of the realities of Indian family laws accompanies such presumptions and strategies, which have meanwhile shown some results in the shape of important new statutory provisions outside the personal law system. Yet as these are not replacing the old system, this complicates the whole scenario. Presently, there is neither conceptual clarity nor agreement on the relationship of personal laws and general laws. As a result, all actors in this densely crowded arena of law reform debate remain confused and edgy, as recent cases confirm.

Secondly, with regard to Hindu divorce, Hindu spouses, both men and women, can today claim divorce on many fault grounds, but there is no effective welfare state system in India to support abandoned women and children. Since around 1988, Indian courts have therefore begun to argue against the 'modern' principle of irretrievable breakdown of marriage, reasoning somewhat tongue-in-cheek that since there is some cruelty in every marriage, 'cruelty' by itself should no longer be a sufficient ground for divorce. This indicates acute sensitivity to social conditions, confirming that India is today working on postmodern country-specific solutions for family law problems which continue to rely partly on 'traditional' religious and cultural norms and duties, rather than insistence on 'modern' individual rights. In India, feminists who support modern reforms have also opposed faultless divorce, as Hindu women would be worse off in such a scenario. In addition, fault-based divorce has given Hindu women a narrow window of opportunity to negotiate divorce in their favour (Solanki, 2011), as they can seek to claim on various grounds that the breakdown of the marriage was the husband's fault. However, as the wider public is not clearly told what the key agenda are (they mainly concern fiscal resources of support for destitute victims of marital breakdown), and the Indian welfare state suffers from a deficit of resources to handle such massive problems of poverty alleviation, many complaints of abuses of human rights in relation to Indian family laws are heard.

The intertwining of general laws and personal laws, including Hindu personal law, shows mixed results. For instance, laws such as section 125 of the Criminal Procedure Code of 1973, which shore up women's access to maintenance and prevent economic distress, have benefitted all women, including Hindu women, as have general laws criminalising domestic violence. However, the impact of civil law governing domestic violence, the Protection of Women from Domestic Violence Act of 2005 has been mixed. It has provided women with access to maintenance and matrimonial residence, and extended some rights of single women, but it has failed to protect the rights of second wives or cohabitating partners.[30]

At present, avoidance of chaos, which often means the day-to-day survival of vulnerable women and children in society, remains primarily a localised, socio-economic challenge. Continued popular resistance to bureaucratised state control of family law thus remains a strong feature of India's scenario today. The limited extent to which Indian state law can provide sustainable remedies for broken marriages leaves the vast majority of Hindu individuals to rely on self-controlled ordering processes. These remain nourished by Hindu concepts, are often surprisingly secular and frequently also not really different from Muslim concepts (Solanki, 2011: 67, 91). Even in the minds of those who are explicitly atheistic, agnostic or secular – and that includes many more Hindus than we realise – this prudent self-sufficiency suggests a policy of keeping one's distance from the bureaucratic modern state and focusing on building strong social relationship to ensure the decent survival of Hindu individuals. While Indian judges have said time and again that they cannot create money to help needy litigants, Sen (2009) sagely advises that real, meaningful justice is not achieved through setting up perfect institutions and rules. What seems to be needed is ethical introspection and consciousness (Sharma, 1996: 60–63) on the part of Hindu individuals to find the right solution at any time of their life and in their specific circumstances. Maybe, then, there is even today some deeper truth in the final ritualised step of the ancient Hindu *saptapadi* ritual that asks spouses at the conclusion of the marriage rituals simply to become each other's best friend (*saptame pade sakhī/sakhā bhava*)!

Notes

1 Vanita and Kidwai (2000) and Vanita (2005) discuss marriage between Aravan, the son of Arjuna, and the Hindu god Krishna in the Tamil version of the Indian epic Mahabharata. This ritual is emulated by the *hijra* in India.
2 Where this leaves same-sex relations, clearly a deviation from this ideal, is a different matter, yet not completely off-radar, as current 'modern' interventions over criminalisation of homosexuality tend to suggest (Vanita, 2005).
3 The other two stages are *vānaprastha* and *samnyāsa*. The former means more or less retirement, figuratively 'moving to the edge of the forest', while the final stage is some kind of 'renunciation', with focus on final release or *moksha*. For details, see Knott (1998: 21–22) and Mees (1980: 74–76).
4 Saying this we should not overlook that low-caste Hindus and untouchables, in particular, and often women, too, were generally prevented from access to education (Gupta, 2016). On India's terrible record in that regard, see Sen (2006: 34).
5 That Dalits claim a share in this, too, is made amply clear in the contributions of the Special Issue on Caste of *South Asia Research*, 36.3 (November 2016).
6 S. 2 of the Hindu Marriage Act of 1955 details that it applies 'to any person who is a Hindu by religion in any of its forms and developments', including many different named Hindu groups, but also Buddhists, Jainas or Sikhs, as well as 'any other person domiciled in the territories to which this Act extends who is not a Muslim, Christian, Parsi or Jew by religion'. The political, much contested nature of such definitions is thus immediately evident. Space constraints prevent further exposition of details.
7 Reports on the honour killing of Manoj and Babli, despite the fact that at least one of the two families was happy with this love match, are now even found on Wikipedia.
8 Polyandry is known in some communities, but peripheral.
9 Sen (2006: 34–35) discusses that the right to custom provides a crucial equity of recognition.
10 See for details, Diwan (1988: 89–103).
11 See Menski (1986: 218–219) and Ross (1973: 266). Kalindi Kokal found during her fieldwork for two separate projects, earlier in 2011 concerning the application of Muslim personal law, and then specifically in her PhD research in India (2014–2015), that marriage of a boy with his paternal aunt's daughter is common among Koḷī people, a lower caste group, and the Dhangar community, a nomadic tribe in Maharashtra.
12 On the world-wide manifestations of dowry among South Asians, see Menski (1998/1999) for further references.
13 In earlier colonial times, vigorous Indian objections arose specifically towards British efforts to stipulate higher minimum ages for marriage and its consummation (Menski, 2003: 334–345; Sarkar, 2001). Such fierce opposition also reduced much of the British appetite for further legislative intervention.
14 Observing that political families prominently engage in such practices, one realises the connections to issues of power and standing in society, rather than 'religion'.
15 See *Latori Chamar v The State of MP*, M.P. High Court, 10 January 2007 (www.indiankanoon.org/doc/701102); *Jitender Kumar Sharma v. State Delhi High Court*, 11 August 2010 (www.indiankanoon.org/doc/1983620/); *T. Sivakumar v The Inspector of Police* AIR 2012 Mad 62 (MANU/TN/3959/2011); *Association for Social Justice & Research v Union of India, Delhi High Court* (W.P. (CRL) 535 of 2010) (www.indiankanoon.org/doc/1652773).
16 *Suo Motu (Lajja Devi, Delhi High Court*, 27 July 2012 (www.indiankanoon.org/doc/41067986).
17 The articles in Shirwadkar (2009) bring out the various tensions indicated here.
18 In many European countries, sometimes with parental consent, young people can marry much earlier than in India. When a UNICEF Report on early marriages suggests that South Asia is today a major problem area for early marriages, giving figures for child marriages in Bangladesh as high as 75 per cent, Nepal 63 per cent and India 57 per cent (www.childinfo.org), subjectivities are strongly evident, also in UNICEF statements that 40 per cent of all child marriages in the world take place in India.
19 In *Naumi v. Narotam* AIR 1963 HP 15, a young Hindu girl was pleading to be freed from an unwanted marriage to a much older man, but was not successful. Today, this kind of case would be decided very differently.
20 See *Sumitra Devi v Bhikhan Choudhary*, AIR 1985 SC 765.
21 See Menski (2003: 445), while Parashar and Dhanda (2008: 203) are clearly wrong. For further details, see Solanki (2014).
22 Kishwar (1994: 2150) correctly observes that the Hindu Marriage Act of 1955 actually has two divorce laws.

23 Menski (2003: 286–293). Section 7(2) of the 1955 Act refers to the ritual of the seven steps as marking the completion of the marriage rituals and its legal effects. However, as many customary Hindu marriages do not contain this ritual, dangerous confusions have arisen in court cases.
24 *Seema v Ashwani Kumar*, 2006 (2) *Supreme Court Cases* 578.
25 For example, section 13 of the Gujarat Registration of Marriages Act of 2006 clearly provides: 'Non-registration not to invalidate marriage'.
26 That this kind of system does not work effectively in European jurisdictions has not escaped the notice of some observers, but state-centric modernists desperately stick to this model as the global gold standard.
27 For a discussion of such cases, see Menski (2001).
28 This happened prominently to Mr Justice Katju of the Indian Supreme Court, specifically in *D. Velusamy v D. Patchaiammal*, 2010(10) SCC 469, which also involved interpretation of the Protection of Women from Domestic Violence Act, 2005, which now competes with the Hindu Marriage Act, 1955. Similar politics appeared again recently when a divorce was granted to a Hindu husband on the basis that his wife had been guilty of cruelty for refusing to live with his parents and to share the family assets with them. See *Narendra v K. Meena*, judgment in the Indian Supreme Court of 6 October 2016 in Civil Appeal No. 3253 of 2008. See also *The Guardian*, 8 October 2016 with typically garbled politicised messages.
29 Lariviere (1991: 38) cites Manusmriti 9.77–84, permitting men to supersede a wife.
30 See *Indra Sarma v. V.K. V. Sarma*, Supreme Court of India, 26 November 2013, https://indiankanoon.org/doc/192421140.

References

Anandhi, S. 2008. 'Women's Question and the Dravidian Movement c.1925–1948' in S. Sarkar and T. Sarkar (eds) *Women and Social Reform in Modern India: A Reader*. Indiana University Press. 389.

Derrett, J. D. M. 1957. *Hindu Law Past and Present*. A. Mukherjee & Co.

Derrett, J. D. M. 1968. *Religion, Law and the State in India*. Faber & Faber.

Derrett, J. D. M. 1978. *The Death of a Marriage Law*. Vikas.

Dhar, R. L. 2014. 'Job Search Processes for Tribal People from Jharkhand and West Bengal'. 34(3) *South Asia Research*. 191.

Diwan, P. 1988. *Modern Hindu Law*. 7th edn. Allahabad Law Agency.

Gupta, C. 2016. *The Gender of Caste*. University of Washington Press.

Holden, L. 2008. *Hindu Divorce. A Legal Anthropology*. Ashgate.

Kakar, S. 1978. *The Inner World*. Oxford University Press.

Kishwar, M. 1994. 'Codified Hindu law. Myth and reality'. 29(33) *Economic and Political Weekly*. 2145.

Knott, K. 1998. *Hinduism. A Very Short Introduction*. Oxford University Press.

Lariviere, R. W. 1991. 'Matrimonial Remedies for Women in Classical Hindu Law: Alternatives to Divorce' in Julia Leslie (ed) *Rules and Remedies in Classical Hindu Law*. Brill. 37.

Mees, G. H. 1980. *Dharma and Society*. Seema Publications.

Menski, W. 1984. *Role and Ritual in the Hindu Marriage*. London: SOAS. Unpublished PhD thesis.

Menski, W. 1986. 'Zur Sozialisation des Kindes bei den Hindus' in J. Martin and A. Nitschke (eds) *Zur Sozialgeschichte der Kindheit*. Karl Alber Verlag. 191.

Menski, W. (ed.). 1998–1999. *South Asians and the Dowry Problem*. Trentham Books.

Menski, W. 2001. *Modern Indian Family Law*. Curzon.

Menski, W. 2003. *Hindu Law. Beyond Tradition and Modernity*. Oxford University Press.

Menski, W. 2006. *Comparative Law in a Global Context*. Cambridge University Press.

Menski, W. 2012. 'The Uniform Civil Code Debate in Indian Law: New Developments and Changing Agenda' in M. McLaren (ed.) *The Many Faces of India: Law and Politics of the Subcontinent*. Samskriti. 136.

Mody, P. 2008. *The Intimate State. Love Marriage and the Law in Delhi*. Routledge.

Pandey, R. B. 1969. *Hindu Samskaras*. Motilal Banarsidass.

Parashar, A. and Dhanda A. (eds). 2008. *Redefining Family Law in India*. London: Routledge.

Ross, A. D. 1973. *The Hindu Family in its Urban Setting*. 2nd edn. Oxford University Press.

Sarkar, T. 2001. *Hindu Wife, Hindu Nation. Community, Religion, and Cultural Nationalism*. Hurst & Company.

Sen, A. 2006. *The Argumentative Indian*. Penguin.

Sen, A. 2009. *The Idea of Justice*. Penguin.
Sharma, A. 1996. *Hinduism for Our Times*. Oxford University Press.
Shirwadkar, S. (ed.) 2009. *Family Violence in India. Human Rights, Issues, Actions and International Comparisons*. Rawat Publications.
Solanki, G. 2011. *Adjudication in Religious Family Laws: Cultural Accommodation, Legal Pluralism and Gender Equality in India*. Cambridge University Press.
Solanki, G. 2013. 'Beyond the Limitations of an Impasse: Feminism, Multiculturalism, and Legal Reforms in Religious Family Laws'. 40(1) *Politikon*. 83.
Solanki, G. 2014. 'Registering Marriage: Debating Legislative and Judicial Efforts' in S. Basu and L. Ramberg (eds) *Conjugality and Beyond: Sexual Economies, Citizenship and Marital Form in India*. Women Unlimited. 218.
Van Gennep, A. 1960. *The Rites of Passage*. Routledge.
Vanita, R. 2005. *Love's Rite: Same Sex Marriage in India and the West*. Penguin.
Vanita, R. and Kidwai, S. 2000. *Same-Sex Love in India: Readings from Literature and History*. St. Martin's Press.

20

Comparative remarks

Religious laws and marriage

Yüksel Sezgin

Across history different societies have exhibited considerable ethnographic, legal, and socio-political similarities in marital and familial customs and patterns. Religio-legal norms and institutions have integrated pre-existing naturalistic, moral, and legalistic ways of thinking about sexuality, reproductive relations, gender roles, and notions, rituals, and markers of identity. As a result, as demonstrated in the preceding chapters, today we observe more convergence than conflict in the teachings of major world religions on marriage and divorce (Browning et al., 2006: xxii). The present chapter will identify main points of agreement (and also disagreement) across major religious traditions in terms of their rules and customs that regulate the formation and dissolution of marital unions within their respective communities. Religious family laws have long been appropriated by governments and integrated into national legal systems in polities all over the world. With this common dynamic in mind, the chapter will also discuss the effects of state appropriation, both on religious traditions themselves and on the rights and freedoms of people who are subject to state-enforced religious family laws.

Comparing religious rules on formation of marriage

All four traditions (Islam, Christianity, Judaism, and Hinduism) examined in the preceding chapters strongly favor the institution of marriage and require their followers to enter into marital unions at a relatively young age in the service of God and community. For instance, Menski and Solanki (Chapter 19, this volume) report that historically Hinduism has considered marriage to be a sacrament, a rite of passage, and thereby a religious duty for all Hindus in order to maintain the balance between macrocosmic order, *rita*, and individual *dharma*. Likewise, as mentioned by Aluffi (Chapter 18, this volume), many Muslim jurists consider marriage as *ʿibāda*, an act of obedience to God, a religious obligation that enhances the spiritual and physical well-being of individual Muslims as well as fosters social harmony among members of *umma*.

Procreation seems to be the primary objective of marriage for all religious traditions. Sexuality is considered to be part of human nature and may be expressed within the legal and moral framework of marriage. Sexuality serves the purpose of expanding the demographic boundaries of the faith by means of procreation. Infertility, or the inability to produce offspring, may be considered a valid ground for dissolution of marriage or bigamy. For instance, both Islamic and Jewish laws allow divorce on grounds of infertility. Likewise, Hindu law, as applied and enforced by the State of Goa in India, allows a Hindu husband to legally take a second wife if the first wife cannot bear a male child by the age of 30 (Mahajan and Jodhka, 2010: 310). Illicit sexual activity outside of marriage is strongly discouraged and in some instances is harshly punished. For example, all Christian churches allow separation or divorce in the event of adultery by either spouse. Similarly, Islam (Morgan, 2010: 210), and Hinduism – since the enactment of the Hindu Marriage Act of 1955 – (Bhattacharyya, 1978) also make provisions for divorce in the case of marital infidelity. However, religious rules pertaining to control of illicit sexual activity seem to discriminate against women more than men. For instance, according to Jewish law, the crime of adultery can by definition be committed only by a married woman. An extramarital affair of a husband with other (unmarried) women is not considered adulterous (Wells, 2015). By the same token, a child born by a married Jewish woman to a man other than her husband is stigmatized as a *mamzer* (illegitimate child), while the child of a married Jewish man from another (unmarried) woman is considered legitimate. A *mamzer* and his/her descendants are not allowed to marry Jews who are not *mamzerim* for ten generations (Sezgin, 2013). Such discrimination, as widely documented in the context of Islamic criminal and family laws in Pakistan, Nigeria and elsewhere, is also experienced by Muslim women who are accused of the crime of *zina*, and even those who have been raped (Ilesanmi, 2010; Quraishi, 1997).

Each tradition regulates entry into and exit from marriage. First and foremost, in theory, all of the traditions reviewed in the preceding chapters require mutual consent of the bride and groom to marriage. However, in many societies, especially where Islamic (and also Hindu) family laws operate, forced marriages, proxy marriages, and underage marriages continue to be widely practiced, mostly due to prevailing cultural norms and customs. Some of the traditions allow a party to exit from marriage if he or she can prove that he or she had not consented to the marriage in the first place. For instance, Carroll (1987) reports that in certain Islamic law jurisdictions the lack of consent by a bride can lead to nullification of the marriage contract by courts. Similarly, as Motilla demonstrates (Chapter 17, this volume), the lack of consent by either spouse is also considered sufficient grounds for nullity by most Christian churches.

Although marriage is consensual and requires the free will of the parties involved, important limitations are placed by religio-legal norms and institutions upon individuals' ability to choose their spouses. Religiously enforced marriageability criteria often include limitations concerning minimum age, consanguinity, civil status, physical, legal, and intellectual capacity, as well as socio-economic status and religious affiliation of prospective spouses.

As noted, all religions set certain age limits for marriage. Classical Islamic law – which sets age limits lower than those in Judaism and Christianity – allows marriage upon attainment of puberty, which is presumed to be reached at the age of 12 years by boys and at the age of 9 years by girls. Today, only a few Muslim countries (e.g., Saudi Arabia) enforce these very low age limits prescribed by classical shari'a. Most other nations set higher minimum ages.[1] For instance, according to the Malaysian Islamic Family Law Act of 1984, the minimum age of marriage is 16 years for girls and 18 years for boys. Ancient Hebrew law sets a marriageable age not too different from that of Islamic law: 12 years for boys and 13 years for girls. The canon law of the Catholic Church is somewhat higher: 16 years for boys and 14 years for girls. While ancient Hindu law did not specify marriageable age (Banerjee and Banerjee, 1923), the Hindu Marriage Act of 1955 prescribes some of the highest minimum ages in the world: 21 years for males and 18 years for females.

Apart from age limits, all four religions also require that prospective spouses meet certain legal, medical, and socio-economic requirements for marriage. As Motilla discusses in detail (Chapter 17, this volume), some Christian churches consider mental illness and contagious or sexually transmitted disease to be impediments to marriage. In other words, prospective spouses must be free of disease that might endanger the well-being of each other and their offspring. Similarly, they should be fertile and of sound mind. Similar requirements can be also found in the personal status laws of many Muslim countries (Nasir, 2002). Other legal impediments to marriage are concerned with the civil or socio-economic status of prospective spouses. For instance, some Christian churches, like the Catholic Church or the Coptic Orthodox Church, do not recognize divorce; as a result, they do not allow individuals who previously divorced to remarry in the church. Individuals who are members of religious orders with a vow of chastity (e.g., Catholic clergy) are also often banned from marriage by their respective religious institutions. Similarly, according to the Jewish law, a *kohen* (a member of a priestly class) is not allowed to marry a woman who is a divorcee or a convert. As mentioned earlier, a *mamzer* and his descendants are also banned from marrying other non-mamzer Jews for ten generations. Similar group- or caste-based restrictions are found in some early historical interpretations of Hindu laws and customs (Sharma, 2004). However, modern Hindu law has abolished caste-based disabilities and allowed inter-caste marriages between Hindus. As Aluffi notes (Chapter 18, this volume), *kafā'a*, or spousal equality, is an integral element of marriage according to Islamic jurists. The bride and groom must be equals with respect to socio-economic status, lineage, nobility, and piety. The doctrine requires the husband to be equal to or superior to the wife, not vice versa. The lack of *kafā'a* between spouses does not render a marriage *batil* (void); however, it is considered critical for the compatibility of spouses and therefore for the success of their marriage (Ziadeh, 1957).

Religious family rules demarcate boundaries of religious communities by regulating who can marry whom, and who can have a child with whom. In this regard, the most rigid rules regulating marital unions across all four traditions concern the religious identity of prospective spouses. Jewish law does not allow interfaith marriages; both spouses must be Jewish. As shown later, the restriction is so rigid that Israeli rabbinical authorities often prohibit Israeli Jews (usually those who migrated from former Soviet republics, India, or Ethiopia) whose 'Jewishness' is contested by halachic criteria, from marrying other Jews in the name of protecting the genealogical purity of the Jewish nation (Hayes, 2002). Although, as Menski and Solanki discuss (Chapter 19, this volume) the cultural and theological diversity of traditional Hinduism in the past allowed inter-religious marriages, and the modern Hindu law closed the door to interfaith marriages between Hindus and non-Hindus, mostly as an attempt by some post-independence legislators to attain religious unity and a 'pure' Hindu majority in the new Indian state. Islam allows Muslim men to marry non-Muslim women who are *kitabiyah* (people of the book, i.e., Jews and Christians). According to some interpretations, however, this permission applies only to Sunni men, while Shi'a men can only contract a temporary (*muta*) marriage with non-Muslim women (e.g., Jews, Christians), not a regular marriage (Kumar, 2002; Singh, 2011). On the other hand, marriage between non-Muslim men and Muslim women is completely prohibited under both Sunni and Shi'a laws. Given the hierarchical and patriarchal nature of marriage, this ban, as Aluffi notes (Chapter 18, this volume), ensures that a Muslim wife is never placed under the authority (*wilaya*) of a non-Muslim husband. Moreover, the ban also ensures that children born in such a union will be Muslim, since according to Islamic law the child's religion follows that of his/her father. Similar genealogical and demographic concerns (i.e., to expand the community of faithful by means of procreation) also inform the Catholic Church's policy towards mixed marriages. According to the Catholic tradition, as explained earlier by Motilla (Chapter 17, this volume), mixed marriages – those between baptized and non-baptized persons – are prohibited if one of the parties has not been baptized in any of the Christian churches. In order to authorize a mixed marriage, a bishop will require the baptized Catholic spouse to make a declaratory promise that he/she will maintain his/her faith and will do whatever is in his/her power to raise the future children as Catholics.

Likewise, all four traditions prohibit marriage within certain degrees of kinship. But, the degrees of prohibited relationships often vary from one religion to another. For instance, Islamic law allows first-cousin marriages, while the modern Hindu law (i.e., Hindu Marriage Act of 1955) prohibits them (Bittles, 2012).

Religions also impose a limit on the number of spouses. Most Christian churches have banned polygamy altogether. Likewise, as Westreich and Westreich note (Chapter 16, this volume), Ashkenazi and Sephardic traditions in Judaism, despite the permission of polygyny (one husband, multiple wives) in Torah, over time have also developed legal tools to restrict polygynous unions, which continued to be practiced among Mizrachi communities in the Middle East and North Africa until the majority of them migrated to Israel and adopted the bigamy ban imposed by the rabbinical authorities in the 1950s. Like ancient Judaism, ancient Hinduism also allowed polygamy and did not set a cap on the number of spouses. Besides unlimited polygyny, some Hindu communities also practiced polyandry (one wife, multiple husbands) (Menski, 2001). The Hindu Marriage Act of 1955 has banned all forms of polygamous unions for all Hindus, except for those in Goa, where the local family laws allow bigamy in the case of the first wife being infertile or failing to deliver a male child. Islamic law allows a Muslim man to take up to four wives. All Muslim-majority nations that formally integrate Muslim family laws into their national legal systems tolerate polygyny, except Tunisia. Most Muslim countries where polygyny is permitted try to limit it by requiring the husband to have financial means to sustain co-wives and their children and to obtain prior permission from the court and/or the consent of the existing wives.

Marriage symbolizes the union of families as well as spouses. It establishes a biological, legal, political, religious, and economic partnership or alliance between two families. In this respect, all four traditions treat marriage as a social and public institution, and over centuries each one has developed its own elaborate rituals, celebrations, and wedding liturgies that emphasize this public and social aspect of marriage. Marriages are usually solemnized by the religious authority of the respective traditions in a public ceremony at a religious venue (e.g., church, temple) attended by members of the community. In some traditions (e.g., Islam, Judaism) marriage contracts serve both a ritual and a legal purpose. In Islam, the wife can insert conditions into her marital contract which may allow her, for instance, to continue her education or prevent her husband from contracting a subsequent marriage (polygyny). In the contract, the husband may also delegate his power of pronouncing divorce (*talaq*) to his wife to allow her to divorce herself (conditionally or unconditionally) (*talaq-e-tafweez*). The Jewish marriage contract (*ketubah*) usually lists the husband's financial obligations towards his wife. However, as shown by Westreich and Westreich (Chapter 16, this volume), in the Sephardic tradition, the Jewish wife, just like her Muslim counterpart, can also insert a monogamy clause, and occasionally a clause against forcible divorce, into her *ketubah*. An Islamic marriage contract (*ʿaqd al-zawāj* or *nikāḫnama*) is a simple legal document in comparison to the Jewish *ketubah*, especially its Orthodox version, which must conform to certain elaborate rules, such as that it has to be written by an expert scribe in Aramaic, using special quill and ink on special parchment. Judaism has a rich culture of wedding ceremonies and rituals, such as the recitation of Sheva Brachot (The Seven Blessings) under the chuppah and the breaking of a wine glass to recall the destruction of the temple in Jerusalem. Christianity is also very rich in terms of wedding liturgies. In the Calvinist tradition, Motilla explains (Chapter 17, this volume), the wedding liturgy – including the manifestation of the consent of the couple before the community, the acceptance and blessing of the union by the pastor – is an indispensable element of marriage. Defective performance of liturgy may nullify the marriage. Likewise, according to modern Hindu law, defective wedding rituals may nullify marriage. In several high-profile cases, Indian high courts have pointed out that two essential ceremonies of a valid marriage (under the Hindu Marriage Act of 1955) were the *Datta Homa* (offering made to the fire-god Agni) and *Saptapadi* (the taking of seven steps by the bride and groom jointly around the sacred fire). Failure to prove the proper and complete performance of either ritual may lead a court to nullify the marriage in question (Sezgin, 2013).

All religions consider marriage to be an economic and a contractual union within which spouses are legally obligated to take care of each other and their offspring. Likewise, many of them also (e.g., Islam, Judaism, Hinduism) require the wife to submit herself to her husband's will and authority. She must be emotionally, physically, and sexually available to her husband and devote herself to his well-being and that of their children. The husband, for his part, must protect his wife's reputation and honor and provide her and their children with housing, food, clothing, and medical care when needed. Some traditions also have detailed regimes of marital property. According to Islamic law, the wife is entitled to acquire, hold, use, administer, and dispose of her own property. She is not required to use her property for or spend her income on household expenses that are the sole responsibility of the husband. No matter how wealthy the wife may be, the husband is under a religious and legal obligation to maintain his wife in a manner suitable to his and her socio-economic status (Sait and Lim, 2006). Judaism also prescribes a regime of separation of property during marriage. However, unlike his Muslim counterpart, the Jewish husband has a right to administer his wife's property, utilize its income, and even prohibit her from disposing of her own property. As Westreich and Westreich explain (Chapter 16, this volume), the Jewish husband, like a Muslim one, must pay maintenance to his wife, but if she has an independent source of income, she must hand over her income to her husband, or else she will no longer be entitled to maintenance from him. In recent years, Israeli courts have also begun requiring Jewish women to make equal contributions to maintenance of their children who are 15 years of age or older (Sezgin, 2018). In most traditions, maintenance of the wife is a religious and legal obligation of the husband. For example, a husband's failure to provide maintenance may be considered grounds for divorce in Islam or Judaism. In this respect, maintenance is a constitutive element of marriage. Similarly, the Islamic *mahr*, the Jewish *mohar*, and the Hindu dowry have also been considered essential for the formation of marriage. For instance, in Islamic marriage, the *mahr* (dower) is an undeniable right of the Muslim wife and absolute obligation of the husband, established by a Quranic injunction (chapter 4, verse 4). That is to say, even if there is no mention of *mahr* made in the marriage contract, it is still a binding obligation for the husband to provide it, unless the wife voluntarily renounces it (Siddiqui, 1995).

Comparing religious rules on dissolution of marriage

In all four traditions, marriage has both sacred and contractual qualities. However, some traditions attach greater importance to the sacred aspects of marriage than to its contractual elements, while others do the opposite. Where one particular religion stands on this question has a direct bearing on the availability, means, and conditions of dissolving or ending marriages within that tradition. Among the traditions examined in the preceding chapters, the Catholic tradition is the most restrictive in terms of the possibility of divorce. The Catholic Church has always proclaimed the absolute indissolubility of the sacrament of marriage. Only the death of one of the spouses can break a consummated marriage between a baptized man and woman. A marriage can be annulled if there was deficiency at the time of marriage in terms of its required elements (e.g., if one of the parties was underage, or if they were within prohibited degrees of kinship) that rendered the holy matrimony invalid in the first place. A decree of nullity can only be issued by a tribunal of the Catholic Church. After annulment, both parties may be allowed to remarry in the church. Other Christian churches have taken stances of varying degrees of toleration towards divorce. For instance, the Coptic Orthodox Church allows divorce only on grounds of adultery and apostasy (Bernard-Maugiron, 2011), while the majority of reform churches permit it on a wide range of grounds, including irretrievable breakdown of marriage.

Like all other traditions, Hinduism is a tradition of great internal diversity. According to its most idealized and purest interpretation, marriage is an indissoluble sacrament, and, as in Catholicism, divorce is not possible under any circumstances. However, as Menski and Solanki explain (Chapter 19, this volume), this definitive position was only a pious ideal; in reality, Hindu customary law has always permitted divorce. After the codification and reformation of Hindu marriage law in 1955 and then again in 1976, divorce on a range of grounds was made available to both Hindu men and women. Currently, adultery, cruelty, mental disorder, desertion, incurable communicable disease, irretrievable breakdown as well as divorce by mutual consent are among the acceptable grounds for divorce under reformed Hindu law. As a result, Hinduism is currently one of the most divorce-friendly religio-legal systems and traditions.

The rules and attitudes regarding divorce in Islam and Judaism are similar to one another. In principle, both traditions discourage divorce and emphasize peace and harmony within the family but allow spouses to exit unhappy marriages by utilizing sanctioned legal mechanisms. Both traditions, and Judaism in particular, favor men and discriminate against women when it comes to dissolution of marriage. In Judaism (particularly in its Orthodox interpretation, which is the official personal status law of the State of Israel), divorce is a private matter between the spouses and cannot take place without the husband's consent and unilateral action. According to Talmudic Law, the husband may divorce his wife for any reason by simply issuing her with a *get*, a writ of divorce, and does not require her consent. Since 1951, under secular Israeli law, divorce against the wife's consent is considered a criminal offense subject to five years in prison. However, in some instances where the husband wants to issue a *get* but the wife refuses to accept it, the rabbinical courts may permit the husband to remarry without the wife's acceptance of the writ of divorce (*get*). On the other hand, no divorce can ever take place without the husband's explicit consent and the issuance of a *get*. Although there is secular legislation from 1995 that allows Israeli rabbinical courts to pressure (by means including cancelling bank accounts, rescinding professional licenses, and jailing) a recalcitrant husband who refuses to issue *get* to his wife, religious court judges (*dayanim*) widely oppose such coercion of the husband. A wife who is denied a *get* by her husband is legally considered an *agunah*, or a 'chained wife'. Chained wives usually purchase their freedom from the marriage by paying their husbands large sums of money or signing up to disadvantageous custody or child support agreements (Sezgin, 2010; Weiss and Gross-Horowitz, 2013). Jewish women, like their Muslim counterparts, can demand divorce on religiously acceptable grounds (e.g., the husband's infertility, cruelty, failure to fulfill duty of sustenance), by filing for a dissolution of marriage at a rabbinical court. The court can decide only whether the wife's request is justified; if so, the court will recommend the husband to issue a *get* – but the court cannot dissolve the marriage itself. A Jewish wife is almost completely powerless vis-à-vis her husband as far as divorce is concerned. However, as Westreich and Westreich remind us (Chapter 16, this volume), historically there was a way to circumvent the requirement for the husband's consent: the law of the rebellious wife[2] (*moredet*). This law required the husband to divorce a rebellious wife who had refused to have sex with him on account of her strong feeling of revulsion towards him. In exchange for the *get*, the rebellious wife was required to forfeit her payment of *ketubah* (i.e., financial settlement needed to be paid by the husband after divorce). However, the *moredet* rule has fallen out of use in the State of Israel.

A similar mechanism that allows a Muslim wife to divorce her husband in exchange for financial consideration also exists in Islamic law. It is known as *khulʿ*. It is simply a no-fault divorce available to Muslim women; that is to say, the woman does not have to prove any fault on the part of her husband or base her request on any grounds. More importantly, in some jurisdictions, such as Pakistan, Egypt, and Jordan, the husband does not even have to consent to the divorce; the court can simply dissolve the marriage whether the husband agrees to it or not. Here Islamic law differs sharply from Jewish law, which does not allow any divorce without the husband's consent. A Muslim wife can also file for divorce in court (*taṭlīq* or *tafrīq*) on a number of grounds (e.g., the husband's absence, cruelty, infertility), again without the husband's consent. Although Muslim wives are better off than their Jewish counterparts under their respective traditions' divorce laws, Muslim husbands are not necessarily worse off than Jewish husbands: they are almost equally as powerful when it comes to their right to unilateral divorce. Indeed, in some respects, Muslim husbands are even more powerful, because in many jurisdictions (e.g., Egypt, Lebanon, Saudi Arabia, etc.) even today, they can divorce (*talaq*) extra-judicially[3] (without appearing at a court) for almost any reason, while Jewish men must appear before a rabbinical court to give a *get*. Like Jewish law, Islamic law also requires the husband to pay his wife, as part of a divorce settlement, compensation (*mata*), her maintenance (*nafaqa* to which she is entitled during her waiting period) as well as the deferred part of her dower (*mahr muw'ajjal*, agreed upon in the marriage contract). Both Islam and Judaism, as well as other traditions, have developed detailed rules and procedures that regulate remarriage, relations between former spouses, as well as the relations between children and parents following divorce.

The etatization of religious family laws and its impact on human rights

All four traditions' religious norms and precepts concerning marriage, divorce, and other aspects of family relations have long histories of directly or indirectly influencing secular state laws and legislations on personal status. The normative, ideological, and historical origins of family law in many Western societies can be traced back to the Christian tradition (Berman, 1993; Witte, 2012). Biblical notions of matrimony, conjugality, patriarchy, and privacy have influenced legislation on family relations in many countries, including England and the United States (Glendon, 1989; Hamilton, 2006). Although after the reformation and secularization of family law in the nineteenth and twentieth centuries, direct religious influence on family law seems to have weakened, religious narratives, values, and notions of family, sexuality, procreation, and womanhood continue to shape public discourse on same-sex marriages, divorce, abortion, and many other issues throughout the Christian world. The legacy of Biblical traditionalism continues to be very strong, especially in Catholic nations like Ireland, Poland, Malta, and the Philippines where divorce is still prohibited under the national family code (Grzymała-Busse, 2015; Miller, 2008; Schembri, 2015).

Christianity's influence on contemporary family law has been more indirect and limited compared to that of Islam, Judaism, and Hinduism, as family laws based on these traditions continue to be officially recognized and applied in various jurisdictions. Today, 53 countries (35[4] Muslim-, 18[5] non-Muslim-majority) apply Muslim family laws within their legal systems. Likewise, Hindu law is applied in state courts by state-appointed judges in India, Pakistan, Bangladesh, Malaysia, and Kenya. Jewish law is primarily applied in Israel by state-appointed judges (*dayanim*) in rabbinical courts. In other words, about one-third of the world's population currently lives under religion-based family law systems where governments hold individuals subject to the purview of ethno-religious rather than secular norms for personal status matters. For various ideological, political, and historical reasons, religious precepts, rules, customs, and narratives have been appropriated by modern governments in many nations and subjected to a process of etatization (Sezgin, 2013).

Etatization, or state appropriation of religious norms, is a violent and invasive process through which the secular authority selectively adopts and codifies certain interpretations and aspects of religious norms, traditions, and narratives, and labels them 'divine law', while leaving out certain other aspects and interpretations of the tradition as unworthy of adoption, since they may not suit the interests and needs of the ruling elite.

Religious traditions and the laws derived from them are multivocal. That is to say, there is no single version of *shari'a* or *halakhah*, but rather multiple versions of each normative system. Competing schools and interpretations offer different notions of family, sexuality, gender, marriage, and divorce. Political actors who have steered and overseen the process of etatization in many nations have often been men, and they have selectively adopted and codified more restrictive interpretations of religious texts and narratives that entrench existing socio-economic and gender disparities and transposed them into the legal arena. Female and subaltern voices and input were rarely sought and almost never taken into consideration, as men continuously negotiated and renegotiated among themselves the rules pertaining to marriage, divorce, and other family matters. As a result, state-enforced religious family laws enable and engender severe discrimination against women. Religion-based laws are also detrimental to the rights of children, religious dissidents, non-religious people, as well as members of heterodox religious communities (Htun and Weldon, 2015; Sezgin, 2012).

State-enforced religious family laws impose a number of limitations and disabilities on four groups of rights and liberties in particular: (1) *the freedom of religion* (which encompasses the right to have religion, the right to change religion, the right not to profess any religion, the right to profess religion without government intervention, and the right to be free from religious coercion); (2) *equality before the law*; 3) *marital and familial rights* (including right to marry and divorce); and (4) *procedural rights* (e.g., right to fair trial, due process, and to seek effective remedy) (Sezgin, 2013: 10).

In religiously based legal systems, religion is a matter not just of personal conviction but of public law and policy. Under such systems, judges who apply state-enforced religious laws, or registrars who register births, marriages, and divorces, are both empowered and required by law to scrutinize and determine which religious community each person belongs to. This requirement often leads to the problem of defining who is a Jew, who is a Muslim, or who is a Hindu, which in turn may push authorities to investigate whether people truly belong to the community whose faith they claim to profess, on the basis of officially sanctioned interpretations of religious laws and precepts. These inquiries threaten the rights of people whose religious identities are in question or contested. For instance, in Israel, rabbinical authorities usually refuse to marry individuals whose Jewishness is uncertain according to halachic criteria (Sezgin, 2010). Given the fact that there is no civil marriage in Israel, these people are permanently denied their fundamental right to marry and establish a family within the country. Due to their forcible subjection to religious law, their freedom of conscience and religion and right to equality before the law are also severely violated. Further, as demonstrated by the infamous Abu Zayd case in Egypt (Sezgin, 2013: 138–142), the inquisitorial powers conferred upon courts or state-appointed religious authorities to determine religious identity can also endanger the lives of the investigated and violate their individual rights and liberties.

Lastly, state-enforced religious laws may also impinge upon an individual's right to fair trial, due process, and to seek effective remedy when his or her rights are violated. For example, in many countries where Muslim family laws are enforced, a husband can unilaterally divorce his wife without appearing in court or providing any legal reason for his action (*talaq*). Since *talaq* is an extra-judicial act, the wife cannot challenge or appeal the husband's pronouncement at a court of law. Similarly, under Egyptian Law No: 1 of 2000, which allows Muslim Egyptian women to seek no-fault divorce from the court without the husband's consent (*khul*ʿ), husbands cannot appeal *khul*ʿ decrees at a court of law. Another procedural concern in religious systems is the relative lack of legal certainty. Religious laws were historically developed as jurists' law (*Juristenrecht*) – a body of law that was formulated by experts and legal scholars rather than the state. Even though in many countries religious rules pertaining to matters of personal status were codified in the late nineteenth and twentieth centuries, many systems continue to recognize unwritten religious rules, narratives, and customs as a source of jurisprudence, which allows both secular and religious judges – à la classical jurists – to find laws and even make new ones by drawing upon classical sources that may previously have been unknown to the parties involved. This approach introduces an element of arbitrariness and legal uncertainty into religious systems and threatens rights to due process and fair trail and the rule of law (Sezgin, 2013). For example, in the aforementioned Abu Zayd case, the Egyptian Court of Cassation's admittance of an ancient legal instrument, the *hisba*, eventually led to the declaration of Professor Abu Zayd as an apostate and subsequently his forced separation from his wife. The story of the late Professor Abu Zayd and his wife is a tragic example of the dangers posed to fundamental rights and liberties by the etatization of religious family laws (Bernard-Maugiron, 1999: 178–182).

Notes

1 Higher age limits do not always mean that underage marriages are void. In fact, in most cases, they mean only that those who contract or facilitate an underage marriage may be subject to civil or criminal sanctions, while the marriage itself may still be valid, especially if the parties have already attained the religiously recognized age of puberty.

2 The concept of rebellious wife also exists under Islamic law. There are important similarities and differences between Jewish *moredet* and Islamic *nashiza*. See Roded (2015).

3 In some Muslim countries, such as Iran, Algeria, Morocco, etc., *talaq* has been judicialized, meaning that the husband has to appear before a court to pronounce the divorce.

4 Afghanistan, Algeria, Bahrain, Bangladesh, Brunei, Comoros, Djibouti, Egypt, Gambia, Indonesia, Iran, Iraq, Jordan, Kuwait, Lebanon, Libya, Malaysia, Maldives, Mali, Mauritania, Morocco, Niger, Nigeria, Oman, Pakistan, Qatar, Saudi Arabia, Senegal, Sierra Leone, Somalia, Sudan, Syria, Tunisia, UAE, Yemen.

5 Cameroon, Eritrea, Ethiopia, Ghana, Greece, India, Israel, Kenya, Mauritius, Myanmar, Philippines, Singapore, Sri Lanka, Suriname, Tanzania, Thailand, Trinidad and Tobago, Uganda.

References

Banerjee, G. K. and Banerjee, S. C. 1923. *The Hindu Law of Marriage and Stridhana*. 5th edn. Cotton Press.

Berman, H. J. 1993. *Faith and Order: The Reconciliation of Law and Religion*. Emory University Studies in Law and Religion. Scholars Press.

Bernard-Maugiron, N. 1999. 'Legal Pluralism and the Closure of the Legal Field: The al-Muhajir Case' in B. Dupret, M. Berger and L. Al-Zwaini (eds) *Legal Pluralism in the Arab World*. The Hague Kluwer Law International. 173.

Bernard-Maugiron, N. 2011. 'Divorce and Remarriage of Orthodox Copts in Egypt: The 2008 State Council Ruling and the Amendment of the 1938 Personal Status Regulations'. 18 *Islamic Law and Society*. 356.

Bhattacharyya, P. 1978. 'Adultery as a Ground for Divorce under the Hindu Marriage Act' in V. Bagga (ed.) *Studies in the Hindu Marriage and the Special Marriage Acts*. N. M. Tripathi. 217.

Bittles, A. H. 2012. *Consanguinity in Context*. Cambridge Studies in Biological and Evolutionary Anthropology. Cambridge University Press.

Browning, D. S., Green, M. C. and Witte, J. Jr. 2006. *Sex, Marriage, and Family in World Religions*. Columbia University Press.

Carroll, L. 1987. 'Marriage-Guardianship and Minor's Marriage at Islamic Law'. 7 *Islamic and Comparative Law Quarterly*. 249.
Glendon, M. A. 1989. *The Transformation of Family Law: State, Law, and Family in the United States and Western Europe*. University of Chicago Press.
Grzymała-Busse, A. M. 2015. *Nations under God: How Churches Use Moral Authority to Influence Policy*. Princeton University Press.
Hamilton, V. 2006. 'Principles of U.S. Family Law'. 75(1) *Fordham Law Review*. 31.
Hayes, C. E. 2002. *Gentile Impurities and Jewish Identities: Intermarriage and Conversion from the Bible to the Talmud*. Oxford University Press.
Htun, M. and Weldon, S. L. 2015. 'Religious Power, the State, Women's Rights, and Family Law'. 11(3) *Politics & Gender*. 451.
Ilesanmi, O. O. 2010. 'Sexual Offences in a Muslim World: A Socio-ethical Reflection on Zamfara State (Nigeria) v. Bariya I. Mugazu'. 14(2) *The International Journal of Human Rights*. 215.
Kumar, H. 2002. *Status of Muslim Women in India*. Aakar Books.
Mahajan, G., and Jodhka, S. S. 2010. *Religion, Community, and Development: Changing Contours of Politics and Policy in India*. Routledge.
Menski, W. 2001. *Modern Indian Family Law*. Curzon.
Miller, A. 2008. '"Until Death Do Us Part?": A Proposal for the Philippines to Legalize Divorce'. 24 *Connecticut Journal of International Law*. 181.
Morgan, D. 2010. *Essential Islam: A Comprehensive Guide to Belief and Practice*. Praeger/ABC-CLIO.
Nasir, J. J. 2002. *The Islamic Law of Personal Status*. 3rd edn. Kluwer Law International.
Quraishi, A. 1997. 'Her Honor: An Islamic Critique of the Rape Laws of Pakistan from a Woman-Sensitive Perspective'. 18 *Michigan Journal of International Law*. 287.
Roded, R. 2015. 'Islamic and Jewish Religious Feminists Tackle Islamic and Jewish Oral Law: Maintenance and Rebellion of Wives'. 11(1) *Comparative Islamic Studies*. 35.
Sait, S. and Lim, H. 2006. *Land, Law and Islam: Property and Human Rights in the Muslim World*. Zed Books.
Schembri, K. 2015. 'The Orthodox Tradition on Divorced and Remarried Faithful: What Can the Catholic Church Learn?' 65(1) *Melita Theologica*. 121.
Sezgin, Y. 2010. 'The Israeli Millet System: Examining Legal Pluralism through Lenses of Nation-Building and Human Rights'. 43(3) *Israel Law Review*. 631.
Sezgin, Y. 2012. 'Triangulating Reform in Family Law: State, Religion and Women's Rights in Comparative Perspective' in C. Raghavan and J. P. Levine (eds) *Self-determination and Women's Rights in Muslim Societies*. Brandeis University Press. 243.
Sezgin, Y. 2013. *Human Rights under State-Enforced Religious Family Laws in Israel, Egypt and India*. Cambridge University Press.
Sezgin, Y. 2018. 'Muslim Family Laws in Israel and Greece: Can Non-Muslim Courts Bring about Legal Change in Shari'a?' 25(3) *Islamic Law and Society*. 235.
Sharma, R. K. 2004. *Indian Society, Institutions and Change*. Atlantic Publications.
Siddiqui, Mona. 1995. 'Mahr: Legal Obligation or Rightful Demand?' 6(1) *Journal of Islamic Studies*. 14.
Singh, R. K. 2011. *Textbook on Muslim Law*. Universal.
Weiss, S. M. and Gross-Horowitz, N. C. 2013. *Marriage and Divorce in the Jewish State: Israel's Civil War*. Brandeis University Press.
Wells, B. 2015. 'Sex Crimes in the Laws of the Hebrew Bible'. 78(4) *Near Eastern Archaeology*. 294.
Witte, J. Jr. 2012. *From Sacrament to Contract: Marriage, Religion, and Law in the Western Tradition*. 2nd edn. John Knox Press.
Ziadeh, F. J. 1957. 'Equality (Kafā'ah) in the Muslim Law of Marriage'. 6(4) *The American Journal of Comparative Law*. 503.

Part V
The legal other

21

Jewish law perspectives

The legal other

Suzanne Last Stone[1]

Introduction

A central feature of Judaism is that the Torah, the law revealed at Sinai, is the exclusive inheritance of Israel (Deuteronomy 33:4; Maimonides, Laws of Kings, chapter 8:9). Only Jews are bound to obey these laws. What, then, is the status of other normative orders, whether religious or secular? Two central doctrines address this question. The doctrine of Noahide law stipulates that there are seven obligations binding on all humanity. Individuals who fulfill these obligations are 'righteous'[2] and merit salvation (Maimonides, Laws of Kings, chapter 8:11).[3] All societies 'constrained by the ways of religion' are valued because they advance the moral and political aims of Noahide law. The second doctrine, referred to as *dina de-malkhuta dina*, confers recognition on the legitimate acts of all governments, religious or secular, because government is necessary for establishing good social order, a pre-condition of spiritual perfection. As we shall see later, these two doctrines were viewed as interrelated by the medieval period. Both served to confer legitimacy on other normative orders and even led to the incorporation of the laws of these normative orders into the Jewish legal system itself.

Other religious traditions and their laws

We begin with the legacy of the Hebrew Bible. The Bible portrays a world populated by morally corrupt societies, on the one hand, and civilized societies, on the other; societies that adhere to basic moral and legal norms. In the Book of Genesis, which tells the history of humanity and of Israel's forefathers before the giving of the Torah, God covenants with Noah, a figure of post-flood humanity, and commands humans neither to murder nor to tear a limb from a live animal, two precepts concerned with blood (Genesis 9:4). Even apart from recorded divine commands, however, humans act in light of a moral and legal order: King Abimelech fears divine punishment for adultery (Genesis 20), rights of property are respected (Genesis 26), and Israel's forefathers are monotheistic.

The rabbinic legal tradition engages in a close reading of Genesis to discern precisely what laws were revealed to humanity before Sinai (B. Sanhedrin 56a–57b)[4] and whether these laws are accessible through reason or solely through revelation.[5] In the Babylonian Talmud, the rabbinic tradition codifies so-called 'Noahide law' as consisting of seven basic human obligations: to refrain from idolatry, blasphemy, homicide, incest and adultery, robbery, and eating the flesh of a live creature, and to establish a system of justice. Each of these laws is further elaborated in the rabbinic corpus so that Noahide law takes on the characteristics of a comprehensive legal order (B. Sanhedrin 56a–59a; Lichtenstein, 1986; Stone, 1991). The nations of the world thus also potentially constitute societies of moral and religious significance, whose basic purpose is to establish justice in the social sphere; they are not merely aggregates of individuals. Only those who do not adhere to the (Jewish) universal code are not members of a true society. They live, instead, in a state of moral chaos.

In the medieval period, rabbinic jurists began to extend the concept of Noahides in novel ways to Moslems and Christians. Maimonides already ruled in the eleventh century that Moslems were monotheists (Blau, 1960: 725–728). Menahem Ha-Me'iri, a thirteenth-century Provencal decisor, extended this ruling to Christians (B. Avodah Zarah 2a; Halbertal, 2000; Katz, 1961). He presented an original synthesis of the entire Talmudic system of discriminatory and exclusionary rules and exceptions, essentially rendering most obsolete. He held that idolaters were pagans of the ancient world, 'who were not bound by proper customs', unlike the people of the medieval era who are disciplined by enlightened religion.[6] The latter share a moral, political, and religious project with Jews: to promote recognition of the one God and to establish moral and just communities. Ha-Me'iri's formulation is of particular importance for two reasons. Although other jurists reached similar legal conclusions with respect to discrete questions touching on joint commerce and neighborly relations, they did so through the traditional Talmudic casuistic method and confined their rulings to the practical needs of the Jewish community. Ha-Me'iri, by contrast, formulated his distinction between the Talmudic era and the medieval world as one of 'principle' (Katz, 1961). Moreover, although Ha-Me'iri compares religiously enlightened non-Jews to Noahides, he does not equate them. Rather, Ha-Me'iri created a new legal category between paganism and Judaism. This category consists of 'nations constricted by ways of religion'. Both Maimonides and Ha-Me'iri reflect the medieval functional understanding of religion as crucial to the creation of well-ordered societies. Societies that fear God are lawful, disciplined societies (Halbertal, 2000).

In the early modern period, with the rise of the civil state and the penetration of the Enlightenment into Jewish spheres, Jewish philosophers turned to the Noahide doctrine to reconceive the relationship between a universal moral law and a particularistic ritual law. Thus, Moses Mendelssohn, in his masterpiece *Jerusalem*, argues that all religions teach a universal truth accessible through plural paths and that the crucial test of religion is conduct (Mendelssohn, 1983: 96–98). Following Mendelssohn, various nineteenth-century reform movements argued that the 'essence' of Judaism is the Noahide, moral, universal religion, while the legal tradition, the halakha, and the ritual law are secondary, at best (Batnitzky, 2011). The Noahide doctrine is invoked as one source, among others, attesting to Israel's mission to spread 'ethical monotheism'. The more traditional streams continue to adhere to the classic division inaugurated in the Talmudic sources: one code for humanity and another for Jews, though the two legal orders may interact in novel ways (see later).

Even from a traditionalist standpoint, however, the existence of universals within Judaism raises the question whether Jews have a religious legal obligation to assure a civilized society by actively promoting observance of Noahide law. Although nominally seven, each Noahide principle is the subject of extensive rabbinic juridical elaboration so that Noahide law potentially covers a large variety of topics, including international human rights, euthanasia, abortion, just and unjust war, and capital punishment. While most rabbinic authorities hold that Jews are not legally obliged to promote observance of Noahide law (Broyde, 1997; Chajes, 1958: 2:32; Weinberg, 2003: 92), the presence of this doctrine within the Jewish legal tradition contributes, along with other doctrines describing Judaism in terms of universal mission, to inter-religious projects to promote a civilized world (Shatz et al., 1997).

The rights and obligations of non-adherents

Observance of the Noahide laws secures non-adherents to Judaism various rights under the Jewish law, including rights of equal treatment under the law and rights of association (B. Bava Kamma 109b). The early Talmudic discussion of non-Jews generally assumed that non-Jews were pagan idolaters and both sanctioned unequal treatment under the law and erected encumbrances against any association with them (B. Bava Kamma 109b; B. Avodah Zarah 35b–40b). Rights of equality under the law were guaranteed only to resident aliens, non-Jews residing in the biblical polity. The rabbinic tradition conceives of the resident alien as a formal status secured by swearing allegiance to the Noahide laws before a formal institution such as a Jewish court, as a condition of remaining on the land and in political association with Israelites. The formal legal institution of 'resident alien' is only possible in the biblical polity. Hence, the medieval turn, in conditions of exile, to a more generalized understanding of membership in other religions, such as Christianity and Islam, as markers of observance of Noahide law entitling their members to rights of equality and association with Jews under Jewish law. The philosopher Hermann Cohen (1842–1918) argued that the Noahide doctrine is the first articulation of the concept of the citizen (Novak, 1983: 105 [1981]).

The most difficult question is whether members of religious traditions or societies who promote observance of the moral law captured by the concept of Noahide law, should be regarded as 'brothers', for purposes of entitlement to the range of social solidarity obligations Jews owe to their 'fellows'. To understand why this is a difficult question philosophically, and not only exegetically, one must return to the early rabbinic discussion of the differences between the Noahide and Sinai regimes. Noahide law and Sinai law are the subjects of extensive comparative jurisprudential inquiry in the Talmud. The Talmud hints that the two legal orders differ because the norms of Jewish law are shaped by the demands of fellowship and solidarity, while the Noahide legal order is framed primarily as a series of negative commandments to prevent harm (Atlas, 1978: 17–40; Stone, 1991). For example, both systems forbid theft but, unlike Noahides, Jews are not punished for *de minimis* theft because Jews 'forgive' one another (B. Sanhedrin 68b; Rashi to B. Yevamot 47b, s.v. 'v'lo nitan l'heishavon'). Sinai law requires the return of lost property, while Noahide law does not (B. Bava Kamma 113a). The various obligations of social solidarity – from returning lost property, forgiving debts, not charging interest, exercising mercy in the sense of waiving rights, as well as specific acts of loving kindness – are aspirational norms for interpersonal relationships modeled along those within a family. As one astute observer commented, the two legal orders reflect different political structures: the former, life in society and the latter, life in a covenantal community (Atlas, 1978: 17–40). Against this backdrop, the various attempts both to expand and contract the category of brother or covenantal fellow reflect different views of what joins people most closely: ethnicity, conduct, shared values, need, or proximity? While the biblical view emphasizes the sharing of space and material need, along with ethnicity, the medieval philosophical view emphasizes moral conduct and proper beliefs.

With the rise of the nation-state, and with it thicker conceptions of what it means to be a citizen-member of the nation-state, Jews were particularly challenged to re-think to whom obligations of special social solidarity are owed. When Napoleon debated whether Jews were capable of becoming citizens in the nation-state, one of the twelve questions he posed to the Paris Sanhedrin was whether, pursuant to the religious legal tradition, Jews could regard their French compatriots as their brothers. The Paris Sanhedrin relied extensively on the concept of Noahide law and its offshoots in its answer (Katz, 1961).

This question of how far the bonds of social solidarity can extend has assumed particular importance in the contemporary State of Israel. The basic laws of the State of Israel, a secular state that defines itself as Jewish (in national-cultural terms) and democratic, guarantee freedom of religious worship[7] and equality under the law to all its citizens. In the wake of the establishment of the State of Israel, rabbinic authorities have struggled with the question whether and to what extent such basic democratic principles are, nonetheless, compatible with the Jewish religious legal tradition. One key issue is, who may hold public office? According to the classic sources of Jewish law, no foreigner, not even a convert, is qualified to hold public office (B. Kiddushin 76b; Maimonides, Laws of Kings, 1:4). Another is the freedom to worship. In addition, an important issue for shaping attitudes within civil society is whether the norms of social solidarity owed to 'fellows' includes non-Jewish citizens of the State of Israel, who share a polity with Jews.

Religious Zionist rabbis have been at the forefront of attempting to synthesize the religious legal tradition with the requirements and sentiments of a democratic state. The concept of Noahides figures prominently in these efforts. Thus, R. Herzog analogizes the Arab and Christian minority to resident aliens who accepted the seven commandments and thus are entitled to freedom to worship as they please and to equal treatment under the law. With respect to holding public office, Herzog makes the novel argument that the State of Israel, in the eyes of the religious legal tradition, is a partnership of Jews and non-Jews, since its sovereignty is dependent on world recognition (1991: 3–9). As with ecumenical business partnerships, each partner has the right to govern. R. HaLevy goes further, insisting that the admittance of Jews into the family of nations, through world recognition of their political rights, ushers in a new phase in which the relationship between Jews and non-Jews has been eased, paving the way for genuine human solidarity (1988: 71–79).

The State and international human rights organizations

The Jewish legal tradition has a longstanding and well-developed doctrine addressing the legitimacy of state law: *dina de-malkhuta dina* (the law of the land is the [legitimate] law; henceforward DDM). DDM was first articulated as a general principle in the Babylonian Talmud (B. Gittin 55b). Although historians tend to identify the principle as an exilic expression of powerlessness and accommodation to the reality of foreign rule, its deployment in the Talmudic discussion follows standard conflict of laws approaches found in virtually all sophisticated legal systems: legitimate acts of government bind Jews and these acts also are entitled to legal recognition within the halakhic system where relevant in deciding matters exclusively between Jews (Stone, 2010: 101). While the original discussion concerned core governmental privileges, such as the taxing power and the power to expropriate land (B. Gittin 55b), the postulate took on a life of its own as the jurists begin to theorize in the Middle Ages about the conceptual basis for the principle.

The Talmud already hints at a close association between the principle of DDM and the custom of the people, and many of the medieval theories revolve around one or other form of popular consent or social contract theory, attesting to the rich interpenetration of the medieval discussions of the rights of kings taking place in the European Middle Ages (Funkenstein, 1993: 158;

Shilo, 1974). Portions of halakha become theoretically optional and not mandatory as the principle is extended through a series of logical progressions and in tandem with the extension of the rights of kings in Europe far beyond the concrete context from which it sprang: taxes and land. In the twelfth century, the Talmudic commentator Rashi proposed a far-reaching and novel theory of DDM, which builds a bridge between the principle and the idea of a universal, divinely ordained law, i.e., Noahide law. Rashi focuses on the one instance in the Babylonian Talmud where DDM functions not as a duty-imposing rule but as a power-conferring rule to Jewish litigants in an intra-Jewish dispute to take advantage of non-Jewish validation of deeds even though the signatories are non-Jews and the method contrary to Jewish law (Rashi to B. Gittin 9b, s.v. 'Kesheirin'). Here, DDM is allowing non-Jewish law to penetrate into Jewish law as an alternative norm. Rashi draws on the Jewish legal principle that only one who is himself under a divine obligation to perform an action can be an effective legal agent for others (B. Berakhot 20a–b). He explains the Talmudic permission as resting on the notion that non-Jews are commanded to 'institute justice', citing the Noahide commandment of *dinim*. Accordingly, they can be effective agents for all matters subsumed under that command.

As noted earlier, from the internal perspective of rabbinic Judaism, this specific Noahide command obligates humanity to preserve social order by enacting systems of law. The kingdom's law is rooted ultimately in divine command and therefore has legal and moral legitimacy equal to that of Jewish law. As the product of divine command, it is, in a sense, sanctified. Accordingly, non-Jewish legal activity can serve here as an alternative norm for Jews to follow even when it is at variance with the norms of Jewish law.

Conversely, Rashi notes, with respect to matters unique to Jewish law and not subsumed under the command of *dinim* – as an example, Jewish marriage and divorce bills – DDM cannot be invoked as a power-conferring rule to utilize alternative norms (Rashi to B. Gittin 9b, s.v. 'Kesheirin'). The implication of Rashi's rationale is that large portions of the halakha are, in fact, replaceable by the law of other civilizations, thus shrinking the scope of halakha to matters of ritual and religious prohibition (Stone, 2008). Over time, these theories subtly undermined the conception of halakha as an all-encompassing legal system. Instead, the sphere of halakha became more and more contracted, so that one could speak of the modern period of a division within halakha between 'religion and state' (Stone, 2008). Thus, DDM became a cornerstone for the successful integration of the formerly legally autonomous Jewish communities into the legal systems of the nation-state.

Facilitating this contraction of the scope of the religious legal tradition is a variety of other *halakhic* doctrines that tacitly recognize a distinction between religious and political spheres. Several were developed in tandem with Islam and Christianity in the twelfth and thirteenth centuries along with the emergence of criminal law as public rather than religious law. Biblical evidentiary restrictions on conviction were jettisoned by all three religions, and various justifications emerged for the assignment of certain extra-legal powers to political authorities not restrained by religious law. Several medieval Jewish legal thinkers imagined the halakha as composed of different jurisdictions generating law in accordance with different principles. The political realm emerges in these writings as a space with its own distinct logic and laws.

The medieval Jewish discussion centers on the rights of monarchs, including the prerogatives of the 'Jewish king' (Blidstein, 1980: 55–56; Gerondi, 1973: Homily 11; Lorberbaum, 2001) and is revived in modern halakhic discussions of the legitimacy of the law of the Jewish state: the State of Israel (Walzer et al., 2000: 463–524). The Hebrew Bible sets up a tension between a model of kingship that is particular and culturally specific, and one that is universal. That tension is fully exploited in the medieval discussion. Strikingly, Maimonides' codification of the laws of Jewish kings seems to transfer over to the Jewish king the precise body of Talmudic law about the universal 'Noahide' laws that bind non-Jewish societies, from the Jewish perspective. For Maimonides, the seventh Noahide command to institute justice, *dinin*, is the requirement to establish governmental structures capable of preserving order. As Gerald Blidstein noted, 'Maimonides' entire edifice of monarchic powers identified Jewish and gentile governance as a single structure possessing similar goals and utilizing similar instruments' (1990: 58–60).

The idea that government is a universal structure subject to the basic logic underlying the Noahide legal order – to secure a minimally just society – facilitates recognition by the Jewish legal tradition of the laws and institutions of the State of Israel. The State of Israel presents a case of first impression because it is a new political structure: a Jewish state, with a Jewish majority population, yet secular. While some rabbinic authorities continue to use the traditional doctrine of DDM (Haddayah, 1958–1959: 37–44), others use the model of Jewish kingship to validate the state and its laws (Washovsky, 1989: 289–310). The choice of halakhic model is primarily driven by ideology. Utilizing DDM implies that the State of Israel is analogous to foreign rulers; whereas analogizing the State of Israel to Jewish kingship imbues the state with some measure of religious significance.

Recognition of international law is a subject of sporadic though intense and fascinating discussion in the Jewish legal tradition (Breuer, 1974: 89–92; Hirschenssohn, 2012 [1926]; Wieder, 2007: 239–265). Modern and contemporary rabbinic discourse is deeply split over the question whether state sovereignty and, especially, nation-state sovereignty, is compatible with the teachings of Judaism. While rabbis associated with religious Zionism valorize state sovereignty, some even viewing Jewish kingship/statehood in messianic terms, others criticize state forms of sovereignty on religious grounds, seeing it as cause of aggression and human suffering (Holzer, 2007: 341–415). R. Breuer, for example, was an intense critic of sovereignty and strongly supported the emerging international law system (Breuer, 1974: 89–92). R. Breuer provides a theological and philosophical defense of international law; R. Hayyim Hirschenssohn engaged in an intricate legal analysis, citing the status of treaties and agreements in the Jewish legal tradition (Hirschenssohn, 2012 [1926]).

One of the most daring legal opinions concerning the status of international law is that of R. Yisraeli, who ruled that, as a matter of religious law, the State of Israel was obligated by – and only by – international standards of war and not the particularistic laws of war to be found in the religious legal tradition. From a technical perspective, he relies on the Talmudic dictum 'the law of the kingdom is the law', but he gives it a radically innovative meaning. Where formerly the dictum governed the obligations and privileges of individual Jews relative to their host states, it now, in the elaboration by R. Yisraeli, governs the obligations and privileges of the Jewish nation acting in the international context. And where formerly the dictum extended only to the laws of a sovereign ruler, such as king or state, it now, in the rabbi's elaboration, extends to international law on the theory that the non-Jewish kingdom could be defined in global terms, as long as the collective will of the world's citizens ratified the laws of the 'global kingdom' (Yisraeli, 1949: 66–78; 1950: 76–88). Yisraeli's opinion, moreover, seems to blend the underlying rationales of the DDM consent school and of Rashi's turn to Noahide *dinim*. Jews can consent to be governed by international norms, just as they can consent to be governed by the civil laws of host states. Consent to laws pertaining to war is legitimate even though war involves the religious prohibition of bloodshed. War, however, is a chosen means to settle disputes in contemporary life and, as such, fulfills the goal of civilizing the world and securing social order, even if such wars are not undertaken for the sake of enforcing Noahide norms. Thus, the link between Noahide law as a universal body of norms that was Jewishly discerned and elaborated and, accordingly, subject to internal standards of some sort – Judaism's contribution to discourse about human rights as a moral theory – becomes reversed. Now at least this one Noahide law is imagined as the tacitly agreed upon practices of conventional societies in pursuit of good governance.

Taken together, the thrust of Rashi, Hirschennssohn, and Yisraeli is that international law is binding on Jews through the complex interaction of Noahide law with the Talmudic principle, 'the law of the kingdom is the law'. While Noahide law was ordinarily thought of as the universal moral law that God gave to humanity – superseded at Sinai for Jews – Noahide law can be seen, instead, as an alternative source of norms even in a purely internal Jewish context, a form of fallback or residual law, which can be invoked when the particular law requires supplementation or functional adjustment (Stone, 1991, 2008, 2010).[8] Paradoxically, although Noahide law is presented as a universal moral code given by God, the content of which is discerned and elaborated by Jewish tradition, the content of Noahide law is increasingly determined by the convention of the nations.

This theory logically can extend as well to the panoply of human rights on which consensus has coalesced. The relationship between the Jewish legal tradition and the contemporary Western idea of human rights is a complex one. On the one hand, through the Hebrew Bible, the Jewish tradition has given to the human rights movement one of its most salient images: the creation of humans in the image of God. Each individual has infinite worth and no one's blood is redder than another (B. Pesachim 25a). This image is elevated to a core legal principle in the Talmud. The Talmud also debates the scope of a cognate legal principle: *kavod habriyyot*, the dignity due to God's creatures (B. Berachot 19b). On the other hand, these principles have thus far generated only a few specific norms, most concerned with the respect owed to the human body, including a corpse (B. Megillah 3b). From a larger perspective, the Western idea of human rights rests on a view of the human as autonomous and possessing rights by virtue of being human. This view is in tension both with the halakhic focus on the heteronomous, commanded individual and with the halakha's view of rights as contingent on conduct (Stone, 2014).

Incorporating norms generated from outside the halakhic world into the halakhic system raises the important question of limits. Contemporary responsa even in the area of private law well illustrate the dilemma. Thus, some rabbinic decisors in the family courts in the State of Israel have held that contemporary practices such as gender equality in splitting marital assets, meet the technical requirements of incorporation doctrines such as DDM and 'customs of the people' (Dichovsky, 1997: 18), while others contend that laws stemming from a 'worldview' or a 'religious or social ideology' cannot be incorporated because the 'religious and social worldview of the Jewish people derives exclusively from the Torah' (Sherman, 1997: 32).

One of the more interesting questions for those observing the Jewish tradition today revolves around this issue of critique. What resources should or could the tradition use to critique the organization of the contemporary political sphere, including the discourse of human rights? Keen observers of the tradition will note that, outside the State of Israel (which presents a unique set of problems), the standards used to judge the political sphere are not, by and large, the particular religious or ethical aspirational norms of the Jewish tradition, but rather they draw on the large body of Jewish sources which develop the universal Noahide code. That body of law is in itself an ongoing project that develops in tandem with developments in the larger political sphere. For example, while the original markers of good government in the service of religion from the Talmudic period through the medieval period cite the Noahide ban on idolatry and blasphemy, over time, these criteria are reinterpreted to fit a secular age. Thus, the ban on idolatry is in the process of reinterpretation in terms of commitment to the rule of law. In short, the tradition continues to provide a standpoint from which to judge the very space it authorizes. In doing so, we can catch a glimpse of what – in the eyes of Judaism – is a well-ordered political space and what is, instead, seen as inimical to the common project of government.

It is here that the turn to the international legal regime is most vulnerable, for it entails abandonment of any standpoint from which criticism is possible. International codes of war, treaties, and so on, govern the State of Israel – from the halakhic perspective – and not indigenous, national-collective norms or particular, aspirational norms developed to govern relations of members within a covenantal community. In his analysis, Yisraeli makes clear that halakhic norms pertaining to use of force developed within the context of individual self-defense could not countenance the manner of conducting warfare acceptable within the international community. But, he argues, halakha permits the incorporation of looser standards of behavior when the nation acts beyond its borders. Should international society adopt more stringent norms than halakha, these too would be binding on the nation acting in the international arena. Contemporary objections to Yisraeli's approach center on the problem of ethical critique, i.e., a failure to contribute a distinctively Jewish ethical voice to society at large.

Notes

1 I wish to thank my research assistant, Tzvi Benoff, for his meticulous attention to detail.

2 The term *tzaddik*, a righteous person, is used in the Talmudic literature, but Maimonides changes the language and refers to such individuals as *hasidei umot ha'olam*. A *hasid* usually connotes a religious virtuoso. There is an extensive literature debating the precise meaning of these terms and why Maimonides altered the rabbinic terminology. For a good summary of the literature, see Rosenthal (2013: 467–490).

3 The early Tosefta records a debate between Rabbi Eliezer and Rabbi Joshua about whether non-Jews merit a portion in the world to come, with each citing competing proof-texts (Tosefta *Sanhedrin*, ed. Moses Zuckermandel, chap. 13, p. 434, para. 2; B. *Sanhedrin* 105a). Maimonides codifies Rabbi Joshua's position in three separate places in his Code of Law but only in Laws of Kings, chapter 8:11 does he specify the criteria for meriting salvation: acceptance of the Noahide laws. One of the most enduring debates among Maimonidean scholars as well as modern Jewish philosophers and theologians is whether this condition, which implies observance of the laws because they are divinely commanded and not solely out of intellectual commitment, represents Maimonides's true views, given seeming contradictions with other Maimonidean passages and manuscript variances (Hartman, 1976; Novak, 1988; Rosenthal, 2013: 467–490).

4 The Talmud here preserves three different lists of laws, each drawing on different proof-texts or different interpretive strategies. Steinmetz has argued that the lists reflect different jurisprudential conceptions as well: one classically positivist, one closer to natural law, and one reflecting a theology of the order necessary to sustain creation (2008).

5 For the debate over Maimonides's views, see *supra* note 2. The Talmud does not allude to knowledge of the law through reason in the *locus classicus* discussing Noahide law. Elsewhere in Talmudic-midrashic literature, however (B. Yoma 67b), there are references to the 'rational' commandments, such as murder, theft, and adultery that could be discovered through reason. Whether and to what extent natural law thinking can be found within the rabbinic legal tradition is a vast, and deeply contested, issue. See Hayes (2015); Statman (forthcoming).

6 This term is mentioned many times throughout his commentary on tractate Avoda Zara of the Babylonian Talmud.

7 The State of Israel allows individuals full freedom of worship, but there are laws that restrict proselytizing. Although proselytizing per se is not illegal, it is illegal to convert a minor from Judaism to another religion unless one of the minor's parents is already an adherent of another religion.

8 Additionally, now see the decision of the Jerusalem Rabbinical Court (R. Dikhovski, Sherman, Ben Shimon) #4276 (citing *Zafnat Paneah*) for the proposition that Jews were given additional obligations at Sinai, including marriage and divorce laws, but were not relieved of their obligations imposed by Hebrew Law on Noahides, which function as fallback law when the former is not applicable

References

Atlas, S. 1978. *Pathways in Hebrew Law* (in Hebrew). American Academy for Jewish Research.

Batnitzky, L. 2011. *How Judaism Became a Religion: An Introduction to Modern Jewish Thought*. Princeton University Press.

Blau, J. (ed.). 1960. *Maimonides Responsa Vol. 1* (in Hebrew). Mekitzei Nirdamim Publishing.

Blidstein, G. J. 1980. 'On Political Structures-Four Medieval Comments'. 22 *Jewish Journal of Sociology*. 52.

Blidstein, G. J. 1990. ''Ideal' and 'Real' in Classical Jewish Political Theory 8. 2(1–2) *Jewish Political Studies Review*. 58.

Breuer, I. 1974. 'Judaism and National Home' in J. Levinger (ed.) *Concepts of Judaism*. Israel University Press. 89.

Broyde, M. 1997. 'Jewish Law and the Obligation to Enforce Secular Law' in D. Shatz, C. Waxman, and N. Diament (eds) *The Orthodox Forum Proceedings VI: Jewish Responsibilities to Society*. Roman and Littlefield Publishers Inc. 103.

Chajes, Z. H. 1958. *Kol Sifrei Maharitz Chayes Vol. 2*, Divrei Hachamim Publishing.

Dichovsky, S. 1997. 'The Shared Assets Rule – Is it Dina De-Malkhuta?'. 18 *Tehumin*. 18.

Funkenstein, A. 1993. *Perceptions of Jewish History*. University of California Press. 158.

Gerondi, N. 1973. *Derashot*. Edited by L. A. Feldman. Shalem Institute.

Haddayah, O. 1958–1959. 'Does Dina De-Malkhuta Dina Apply to the State of Israel?' 9–10 *Hatorah Vehamedinah*. 37.

Halbertal, M. 2000. *Between Torah and Wisdom: Menachem ha-Meiri and the Maimonidean Halakhists in Provence* (in Hebrew). Magnes Press.

HaLevy, H. D. 1988. 'Ways of Peace in the Relationship of Jews and Non-Jews'. 9 *Tehumin*. 71.

Hartman, D. 1976. *Maimonides: Torah and the Philosophic Quest*. JPS Press.

Hayes, C. 2015. *What's Divine About Divine Law? Early Perspectives*. Princeton University Press.

Herzog, I. H. 1991, 'Towards a Jewish State' (in Hebrew). 1 *Betzomet Hatorah Vehamedinah*. 3.

Hirschenssohn, R. H. 2012 [1926]. *Responsa Malki BaKodesh*. ed. D. Zohar. The Shalom Hartman Institute (in Hebrew).

Holzer, E. 2007. 'Attitudes Towards the Use of Military Force in Ideological Currents of Religious Zionism' in L. Schiffman and J. B. Wolowelsky (eds) *The Orthodox Forum: War and Peace in the Jewish Tradition*. Yeshiva University Press. 341.

Katz, J. 1961. *Exclusiveness and Tolerance: Studies in Jewish-Gentile Relations in Medieval and Modern Times*. Oxford University Press.

Lichtenstein, A. 1986. *The Seven Laws of Noah*. 2nd edn. The Rabbi Jacob Joseph School Press.

Lorberbaum, M. 2001. *Politics and the Limits of Law Secularizing the Political in Medieval Jewish Thought*. Stanford University Press.

Mendelssohn, M. 1983. *Jerusalem: Or On Religious Power and Judaism*. Translated by A. Arkush. Brandeis University Press.

Novak, D. 1981. 'Universal Moral Law in the Theology of Hermann Cohen'. 1 *Modern Judaism*. 101–117; Rev. edn. in Novak, D. 1983. *The Image of the Non-Jew in Judaism: A Historical and Constructive Study of the Noahide Laws, Toronto Studies in Theology*, vol. 14. Edwin Mellen Press; Second rev. edn. in Matthew LaGrone (ed.) 2011. Littman Library of Jewish Civilization.

Novak, D. 1988. *The Image of the Non-Jew in Judaism*. The Littman Library of Jewish Civilization.

Rosenthal, G. S. 2013. 'Hasidei Umot Ha-Olam: A Remarkable Concept'. 48(4) *Journal of Ecumenical Studies*. 467.

Shatz, D., Waxman, C. and Diament, N. (eds). 1997. *Tikkun Olam: Social Responsibility in Jewish Thought and Law*. Jason Aronson Inc.

Sherman, A. 1997. 'The "Shared Assets" Rules in Light of the Laws of the Torah'. 18 *Tehumin*. 32.

Shilo, S. 1974. *Dina D'Malkhuta Dina* (in Hebrew). Hotsa'at Defus Aḳademi bi-Yerushalayim.

Statman, D. (forthcoming). 'Judaism and Natural Law' in Y. Lorberbaum, A. Mermelstein and S. Stone (eds) *The Jewish Legal Tradition*.

Steinmetz, D. 2008. *Punishment and Freedom: The Rabbinic Construction of Criminal Law*. University of Pennsylvania Press.

Stone, S. L. 1991. 'Sinaitic and Noahide Law: Legal Pluralism in Jewish Law'. 12(3–4) *Cardozo Law Review*. 1157.

Stone, S. L. 2008. 'Religion and the State: Models of Separation from Within Jewish Law'. 6(3–4) *ICON*. 631.

Stone, S. L. 2010. 'Law without Nation? The Ongoing Jewish Discussion' in A. Sarat, L. Douglass and M. Umphrey (eds) *Law Without Nations*. Stanford University Press. 101.

Stone, S. L. 2014. 'Religion and Human Rights: Conflict or Convergence, Babel or Translation?' *Proceedings of the International Democracy Institute*. 524.

Walzer, M., Lorberbaum, M. and Zohar, N. (eds). 2000. *The Jewish Political Tradition: Volume 1 – Authority*. Yale University Press.

Washovsky, M. 1989. 'Halakah and Political Theory'. 9(3) *Modern Judaism*. 289.

Weinberg, Y. Y. 2003. *Shut Sridei Eish vol. 2*. Mosad Harav Kook.

Wieder, J. 2007. 'International Law and Halakhah' in L. Schiffman and J. B. Wolowelsky (eds) *The Orthodox Forum: War and Peace in the Jewish Tradition*. Yeshiva University Press. 239.

Yisraeli, S. 1949. 'Samkhut HaNasi uMosedot Mimshal Nivharim BiYisrael'. 1 *Hatorah Vehamedinah*. 67.

Yisraeli, S. 1950. 'Tokef Mishpat HaMelukhah BiYameinu'. 2 *Hatorah Vehamedinah*. 76.

22

Christian law perspectives

The legal other

Norman Doe

The treatment of the 'legal other' in the laws and legal thought of Christians is illustrated well in terms of their approaches to: (1) natural law, as it applies to human beings regardless of their religion; (2) the State, and its relationship with institutional churches; and (3) human rights, and their promotion by the churches. Natural law has played a pivotal but much contested role historically in Christian thought. At its core is the divine commandment to love our neighbours as ourselves. Historically, Christianity has grappled with the scriptural principle to render to Caesar that which belongs to Caesar (Matthew 22.21). Today, churches employ a range of distinct but related approaches in order to work out the implications of this principle for the relations between churches and the States within which they carry out their mission. The emergence of human rights discourse has also stimulated churches to develop their own particular positions on the fundamental rights of the other in terms of the equality of all humans who are understood theologically to be created in the image or likeness of God. What follows examines comparatively the presence of these ideas in the laws and legal thought of Christians across a range of ecclesial traditions in global Christianity today. In so doing, it explores whether it is possible to identify principles of Christian law on 'the other'.

Natural law: the Golden Rule

In Christianity, natural law discourse concerns, at its core, the existence of God-given universal principles which God 'revealed' to humankind at creation. This original revelation has to do with what it means to be human and is related, therefore, to the social character of human nature and life. It may be contrasted with the 'special' revelation of God in Christ, which is about our relation with God, the perfection of natural law, and, ultimately, salvation. With natural law, a form of divine law, God implanted in the minds or hearts of every human the capacity to know right and wrong and thus to discern these universal principles, which are normative, which provide moral standards, or ethical constraints on human behaviour, and which determine what actions are right and wrong in our relations with others. These standards are applicable to all humans, discoverable through the use of reason, and the exercise of conscience, and should be used as a source of and criterion to assess the legitimacy of action. Views of what natural law contains vary widely and often depend on prior ideas about 'nature' and perhaps the physical laws of cause and effect – natural law is its order or the sphere of rationality; and so natural law is rational law deducible from rational principles. However, within Christianity, natural law has been contested for many reasons: that it proceeds from facts to normativity; how it may be seen as a species of divine law; and that its precepts of love for God and neighbour are too diffuse to be of practical value.

Natural law doctrine historically has enjoyed a prominent place in Christian thought. Many scholars see Paul's Letter to the Romans as containing a germ of the doctrine: 'When Gentiles who have not the law do by nature what the law requires, they are a law to themselves, even though they do not have the law. They show that what the law requires is written in their hearts' (Romans 2.14–15) (see e.g. Contreras, 2013). The doctrine was developed by the early Fathers of the Church (though some today think its role in patristic writing was minimal) (see e.g. Wilken, 2003: 320). For example, according to Origen of Alexandria (185–254), natural law is the physical law governing the cosmos and the law of reason binding humans as universal ethical norms and following from the Golden Rule – do to others as you would have them do to you (Luke 6.31); moreover, all humans are able to obey natural law, but need Christ the redeemer who teaches a morality going beyond natural law, otherwise our sin would not be expiated and we could not have a share in God's righteousness (Dunkle, 2004). Similarly, for Augustine (354–430) there is a 'law which is called supreme reason, which must always be obeyed, by which the evil deserve an unhappy life and the good a blessed life'; this law is the eternal law: 'the divine reason or will of God which commands that the natural order be preserved and forbids that it be disturbed'. However, unless humans are united to the salvation won by Christ with the grace of the Holy Spirit, they cannot sufficiently obey natural law (see generally Levering, 2014).

In the medieval period, Aquinas famously argues (along Aristotelian lines), that humans are rational creatures, with the capacity to reason, and that by using reason to reflect on human nature, we may discover the specific ends towards which we naturally tend (e.g. to live, reproduce, have an ordered society, and worship God), and the general end for which God created us, i.e. salvation in eternal communion with God. When we have discovered these ends, it is possible for us to determine the means required to achieve them. This understanding of God's plan for humans, implanted in us by His act of creation, is natural law – it is a participation in the eternal law of God – and from natural law precepts may be induced moral duties (and rights) (see generally Finnis, 1980). Some elements of the theory were retained at the Reformation. For example, according to Calvin:

> It is a fact that the law of God which we call the moral law is nothing else than a testimony of natural law and of that conscience which God has engraved upon the minds of men. Consequently, the entire scheme of this equity of which we are now speaking has been prescribed in it. Hence, this equity alone must be the goal and rule and limit of all [positive] laws.[1]

For Luther, the commandment of love, the Golden Rule, and the Decalogue all provide for the same thing concerning love of God and neighbour – as expressions of natural law they concern *both* the inner orientation of a person and external action, and they demand selfless, divine love; however, for Melanchthon, natural law consists of precepts, resembling the Ten Commandments, which demand *only* external action, not an inner disposition of love. In turn, Lutherans in the seventeenth and eighteenth centuries echo these two approaches. For instance, Leibniz follows Luther and combines natural with the idea of divine love, whereas the approach of Pufendorf resembles that of Melanchthon (Raunio, 2006).

However, later Reformation theology generally rejected the competence of fallen human reason to engage in natural theology, a view asserted by Karl Barth (1886–1968):

> What is pleasing to God comes into being when all human righteousness is gone, irretrievably gone, when men are uncertain and lost, and when they have abandoned all ethical and religious illusions, and when they have renounced every hope in this world and in this heaven.

Indeed, when Gentiles 'show that what the law requires is written on their hearts' (Romans 2.15), they show precisely that they no longer cling to any human resources, including 'natural law' (Barth, 1933: 68). Generally, therefore, arguments against natural law theory typically include the propositions that: (1) natural law theory is flawed because it moves from observable facts to moral principles; it attempts to base ethics (ought) on a non-moral account of what human beings are like (is) – what humans are like does not tell us what they ought to be like morally; (2) the picture of human nature is likely to be as controversial as the moral conclusions at which it arrives – that picture is itself the product of a moral outlook rather than an independently established basis by which a moral outlook can be supported; (3) that human reason alone (and fallen human reason at that), reflecting on human nature, can understand God's will for us, undermines the need for God's grace, and so devalues the revelation in Christ – if humans can know what is good in God's eyes, this unacceptably exalts human reason; and (4) natural law theory plays down or denies specifically Christian ethics – whereas Christianity actually requires a radically new set of imperatives instituted by the ministry of Christ (Hauerwas, 1983; Hughes, 1986; Ramsey, 1993: 84–85).

Nevertheless, there are today Catholic (Grisez, 1965; Hervada, 2006), Orthodox,[2] Lutheran (Braaten, 2011), Reformed (see e.g. Van Drunen, 2006; 2010: 95), and other scholars (Charles, 2008; Porter, 1999) who propose natural law theory, rooted in the idea that God imprints upon all a capacity to discern through our natural inclination and human reason the ordering which God has given us, whether the discoverability of universal ethical principles is affected by sin (Hittinger, 2003: 3–37, 63–91, 93–112), or not (Porter, 2009). For example, the Anglican theologian Nigel Biggar proposes that to 'affirm natural law' means that: there is a form of flourishing given in and with the nature of human beings; reflection on human nature can achieve an understanding of that flourishing and its basic goods; reflection on our experience can produce a grasp of kinds of disposition and action that respect and promote those goods in our relations with others; all humans are, despite their sinfulness, *somewhat* capable of an accurate grasp of basic goods and their practical requirements; and, therefore, there are sometimes areas of ethical agreement between Christians and others. However:

> None of this . . . makes the Christian theological salvation narrative ethically irrelevant. It does not say that sinful humans have the motivation to do sufficiently what they know to be right, apart from penitence, faith, gratitude, and hope that the story of God's salvific initiative inspires. . . [nor] . . . that they have the power, unaided by biblical tradition, to know completely what is good, what is virtuous, or what is right.
>
> *(Biggar, 2011: 41–42)*

Similarly, for Matthew Levering, the principles of natural law are capable of specific articulation and should function as the basis for any just legal system which seeks to recognize the dignity of the human person and to maintain justice. He proposes:

(1) Natural law does not obviate the need for the grace of the Holy Spirit and the work of Jesus Christ. Knowing its precepts does not mean that we will observe them, or that our observance will be matched by our interior attitude (which should be that of love). As human sinfulness obscures natural law and makes it impossible to know its precepts adequately and observe them rightly, so we need to be transformed by the grace of the Holy Spirit and the redeemer Christ to be reconciled to God and become the righteous people God intended.

(2) In following conscience and striving to act justly to God and neighbour, humans may be moved by grace that unites them to the salvation won by Christ, even without knowing God explicitly. This explains the presence in the Bible of righteous gentiles. God cares for all humans not just the people of God. The people of God (e.g. Israel/Church) are cared for by God in various ways, including natural law that enables them to distinguish right from wrong.

(3) Like all humans, Christians possess natural law and are required to live by its precepts. Imitating Christ would not suffice - indeed it would not be possible, if Christians lacked natural law. That is the 'moral path of Christians should not be set at odds with the natural law precepts one finds in the Golden Rule and Decalogue, as Jesus affirmed. Part of the task of Christian [approaches to] natural law . . . is to remind Christians of what Christians should be doing, rather than solely to call upon others to value the dignity of all human persons'.

(4) Natural law doctrine helps to affirm God's universal providence and desire to save all humans (I Timothy 2.4), affirms the worth of each, and shows that there are certain things that no human may do to other humans. It also upholds the value of free choice: 'Since God will render to every man according to his works (Romans 20.6), natural law doctrine supports the obvious point that knowledge and good works are by no means limited to Christians'.

(5) Natural law is our participation in God's eternal law, and it is constituted and promulgated by the Creator God, who imprints it on our hearts. It requires recognition of a divine lawgiver. As a rational sharing in God's providence, natural law is ordered toward human fulfilment, which involves hierarchically ordered ends or goods. Its teleological character, and its rootedness in human inclinations (shaped by rationality), follows from the fact that God creates humans in his image for the good of communion with God and with fellow humans.

(6) Human positive law is properly grounded on natural law. Murder would still be wrong even if positive law approved it. People know by natural law, e.g., that preservation of human life is good and murder is evil. Law is not a solely cultural constraint, according to which some actions are right or wrong depending on time/place. Some actions are simply wrong because they violate God's law which we know however imperfectly by natural law.

(7) Human sinfulness obscures but does not eliminate our ability to perceive the precepts of natural law. One of the common rebuttals to natural law doctrine is that humans have not been able to agree on its content. With the exception of certain basic precepts (e.g. the prohibition against murder), people often disagree about what natural law entails. Even with regard to murder, people differ as to what is 'murder'. People also have different ideas as to what human flourishing involves. The fact that sin obscures but does not obliterate the perception of natural law makes sense of what would otherwise be a strange paradox i.e. that both the Torah and Jesus Christ reveal precepts that belong to natural law. The obscuring of natural law also helps to explain the historical

> variance with respect to what has counted as the content of natural law. Over the course of history, and for all sorts of reasons, different individuals and societies will perceive the precepts of natural law more or less clearly.
>
> *(Levering, 2014)*

Christian churches also address natural law in their official teaching.[3] For example, in the Roman Catholic Church, the International Theological Commission in 2009 proposed that 'natural law is the basis of collaboration among all persons of good will, whatever their religious convictions'. Indeed, there are 'convergences' in the great religious traditions that 'bear witness to a largely common moral patrimony that forms the basis of all dialogue on moral questions'. So it is possible to speak of the perception of common moral values, beginning with their insertion into a network of human relationships from birth, which allow individuals to become aware of themselves, of others, and of the context within which they live. In turn, natural law is: the foundation of a universal ethic and yardstick against which to measure the political order, discoverable from observing and reflecting on a common human nature; inscribed on the human heart; dynamic rather than static; and, instead of being a list of definitive and immutable precepts, 'a spring of inspiration always flowing forth for the search for an objective foundation for a universal ethic'.[4] Unsurprisingly, natural law has also emerged as a subject in ecumenical dialogue between Christians; for example, dialogue between Anglicans and Roman Catholic has addressed how:

> Reflection on experience of what makes human beings, singly and together, truly human gives rise to a natural morality, sometimes interpreted in terms of natural justice or natural law, to which a general appeal for guidance can be made. In Jesus Christ this natural morality is not denied. Rather, it is renewed, transfigured and perfected, since Christ is the true and perfect image of God.[5]

However, natural law does not generally appear explicitly in the modern juridical texts of churches worldwide, though they do invoke concepts of divine law, the revealed law of God, as well as large moral ideas rooted in ethical standards perhaps conceivable as universal.[6] Nevertheless, the juridical instruments of churches place great emphasis on the pursuit of philanthropic activities in society for the good of the other; they oblige or exhort care for others on the part of the faithful individually and/or collectively. For example, in the Roman Catholic Church, all the faithful must promote social justice and help the poor, and they may establish associations for charitable purposes;[7] and each parish priest is 'to help the sick and especially the dying in great charity' and he is 'to endeavour to ensure that the faithful are concerned for the community of the parish', and 'to foster works which promote the spirit of the gospel, including its relevance to social justice'.[8] Social responsibility is also a key value in Orthodox law. For instance, several institutions in the Russian Orthodox Church are to 'express, if need be, concern for contemporary problems' and 'pastoral concern for social problems'.[9] The Holy Synod may establish commissions on 'works of charity and social ministry'.[10] The bishops should promote (and establish) charitable institutions, and dioceses must have departments for the promotion of social and charitable activity.[11] At parish level, the rector has a responsibility for 'organizing activities in the public domain' including the 'charitable' and associated activities of the parish;[12] and property may be put to social and charitable uses.[13] Similarly, in Anglicanism, the objects of a church may include the duty to contribute to the 'moral and spiritual' welfare of society,[14] to promote justice in the world,[15] 'to transform unjust structures of society, caring for God's creation, and establishing the values of the Kingdom',[16] and to engage in 'educational, medical, social, agricultural and other service'.[17] Consequently, for example, the governing body of each parish must 'promote the whole mission of the church, pastoral, evangelistic, social and ecumenical'.[18]

Care for the other is contemplated in various forms by Protestant laws. The Evangelical Lutheran Church in America (ELCA) is typical of Lutheranism. One object of the Church is 'to meet human needs, caring for the sick and the aged, advocating dignity and justice for all people, working for peace and reconciliation among the nations, and standing with the poor and powerless and committing itself to their needs'.[19] Moreover, the Church 'shall seek to meet human needs through encouragement of its people to individual and corporate action, and through establishing, developing, recognizing, and supporting institutions and agencies that minister to people in their spiritual and temporal needs'. Through affiliated social ministry organizations, it must also 'establish affiliations and alliances within this church and within society, and carry out a comprehensive social ministry witness'.[20] As such, its central organization must respond to 'human need, caring for the sick and suffering, working for justice and peace, and providing guidance to members on social matters',[21] and its Church Council 'shall have responsibility for the corporate social responsibility of this church'.[22]

It is a principle of Methodist social responsibility that the Church has a duty 'to apply the Christian vision of righteousness to social, economic and political issues'; as such, a local church council is to 'give attention to local and larger community ministries of compassion, justice and advocacy' including 'religion and race, and the status and role of women'; moreover, the faithful individually should engage in 'healing the sick, feeding the hungry, caring for the stranger, freeing the oppressed, being and becoming a compassionate caring presence, and working to develop social structures that are consistent with the gospel'.[23] Similarly, in Presbyterianism, a national General Assembly may take action for 'the well-being of the community';[24] the regional Presbytery must provide for pastoral care 'within the wider community';[25] the local Kirk Session must seek to further Christian witness and service in the local community and raise funds for prescribed 'philanthropic objects';[26] ministers must visit the sick and provide leadership in the humanitarian activity of the local Church;[27] and Church members must themselves witness to society.[28] Likewise, according to the North American Baptist Conference: 'Christians, individually and collectively . . . [must] promote truth, justice and peace', and 'aid the needy and preserve the dignity of all races and conditions'.[29] Increasingly, churches are also developing norms on interfaith relations as to their engagement with other major world religions represented in wider society.[30]

In Christianity, then, natural law has a wide variety of meanings, but it is generally seen as the law implanted in nature by God, which rational creatures can discern through the use of natural reason; it is thus contrasted with the revealed law, though aspects of divine law may also be precepts of natural law. At its core is the Golden Rule which applies to all human relations regardless of religion. However, there are differences of opinion about the content of natural law beyond broad agreement that good is to be done and evil avoided. This suggests that natural law underwrites morality as such, rather than any particular moral code. Nevertheless, Christians across the traditions in the regulatory instruments of their various churches oblige or exhort the engagement of the faithful in pastoral care for the other.

Church and State relations

The State is our second legal other for Christians and their institutional churches. As a general pattern, the juridical instruments of the churches address: the nature and purpose of the State; the distinct identity and functions of the Church as against those of the State; the need for cooperation between Church and State; the recognition and applicability of civil law to the Church; Christian involvement in politics; disobedience by the faithful to unjust laws; and the avoidance in disputes among the faithful of recourse to the courts of the State (see Doe, 2013: 346–356).

The Catholic Church teaches that: there is no authority except from God (Romans 13.1); the 'political community and public authority are based on human nature and therefore . . . belong to an order established by God'; political authority must be exercised within the limits of the moral order; and it is 'the role of the State to defend and promote the common good of civil society', namely: 'the sum total of social conditions which allow people, either as groups or individuals, to reach their fulfilment more fully and more easily'. However, 'in their own domain, the political community and the church are independent from one another and autonomous', but they should develop a 'mutual cooperation' in favour of the welfare of all human beings.[31] Indeed, the Latin Code recognizes the qualified applicability of the law of the State to the Church:

> When the law of the Church remits some issue to the civil law, the latter is to be observed with the same effects in canon law, in so far as it is not contrary to divine law, and provided it is not otherwise stipulated in canon law.[32]

In other words, for the faithful, 'unjust laws . . . would not be binding in conscience'.[33] Moreover, Catholic canon law provides for the appointment of papal legates to States,[34] forbids clerics 'to assume public office whenever it means sharing in the exercise of civil power',[35] asserts that 'no rights or privileges of election, appointment, presentation or designation of bishops are conceded to civil authorities',[36] and enables an ecclesiastical tribunal to refrain from imposing a penalty if the offender in question has been or will be 'sufficiently punished by the civil authority'.[37]

The Orthodox canonical tradition proposes that: 'The Church was founded by God, the birth of the State is a product of the will of Divine Providence for the world' but each is 'self-sufficient and independent in the sphere of its jurisdiction'; the Church seeks the salvation of souls, the State, peace, and order; and the Church has at its disposal spiritual means, the State, material means.[38] Thus, the Church should not be subject to the State, nor the State to the Church, but they should co-exist in harmonious cooperation – 'the *symphonia* of the sacred and secular power' (Patsavos, 1984: 137). In turn, the juridical instruments of Orthodox churches deal with, typically, cooperation with the State and its authorities,[39] the applicability of civil law to the Church,[40] the registration of a church as a legal entity in civil law,[41] and the determination of Church-State relations by a church assembly.[42] Orthodox laws also deal with recourse to civil courts and engagement in politics. For instance, the ordained and lay members of the Russian Orthodox Church 'cannot apply to the authorities of the State or to the civil courts on matters which pertain to the internal life of the church, including canonical governance, church order, liturgical or pastoral activities'; also: 'The canonical units of the [Church] shall not engage in political activities and shall not rent their premises for political events'.[43] Clergy must not seek political office.[44] This stance is shared broadly by Anglicans in terms of how they view the State, cooperation with it, the applicability of civil law, political activity,[45] recourse to the courts of the State with regard to church disputes,[46] and deference to the State in its domain.[47]

The Protestant Reformation in northern Europe saw the development of the principle that subjects should follow the religion of their ruler: *cuius regio eius religio* (Witte, 1990). Today, the juridical instruments of Lutheran Churches refer to the doctrine of the 'two kingdoms' – earthly and heavenly – designed *inter alia* 'to guide the church in its relations with the world, especially government'. Firstly, the doctrine 'does not call for a separation of church and state but for a proper distinction between them': God rules 'all people, Christians and non-Christians, in his earthly kingdom through the agency of secular government [and] law' and 'he rules all Christians in his spiritual kingdom . . . through the gospel [and] grace'.[48] Secondly, Christians are 'citizens of two kingdoms': 'The two reigns of God are also mutually dependent'; the Church needs the State to ensure freedom of religion and the State needs 'the prayers and intercessions of the church (whether it realises it or not)' to fulfil its tasks properly.[49] Thirdly, while the Church 'is not called to develop and implement policies for a more just and equitable society', the Church has 'every right' to be 'the conscience of society' and 'hold governments . . . accountable to the public, and ultimately to God'. Fourthly, 'church and state must be clearly distinguished but not separated' though 'each has its own area of competence and responsibility': secular government must not interfere with the proclamation of the gospel, and 'the church must not use the agency of the state . . . to promote the gospel or Christianise society'. Thus:

> The Church . . . ought not to interfere . . . in the affairs of the State: but it must bear witness to the truth . . . and may therefore, for the instruction of its members and as a public testimony, have to condemn or approve acts of the State . . . [even if the consequence is] . . . oppression and persecution on the part of the State.[50]

Fifthly, while Lutherans are subject to 'the laws of the land', 'Obedience to all forms of human government is never absolute but always limited and conditional. If it means disobedience to God, our allegiance to God must come first'.[51] In turn, while there should be 'institutional separation' of Church and State: both need to cooperate in matters of common concern;[52] church bodies may have personality under civil law;[53] central assemblies are to 'determine and implement policy for [a] church's relationship to governments';[54] civil laws apply to the Church;[55] ministers must obey State law unless there are grounds in conscience for civil disobedience to 'unjust law';[56] and recourse should not generally be made to secular courts:

> It is the policy of this church not to resort to the civil courts . . . until all internal procedures and appeals have been exhausted, except for emergency situations involving a significant imminent risk of physical injury or severe loss or damage to property.[57]

The Methodist position on Church and State is similar to the Lutheran. A particularly full treatment of the subject is found in the United Methodist Church. Firstly, 'civil government derives its just powers from the sovereign God', is a 'servant of God and human beings', and should be 'based on, and be responsible for, the recognition of human rights under God'. Secondly, 'Separation of church and state means no organic union of the two, but it does permit interaction. The state should not use its authority to promote particular religious beliefs' nor 'attempt to control the church, nor should the church seek to dominate the state'; rather: 'The rightful and vital separation of church and state, which has served the cause of religious liberty, should not be misconstrued as the abolition of all religious expression from public life'. Thirdly, the strength of a political system depends upon the participation of its citizens; as such: 'The church should continually exert a strong ethical influence upon the state, supporting policies and programs deemed to be just and opposing policies and programs that are unjust'. Fourthly, Christians must obey the law of the State:

> It is the duty of all Christians, and especially of all Christian ministers, to observe and obey the laws and commands of the governing or supreme authority of the country of which

> they are citizens or subjects or in which they reside, and . . . to encourage and enjoin obedience [to them].

However, fifthly, 'governments, no less than individuals, are subject to the judgment of God'; the Church recognizes therefore, 'the right of individuals to dissent when acting under the constraint of conscience and, after having exhausted all legal recourse, to resist or disobey laws that they deem to be unjust or that are discriminately enforced' – but this requires 'refraining from violence' and 'being willing to accept the costs of disobedience'.[58] Some ministers make the declaration: 'While respecting the law, I will act to change unjust laws'.[59]

In turn, Methodists recognize the general applicability of civil law to the Church.[60] They may also: assign functions to prescribed bodies to engage in dialogue with civil government; permit ministers to participate in the work of political parties and stand for civil office (but no church property may be used for any form of political electioneering); and: 'No lawsuit relating to churches, schools or other Trust property shall be commenced without the consent of the General Committee through the Property Board, except by direction of the Conference'; in the event that no such consent or direction is obtained, 'the parties proceeding shall be held responsible for all expenses incurred by such lawsuit'.[61]

The Lutheran and Methodist approaches are broadly replicated in the Presbyterian tradition. The classical Presbyterian position is stated in the Book of Church Order of the Presbyterian Church in America:

> The power of the Church is exclusively spiritual; that of the State includes the exercise of force. The constitution of the Church derives from divine revelation; [that] of the State must be determined by human reason and the course of providential events. The Church has no right to construct or modify a government for the State, and the State has no right to frame a creed or polity for the Church.[62]

Therefore: 'No religious constitution should be supported by the civil power further than may be necessary for the protection and security equal and common to all others'.[63] However, the Church must comply with the law of the State (particularly in matters of property and finance).[64] Presbyterian laws also sometimes assign to the Moderator the function of representing the Church in public affairs.[65]

For the Reformed Churches:

> Christ, the only ruler and head of the Church, has therein appointed a government distinct from civil government and in things spiritual not subordinate thereto, and that civil authorities, being always subject to the rule of God, ought to respect the rights of conscience and of religious belief and to serve God's will of justice and peace for all humankind.[66]

The Church should therefore exercise no authority over the State, neither should the State over the Church.[67] Nevertheless, some churches have State law devoted exclusively to them,[68] and generally churches must comply with State law.[69] Baptist instruments also propose the separation of Church and State. For example, the Baptist Union of Southern Africa affirms 'the principle of separation of Church and State, in that, in the providence of God, the two differ in their respective natures and functions'. Thus:

> The Church is not to be identified with the State nor is it, in its faith or practice, to be directed or controlled by the State. The State is responsible for administering justice,

> ensuring an orderly community, and promoting the welfare of its citizens. The Church is responsible for preaching the Gospel and for demonstrating and making known God's will and care for all mankind.[70]

Similarly, for the Canadian National Baptist Convention: 'Church and state should be separate'; moreover: 'The state owes every church protection and full freedom in the pursuit of its spiritual ends. In providing for such freedom no ecclesiastical group or denomination should be favoured by the state more than others'. Also:

> Civil government being ordained of God, it is the duty of Christians to render loyal obedience thereto in all things not contrary to the revealed will of God. The church should not resort to the civil power to carry out its work.[71]

A Baptist Union is sometimes the subject of State law exclusively devoted to it,[72] but some churches refuse submission to State laws as to matters properly pertaining to the autonomy of the Church.[73] Sometimes instruments also forbid recourse to the civil courts,[74] and provide for civil disobedience: a minister should undertake to be a 'good citizen' and 'to obey the laws of [the] government unless they require disobedience to the law of God';[75] 'God alone is Lord of the conscience, and He has left it free from the doctrines and commandments of men, which are contrary to His Word or not contained in it';[76] and: 'Christians should pray for civil leaders, and obey and support [the] government in matters not contrary to Scripture'.[77]

In sum, principles of Christian law emerging from similarities between the legal instruments of churches with regard to the State as other include: the political community is instituted by God; its function is to promote the temporal and common good of society; State functions are fundamentally different from those of the Church; there should be an institutional separation between Church and State; Church and State should cooperate in matters of common concern; the faithful may participate in politics to the extent permitted by Church law; the Church should comply with State law but disobedience by the faithful to unjust laws is permitted; and the faithful should not resort to State courts unless all ecclesiastical process has been exhausted.[78]

Human rights and religious freedom

The teaching and laws of Christians seek to promote human rights (including religious freedom) in society not only for themselves but also for others regardless of religion. These instruments deal variously with the basis of human rights (the idea that all humans are equal being made in the image of God), the nature of human rights, the corporate duty of a church to promote them in civil society, the establishment of institutions to work in the human rights field, and the obligation of the faithful as individuals to respect the human rights of others (Doe, 2013: 362–368).

The Catholic Church teaches that the role of the State is 'to defend and protect the common good of civil society', which consists of 'respect for and promotion of the fundamental rights of the person, prosperity, or the development of the spiritual and temporal goods of society, and the peace and security of the community and its members'.[79] Equally, the Church claims for itself a right:

> [t]o true freedom to preach the faith, to proclaim its teaching about society, to carry out its task among people without hindrance, and to pass moral judgments even in matter relating to politics, whenever the fundamental rights of man or the salvation of souls requires it.

Its canon law also recognizes the inherent right of the Church to own and administer property 'independently of any secular power'.[80] The rights and duties of the faithful, as enumerated in the Code of Canon Law, derive from the fundamental dignity of the individual as a human person and include inalienable and inviolable human rights.[81]

Whereas the laws of some Orthodox churches expressly assert their right to their own freedom of religion or institutional autonomy,[82] those of Anglicanism generally do not. However, there is a large body of Anglican teaching and quasi-legislation on the promotion of human rights; much of it is in resolutions of the Lambeth Conference (see generally Doe, 2002). Five themes emerge. Firstly, the Conference recognizes the existence of human rights and regards them as of 'capital and fundamental importance' not least in the context of the effects of their abuse and attacks upon human dignity.[83] It calls upon 'all the Churches to press upon governments and communities their duty to promote fundamental human rights and freedoms among all their peoples'.[84] Secondly, for the Conference, human rights involve freedom to enable humankind to develop its relationship with God, to ensure that 'the divine dignity of every human being is respected and . . . justice is pursued'.[85] Thirdly, it classifies human rights in terms of political rights, which include 'a fair and just share' for people in government, and economic rights, in so far as 'human rights must include economic fairness and equity, and enable local economies to gain greater control over their own affairs'.[86] Fourthly, 'the Christian must . . . judge every social system by its effect on human personality'.[87] Fifthly, member churches are 'to speak out' against breaches of human rights, 'support all who are working for [the] implementation of human rights instruments',[88] and urge compliance with international human rights law.[89] Individual Anglicans also have a responsibility to promote and protect human rights.[90] The principles of canon law common to Anglican churches also state that: 'All persons are equal in dignity before God'; and that: 'All persons have inherent rights and duties inseparable from their dignity as human beings created in the image and likeness of God and called to salvation through Jesus Christ'.[91]

Promotion of human rights and religious liberty is also pivotal in the doctrinal and juridical instruments of Protestants. At international level, one function of the Lutheran World Federation is to further 'worldwide among the churches diaconic action, alleviation of human need, promotion of peace and human rights, social and economic justice, care for God's creation and sharing of resources'.[92] At national level, typically: 'This Church affirms the God-given human dignity of all people, rejoicing in the diversity of God's creation', and commits itself to 'struggle for justice, peace and the integrity of creation'.[93] The Lutheran Church in Australia has a particularly full treatment of the subject: 'The concept of human rights is based on two convictions: that certain actions against other human beings are wrong no matter what; and that in all circumstances all people are entitled to respect and proper treatment as human beings'. The preservation of ordered human society belongs to the earthly kingdom in which God rules the world through the law: governments, as 'ministers of God', have the duty to preserve the life, liberties, property, prosperity, and honour of each citizen. Christian citizens have the duty to urge their governments to honour human rights, and to protest where they are either ignored or violated; and the foundation for Christian involvement in human rights is both the fundamental dignity of all human beings as creatures of God and the divine command to love their neighbour. Consequently, in accordance with the following 'guidelines', Christians should *inter alia*: (1) become informed about situations, at home and abroad, where people's human rights are being threatened or human rights abuses are taking place; (2) develop an attitude of concern and compassion toward victims; (3) increase community awareness of the need to safeguard human dignity; (4) intercede for those who suffer, especially those who cannot pray for themselves; and (5) investigate particular situations, study human-rights questions, contact politicians and embassies, organize petitions, distribute information, and support or join human rights organizations.[94]

The United Methodist Church has a similarly robust approach to human rights. Firstly, as 'all persons as equally valuable in the sight of God', governments should respect 'human rights under God'.[95] Civil government is 'a principal vehicle for the ordering of society', and it is responsible for 'the protection of the rights of the people' to, e.g. free and fair elections, free speech and assembly, redress of grievances without fear of reprisal, privacy, adequate food, clothing, shelter, education, and health care.[96] Secondly, recognizing the 'inherent dignity of all persons', the Church should: 'transform social structures';[97] support 'the basic rights of all persons to equal access to housing, education, communication, employment, medical care, legal redress for grievances, and physical protection'; combat acts of hate or violence against groups or persons based on race, ethnicity, gender, sexual orientation, religious affiliation, or economic status'; and work for 'the recognition, protection, and implementation of the principles of the Universal Declaration of Human Rights so that communities and individuals may claim and enjoy their universal, indivisible, and inalienable rights'.[98] Thirdly, the Church should support 'policies and practices that ensure the right of every religious group to exercise its faith free from legal, political, or economic restrictions' and condemn 'all overt and covert forms of religious intolerance'. The Church asserts 'the right of all religions and their adherents to freedom from legal, economic, and social discrimination', and should 'defend religious freedom' and other freedoms; indeed: 'the rightful and vital separation of church and state, which has served the cause of religious liberty, should not be misconstrued as the abolition of all religious expression from public life'.[99] These principles are echoed in other Methodist laws, which rest human rights on the equality of all,[100] promote human rights in society,[101] forbid discrimination,[102] and advocate freedom of belief and conscience.[103]

Like the Lutheran World Federation, the World Communion of Reformed Churches is to work for justice and promote 'the full and just partnership of men and women in church and society', 'diaconal service in church and society', and it is to engage in 'promoting and defending religious, civil, and all other human rights wherever threatened throughout the world'.[104] Similar functions are assumed by individual churches at national level. For instance, as to religious freedom, the United Reformed Church in Great Britain declares that 'civil authorities, being always subject to the rule of God, ought to respect the rights of conscience and of religious belief and to serve God's will of justice and peace for all humankind'.[105] The Presbyterian churches also hold to the view that (typically): 'although civil rulers are bound to render obedience to Christ in their own province, yet they ought not to attempt in any way to constrain anyone's religious beliefs, or invade the rights of conscience'.[106] Thus: 'the rights of private judgment in all matters that respect religion are universal and inalienable'.[107] In like fashion, the United Church of Christ in the Philippines 'affirms and upholds the inviolability of the rights of persons as reflected in the Universal Declaration of Human Rights and other agreements on human rights, [and] the international covenants on economic, social and cultural rights and on civil and political rights'.[108]

There is very little to distinguish these Reformed approaches to human rights and religious freedom from those which appear in the legal instruments of Baptists. As the World Baptist Alliance is to defend human rights at global level,[109] so too at national level Baptist Conventions and Unions recognize fundamental human rights and are 'to maintain religious liberty'.[110] For instance, the Baptist Union of Southern Africa accepts 'The principle of religious liberty, namely, that no individual should be coerced either by the State or by any secular, ecclesiastical or religious group in matters of faith'; as such: 'The right of private conscience is to be respected. For each believer this means the right to interpret the Scriptures responsibly and to act in the light of his conscience'.[111] Again, for the North American Baptist Conference religious freedom is an 'inalienable right'; and: 'The state should guarantee religious liberty to all persons and groups regardless of their religious preferences, consistent with the common good';[112] in consequence, the State has 'no right to impose penalties for religious opinions of any kind'.[113]

Conclusion

Natural law continues to play an important part in Christianity across the various ecclesial traditions in terms of how Christians should treat others (irrespective of their religion). With natural law, a form of divine law, God implanted in the minds or hearts of every human the capacity to know right and wrong and thus to discern universal moral principles. These standards are applicable to all humans, discoverable through the use of reason, and the exercise of conscience, and should be used as a source of and criterion to assess the legitimacy of action. At their core is the Golden Rule: do to others what we would have them do to us. In turn, juridically, a church must engage directly in works of pastoral care, charity, and social justice; the faithful must do likewise, and the ordained ministers must provide leadership in this.[114] With respect to the State as a legal other, the regulatory instruments of churches indicate that for Christians the State is instituted by God. Church and State are distinct and discharge separate functions. Church and State must cooperate with each other in matters of common concern. The faithful, both lay and ordained, may engage in political activity in wider society to the extent permitted by the law of a church. Each church and its faithful must comply with State law in so far as obedience is just and conscionable.[115] The concept of the legal other also surfaces in Christian teaching and law on human rights. All humans are created in the image of God. They are therefore equal and bearers of fundamental or human rights. The State should uphold human rights – including religious freedom – and the Church corporately and the faithful individually should promote them.[116]

Notes

1 *Institutes*, 4.20.16.
2 See Babie, 2017: this explores various 'disputes' in Orthodoxy about natural law in terms of its existence, its definition, its structure, and its relevance.
3 For instance, the American Methodist Church's conference declared in 1780: 'Slavery is contrary to the laws of God, man and nature, and hurtful to society; [and] contrary to the dictates of conscience'; and this is echoed by Wesley himself: 'Can law, human law, change the nature of things? . . . Notwithstanding ten thousand human laws, right is right and wrong is wrong still': See Harrod, 2017.
4 *In Search of a Universal Ethic: A New Look at Natural Law*. International Theological Commission of the Roman Catholic Church (2009) pars. 9, 11, 38, 113: see Costigane, 2017.
5 The Second Anglican-Roman Catholic International Commission (ARCIC II) report *Life in Christ: Morals, Communion and the Church* (1994) par. 9: see Koffeman, 2017.
6 For concepts of divine law, moral law, conscience, and equity, see Doe, 2013.
7 Code of Canon Law 1983, *Codex Iuris Canonici* (CIC), c. 215: the faithful; c. 222.2: social justice.
8 CIC, cc. 528–529.
9 Russian Orthodox Church (ROC): Statute, II.5(h): Local Council; III.4(g): Bishops' Council.
10 ROC: Statute, V.28(i)–(j).
11 ROC: X. 48.
12 ROC: Statute, XI.20(e).
13 ROC: Statute, XV:4, 5, 10, 17, 18, 23.
14 Anglican Church in Venezuela: Constitution, II.
15 See e.g. Episcopal Church in the Philippines: Constitution, 1.1; Canons 1.2.2(d): one of the functions of the Provincial Synod's Commission on Social Concerns is 'to study the nature and root causes of poverty and underdevelopment in the country and review the participation of the Church in the development process'.

16 Anglican Church in Aotearoa, New Zealand and Polynesia: Constitution, Preamble.
17 United Church of North India: Constitution, II.I.II; see also Anglican Church of Chile: Statutes, 2.
18 Principles of Canon Law Common to the Churches of the Anglican Communion (London: Anglican Communion Office, 2008) (PCLCCAC): Principle 21.6.
19 ELCA: Constitution, 4.02.
20 ELCA: Constitution, 8.33.
21 ELCA: Constitution, 11.20–21
22 ELCA: Constitution, 14.21.10–16.
23 United Methodist Church in Northern Europe and Eurasia (UMCNEAE): Book of Discipline (BOD), pars. 101, 122 and 252.
24 Presbyterian Church in Ireland (PCI): Code: Book of the Constitution and Government (Code), VII. II.104; Presbyterian Church of Wales (PCW): Handbook of Order and Rules (HOR), 3.4.2: social issues; Presbyterian Church in America (PCA): Book of Church Order (BCO): General Assembly is 'to recommend measures for the promotion of charity . . . through all the churches under its care'.
25 Presbyterian Church of Aotearoa New Zealand (PCANZ): Book of Order, 8.4(4).
26 PCI: Code, II.II.35 and 38; PCA: BCO, 4.4: the local church must make offerings 'for the relief of the poor'.
27 PCI: Code, IV.73: Presbytery must ensure that visits to the sick are carried out; PCW: HOR, 4.2: humanitarian activity in 'the local community, nation and world'; PCA: BCO, 8.4: pastors; 9.2: deacons.
28 PCW: HOR, 2.2: members must 'give freely of their service to society'.
29 North America Baptist Conference (NABC): Statement of Beliefs, 8: this cites e.g. Matt. 5.13–16, Hebrews 13.5, Luke 9.23, and Titus 2.12.
30 See e.g. CIC, c. 1086: interfaith marriages; Romanian Orthodox Church (ROMOC): Statutes, Art. 14(s): the Holy Synod governs 'inter-religious cooperation'; Art. 37(f): the Department for Interreligious Relations; (Anglican) Lambeth Conference 2008, Reflections, Section F: Relations with Other World Religions: mutual respect, dialogue and cooperation; the Anglican Communion's Network for Inter-Faith Concerns (NIFCON) is to e.g. develop relations with other faiths; ELCA: Constitution, 4.03(f), 8.60, 11.20–21, 15.12.B10: the church should have a 'policy' towards other faiths and 'interfaith activities'; Evangelical Lutheran Church in Ireland (ELCIRE): Constitution, 3(4): the church is to engage in 'interreligious dialogue'; UMCNEAE: BOD, pars. 121, 252, 340, 2001–2008: 'respect for persons of all religious faiths'.
31 Catechism of the Catholic Church (CCC), pars. 1918–1924, 1927.
32 CIC, c. 22; for other references to civil law, see e.g. cc. 98.2, 110, 197, 1059, 1062, 1284, 1290.
33 CCC, pars. 1897–1942; GS 29–31.
34 CIC, c. 362–367.
35 CIC, c. 285.3; CLLS, par. 593: if 'it would serve a spiritual purpose' a bishop could (under c. 87) 'dispense' from c. 285.3 'in a particular case' for a 'just and reasonable cause' as demanded by c. 90.
36 CIC, c. 377.
37 CIC, c. 1344.2.
38 Rodopoulos, 2007; (OOCL): 205–210 (citing Matthew 22.21): 'Render unto God that which is God's and unto Caesar that which is Caesar's'.
39 See e.g. ROMOC: Statutes, Art. 4.2: the church 'establishes relations of dialogue and cooperation with the State' to accomplish its 'pastoral, spiritual-cultural, educational and social-charitable mission'.
40 Ukrainian Orthodox Church in America (UOCIA): Instructions, Policy on Marriages, 2: 'A civil marriage licence must be obtained from the appropriate civil authorities' prior to church marriage; Code of Pastoral Conduct, 2.1: information obtained by counselling is confidential, 'except. . .as required by law'; ROC: Statutes, XI.13: brotherhoods are subject to e.g. 'the civil statutes' of the church, diocese and parish; XI.45: dismissal from a Parish Council for breach of the parish 'civil statutes'.
41 ROC: Statute, I.5.
42 ROC: Statute, II.5(g): the Local Council is to 'determine and adjust the principles of relations between the Church and the State'.
43 ROC: Statute, I.9–10.
44 Orthodox Church in America (OCIA): Guidelines for Clergy, A Selection of Clergy Discipline, 8: 'Clergy must not run for political office'.
45 PCLCCAC, Principle 46.2–3: processing data is subject to civil law; 71.1–3: ministers and parties must comply with civil law as to marriage formation; 77.5–7: civil law on disclosure of information in breach of the seal of the confessional; 80.1–2: trustees must comply with civil law.

46 E.g. The Episcopal Church (USA) (TEC): Canon IV.14.2: 'No Member of the Clergy ... may resort to the secular courts for the purpose of delaying, hindering or reviewing any proceeding' of the church's tribunals; 'no secular court shall have authority to review, annul, reverse, restrain or otherwise delay any proceeding' of these tribunals.
47 E.g. Church of Ireland: Constitution, VIII.26.4: the Court of General Synod must not determine 'any matter ... which, in the opinion of the lay judges, is within the jurisdiction and more proper to be submitted to the ... decision of a civil tribunal'.
48 LCA: Statement on the Two Kingdoms, 1–2: Romans 13:1–5 and 1 Peter 2:13–14 are cited.
49 LCA: Statement on the Two Kingdoms, 1–2: 'when the state becomes tyrannical ... it exceeds its God-given bounds. Then we are freed from our obligation to obey it' (1 Peter 2:13; 1 Tim. 2:1–2).
50 LCA: Theses on the Church, par. 16: 'The Church must act according to the instruction ... "Render unto Caesar the things which are Caesar's, and unto God the things that are God's" (Matt. 22:21) ... "obey God rather than men"' (Acts 5:29); John 18:36: 'the Lord has removed the Church from the sphere of earthly dominion, political activity, and the like, and assigned to it the spiritual sphere, with the Word as its only weapon'.
51 LCA: Statement on the Two Kingdoms, 3: this cites Acts 5:29.
52 ELCA: Constitution, Ch. 4.03: the church must e.g. 'work with civil authorities in areas of mutual endeavour, maintaining institutional separation of church and state in a relation of functional interaction', and institute processes to 'foster mutuality and interdependence' to involve people 'in making decisions that affect them'.
53 ELCA: Articles of Incorporation, Art. II (under 'the laws of the State of Minnesota'); LCA: Constitution, Art. I: the church is 'An association incorporated under the Associations Incorporation Acts 1956–1965 of the State of South Australia'.
54 ELCA: Constitution, 11.20–21.
55 ELCA: Constitution, 17.60–61: the Board of Pensions must 'comply with federal and state law'; Lutheran Church in Great Britain (LCGB): Rules and Regulations, Congregations, 3: a congregation is 'to comply with legal requirements, for example those concerned with charity, employment and taxation law'.
56 North American Lutheran Church (NALC): Standards for Pastoral Ministry, B.7: 'The society in which the Church ministers, has placed a high premium on the rule of law in regulating the rights and duties of individuals to promote the common good'; thus: 'being convicted ... is grounds for discipline as conduct incompatible with ... ministerial office but may not be grounds for discipline ... where the violation of law was to protest or to test a perceived unjust law or as an expression of civil disobedience'.
57 ELCA: Constitution, Ch. 20.16; 5.01: the composition and actions of a church assembly, council, and committee must not 'be challenged in a court of law'; LCA: Constitution, Art. IV.1: in property disputes a congregation must (under 1 Cor. 6) 'make every effort to avoid action in the civil courts'.
58 UMCNEAE: Book of Discipline (BOD), pars. 103 and 164: but, the norm is that 'Citizens have a duty to abide by laws duly adopted by orderly and just process of government'; prayers should be offered 'for those in rightful authority ... and we support their efforts to afford justice and equal opportunity for all people'.
59 Methodist Church of New Zealand (MCNZ): Laws and Regulations, Introductory Documents, III Ethical Standards for Ministry, Responsibilities to the Wider Community, 2.
60 Methodist Church in Great Britain (MCGB): Constitutional Practice and Discipline (CPD), Standing Order 018: in employing lay persons, every church body must comply with the civil legislation; Church of the Nazarene (COTN): Manual, par. 113.4: 'where the civil law requires a specific course of procedure in ... church meetings, that course should be strictly followed'; par. 142: 'where the civil law requires a specific mode of election of church trustees, that mode shall be strictly followed'.
61 Methodist Church in Ireland (MCI): Regulations, Discipline and Government (RDG), 8.10, 4D 19–24, 29.20.
62 PCA: BCO, 3.4.
63 PCA: BCO, Preface I.1–3; Preamble, II.1; II.8: ecclesiastical discipline is 'not attended with any civil effects'.
64 PCA: BCO, 59.1: 'It is proper that every commonwealth, for the good of society, make laws to regulate marriage, which all citizens are bound to obey'.
65 PCANZ: BO, 14.17(4): the moderator also makes 'statements' on behalf of the church.

66 URC: Manual, Basis of Union, A, Sch. D, Version I, 8.
67 Reformed Church in America (RCA): Book of Church Order (BCO), Preamble: 'The church shall not exercise authority over the state, nor should the state usurp authority over the church' – Christ is 'the only Head of the Church'.
68 URC: United Reformed Church Acts 1972, 1981 and 2000: these set out, e.g. the trusts for places of worship and manses; RCA: the General Synod of the Reformed Protestant Dutch Church was incorporated 'by an Act of the Legislature of the State of New York ... 1819'; an Act of 1920 changed its name to its current name.
69 RCA: BCO, Ch. I, Pt. II, Art. 14.5: pastors must perform marriages 'subject to state and provincial law'.
70 Baptist Union of Southern Africa (BUSA): Model Constitution for a Church, 4.2.7.
71 CNBC: Constitution, 3, Statement of Faith, Art. XVII: 'The state has no right to impose taxes for the support of any form of religion. A free church in a free state is the Christian ideal, and this implies the right of free and unhindered access to God on the part of all men ... without interference by the civil power'.
72 Baptist Union of Great Britain (BUGB): Baptist and Congregational Trusts Act 1961.
73 Bethel Baptist Church (Choctaw): Constitution, Art. XI: 'While Bethel Baptist Church recognizes the authority of the state over members of the church in those areas in which God has specifically granted the state authority in His Word (the Bible), the church maintains it is not subject to the state or any of its officers in its doctrines, offices, government, discipline, property, and practices. The state has no business in the affairs of the church other than what pertains to property, buildings, and codes affecting the same'. Asserting its rights under the US constitution, 'Bethel Baptist Church refuses to incorporate as a corporation under the laws of the State of Oklahoma, since such an incorporation subjects the Church of Jesus Christ to the laws of the state'.
74 National Baptist Convention (USA) (NBC-USA): Constitution, Art. IV.8: 'Under no circumstances shall a member [church] or group of members have the right to litigate, adjudicate, or arbitrate disputes and questions regarding membership rights, privileges, and procedures of this Body in the secular courts or any other forum other than that prescribed by this constitution'.
75 Baptist Union of New Zealand: Ethical Principles and Guidelines for Pastors, 6: 'I will be a good citizen'; 'I will endeavour to obey the laws of my government unless they require disobedience to the law of God'; North American Baptist Conference (NABC): Code of Ministerial Ethics: 'I will obey the laws of my government as long as they do not conflict with the laws of God and will practice Christian citizenship without engaging in partisan or political activities that would discredit the integrity of the ministry'.
76 Canadian National Baptist Convention (CNBC): Constitution, 3, Statement of Faith, XVII.
77 NABC: Statement of Belief, 7: this cites 1 Timothy 2.1–4; Romans 13.1–7; 1 Peter 13–16.
78 For the position of churches from the perspective of State law, see Doe, 2103: 356–362.
79 Catechism of the Catholic Church (1994), pars. 1925–1927; GS 26, 84.
80 GS 76; DH 14; CIC c. 1254.1: property; see also cc. 1311, 1401 on the right to discipline and conduct trials.
81 CIC, c. 204: equality and dignity; c. 747: 'fundamental human rights'.
82 ROMOC: Statutes, Art. 4.1: the church is 'autonomous in regard to the State and other institutions'.
83 See e.g. LC 1998, res. 1.1: the Conference affirmed and adopted the UN Declaration of Human Rights.
84 LC 1968, Res. 16.
85 *The Official Report of the Lambeth Conference 1998* (Morehouse Publishing, 1999) 77.
86 LC 1920, Res. 75; 1920, Res. 78; 1958, Res. 110; *Called to Full Humanity*, LC 1998, *Official Report*, 79.
87 LC 1948, Res. 5.
88 LC 1988, Res. 33.
89 LC 1998, Res. 1.1(a).
90 LC 1920, Res. 77; however, 'the Church is not to be identified with any particular political or social system': LC 1958, Res. 104.
91 PCLCCAC, Principle 26.1 and 2.
92 LWF: Constitution, Art. III.
93 LCGB: RAR, Statement of Faith, 9.
94 LCA: Human Rights, adopted by the Commission on Theology and Inter-Church Relations, 1994, edited 2001, Introduction: this sets out the history of international human rights instruments and cites Rom. 13:1–7 and 1 Peter 2:13–14; Christian Perspectives: 'Although the human rights movement has secular origins, 'justice' and 'right' are concepts which have a biblical basis'; Practical Considerations: these contain the 'guidelines'.
95 UMCNEAE: BOD, par. 103, Confession of Faith, Art. XVI; par. 161: the equality of humans and genders.

96 UMCNEAE: BOD, par. 164.
97 UMCNEAE: BOD, par. 121.
98 UMCNEAE: BOD, par. 162: it also rejects 'inequalities and discriminatory practices [in] Church and society'.
99 UMCNEAE: BOD, pars. 121, 162 and 164.
100 Free Methodist Church of North America (FMCNA): Book of Discipline (BOD), par. 111: 'God created human beings in His own image, innocent, morally free and responsible to choose between good and evil, right and wrong' but 'humans are corrupted in their very nature so that from birth they are inclined to sin' though by 'God's grace and help people are enabled to do good works with a free will'; par. 112: under the law of God humans 'should strive to secure to everyone respect for their person, their rights and their greatest happiness in the possession and exercise of the right within the moral law'.
101 MCNZ: LAR, Introductory Documents, V: Some Social Principles of the Methodist Church: the 'right to freedom of conscience, constitutional liberty, secrecy of the ballot and access to the Courts'; Christians should influence 'the politics of human rights'.
102 MCNZ: LAR, Introductory Documents, II, Pastoral Resolutions: the pledge to 'breaking down all racial, political and religious barriers, and of confronting all people' with fullness of life in Christ; III, Ethical Standards for Ministry, 3: human dignity and a prohibition against discrimination of grounds of 'race, colour, gender, sexual orientation, socio-economic group, disability, age, religious, theological or political belief'; COTN: Manual, par. 903.2: the church promotes equality and prohibits discrimination.
103 COTN: Manual, par. 903.8: the church does not 'bind the conscience of its members relative to participation in military service ... although ... the individual Christian as a citizen is bound to give service ... in all ways that are compatible with the Christian faith and ... way of life'; the church claims for 'conscientious objectors within its membership the same exemptions and considerations regarding military service as are accorded members of recognized non-combatant religious organizations'; FMCNA: BOD par. 3331: 'It is our firm conviction that the consciences of our members be respected (Acts 4.19–20; 5.29). Therefore, we claim exemption from all military service for those who register officially with the church as conscientious objectors to war'.
104 WCRC: Const., Art. V; see also Art. IV: its values include 'the dignity of every person'.
105 URC: Manual, Basis of Union, A, Sch. D, Version I, 8.
106 PCI: Code, I.III.13; this cites the Act of the Church of Scotland 1647.
107 PCA: BCO, Preamble II.1.
108 UCCP: Constitution, Art. II.11.
109 BWA: Constitution, Art. II. See also Pierard (2005: 281): 18th Congress, Melbourne: 'human rights are God-given and that violations of human rights are violations of the laws of God'.
110 BUSA: Constitution, Art. 5.3; Nigerian Baptist Convention: Policies and Practices, Ethical Behaviour of Baptists in Public Life: 'it is the inalienable right of every citizen to take part in the government of the country through ... his civic rights'; church members may enter 'fulltime politics' but are 'under divine obligation to influence [their] party to embrace principles of morality and righteousness'; if a political party acts 'in a way displeasing to God and contrary to Christian teaching' the member should dissociate himself 'until the policies and practices are made right'.
111 BUSA: Model Constitution, 4.2.7.
112 NABC: Statement of Beliefs, 7: 'religious liberty, rooted in Scripture, is the inalienable right of all individuals to freedom of conscience with ultimate accountability to God (Genesis 1.27; John 8.32; II Corinthians 3.37; Romans 8.21; Acts 5.29)'; Riverside Baptist Church (Baltimore): Constitution, Preamble: the constitution is designed e.g. for 'preserving the liberties inherent in each individual member of the church'.
113 CNBC: Constitution, 3, Statement of Faith, Art. XVII.
114 See also A Statement of Principles of Christian Law Common to the Component Churches, Christian Law Panel of Experts, 2016, Principle X.3. Social Responsibility: 1. A church should promote social justice. 2. The faithful should promote social justice and charitable work as regulated by their church.
115 *Ibid.* X: The churches have a wide variety of legal experiences in terms of their relationship to or institutional separation from the States in whose territorial boundaries they function. 1. Church-State Relations: 1. A church should cooperate with the State in matters of common concern, but each is independent in its own sphere. 2. The faithful may participate in politics save to the extent prohibited by church law. 3. Cooperation between a church and the State may be exercised on the basis of: (1) The establishment of, or other formal relationship between, a church and the State; (2) An agreement

or civil legislation negotiated freely with the State; (3) The juridical personality which a church or institutions within it may enjoy under civil law; (4) The registration of a church in accordance with the provisions of any applicable State law; (5) The fundamental institutional autonomy of a church in carrying out its lawful objects and its freedom in these areas from intervention by the State.

116 *Ibid.* Principle X.2. Human Rights and Religious Freedom: 1. All humans, having been created in the image of God, share an equality of dignity and fundamental human rights. 2. A church should protect and defend human rights in society for all people.

References

Babie, P. 2017. 'Natural Law in the Orthodox Tradition' in N. Doe (ed.) *Christianity and Natural Law: An Introduction*. Cambridge University Press. 36.

Barth, K. 1933. *The Epistle of Paul to the Romans*. Oxford University Press.

Biggar, N. 2011. *Behaving in Public: How to Do Christian Ethics*. William B. Eerdmans.

Braaten, C. E. 2011. 'A Lutheran Affirmation of the Natural Law' in R. C. Baker and R. C. Ehkle (eds) *Natural Law: A Lutheran Reappraisal*. Concordia Publishing House. 3.

Charles, J. D. 2008. *Retrieving the Natural Law: A Return to Moral First Things*. William B. Eerdmans.

Contreras F. J. (ed.). 2013. *The Threads of Natural Law: Unravelling a Philosophical Tradition*. Springer.

Costigane, H. 2017. 'Natural Law in the Roman Catholic Tradition' in N. Doe (ed.) *Christianity and Natural Law: An Introduction*. Cambridge University Press. 17.

Doe, N. 2002. 'Canonical Approaches to Human Rights in Anglican Churches' in M. Hill (ed.) *Religious Liberty and Human Rights*. University of Wales Press. 185.

Doe, N. 2013. *Christian Law: Contemporary Principles*. Cambridge University Press.

Dunkle, B. L. 2004. 'A Development of Origen's View of the Natural Law'. 13 *Pro Ecclesia*. 337.

Finnis, J. 1980. *Natural Law and Natural Rights*. Clarendon Press.

Grisez, G. 1965. 'The First Principles of Practical Reason: A Commentary on the *Summa Theologiae*, 1–2, Question 94, Article 2'. 10 *Natural Law Forum*. 168.

Harrod, J. 2017. 'Natural Law in the Methodist Tradition' in N. Doe (ed.) *Christianity and Natural Law: An Introduction*. Cambridge University Press. 98.

Hauerwas, S. 1983. *The Peaceable Kingdom: A Primer in Christian Ethics*. University of Notre Dame Press.

Hervada, J. 2006. *Critical Introduction to Natural Law*. Translated by M. Emmons. Wilson and Lafleur.

Hittinger, R. 2003. *The First Grace: Rediscovering the Natural Law in a Post-Christian World*. ISI Books.

Hughes, G. J. 1986. 'Natural Law' in J. F. Childress and J. Macquarrie (eds) *A New Dictionary of Christian Ethics*. SCM Press. 412.

Koffeman, L. 2017. 'Natural Law in the Ecumenical Movement' in N. Doe (ed.) *Christianity and Natural Law: An Introduction*. Cambridge University Press. 162.

Levering, M. 2014. 'Natural Law and Christianity' in A. M. Emon, M. Levering and D. Patsavos, L. J. 1984. 'The Canonical Tradition of the Orthodox Church' in F. K. Litsas (ed.) *A Companion to the Greek Orthodox Church*. Greek Orthodox Archdiocese of North and South America. 137.

Pierard, R. V. (ed.). 2005. *Baptists Together in Christ 1905–2005: A Hundred Year History of the Baptist World Alliance*. BWA.

Porter, J. 1999. *Natural Law and Divine Law: Reclaiming the Tradition for Christian Ethics*. William B. Eerdmans.

Porter, J. 2009. 'Does the Natural Law Provide a Universally Binding Morality?' in L. S. Cunningham (ed.) *Intractable Disputes about Natural Law: Alistair MacIntyre and Critics*. University Press of Notre Dame.

Ramsey, P. 1993. *Basic Christian Ethics*. John Knox Press.

Raunio, A. 2006. 'Divine and Natural Law in Luther and Melanchthon' in V. Mäkinen (ed.) *The Lutheran Reformation and the Law*. Brill. 21.

Rodopoulos, P. 2007. *An Overview of Orthodox Canon Law*. Orthodox Research Institute.

Van Drunen, D. 2006. *A Biblical Case for Natural Law*. Studies in Christian Social Ethics and Economics, No. 1. Acton Institute.

Van Drunen, D. 2010. *Natural Law and the Two Kingdoms: A Study in the Development of Reformed Social Thought*. William B. Eerdmans.

Wilken, R. L. 2003. *The Spirit of Early Christian Thought: Seeking the Face of God*. Yale University Press.

Witte, J. Jr. 1990. *Law and Protestantism: The Legal Teachings of the Lutheran Reformation*. Cambridge University Press.

23

Islamic law perspectives

The legal other

Anver M. Emon

Introduction

There are two different and distinct ways to address the legal other in Islamic law. The first, which is animated by the concept of 'jurisdiction', concerns the place of other legal traditions within Islamic law. A typical situation might involve whether and to what extent an imagined 'domestic' Shari'a court would resolve a dispute that originated in a foreign jurisdiction. The second concerns the 'religious other' living in Islamic lands governed by Islamic law. In both cases, premodern Muslim jurists imagined the foreign law and the religious other as appearing before a 'domestic' court in Islamic lands. This chapter will examine both approaches to the 'legal other' in Islamic law.

Islamic law's legal other: a jurisdictional analysis

Muslim jurists had a monist, imperial vision of the enterprise of governance, which was captured by reference to Islamic lands as 'the abode of Islam' (*dar al-Islam*). Everything outside of that was the world of non-Islam or the *dar al-harb* (lit. abode of war). Pre-modern Muslim jurists promoted an ideal of governance as led by a single authority, the caliph. As H.A.R. Gibb (1955: 17) argued, pre-modern Muslim jurists imagined a governing enterprise 'in which all political authority was centered in the caliph-imam, and no authority was valid unless exercised by delegation from him, directly or indirectly'. As much as the empire might expand, so it was argued, it was always to be ruled by a single caliph. Remarking on the early history of the Islamic ruling authority, Muhammad Hamidullah (1945: 46) noted: 'although the Muslim empire soon spread far and wide outside its birthplace, Arabia, yet practically for more than a hundred years the unity of the Muslim remained intact'.

The possibility that the Muslim world might be fractured into territorially based polities was a form of non-ideal politics that jurists considered unworthy of the Islamic mandate. That non-ideal politics became a reality in the 10th century, when three rulers proclaimed themselves caliphs of the Muslim world, creating the 'Abbasid caliphate in Baghdad, the Fatimid caliphate in Egypt, and the Umayyad caliphate in Spain. These caliphates eventually lost effective control of their lands as princely rulers gradually gained and exercised greater control of the once-caliphal territory, rendering the caliph more a symbolic office holder than effective executive (see generally, Emon, 2012a).

The juristic imagination of a monist, imperial governance system ruled by a single caliph was ultimately forced to confront the reality of regional fracturing of political authority. In some cases, jurists distinguished between spheres of authority held by different office holders, whether caliph or sultan, in the service of their monist commitments (Gibb, 1955: 20). In other cases, they held that regional princes exercised legitimate claims to authority by virtue of caliphal delegations of authority, or by virtue of their adherence to the Shari'a as devised by jurists (Crone, 2004: 233).

But what remains important for our purposes is to appreciate the significance of this monist, imperial vision as an ideal politics that renders contemporary state practices as non-ideal forms of governance. The political thought of the pre-modern jurist al-Juwayni (d. 1085) offers an example of this imperial vision. For al-Juwayni, the singular caliphate represented the aspirational model of leadership for the Muslim *umma* writ large. Its legitimacy was derived from historical precedents and a theory of politics that demanded checks on princely rulers whose authority relied on coercive force.

Al-Juwayni, who lived in the era of the three caliphal contenders, argued against the appropriateness of having more than one caliph. Al-Juwayni (1997: 80) stated that in cases where a single *imam* can observe, manage, and control Muslim lands from the east to west, no second *imam* is permitted. Reflecting on the post-prophetic history of the first four caliphs of Islam, al-Juwayni (1997: 80) claimed that the *imamate* is singular, not plural; any other position is based on ignorance (*ba'id al-fahm*). He believed a single caliph was necessary to maintain social order: 'polities become unstable as princely rulers become partisan, opinions diverge, and desires compete' (al-Juwayni, 1997: 80). The caliph, on the other hand, offers a uniting thread by which to guide regional rulers. If regional rulers:

> [d]o not have a rope to follow, [and] a particular aim to which to adhere, they will compete, become insolent, struggle with each other, vie against each other, and indulge the desires for conquest and regal authority. They will jockey with each other without paying any heed to the ruin of the multitudes and masses.
>
> *(al-Juwayni, 1997: 80)*

Although al-Juwayni was unflinching in his advocacy of the monist, imperial political ideal, he also recognized it as a form of ideal theory from which reality all-too-often departed. 'It may be', he suggested, 'that a group of people reside on a portion of land to which the [caliph's] oversight does not reach' (al-Juwayni, 1997: 81). But even in this case, al-Juwayni rejected the possibility of two or more caliphs. His rationale, more than his specific answer, is especially important for appreciating the power and significance of this imperial vision on Muslim jurists' imagination. He held that a governor (*amir*) may rule over certain regions. But the *amir* would not assume the title of caliph. Rather, the office of the *amir* is an administrative position that provides order and stability for Muslims outside the control of the ruling caliph. If there is no caliph, and instead Islamic lands are divided into smaller units – as is the case in the modern state system – al-Juwayni argued that the people of those regions can appoint *amirs* to govern each area. In this case, the imperative to appoint an *amir* is a matter of necessity (*darura*), for without an *amir*, chaos prevails. But at no point can the *amir(s)* presume to hold the title of caliph. There may be many *amirs*, but none can claim to be the caliph, since the caliph is strictly understood by al-Juwayni as the one around whom all Muslims are united. As al-Juwayni said:

> I do not reject the permissibility of establishing [two *amirs*] according to what is needed, and enforcing their commands in accordance with the demands of the law. But [that] is a time without an *imam*[1] . . . If the *imam* is agreed upon, then the two amirs must submit to him.
>
> *(al-Juwayni, 1997: 82)*

Territorial leadership does not render one an *imam*: the office of the *imam* transcends territorial boundaries and instead embodies community leadership.

Al-Juwayni's doctrine of the *amir* revealed both his willingness to be pragmatic, as well as his commitment to an ideal theory that cautions against granting too much legitimacy to multiple sovereign powers. The plurality of polities was a reality he could not avoid. But their existence should not be mistaken as evidence of the legitimacy of their authority over the *umma*. Guiding the Muslim *umma* requires a type of legitimacy and authority that ruling a territory through coercive force alone cannot and does not confer. In this sense, al-Juwayni is not opposed to political pluralism. His theory acknowledges the reality of regional polities and conditions the exercise of power within this context to ensure order and stability. Instead, he cautions the various claimants to worldly, territorially based authority not to mistake the circumstances of their power and dominance for the constitutive features of legitimacy and authority that extend beyond their borders.

The ideal theory of an imperial monist form of governance directly affected how jurists imagined legal doctrines and the possibility of jurisdictional conflict. If legitimacy runs from the singularity of the caliphal office and not from the *amir* or *sultan*, then how might this affect the way jurists imagined the existence of competing jurisdictions? In a context of diverse regional authorities, Muslim jurists crafted a legal tradition that relied on an imagined imperial mode of governance. Doing so allowed them to create unity among Muslims through law where politics had failed to create such unity. Certainly there may be different regions with different rules. But the legitimacy of those legal rules was premised upon whether the region itself fell inside or outside the imperial Muslim regime. However as the next section will show, unity through law precluded their recognition of laws from foreign jurisdictions. A Manichean world view of politics, we argue, informed a legal tradition that did not make substantial allowances for multiple, equally legitimate, but at times foreign, law.

Foreign law in an Islamic court

To appreciate how an imperial vision of Islamic law precluded a robust private international law regime requires understanding how pre-modern Muslim jurists classified possible litigants. There were four possible categories: Muslim, *musta'min, dhimmi*, and *harbi*. Each of these terms will be described below, after which will follow a brief analysis of the jurisdictional issues they posed for jurists.

'Muslim' denotes the person who is most closely considered part of the Islamic 'us' or 'we' for the purposes of Islamic law and its application. Whether the Muslim is located inside the Muslim polity or outside, he or she falls under the legal authority of Shariʿa. There are of course differences among Muslims, e.g. gender or age, that might alter the degree to which any particular person is subject to the law fully (see for instance, Emon, 2013).

Dhimmi refers to the non-Muslim permanent resident in Muslim lands. According to Islamic legal doctrines, the *dhimmis* would enter a 'contract of protection' (whether express or implied) with the ruling Muslim authorities. Under the terms of this contract, *dhimmis* agreed to live by certain conditions in return for maintaining their distinct faith traditions and residing peacefully in Muslim lands. The *dhimmi* rules were those conditions. Hence, the *dhimmi* rules were part of the political compromise made between the ruling Muslim authorities and the minority religious groups. These rules rendered minority religious groups as both insiders and outsiders to the Muslim polity.[2]

Harbi refers to the person who resides in what jurists called the *dar al-harb*, literally translated as the Abode of War. As many scholars have noted already, Muslim jurists viewed the world in a nearly dichotomous fashion, comprising the Abode of War and the Abode of Islam (*dar al-islam*).[3] Many also write about a third region, namely the Abode of Treaties (*dar al-sulh*), or regions that have treaties of peace with the Muslim empire (see for instance, Bsoul, 2008a). On first appearance, the language of these terms seems to imply a state of perpetual war and, by implication, imperial expansion. Indeed, those implications have been used by many to characterize Islam and Muslims as intolerant of religious others;[4] as incapable of enjoying meaningful peace with other nations and peoples (Sharify-Funk, 2013); and as set in an interminable clash with the non-Muslim West.[5] However, from a legal perspective – specifically, when it comes to jurisdiction – the *harbi* is the quintessential foreigner who lives under a foreign law, and whose presence in an Islamic court in Islamic lands posits a foreign element that we in the contemporary context might frame in terms of jurisdiction and private international law. For that reason, this report will depart from a literal translation of *harbi* and instead cast him or her as a foreigner subject to a foreign law.

The final term, *musta'min*, refers to someone who has a temporary license (*aman*) to reside in a land not his own. The *aman* could be understood as the pre-modern analogue to a visa.

> Technically, the term *aman* signifies a safe conduct or pledge of security given by a Muslim to a non-Muslim alien upon the termination of hostilities or, more often, to an outsider visiting the Abode of Islam (*dar al-Islam*) for a limited period of time.
>
> *(Khalilieh, 2014)*

Generally, any *harbi* who wishes to enter Muslim lands can do so safely as long as he or she has an *aman*. As much as the *harbi* was the quintessential outsider to the world of Islam, the *harbi* might still engage in various sorts of relationships with people in the Abode of Islam. The *harbi* may be a foreigner or a stranger, but that does not preclude relationships that might have attendant legal dimensions to them, such as contracts of trade and exchange.

From a jurisdictional perspective, it is fruitful to view the *dar al-islam* as the 'domestic' jurisdiction, and the *dar al-harb* as the foreign jurisdiction. A jurisdictional lens promises compelling insights into the formation of Islamic law's legal other. As jurists determined whether an Islamic court had jurisdiction over a case, the status of the litigant in relation to the Manichean imaginary of the world informed their decisions. To explore this complex dynamic, we review hypothetical legal disputes that involve a foreign element (either foreign law or a foreigner) before an Islamic (domestic) court. The examples are drawn from a premodern treatise that many consider a work on 'international law', specifically the Hanafi jurist al-Sarakhsi's (d. 483 AH/1090 CE) commentary *Sharh Kitab al-Siyar al-Kabir*. This particular text is a commentary on the early Hanafi text *al-Siyar al-Kabir* by Muhammad b. al-Hasan al-Shaybani (d. 189 AH/805 CE). It is offered here as an example of the nature of the pre-modern debates that are both relevant for issues in private international law, as well as the subject of this section of this volume.[6] Given space limitations, two examples will be addressed for illustrative purposes. The first example concerns marriage law and whether the foreign status (*harbi*) of the one of the parties precludes the court from assuming jurisdiction. The second example concerns trade and contract law, and whether a judge sitting in the Islamic empire can adjudicate the terms of an agreement made in foreign lands.

Marriage law hypotheticals: upon whom is Islamic law operative?

Hypothetical 1: foreign, non-Muslim spouses in Islamic lands

Suppose a *harbi* husband had two wives who were also sisters. Subsequently the husband converted to Islam, as did his wives. Under Islamic law, while a man can have up to four wives, he cannot marry sisters simultaneously, thus putting this new Muslim husband in a legal predicament with respect to his two wives. Hanafi jurists disagreed on the resolution. One approach focused on the nature of the marital contract. If the original marriages were conducted pursuant to a single contract, the entire contract is void and the marriages to the two sisters are invalid. However, if the original marriages were contracted through two separate contracts, then the sister whom he married first will remain his wife, and the marriage to the second sister is void. The second approach required the husband to choose which wife to retain and which to divorce, without reference to the marital contracts.

To harmonize the difference within the Hanafi School, al-Sarakhsi contrasted this case by reference to the figure of the *dhimmi*. Suppose a *dhimmi* husband residing in Islamic lands was married by separate contracts to two sisters (neither of whom were Muslim at the time of marriage). Later, all three of them convert to Islam, raising the question of the marital restriction. According to al-Sarakhsi, the *dhimmi* would be held to Abu Hanifa's first-in-time rule, while the *harbi* would exercise a choice pursuant to al-Shaybani's rule. The reason for the discrepancy between the *dhimmi* and *harbi* in this case has to do with what it means to be obligated under the law. The *dhimmi* entered into a contract of protection (*'aqd al-dhimma*) that permitted him to retain his distinctive faith and remain secure in Muslim lands. That contract also required him to abide by the laws of Islam. In other words, the *dhimmi* husband was always and at all times subjected to Islamic law when he got married to the two sisters through the two separate contracts. Since Islamic law prohibits being married to two sisters simultaneously, the second contracted marriage was legally void from the outset, even though none of the parties was Muslim when they married. The *harbi* on the other hand was never obligated to the laws of Islam at the time he entered the separate contracts of marriage with the two sisters. Consequently, for the *harbi* who later converted to Islam, he had the power to simply choose which wife to divorce. Since the original contracts were never subject to the laws of Islam, the second contract was not void at the outset. The issue of validity and invalidity only arose because the *harbis* converted to Islam.

Of particular importance in this discussion is the way in which jurists such as al-Sarakhsi understood the scope to which Islamic law was applied and to whom. The foreigner was never obligated to the laws of Islam. As a foreigner, he or she was the quintessential outsider governed by a different, foreign law, which precluded any *post hoc* application of Shari'a to his or her situation.

Hypothetical 2: foreign, non-Muslim spouses litigate in an Islamic court

Suppose a *harbi* married couple temporarily entered Muslim lands, such as for trading and business purposes. Neither the husband nor the wife was Muslim, but the wife was a Jew or Christian. Later, the husband converted to Islam, while the wife did not alter her faith. After a certain point in time, the wife wanted to leave the Islamic lands to return to her home in foreign lands (i.e. the *dar al-harb*), but the husband refused. According to al-Sarakhsi, the wife cannot leave and the husband's wishes are vindicated. Drawing upon a highly gendered mode of legal reasoning, he argued that under Islamic law the wife is presumed to follow the husband, thus precluding separate travels. But this legal conclusion is only possible because the husband converted to Islam and thereby 'domesticated' himself sufficiently for the court to take jurisdiction and apply Islamic law as if it were operative when they first got married.

Suppose, on the other hand, the husband did not convert to Islam, and the wife, who wanted to return to her homeland over her husband's objection, said that they were never married at all. On these facts, al-Sarakhsi precluded an Islamic court from taking jurisdiction of the case. 'The judge does not judge between two temporary visitors in accordance with underlying claims that apply in foreign lands' (Al-Sarakhsi, 1:97). In this modified scenario, two foreign elements appear. The first is the fact that both parties are deemed foreigners. The second is that the two are disputing their original marriage, which if it took place, would have occurred in a foreign jurisdiction under foreign law. The foreign nature of the parties and the legal action render the Islamic court unable to assume jurisdiction.

Trade and contract law hypotheticals: foreigners, foreign law, and Islamic courts

Hypothetical 1: non-Muslims in Islamic lands and domestic courts

Suppose a sale of goods occurs in foreign lands between parties who are not Muslim. Later, all the parties convert to Islam and travel to Islamic lands. While residing in Muslim lands, the original purchaser finds a defect in the product he purchased. Can the purchaser claim that the contract was breached, return the defective property, and get his money back? According to al-Sarakhsi, an Islamic court cannot take jurisdiction of the case because the transaction occurred in foreign lands and because the contracting parties were not even subject to the laws of Islam when they entered the original agreement (Al-Sarakhsi: 1:129).

Hypothetical 2: Muslims in foreign lands and 'domestic' courts

Suppose two Muslims contract for an exchange of good while visiting foreign lands. Upon their return to Islamic lands, one of them filed suit against the other for breach of contract. According to al-Sarakhsi, the court can assume jurisdiction because Muslims are subject to the laws of Islam wherever they might be. Despite entering into the agreement in a foreign jurisdiction, the two parties' Muslim identity renders the foreign venue irrelevant for jurisdiction purposes. 'Their [legal] situation in non-Islamic lands is like their [legal] situation in the lands of Islam' (*kana haluhuma fi dar al-harb ka-haluhuma fi dar al-islam*) (Al-Sarakhsi: 1:129–130). Whether entered into in Muslim lands or non-Muslim lands, transactions between Muslims remain governed by Islamic law and subject to Islamic court jurisdiction (Al-Sarakhsi: 1:132). In this example, we see the universalist ethos of an Islamic empire inform a jurisdictional rule concerning Muslims abroad.

Reflections on the jurisdictional analysis

In these two sets of examples, we consistently find a limit to an Islamic court's capacity to assume jurisdiction when a foreign element is present. That foreign element is not merely the fact that a particular person or claimant is foreign (i.e. a *harbi*). Rather, the foreigner is presumed to be subject to a law other than the Shari'a. The Muslim judge (*qadi*) is not the appropriate officiant to resolve the conflict and settle the dispute. Institutionally and substantively, the *qadi*'s court is the wrong forum.

It is not the case that the *qadi* cannot *factually* inquire into a law other than Shari'a. Indeed, an early example from the Prophet Muhammad's life attests to the fact that he adjudicated a matter of Jewish law concerning a case of two alleged adulterous Jews.[7] But his inquiry into the Jewish tradition was to determine, as a *matter of fact*, what the Jewish law on adultery was so that he could apply, as Muslim jurists argued, the Islamic law on adultery. The inquiry into Jewish law was not to be viewed as an elevation of a 'foreign' law to the same or equivalent status of Shari'a.

Al-Sarakhsi's judicial restraint in the above examples involving foreign law is consistent with the imperative to ensure the primacy of Shari'a (coded here as 'domestic law'). These hypotheticals represent a zero-sum conflict of laws regime that tracks the Manichean world view of the abode of Islam and foreign lands. An imperial logic demands that a *qadi* court either apply Shari'a or deny jurisdiction entirely. If a *qadi* were to assume jurisdiction to apply foreign law, the *qadi*'s court would implicitly serve the sovereign interests of a foreign regime, thus recognizing its validity and legitimacy. Consequently, when al-Sarakhsi held that courts must refuse jurisdiction in cases involving foreign elements, it is unlikely that the reason had to do with judicial inability to know or understand foreign law. Rather, what was at stake was the sovereign integrity of the institutions of an Islamic empire.

This interest in the sovereign integrity of Islamic law and legal institutions is not unique to Islamic law. It is a feature of any domestic legal enterprise, which comes into stark relief when faced with jurisdictional questions. The challenge, therefore, is to determine whether and to what extent issues of comity may implicitly inform legal analyses about jurisdiction when a foreign law is at issue.

The Muslim's other: dhimmis in Islamic law

As noted earlier, the *harbi* is the foreigner, and the *musta'min* is the temporary visitor. These two legal categories pose important vehicles for reflecting on jurisdiction. But to examine the status of the non-Muslim under Islamic law, the most salient conceptual site of analysis involves the non-Muslim who permanently resides in the Islamic polity, known as the *dhimmi*. As a matter of law, the *dhimmi* pays a poll tax (*jizya*) to enter into a contract of protection (*'aqd al-jizya*) under which he is permitted to permanently reside peacefully within Muslim lands and preserve his faith commitments. The contract of protection was the device through which jurists used to debate the rights and obligations of religious minorities living under an Islamic imperium, or the *dhimmi* rules. Premodern Muslim jurists articulated various rules regulating the scope of freedoms *dhimmis* enjoy, whether to manifest their religious beliefs or to act in ways contrary to Islamic legal doctrines but in conformity with their own traditions.

It would be naïve to address these rules without also recognizing that they are currently part of an ongoing political debate in Europe and the United States about whether and to what extent they can trust their Muslim residents or subject them to security-based modes of surveillance. These debates are often framed around a single question, namely whether the Islamic faith (and those who adhere to it) is tolerant or intolerant of non-Muslims. Some suggest that the *dhimmi* rules are positive proof that intolerance is inherent to the Islamic tradition.[8] Others suggest that these rules had limited real-world application and were mere academic exercises of little historical import to the lives of non-Muslims in Islamic regimes. Both sets of arguments are not without evidence. The first view is supported by historical incidents of persecution, premodern rules that discriminated on religious grounds, and, more recently, reports of human rights monitoring groups that detail incidents of persecution (both official and unofficial) against non-Muslim citizens of Muslim-majority states today. The second view finds support in historical records that illustrate the important role non-Muslims played in Muslim-ruled lands, whether economically, politically, or otherwise.

This chapter takes issue with the use of 'tolerance' to inform debates about the *dhimmi* rules. Philosophers and political scientists describe 'tolerance' as a cover that hides the underlying dynamics of governance amid diversity that is often quite coercive (see for instance, Brown, 2008). This chapter will instead address the *dhimmi* legal doctrines both to illuminate their internal logic and to situate them more broadly in contemporary debates about tolerance, pluralism, and the challenge of governing a diverse polity.

The dhimmi rules: a framework of analysis

Jurists utilized a range of legal arguments to justify the rules that governed the rights, duties, and restrictions on *dhimmis* living in a Muslim polity. A close analysis of this range of arguments shows that they cannot be easily reduced to the binary of tolerance or intolerance. Rather, the different arguments reveal how the concept of 'minority' is more than a reference to a particular demographic. Instead, I will reflect on certain *dhimmi* rules in order to posit 'minority' as a conceptual standpoint from which to observe the complex dynamics of governing a diverse setting. Consequently, this section of the chapter will not so much list the various rules and regulations that pertained to *dhimmis*. There are other studies that can provide such positivist accounts of the law.[9]

Accommodation and its limits: alcohol and pork as contraband or consumer goods?

As noted earlier, *dhimmis* paid the *jizya*, or poll tax, to enjoy the freedom to reside in the Muslim polity. However, the scope of their freedom was conditioned by their status as a religious minority, as reflected in the *dhimmi* rules. For instance, the contract of protection required the governing regime to protect the property interests of *dhimmis*, just as it protected those of Muslims. But does all property qualify for full, robust protection, or are certain kinds of property suspect under Islamic law, such as wine or pork? Both wine and pork are forbidden to Muslims; they cannot consume either. But *dhimmis* were presumed by Muslim jurists to be free under their own traditions to consume such items. What kind of property protection could the *dhimmi* expect from the Muslim regime when the property in question was illicit for Muslims under Islamic law?

Not all things that can be owned necessarily qualify as property under the law. Only certain types of things are legally recognized as conveying rights of exclusive use and enjoyment. For the Hanafi al-Kasani (1997: 9:292), a thing that conveys such legal benefits is considered *mutaqawwam*, or legally protected. Determining which things could be designated as *mutaqawwam* had potentially adverse effects on the scope of a *dhimmi*'s property rights. Specifically, in the case of wine and pork, *dhimmis* could consume them even though Islamic law prohibited their consumption for Muslims. But that did not mean *dhimmis* enjoyed the full protection of their property interests in wine and pork products, such as in cases when their items were stolen. Rather, the legal debate about protecting the *dhimmis*' property interest in wine and pork illustrates how Muslim jurists used the law inclusively by protecting aspects of *dhimmi* ownership in prohibited products, but only to a certain extent.

Consuming alcohol (*shurb al-khamr*) was a crime under Islamic law, with a penalty of 40 or 80 lashes, depending on which school of law is referenced.[10] Consuming pork was also prohibited to Muslims under their dietary laws. However, neither of these prohibitions applied to *dhimmis*: premodern jurists allowed *dhimmis* to consume both items. This begs the questions of why, on what basis, and with what limits? For jurists such as al-Ghazali and al-Kasani, *dhimmis* were entitled to have their own traditions respected under the contract of protection. Since their traditions allowed them to consume wine and pork, *dhimmis* should be allowed to consume such items in an Islamic polity, despite the general prohibition for Muslims (al-Ghazali, 2001: 4:152; al-Kasani, 1997: 9:292).[11]

As much as jurists permitted *dhimmis* this liberty, the jurists were nonetheless aware that they might have to limit their accommodation in light of other issues of law and legal order. For instance, although jurists agreed that *dhimmis* could consume alcohol, they nonetheless were concerned that unrestricted alcohol consumption might endanger the public welfare, which they presumed reflected the majoritarian values of the Muslim polity. Consequently, though they permitted *dhimmis* to consume alcohol, they developed legal rules banning public drunkenness or public displays of alcohol (al-Mawardi, 1994: 13:328; al-Shirazi, 1995: 3:317; al-Muzani, 1990: 5:385; al-Kasani, 1997: 9:214).[12] While the *dhimmi* enjoyed an exception to a rule of general application, that general rule was nonetheless circumscribed by abstract notions of the public good, as expressed in legal rules banning public drunkenness.

Suppose, however, that someone steals a *dhimmi*'s supply of wine or pork. Could that *dhimmi* petition the governing authorities to punish the thief? As the Hanafi al-Kasani recognized, under the *dhimmis*' law, the items are rights-conferring. But under Shari'a-based doctrines, such items are not necessarily rights-conferring, and thus not legally considered property, since neither are *mutaqawwam*. If the wronged *dhimmi* seeks redress under Shari'a against the thief, what ought to be the claim and potential sanction? For instance, should the Muslim judge sentence the thief to the Qur'anic punishment of hand amputation? If the judge does so, would that effectively be using a Shari'a-based legal system to enforce a right to a thing that is not regarded as *mutaqawwam* under Shari'a norms, despite being valuable under the *dhimmis*' tradition? This issue does not merely present a conflict of law issue about which doctrine to rely upon. Instead, it shows how *dhimmi* doctrines are part of a larger political contract, the latter of which gives the *dhimmi*'s tradition some, but not absolute, normative significance in a legal system that is deeply wedded to the Shari'a as a tradition and source of legitimacy. Certainly, the *dhimmi* enjoyed legal protection under the contract of protection, but at what cost to the gravitas of the Shari'a-based legal system? At first glance, redressing the wronged *dhimmi* seems consistent with a commitment to protect people from theft. But on further reflection, there is a fundamental inconsistency when upholding the *dhimmi*'s tradition requires violating a rule of Shari'a.

According to the Hanafi al-Kasani, wine and pork are not *mutaqawwam*. Consequently, if a *dhimmi* steals wine from another *dhimmi*, the former will not suffer the Qur'anic punishment for theft, despite having stolen something that does not belong to him (al-Kasani, 1997: 9:292). Under a Shari'a analysis, if such property has no value, then no theft has occurred. To view al-Kasani's position from the systemic level, though, one can appreciate that, for al-Kasani, to use the coercive power of Shari'a to redress the theft of a thing that is condemned under Shari'a might appear to 'over-accommodate' the *dhimmi* at the expense of legal consistency and the public good sought through Shari'a regulations.

This is not to say, however, that a *dhimmi* whose pork or wine is stolen by another is without recourse. Although the *dhimmi* may not be able to pursue a criminal action against the thief on Qur'anic grounds, some (but not all) jurists awarded the *dhimmi* financial compensation for the value of his lost property. As the Maliki Sahnun (n.d.: 6:278) held, the thief should not suffer the Qur'anic punishment but can be required to pay damages (*aghrama thamnahu*) for the value of the stolen items.

Of course, the jurists were not unanimous in their approach. According to Ibn Hazm (n.d.), some held the thief liable to both the Qur'anic punishment and financial compensation, given that the item in question was *mutaqawwam* under the *dhimmi*'s tradition. Others held that the thief had no liability whatsoever (Hazm, n.d.: 12:321–322). Nonetheless, the fact that jurists might deny corporal sanction but impose compensatory liability on the thief illustrates a crucial negotiative feature of governing in a diverse environment.

The general bans on the consumption of alcohol and pork, coupled with the exceptions derived from the contract of protection, provide important insights into how jurists used legal argument both to accommodate *dhimmis* and to limit the scope of that accommodation in the interest of the social good. The legal debates are interesting not so much for the content of the doctrine, but rather for illustrating the strategies and scope of legal accommodation.

Property, charity and security: the case of charitable endowments (awqaf)

As discussed in the previous section, a *dhimmi* who consumes alcohol is exempted from the general rule prohibiting alcohol consumption under the contract of protection. This accommodation is an exception that does not alter the general nature of the ban nor the general public policy concern about public drunkeness. Though the contract of protection accommodates the *dhimmi*'s difference, it also constrains the scope of his liberty interest to give effect to an ambiguously defined public good.

This section addresses whether *dhimmis* could create charitable endowments, or *awqaf* (singular *waqf*), for the purpose of teaching the Bible or Torah. Creating a charitable endowment is a right that accrues to private property owners. However, under Islamic law, charitable endowments are meant to support the public weal. Does a *dhimmi*'s desire to endow a Torah or Bible reading school benefit an Islamically defined public weal? As will be shown, private rights of ownership and bequest raise concerns when property is donated for purposes that may contravene what jurists considered the public good. Consequently, the debate about whether and to what extent a *dhimmi* could endow a charity pitted respect for the *dhimmi*'s private property interests against an Islamically defined public good. Identifying the appropriate balance was not easy. Jurists examined a range of factors that contributed to the public good, those that diminished it, and how best to strike an appropriate balance in pluralist settings where not all members of the polity shared the same set of core values.

Shafi'i and Hanbali jurists generally agreed that *dhimmis* could create trusts and issue bequests to any specified individual (*shakhs mu'ayaan*), regardless of religious background, although some jurists limited the beneficiaries to one's kin group (al-Ghazali 2001: 2:397–398).[13] This permissive attitude was based on legal respect for private ownership (*tamlik*) (al-Ghazali, 2001: 2:397–398; Muflih, 1997: 4:513; Qudama, n.d.: 5:646). For Shafi'i and Hanbali jurists, the *dhimmi*'s private property interest was sufficiently hefty to warrant the right to bequest property to other individuals.

However, if the *dhimmi*'s bequest was for something that might adversely affect the public interest, then the bequest was a sin against God and could not be valid under the Shari'a.[14] To hold otherwise would be to use the doctrines and institutions of a Shari'a-based governance system to legitimate practices that contravene an Islamically defined public good. Consequently, if a *dhimmi* created a charitable trust to support building a church or a school for Torah studies, Shafi'i jurists would invalidate the *waqf*, because it constituted a sin (*ma'siya*) that the law could not allow (al-Ghazali, 2001: 2:397; al-Ramli, 1992: 5:366).[15]

The Shafi'i jurist al-Shirazi offered a striking analysis that reveals the public policy and security concerns implicit in debates (even today) about philanthropy, endowments, and non-governmental organizations. First, as a matter of law, a charitable endowment is designed to bring one close to God (*qurba*). Second, anyone who creates a charitable endowment creates an institution that, by its very nature, brings benefit to others (and society at large). Lastly, any charitable endowment that facilitates sin (*i'ana 'ala ma'siya*) cannot be a charitable endowment and thereby cannot benefit from the legal doctrines of *waqf* (Al-Shirazi, 1995: 2:323–324). For al-Shirazi, a Torah or Bible reading school would perpetuate disbelief in the land of Islam, which was tantamount to sin. Moreover, he argued that such endowments were fundamental threats to the Muslim polity. For instance, he likened a charitable endowment for a church or synagogue to a bequest that arms the Muslim polity's enemies.[16] In other words, charitable endowments that perpetuate value systems other than Islam are security threats that must be eliminated. To allow such charitable endowments as a matter of law would be to use the Shariʿa rule of law system, both in terms of its doctrines and institutions, in a manner contrary to the public good.

Not every school of law viewed such bequests through the lens of security. Hanafi jurists addressed the power to bequest using a hypothetical about a *dhimmi* who bequeaths his home to a church, as opposed to leaving it to a specifically named person. Abu Hanifa held this bequest lawful on the ground that this act constitutes a pious, devotional act for the *dhimmi* (i.e. *qurba*) and must be respected just as Muslims respect the *dhimmi*'s faith in other regards. In other words, both al-Shirazi and Abu Hanifa understood charitable endowments as bringing one closer to God. However, Abu Hanifa also appreciated that what it means to bring someone closer to God cannot be defined only in Islamic terms, especially when the contract of protection gives legal cover for *dhimmis* to practice their faith. Abu Hanifa's students, Muhammad al-Shaybani and Abu Yusuf, however, disagreed with their teacher because they (like al-Shirazi) deemed its subject matter sinful (*maʿsiyya haqiqa*) despite the *dhimmi*'s belief that it is a pious act (al-ʿAyni, 2000: 13:495; Nujaym, 1997: 9:302; al-Kasani, 1997: 10:500–501).

To further complicate matters, the Malikis analyzed a *dhimmi*'s charitable endowment by reference to Islamic inheritance law, the *dhimmi*'s community leadership, and the prevailing tax regime. Under Islamic inheritance law, two-thirds of a decedent's property is distributed to pre-designated heirs. The decedent can bequeath the remaining one-third to non-heirs.[17] Malikis asked, though, whether a Christian *dhimmi* with no heirs could bequeath all of his property to the church, namely the Patriarchate.

The answer depended on the mechanism used to collect the *jizya* tax payments. Specifically, Malikis asked whether the *dhimmi* is personally liable to the governing regime for the *jizya*, or whether the *dhimmi* community, via the office of the Patriarch, is collectively liable for the tax payment. If the *dhimmi* is personally liable for paying the *jizya* directly to the government, he can only give one-third of the estate to the Patriarchate. The remaining two-thirds escheats to the Muslim polity, which is considered his lawful heir in this case (al-Jadd, 1988a: 13:326–327). Malikis reasoned that with the death of the *dhimmi*, the ruling regime would lose its annual tax revenue from him. Consequently, the escheat of his estate is designed to account for the regime's lost revenue (al-Jadd, 1988a: 13:326–327; see also al-Qarafi, 1994: 7:35). This arrangement is to be carried out even if the testator leaves a testamentary instrument that transfers his whole estate to the Patriarchate (al-Jadd, 1988a: 13:326–327).[18]

On the other hand, if the Patriarchate collects the *jizya* from its members, where the rate of tax is a pre-set amount that does not decrease with deaths of community members, many Malikis allowed individual *dhimmis* (presumably without heirs) to bequest their entire estate to the Patriarchate (al-Jadd, 1988a: 13:326–327).[19] In this scenario, the regime receives the same *jizya* tax returns, suffering no diminution in tax revenue with the death of individual *dhimmis*. Any financial loss is distributed to the Patriarchate, since its tax liability does not diminish with the death of its community members. To offset that financial loss, the Malikis permitted *dhimmis* who lacked heirs to bequeath their entire estate to the Patriarchate.

This analysis shows that when a *dhimmi* sought to endow a religious institution, Muslim jurists were concerned about giving such charitable institutions legal recognition. The divergences between the schools reflect juridical attempts to account for and respect (a) the *dhimmi*'s religious freedom and property, and (b) the public good, which for some was tied directly to security concerns. Regardless of the analytic route any particular jurist adopted, the legal debate shows that the *dhimmi* rules are hardly clear cut indices of tolerance or intolerance. Given the current climate in Europe and North America concerning the specter of the 'Muslim', we can appreciate the *dhimmi* rules as symptoms of the shared challenge of governing diversity.

The *dhimmi* rules today

Islam's historical doctrine remains a point of debate in both Muslim states that rely on Shari'a in their legal system, and in liberal constitutional states where Muslims live as a religious minority (see for instance March, 2009). For example, politicians capitalized on the fear of Muslims as terrorists during the Brexit referendum in the UK as well as in the US presidential election. At the heart of much of this fear-mongering is an assumption that Muslims, because of their commitment to Islam, cannot and will not tolerate a polity made up of a diverse array of religious groups. Islam generally, and Muslims specifically, are represented as a threat to liberal democracy in part because the *dhimmi* rules sanctify discrimination on grounds of religious belief.

Before addressing examples from Europe and the United States, though, it is useful to illuminate how the *dhimmi* rules serve pedagogic functions in Muslim majority countries contending with their own place in a global community of states and transnational capital flows. For example, elsewhere I have written about the operation of certain *dhimmi* rules in the modern state of Saudi Arabia, in particular, the rules governing the measure of wrongful death damages (*diyya*) (Emon, 2008). According to the Philippines Consulate in Jeddah, Saudi Arabia, the families of Philippine expatriates working in the Kingdom can claim wrongful death compensation pursuant to a schedule of fixed amounts. However, the amounts vary depending on the victim's religious convictions and gender. If the victim is a Muslim male, his family can claim SR100,000. But if the victim is a Christian or Jewish male, the family can only claim half that amount, namely SR50,000. Further, if the victim belongs to another faith group, such as Hinduism, his family can claim only approximately SR6,666. The family of a female victim can claim half the amount allowed for her male co-religionist.[20]

Arguably, Saudi Arabia patterns its wrongful death compensatory regime on early Hanbali rules of tort liability. Premodern Muslim jurists held that the *diyya* or wrongful death compensation for a free Muslim male was 100 camels (al-Ghazali, 2001: 4:64; al-Shirazi, 1995: 3:210). But if the victim was a Jew or Christian male, his family could only claim a percentage of that amount. The Shafi'is held that the family was entitled to one-third of what a free Muslim male's family would receive (al-Shafi'i, 1990: 3:113; al-Mawardi, 1994: 12:308; al-Nawawi, 1991: 9:258; al-Ramli, 1992: 7:320). But the Malikis and Hanbalis granted them one-half of what a Muslim's family could obtain.[21] Furthermore, Sunni and Shi'a jurists held that if the victim was a Magian (*majus*), his family received even less at just 1/15th of what a Muslim family would obtain.[22] Importantly, 1/15th of SR100,000 is approximately SR6,666, the amount a Hindu male's family, for instance, can claim under Saudi law.

What is the significance of the *dhimmi* rules in a modern state such as Saudi Arabia? On the one hand Saudi Arabia is exceptional in its implementation of these rules as a matter of law. But that the *dhimmi* rules are still invoked outside the legal sphere, such as educational and cultural programming, is not exceptional. For instance, in her analysis of Saudi Arabian high school textbooks, Eleanor Doumato notes that some lessons use the *dhimmi* rules to instruct Muslim students on how to best position themselves in the world:

> With no mediating discussion or attempt to place the restrictions in historical context, the chapter ends with questions posed to the students such as 'What is the judgement about greeting the ahl al-dhimma on their holidays?' . . . leaving the impression that the historical

> relationship of inferior subject people to superior conquering people is meant as a model with contemporary relevance.
>
> *(Doumato, 2003: 237–238)*

According to Doumato, the textbook does not aim to incite aggression against non-Muslim others. Instead it adopts a pedagogy based in a post-colonial angst and defensiveness of a people who face existential threats to their wellbeing. The Saudi textbooks inculcate a traditional set of values for a people who feel 'they have inherited an ancestral past, but then experience[d] a sense of being threatened. The threat may be something vague such as a fear of "identity diffusion" or secularism, or it might be quite concrete, such as assault by outsiders' (Doumato, 2003: 233).

Across the ocean, the *dhimmi* rules inform a security industry that seeks to influence official policy in Europe and the United States. In a post-9/11 security environment, when we have moved from a sole focus on the hydra-headed al-Qaida to a wider range of actors (e.g. ISIS, Boko Haram, al-Shabaab) who are recruiting from around the world, how might one understand the end-game of these extremist groups? In a report issued by the Center for Security Policy (2010: 1) entitled *The Shari'ah: The Threat to America*, a team of security experts, led by Lt. Gen. William Boykin (ret.) and Lt. Gen. Harry E. Soyster (ret.), spent months studying and assessing the 'preeminent totalitarian threat of our time: the legal-political-military doctrine known within Islam as shariah'. The Boykin-Soyster team concluded that since our enemy cites doctrines from within the rich tradition of Shariʿa, then Shariʿa (whatever that might be) is the problem. 'Shariah is the crucial fault line of Islam's internecine struggle' (Center for Security Policy, 2010: 6). Indeed, the report proclaims: '7th Century impulses, enshrined in shariah, have reemerged as the most critical existential threat to constitutional governance and the freedom-loving, reason-driven principles that undergird Western civilization' (Center for Security Policy, 2010: 10). Curiously, the authors expressed their concern about Shariʿa in part by reference to the *dhimmi* rules. Critical of Western diplomats who don Islamic attire on diplomatic missions, the authors state: 'this sort of behavior demonstrates a kind of pre-emptive submission on the part of non-Muslim Westerners who adopt a subservient mentality of *dhimmitude*, erroneously believing their diplomacy, interview or outreach will go the better for it' (Center for Security Policy, 2010: 56).

Ironically, the *dhimmi* rules perform for American security pundits the same pedagogic function as they do for school children in Saudi Arabia. Whether or not the *dhimmi* rules are ever applied formally or even operate informally, they are invoked in both contexts to inform the relative position between Muslims and others. In neither context are they historicized or subjected to legal analysis and critique. They are read as if their meaning is transparent, as if the words of a treatise (whether in Arabic or translated) speak with clarity and precision to a present that is politically organized in ways that were unforeseeable when these rules were crafted centuries ago. To move beyond this polemic requires that we examine the *dhimmi* rules in terms of what Pierre Bourdieu would call the 'juridical field' or the various empirical and material practices and assumptions that make certain understandings of the *dhimmi* rules possible, meaningful, and responsive (Bourdieu, 1987).

Conclusion: regulating difference

The above legal analysis of premodern *dhimmi* rules showed that the conceptual lens of tolerance misses how these rules are symptoms of the shared, and increasingly apparent, challenge of governing a diverse demographic. Whether framed in terms of racial politics (Omi and Winant, 2015), multicultural governance (Kymlicka, 1995), or reasonable accommodation (Bouchard and Taylor, 2008), contemporary debates about managing diversity have more in common with the premodern *dhimmi* rules than most commentators on the historical tradition have noticed.

Of course, there is no denying that the *dhimmi* rules differentiated between people in ways that many today would describe as outright discriminatory. But as we all too painfully know, the regulation of minorities often indulges in discrimination in the service of some presumed broader goal, often defined along majoritarian lines. For instance, countries in Europe and North America are increasingly issuing (and passing) legislation that bans certain forms of veiling for Muslim women. Summer 2016 witnessed the controversy in France about Muslim women who wear the *burkini* on French beaches. Mayors persisted with enacting bans even as the courts invalidated them. As Cannes official Thierry Migoule argued, the burkini is 'clothing that conveys an allegiance to the terrorist movements that are waging war against us'.[23]

Beyond individual fashion, governments are increasingly directing regulatory efforts against mosques in Europe and the United States. In Switzerland, a popular referenda led to the successful constitutional ban on minarets. Notoriously prominent during the referendum campaign were posters that featured an ominous image of a niqab wearing woman standing next to missile-like minarets emanating from the Swiss flag (Caldwell, 2009; Nurrohman, 2009: 7). In New York City and Murfreesboro, Tennessee, debates about zoning permits turned into protests over the erection of mosques.

Majoritarian governance will often cause hardship for minorities. It is hard to ignore that the Muslim today is securitized at a time when the so-called War on Terror has infected the halls of government and the corners of high streets around the world. The language of justification may invoke 'security', but more often than not, the promotion of 'security' is meant to promote the presumed core values that some believe are under threat from foreign interests positioned both externally and internally. Whether under premodern Islamic law or more contemporary constitutional legal systems, legal and political arguments are used to regulate the bodies of the 'other'. But as this chapter shows, in the Islamic and liberal constitutional case, both legal systems address anxieties about the public good by targeting those who are different and, quite often, powerless to resist.

Notes

1 Al-Juwayni's use of 'imam' coincides with the usage of caliph in this report.
2 For an extended study on the *dhimmis* and the *dhimmi* rules as symptoms of the larger challenge of governing a diverse polity, see Emon, 2012b.
3 For a discussion of this dichotomous world view and its limitations, see El Fadl, 1994.
4 For a discussion of this literature, see chapter 1 in Emon, 2012b.
5 Of particular note here is Huntington's (1993, 1996) well-known 'clash of civilizations' thesis, though Huntington was less interested in pre-modern Islamic intellectual history and more interested in geo-political predictors.
6 For an overview of the field of *siyar* in Islamic law and history, and its invocation as an 'Islamic law of nations', see Bsoul, 2008b.
7 For a more extensive analysis of his case, see chapter 4 in Emon, 2012b.
8 For a concise overview of the myths and countermyths, see Cohen, 1996.
9 For books in Arabic and English that provide an introduction and overview of the *dhimmi* rules, see Zaydan, 1988 and Friedmann, 2003.
10 The punishment for consuming alcohol is generally held to be 40 lashes, although some schools such as the Malikis required 80. For a discussion of this debate, see Hassan, 1971: 73.
11 See also, al-Tanukhi, n.d.: 6:270, who does not apply the punishment for consumption of alcohol to the *dhimmi*.
12 For a general discussion on the exception to the punishment for alcohol consumption, see Zaydan, 1988: 179–180.
13 Al-Mawardi (1994: 8:328–330) wrote that there is a dispute about whether a non-Muslim can make a bequest to anyone other than a free Muslim of legal majority. Al-Nawawi (1991: 5:317) held that a *waqf*

could be for the benefit of a *dhimmi*, but not for an enemy of the state (*harbi*) or apostate. Al-Shirazi (1995: 2:323–324) allowed *waqfs* for specified *dhimmis* but noted the debate about *waqfs* for the benefit of apostates or enemies of the state.

14 Al-Ghazali, 2001: 3:41–42; al-Nawawi, 1991: 6:107, allowed a *wasiyya* to be for the benefit of *dhimmis, harbis*, and apostates; Qudama, n.d.: 6:103, analogized a *wasiyya* to a gift, and said that both could be given to *dhimmis* and *harbis* in the *dar al-harb*; Abu 'Abd Allah b. Muflih, 1997: 4:513l; al-Bahuti, 1997: 4:442; al-Hilli, 1998: 1:482.

15 The Ja'fari al-Muhaqqiq al-Hilli interestingly held that a *Muslim* could not create a *waqf* to support a church, synagogue, or schools for studying the Torah or Bible. However, he allowed a non-Muslim to do so, thus introducing yet another complicated piece into the debate. See al-Hilli, 1998: 1:459.

16 For another argument, the Hanbali Ibn Qudama (n.d.: 6:105) argued that a bequest could not be made to support schools for teaching the Torah or the Bible because both had been abrogated by the Qur'an and contain corruptions. See also al-Bahuti, 1997: 4:442.

17 On the rules of inheritance in the Qur'an and Islamic law, see Q 4: 11–12; Powers, 1986.

18 See also al-Hattab (1995: 8:515) who relates this view and critiques another that upholds the validity of any *wasiyya* by a *kafir*; al-Qarafi, 1994: 7:12.

19 However, Ibn Rushd did note others who disagreed with him, and held that the estate escheats to the state when there is no heir. Al-Qarafi (1994: 7:12) held the same view as Ibn Rushd al-Jadd but also noted the disagreement on this issue.

20 Philippines Consulate General, http://jeddahpcg.dfa.gov.ph/qisas-and-diyya-or-blood-money (accessed January 11, 2017).

21 Anas (1997: 2:434–435) related that 'Umar II decided that the *diyya* for a killed Jew or Christian is half the *diyya* for free Muslim male'. See also al-Jadd, 1988b: 3:295; al-Hafid, 1997: 2:604–605; al-Qarafi, 1994: 12:356; Qudama, n.d.: 7:793–794, who said that Ahmad b. Hanbal held the amount was one-third, but then changed his position to one-half. Muflih (1997: 6:16) also indicated some would provide the Muslim *diyya* for *dhimmis* if the latter were killed intentionally. However, Maliki and Hanbali jurists held that in personal injury cases (*jirahat*), the *diyya* for the injury is whatever a free Muslim male would get (Anas, 1997: 2:434–435; Sahnun, n.d.: 6:395; Qudama, n.d.: 7:795; al-Bahuti, 1997: 6:23–24).

22 Al-Shafi'i, 1990: 3:113; al-Ghazali, 2001: 4:67; al-Mawardi, 1994: 12:311; al-Nawawi, 1991: 9:258, who said that the *majus* get *thultha 'ushr* of the *diyya* for a free Muslim male; al-Ramli, 1992: 7:320. Notably, Ibn Qudama (n.d.: 7:796) related a minority opinion held by al-Nakha'i and others who equated the *diyya* for the *majus* and free Muslims because both are free and inviolable human beings (*adami hurr ma'sum*). The Ja'fari al-Muhaqqiq al-Hilli (1998: 2:489) related three views, namely that Jews, Christians, and Magians are valued at 800 *dirhams*, or all enjoy the same *diyya* as Muslims, or that Christians and Jews are entitled to 4,000 *dirhams*. According to the Ja'fari al-'Amili (nd: 19:141–142), the *diyya* of a free Muslim male is roughly 10,000 *dirhams*, while the *diyya* of a *dhimmi* Jew or Christian is 4,000 *dirhams*, and the *diyya* of the *majus* is 800 dirhams, roughly 40% and 8% respectively of the *diyya* for a free Muslim male.

23 New York Times Editorial Board. 'France's Burkini Bigotry'. *The New York Times*, August 18, 2016. Available at www.nytimes.com/2016/08/19/opinion/frances-burkini-bigotry.html?_r=0.

References

Al-'Amili, a.-H. nd. *Wasa'il al-Shi'a ila Tahsil Masa'il al-Shari'a*. Beirut: Dar Ihya' al-Turath al-'Arabi.

Al-'Ayni, B. al-D. 2000. *al-Binaya Sharh al-Hidaya*. Dar al-Kutub al-'Ilmiyya.

Al-Bahuti. 1997. *Kashshaf al-Qina' 'an Matn al-Iqna'*. Dar al-Kutub al-'Ilmiyya.

Al-Ghazali, A. H. 2001. *al-Wasit fi al-Madhhab*. Dar al-Kutub al-'Ilmiyya.

Al-Hafid, I. R. 1997. *Bidayat al-Mujtahid wa Nihayat al-Muqtasid*. Dar al-Kutub al-'Ilmiyya.

Al-Hattab. 1995. *Mawahib al-Jalil*. Dar al-Kutub al-'Ilmiyya.

Al-Hilli, a.-M. 1998. *Shara'i' al-Islam fi Masa'il al-Halal wa al-Haram*. 10th edn. Markaz al-Rasl al-A'zam.

Al-Jadd, I. R. 1988a. *al-Bayan wa al-Tahsil*. Dar al-Gharb al-Islami.

Al-Jadd, I. R. 1988b. *al-Muqaddimat al-Mumahhidat*. Dar al-Gharb al-Islami.

Al-Juwayni. 1997. *al-Ghiyathi: Ghiyath al-Umam fi Iltiyath al-Zulam*. Dar al-Kutub al-'Ilmiyya.

Al-Kasani, A. B. 1997. *Bada'i' al-Sana'i' fi Tartib al-Shara'i'*. Dar al-Kutub al-'Ilmiyya.

Al-Mawardi, A. a.-H. 1994. *al-Hawi al-Kabir*. Dar al-Kutub al-'Ilmiyya.

Al-Muzani. 1990. 'Mukhtasar al-Muzani' in al-Shafi'i (ed.) *Kitab al-Umm*. Vol. 5. Dar al-Fikr.

Al-Nawawi. 1991. *Rawdat al-Talibin wa 'Umdat al-Muftin*. 3rd edn. Al-Maktab al-Islami.
Al-Qarafi, S. a.-D. 1994. *al-Dhakhira*. Dar al-Gharb al-Islami.
Al-Ramli, I. S. a.-D. 1992. *Nihayat al-Muhtaj ila Sharh al-Minhaj*. 3rd edn. Dar Ihya' al-Turath al-'Arabi.
Al-Sarakhsi. 1997. *Sharh Kitab al-Siyar al-Kabir*. Dar al-Kutub al-'Ilmiyya.
Al-Shafi'i, M. b. I. 1990. *Kitab al-Umm*. Dar al-Fikr.
Al-Shirazi, A. I. 1995. *al-Muhadhdhab fi Fiqh al-Imam al-Shafi'i*. Dar al-Kutub al-'Ilmiyya.
Anas, Malik b. 1997. *al-Muwatta'*. Dar al-Gharb al-Islami.
Bouchard, G. and Taylor, C. 2008. *Building the Future: A Time for Reconciliation*. Government of Quebec.
Bourdieu, P. 1987. 'The Force of Law: Toward a Sociology of the Juridical Field'. 38 *Hastings Law Journal*. 805.
Brown, W. 2008. *Regulating Aversion: Tolerance in the Age of Identity and Empire*. Princeton University Press.
Bsoul, L. 2008a. *International Treaties (Mu'ahadat) in Islam*. University Press of America.
Bsoul, L. 2008b. 'Historical Evolution of Islamic Law of Nations/Siyar: Between Memory and Desire'. 17(1) *DOMES*. 48.
Caldwell, C. 2009. 'No Minarets, Please'. 15(3) *The Weekly Standard*.
Center for Security Policy. 2010. *Shariah: The Threat to America: An Exercise in Competitive Analysis: Report of Team 'B'II*.
Cohen, M. 1996. 'Islam and the Jews: Myth, Counter-Myth, History' in S. Deshen and W. Zenner (eds) *Jews among Muslims: Communities in the Precolonial Middle East*. New York University Press. 50.
Crone, P. 2004. *God's Rule: Government and Islam: Six Centuries of Medieval Islamic Political Thought*. Columbia University Press.
Doumato, E. 2003. 'Manning the Barricades: Islam According to Saudi Arabia's School Texts'. 57(2) *Middle East Journal*. 230.
Emon, A. M. 2008. 'The Limits of Constitutionalism in the Muslim World: History and Identity in Islamic Law' in S. Choudhry (ed.) *Constitutional Design for Divided Societies*. Oxford University Press. 258.
Emon, A. M. 2012a. 'On Sovereignties in Islamic Legal History'. 4(2–3) *Middle East Law and Governance*. 265.
Emon, A. M. 2012b. *Religious Pluralism and Islamic Law: Dhimmis and Others in the Empire of Law*. Oxford University Press.
Emon, A. M. 2013. 'The Paradox of Equality and the Politics of Difference: Gender Equality, Islamic Law and the Modern State' in Z. Mir-Hosseini et al. (eds) *Gender and Equality in Islamic Law: Justice and Ethics in the Islamic Legal Tradition*. IB Tauris. 237.
El Fadl, K. 1994. 'Islamic Law and Muslim Minorities: The Juristic Discourses on Muslim Minorities from the Second/Eighth to the Eleventh/Seventeenth Centuries'. 1(2) *Islamic Law and Society*. 141.
Friedmann, Y. 2003. *Tolerance and Coercion in Islam*. Cambridge University Press.
Gibb, H. A. R. 1955. 'Constitutional Organization' in M. Khadduri and H. Liebesny (eds) *Law in the Middle East: Origin and Development of Islamic Law*. Middle East Institute. 3.
Hamidullah, M. 1945. *Muslim Conduct of State*. Sh. Muhammad Ashraf.
Hassan, H. 1971. *Nazariyyat al-Maslaha fi al-Fiqh al-Islami*. Dar al-Nahda al-'Arabiyya.
Huntington, S. 1993. 'Clash of Civilizations?' 72(3) *Foreign Affairs*. 22.
Huntington, S. 1996. *The Clash of Civilizations and the Remaking of World Order*. Simon & Schuster.
Ibn Hazm. n.d. *al-Muhalla bi'l-Athar*. Dar al-Kutub al-'Ilmiyya.
Ibn Nujaym. 1997. *al-Sharh al-Bahr al-Ra'iq*. Dar al-Kutub al-'Ilmiyya.
Ibn Qudama. n.d. *al-Mughni*. Dar Ihya' al-Turath al-'Arabi.
Khalilieh, H. 2014. 'Aman' in K. Fleet et al. (eds) *Encyclopaedia of Islam*. Brill. Online version at http://dx.doi.org/10.1163/1573-3912_ei3_SIM_0048
Kymlicka, W. 1995. *Multicultural Citizenship*. Oxford University Press.
March, A. F. 2009. *Islam and Liberal Citizenship: The Search for an Overlapping Consensus*. Oxford University Press.
Muflih, A. 1997. *al-Furu'*. Dar al-Kutub al-'Ilmiyya.
Nurrohman, B. 2009. 'A Lesson to Draw from the Swiss Ban on Minarets'. *The Jakarta Post*. 15 December. 7.
Omi, M. and Winant, H. 2015. *Racial Formation in the United States*. 3rd edn. Routledge.
Powers, D. 1986. *Studies in Qur'an and Hadith: The Formation of the Islamic Law of Inheritance*. University of California Press.
Sahnun b. Sa'id. n.d. *al-Mudawwana al-Kubra*. Dar Sadir.
Sharify-Funk, M. 2013. 'Pervasive Anxiety about Islam: A Critical Reading of Contemporary "Clash" Literature'. 4 *Religions*. 443.
Zaydan, 'A. a.-K. 1988. *Ahkam al-Dhimmiyin wa al-Musta'minin fi Dar al-Islam*. Mu'assasat al-Risala.

24

Hindu law perspectives

The legal other

Werner Menski and Zoe Headley

This contribution relies on our respective strengths as two very different scholars on India and specifically Hindu law, religion and society. It answers the three questions put to us by indicating considerable reservations about whether such questions would make sense to most Hindus, either earlier or today. With regard to Hindu 'religion' (Knott, 1998), not even to speak of Hindu 'law' (Menski, 2003), the ubiquitous phenomenon of co-existence of multiple normative orders and the diversity of the nature of their interactions with each other (which may be cooperative, antagonistic or indifferent) within its fold forces observers and analysts, insiders and outsiders alike, to be intensely plurality-conscious. However, in the available literature, blatantly reductionist assumptions about the uniform nature of Hindu law are often forcefully expressed by scholarly imaginations,[1] powerfully pitted as some kind of essentialised 'Hindu' construct against the lived experience of most Hindus themselves, who constantly find themselves required to navigate and balance many competing expectations and often completely contradictory assumptions. While the internally pluralistic nature of Hinduism is actually well known (Sharma, 1996: 61), it remains thus true today that 'the private law of the Hindus is one of the most complicated in the world' (Derrett, 1957: 3). In addition, it is a global truism that times constantly change (Sharma, 1996: 5, 7) and that everything is highly dynamic. Change is powered by multiple processes of interaction (Chiba, 1986: 5), not only between indigenous and received elements but also individual needs and rights and cosmic concerns (Sharma, 2004: 36), to which one should today add group rights and human rights concepts. Everything is, following Deleuze and Guattari (1994), constantly becoming something, forever negotiated and contested through multiple engagements of various actors/actants. Aware of such volatile multilayered processes of development and constant argumentative discussions about them, Amartya Sen (2006: xii) highlights specifically the importance of understanding the long tradition of accepted heterodoxy in India:

> In resisting the attempts by the Hindutva activists to capture ancient India as their home ground (and to see it as the unique cradle of Indian civilization), it is not enough to point out that India has many other sources of culture as well. It is necessary also to see how much heterodoxy there has been in Indian thoughts and beliefs from very early days. Not only did Buddhists, Jains, agnostics and atheists compete with each other and with adherents of what

> we now call Hinduism (a much later term) in the India of the first millennium BCE, but also the dominant religion in India was Buddhism for nearly a thousand years . . . Ancient India cannot be fitted into the narrow box where the Hindutva activists want to incarcerate it.

Similarly, current discussions about Hinduism, Hindutva and Hindu law cannot just be neatly fitted into the globally dominant eurocentric parameters of 'model jurisprudence', in clearer language, assumptions about positive law, since these are actually themselves culture-specific (Chiba, 1986: 1–2) and tend to disrespect the perceptions of other legal cultures, particularly so-called 'Asian values'.[2] Neither can present global human rights discourses simply and uncritically presume a right to relegate Hinduism 'to the status of a permanent delinquent in the race of modernity' (Sharma, 1996: 2). Avoiding various forms of epistemic violence and intellectual colonialism through partial and elitist claims to supremacy of certain opinions and strategies, both in the camps of 'tradition' and 'modernity', and in the interface of law and society, as shown further later, requires great caution. This is necessary especially regarding often well-sounding and well-meaning suggestions for reform and improvement,[3] rather than accepting and respecting 'the other' on its own terms.[4]

Conflicts and tensions over drawing boundaries and managing difference in all domains (on caste, see Menski, 2016a) are hardly new. Given that Hinduism is a family of culturally similar traditions (Lipner, 1998: 6) marked by unity-in-diversity, it has been impossible to neatly define 'Hindu', 'Hinduism' or 'Hindu law'. The present contribution, perhaps more than others, therefore needs to break down the often alleged and perceived monoliths of Hinduism and Hindu law. Above all, it must discuss 'the other' also as a 'Hindu other', prominently in terms of sect, caste, class and – very importantly – regional differences, which now extend to the global Hindu diaspora. Hinduism as 'a potpourri of religions, doctrines and attitudes towards life, rites and cults, moral and social norms' (Michaels, 2004: 3) generates many messy, chaotic and highly contested socio-cultural and legal conflict scenarios within itself. The differing dispute settlement mechanisms observable in India, as many legal scholars know, but have too rarely researched in detail, are often matters of social re-balancing and stress management, not immediately subject to state-centric legal regulation. Studies by anthropologists on widespread recourse to forum shopping strategies in conflict management,[5] earlier as well as today, confirm that state law is only one among several forms of law. For the sake of conciseness and clarity, these differing legal orders can be condensed into four competing sets of internally plural legal expectations in constant need of dynamic balancing: (1) traditional forms of ethics/values/morality; (2) various social normativities; (3) state-centric laws; and (4) the principles and structures of modern human rights laws and international laws.[6]

Since Hindu law is clearly not primarily state law, much of it remains regulated within the private informal sphere. Contests over private/public boundaries prominently manifest in the continuing huge role given to customary laws in Hindu marriage and divorce laws. Assessments of what may or may not be legally valid are highly sensitive to situation-specificity. Social control and personal agency remain important, reflected in the fact that the Hindu key concept of sanctions, *danda* ('punishment' by a stick) in Sanskrit, is itself so internally plural that it includes malicious gossip and tongue-lashing (*vakdanda*), instead of state-imposed, criminal penalties. The highest social sanction, based on early writings such as the *dharmasūtras*, is still found today, albeit episodically. It involves excluding and 'othering' the guilty individual or group from the community, often through severance of all religious, social and economical ties from the birth group.

In such highly contested plural contexts, where state law is itself primarily an outsider, state intervention may be called for by interested stakeholders. These may be individuals or private bodies, nowadays often NGOs, rarely without their own socio-political agenda. Recent pressures from international legal actors may, however, create additional chaos and disorder locally, rather than securing peace, harmony and/or justice among and between Hindus as individuals or groups through subtly negotiated processes of dispute settlement. A striking example of battles over the endurance of unrecognised legal fora is the recent 're-discovery' and purported shock by the press, and partly by the judiciary, of the pervasive hold of caste judicial assemblies (*khap panchayats*) in numerous, mostly rural, regions of India.[7] This illustrates in abundance that law (both national and international), local norms/traditions and 'religion/ethics' may conflict, or they may be mutually supportive, ignorant of each other, or complementary. The potential for competitive relationships has manifestly grown over time (Williams, 2006: 38–42). In such complex culture-related wars, the huge banyan tree of Hinduism (Lipner, 1998: 5) cannot be simply cut down, defined away, or just 'othered' as something 'extra-legal' by secularising reforms and aggressive legal interventions. It will always grow new shoots in response to regulatory efforts and give rise to new 'living laws'.

Since 2014, India is again ruled by a so-called Hindu nationalist government, which seems to have its own ideas about what 'Hindu law' is or may be, but also claims to recognise its constitutional obligations as a government for all Indians, not just for Hindus. In this highly politicised scenario, serious limitations exist for ignoring or sidelining non-Hindu 'others', especially in a lively democracy with more than 180 million Muslims and many other minorities, which increasingly claim recognition of their presence through the ballot box. Moreover, India has one of the most powerfully worded constitutions in the world,[8] which includes as a basic principle that Hindu-dominated India is not to become a Hindu state. While such legal guarantees are not trusted by human rights activists (on this predicament, see Baxi, 2008), it complicates discussions about 'otherness' within the global predominantly secular space that 'Hindu law' continues to exist as a viable, lively entity (Menski, 2003). In legal discourses about Hinduism and the related laws as 'the West's other' (Flood, 2003: 3), this comes out prominently today in fierce ideologically grounded battles over the continued recognition of personal law systems. Connecting law and religion with social structures, this ancient and well-tested method of legal regulation deeply upsets all those who seem to think that the post-modern world of law ought to be a purely secular space reserved for state law, inspired by global visions of human rights. In this scenario, an entity like Hindu religion is sought to be banished into a tight corner, kept as separate and as irrelevant as possible from legal regulation.[9] It needs to be clearly stated upfront that this is simply not a realistic basis or feasible strategy for debating or regulating the relationship of law, religion and society in South Asia today,[10] let alone assessing the place of Hindu law.

Other religious traditions and their laws

While, as indicated earlier, many different legal perspectives and jurisdictions exist within the broad 'Hindu' framework itself, there is also much to say about the treatment of non-Hindu legal others in Indian laws.[11] Since its earliest conceptual beginnings, Hinduism has always encountered multiple manifestations of internal difference and otherness. Hence, not only today are Hindus themselves, both as individuals and/or as groups, frequently 'others', even 'legal others', for other Hindus. This 'otherness' unfolds in so many different ways that it is impossible to review all of them here.

Many studies attest widespread syncretic practices among Hindus, Muslims, Sikhs and Christians throughout India. Much-cited examples are Hindu-Christians in various parts of South India. Derrett (1968: 49) noted that 'a Hindu may accept Christianity, and, in these days, even undergo baptism, without ceasing to be a Hindu in both social and spiritual terms'. Further examples are provided by Derrett (1968: 59–60) and many others. Among diasporic Hindus, too, one observes that many place Christ's image among various Hindu deities. Hindu-Muslim syncretisms are prominent, too. Sharma (1996: 23) alludes to a familiar phenomenon when he recounts how a Hindu man used a Muslim healer in a moment of crisis. Similarly, especially in Punjab,[12] one can see Hindu Sikhs, basically clean-shaven Hindus who perform Sikh rituals, as well as Sikh Hindus, turban-wearing Sikhs with Hindu surnames such as Ram, Pal, or Das.[13] Such hybrid socio-cultural arrangements may carry important legal consequences, associated with inheritance, property rights, or access to the much-debated reservations in education and employment under policies of positive discrimination or affirmative action for various communities, mainly, but by no means only, for Scheduled Castes and Scheduled Tribes.[14] Marking differences in a variety of ways to assert one's own culture and/or reconstruct one's heritage (Singh, 2016) shows that being 'other' increasingly becomes a matter of pride and a sign of communal and individual self-confidence.

In explicitly legal contexts, questions arise about how each religious legal system (which is anyway never just purely 'religious') considers other normative orders and how this influences relations to individuals who are not members of the respective religious group, or are members of non-dominant Hindu groups. The main observation to make here is that India's personal law system actually secures normative acceptance of the long-established fact that Hindu law co-exists with Muslim, Christian, Parsi and Jewish personal laws. Smaller groups like the Bahais do not have their own recognised legal space, but can, like atheists or anybody who wishes to, use the optional parallel secular legal provisions, such as the Special Marriage Act of 1954. However, since use of such formal laws is also not unproblematic (Mody, 2008), staying away from state law and legal formality and relying on informal customary norms may be preferred. Precisely related to this, particularly the legal position of many peripheral tribal communities remains deeply contested (Solanki, 2011). Much could also be said about the post-colonial inclusion of Sikhs, Buddhists and Jains under the umbrella of Hindu personal law (Menski, 2003: 293). This has led to ongoing anguished debates over community identity, presently especially among Jains (Sethi, 2016).

It is important to note that the immensely broad conceptual framework of Hindu law has resulted in practice-focused principles to the effect that 'custom is and remains king'.[15] The rhetorical pre-eminence of custom during the colonial period mingled with another prominent feature of the British administration of justice to reinforce the recognition of diverse socio-legal normative orders among Hindus. The principle of non-cognizance of caste questions, which dates back to the Elphinstone Code (1827), enshrined the recognition of socio-cultural diversity among Hindus along caste lines (Headley, 2018). Though this principle was mitigated over time through several legislations, it loomed large in colonial court rooms, serving to dismiss a vast number of cases as beyond the purview of the court. While it was made virtually impossible for many litigants to satisfy the high formal standards of proof to establish custom, Hindu law has maintained strong presumptions about marriage and divorce to keep law and society in harmony (Desai, 1998, 65–68). Such problems persist in administering Hindu law today, causing disastrous results for women if judges are not alert to social reality.[16] Sen (2006: 34–35) emphasises that the right to custom established what may be called 'equity of recognition', reflecting the impossibility of imposing uniform standards that could bind Hindus of all kinds. As a consequence of such deep-rooted recognition for the customs of Hindu 'others', on the basis of principles of equity, the respective customs of non-Hindu 'others' are then also entitled to recognition as appropriate regulatory mechanisms for such people.

Historically, such struggles of diversity management are not new at all. The most ancient antecedents of the cosmic Vedic visions of a holistic macrocosmic Order (Miller, 1986) were already characterised by much internal plurality. Awareness of the presence of local religious traditions, apart from the emerging Vedic conceptualisations, led to incorporation of many local concepts. While this emerging ancient hybrid vision of Order emphasised a convergence-inducing interconnectedness of everything that exists, this also posits significant divergences, since internal otherness and differentiation based on many kinds of criteria, including later of course caste, is not excluded.[17] Ultimately, then as now, 'every Hindu decides what is Hinduism' (Sharma, 2003: 13) and this 'liberal space within Hinduism' (Sharma, 2003: 2) cannot be defined away today by boisterous Hindutva ideologues and their aggressive use of surprisingly modern, positivistic strategies to claim power over minds and bodies.

Since the ancient Vedic Order as a symbiotic whole was manifestly made up of many interconnected parts, Raimundo Panikkar observed while discussing intellectual colonialism (see Miller, 1986: xv) that 'the modern western individualistic perspective is foreign to vedic culture in which all is interconnected and the function of a bigger complex'.[18] Philosophy in ancient India grappled with identifying – indeed imagining – the nature of the Absolute, coming up with several explanatory models, exemplified in the well-known Upanishadic phrase that the highest Absolute is neither this nor that (*neti-neti*), but still exists, visibly and invisibly.[19] These are ardently rational efforts, but since that super-human higher force could never be fully identified in any universally agreed form, early Hindus as a 'religious' imagined community never developed a central belief structure, with one dominating God, but stressed instead the importance of right consciousness and appropriate action. Early Hindus, well before that term itself existed, thus figured out the rational necessity to be prepared to disagree in order to survive harmoniously, allowing multiple ways of life, long before the term 'Hinduism' was coined. Hence the imagined world religion of Hinduism took a rather different shape than other 'religious' traditions and specifically traditions of 'the Book'. While 'Hinduism has many sacred texts' (Smith, 2003: 33), that certain groups of Hindus claim adherence to specific sacred texts or even a particular 'Holy Book' merely reinforces evidence that Hinduism is a collection of religions (see Knott, 1998).

Later efforts to circumscribe specific human duties, and more generally to denote various specific obligations in highly differentiated forms (the collective key term here is *dharma*), are recorded in abundance. None of this, though, amounts to universally binding norms. Instead, many situation-specific expectations and recommendations are coupled with many exceptions introduced by time-space contexts. Such suggestions and prescriptions are as much about the self as 'the other', the latter often ritually distinguished.[20] The ancient texts, but more significantly our modern interpretations, frequently attempt(ed) to sideline or even silence the power of individual discretion in favour of formal texts and rules.[21] These tend to be male-centric, heterosexual and patriarchal. For many observers, they also seem to dictate misogynistic patterns, so that partial citations from such texts can be used to prove anything to critique Hindu concepts as a primitive 'other'. Yet this amorphous textual mass could never have become a completely agreed, universally binding framework of reference for all Hindus and indeed provided rich foundations for constant argumentation (Sen, 2006).[22] The (however reluctant) agreement to disagree, very early on, always left huge spaces for negotiation and much scope for many types of 'the other' within Hinduism itself, not to speak of boundaries and overlaps with other religious traditions, as already discussed.

More recently, reformative state intervention in India, in Hindu law itself as well as the general constitutional and criminal law,[23] thus credibly appeals with some justification to individuals' awareness of specific duties, addressing equal citizens of a modern state. Most notably, Article 51A(j) in the Indian Constitution of 1950, as amended in 1976, makes it a duty of every citizen of India:

> [t]o strive towards excellence in all spheres of individual and collective activity so that the nation constantly rises to higher levels of endeavour and achievement.

Many scholars doubt whether this can be read, let alone trusted, as a secular re-phrasing of ancient Hindu core principles of *dharma* and even Order, now presented as obligations to a state entity. Was this not rather, as Sharma (2004: 19) observes, a dictatorial device to restrain common people's basic rights? Indeed, these provisions were introduced at a moment of crisis in the Indian legal system (Sharma, 2004: 19), after the Emergency declared by Indira Gandhi, amidst growing awareness that the contract-based system of early post-colonial governance had led to ever larger discrepancies between rich and poor. While this complex Article 51-A on Fundamental Duties as part of the Indian Constitution is manifestly not a rule of Hindu law, it seems inspired by Hindu but also humanitarian principles. Intriguingly, in a few well-chosen words, Article 51-A connects individual rights and obligations to group rights and legitimate expectations of positive collective action to the wider global context, suggesting the need for awareness of a kind of higher public interest than the secularly worded Indian Constitution may dare to express explicitly. This could, then, be read as a remarkably secular Indian statement of post-colonial legal consciousness feeding on ancient Hindu roots.

While such carefully chosen phraseology of basic duty effortlessly also includes all Muslim, Christian and other citizens of India,[24] this wording could not be interpreted as a deviously constructed effort at Hinduisation of India's whole body politic. Rather, this constitutes a sophisticated rephrasing of the ancient principle that everything – and everyone – should be imagined as connected and interactive, also in today's post-colonial contexts. There is, in that sense, no 'legal other'. This constitutional reminder of duties for all, rather than rights, indicates efforts to place fresh reliance on holistic self-controlled ordering principles. It suggests inclusion rather than exclusion, more respect and consideration for any potential 'other', ultimately to avoid total chaos (Menski, 2016a). While specific Hindu key terms like *karma* and *dharma* are studiously avoided in such highly sophisticated legal restructuring, culture-sensitive reading of these provisions identifies Hinduism-inspired hidden subtexts. Hindu terminology, however, would not even need to be used explicitly, as the idealistic message that public interest should prevail over private interest is actually shared by all religions within their specific visions of the cosmos.

The ease with which such inclusive messages continue to be emitted in India today, even in the new era of Hindu nationalist governance, seems remarkable. Unsurprisingly, as noted, this is not trusted by rights-focused critical observers. Yet despite reliance on effectively culture-specific basic claims as an interconnected cosmic system, these Hindu law perspectives necessarily involve recognition of various forms of the 'legal other', both Hindu and 'non-Hindu', built into the system since ancient times and continued today, subtly serving as one of the vitamins allowing India's multicultural democracy to remain stable, despite repeated predictions of disaster by detractors.

However, the highly politicised nature of global debates about Indian laws and religions largely overlooks and/or elides such finer points. Oddly, while equality has become the new guiding principle in the global language of constitutional rights, some forms of respect for diversity are seen as problematic by many modernist scholars. Certain elements of difference, prominently the personal law systems, are sought to be removed. In other respects, for example sexual orientation, difference is however sought to be protected, albeit on the basis of equality arguments. Moreover, India's various acknowledged differentiations do not stop at the human/non-human border, since the holistic Hindu value system seeks to include all aspects of creation. Often deliberately ignoring this, numerous partial assertions and counter-assertions dominate current highly contested academic discourses, preventing deeper conceptual debates. Indian laws, not afraid to name and identify such differences, are globally criticised for this approach.[25]

Significantly, resistance to such culture-conscious debates is also deeply entrenched in comparative law discussions. Western assertions of knowing better how to handle difference have been politely critiqued by some early comparative legal scholars from Asia, yet not from India.[26] Maybe this lack of critical voices from within India reflects the suppressive forces of colonialisation of minds in British India and its impact on subsequent law-related scholarship, which remains seriously underdeveloped in studies of law and society, and law and religion (see Baxi, 1986). Professor Masaji Chiba from Japan, whose work is largely unknown in Indian law schools, focused on socio-legal approaches, prominently the reception of foreign laws in Asia and the intense impact of value pluralism which resulted in new forms of legal hybridisation.[27] Chiba (1986: v) strongly critiqued Western presuppositions about the superiority of state-centric models of law and emphasised that Asian voices were deliberately silenced and simply not wanted at the debating table. His key message was, basically, that the legal systems of Asian countries remained Asian legal systems, even if they had imported or created large sets of rules that originated from Europe. That, of course, directly contradicts dominant presuppositions of the global domination of Western legal orders. Baxi (2008: 17) more recently added further doubts about the globalised effects of human rights activism, noting in his typically elaborate style that 'there is no assurance that rights-integrity governance structures, normatively blueprinted by the language of human rights, may anywhere fully translate into prospects of lived human rights for all'.

For the present discussion, this means that for Hindu-dominated secular post-colonial India, one wrongly presumes that either Hindu domination or the continued presence of the personal law system are per se problematic, unless we treat all laws as problematic. India's current legal system is not merely an inferior copy of English common law; rather, it has developed into a hugely sophisticated multi-cultural entity. This legal system evidently continues to face huge challenges in handling the living laws of the various people of India, especially their connections to various social and religious concepts. While 'the great chasm between custom and law remained' (Derrett, 1968: 305), formally unrecognised customs, which continue to be much more dynamic than lawyers realise, have quite evidently not ceased to exist in social reality, and they cannot be just 'othered'. Given that only about 5 per cent of cases, even today, reach the High Courts (Solanki, 2011: 32), informal customary, indeed 'living' Hindu law has neither been completely displaced nor abolished. It has remained a socio-legal phenomenon, which needs to be more fully researched.

An early prominent example of complete confusion was the litigation concerning Self-Respect Marriages (*suyamariyadhai*) in Tamil Nadu,[28] which do away with several key features of Brahmin-dominated Hindu weddings and were conducted without a Brahmin priest, the holy fire and the seven step ritual (*saptapadi*). This meant that thousands of such simple marriages risked being invalidated. It took the state law many years to introduce a formal legal amendment, the Hindu Marriage (Madras Amendment) Act of 1967, to revise the formal law by explicitly recognising the modified modern local customary practices. By and large, Indian lawyers have remained ignorant of Hindu customary law (Kishwar, 1994: 2160), resulting in important discrepancies in the legal management of cases involving so-called 'customary practices'. Indian law students are not sufficiently trained to analyse the many complex cases arising in their country. Any complications caused by the existence of minorities within various groups or reform efforts then allow instant politicisation of any contested boundaries. While some remedies to deficiencies in education and lack of practical handling of such cases may be offered by the various Judicial Academies at central and state levels, Indian family law teaching is generally undervalued. Most damagingly, it tends to keep complex socio-cultural questions of religious and customary norms out of most classrooms. The resulting gaps of knowledge about the spaces between law and society, and law and religion, are ruthlessly exploited when often highly politicised cases are brought to courts.[29] Often these are then milked by a sensationalising press, in India and abroad, which does not hesitate to 'morph' judgments through their own interpretations of what a case actually said.[30] Similarly a much-cited Supreme Court case, demanding compulsory registration of all marriages in India,[31] may have led to much agitated legal activity, but the current law of India remains plural, in that primarily the performance of religious rituals determines whether a marriage between two Hindus is legally valid or not.

Detailed research reports on this would go too far here, but the evidence confirms, in line with the above-cited argument of Baxi (2008: 17), that highly politicised formal processes of law making, especially in family law, cannot be trusted to take sufficient account of all stakeholders. Particularly, undue focus on middle class concerns and certain agenda of feminist activists may actually damage the basic rights of India's most disadvantaged citizens, including Dalits and many women and children (Menski, 2016b). Fortunately, common sense still prevails, so that the reformed Hindu law of 1955 continues to support strong presumptions of the legal validity of simple, customary Hindu marriages and divorces. While important protective mechanisms for the legal recognition of Hindu marriages and divorces exist, these are hidden away in section 29 of the same Act and are often more or less deliberately overlooked, but can be activated.[32]

These are not just matters of religion, then, but practical management problems related to religious and cultural value pluralism, diversity and resulting politics (Menski, 2016a). It is hence completely unsurprising that recent research identifies people's inclinations to keep as many disputes as possible out of the official courts and to use informal dispute settlement processes. Solanki (2011: xxii) even found that legal recognition of cultural pluralism through respect for local patterns of dispute settlement can facilitate gender equality. This is assisted by self-controlled ordering as an integral part of the lived experience of most Indians, for whom multi-locational justice is prominent (Solanki, 2011: 60). Solanki (2011: 67, 91) also found among a particular multi-religious caste community in Mumbai that Hindu concepts are often not that different from Muslim notions, confirming that the much-politicised major differences of the various personal law systems are not actually that great. The 'othering' itself is a deeply problematic act of devious construction.

Certain boundary problems may arise in mixed marriages, or when someone converts to a different religion, which may or may not have significant impacts on other members of the family. Given the hugely important arena of affirmative action policies in India, there is also much evidence that high caste and upper/middle class Hindus have become upset about excessive concessions being given to 'others'. Yet there is also much evidence that the structural need for such provisions is accepted. What irks such privileged Hindus, then, apart from often vile denigrations of Hinduism itself as a false religion and an inherently cruel form of culture, are perceived abuses, including efforts to pull low caste Hindus away from Hinduism by offering them various benefits. Current controversies over re-conversions, with the prominent term *ghar vapsi* denoting bringing such people 'back home', indicate further politics of difference that are not only related to questions of 'religion' and the 'othering' of religious minorities.[33]

Rights and obligations of non-adherents

The resurgence of local cultural and religious consciousness in India under the influence of modernity and globalisation has resulted in increasing complications in relation to the interaction between religious traditions (Anthony et al., 2005; Williams, 2006). We have already seen how strongly, at least on paper, the protective umbrella of the Indian Constitution of 1950 seeks to secure the rights and obligations of Indian citizens of all backgrounds and religions. While there is still sometimes claimed to be considerable disquiet on the part of the Indian state about defeat for the 'pious concept of WE THE PEOPLE' (Sethi, 2016: 59), India's democracy has remained strong also in times of adversities (Khilnani, 2012). The arduous management problem lies in the inherent tension between guaranteeing freedom of religion (Article 25) and then safeguarding the cultural and educational rights of minorities in India in terms of admissions to institutions (Article 29(2)) and the right to establish and administer minority educational institutions (Article 30(1)). These are ongoing, highly convoluted battles, in which both 'Hindu others' and non-Hindu minorities feature prominently.

A major concern should be to ensure safe spaces for adherents of different religious traditions in India to enjoy freedom of religion and basic rights connected to it, as individuals and as groups. These rights, however, as recent jurisprudence has established with increasing clarity, do not include the right to violate the basic rights of others. Some kind of higher public interest, that means, prevails over private interest and selfishness. Thus, a husband of whatever religious background who fails to provide for his wife, whether the couple is married or divorced, and provided he has the means to do so,[34] has a moral as well as legal obligation to maintain the woman.[35] There is also no doubt that fathers from all religious communities have to provide for their children. India is not a state-funded welfare state like Finland or Switzerland that would step in to provide remedies in such scenarios. These examples confirm that modern India needs its personal law structures to maintain the family-based Indian version of a post-modern welfare state system (Menski, 2001). Despite much disbelief, this goes also for Indian Muslims (Menski, 2008).

As noted, the management of religious institutions is sometimes contested as an aspect of freedom of religion. Since temple rituals became all-pervasive markers of social boundaries, high caste and low caste temple offerings may vary significantly, and exclusion of low caste people has been a frequent pattern (Flood, 2003: 7). Disputes may also arise over access to non-adherents of a particular religion; in numerous Hindu temples, access to the sanctum sanctorum is denied to non-Hindus. Sometimes, even Hindu women are banned from access to religious buildings on ritual grounds.[36] In efforts to strengthen provisions of equality, such forms of 'othering' are today treated as unacceptable, and even proof of custom may be challenged as constitutionally invalid by judges, as in the case of the Sabarimala temple barring women of reproductive age.

The modern state is here being involved in power struggles within certain societies and particular communities. This field, again, is highly politicised, so that in some cases there is coherent long-term evidence of more or less completely syncretic practices, such as Hindus going to mosques, *dargahs* and cathedrals to seek blessings (Mohammad, 2013). Some Muslims and Christians may attend Hindu festivals and visit Hindu places of worship (Lynton, 2009: 171–180 offers some anecdotal evidence). However, restrictive 'othering' practices are also reported, and from time to time riots break out when one religious community, often with much noise and provocative gestures, makes a public show of its strength and maybe claims domination of a particular facility or locality. Such activities indicate ongoing multi-level competition in India today over resources, but also over the definition of religion as a way of life rather than a 'religion'. In these ongoing struggles, it seems pointless to call for a complete segregation of law and religion. Prominent efforts by scholars and commentators to engage in partial politics to such effect often look like publicity stunts.

However, as indicated, the nature of complaints is often that certain 'others' (mainly Muslims and Christians, but also Dalits) have been given undue favours by the supposedly 'neutral', so-called secular state law. Hence, legal battles over affirmative action and India's powerful quota systems remain prominent. Another example is the constantly raised assertion that granting Indian Muslims continued rights to have up to four wives constitutes unlawful discrimination against Hindus. In practice, however, as diligent case analysis rather than journalistic assertion quickly confirms, the rhetorical formal criminalisation of Hindu polygamy is not actually implemented in practice. There are many Hindu polygamous marriages, too, and a Hindu woman in a polygynous marriage is still treated as party to some kind of marriage, whether sacramental or not. Hence she is also entitled to maintenance (Menski, 2001, 2003, 2006; Solanki, 2011: 198, 209), while the husband is unlikely to be criminalised, let alone jailed. Rather, as an 'able-bodied citizen', which is the relevant constitutional term of art, he is expected to make sufficient money for the privilege to be polygamous.

Clearly, to simply expect Hindus or Hindu-dominated India to shed the social and cultural elements that form the fabric of various hybrid Indic cultures and current Indian laws effectly asks several hundred million people to disown their identity. As Chiba (1986) seminally identified, many Western observers and their acolytes still struggle with accepting the Oriental 'other' as a legitimate socio-legal actor. Such approaches deny agency to non-Western people to operate their own legal systems, and to do so, as the social anthropologist Roger Ballard (1994: 8) has called this, 'on their own terms'. Deep-rooted resentment of the fact that contemporary non-Western societies engage in ongoing processes of self-developing their indigenous law, whether successfully or not, as Chiba (1986: v) pointedly noted, rather than treating their laws as received legal systems, seems to underlie much of the current hostility and critiques of Indian laws and particularly Hindu law.

The state and international human rights obligations

In Indian law, there are no serious indications of Hindus refusing to recognise the superiority of state law and democracy, as an idea, 'has irrevocably entered the Indian political imagination' (Khilnani, 2012: 60). Centuries of colonial subjugation probably settled that particular issue, though adherence to a plethora of highly diverse customs remains strong. Wood (2004: 39) rightly states that 'a balanced assessment of something so complex as democracy in India is not easy'. This sums up, to some extent, what the previous sections have already documented in various ways, namely that the global scholarship on international law and human rights frequently fails to understand even the most basic elements of India's extremely hybrid cultural foundations, socio-religious orientations and Hindu domination.

We have already identified and critically highlighted the prominent global view that 'Hinduism' – and by implication the state of India – is widely treated as a virtual serial offender in the global ranking systems of compliance with international laws and human rights norms. The shelves of libraries worldwide are filled with books which aim to criticise everything that goes on in India, either blaming 'tradition', 'religion', or nowadays the Indian state, more so since a 'Hindu nationalist' leadership gained power in 2014. Like previous Indian governments, it refuses to fall into line with many international law principles held up as the global gold standard.[37] The availability of internet facilities has made these largely media-based battles even more aggressive. India is frequently being framed as though state law had no space in Indian law today, and rabid Hinduisation was rampant. It is notable how the term *hindutva* is being employed in such contexts. Deeply contested (see in detail Sharma, 2003), it really means 'Hinduness' first of all, a commitment to Hindu identity, not immediately enforced Hinduisation of 'others', and there is 'soft' and 'hard' Hindutva (Sharma, 2003: 7–8). Deliberate misuse of such terminology is giving away the underlying agenda that any commitment to Hindu identity per se, as already identified earlier, is widely perceived and portrayed as an act of political incorrectness and violence. Muslims, too, are often happy to engage in similar anti-Hindu arguments.[38] By claiming that so-called Hindu fundamentalists are arguing for certain completely unacceptable positions, global scholarship, perhaps largely inadvertently, endorses and thereby actually encourages certain radical Hindu perspectives (Sarkar, 2001), which are not even maintainable on closer inspection of what Hinduism actually is and stands for. It does not help that similar accusations can be levelled against abuses of global rhetoric relating to Islamic law and religion. The key argument here would be that many so-called Islamic views and perspectives are not in fact truly Islamic, but man-made constructs, unsupported by the wider ethical framework of the divine sources of Qur'an and Sunna. In view of the much deeper historical roots of Hinduism, the structural implausibility for relying on divine Hindu revelation makes it even more evident that 'hard' forms of Hindu fundamentalism are politicised aberrations, sad reflections of the current global chaos caused by new forms of culture wars. Claims that certain leaders of Hinduism, whether as heads of mutts (*mattas*), caste gurus, or certain leaders of caste and village *panchayats* represent 'the law', rather than the Constitution and the courts of the country, are thus inflated, to say the least.[39]

In legal terms, ultimate formal and unifying authority rests with the judges of the Indian Supreme Court, while from a bottom-up Hindu perspective, the ultimate moral authority remains, to reiterate, the conscience of the individual Hindu (Menski, 2003: 125–127; Sharma, 2003: 2). This is one reason why self-controlled action, through widespread recognition of customary laws, and much respect for local patterns of 'living law' have remained so strong within the Indian legal system. If for a self-conscious Hindu 'the other' is already an inseparable part of the self, not just the person in the next hut or apartment, then there is of necessity limited scope for legitimate 'othering' and little reason for state involvement in the daily religious politics of Indian citizens.

At the same time, the Indian state as a member of the international community cannot – and does not – completely divorce itself from the agenda and expectations of the international community. There is ample evidence from recent Indian jurisprudence of efforts and well-considered readiness to take account of international law principles.[40] The properly balanced strategy, however, is to be selective and circumspect in what one seeks to adopt and/or copy from others. At the same time, India's (often rather too idolised) vision of its own contribution to the global process of developing a sustainable future for mankind, while much-debated, cannot be completely unsettled by inflammatory arguments that there are incontrovertible discrepancies between Hinduism and human rights. The major study that tackles this particular issue explains well that the dominant Hindu perspective is grounded in a dialectic of duty (Sharma, 2004: 33), which approaches basic common questions about human rights from a different perspective, but has ultimately the same aims as so-called 'Western' human rights discourses (Sharma, 2004: 30).

Constant allegations that non-Western state laws such as those of Hindu-dominated India violate international human rights norms thus generate, as noted, not only self-serving forms of defensiveness (Sarkar, 2001). They risk metamorphosis into self-righteous forms of resentful overreaction, defending an imagined 'self' and opposing any equally legitimately constructed 'other'. This dichotomous process of assembling a threatening, feared and hated 'other' is then rhetorically or even physically taken out against such 'others', manifesting as individual violence or full-scale 'communal riots'. A plural nation such as India seems to be innately aware that such frightful conflict scenarios are not conducive to building a massive country into a viable democracy. Many Indians seem engaged in learning to be better Indians, no matter how peripheral they may be or are perceived to be.[41]

Faced with rather more unsuccessful models next door on either side,[42] India seems to be aware of the need to fly its own kite of law, with all the accompanying conflicts and tensions, continuously hoping to achieve better justice. This can only happen through explicit commitment to its own hybridity and internal plurality, rather than processes of discarding some people's culture and religion in efforts to construct a purportedly value-neutral or even secular 'rule of law' to fit purported global templates of imagined firm walls between law and religion. Indian secularism, for that reason, constitutes a firm commitment to respect and include 'the other', but it then also demands respect from those others. Panjabis in particular seem to have experienced the chasms of impending destruction of India from within (Singh, 2016). Fortunately, maybe because Hindu conceptual roots have not been completely forgotten, India is presently a unique model of a highly plural state-nation (rather than a nation-state). In a category of its own, it forms an entity that needs to be studied and engaged with, rather than being bullied and dictated to by others. This does not mean to say there are no confusions, abuses of power, or continuing problems over selective and often discriminatory 'othering' in India and/or among Hindus. But this innate awareness of being linked into a deeply plural larger entity somehow still holds water today. Provided one finds the right language to convey the need for balance and avoidance of chaos (see Menski, 2016a), reminders of 'tradition' can serve as corrective devices in times of chaos. Managing such wide-ranging diversity could never be a simple game of joyful, care-free kite flying. Rather, it is hard work, but that is precisely what India is currently engaged in, not only making remarkable economic progress but also working assiduously on reconstructing and re-imagining itself as a uniquely plural place, with Hindu principles as *Grundnorms*. In that internally plural space, being 'other' as part of this larger whole is simply part of being oneself. This self can be a rights-holding citizen of any kind under the protective umbrella of a Constitution that is, to reiterate, not merely a document in English but a restatement of what it means to be Hindu in the 21st century, not only living with Hindus but together with all kinds of people who are prepared to share that holistic vision.

Notes

1 The most obnoxious key example simply remains that Manu, as the ancient lawgiver of Hindus, acted like some kind of Napoleon to 'give' Hindus their law.
2 While there is little unanimity regarding the precise nature of Hindutva (Sharma, 2003: 1), the Asian values debate in comparative law analysis related to the interaction of law and culture (see Engle, 2000), remains undeveloped for Hindu law, but seems relevant (see Menski, 2003: 511; 2006).
3 Problems of reform arise not only in interaction between Western and non-Western actors, often in terms of reception of laws (Chiba, 1986: 5), but also within various discourses about gender and caste (Gupta, 2016) and even within lower castes (Gundimeda, 2016: 329–330).
4 For deep personal insights into such predicaments, see Lynton (2009).
5 The precursors in this field are the many writings of Srinivas since 1959 (see Srinivas, 1998) and Cohn (1965). More recent studies are Ananth Pur and Moore (2007), Hayden (1984, 1999), Holden (2003), Vincentnathan (1996), Chowdhry (2004) and Nagaraj (2012).
6 Inspired by Chiba (1986), and building on Menski (2006), this competitive scenario is now illustrated graphically as a kite flying in the air (Menski, 2014a, 2014b, 2014c).
7 The much-debated honour killing case of Manoj and Babli in 2007 is now a prominent feature on the global web. For spurious press-driven constructions of *panchayats* in South India, which set in motion a wave of criminalisation of village judicial practices, see Headley (2015).
8 The Indian Constitution of 1950 contains both a catalogue of Fundamental Rights and a today equally important set of Directive Principles of State Policy, whose implementation continues to pose major challenges, given the sheer size of the Indian Republic, with more than 1.2 billion very diverse people.
9 Evidently, this runs counter to the interactive pluralist model outlined in note 6 above.

10 See, however, the important recent article on the personal law system by Farrah Ahmed (2016) and the references contained therein. Ahmed (2016: 2) claims that 'personal law systems generally raise serious concerns relating to religious freedom; equality and non-discrimination; marital and family rights; and procedural rights'. In other words, personal laws are portrayed as a somewhat seriously wrong 'other', while there is no recognition that all forms of legal arrangements may be challenged on each of those grounds, for no law anywhere is just working perfectly. While Ahmed rehearses a politically attractive argument, her article runs the risk of ignoring the dangers of intellectual colonialism or simply the claim that 'the other' is misguided, hence displaying plain contempt for 'the other', or *Besserwisserei*, as one would say more succinctly in German.

11 The Indian state's deep disquiet about the idea of minority rights as a divisive fissiparous tendency is discussed by Sethi (2016) through cases of Jain claims for recognition as a separate minority.

12 The 1921 Census for Punjab returned the 'curious category' (Sethi, 2016: 55) of 'Jain-Hindus'.

13 We thank Surinder Singh for these details. He also confirms that in Punjab today, despite some reservations about intermarriages between Sikhs and Hindus, one still often sees that male children in the same family may be brought up either as Sikhs or Hindus. Some groups, such as the Kamboj caste of Ferozepur and Fazilka districts, perform the rituals and traditions of Sikhism, but identify themselves as Hindus.

14 On affirmative action in India, see Galanter (1984). This topic of 'reservations' for legal others is so complex that we cannot cover it here.

15 This principle was formally acknowledged in the Privy Council case of *Collector of Madura v. Moottoo Ramalinga* (1868) 12 MIA 397, holding that 'under the Hindu system of law, clear proof of usage will outweigh the written text of the law'.

16 For details see Menski (2001, 2003). In *Surjit Kaur v. Garja Singh*, AIR 1994 SC 135, the highest Court of the land failed to produce a correct situation-specific decision on the legal validity of a Sikh marriage, where the parties were remarrying and rituals would thus be minimal.

17 The precise nature of the relationship between Vedic Hindus and others around them remains contested, but undoubtedly such others existed and were gradually incorporated, more or less incompletely, into the Vedic framework (Zaehner, 1975 [1962]). See in this regard Miller (1986: 195) on the first references to *śūdra*, then still 'worker' or 'tiller of the soil', rather than the later Dalits.

18 This rootedness in cosmic links seems similar to African *Ubuntu* principles, which tend to stress 'we-ness' in social but also spiritual contexts.

19 Naipaul (2011: 13) identifies the need to remain somehow linked to 'religion' as a back-up insurance mechanism, given the often vague recognition of 'something you think of who's controlling the world'.

20 There is no space here to elaborate on the abundantly documented plurality of ritual diversities in the ancient texts themselves.

21 For a telling example concerning individual duty, see Menski (2006: 215–217). Knott (1998: 40) strongly supports the theorising of Sharma (1996) that the concept of *karma* actually signifies the free will of the individual rather than fatalistic pre-determination.

22 Recent work on Islam now brilliantly theorises the 'hermeneutical engagement with Revelation as Pre-Text, Text, and Con-Text' (S. Ahmed, 2016: 492), in a way that Hinduism could never even credibly claim to do, but this methodology needs to be also applied to future studies on the emergence of perceptions of Hindu law.

23 The most prominent example here would be the highly complex laws on post-divorce maintenance, treating all divorced Indian wives still as 'wives' to protect their financial position (see Menski, 2001: chapter 4; 2003: chapter 12; 2008).

24 Space restraints do not permit analysis of how these provisions have been used by Indian courts to remind individuals of their duties to others.

25 Opposing what one may call a 'jurisprudence of hope', which simply demands perfect legal rules, because that is seen as desirable and morally right, and asking instead for more plurality-conscious realism, Menski (2016a: 303) notes that Amartya Sen (2009) has seminally pointed out the deeply problematic nature of methodological efforts to secure justice through making perfect rules, rather than arduous efforts to manage diversity sustainably. Actually, Baxi (2008) argues along similar lines, as shown later.

26 The preface in Chiba (1986) is quite clear on this. On the 'Asian values' debate see above, note 2.

27 For a succinct summary of his main arguments, see Menski (2006: 119–128).

28 See *Deivaini Achi v Chitambaram Chettiar*, AIR 1954 Madras 657.

29 The world-famous, highly politicised case of *Sarla Mudgal v. Union of India*, AIR 1995 SC 1531, concerns the legal effects of a Hindu husband converting to Islam to allow himself a polygamous marriage.

30 A typical case of this kind is *D. Velusamy v. D. Patchaiammal*, AIR 2011 SC 479, which also concerns the largely unexplored politics between India's system of personal laws and the new class of general legislation within the same sphere, prominently the Protection of Women from Domestic Violence Act, 2005.
31 *Seema v Ashwani Kumar*, 2006 (2) *Supreme Court Cases* 578.
32 See on this Menski (2003: 445). Kishwar (1994: 2150) notes astutely that the Hindu Marriage Act of 1955 actually has two divorce laws.
33 For a number of heated exchanges on *ghar vapsi*, see the prominent journal *Economic & Political Weekly* between 2014 and 2015.
34 Indian courts have been quite clear that impecunity is a misfortune to be borne by both parties together, as the courts cannot magically produce maintenance from state funds.
35 Significantly, under the modern Hindu law, in section 25 of the Hindu Marriage Act, either spouse may seek maintenance payments from the other spouse. However, able-bodied Hindu husbands seeking to take advantage of this rule have been laughed out of court and were told to go and earn their own income.
36 Recently, the Shani Shingnapur temple (Maharashtra), the Haji Ali Dargah (Mumbai) and the Sabarimala Temple (Kerala) have been in the limelight over ongoing legal battles to allow women to enter these holy places.
37 Major examples would be India's refusals to strictly implement compulsory registration of all marriages and to introduce a minimum age of marriage which would be the same for both genders, namely 18 years. The resulting assertions of human rights abuses are frequently put-up claims to blacken the reputation of India and reflect resentment that a major Asian democracy is unwilling to simply follow western-led prescriptions of governance and 'rule of law'.
38 Mainly Muslims, rather than Hindus, seek to claim that God's law is superior to man's law, and then feel entitled to challenge state-made legal rules, much more aggressively than Hindus could ever credibly do. On misuse of such arguments to justify Taliban violence, see Watts (2015: 23).
39 On the mischief of such actors, see Menski (2006: 198).
40 One much-cited case, marking a shift towards a more liberal and gender-sensitive position, is *Vishaka v. State of Rajasthan* (1997) 6 SCC 241.
41 Several articles in *South Asia Research* over the past few years have picked up this theme, specifically for India's North-East.
42 However, also Pakistan and Bangladesh are painfully learning that self-destruction through excessive othering is a form of self-harm that can be avoided. For Pakistan, see Watts (2015); in Bangladesh the message is far less clearly stated.

References

Ahmed, F. 2016. 'Remedying Personal Law Systems'. 30(3) *International Journal of Law, Policy and the Family*. 248.

Ahmed, S. 2016. *What is Islam? The Importance of Being Islamic*. Princeton University Press.

Ananth Pur, K. and Moore, M. 2007. *Ambiguous Institutions: Traditional Governance and Local Democracy in Rural India. IDS Working Paper 282*. Institute of Development Studies of the University of Sussex.

Anthony, F.-V., Hermans, C. A. M. and Sterkens, C. 2005. 'Interpreting Religious Pluralism: Comparative Research among Christian, Muslim and Hindu Students in Tamil Nadu, India'. 18(2) *Journal of Empirical Theology*. 154.

Ballard, R. (ed.). 1994. *Desh Pardesh. The South Asian Presence in Britain*. Hurst & Co.

Baxi, U. 1986. *Towards a Sociology of Indian Law*. Satvahan.

Baxi, U. 2008. *The Future of Human Rights*. 3rd edn. Oxford University Press.

Chiba, M. (ed.). 1986. *Asian Indigenous Law in Interaction with Received Law*. KPI.

Chowdhry, P. 2004. 'Caste Panchayats and the Policing of Marriage in Haryana: Enforcing Kinship and Territorial Exogamy'. 38(1–2) *Contributions to Indian Sociology*. 1.

Cohn, B. S. 1965. 'Anthropological Notes on Disputes and Law in India'. 67(6) *American Anthropologist*. 82.

Deleuze, G. and Guattari, F. 1994. *What is Philosophy?* Verso Books.

Derrett, J. D. M. 1957. *Hindu Law Past and Present*. A. Mukherjee & Co.

Derrett, J. D. M. 1968. *Religion, Law and the State in India*. Faber & Faber.

Desai, S. A. 1998. *Mulla's Principles of Hindu law*. 15th edn. N. M. Tripathi.
Engle, K. 2000. 'Culture and Human Rights: The Asian Values Debate in Context'. 32(2) *NYU Journal of International Law & Politics*. 201.
Flood, G. (ed.). 2003. *Hinduism*. Blackwell.
Galanter, M. 1984. *Competing Inequalities: Law and the Backward Classes in India*. University of California Press.
Gundimeda, S. 2016. 'Dalit Activism in Telugu Country, 1917–30'. 36(3) *South Asia Research*. 322.
Gupta, C. 2016. *The Gender of Caste*. University of Washington Press.
Hayden, R. M. 1984. 'A Note on Caste Panchayats and Government Courts in India: Different Kinds of Stages for Different Kinds of Performances'. 22 *Journal of Legal Pluralism*. 43.
Hayden, R. M. 1999. *Disputes and Arguments Among Nomads: A Caste Council in India*. Oxford University Press.
Headley, Z. 2015. 'The Devil's Court! The Trial of "Katta Panchayat" in Tamil Nadu' in D. Berti and D. Bordia (eds) *Regimes of Legality. Ethnography of Criminal Cases in South Asia*. Oxford University Press. 227.
Headley, Z. 2018. 'Adjudicating Social Death. Caste Exclusion, Civil Rights and the Colonial Court'. 17 *SAMAJ*. 1.
Holden, L. 2003. 'Custom and Law Practices in Central India: Some Case Studies'. 23(2) *South Asia Research*. 115.
Khilnani, S. 2012. *The Idea of India*. Penguin Random.
Kishwar, M. 1994. 'Codified Hindu law. Myth and Reality'. 29(33) *Economic and Political Weekly*. 13 August. 2145.
Knott, K. 1998. *Hinduism. A Very Short Introduction*. Oxford University Press.
Lipner, J. 1998. *Hindus. Their Religious Beliefs and Practices*. Routledge.
Lynton, H. R. 2009. *Veiled Destinies. Learning to Live in India*. Xlibris Corporation.
Menski, W. 2001. *Modern Indian Family Law*. Curzon.
Menski, W. 2003. *Hindu Law. Beyond Tradition and Modernity*. Oxford University Press.
Menski, W. 2006. *Comparative Law in a Global Context. The Legal Systems of Asia and Africa*. Cambridge University Press.
Menski, W. 2008. 'The Uniform Civil Code Debate in Indian Law: New Developments and Changing Agenda'. 9(3) *German Law Journal*. 211.
Menski, W. 2014a. 'Legal Simulation: Law as a Navigation Tool for Decision-Making'. 59(2/1) *Report of Japan Coast Guard Academy*. 1.
Menski, W. 2014b. 'The Liquidity of Law as a Challenge to Global Theorising'. 11 *Jura Gentium*. 19.
Menski, W. 2014c. 'Remembering and Applying Legal Pluralism: Law as Kite Flying' in S. P. Donlan and L. Heckendorn Urscheler (eds) *Concepts of Law: Comparative, Jurisprudential, and Social Science Perspectives*. Ashgate. 91.
Menski, W. 2016a. 'Justice, Epistemic Violence in South Asian Studies and the Nebulous Entity of Caste in Our Age of Chaos'. 36(3) *South Asia Research*. 299.
Menski, W. 2016b. 'Still Asking for the Moon? Opening Windows of Opportunity for Better Justice in India'. 49(2) *Verfassung und Recht in Übersee*. 125.
Michaels, A. 2004. *Hinduism Past and Present*. Orient Longman.
Miller, J. 1986. *The Vision of Cosmis Order in the Vedas*. Routledge & Kegan Paul.
Mody, P. 2008. *The Intimate State. Love Marriage and the Law in Delhi*. Routledge.
Mohammad, A. 2013. *The Festival of Pirs: Popular Islam and Shared Devotion in South India*. Oxford University Press.
Nagaraj, V. 2012. 'Local and Customary Forums: Adapting and Innovating Rules and Formal Law'. 17(3) *Indian Journal of Gender Studies*. 429.
Naipaul, V. S. 2011. *India: A Million Mutinies Now*. Vintage International.
Sarkar, T. 2001. *Hindu Wife, Hindu Nation. Community, Religion, and Cultural Nationalism*. Hurst & Company.
Sen, A. 2006. *The Argumentative Indian*. Penguin.
Sen, A. 2009. *The Idea of Justice*. Penguin.
Sethi, M. 2016. 'Majority Claims and Majoritarian Anxieties'. 51(4) *Economic and Political Weekly*. 55.
Sharma, A. 1996. *Hinduism for Our Times*. Oxford University Press.
Sharma, A. 2004. *Hinduism and Human Rights. A Conceptual Approach*. Oxford University Press.
Sharma, J. 2003. *Hindutva. Exploring the Idea of Hindu Nationalism*. Penguin.

Singh, S. 2016. 'Dalits in Punjab: Cultural Assertion and Heritage Reconstruction'. 36(3) *South Asia Research*. 356.
Smith, D. 2003. *Hinduism and Modernity*. Blackwell.
Solanki, G. 2011. *Adjudication in Religious Family Laws*. Cambridge University Press.
Srinivas, M. N. 1998. *Indian Society Through Personal Writings*. Oxford University Press.
Vincentnathan, S. G. 1996. 'Caste Politics, Violence, and the Panchayat in a South Indian Community'. 38(3) *Comparative Studies in Society and History*. 484.
Watts, D. 2015. 'Pakistan's Home Truths on Terror'. 19(5) *Asian Affairs*. 23.
Williams, R. V. 2006. *Postcolonial Politics and Personal Laws*. Oxford University Press.
Wood, A. T. 2004. *Asian Democracy in World History*. Routledge.
Zaehner, R. C. 1975 [1962]. *Hinduism*. Oxford University Press.

25

Comparative remarks

Religious laws and the legal other

Adam B. Seligman

Introduction and background

Today, the effects of globalization, the enmeshment of world-wide economies, the massive movements of population across the globe, including the growth in Europe of its non-Christian populace, have all led to a questioning of conventional understandings in the social and historical sciences, political thought, religious studies, literature, and law. In the latter field, this has found expression in the growing debate over legal pluralism (De Sousa Santos, 1987; Tamanaha, 1993, 2000; Teubner, 1991–1992), that is, in a growing recognition that the centrism characterizing the legal order of the State was not as unproblematic as it was once thought to be. With the growth of the nation-state during the nineteenth century, and with the extension of its power and hegemony over ever more arenas of human action and interaction, the law of the State came to be seen as the only source of legally valid normative orders. The legal system of the State attained its apogee in the formulations of positivistic legal thought, procedural in nature, which made nary a claim to transcendent, revelatory or otherwise other-worldly or ultimate sources of their authority.

This picture began to change in the early 1990s. The publication of Robert Cover's (1992) *Nomos and Narrative* made clear the existence of very different 'interpretive communities' within the boundaries of the nation-state that did not necessarily share the same 'narrative' of meaning-giving order which was represented in and through the legal codes of the state. At roughly the same time the idea of legal pluralism had begun to take root. It argued for the existence within one country of multiple legal orders and normative frameworks; that is, of communities that regulated their lives according to different (often hierarchically ordered) sets of legal criteria, not all of which could be subsumed within the logic of the law of the State. Debates abound within the literature devoted to legal pluralism over the existence of weak vis à vis strong forms of pluralism (Griffiths, 1986). Weak legal pluralism is, here, understood as the delegation by the State of a particular area of legal adjudication to a system of law that is autonomous of State principles and codes. The existence of rabbinic courts or Muslim Shari'a courts in Europe and North America are examples of this type of legal pluralism – in which the State, while granting a certain degree of legal autonomy to an alternative system, ultimately maintains its hegemony. Thus, one can marry according to Jewish ritual law, but what makes the marriage legally valid is the signing of a certificate issued by the secular authorities. Strong legal pluralism implies the de facto existence of alternative legal orders that effect compliance by a certain populace and exist independent of the State's legitimizing mechanisms (if not, of course, of its coercive force). If anything, this debate, its social correlates and, crucially, its prescriptive dimensions, have only intensified following September 11, 2001 and the endless debates over Islam in Europe, Sha'aria courts, the veiling of women, polygamy, etc.

Whatever else the Islamic presence in Europe has led to, it has evoked serious debate concerning the legal orders of EU member states (Foblets and Renteln, 2009; Foblets et al., 2010). How Islam and Islamic practices (from family law, to dietary restrictions, to personal codes of behavior) can or cannot be accommodated under current European law has become an enormously important issue and has already generated a vast and important literature, not to mention conferences, colloquia, courses, and degree specializations.

Most of the debates concerning Islam in Europe and about legal pluralism have focused on the State and have wrestled with the ability, willingness (or not) of its legal orders to accommodate alternative, sometimes opposed modes of legal ordering. Central to these discussions has been the debate over colonialism and post-colonial studies which have contributed greatly to our understanding of how customary law was, and was not, accommodated by colonizing Empires in the nineteenth and early twentieth centuries.

Little discussion however has focused on the other side of the issue, though this approach was already present in Cover's seminal essay of 1983 (Cover, 1992). That is to say, there seems to be much less work on just how non-State legal traditions – or perhaps it is better to phrase it as the legal traditions of non-State actors – accommodate themselves to the laws and hegemonic demands of the State as well as to their own legal other. After all, if a modus vivendi is to be found between different juridicially constituted communities, it will demand accommodation from all sides. And while it is perhaps quite justified to focus our analytic attention on the State, on that entity which, in Max Weber's telling phrase 'has the monopoly on the legitimate use of force' in society, it is no less the case that – unless particularistic or segmented 'enclave legal-cultures' can, each from their own perspectives, recognize a legal other – no reasonable way will be found to reach that overlapping consensus necessary to accommodate the existence of diverse normative orders within either the State or such legally coordinated multi-State frameworks as the EU. In brief, not only must the State recognize the existence of alternative legal orders, but these alternative legal orders must also recognize the existence (and perhaps even the legitimacy) of both the State and their own legal other, and do so from within their own emic legal assumptions (as well, in Cover's terms, from their own narrative assumptions). This will be the rule if a way is to be found to 'live together differently' and accommodate the multi-cultural, multi-religious, and multi-communal nature of our cities and towns within which diversity is more and more the norm.

Traditional law and their legal other

The four chapters in this part take up this challenge in different religio-legal traditions. They deal with the place of the legal other within the Jewish, Christian, Muslim, and Hindu legal traditions respectively. They move beyond this question, however, to view the different ways these traditions accommodate international human rights law and the more generally accepted legal notions such as religious freedom which define contemporary Western, democratic, legal orders.

The different traditions studied here approach the challenge of the legal other from markedly different philosophical, religious, and juridical perspectives. So much is this the case that it is difficult to argue for a common approach that applies to all four. Closest in nature are the Jewish and Christian perspectives where the Jewish idea of the Noahide laws and the Christian concept of natural law have some overlapping features. Both rest on the idea of a universal and transcendent fount of law which provides a universal code of conduct accessible though reason and obligatory on all human societies.

In their universality, both provide a principled recognition of the 'other' as a morally responsible and ethical being capable of existing in some relation of solidarity and mutuality – and hence in a principled relation of peace – with members of the Jewish or Christian societies respectively. As developed in the chapters of both Suzanne Stone (Chapter 21, this volume) and Norman Doe (Chapter 22, this volume), the extent of this mutuality, the nature of the obligations it entailed, and its specific enactments, changed over time and with different legal decisors and depended not a little on the changing social and political environments in which the traditions found themselves. Thus, and as we have seen earlier, the emergence of the modern state clearly had significant implications on how these obligations to mutuality – now understood in terms of rights as well as of Church-State relations – were conceived.

Moreover, the more modern move from a transcendentally constituted system of laws to one predicated on the idea of rights progressed very differently in these two traditions. The move to rights in the Christian tradition follows more or less seamlessly from the idea of natural reason, always a predicate of natural law doctrine. The various permutations of rights in terms of relations between Church and State and of religious freedom within different Christian traditions are adumbrated in a most useful manner in Norman Doe's contribution.

The Jewish tradition however is somewhat different. Arguments providing for different sets of modern freedoms and recognition of rights, rest, not on a shared reason, but on ever expansive interpretations of those societies obligated by the Noahide laws. This, as Suzanne Stone has argued, has provided a strong basis for recognition of minority rights (among religious decisors) within the Jewish state. Moving further towards a principled appreciation of alternative legal systems is, within the Jewish tradition, the general legal principle of *dina de-malkhuta dina* (the law of the land is the law) which appeared first in the Babylonian Talmud and has provided a foundation for recognition of a type of legal pluralism ever since. Tracing the development of this concept over medieval, early modern, and more contemporary legal traditions, Stone makes an admirable case for its critical role as an anchor for the status of international law within contemporary religious thought in the State of Israel.

In earlier times, however, the very same concept provided the grounds for dealing with the legitimacy (as well as limits of legitimacy) of gentile courts (*arka'ot shel goyiim*). While Jewish law from the Amoraic period onward has included the dictum of *dina de-malkhuta dina*, the understanding, circumscription, interpretation, and enactment of this legal principle has, as shown in the monumental work by Shmuel Shilo (1974), varied in different periods. How, for example to accept its principle implications but not, at the same time, lose the specificity of one's own legal system has been much debated over the generations of legal theorists from the seventh century until today. Does the law pertain only to matters between the king and his subjects (and not for example in matters of tort or family law)? Is it restricted to matters of taxation, punishment, or eminent domain? Do such laws apply to returned property, if so when and in which circumstance?

Further complications arise in matters of contracts. Contracts drawn up in gentile courts are valid, with the exception of divorce decrees and those of freeing slaves. Yet the scope of these exceptions and their meaning have been given to very different understandings at different times and in different places of the Jewish Diaspora. All these matters and more were thus the subject of continual debate and contestation within circles of Jewish legal decisors from early medieval into modern times.

The generally accepted view – as evinced clearly in the legal codes of Moses Maimonides (*Mishneh Torah*), Jacob b. Asher (called *Ba'al HaTurim* or often just the *Tur* for the name of the code of law he assembled), Joseph Karo (*Shulhan Arukh*), and others – is that recourse to gentile courts is prohibited in the strictest of fashions. Yet a closer reading of texts and commentaries tends to mediate this harsh view and comes to recognize that the very different sets of extenuating circumstances, exceptions to the rule, and principled recognition of non-Jewish courts add a complexity to the binary view that has dominated much of medieval and modern understandings.

So, for example, in matters of damages (*dinei mamonot*) it is, in the general run of things, strictly forbidden to have recourse to a gentile court (such recourse is likened to a revolt against and desecration of the Law of Moses). Yet, despite this rhetoric it appears that this prohibition is based more on an incongruity of procedure between gentile and Jewish courts than – what is so often assumed – a categorical condemnation of gentile judicial systems. For, whereas in Jewish courts two witnesses are needed to effect the transfer of property from defendant to claimant, in gentile courts one witness is sufficient. In those situations where Jewish law admits the evidence of only one witness (as in the case of a witness for the defense), a Jew is permitted to give testimony in a gentile court because in such a case the requirements of Jewish law are fulfilled (*Tur*, § 281990). Accordingly, parsing the problem in procedural terms forces us to rethink our understanding of the broader rhetorical tropes and condemnations. It also raises interesting possibilities for how different legal systems may accommodate one another. Moreover, and somewhat surprisingly, at certain points and among certain decisors, there seems to be a willingness to adopt (or accede to) discrete non-Jewish practices, such as the swearing in of witnesses which, according to the Beit Yosef (1990, § 28), is a Christian practice that certain Jewish communities, knowing no better, accepted as the law and in such circumstances could be practiced in Jewish courts.

All such features of the law, as well as the exceptions to the blanket prohibition on gentile courts (the most important being the permission to go to gentile courts when dealing with a man of known violent inclinations), should lead us to recognize that we are looking at a number of critical mechanisms of accommodation and even (partial) legitimation that are useful and just possibly transferable to other legal systems at other times. To support this claim, however, much further study is necessary. More detailed exploration of the Jewish law on these matters is needed, as is a wider, comparative perspective that will help highlight the uniquely singular and the more broadly shared components – and potentialities – of different systems.

For, at the end of the day, whatever their similarities, the Christian notions of universal natural law and Jewish ideas of the Noahide commandments or of the legitimacy of gentile courts are not easily translatable. The Noahide laws are a specific legal code, revealed by God after the flood, and obligatory on all mankind. Those who accept these obligations are, in the Jewish tradition, granted what may be thought of as the highest good a religious tradition can grant – a place in the scheme of salvation. As argued by Stone (1991), the development of Jewish legal thought has seen a gradual extension of those societies included in those who are obligated by a legal order – and so, viewed as potential partners in the process of world building. The legitimacy granted to gentile courts by the Talmudic dictum of *dina de-malkhuta dina* is moreover not – as far as we can see – rooted in the same universalist assumptions of reason that we can find in the natural law tradition. And this is a difference well worth exploring.

The approaches to the legal other taken in Anver Emon's contribution on Islam (Chapter 23, this volume) as well as in the chapter by Werner Merski and Zoe Headley (Chapter 24, this volume) are moreover different yet again, both from the Jewish and Christian perspectives as well as from one another. Striking in both is the absence of any principled recognition of alternative legal orders. Neither recognizes any meta-legal frame within which its own legal order resides and which, in principle (if with various caveats and exceptions), could accommodate alternative legal dictates. While the Islamic perspective does not seem to recognize the metaphysical legitimacy of any legal order outside of Islam, the Hindu framework does not seem to recognize any over-arching order at all. In Menski and Headley's terms 'custom is and remains king' in a legal system that remains primarily 'regulated within the private informal sphere'.

The Islamic framework as presented by Emon focuses its attention solely on the political dimension or, to put it differently, on the limits of Islamic jurisdiction. The fundamental distinction here, as he points out, is between the realms of *dar al-Islam* and *dar-al harb* – with the case of the *dhimmi*, the resident (but monotheistic) alien as a third and critically important category (in that the *dhimmi* is subject to Islamic law, while the *harbi* is not). Emon's various hypotheticals make clear that the issues at stake in terms of the legal other are solely those of jurisdiction and, therefore, the boundaries of the Islamic legal enterprise. The *dhimmi* is included within this project as a resident in Islamic lands – he had entered into a contract that obligated him to abide by Islamic law. The *harbi*, on the other hand, is not so included even if for various reasons he may have entered in and resided in Islamic lands. The issue debated by Islamic jurists is the limits of Islamic legal jurisdiction, not the relative legitimacy of a foreign legal order (as is the case for example in the Jewish notion of *dina de-malkhuta dina*). What is enacted is, as Emon makes clear, a 'zero-sum' conception of contesting legal orders, and at no point were foreign legal codes granted the legitimacy granted to Islam – as he discussed in the case of the prophet and Jewish laws of adultery.

As Emon claims, the sovereignty of imperial Islamic institutions necessitated an approach to foreign legal orders in binary terms that either applied Shari'a law or denied its jurisdiction. Emon's fascinating discussion of a *dhimmi*'s theft of pork or wine from another *dhimmi*, and if such property was legally protected under Islamic law (making it *mutaquwwam*), and the nature of recourse left to the person whose property was stolen, is however illustrative of the inherent problems of such an approach to the legal other, resident in Islamic lands. The different approaches of different legal decisors and attempts to find what is essentially a compromise between different aspects of public ordering (defined strictly in terms of particular Islamic orders – thus excluding wine or pork from the category of valued property or in more general terms of stolen goods, for which restitution must be made) is a wonderful example of the limits to any imperial project in a world that is, always, of necessity, more diverse than its systemic definitions allow. As Emon makes clear, similar tensions existed as well in respect of endowments to charitable institutions by *dhimmis*. Here, as earlier, what was at stake was the conception of the public good, and so the questions arise: is a pious act only conceivable by Muslims; is a non-Islamic religious institution a threat to the Islamic community; what of lost income to public coffers, etc? As Emon shows, different Islamic legal schools approached these issues differently – though in all, either the issue was removed from the legal sphere per se (endowing a charitable institution may bring one closer to God but does not as such raise a legal claim) or was understood in financial rather than principled terms (calculating for example how the *jizya* would be paid).

Nowhere however do we move beyond the logic of a very particular imperial project making universalist claims (as indeed is the case with most imperial projects) and facing a more complicated and diverse social reality than it can accommodate on the principled level of Shari'a law. Such challenges are inherent in a system that does not recognize any meta-legal order beyond its own – though this is not a claim that systems (such as the Jewish or Christian) that do recognize such an order are free of tensions and contradictions – as we just saw in our brief discussion of *dina de-malkhuta dina*.

A rather different situation is encountered in the case of Hindu law as presented by Menski and Headley. Rather than an imperial project that recognizes only the limits of its own jurisdiction and no meta-legal framework within which other legal frameworks can be conceived, we have instead an interconnected legal space defined by its own multiplicity. Neither the extra-legal frameworks of reason (Christian, natural law) nor of revelation (Jewish Noahide commandments), nor of a bounded jurisprudence with the legal other existing beyond its purview (Islam), we have instead a system of infinite, internal pluralism where most (Hindu) law exists, as our authors state 'within the private informal sphere'. Personal law rather than state-centered law is the touchstone of Hindu legality – not just for Hindus but for all others within the polity. Multiplicity and with it the recognition of multiple others is its defining feature – reflecting in many ways the hybridity and diversity of the society at large. A society then of particularly constituted legal individuals – connected to one another, 'interactive' (in our authors' words) but always within specific, concrete, and local situations: with their own expectations, obligations, and interpretations. Internal otherness and broad social differentiation rather than any specific 'legal other' are the defining traits of the legal order here.

Of special relevance to the comparative perspective are the (perhaps counterintuitive) manner in which such a legal orientation may foster values that one would hardly associate with Hindu law – such values as gender equality, multicultural jurisprudence, religious freedom and its attendant rights, for example. While contested and challenged by some human rights activists, and other uncritical champions of Western legal orders, Hindu law has, as our authors are at pains to point out, its own resources with which to address contemporary concerns – often achieving some sort of 'Rawlseian' overlapping consensus with modern Western ideas of human rights and individual autonomy.

Duties and obligations, rooted in the moral authority of individual conscience, form the basis of a huge interconnected and inclusive system of custom and law towards which none is a total stranger, or absolute other. The skein of interconnected socially obligated individuals of the Hindu legal enterprise rejects neither the principles of democracy nor of state law; though, they are often conceived of as in violation of international legal codes and principles. This, however, as our authors imply, has much more to do with the projection of otherness by Western legal thought than any characteristic inherent to Hindu law per se.

At the end of the day, much of the discussion around the legal other comes down to the issue of borders, boundaries, and how we conceived of that whole which a system's (including a legal system's) boundaries define. Diversity, multiplicity, and a capacity to abide with ambiguity seem to define the Hindu systems in ways that Western legal orders can hardly countenance or manage. Its challenges are, therefore, different from those of the Western legal orders – as are its solutions.

Conclusion

With this in mind, it is therefore perhaps fitting to end this reflection on the legal other by considering the issue of boundaries – not least in the Western context – and as a case in point, to review the position of Jews and prostitutes in medieval Europe, whose acceptance as the legal other par excellence in Medieval canon law was the cause of their tolerance within society (Bejcz, 1997; Seligman, 2004). Jews and prostitutes, we would do well to recall, were the marginal or liminal people par excellence of medieval Christian society. They existed very much on its boundaries (not, I hasten to point out, totally beyond them). Existing at the boundaries, however, also meant that in a sense, they patrolled these boundaries. Their existence on the margins did not make of them marginal categories. Quite the opposite, for on the margins the 'whole' was represented. In general terms this is a truism we know well from the anthropological work of Victor Turner (1995) on liminal or marginal states and statuses. Marginal states, of pilgrimage or of a change in social status and so on become precisely those social spaces where the whole of society is represented and the solidarity of the group as a whole expressed. It is in that role that the margins carry the potential to provide an ongoing challenge and critique to society and its received opinions.

David Nirenberg illustrates this issue wonderfully in the case of prostitutes in the Christian Middle Ages. The prostitute who belonged to no man, neither father nor husband, but was the receptacle of all men's lust thus became:

> [a] concrete representation of a community of men united to each other by a common sexual bond. In the case of the fourteenth century Crown [of Aragon] this was a community delimited in terms of religious identity. All Christian males could, in the words of St Paul, 'become one body' with a Christian prostitute, but through her (and this St. Paul did not say) they also became one with each other.
>
> *(Nirenberg, 1996: 155)*

It is no wonder that prostitutes were known (and continue to be known in certain societies) as public women, *les femmes publique*. It is also no wonder that, as Nirenberg makes clear, concerns with miscegenation across the lines of religious communities (those of Christians, Jews, and Moslems) was of such great concern in the fourteenth century Kingdom of Aragon – especially in terms of the prostitutes. The different communities maintained their own prostitutes, and the granting of sexual favors across confessional lines was punished by death. The prostitute, the public woman, whose public nature was itself a function of her marginality, thus in a sense patrolled the boundaries of the community – that very community or public that in a strange, counter intuitive way she came to represent. Note the irony, that it is precisely the marginal or peripheral prostitute who plays a role in defining and maintaining the boundaries of the center and of the community. Perhaps though the irony is more apparent than real, for indeed there is no center without its boundaries, and no public without its margins within which its very own definition resides. The point is that the prostitute who could deny her sexual favors to no man within the community, was barred on pain of death from granting them to anyone beyond the community. Prostitutes had to be tolerated precisely because their role on the boundaries of the public defined and in some sense maintained that very public.

And here the case of the Jews, that most significant other of Christian civilization, comes to mind as playing a somewhat similar role. For the Jew also, as it were, patrolled the boundaries of Christendom. The Jew did not so much define the Christian other as define the Christian self (Flusser, 1979; Rokeah, 1982; Taylor, 1995; Yuval, 2001). Christianity had, after all, defined itself in terms of the rejection of Judaism and of Jewish law and posited alternative terms of fulfillment in the form of Jesus as Christ. More importantly, Christianity itself could only be realized at the eschaton when the Jews came to accept Jesus as Messiah. In some sense then the final triumph of Christianity did indeed rest (in fact until the Second Vatican Council) on the elimination of the Jews – not their corporeal elimination (which was why Jews were protected by canon law edicts on toleration) but their ideal or symbolic elimination in accepting the tenets of the Christian faith. Again, we see how the very core of a community (the Christian ecclesia) is intimately tied to and dependent upon those existent on its boundaries. Christians cannot be free of the Jews whose final eschatological acceptance of Jesus as Christ will prove the truth of Christianity. This was, in turn, precisely the reasoning behind medieval canon laws on tolerance – the need to maintain the Jewish presence as witness to the Second Coming. The Jew was hated, reviled, demeaned, and often attacked. But he could not be destroyed, precisely because of his role vis à vis the very central tenets of Christianity (Seligman and Weller, 2018).

Both Jews and prostitutes – the quintessential legal other – in different ways did provide a similar function – both patrolled (to continue the metaphor) the boundaries of the Christian community. Precisely their existence on the boundaries is what defined them as existing in Freud's (1945: 113–115) 'small difference' to the majoritarian society. Existing on the margins, the boundaries in a sense maintain the center. To do away with the other, either by eliminating him (or her) or incorporating them within us thus allows us to patrol our own boundaries. However, doing so means, by definition, destroying the other who is necessary for the very constitution of self. The move to incorporate the other grants us perhaps safety (and control) but not recognition. Living with the reality of other's control is thus a situation of great fragility and uncertainty. The fact that our own boundaries are in the hands of another, presents us with a frightening situation: less than total control over our very own constitutive terms of ordering, meaning, and integration (Seligman et al., 2016).

There is, I believe, no final way out of this tension, and the burden of living with the uncertainty of the other patrolling the boundaries of our own selves, whether collective or individual, is not easy to bear. All attempts at foreshortening this tension have led either to the physical elimination of the other, or, what was sometimes only slightly less horrible, the myriad attempts to incorporate the other by denying his or her *existence* as other. What is fascinating in the studies presented in this part is the seemingly inherent recognition of this fact. In different manners and through different mechanisms, all the legal systems presented recognize the pervasive existence of the legal other and the need to accommodate this difference. In the Jewish and Christian traditions this is achieved through the application of a meta-legal framework or ontology: a set of principles either revealed to all mankind (Noahide commandments) or accessible to all by virtue of their reasoning capacity (natural law). In the Islamic case it is achieved through a careful parsing of the rights and obligations of the legal other resident within the *dar-al Islam*, not to mention of those residing beyond the jurisdiction of the Shari'a (those residents of *dar-al harb*). In the Hindu tradition, it is, in fact, the reducibility of all legal frames to their concrete particularities that inherently recognizes the 'otherness' in and of all others.

It may be fair to assume that this very recognition of the other is rooted in the Axial nature of these traditions and so in their recognition of a transcendent dimension to existence and with it the necessary existence of the stranger or legal other as fellowman (Eisenstadt, 1982, 1986; Jaspers, 1953). In the early decades of the twentieth century the philosopher Hermann Cohen (1995: 120) noted in terms of the injunctions of the Book of Exodus: 'Humanity is already so rooted in the stranger, that the slave, as stranger can be admonished to the bond of gratitude'. The stranger or legal other is, in this reading, incorporated within that shared reciprocity that is the basis of all legal systems.

It may be most fitting, to end on this note with the observation of Karl Jaspers (1955: 103) on the role of transcendence in making possible the principled existence of the other among us:

> The plurality of truths is untrue at the moment when they are seen externally as many, as determinable standpoints; for every standpoint can also absorb him who thinks it. They become even more untrue when they become mutually indifferent and simply rest alongside one another. What will not and what can not become the same, nevertheless, become related through Transcendence which touches the One, which, even if our gods be different, discovers the God, which requires of us not to relapse into the distraction of warring multiplicities related only by indifference or the struggle over room to exist. There is the sophistry of easy tolerance which wishes to be valid, but not to be really touched. On

> the other hand, there is the truth of tolerance which listens and gives and enters into the unpredictable process of communication by which force is restrained; in such a process, man reaches from his roots to the heights possible for him.

Recognizing the other, as a *legal other*, is perhaps the first and most crucial step in this process of circumscribing the use of force and recognizing the mutuality of our existence.

References

Bejcz, I. 1997. 'Tolerantia: A Medieval Concept'. 58 *Journal of the History of Ideas*. 365.
Cohen, H. 1995. *Religion of Reason Out of the Sources of Judaism*. Oxford University Press.
Cover, R. 1992. *Narrative, Violence and the Law: The Essays of Robert Cover*. University of Michigan Press.
De Sousa Santos, B. 1987. 'Law: A Map of Misreading. Towards a Postmodern Conception of Law'. 14 *Journal of Law and Society*. 279.
Eisenstadt, S. N. 1982. 'The Axial Age: The Emergence of Transcendental Visions and the Rise of Clerics'. 23(2) *European Journal of Sociology*. 294.
Eisenstadt, S. N. (ed.). 1986. *The Origin and Diversity of Axial Age Civilizations*. State University of New York Press.
Flusser, D. 1979. *Jewish Sources in Early Christianity* (in Hebrew). Sifriat HaPoalim.
Foblets, M. C., Gaudreault-Desbiens, J. F. and Renteln, A. D. (eds). 2010. *Cultural Diversity and the Law*. Bruylant.
Foblets, M. C. and Renteln, A. D. (eds). 2009. *Multicultural Jurisprudence: Comparative Perspectives on the Cultural Defence*. Hart Publishing.
Freud, S. 1945. *Civilization and its Discontents*. Hogarth Press.
Griffiths, J. 1986. 'What is Legal Pluralism?' 18 *Journal of Legal Pluralism and Unofficial Law*. 1.
Jaspers, K. 1953. *The Origin and Goal of History*. Yale University Press.
Jaspers, K. 1955. *Reason and Existenz*. The Noonday Press.
Nirenberg, D. 1996. *Communities of Violence: Persecutions of Minorities in the Middle Ages*. Princeton University Press.
Rokeah, D. 1982. *Jews, Pagans and Christians in Conflict*. Magnes Press.
Seligman, A. 2004. *Modest Claims: Dialogues and Essays on Tolerance and Tradition*. Notre Dame University Press.
Seligman, A., Wasserfall, R. and Montgomery, D. 2016. *Living with Difference: How to Build Community in a Divided World*. University of California Press.
Seligman, A. and Weller, R. 2018. *What Counts as the Same: Memory, Mimesis and Metaphor in Social Life*. Oxford University Press.
Shilo, S. 1974. *Dina de-Malkhuta Dina [The Law of the State is the Law]* (in Hebrew). Academic Press.
Stone, S. 1991. 'Sinaitic and Noahide Law: Legal Pluralism in Jewish Law'. 12 *Cardozo Law Review*. 1157.
Tamanaha, B. 1993. 'The Folly of the "Social Scientific" Concept of Legal Pluralism'. 20 *Journal of Law and Society*. 192.
Tamanaha, B. 2000. 'A Non-Essentialist Version of Legal Pluralism'. 27 *Journal of Law and Society*. 296.
Taylor, M. 1995. *Anti-Judaism and Early Christian Identity*. Brill.
Teubner, G. 1991–1992. 'The Two Faces of Janus: Rethinking Legal Pluralism'. 13 *Cardozo Law Review*. 1443.
Tur, Beit Yosef in. 1990. *Hoshen Mishpat [Laws of Testimony]* (in Hebrew). H. Vashal.
Turner, V. 1995. *The Ritual Process: Structure and Anti-Structure*. Aldine de Gruyer.
Yuval, Y. 2001. *'Two Nations in Your Womb' Perceptions of Jews and Christians* (in Hebrew). Am Oved.

Index

FSC
www.fsc.org
MIX
Papier | Fördert
gute Waldnutzung
FSC® C083411

Kolibri 360 GmbH
Ferdinand-Jühlke-Straße 7
99095 Erfurt, Deutschland
produktsicherheit@kolibri360.de